Alice Paul

Alice Paul

Claiming Power

J. D. ZAHNISER

&

AMELIA R. FRY

OXFORD
UNIVERSITY PRESS

OXFORD
UNIVERSITY PRESS

Oxford University Press is a department of the University of
Oxford. It furthers the University's objective of excellence in research,
scholarship, and education by publishing worldwide.

Oxford   New York

Auckland   Cape Town   Dar es Salaam   Hong Kong   Karachi
Kuala Lumpur   Madrid   Melbourne   Mexico City   Nairobi
New Delhi   Shanghai   Taipei   Toronto

With offices in

Argentina   Austria   Brazil   Chile   Czech Republic   France   Greece
Guatemala   Hungary   Italy   Japan   Poland   Portugal   Singapore
South Korea   Switzerland   Thailand   Turkey   Ukraine   Vietnam

Oxford is a registered trademark of Oxford University Press
in the UK and certain other countries.

Published in the United States of America by
Oxford University Press
198 Madison Avenue, New York, NY 10016

Library of Congress Cataloging-in-Publication Data
Zahniser, Jill Diane.
Alice Paul : claiming power / J. D. Zahniser & Amelia R. Fry.
pages cm
Includes bibliographical references and index.
ISBN 978-0-19-995842-9 (alk. paper) 1. Paul, Alice, 1885–1977.
2. Suffragists—United States—Biography. 3. Women—Suffrage—United States—History.
4. Womens rights—United States—History. I. Fry, Amelia R. II. Title.
HQ1413.P38Z34 2014
324.6'23092—dc23
[B]
2013050418

1 3 5 7 9 8 6 4 2
Printed in the United States of America
on acid-free paper

Alice Paul raises a glass to celebrate winning the vote for American women in August 1920. *Library of Congress, Prints & Photographs Division, LC-DIG-ds-00180*

Contents

Acknowledgments

THE PATH TO completing this book became as complicated as its subject. Amelia Fry began researching Alice Paul's life a decade after her extensive interview with Alice completed under the auspices of the Suffragist Oral History Project, based at Berkeley's Bancroft Library. Beyond this oral history, Amelia found personal information about Paul difficult to acquire because an uncooperative nephew held the suffrage leader's private papers. Amelia therefore talked to as many former friends, relatives, neighbors, and compatriots as she could locate.

She spent the next twenty years excavating Alice Paul's past and maintaining her historical memory. She dipped into the National Woman's Party (NWP) papers and traveled to Great Britain and Europe to trace Alice's footsteps. As she worked, Amelia regularly assisted other historians who were working on the NWP or related topics. She often appeared at conferences and before other interested audiences as she developed resources, living her commitment to the legacy of Alice Paul. Her health failed as another new century dawned and the progress of her book stalled. In 2005, I agreed to complete the biography of Alice Paul's early life and suffrage years, utilizing Amelia's partial draft and research files. Amelia Fry died in 2009.

Many people contributed to Amelia's work. Corona Machemer, an editor at Harper & Row, initiated the discussion of a biography and assisted Amelia for many years. Amelia's research assistants included Amy Butler, Susan Hines, and Kristy Nishimoto. Amelia used the resources of the Sewall-Belmont House and the Library of Congress extensively. Smithsonian curator Edie Mayo became an important resource on Paul memorabilia. The late British filmmakers Midge MacKenzie and Stephen Peet offered their knowledge and insight about the Pankhursts and Edwardian England. Margaret Hope Bacon, the late historian of Quakerism, became a touchstone for Quaker history and values. Paul relatives like John and Anita Parry and Lew Robbins and wife Jean (now Stratton) volunteered family photos and memories. Barbara Irvine, then of the Alice Paul Centennial Foundation (APCF), provided early access to Paul's personal papers and years of

moral support. Amelia's husband, Rex Davis, supported her financially and emotionally as she worked on the biography. After both Amelia and Rex died, her
sons Randy, Gary, and Byron championed the completion of the work.

My own interest in Alice Paul, which began in graduate school, was rekindled
in 1987 when I joined an ambitious and successful effort by the recently formed
APCF to purchase Paul's private papers and memorabilia and donate them to the
Smithsonian Institution and Harvard's Schlesinger Library. The APCF, now the
Alice Paul Institute, went on to purchase the former Paul family home in order to
create a leadership institute for women and girls.

I am indebted to many individuals though, of course, responsibility for any
errors is entirely my own. I thank each and every person who contributed to this
biography, including those who helped Amelia but whose names were lost over
time and other people I have inadvertently forgotten.

My greatest appreciation goes to the distinguished historian Linda K. Kerber,
once my thesis advisor, who encouraged my efforts and graciously introduced me
to publishers. Women's history is thriving because of scholars like Linda doing
superior work of their own and sustaining other historians of women as well.
My longtime friend Barbara Irvine played this role on the activist side, sharing
her enthusiasm, experience, and contacts, and going out of her way to help this
project along.

Other friends and colleagues served as sounding boards. Early readers Betty
LaSorella and Julie Goldstein applauded my first drafts, and historian Betty
A. Bergland took time from her own work to read chapters and listen to my frus-
trations. Lucy Burns's grand-niece, Janet Campbell Burns, kindly obliged all my
questions. Sidney R. Bland conversed with Amelia for years, initially about his
thesis, one of the first about the NWP; he kindly delved into his files at my request,
became another early reader, a reference, and eventually a valued colleague.

My siblings all contributed to this project. My sister Judy Voshell pitched in
to help with microfilm research. My brother Rick offered financial advice and an
ear to bend, while brother Bert found opportunities to publicize the book and
helped me sort out technological puzzles.

Historical accounts of the NWP and its leader paved the way for this book.
Most sources still cite Sidney Bland's 1972 dissertation and subsequent article on
the 1913 parade; his article on Lucy Burns remains the best source of information about her. Christine A. Lunardini brought her incisive political acuity to two
books about the NWP. Linda G. Ford's examination of militancy drew attention
to the political and cultural diversity in the ranks of the NWP pickets. Ford inadvertently gave HBO producers the title for their docudrama on Alice Paul and
the NWP, *Iron-Jawed Angels*. While popularized to a fault, *Angels* nevertheless
introduced Alice Paul to millions.

Research librarians and curators are a godsend for historians. Sarah Hutcheon and the staff at the Schlesinger Library were unfailingly helpful with the Alice Paul Papers. Lily Pforzheimer Foundation Director Nancy Cott and executive director Marilyn Dunn obligingly gave me access to closed files on the library's history. Rhonda DiMascio and Lucy Beard, successive executive directors of the Alice Paul Institute, offered Amelia's files a home, and program director Kris Myers patiently dug into her files to find photographs and answer queries. Edie Mayo, now retired, and current curator Lisa Kathleen Graddy lent moral support and enthusiastically walked me through the Alice Paul collection in the Political History Division at the Smithsonian. Elspeth Kursh at the Sewall-Belmont House and Museum tracked down photographs and copyrights. Christopher Densmore of the Friends Historical Library at Swarthmore College unfailingly provided details and tracked down obscure documents. Likewise, Nancy R. Miller of Penn's archives helped me pin down important details about Penn's early graduate women. Ian C. Jackson, librarian at Woodbrooke, clarified my understanding of the Quaker study center; his precedessors had opened their files to Amelia Fry. The librarians and staff at the Moorestown Friends School also graciously offered their records and expertise on Alice Paul and the school to both myself and Amelia.

My research assistants completed the daunting and tedious microfilm work for this book. The amazing Lin Salisbury scanned every page of the NWP records between 1913 and 1920; Christine Manganaro efficiently examined a wide range of other records. I am deeply appreciative of their diligence.

I often worked out ideas while lecturing about Alice Paul and women's history to K–12 teachers for the American Institute for History Education (AIHE). I thank Kevin T. Brady, AIHE president, for those opportunities and his support of this project. I am grateful to my audiences for helping me refine the themes of this book.

The New Jersey Historical Commission, a division of the New Jersey Department of State, generously supported the final stages of writing with a grant.

Once the book was in production, Molly Morrison expertly led me through the process. Heather Hambleton's careful eye for copyediting eased my review considerably.

It was great good fortune that I was introduced to Nancy Toff, who became my editor. Her ready interest in Alice Paul and willingness to advocate for a focused political biography were essential to the completion of the book. She insisted I clarify ideas and refine expressions to keep this book accessible. I am in debt to her.

J. D. Z.

A Note about Naming

THE TEXT REFERS to Alice Paul by her given name, since the late Amelia Fry knew the elderly Miss Paul as "Alice." "AP" is also used, as Alice Paul regularly signed her initials on letters to both family and colleagues. The close connection between Alice and Lucy Burns prompted the use of Miss Burns's given name as well. For other key players, we use given names plus surnames, even though many married women at the time used their husbands' names socially, as in Mrs. Lawrence Lewis. Single women and the vast majority of married women used their given names to sign correspondence.

Alice Paul

Introduction

"I REMEMBER HESITATING the longest time and writing the letter and not being able to get enough courage to post it and going up and walking around the post office, wondering whether I dare put this in." The turning point of Alice Paul's life occurred in London in June 1909. She suddenly faced a stark choice: return to America or risk arrest and imprisonment by joining a British woman suffrage protest. "While I didn't object" to joining the protest, she told Amelia Fry many years later, "I thought all my family and everybody I knew would object." Yet her Quaker forebears imperiled life and limb to secure their religious freedom; her American progenitors risked their lives for liberty. In the moment, she "longed to be one of those who had fought in the revolution instead of being merely a descendant." She shrank from personal glory but hungered to join her ancestors in the making of history. She thought long and hard, sensing the moment was critical. "At last I got up enough courage to post my letter, saying I would go." Her life would never be the same.[1]

The decision Alice Paul made in 1909 not only transformed her life; it ultimately changed the course of the American votes-for-women campaign and subsequent efforts to secure women's rights. She became the soul and guiding spirit of the final years of the American suffrage movement, transforming that long-standing struggle with bold and controversial action. She raised the constitutional campaign for women's enfranchisement to national prominence and publicly held politicians' feet to the fire, obliging other suffragists and lawmakers to reshape their postures. She captured the narrative of the American movement and, in today's parlance, made suffrage "cool," at least for the young and the young at heart. Thus, she drove the final campaign to win the vote for women.

She understood the signal importance of woman suffrage. "It has become impossible to forget 'votes for women,'" she declared in 1910, "just as it was impossible to forget the reformation of Luther." Alice Paul recognized that the vote embodied the very foundation of citizenship—the right to consent. The notion of thus including women—half the population—in the body politic countered elemental understandings of the nature and function of womanhood; hence, the idea of giving women the vote was a radical prospect. Even today, our anxieties and ambivalence about women's political agency, indeed about women and power, are rooted in the struggle for the vote. Alice Paul's groundbreaking strategy became crucial at that first moment when women asserted their collective power as a political force.[2]

Her negotiation of gender boundaries and political frontiers stands among the most significant chapters of women's political history. Her experience as a suffrage leader illuminates the difficulty of navigating life as a woman in the early twentieth century; unlike many, she saw no contradiction between womanliness and the exercise of raw political power. She subverted propriety to employ a kind of pressure politics wholly new to women; for her trouble, she earned both praise and lasting censure.

Today, we remember Alice Paul as a woman who staged spectacular protests, sent pickets to the White House, and endured prison—all to win the vote for women. The broad strokes of her life and work (the two are usually equated) are now familiar to many because of popular and scholarly accounts of the dramatic suffrage protests she launched. However, we know little more than generalities about her path to power or about the historical circumstances that allowed her to emerge and construct herself as an influential political leader. Her persona and leadership style divided suffragists and historians, yet we understand the woman only dimly.

In every era, the nexus of women and power has been fraught with peril. Historical assessments of Alice Paul's political acumen improved after the late twentieth century's successive waves of social movements, including a re-emergent feminism, remolded American assumptions about acceptable political protest and gender. Assessments of her leadership style and personal qualities proved more resistant: she was consistently painted as ruthless, dictatorial, elitist, and devoid of personal connections.[3]

This book attempts to untangle gender-bound notions of power from our understanding of Alice Paul so we can gaze at her with a fresh eye. For the first time, her story is told from her point of view. We examine her upbringing and education to trace her personal growth and the development of her political consciousness, exploring how her public and private journeys intertwined. We reconstruct her road to leadership and investigate the source and contours of her charismatic authority and strategic ingenuity. As we analyze her leadership abilities, we highlight relations with her most important political adversaries, Woodrow Wilson and rival suffrage leaders Anna Howard Shaw and Carrie Chapman Catt.

To be sure, Alice Paul chose to remain elusive. She readily agreed that the personal is political. However, in her world, the personal was also private; she deliberately sheltered her personal life from public view. She never wrote a memoir and she balked at discussing personal matters with interviewers; we know almost nothing, for example, about her sexuality. She culled the National Woman's Party

(NWP) papers to banish lingering evidence of her life beyond her work, and left precious few clues in her personal papers.[4] Thus we will never know Alice Paul as fully as we would like. We respect her choice, but attempt to nudge open the door to her sanctum sanctorum in order to humanize her.

All her life, Alice Paul proudly claimed her Quaker heritage as motivation for her commitment to women's rights. Indeed, her social conscience and her belief in equality emerged from her upbringing among the Friends. These beliefs, however, were necessary but not sufficient causes of her subsequent undertakings. By virtue of parental example and encouragement and the educational opportunities afforded her in Quaker institutions, she acquired a fluid gender role repertoire that enabled her youthful explorations and facilitated her emergence as a leader. She also developed a sense of self that became the touchstone of her political involvement. Nonetheless, her suffrage zeal soon challenged the constraints of turn-of-the-century Quakerism and she stepped beyond its protective hedge. She eventually became a rather unQuakerly Friend.

Most pioneers capitalize on good historical fortune, and Alice Paul was no exception. She came of age in dynamic times, along with a critical mass of women, "new women" whose rising expectations held enormous political promise for the newborn twentieth century, a promise from which Alice Paul drew and benefited. Likewise, when she ventured abroad, she encountered the militant British suffragists Emmeline and Christabel Pankhurst at an auspicious time, as they neared the peak of their influence. Paul built on her failures as well as her fortunes. Turning to militant activism after a crushing loss, she unexpectedly found her life's passion. A lesser failure after her return to America prompted her to hazard leadership at a propitious moment in the suffrage campaign.

The term *charismatic authority* describes the power of leaders who hold exceptional gifts and inspire the devout loyalty of followers; often, such leaders arise from religious crusades or cults.[5] In Great Britain as well as America, many suffragists viewed their movement reverently and so it hardly seems surprising that charismatic yet controversial leaders came to the fore in both countries. The Pankhursts gave Alice her first glimpse of how women could wield power. She shaped her own brand of leadership in distinctive ways, ways nevertheless rooted in the Pankhursts' complex braiding of masculine and feminine ways of acquiring power.

Alice Paul's overarching ambition fueled her leadership. Her drive was charged by a Quaker culture that treated women equally enough, if not equally, and that valued public service for both sexes. The premature death of her successful and strong-willed father enlarged her possibilities and magnified her worldly desires. She employed her privilege together with the dynamism of her time to serve her ambition, which she expressed—in socially acceptable fashion—as feminine selflessness rather than manly egoism.

Her leadership of the suffrage movement displayed three paramount qualities, all fed by her ambition and each feeding on and into the others. First,
Alice Paul seemed utterly fearless, though not reckless. As a young girl, she
revealed an enthusiasm for testing her physical and intellectual limits; she
gained a facility for melding book and experiential learning. She immersed
herself in a series of new places of encounter, crossing cultural, class, political,
and gender boundaries; taking her own measure; crafting a mature identity.
Her engagement with radical British politics gave her insight into how women
wielded power and tested her courage in another uncharted territory: political
protest. When she finally stepped into the leadership vacuum of the American
suffrage movement, she stood ready to sow the wind. She gathered up the
pent-up energy of those who chafed under the existing suffrage leadership and
began to redirect it.

Alice Paul's strategic capacity wedded resourcefulness and adaptability;[6] her
fearless nature abetted both attributes and even fed arrogance. Her constant urge
for self-improvement fostered, and was fostered by, her native intelligence. Her
willingness to venture onto untested ground developed her adaptability, which
led to more adventuring. By the time she became an American suffrage leader,
she could draw on years of experience with social activism. The inventiveness of
her suffrage campaign became possible because of her wealth of empirical knowledge and her creativity in refashioning strategy and tactics learned elsewhere to
meet her own ends. She drew and kept followers because she became a leader who
always knew the next move.

Alice Paul thrived on self-mastery, her ambitiousness directed inwardly.
The courage which sustained her through imprisonment and hunger strikes
required extraordinary willpower. Years of silent Quaker worship honed her
discipline, and her sheltered religious upbringing developed a sense of caution that tempered her fearlessness. Her ambition drove her to demand the
utmost of herself, physically, emotionally, and intellectually; it also led to
unrealistic expectations of others. As a suffrage leader, she exhibited a watchful anxiety that anticipated potential roadblocks, a mindfulness which held
her outside the moment. One admirer called it "the quiet of the spinning top."[7]
Some found her remote, even cold; however, that watchfulness deepened her
self-command, resulting in a prodigious capacity for work and the discipline
to withstand—even deny—physical privation as well as vilification. The pursuit of self-mastery forged her indomitable spirit, which helped propel the
suffrage cause to victory.

I

"Mind the Light"

IN 1885, THE Paul Road led southeast from the historically Quaker village of Moorestown, New Jersey, to a commodious century-old farmhouse surrounded by a sweeping wooded lawn. There, on an unseasonably warm January 11, 1885, Alice Paul was born. She joined a family proud of its deep roots in the Religious Society of Friends. "I have practically no ancestor who wasn't a Quaker," the aged Alice remarked. "My father and mother were, and *their* fathers and mothers were."[1]

Alice Paul spent the first twenty years of her life in cohesive Quaker communities; they indelibly shaped her ideals, her possibilities, and her passions. She developed a sense of self out of her Quaker and family past and present. Her adult identity incorporated a deep appreciation of history and core beliefs in social justice alongside such values as self-reliance, humility, probity, and service; all these sustained her longer than her religious commitment to the Friends. Her defining character traits emerged in childhood—a nimble intelligence abetted by voracious curiosity, emotional intensity masked by outward stoicism, and competing desires for self-command and self-effacement. She also gained an expansive view of appropriate female behavior from her Quaker milieu, which, while conservative in some respects, embraced academic excellence and athleticism for women ahead of mainstream society.

Late in life, Alice developed an avid interest in her forebears and sought out information that fleshed out stories she heard growing up about notables on the Paul family tree, some of whose portraits graced the walls of her family's home. Ancestors from one branch helped shape the 1657 Flushing Remonstrance, one of the earliest cries for religious liberty in America. Another branch of the family claimed a member of the New Jersey colony's pre-Revolutionary Committee of Correspondence. Through her mother, Alice traced her progenitors back to William Penn and even further to the creators of the Magna Carta.[2]

In more recent memory, her grandfather and great-grandfather advocated historic changes while upholding Quaker principles. The popular image of Quakers links the faith with social and political action; however, by the 1800s, the Friends turned inward and regarded mainstream reform work and public service warily. Nonetheless, the Quaker emphasis on individual conscience tolerated individuals like Charles Stokes and, later, his son-in-law William Parry. Alice's great-grandfather Stokes, a mid-century Republican legislator, urged temperance and abolition but also shared the Quaker commitment to consensus; he "was willing to wait until the minds of the people were prepared" to act, said one history. Continuing Stokes's legacy, young William Parry became speaker of the New Jersey Assembly in 1855 and a year later presided over the first Republican state convention, where he supported a nationwide emancipation of slaves. Beyond political success, Parry's business acumen translated into considerable wealth and influence.[3]

Alice Paul's extended family hewed to a belief system that retained the distinctiveness of its seventeenth-century English beginnings but, as with any faith, evolved with historical circumstance. Friends spurned a fixed creed, convinced that every person could find God directly, in any setting, continuously throughout life; their belief in the spiritual (as distinct from social) equality of all peoples necessarily followed. An Inner Light guided each soul to the Divine Will or the way forward. These fundamental principles led Friends to abjure sacraments and ceremony for silent, inner-directed group worship. As their numbers grew, the emphasis on individual conscience did not preclude Quakers deeming some members Elders and governing themselves through regional bodies called Yearly Meetings. Through the Yearly Meetings, Elders periodically published the *Rules of Discipline*, which codified current Quaker understanding for local meetings. The rules underscored the conviction that a Quaker life involved every aspect of one's existence, its faith embodied in folkways and cultural practices.[4]

Friends valued a simple life beyond reproach that transcended notions of sacred or secular. Quakerism conflated the public and private spheres, which in the dominant culture grew increasingly separate in the nineteenth century as the Industrial Revolution pulled work apart from home life. Like the Puritans before them, Friends became identified with plain dress, but simple garments formed only one aspect of their style of living. Indeed, by the 1880s, use of plain dress declined, though Alice's mother dressed traditionally into the twentieth century.[5]

Though Alice discarded religiosity early in adulthood, she retained many Quaker ways of being. Ideally, the Quaker life joined meetinghouse and home, work, and family in a communal conversation with revelation. The faith's principles could be contradictory: Friends sanctified conscience while at the same time emphasizing humility and a lack of pretentiousness. Simplicity in speech meant avoiding honorific titles like "Dr." in favor of given names or "Friend"; among themselves, Quakers used *thee* and *thy* instead of *you* and *your*, usage harking back to a time when *you* connoted superiority. Living simply led to the construction of meetinghouses without steeples or stained glass and home architecture and furnishings that ran counter to the prevalent Victorian ostentation. Outside the home, Friendly simplicity often read as integrity; Quakers emphasized diligence in practical, useful work; scrupulous conduct in business affairs; and service to the community. Quaker meetings disowned members for serious infractions including marrying outside the faith, but by the nineteenth century, membership began to dwindle and the drawbacks of such a rigorous approach became apparent. For adherents like the Parrys and the Pauls, however, the bonds of faith strengthened family and Quaker family bound the community.[6]

Alice Paul was descended on both sides from Hicksite Quakers, the name for Friends who followed Elias Hicks in the Quaker schism of the 1820s. Hicksites believed that they, not the so-called Orthodox branch, upheld the very foundations of Quakerism, particularly the weight accorded individual conscience, a concept which loomed large in Alice's life. After several years of turmoil, 70 percent of Quakers in the region—among them the Stokeses and Pauls—severed connections with the Philadelphia Yearly Meeting and established a separate Hicksite meeting structure. In Moorestown and other small towns where both sides of the divide were represented, two Quaker meetings now convened and two discrete populations of Friends each regarded the opposite faction as Other. The discord remained so profound that young Alice would not interact with an Orthodox Quaker until she reached her twenties. The faith remained divided until the 1950s.[7]

Even Hicks's followers were not of one mind. More conservative Hicksites viewed those drawn to reform movements, like those supporting abolition and women's rights, suspiciously, uncertain that God led Friends to such public stances away from their distinctive communities. Other Hicksites, like Philadelphian Lucretia Mott, felt certain their own way forward included social activism. Ironically, Quakerism, the fount of their beliefs, now confined them. Hicksites disowned some reform pioneers, while others—notably Mott—tenuously retained their Quaker standing. Still other Hicksites, like suffrage leader Susan B. Anthony, became alienated; she remained a Friend but avoided attending meeting. By the 1880s, the more worldly Hicksites gained sway, due to generational forces as well as influences from mainstream society. Posthumously, Lucretia Mott became a revered Quaker figure. As Alice Paul discovered, tensions between conservative and progressive Hicksites over issues like women's rights continued into the twentieth century.[8]

Hicksite beliefs countered mainstream society's ideas about women's inequality, but the faith had not completely shaken off the notion of female subordination. Despite their spiritual equality, Quaker women historically lacked equal authority within Friends' guiding or social structures. Within marriage, however, women were considered equal. When Alice Paul's parents, Tacie Stokes

Parry and William Mickle Paul II, married in the fall of 1881, they spoke identical one-sentence vows to be loving and faithful, quite unlike conventional vows that directed women to serve and obey. After marriage, Friends charged both spouses with responsibility for holding themselves and each other in the Light. Real marital relations often fell short of the ideal, much like Quaker administrative councils. Over the decades, however, as Hicksites conversant with the mainstream women's rights movement gained influence, women like those in the Parry and Paul families exercised increasing equality in their meetings and, possibly, at home as well.[9]

Tacie Paul's age at marriage—twenty-two—typified her generation, yet her class and education lent her considerable privilege. She attended Swarthmore, the Quaker college south of Philadelphia founded by her grandfather and other Friends, but left before her senior year to marry. Nevertheless, even three years of college made Tacie Parry more highly educated than nearly all her contemporaries; fewer than 2 percent of women went on to higher education in her time. Most of their fathers, like Tacie's, had the wealth and social prominence of the upper middle class.[10]

Tacie was the baby of the Parry tribe and the only surviving girl. Photographs reveal a handsome woman with abundant dark hair and large, steady, deep-set eyes, features Alice inherited. Growing up with five older brothers no doubt shaped Tacie's manner: most remembered her as gentle and intelligent. The youngest child of the influential William Parry shared his civil conscience and expressed it in gender-appropriate ways. As a young woman, Tacie joined the local woman suffrage group and continued attending meetings after her marriage; she gave Alice an early example of a woman whose interests extended beyond the home.[11]

Perhaps William Paul reminded Tacie of her capable father. She had known him since their youth, when he boarded with an aunt near her father's nursery. He taught briefly at the Chester Friends School when she attended the early grades and he, in his late teens, took charge of older children. William was slim and a bit shorter than average. He wore no beard, though a generous, drooping mustache adorned his oval face. His straight, neatly trimmed dark hair parted to one side. Many around Moorestown viewed the adult William as remote and stern; they also acknowledged his victory over an unsettled childhood. Orphaned as an infant, William was raised apart from his three siblings by two consecutive families and spent years in boarding school. However, he left adolescence with a drive like that his eldest daughter would later exhibit.[12]

William Paul became determined to establish himself. In the 1870s, young men and women just out of high school commonly taught in small communities, but William soon tired of teaching. He moved to Philadelphia to learn the shoe business, a leading industry there. In 1875, he partnered with his brother Mickle, thirteen years his senior, to establish a wholesale shoe dealership. A few years later, William's health failed and he withdrew from the partnership, albeit with substantial assets. After his recovery, he changed course again, returning to the Moorestown vicinity to become a gentleman farmer and invest in real estate. He chose a mate whose family embodied the stability and economic security denied him as a child.[13]

The wealth of Friends like Tacie's father and William Paul became another apparent contradiction of a simple life. Over the years, however, some Quakers, following the faith's ethics, built reputations for upright business dealing that became the foundation of wealth. William Paul, like the Parry men, became one of the beneficiaries of this unsought consequence of the plain life. (The unease in Quaker circles with their wealth is suggested by the aphorism, "The Quakers came to America to do good, and they have done very well indeed."[14])

William Paul soon continued his pilgrimage to business success. In 1883, he and Tacie moved into the commodious farmhouse anchoring three adjoining tracts of farmland in Mount Laurel Township. Over the next seventeen years he purchased eight more parcels of land, some of which extended his property (three hundred acres all told) to the edge of Moorestown. One relative recalled that the mature "Paulsdale"—as they called it—became a showplace with numerous outbuildings housing the best equipment available and an expansive lawn where peacocks strutted and sheep grazed. Within a few years, William Paul joined others to found the Moorestown National Bank and became its vice president and later president.[15]

Settled in their own home, the Pauls built their married life together. William's drive and sternness inspired respect and admiration more than affection within the family and community; some believed his wife feared him. However, Tacie's education, community participation, and social advantage suggest a more complex relationship. They stood equally charged with parenting. For in an age when many young Friends increasingly fell away from the faith, children became central to the sustenance of Quakerism.[16]

Alice's distinguishing personal characteristics began to emerge during the two years she spent as an only child. Both parents' reserve plus her father's forbidding temperament shaped her own stoic demeanor, prompting early attempts at self-mastery. She eventually found an outlet for her emotions in athleticism and in reading. As her father spurred himself toward greater achievement, the young girl found a way to find favor with her own small successes. Her persistence drew his praise. Years later, Tacie Paul hinted at this relationship between her daughter and husband; she remembered William Paul's adage, "When there is a job to be done, I bank on Alice."[17]

Alice's sense of Quaker distinctiveness as well as her class consciousness began at home. Early memories harked back to the family's Irish Catholic maids, who lived on the third floor and relieved Mrs. Paul of physical work. Servants were commonplace at the time for families with any discretionary income. Alice remembered "these gay maids…going off to dances and [having] a different life than we did. We just felt that was a sort of common people who did these things." She had clearly internalized a sense of superiority about her own family's lifestyle, a view born of her privilege and her faith. The aura of condescension in this memory points up the limits of Quaker egalitarianism. Alice's more distant contact with the one or two, sometimes African American, hands living on the property also deepened her sense of class, as did parental remarks about Catholics and indigents.[18]

Like most American and Quaker couples of the time, Tacie and William Paul decided to have a smaller family than their parents had, thus allowing them to invest more time and resources in their progeny. A few months before Alice's second birthday, she became a big sister. Brother Will was born in October 1886, and Helen two years later. By the time baby Parry joined the family in 1895, Alice was attending school.[19]

In later life, Alice Paul discussed her childhood with great reluctance, so we have little direct knowledge of Paul family life. Relatives remembered the familiar routines that punctuated the Paul children's days, time immersed in a bucolic environment that nurtured the adult Alice's love of nature. Mr. Paul strode out most days to give orders to his overseer and then ride off on his horse to town and his work at the bank. Mrs. Paul supervised the maids' work; the children had their own chores. Alice, for example, tallied up duck eggs for her mother. After chores, the farm offered plenty of opportunities to explore. One visitor remembered rushing to gather new-fallen peaches from the orchard before the chickens descended and sitting on the wraparound porch to eat peaches and cream.[20]

In the late nineteenth century, Quakers encouraged their children to play, much like middle-class children in the wider society. The Friends' Rules of Discipline no longer discouraged nursery rhymes and make-believe. The Pauls eschewed card games and music, though many Hicksites enjoyed the latter. Among her own set, Alice recalled, "You didn't regard it as oppressive, you know, you just didn't know there was such a thing." The children played checkers instead and "all the little things that people play." In later years, they played tennis on the grass court laid out on the great lawn and sledded down the slope in winter.[21]

Reading became the childhood pastime Alice most remembered. The Pauls owned an extensive home library. At least one parent shared the cosmopolitan reading appetite becoming more common among younger Hicksites: the Paul library included fiction and plays, genres that, before the mid-1890s, Elders officially deemed impractical. The children also received books from relatives as gifts. The home library included tales of Shakespeare's heroines, the yarns of that new British author Rudyard Kipling and the trickster fables made popular by Joel Chandler Harris (neither author yet controversial), and the timeless weavings of Scheherazade. Alice acquired a lifelong habit of devouring the newspaper, perhaps from her parents reading aloud the weekly Hicksite *Friends' Intelligencer* compendium.[22]

Her parents also taught her what it meant to be Quaker. The children assumed the gentle *thees* and *thys* and mastered the silent grace before meals. They learned to number the months and days and attend meeting on First Days. Mrs. Paul did not insist that Alice and Helen adopt the plain costume she wore (few Quakers of the girls' generation would), but she preached frugality about their wardrobes as in all things. Chores taught them the importance of a useful life, a concept Alice internalized deeply.[23]

Attending meeting in Moorestown rounded out Alice's Quaker being. The Pauls knew many of the families who gathered inside the simple brick edifice at the center of town; quite a few were relations. They sat in the unadorned room on long facing benches for a service focused on the inner experience of worship, rather than any outward performance. The meeting communed silently, each member listening for the Light Within and hearing those individuals moved to testify. A small, serious girl could grow comfortable with silence in these hours, year after year, willing herself to reach down into her soul for guidance or simply stay quiet and still. The adult Alice impressed many with her serenity, a quality shaped by Quaker meetings. Her self-possession also deepened there.[24]

Quaker and family history surrounded young Alice, shaping her understanding of generational ties and commitment. The Pauls steeped Alice and her siblings in the Quaker subculture through their large extended family in which aunts, uncles, and cousins abounded. Complex family networks were the legacy of Quaker intermarriage. Relatives and friends easily visited back and forth, as most were only a short buggy ride away. Even after visitors left Paulsdale, the house brimmed with family: records, portraits or photographs of deceased relations, and also chairs, tables, beds, and even an old Paul sampler bequeathed or presented by kin as wedding gifts.[25]

The wider opportunities Hicksite Quakers offered women nurtured Alice and developed her sense of history. The community encouraged, to a point, what few in the larger culture supported: accomplished women. Hicksite belief in gender equality meant Alice enjoyed the same educational opportunities as her brothers. She also experienced women, including single women, playing leadership roles. Her Aunt Abigail Paul, for example, served as a teacher and later a traveling minister; in Abigail's late fifties, Hicksites appointed her assistant clerk of the Yearly

Meeting, the first woman to hold that position. As Alice learned the history of her faith, Lucretia Mott and others provided inspiration beyond her immediate family.[26]

Alice Paul started school at age six, walking or biking the mile into Moorestown. Her photograph that year shows a little girl with a serene look in her big eyes. Her dark hair with a hint of wave parts in the middle and pulls severely back from her face and behind her ears. She wears a high-necked, dark plaid blouse under an ankle-length cotton jumper with ruffled straps. Dark cotton stockings and sturdy black lace-up shoes peek out beneath her skirt hem.[27]

She attended the private Moorestown Friends School, the Hicksite institution built by local members. Indeed, both of Alice's parents helped finance the school and soon sat on its governance committee, one sign of their encouragement and involvement. The school enrolled about 125 students during Alice's years there; her kindergarten class of eleven boys and girls gave Alice her first sustained exposure to non-Quaker children. Orthodox Quakers had established their own academy, and the populations of the Orthodox and Hicksite schools nearly equaled that of the town's public school. The Hicksite school accepted anyone who could pay tuition, though no black children attended until decades later. The weekly tuition—$1.25 for seniors in 1891—kept the school relatively exclusive.[28]

Co-education at the school encapsulated the complexities of the Friends' belief in gender equality. Equality did not mean sameness. As in most public schools of the day, Quakers educated girls and boys in the same classrooms at primary and secondary levels but otherwise preferred to separate the two groups. Any mixing of the sexes outside class was supervised. That left Alice and other students sorting out mixed messages. In truth, Hicksite practices resembled the views of most women's rights activists of the time, who sought legal equality for women while simultaneously believing men and women to be innately different.[29]

Alice received what Quakers called a "guarded" education, a course of study aimed at inculcating "the principles of true religion and virtue." In this age before American education became standardized, the Friends designed and redesigned programs as they wished. They fashioned a nurturing and protective environment. Small school size allowed lots of individual attention, essential to "complete development of the children, physically, morally, and mentally." Students moved through grade levels K–A when teachers believed them ready: Alice would graduate at age sixteen.[30]

Alice Paul's sense of herself as exceptional probably began at the Friends School. She excelled from the early grades, an indication of a native intelligence as well as parental encouragement and example. The curriculum emphasized the "three Rs" and geography. Hicksites had reconsidered earlier bans on art in the schools; elementary students learned to draw. The young scholar Alice tended to procrastinate, perhaps a sign of overconfidence. Cramming for exams became a habit.[31]

The two-hundred-year-old town of three thousand residents around Alice's school changed as she grew up, though her world remained much like the gracious, tree-shaded Quaker community of old. By 1895, the wider world reshaped the town. Though it was still a hub for area farmers, rail connections to Philadelphia drew a thousand new residents, not all the "right kind of new elements," in one chronicler's view. Quakers still dominated many civic institutions and philanthropic efforts, though they now comprised only 15 percent of the population. So they welcomed Philadelphia Quakers seeking respite from the dust and hubbub of city life. Less welcome were black and Irish settlers who followed the well-to-do out of the city for jobs in newfangled industries such as electric lighting and steam heating. Soon Irish families crowded into one neighborhood, blacks into another. Alice interacted mostly with other Hicksites, so she stood largely apart from the diversity, a distance that reinforced her sense of Quaker Otherness.[32]

By her high school years, Alice began to exhibit a voracious desire to pack in as many experiences as she could, both inside and outside the classroom. She struggled to reconcile her ambition with her equally intense reticence. Now a young woman of average build with thick chestnut hair, an oval face, and deep-set blue eyes, Alice felt self-conscious about her "buck" teeth but did not let insecurity deter her activities. She benefited from the Friends' progressive thinking about vigorous exercise for girls—still a controversial idea in mainstream society. Alice loved the physical challenge of sports and became "one of the best batters," one relative recalled; she took up basketball and hockey too. Her athleticism eased her later entry into vigorous social protest.[33]

The leadership capacity so evident in Alice's later life surfaced in more cerebral pursuits. She became an officer of the school literary society and edited the group's magazine. Though constitutionally averse to public speaking, she nevertheless engaged in debate activities, showing an early interest in public policy and beginning a lifelong predilection for testing her limits. She also joined her mother at woman suffrage meetings and probably assisted with local plans to host the state suffrage convention in 1900, the same year the Hicksite Yearly Meeting encouraged individuals to support the cause (although avoided any official endorsement). Suffrage failed to draw Alice's attention.[34]

More than anything else, reading captivated her. The activity appealed to her retiring nature and need to explore. Even in later life, she recalled her passion: "I read just endlessly, ceaselessly, almost every book it seems!" She bragged, "I took out every book in the library." She explored both the Hicksite and public libraries, taking imaginary voyages of self-discovery, journeys the young girl hardly realized she wanted to take. Many in the dominant culture considered too much reading dangerous for the supposedly delicate adolescent female brain; Alice's reading again suggests strong parental and community support. "We just read whatever books there were," she marveled. "And there was pretty nearly everything I can remember. It was a wonder."[35]

The 1,500-volume public library, like the school library, fostered and sheltered her reading. The young adventurer ingested fare that the founding Orthodox Friends deemed educational. Alice found plenty of books on history, biography, and travel, including female-authored titles by renowned Quakers like Lucretia Mott and Sarah Grimke and biographies of heroic women such as Florence Nightingale. She found models of achievement as well as exciting lives to ponder. Not too exciting, though: until 1895, the library constitution banned any "novels, romances, or any works of an immoral tendency."[36]

Nonetheless, Alice found novels at home. In later life, she remembered "reading every single line of Dickens as a child over and over and over and over again." The Pauls owned a full set of the popular English novels; those Hicksites who read fiction embraced Dickens for his moral compass. Alice's adolescent highs and lows harmonized with his larger-than-life characters and emotional drama; she could try on many exotic roles there, roles of either gender. The insatiable young reader ventured beyond Dickens and began developing her personal library. She purchased few books, thinking it impractical to buy when libraries offered access, but treasured those given by family and friends.[37]

She sandwiched her reading between her homework hours. Her studies included four years of Latin, and three each of French and German, plus math, science, composition, history, and drawing. English classes introduced her to new American and British authors; she carried a love of popular Victorian poets Tennyson, Browning, and Longfellow into later life.[38]

Alice prefigured her own future in the valedictory speech she gave at her graduation in the spring of 1901. Drawing on her reading of many biographies, she chose to talk about living legend Florence Nightingale. Her choice of subject indicates that as she looked toward her future, Alice saw no barrier between women and heroic endeavor. Nightingale felt called to serve and refused to accept her society's expectations of her class and gender.[39]

More than eighty thousand American women—double the number in Tacie Paul's years—headed to college in 1901. Still, the number represented fewer than 5 percent of college-aged women. Questions lingered about the value of a higher education for females. Studies of the first two generations of college-educated women showed that a significant proportion remained unwed, suggesting that higher education undermined traditional ideas about a woman's role. Indeed, college graduates sought meaningful, though often unpaid, work in the public sphere; their visibility led observers to dub them "new women." Paid work still held an undesirable taint for elite women, although teaching had acquired some respectability. For women privileged enough to attend, college more often served as a finishing school or a chance to meet potential husbands. Marriage or lack of purpose ultimately derailed many women who, like Tacie Paul, never graduated.[40]

The Pauls fit the usual profile of upper-middle-class families who could afford college. Like many Hicksites, they had long abandoned their prejudice against post-secondary education, historically held as impractical by Quakers. Indeed, Tacie Paul's own college years fueled her enthusiasm for her daughter to attend, particularly at her alma mater Swarthmore, the only Hicksite institution in the nation. Her mother's experience raised Alice's sights. She remembered in later life that her mother told her about the school, how her father William Parry "collected the money with this little committee and founded Swarthmore" in 1864, how he then sent her there to join others in the family. Attending Swarthmore reminded Alice at many levels of the family pedigree and expectations.[41]

The expense of a private college was considerable: in Swarthmore's case, tuition and board cost $400 each year. The Pauls' financial burden eased when Alice won a $150 Williamson Scholarship, an award given to the top student from each of thirteen Quaker high schools in the region. Moorestown Friends presented little competition: the graduating class of '01 numbered five students.[42]

Any trepidation Alice and her parents felt about her leaving the cocoon remained unrecorded. At sixteen, she would join the youngest Swarthmoreans. A June letter from Swarthmore dean of women Elizabeth Powell Bond assured Alice's parents that her education would continue to be "guarded"; she sought the Pauls' assistance in keeping it so. "Inasmuch as one of the chief advantages to students of absence from home is to secure freedom from the nervous strain of combining social pleasures with study," Bond wrote, "it is desired that thy daughter have permission to attend only such social gatherings as are approved by the Faculty." Dean Bond also outlined the limits of female respectability. "It is also expected," she continued, "that permission to visit the city shall not include the privilege of attending the theatre with the young men of the College." Alice saved the letter in the journal she packed, but, judging from her later pursuits, took Bond's admonitions against social pleasures rather lightly.[43]

Though Swarthmore College offered Alice another, if different, Quaker environment, it also added a critical enrichment to her life: the intimacy and woman-centered space afforded by female community. Swarthmore gave Alice Paul the first glimpses of her future, though she hardly realized that at the time. She later regretted spending four years there, wishing she had experienced more than one college. Many features of her Quaker existence carried over to Swarthmore; indeed, the college motto was "Mind the Light."[44] At the time, however, she dove into the new undergraduate experience with gusto, quickly reconstituting a whirlwind schedule for herself. She reveled in her first women's community and tried out dating. Swarthmore introduced her to a number of "new women," some of whom became role models, particularly for the teaching career she later considered. Her freshman journal, the only surviving diary, offers a window on her Swarthmore life and times.

On a rainy afternoon in mid-September 1901, Alice boarded the 2:18 p.m. train to Philadelphia to begin the journey to Swarthmore College. Cousin Mary Parry, a sophomore, joined her; Alice had probably quizzed Mary about college life for months. Switching trains in the city, the two girls settled themselves for the eleven-mile trip south to Swarthmore, the village surrounding the college. They disembarked a half hour later, opened their umbrellas, brushed off the soot, and looked up the grassy sweep to a campus that, to Alice, probably seemed awfully large.[45]

The two young Quakers began the wet trudge up the broad tree-lined walkway to the gray stone edifice dominating the campus. Like other private colleges built in the 1860s, one roof covered much of the institution. Ivied Parrish Hall reached up four grand stories to a mansard dome, then spread east and west into wings housing girls and boys, respectively. As the Moorestown girls reached the crest of the slope, Alice could see the gracious president's house to the left and leafy woods shading the campus on its east flank. To the right, she glimpsed the women's gymnasium. The meetinghouse, science building, and playing fields stood further back, barely visible through the rain and mist.[46]

Alice and Mary climbed the steps and walked into Parrish Hall. They made their way to the third floor, past the dining hall and laundry on the first floor and classrooms and professors' offices on the second. Arriving at Alice's room, they found her roommate, Edith Powell, also sixteen, a brunette with upswept hair and an upturned nose, who spoke with the unusual accent characteristic of Maryland's Eastern Shore.[47]

The crowded room, though smaller than Alice's room at home, mirrored its Quaker plainness. She chose room 90 for its privacy (tucked away at one end of third floor east), convenience (near the back stairs), and frugality (twenty-five dollars cheaper than front rooms). The space crammed in two beds, an armoire for both girls' clothing, and two dressers; a china wash bowl for shampooing hair or washing up rested atop one dresser. Under one bed sat the slop jar, a lure for curious mice. Gas jets provided light, as at home; a newfangled steam heating system generated warmth. Alice looked around for her trunk.[48]

She unpacked a wardrobe suggestive of both the Friends' simplicity and her own generation's movement away from plain dress. By 1901, college girls had appropriated the shirtwaist from laboring women and wore the man-tailored, often high-necked blouses with ankle-length trumpet skirts for classes and casual wear. Much like other collegians, Swarthmore co-eds donned fine dresses for dinner and social hour, a practice underscoring their privileged backgrounds. Ready-to-wear clothes were beginning to compete with the custom creations of local dressmakers or tailors; many households still made women's clothing, but the affluent Pauls did not. Alice wore both manufactured and custom-made clothing.[49]

She cared about both personal style and fashion but pursued them with practicality. Her favorite skirt for college was a custom-made white mohair, which she serviceably dressed up or down with a shirtwaist. She wore fashionable sailor-dress suits for classes along with shirtwaists and skirts, while she used modish dresses of gauzy cotton or linen for meals and a tailor-made suit and ribbon-trimmed hat for train travel. She embraced color, favoring deep red—not coincidentally the college hue—for her suit, hat, and bathrobe. She thought frugally of adapting boys' shirts or buying cheap white gloves; nevertheless, for some essentials like her suit, she chose custom clothing that would last for years. She favored simple lines and pintucks and avoided lace altogether ("Cheap lace is an abomination and good lace is too expensive," she told Helen). Her necklines occasionally stood high, but more often she wore simple linen collars that could be changed out and washed.[50]

Alice eased quickly into college life, the first sign of her adaptability to new environments, despite some social immaturity. At dinner that first evening, she clicked immediately with Serena Miller (Rena), another small-town girl and sixteen-year-old freshman. Rena's joie de vivre and risk-taking captivated Alice. A circle of a dozen or so first-year women evolved in short order, and Alice embarked on a college life focused more on socializing than study. The circle of friends excluded her roommate, whose unfamiliar accent and social awkwardness soon left her an outcast, a state of affairs Alice at first accepted or even encouraged.[51]

Swarthmore meals gave Alice her first taste of the pageantry at which she later excelled. The bells summoning everyone to breakfast, lunch, and dinner in the Parrish dining room signaled the beginning of that most familiar of Swarthmore rituals. Alice recalled the impressive decorum of every meal, notwithstanding the laggards' wild rush downstairs to squeeze in before the doors closed. Each table brought together a few girls, a few boys, and one professor, a group that offered opportunities to engage the opposite sex in conversation on an ongoing basis but discouraged intimacies.[52]

Dean Elizabeth Bond presided at the head table "as though it were her own private dining room," Alice recalled. "You all came in together, you all sat down together; [all observed] grace together, then the boys arose and went out and brought in the food and placed it on the table." The use of student servers was both economical and superficially democratic; it also reversed the usual gender roles by giving boys a domestic role. At the meal's close, "the dean arose," Alice noted, then "all the students arose and with great ceremony walked out behind her." Alice thought, "It was a very dignified and very lovely regime that she had."[53]

She admired the dean of women, who became her first real-life model for a woman-centered life of service. She remembered Bond as a distinguished woman who brought a greater touch of class to the college. In 1901, the sixty-year-old Elizabeth Powell Bond was nearing the end of her many years at Swarthmore. A dignified, sympathetic woman with intense, lively eyes, she unvaryingly appeared in black or gray silk, adorned with a cameo opening to a likeness of her late husband. In Alice's time at the college, Bond led a woman-centered life; she not only served as dean, but enjoyed an intimate friendship with Swarthmore's librarian Sarah Nowell.[54]

Bond cloaked her ambitions for modernizing student life within her poised, gracious manner—a feat that Alice likely noted. The dean of women believed as staunchly in co-education as in good breeding; she knew emphasizing propriety helped offset concerns about college girls becoming mannish. Bond sought to instill proper relationships by mutual respect rather than stern directives. Over her fifteen years in office, she moved the college toward student self-governance and refined intermingling, introducing such rituals as the nightly social hour following the evening meal. She introduced music and dancing to Swarthmore, as well as literary readings—such innovations made her cutting-edge in the Hicksite Quaker world.[55]

Bond's disciplinary responsibility for female students allowed her to exert her influence one-on-one, and her residence in the women's wing strengthened her impact. Alice recalled that she "made it her business to know every girl personally," though we know nothing of the Bond-Paul relationship beyond Alice's admiration and vivid memory of the dean. Bond made herself available to Swarthmore's women during her frequent "at homes," small group meetings in her private quarters where she reminisced about her abolitionist roots or relationships with Louisa May Alcott and famed astronomer Maria Mitchell. Endlessly enthusiastic for reform movements like woman suffrage, she often urged students, "Ally thyself with some great cause." Toward this end, Bond brought activists to speak at the college and forged ties with a Philadelphia settlement house.[56]

If Bond enlarged Alice's sensibilities, she also assisted in circumscribing her world as a young woman. As at Moorestown Friends, Alice learned that the equality of the classroom stopped at the academy door. And Swarthmore limited same-sex as much as opposite-sex social interactions, reacting to cultural fears about unseemly attachments. Girls were expected to keep to the east side of campus and stay out of the parlor and public hallways except at social hour. The dean warned against improper displays, like "girls promenading in public places with arms wrapped about one another" or lingering near the parlor to attract male attention. But some rules proved hard to enforce, including those that stipulated girls walk outdoors in groups rather than pairs.[57]

Bond communicated the gender role prescriptions of both mainstream and Quaker cultures. She delineated the special rules for co-eds as well as general advice on ideal female deportment during her at-homes. She expected rooms quiet after ten thirty each evening, gas jets out by eleven o'clock. She preached hygiene: "Maidens should be as sweet as roses and violets." She believed gossip and "forming the coffee habit" dangerous. She recommended "running on the toes."[58]

The egalitarian academic arena at Swarthmore contrasted with the social sphere: women and men chose from the same four courses of study, a standard in place since 1864. While some universities vacillated over admitting women or belatedly tried to squelch co-education, Swarthmore remained constant, welcoming roughly equal numbers of women and men each year. Of four possible course tracks, nearly half the students chose "letters," essentially a humanities or "arts" program without classical languages. Swarthmore's women, through the years, overwhelmingly preferred arts or letters; fewer than 10 percent opted for science, and none for engineering. Their selections reflected the norms of the prevailing culture, including the few careers open to and the tentative acceptance of paid work for "respectable" women. Most presumed their life's work to be in the home and community. As Bryn Mawr's Quaker president M. Carey Thomas observed, "Until all women become self-supporting, more women than men will go to college for culture."[59]

Alice's uncommon choice of a science major suggests a degree of independence unusual among even her Quaker peers. Like most women, however, she did not consider future careers; she based her choice solely on her own avid love of literature. Nevertheless, "the one thing I don't know anything about," she thought, "and I never would read and I can't understand it or comprehend it or have any interest in it are all the things in the field of science." The voracious Alice signed up for a heavier course load than most of her newfound friends: biology, chemistry, and math classes, as well as three required courses: Bible literature, a language (she took French), and composition. She treated herself to two electives: drawing and painting and elocution, the latter building on her high school interest in debating. As with science, she might not have liked public speaking, but she strove to master it.[60]

As she settled into the Swarthmore routine, Alice resumed her prep school pattern of studying intermittently, then cramming intensely a few days before examinations. Bible literature and elocution proved to be her strengths, while

math became her toughest subject and earned her only failing grades. Her geometry class, taught by Susan Cunningham, presented unique challenges.[61]

Students knew Professor Cunningham as a rigid disciplinarian and, one
recalled, the "terror of timid souls and shirkers." A large, no-nonsense woman, she
sailed the corridors in high-necked plain gowns. Students mimicked her emphatic
catchphrase "Use thy gumption!" in admiration as much as fear, for Cunningham
devoted herself to teaching and to Swarthmore. No matter how qualified, women
found faculty positions hard to come by, especially at co-educational institutions;
most either accepted being channeled into home economics departments or
found a home at a women's college. Swarthmore had hired not only Cunningham
but six other female faculty members, all in the humanities or physical education, a quarter of all teaching positions. Cunningham had earned her doctorate
at Swarthmore and relished the opportunity to lead others down a similar path.[62]

Few students tested their will against Cunningham. Alice crossed her inadvertently after falling asleep while studying for afternoon geometry. In the small class,
Cunningham quickly noted her absence. Alice recorded Cunningham's response
in unusual detail in her journal and took the opportunity to mock her roommate
at the same time:

> Miss Cunningham inquired where I was and [roommate] Edith said,
> "Oh, she's a-coming!" In about ten minutes Miss C. said "Edith, go up
> and tell Alice P. to come right down to Geometry." Edith came trotting
> up and woke me and then trotted back and informed Miss C. that I "was
> a-comin."

After another prompt from Edith fifteen minutes later, the dawdler's defiant posture collapsed. "Hadn't nerve enough to stay away this time," Alice wrote, "so went
down and felt like a fool." The sleepy laggard later "nearly went into spasms" with
her friends. Despite the cattiness, Alice rued the embarrassment and resolved not
to appear foolish again.[63]

Three weeks later, Alice's bluster proved stiffer. After again falling asleep
studying geometry before class, her roommate once more appeared on command
to wake her. Alice told Edith to advise Cunningham she was "suffering from some
disease." The young Quaker's bravado had limits, however; she avoided her other
afternoon class. Cunningham's manner, alone among her professors, continued to
annoy Alice, judging from several further journal entries.[64]

The Cunningham chronicles illustrate Alice's emerging will; moreover, they reveal
the young Quaker coming to terms with her own presence as a woman. Her objections to Cunningham's blunt speech and manner reflected campus sentiment: students made much of differences between Cunningham and the ever-gracious Dean

Bond. Even in a Quaker environment, abruptness in women rankled. Perhaps the professor became a mirror for Alice, an image that discomforted her. When criticized herself for brusqueness in later years, she quickly apologized. Yet Cunningham's strength as well as Bond's refinement shaped Alice's adult persona.[65]

Alice's freshman diary offers a glimpse of a socially active co-ed, a quite different depiction than her historical image as a remote loner. Writing in a spare, reportorial style, she recorded the facts of youthful explorations though little about her motivations or emotions. Her mother wrote in a similar style, judging from one surviving reminiscence. In Alice's journal, notes about social pursuits and college activities predominate. Her interest in socializing prompted a movement away from the Quaker life of her parents: at times she skipped the required First Day meeting to sleep in after a late night or accompany non-Quakers to their church. She often avoided pre-meeting Bible classes and Sunday night hymn-singings.[66]

Alice enthusiastically participated in the female-centered life that flourished amid all the rules and restrictions for Swarthmore's women. Intimate friendships still animated many undergraduates' experiences—indeed their lives—in this era; the crushes on older girls or women commonplace at home developed greater intensity in a dormitory setting. Alice socialized with nearly all the female freshmen at one time or another. She spent the most time with her special friends, including Rena Miller, Anna Holme (Rena's roommate), Ethel Close, and a few others. They talked for hours in the evenings. They played pranks and flaunted the rules by making fudge over the gaslight.[67]

Alice preferred the intensity of one-on-one encounters, which agreed more with her personal modesty. Her diary mentions walks in the woods, tennis games, and rowing on the campus creek, usually with one companion. Close friends commonly shared a bed on campuses at the turn of the twentieth century. Alice carefully noted her sleeping companions, as if she was logging her own popularity or lack thereof. She often slept with Rena during their first months and with Anne or Ethel later in the year. Alice wrote nothing beyond the fact of the bed-sharing, so the meaning of these intimacies to her beyond physical comfort and enjoyment is unclear. However, the young Quaker's love of athleticism hints that other forms of physicality came easily to her too.[68]

If any college relationship moved beyond physical to erotic, it was likely Alice's abbreviated fling with the irrepressible Rena Miller, who truly delighted her, perhaps by contrast with herself. Rena was outgoing, even brash, and full of creative mischief, and Alice quickly became willing to take risks for her. Before the end of their first week, the two girls stood out on the fire escape singing. "At ten Rena & I climbed down the fire escape and then down the ladder & went to the village," Alice reported in her journal. Their after-hours adventure went undetected and the two continued to skirt rules and pull pranks.[69]

Six weeks later, Alice sensed the delicate balance required to pursue her own life while dependent upon parental funds. She distanced herself from Rena rather than test parental forbearance. Apparently the Pauls admonished their daughter to behave better after receiving notice that Alice often was tardy to meals and retired too late at night. Though Alice reduced her socializing with Rena, she could not resist recording her chum's exploits occasionally. While everyone crammed for finals, for example, she reported that Rena "[tore] down every 'busy' sign on every hall because she doesn't believe in studying and thinks fresh air much more important." But now, Alice admired such insouciance from afar.[70]

As Alice adopted a more cautious tack, a less iconoclastic friend replaced Rena in her life. The Quaker Ethel Close, from New York City, was four years Alice's senior and another science major. They could study together and make common cause in a subject area that few women chose. The two took long walks, shared a bed occasionally, and even ventured into Philadelphia, sharing more tame adventures rather than pranks. In the spring, Alice wrote, "Ethel and I sat up in the moonlight til 12:00 o'clock in hall window."[71]

Alice's relationship with her roommate Edith matured along with her friendships. At first, she avoided Edith or joined in the ridicule of the young Quaker with the unusual accent and dialect, her behavior underscoring the distinction between spiritual and social equality among Friends. After one such prank, Alice impassively reported, "In the morning, Edith wept and lamented on the way she was treated." As the year progressed, Alice began to accept, if not appreciate, Edith's differences. In the winter, she began socializing occasionally with her roommate. Edith Powell never entered the special circle, but the two young women apparently made their peace.[72]

Alice and her circle happily fell in with the larger social whirl of Swarthmore, from football games to receptions and club activities. In these mixed-sex venues, Alice explored the world of heterosexual relationships in supervised settings. She shared her dining table with several young men, including the other Moorestown Friends grad and fellow science major, Will Linton. Alice received fewer invitations to social hour than some of her classmates, but she attended once with Linton and several times each with two other boys. Alice tallied up the boys she dated or refused, recording her interest in exploring opposite as well as same-sex relationships.[73]

By contrast with Alice's female friendships, young men became only a footnote in her Swarthmore experience. Her combination of reticence and self-assurance may have confused young men; she felt little need to flatter potential suitors, it seemed, though her diary entries seem more blunt than her conversations with male companions. She noted an ice-skating excursion one December day, during which she had the "misfortune to skate three times with Hansell," a boy she also knew from home. Alice kept trying to discourage him by feigning fatigue, but the boy—oblivious—sat down to wait with her until her weariness passed. "So obliging," she later wrote dryly. She resisted one invitation to social hour, offering an excuse; the boy promptly asked her for the following night and "there was nothing to do," she groaned, "but accept." Her same-sex relationships remained her priority.[74]

Alice became increasingly invested in Swarthmore, while her Moorestown existence receded inexorably. She returned home only once beyond school holidays. Her mother visited a few times, as did other Moorestown friends or relatives. Alice felt warmly enough about her old high school to visit on her way home for Thanksgiving. She never mentioned home or family in the journal beyond these times, though letters probably passed back and forth. The Pauls had now acquired a telephone, but long-distance calling remained prohibitively expensive with dicey connections. Clearly, though, Alice gave herself over to the crowded days and festive nights of college.[75]

She made up for all the socializing with long cram sessions. Even those failed to improve her scores in the male-identified subjects like chemistry, despite her desire for mastery. One midyear cram involved making strong coffee to study algebra and geometry through dinner until two thirty in the morning and again starting at dawn. "Have never studied so in my life," she declared. Her grades ended up fine in Bible literature, elocution, and French, less so in the science and math classes.[76]

She gave more of herself to physical activity. Like Moorestown, Swarthmore encouraged exercise, including dancing. Alice picked up dancing quickly (single-sex only) and loved it. Her first Saturday night, she "danced whole evening and had glorious time." She joined spontaneous dancing in the dorm hall, the informal dances in the gymnasium, and the dances for more formal occasions. At the Halloween dance, she waltzed and two-stepped with Rena, Ethel, and eleven other girls, tucking her dance card into her diary to treasure.[77]

Alice continued to delight in sports as well. When Crum Creek froze over, she took every advantage of the all-too-brief skating season. Like others, she endured the awful bloomer suits required for gym class—one classmate wailed, "We looked like elephants!"—but enjoyed getting back to the games she played in high school. She joined the basketball team in February. Between that and tennis, rowing, and long walks (and rushing up and down the Parrish Hall stairs), Alice kept herself fit despite gaining twelve pounds her first year.[78]

On the last Saturday in April, a telegram arrived telling Alice to return home. She hurried past the fragrant cherry trees blooming on the great lawn and rushed down the hill to the train station. Unbeknown to her, her mother had cranked the big telephone box at Paulsdale a day earlier to tell the bank trustees that her husband's cold had progressed to pneumonia. Tacie Paul phoned her best friends, William and Tacy Lippincott, on Sunday. Young Engle Conrow, who lived with the Lippincotts, heard the new telephone ringing. Then, he later recalled, "I remember William saying, 'I am very sorry indeed.'"[79]

2

"We Will Find a Way, or We Will Make One"

ALICE MAY NOT have reached her parents' hushed bedroom in Paulsdale before her father died that Saturday in April. In 1902, death commonly arrived at any age; pneumonia claimed lives with breathtaking speed. William Mickle Paul's passing at fifty-three mirrored the premature death of his father and presaged the early demise of his two sons. Alice had already experienced death in the family: two maternal uncles and the revered Aunt Abigail Paul had died in her youth, but these were all relatives at a greater emotional remove than her father.[1]

Family support helped Alice, her mother, and her siblings confront the vacuum left without her father's strong presence. Extended family rallied around the stricken Pauls, forming a circle of psychological comfort and practical aid that continued for years. Unlike many widows, Tacie Paul was spared financial worries: William Paul left a considerable estate in land, real estate, and stocks; his salary from the bank did not provide their primary source of wealth. In the aftermath of his death, his wife learned to effectively manage the Paul assets, with assistance from a brother and cousin. Tacie soon made one change that hinted at marital differences: she purchased a piano in order to grant Helen's long-standing request for lessons.[2]

Alice returned to Swarthmore a week after her father's death and chose not to grieve for him in her journal, both facts underlining the Pauls' stoicism as well as the Quaker practical-minded focus on the living. In old age, she reflected dispassionately, "I was too young for [my father's death] to be much of a blow to me. Life went on just the same." At the time, however, the shock of his sudden death undoubtedly resonated; the long walks with a friend she noted on her first days back hint at her struggle to adjust to the loss.[3]

Her father's death shaped Alice's prospects, perhaps without any realization on her part. Her trauma was lessened by its timing. She had already separated, physically and psychologically, from her parents. Her father had ample opportunity to influence her character; indeed, her two siblings who came of age after William Paul's death turned out to be far more gregarious than Alice, which suggests the impact of his sternness on her personality. The family wealth ensured that her life continued much as before. Her father's strong presence as she matured might have become a roadblock for Alice; but in his absence, his daughter became free to invent her own future. Moreover, as the eldest, she may have felt some responsibility to familial history to continue his record of achievement, in a sense retrieving his fallen standard.[4]

In the few weeks remaining of Alice's freshman year, she resumed her college routines. Despite the crush of finals and the lingering memories of her father, she seemed serene. "Went walking with Ethel in evening and sat on Meeting House porch till late at night—was moonlight and glorious," she wrote. After year-end revelries and posing for newfangled Brownie snapshots with friends, Alice rode the train with Rena into Philadelphia, then headed for home, one emptier than in memory. Her journal noted simply, "Freshman year over." She clipped and pasted an epilogue on her first college year: "the dear, free days that slip away but too soon," a sentiment that could also serve as a valediction for her father.[5]

When Alice returned to Swarthmore in the fall, she found a campus reorienting itself to the new century. College trustees persuaded the highly regarded Quaker Joseph Swain to take on the task of making Swarthmore the equal of prestigious private eastern colleges. Students quickly rallied behind his efforts, as he promised self-government and fewer restrictions; nevertheless, he reassured parents and patrons that female students still required a guarded education. So Dean Bond acquired an ally in loosening some constraints on women, though in Alice's time the changes proved slight.[6]

Alice studied in earnest now, perhaps sensing wider possibilities. She searched for her place in the world. No journal beyond the first year survives, but her student record tells the tale. Her grades improved steadily until, in her last two years, she achieved all As (save one B in chemistry). She excelled equally at stereotypically male and female subjects. She hung a busy sign on her door more often, studying into the night and acquiring a reputation as a serious scholar. Her voracious curiosity persisted: she took on extra courses, considered going into medicine—she cheekily thought doctors always seemed so ill-informed—and signed up for anatomy and physiology courses as well as German and art history. College requirements exposed her to political science for the first time and more courses in public speaking as well.[7]

Two professors exerted the most influence on her education. Alice took every class the beloved Jesse Holmes offered. A maverick even in liberal Hicksite circles, the rumpled Holmes acquired a reputation for influencing students profoundly. His Socratic teaching methods—in Bible literature, philosophy, history, or psychology—whirled young minds around in a shared inquiry, "fascinating and often scandalizing his students," according to one Swarthmore history. "There were few like him on any college campus anywhere." One classmate recalled his forward-looking mind and technique, saying he "made more impression on me than any of the rest." Indeed, Alice began considering teaching as a vocation.[8]

Jesse Holmes introduced students to the new "Progressive" ideas about social and political reform, connecting them with Quakerism. He agreed with mainstream reformers that "old formulas [had] lost their power and the new faith [was] yet 'without form.'" He favored woman suffrage activism and embraced socialist ideas about property and race relations, notions disdained by most Hicksites. He lived his principles by standing for public office several times. Holmes became a controversial figure among the Friends. Alice later came to understand his frustration as he tried to encourage Quakers to shape a world fast remaking itself.[9]

Alice gained a heightened social conscience from Holmes's classes, and these principles were strengthened and enlarged by her political science and economics classes with Robert C. Brooks. She took political science only to meet Swarthmore requirements, but unexpectedly loved Brooks's classes. Purely by happenstance, Alice encountered two men deeply engaged in shaping the emerging field of political science. The first, Brooks, was one of President Swain's new faculty recruits. His interest in combining political work and social activism to effect change represented the leading edge of his field. Only ten years Alice's senior, Brooks honed his pragmatism during a year of settlement house work and later explorations of social reform in Germany. His remarks about the benefits of living abroad gave Alice's German-language classes a new dimension.[10]

Celebrated visitors sowed more Progressive ideas into collegiate life. Swain's good friend and president of Stanford University, David Starr Jordan, blew in with a snowstorm to speak about the "Call of the Twentieth Century." Striking a Quaker chord, he told students the new century valued usefulness not to oneself but to the larger world. Pacifist Bertha von Suttner and social work pioneer Florence Kelley also spoke on campus. Alice recalled her youthful Moorestown activities when the college opened its doors to woman suffrage leader Carrie Chapman Catt in late 1902, six weeks after the death of pioneer Elizabeth Cady Stanton. One student wrote Catt had "such a commanding presence that we could not help listening to every word she said," but few students had any interest in the suffrage cause. Alice felt no urgency about the issue; like most Quakers, she assumed its eventuality.[11]

Alice engaged in a wide variety of extracurricular pursuits, her college days the antithesis of the single-mindedness that later became her hallmark. She continued playing basketball and hockey and kept up debate activities as well. As a consequence of Swarthmore's small size, most students active in campus life assumed one or more leadership roles during their college years. Alice, clearly moving in the thick of things, helped lead the literary society, the Girls' Athletic Club, and the new student government.[12]

Her peers took note of the self-assurance young men found intimidating. When the members of her own junior class published the college yearbook, Alice found herself taken down a notch. The irreverent "Knocks" column borrowed from Shakespeare to advise her, "Mend your speech a little/Lest it mar your fortunes." Her willingness to speak her mind apparently startled more than just potential suitors. While such criticisms failed to tamp down Alice's candor, she undoubtedly came to understand that most people preferred women who minded their tongue.[13]

Alice's circle of intimates widened to include Moorestown friends and relatives. Susanna Parry arrived in Alice's junior year. A favorite cousin, Susanna brought a sense of home, and the two cousins shared some classes after Susanna also chose biology as her major. Elizabeth Lippincott, a Moorestown School and meeting acquaintance, also arrived in 1903. Decades later, she still felt grateful for Alice teaching her the art of the two-step and the waltz so unfamiliar to Moorestown Friends.[14]

The second semester of her junior year, Alice befriended classmate Mabel Vernon when both girls entered a campus extemporaneous speaking contest. Vernon recalled, "My whole future was affected, although I didn't know it at the time." The two strolled along Crum Creek and talked. Like Alice, Mabel had lost her father suddenly. Alice began to grasp her own privilege when she learned that financial and other consequences of Mr. Vernon's death kept Mabel from college for a year. A plain young woman whose warmth and dynamism radiated from her intense blue eyes, Mabel won the speaking contest, while Alice—who predicted Mabel's win and her own lesser success—scored a finalist rank. The two became best friends at Swarthmore and colleagues in later years.[15]

By senior year, Alice began to think about life after Swarthmore. Change surrounded her, from the freshmen arriving at a newly vigorous college, to the electric lights that began to illuminate the classrooms, to President Swain's opening-day exhortation to "put away childish things." Alice had discarded the idea of a medical career and now considered something more female-appropriate. Dorm mates who needed paid work began writing to schools about teaching positions. Alice did not need to work—she apparently felt confident of her mother's financial support—but contemplated teaching in the absence of clear alternatives. She loved learning and had enough ease in a school setting to teach. Unexpectedly, Professor Brooks led her in another direction.[16]

As with the selection of her science major, Alice found direction by dint of her own curiosity. Late in her senior year, she recalled, Brooks offered her a College Settlement scholarship; her memory downplays any ambition on her part. In reality, she may have applied. The College Settlement Association had chapters at more than a dozen colleges; it gave one of its scholarships to Swarthmore, sponsoring a year's work for a graduate based at one of their three settlement houses. When the professor told Alice she could both work in New York City and simultaneously attend the School of Philanthropy, the only institution attempting to teach social work, the young lover of learning embraced the idea. The scholarship aspect not only appealed to her frugality; it provided a ready excuse to any objections her mother might raise. She appreciated the scholarship far more than another honor that soon came her way.[17]

"To my great horror and amazement," the elderly Alice recalled, "suddenly I was told that I was the Ivy Poet," the student selected to compose and deliver the annual pre-commencement poem. The planting of a sprig of ivy, a Swarthmore tradition, accompanied recitation of a ceremonial poem and oration. In her habitually self-deprecating way, Alice claimed she found the honor "a great tragedy." Reminiscing about the event offered her an opportunity to underscore how much she always disliked public speaking and minimize the presentation skills she had honed since high school. "I struggled away and I struggled away" with the poem, she remembered. She then appealed to Mabel for help, who "undertook very religiously to have me practice and practice and practice my poem." Her reading of the poem at Class Day went well; she ended with the age-old promise to be steadfast: "Keep our heart ever loyal to classmates,/In a friendship that time shall not chill."[18]

At a rain-soaked commencement the following day, Alice and thirty-six others officially completed their Swarthmore years. About half of Swarthmore's freshmen persisted until graduation, women in parity with men. This fact suggests that, despite the societal pressures against achievement on even Quaker women, they embraced higher education. Rena Miller and Ethel Close also graduated. Alice did not bid farewell to all: she planned to see Ethel in the fall as she began her settlement house year in New York City, the latter's hometown. Some women in her graduating class "planned to start in and support themselves," Alice recalled, while those without a financial imperative "just supposed they'd go home, live at home and maybe they would marry." In fact, most of her Swarthmore circle of friends, with the notable exception of 1906 grad Mabel Vernon, married within a few years, a fact suggesting they welcomed equal opportunity but not unorthodox paths in life. Alice heeded the call to serve, though in the spring of 1905, she scarcely knew where that might lead her. For the time, she set her sights on New York and social work, both well outside of the guarded Quaker realm.[19]

Home in Moorestown for the summer, Alice read with an eye to her future. She refreshed her enjoyment of lyrical poetry about nature with a book by Sidney Lanier. Her most telling choice, however, was a novel by George Eliot, whose books, a young Jane Addams wrote in 1885, gave "me more motive power than any other books I read." The title character in *Romola* struggles with duty to family and religion, finally casting off strictures to forge an independent life for herself. As later events would show, Alice faced much the same dilemma.[20]

She saved a sojourn at Squirrel Inn in the Catskill Mountains for her last summer days. Her capable Aunt Hannah Paul had established the resort inn a few years back; it catered primarily to Quakers. Alice and her siblings loved spending time in the mountains. She picnicked and walked in the woods, learned bridge and lawn bowling, with lodgers both young and older. Many knew her relatives or friends, and others lived in the city soon to be her new home.[21]

In the few letters home that survive from this year, Alice betrayed little trepidation about living in a non-Quaker environment for the first time. However, she seemed grateful when the opportunity arose for her to have an escort into New York. She wrote her mother, "A good many N. York people have given me their addresses & asked me to visit them." One couple extended themselves: "Mr. and Mrs. Hedrick—two people of about 30 yrs. Asked me to go home with them yesterday & spend the night & then they would take me to the Settlement." Easing Alice's entry further, Ethel Close had promised to meet her that first day.[22]

Alice Paul's year in New York City drew her, like Romola, into an exotic and turbulent environment unlike anything she had experienced before. Only letters and a year-end thesis offer clues about her response to her first taste of an adult life outside a Quaker community. Certainly, the strangeness of the territory was softened by the settlement house community, an even more woman-centered world than her Swarthmore dormitory. She would interact with pioneer "new women," including leading figures in social reform, as well as other young women fresh from college and searching for a path in life. She found opportunities to gauge her own worth and weigh her life choices. What she discovered led her to a new appreciation of politics.

As Alice rode with the Hedricks to the College Settlement House on New York's Lower East Side, she looked out at territory quite foreign to her experience. A cacophony of sound exploded as they neared Rivington Street, which ceaselessly swirled with activity. Masses of people converged, congregating around pushcarts piled with glistening fish or colorful vegetables, peddlers bawling, customers haggling. Above the teeming street, women hung out wash and called from windows. The energy and the sounds of survival mingled with a profusion of smells: from sweat and garlic to baking bread, overripe produce, offal, and horse dung.[23]

She came among people who, like her own ancestors, reached out for religious and political freedom. The neighborhood around the settlement house at 95 Rivington Street had filled with immigrants in recent years; during Alice's time, many were Jews fleeing pogroms in Russia or persecution in eastern Europe.

Whatever their ancestry, most around Rivington Street lived in dire poverty or one notch above it. Yet the vitality of the neighborhood was undeniable.[24]

Walking into the settlement house, Alice found a more familiar world, one physically and emotionally reminiscent of Swarthmore. The lovely old mansion, like Parrish Hall, housed residents as well as work spaces. Spacious rooms with sliding doors accommodated resident dining, large assemblies, and parties. Alice loved her assigned room: "On 3rd floor—one large window—it is the nicest room in the house except the head workers for it has the best light, biggest mirror etc," she wrote her brother Parry. "The light is perfect—better than I ever had at college." As at Swarthmore, servants shielded the elite residents from the mundane: cooks prepared residents' meals and washerwomen did the laundry. The resident community of women at the core of the settlement house replicated many aspects of Swarthmore living, easing the young Quaker's way into her first "unguarded" experience. "This is a grand place," she proclaimed.[25]

Her letters, most from the early months, are crammed as much with tourist activities as with her settlement work or schooling. Despite her sheltered past, she expressed no anxiety but thrived on exploring her new world, adapting as easily as she had to college. Her chum Ethel Close helped smooth her initiation. The very first day, Ethel "took me all over N. York—through stores, restaurants, everywhere," Alice wrote her mother. Other days, they attended meeting and dined at Ethel's home. One afternoon, "we went to the Metropolitan Art Museum & then rode from one end of 5th Ave. to the other in the 5th Ave. stage—sitting up on top." With Ethel to abet her, Alice ventured into worlds beyond what Dean Bond (or her mother) might approve. The two girls joined another Swarthmore alum one afternoon to visit the Yiddish theater and, later that evening, the Italian theater: "We were the only women in the house," Alice crowed, exulting in the thrill of erasing earlier boundaries.[26]

She welcomed visitors. Ethel remained her closest companion, and she came every Sunday to play the house piano for guests and share Alice's bed. Other friends from Swarthmore and home also stopped by when visiting the city, including her mother and Aunt Hannah.[27]

She readily socialized with other residents, though twenty-year-old Alice was several years younger than most. The other scholarship women hailed mostly from single-sex colleges like Smith, Vassar, and Wellesley. One woman showed her around Chinatown and another corralled her into a double date with two visiting collegians. The four hopped the boat to Staten Island, then the trolley for an island tour, returning to Rivington Street at one o'clock in the morning. Alice wrote more enthusiastically about the excursion than about the men, whom she found "quite nice." Her interest in social life soon became secondary.[28]

Her work for the settlement house immersed her in ongoing efforts at social reform as well as worker activism. She particularly remembered helping working women form a union and likely witnessed the growing pains of the New York chapter of the Women's Trade Union League (NYWTUL). These women had not gained the visibility of the more privileged "new women"; however, for decades, industrialization had opened new categories of work to women, particularly in factories and, increasingly, offices. Now, they were starting to organize to gain better working conditions.[29]

Alice felt intrigued by the expressions of Judaism in the neighborhood. During the High Holidays, she sent her younger brother a Jewish New Year's card, telling him about shops closing and pushcarts leaving for the holiday. "From our bathroom," she wrote Parry, "we can look into the window of the synagogue. It is crammed with men and women—singing & chanting." She recommended two books to her brother, if he wanted to learn more, as she scrambled to do herself.[30]

The settlement house's fall election activities became Alice's introduction to political work, in those days before the tax code forbade combining social service with politics. Workers sent children out with campaign literature, then charged Alice and others with double-checking poster displays. She gamely walked miles through the teeming streets, tipping her head back to see posters high atop buildings. "People thought we were intoxicated," she told her mother. "It was the most absurd thing to do but somebody had to do it." As election day arrived, she dryly noted that "votes were five dollars apiece around here." A settlement house group trouped sixty blocks to see election returns. "It was like a carnival night," Alice rhapsodized. "The streets were so crowded that policemen on horseback had to force a path for the street cars." New York was a far cry from Swarthmore or Moorestown.[31]

Alice chose the College Settlement House because of its proximity to the New York School of Philanthropy (NYSP). Just as she shared in Swarthmore's maturing under President Swain, now she experienced a pioneering institution coming into its own. Founded in 1898 to train social service professionals and volunteers, the NYSP combined lectures with social agency visits and fieldwork. Progressives engaged in social action around the country signed on as lecturers, eager to professionalize their passions. The course of study had expanded just a year earlier from a summer lecture series to a full-year course, a change sustained by a 66 percent increase in registrations from forty-six to sixty-nine students in Alice's year. The NYSP eventually became the School of Social Work at Columbia University, but in Alice's day, the school was still in pursuit of academic respectability.[32]

Most students were college-educated women like her, many expecting to volunteer rather than seek paid work. She struck up a friendship with socialite and social reformer Mary Dreier, a founder of the NYWTUL. Older than most students at thirty, Dreier already worked organizing factory girls; Alice probably saw her at union meetings as well. Mary Dreier, like most NYSP students, did not complete the NYSP course of study—a fact that underlined its ambiguous academic status.[33]

Nonetheless, NYSP introduced Alice to some of the movers and shakers in social reform, including settlement house directors and Progressive academics who encouraged this new social work in their classrooms. In her later endeavors, she reconnected with quite a few, underscoring the tightly woven elite reform networks of the era. Jane Addams was among the school's lecturers, although apparently not in the year Alice attended. However, Addams's former co-worker Florence Kelley (a one-time Swarthmore speaker) gave impassioned lectures on urban destitution; she had founded the National Consumers' League to lobby against sweatshops and child labor. Public health activist Lavinia Dock offered talks on nursing and social work; Dock lived at the Nurses' Settlement around the corner from the College Settlement and occasionally asked Alice to join her canvassing in the neighborhood. Alice came to know Dock and Kelley well enough to call on them for help a few years later. Noted Progressive and political economist Simon Patten gave a special series of lectures on social reform. Patten and his young University of Pennsylvania colleague, sociologist Carl Kelsey, influenced Alice's later academic choices.[34]

Alice probably stood out to the NYSP faculty as one of the more serious students. She piled up two dozen credits beyond the requirements, replicating her Swarthmore pattern of exceeding expectations. Her demanding schedule included making her way uptown to the United Charities building at Park and 22nd for morning lectures, periodic field trips to social agencies, studying, examinations, and eventually a short thesis, all in addition to her work at the settlement house. She tried to cover all bases with her courses, taking on basic social work methods and the administration of agencies, plus specialized treatment for families and criminals.[35]

She returned to the settlement house to take on multiple, ongoing tasks, a challenge that helped prepare her for administrative work. She primarily assisted the paid workers with running clubs for local residents, but sometimes took up clerical duties in addition to political errands. The College Settlement House saw its mission as social and intellectual as opposed to the intensive family intervention focus of other settlements in the neighborhood. Its program concentrated on classes and related clubs providing "wholesome recreation," including three dozen choices in cooking, manual arts and trades, and dressmaking. Though unused to stitchery beyond simple mending, Alice took over a sewing club and probably learned more than she taught, though she hustled to keep ahead of club members.

She happily took the gymnasium club and purchased a gym suit so she could enjoy the physical activity too. Alice no doubt spoke of herself as much as the boys in the club when she later wrote of the new gym, "Nothing had been more needed...[or] more appreciated."[36]

Her Quaker affiliation lent her some perspective about the neighborhood. In New York, she grew conscious of the uncommonness of her faith. She knew of the historic Quaker struggle for acceptance and the contemporary concerns about dwindling membership, and these were potential connections to the surrounding Jewish community. Indeed, there is no trace in her letters of the anti-Semitism with which some historians have charged her. Her attitude implicitly rejected both the condescension often reported of settlement house workers and the disdain for Others evident in the Paul home. Instead, she allowed her native curiosity to lead her; she maintained the professional distance her classes encouraged and surely felt the class distinction as well, but her openness to learning steered her toward identifying with, rather than objectifying, community members.

She realized that the Americanizing forces of the settlement house and the larger culture threatened Jewish immigrants' way of life. Her thesis applauded a settlement house effort to maintain personal dignity: members paid a small fee for each club, "so that the idea of charity is avoided." She noted, "Each member feels a sense of possession in the House and contributes what he can toward its improvement." Alice further commented on a misguided College Settlement House effort to take children to see a Broadway show one Friday evening. "It was with difficulty that forty were found who could go, owing to the Jewish custom which forbids the riding on the cars on 'Shabba,'" she wrote. "Child after child that had joyfully accepted the invition [sic] came back to say that her father would not allow it." Alice understood the fathers' dilemma and wrote about "the loyalty with which the old Hebrew traditions are preserved in the neighborhood."[37]

By the summer of 1906, Alice believed that settlement houses were ultimately not "doing much good." Her thesis declared:

> Twelve women, even though aided by a large body of associate workers, can make no impression on a neighborhood as a whole where there are from two to three thousand in a block and where moving is constant. The College Settlement finds its district more congested than seventeen years ago, its streets as filthy as ever, its children still turned away from school. Nothing fundamental seems to have been accomplished.

Alice became convinced that municipal governments were better equipped to handle the volume of need settlement house workers struggled to meet, a conclusion many Progressives shared and had already acted upon. Indeed, she saw this already happening, as schools began to embrace some of the educational work of the settlements.[38]

Alice's assessment of her own experience underlies the settlement house appraisal presented in her thesis. She found the settlement's value in the awakening political consciousness of its residents, a judgment suggesting that her political work in New York influenced her the most. "Gradually [residents'] whole point of view is changed by the impressions constantly pouring in on their subconscious selves," she concluded. "This new sympathy impels them to work more earnestly, the new understanding enables them to work more effectively, for the social wellfare [sic]." The settlement house should exist, Alice decided, in order to "move public opinion."[39]

As the school year ended, Alice took on her first paid job, more rewarding work which also allowed her to try on a new identity. She accepted a job as a "visitor," a sort of caseworker (a term not yet coined) for the Charity Organization Society (COS), a precursor to the United Way as a social service clearing house. She had taken on similar, but unpaid, work in the spring. Taking the COS job indicated her willingness to present herself as a less privileged woman than she actually was. She began occasionally signing letters with the more professional-sounding "AP," one hint to her evolving self. Her salary—$45 a month —was "not munificent," she told her mother, "but the experience will be valuable."[40]

Compared to her club work at the College Settlement House, Alice felt a sense of accomplishment and remembered the experience as "marvelous." "I was assistant to an exceedingly experienced social worker," she recalled. In an age before public assistance, private organizations worked together to provide social services to the poor. As she recalled, "So you would be sent to somebody who was needing medical attention and then you would try to call up the hospitals and so on that she might be eligible for and get her in and get it for her. Just all day long. So you got to know the city of New York in places which were sort of the underground places—not *underground*, but the underlayer of people who were up against it." Visiting provided the first extended opportunity for AP to observe living conditions in the tenements and meet women with meager resources. Her contemporary Margaret Sanger found her life calling in similar circumstances a few years later. Alice did not share Sanger's epiphany, but she began to feel more hopeful about social work, though not enough to make a career of it. At summer's end, she headed home to Moorestown, feeling unsure about her next step.[41]

"I had learned enough to know that I didn't know anything," Alice remembered. Her interest in politics, sparked at Swarthmore by Robert Brooks, surged with the new political consciousness she gained during her settlement house year. She wanted to know more, and the obvious place for her to learn, she decided, was graduate school, studying political science. Most graduate schools admitted

women by 1906, though some still refused to grant women degrees. AP could
return to New York and attend New York University or Columbia. Her mother
agreed to finance her studies but may have insisted her daughter study closer to
home. Nearby Princeton did not accept women, but Philadelphia's University of
Pennsylvania did. Alice began graduate school there in October 1906.[42]

Alice's first year at the University of Pennsylvania laid the foundation for her
later conversion to woman-centered political reform. The little we know about
Alice Paul's master's work hints at its importance for her later interest in suffrage.
In her first experience of an institution that marginalized women, she devoted
herself to political inquiry.

At the University of Pennsylvania, Alice quickly reconstituted a semblance
of a women's community. Since no campus housing existed for female graduate
students, AP and a NYSP classmate, Carrie Gauthier, found rooms in one of the
university-sanctioned boarding houses, this one at 330 South 42nd Street, a half
mile west of campus. Clara Thompson, a classics student from St. Louis, joined
them. Thompson became "the friend I knew best" at Penn, Alice remembered. An
outstanding scholar, Thompson went on to a teaching career at several small colleges. Unfortunately, little direct knowledge of AP's year at Penn is available: only
one letter survives. Later records make clear, though, that Alice, Carrie, and Clara
stayed in contact long after they had all left Philadelphia.[43]

The Penn administration educated women only grudgingly. Certain departments of the university had admitted graduate women on an equal basis with
men since the 1880s; yet in the fall of 1906, women comprised fewer than 15 percent of the 339 graduate students. A barely functioning Graduate Department of
Women offered scant guidance to these intrepid souls. Undergraduates fared even
worse. Despite attempts from within and without the university to introduce
co-education, only Penn's music and biology departments admitted undergraduate women, though some individuals gained admission through special petition.
Nationally, however, women comprised more than a third of all collegians.[44]

Thus, among the nearly four thousand students on the entire campus, the
fifty women in master's or doctoral programs barely registered amid the whole,
while at the same time individual women sat conspicuously in classes filled with
men. Graduate women felt the need to carve out their own literal and symbolic
space and turned to each other for support. As Alice Paul later remarked, "We
got to know each other very well." In addition to her roommates, Alice already
knew three of the seven Swarthmore alumnae. Nearly half of the remaining
female grad students hailed from women's colleges, with Wellesley especially well
represented.[45]

Alice's academic choices made female friendships particularly difficult to nour-
ish. At Swarthmore, while women were a minority in some classes, the smaller

and gender-balanced student body mitigated isolation. At Penn, only one other graduate woman majored in political science; Carrie Kilgore (Swarthmore '03) joined AP in those classes. Alice's sociology and economics classes did include a few women, however.[46]

The campus combined the rural peace of Swarthmore and the relentlessly urban NYSP non-campus: Penn thrived with activity, though it was sheltered in some corners from the city's hubbub. The roommates walked to class along Spruce Street and busy Woodland Avenue. They strolled beneath memorial gates leading onto campus; one inscription read, as if directed at women, "In Veniemus viam avt facimus" ("We will find a way, or we will make one"). On land sloping gently toward the curving Schuylkill River, nearly a dozen massive more-or-less Gothic structures silhouetted the campus. Alice usually threaded her way to class through groups of young men to Logan Hall, the former medical school.[47]

Moving in an ambiguous campus space, Alice inevitably became more conscious of her gender identity. Now twenty-one, she lived more independently than ever before, no longer subject to the eagle eye of a dean or even a head settlement house resident. She knew the differential constraints on women in terms of social mores and career aspirations. She had seen at close range in New York the ways poverty cinched women in. Now, for the first time, she likely realized that knowledge itself, the learning she voraciously pursued since childhood, this could be denied her. A number of her professors and fellow students no doubt mirrored the institutional doubt about women's capacity. AP had never experienced minority status in the way she stood out in Penn's political science courses, an exceedingly uncomfortable visibility for one who disliked the spotlight. Perhaps unsurprisingly, the two mentors she found among her professors were both in sociology, a specialty that recognized how women's contributions in the form of settlement work were shaping applied sociology.

Seventy years later, Alice seemed to forget the barriers she faced and remembered receiving "great joy" from her coursework at Penn. Professor Simon Patten influenced her profoundly; his lectures at NYSP may have drawn her to Penn. She took only two classes from the German-trained Patten. Alice recalled, "Patten was a great, great, great teacher," a sentiment often voiced by his students. He probably reminded AP of Jesse Holmes at Swarthmore; Patten's rural upbringing and Republican loyalties also linked to her past. By the end of the year, she decided to follow his career path.[48]

Twice a week, Alice listened, or rather experienced, the awkward, gangling fifty-four-year-old Patten challenging students to pit their callow minds against his. Patten's forthcoming Progressive masterwork, *The New Basis of Civilization* (1907), foresaw an economy based not on production, but consumption, an economy producing enough wealth to eliminate poverty and turn surpluses not to materialistic indulgence but to the greater good of meeting social needs. Patten's vision squared with Alice's Quaker notions of frugal and ethical living and embraced the hands-on social casework that she enjoyed the previous summer. At the same time, Patten's work reminded her how rewarding a teaching career might be.[49]

Patten's focus on change carried over into Alice's political science course with a professor whose ideas re-emerged in her later work. AP's insight into the political process matured in his classes, though he probably did not serve as a mentor. Henry Jones Ford, a fifty-six-year-old author and newspaper editor-cum-academic was, like Robert Brooks at Swarthmore, actively shaping his emerging field. The American Political Science Association, founded only three years earlier, framed its mission as studying workaday politics. Brooks at Swarthmore exemplified the new interest in how the public in a democracy expressed its will through political parties, social activism, and elections. Ford's approach, simply his accumulated political wisdom, was equally pragmatic and path-breaking.[50]

Alice's conspicuous, if not unwelcome, presence in Ford's classes deepened her nascent awareness of how gender was shaping her life. Like most men and women, reformers included, Ford believed politics a dirty business, especially unsuitable for women, who had a "higher vocation." Women like Jane Addams and Florence Kelley had long advanced the concept of politics and government as "municipal housekeeping," an idea that opened the door for women's reform work. This definition consciously built on prevailing notions of proper and separate spheres for men and women; however, absent the vote and a full range of respectable paid work for women, most female reformers grew more interested in the social welfare of the needy than in municipal administration or political parties. The political consciousness AP had acquired in New York primed her for Ford's ideas. If his lectures or the occasional glare failed to warn her of political science as a male preserve, her status as a minority of one or two in the class surely did. Nevertheless, her imperturbability and enthusiasm for the subject matter provided bulwarks against discouragement. And Ford's approach to political science suited Alice's pragmatic mind.[51]

His blunt talk about the world of politics dovetailed with her interest in practical solutions. She understood why Ford believed boss systems indispensable, recalling how College Settlement House workers relied on Tammany Hall to help solve problems. Ford's take on the civic temperament recalled her own thesis view that settlement workers needed to lobby for community support. "The true public opinion of the nation is ordinarily in a state of suspense. The minds of people are preoccupied by too many interests," he maintained. "Not until the issue is thrust upon the public in a definite form by some pressing emergency is the genuine expression of public opinion evoked."[52]

In America, Ford said, the president became the key to moving the public. Only the president held the power to "end party duplicity and define issues in such a way that public opinion can pass upon them decisively." President Roosevelt, Ford no doubt pointed out, became a master at using what the former Rough Rider called the "bully pulpit." This view of the presidency would prove useful to Alice when she jousted with the complicated political arena of Washington. Ford believed the White House could wield an authority greater than that of political parties or Congress, for only the president represented and held a national mandate from the entire populace. Any political party would be stymied, Ford asserted, unless its program "embodie[d] a policy accepted by the President and sustained by the influence of his office."[53]

Campus activities underscored Penn's indifference to women. The all-male Mask and Wig Club offered an occasional production; the club only permitted women to join the club's "patronesses" in the audience. They could watch football and other athletic matches as well, but the university excluded them from playing sports or even using the gymnasium. Alice had reveled in sports at Swarthmore and no doubt felt this barrier keenly. On a more intellectual front, the discussions and debates she enjoyed as an undergraduate were organized at Penn by private student clubs and closed to non-members. She could attend lectures given by visiting notables on campus, however.[54]

Graduate women looking for male companionship enjoyed ample opportunities to meet men in classes as well as around campus. Alice met some like-minded men in her classes, though we know nothing of their interaction at Penn. Carl Linn Seiler, also Quaker, studied both political science and sociology; another, Scott Nearing, felt as enamored with Simon Patten as AP and shared her enthusiasm for reform. She encountered both men again in later years. As she talked with male classmates, she could not fail to notice their eager anticipation of careers and, often, families. Most of the career women she knew chose to remain single and, in those days, presumably childless. They recognized, as Alice began to, that for women, combining family with a career became professionally and personally difficult, perhaps impossible.[55]

Alice's burgeoning interest in political science found plenty of nourishment, though her curiosity did not spill over into activism. Locally and nationally, she witnessed Progressive ideals inching toward reality. Keeping abreast of news in the Philadelphia papers proved necessary to stay current with courses like Ford's and Patten's. In fact, Alice may have acquired her habit of devouring several morning newspapers while at Penn. In Philadelphia itself, the struggle of the new anti-machine City Party against entrenched interests drew some Penn students to actively campaign for it. Nationally, the exuberant presidency of Theodore Roosevelt became a subject of endless fascination for anyone

interested in social change. By dint of her burgeoning gender awareness, Alice
followed the shocking news of the arrest of sixty British suffragists in February
1907 as they marched on Parliament. She and her mother, with whom she had
attended suffrage meetings long ago, shared their amazement about the aggressive British tactics.[56]

Living in Philadelphia also offered easy access to her family once more. Her
mother had adjusted to life as a widow, becoming increasingly engaged with
the Moorestown Friends School. Helen, nearing the end of her high school
years, contemplated her own future, one that her mother stressed included
Swarthmore. Alice could play big sister much more now, proffering advice and
detailing her adventures, suggesting books to learn more. Brother Will studied only a few blocks away at Philadelphia's Drexel Institute. But Will lacked
Alice's adaptability and, perhaps trying to step in for his absent father, looked
askance at Alice exploring the world. Though closest in age, the two would
never have much in common. AP's politically active Uncle Mickle Paul proved
much more supportive. He and his non-Quaker wife lived in town and Alice
probably spent some weekend afternoons chatting with the two about family,
as well as local and Quaker politics.[57]

Alice knew she was headed abroad by the time she finished her master's work
in June 1907. *Friends' Intelligencer* articles drew her attention to Woodbrooke, a
new British Quaker-founded study center in Birmingham, England, which offered
the chance to study and travel at the same time. Fortunately, local Quakers put
together scholarships to encourage American students to attend Woodbrooke.
Alice recalled being sought out for such a gift; more likely, she applied and won
it based on her references. Anxious to depart, she skipped Penn's commencement
and headed home to unpack, mend and clean, then quickly repack for a summer
in Germany before going on to England. She now saw herself more in a teaching career than in social work and, toward that end, she thought perfecting her
German might help her finance studies for a doctorate at a prestigious German
university (Patten and Brooks had studied in Germany). A postcard from her
roommate Carrie followed her: "Going to commencement the 15th. Sorry not to
see you once more."[58]

Her departure proved so rushed that Alice left a trail of messages after the ship
steamed away from the Philadelphia dock on June 21. As the *Manitou* reached the
Delaware Breakwater, she scribbled out a hasty note to her mother and gave it to
the pilot to mail. Then Alice Paul looked out at the wide Atlantic; she was off, she
recalled, to "see something of the world."[59]

3

"Heart and Soul Convert"

ALICE MADE SHIPBOARD friends easily on her voyage across the Atlantic. In an age when Britain and Europe dominated the world, when the Old World towered over an American culture still perceived as jejune, some sort of European experience became requisite for privileged young people. Aboard ship, Alice enjoyed "about the happiest two weeks I've ever spent," connecting with other collegians of similar background, young men and women including several Quakers and two other Swarthmore graduates. They disembarked at Antwerp on the Fourth of July. Despite wishing she was "still on the boat," she set off on the twenty-hour train ride to Berlin.[1]

Alice Paul's years abroad became the crucible forging her leadership potential. She made the most of her time in Europe and lived a vigorous life filled to the brim with work, study, touring, and socializing. Her voracious curiosity and desire to excel drove her explorations, which in turn deepened her confidence and shaped her outlook on the world. Her flexible notion of female-appropriate behavior allowed her to venture places many women of her background would avoid; these undertakings were early glimpses of the audacious leader she would become.

Alice's cultural and class sensibilities were immediately challenged in the German capital. She had encountered many foreign-born women in New York City but never lived with them; as she struggled to acclimate to German customs, she faced the proximity of many women who lacked her advantages. She stayed first at the centrally located Heimat, a low-cost Lutheran residence for visiting women, "something like a YWCA, I guess," she wrote her mother. The sole American on the premises, she joined nearly a hundred mostly European lodgers. She found the Heimat residents rather coarse, "but I am going to try to stand it."[2]

The experience deepened her self-awareness. "I thought it was the worst place in the world at first," she admitted after a while, "because of the food & the people." She recognized how much the language barrier affected her perceptions, however, writing that "the people would probably be quite interesting if I could talk to them."[3]

Her roommate became her German tutor and guide. She wrote that Frau Heick, an "unusually well-read" fortyish former schoolteacher, "tells me that I don't pronounce a single word correctly!" Heick gave Alice daily lessons and the two women also walked about each day: "So I am getting to see all sides of Berlin—things I would never know about otherwise." Heick charged her pupil twelve cents per lesson, by Alice's lights "ridiculous!" "I'm going to pay her twice that, I think," the frugal Quaker wrote her mother, "for she is exceedingly poverty stricken it seems." From Frau Heick, Alice also gleaned something of life in Germany for independent women. The widowed Heick could not teach in a school because authorities did not deem her single.[4]

Their visit to the University of Berlin enlarged Alice's sense of the challenges educated women faced. She knew that many Americans considered German universities preeminent for advanced scholarship. One day, Frau Heick accompanied her to two lectures. "There were a great number of women at the university—most of them seemed to be Americans," Alice wrote home. She knew two of the latter, a fact underscoring the small number of female scholars. Penn's graduate women seemed fortunate in comparison; although women had audited courses at Berlin for fifteen years, the university refused to admit them officially. They endured repeated indignities, including being barred from class outright on any professor's whim.[5]

Alice seemed to think she could overcome the barriers, judging from her comments about another of the university women at the Heimat. She found the woman "superior" to most residents, but also "*so* queer—about 6 feet broad" with irritating mannerisms. "When I watch her," Alice wrote, "I don't wonder that men don't like co-education." The remark suggests that her fluid conception of gender roles allowed her to identify with Brooks and other male professors who encouraged her. She now saw herself as an exceptional woman—both feminine and scholarly (that is, masculine), a woman versatile enough to evade frustrating restrictions.[6]

After a month at the Heimat, Alice's class and generational sensibilities won out over her frugality. She moved into a private room in a nearby rooming house where one of her shipmates lodged. "She is paying just twice as much board," Alice explained her decision to her cost-conscious mother, "but food is 40 times as good." Other boarders were mostly in their twenties and she felt more at ease. "The people here are delightful," she wrote.[7]

From the first, Alice denied homesickness, while craving news from home. The pace of overseas mail frustrated her. "No letter came this morning," she fretted to her mother, "Why don't you write? I haven't had a letter since I've been here." She sought family news and more: her *Friends' Intelligencer* had not arrived either. "I wish you would write to me about the political news."[8]

She displayed her growing self-regard to her family from afar. For the Swarthmore-bound Helen, she composed an eight-page treatise on the college wardrobe, emphasizing frugality and hues of red ("to give thee more color"). She tried to mold her more effusive sister in her own image. "I should like to suggest to Helen that she cut out superlatives—it weakens her style. In her letter," Alice noted, "the word 'exceedingly' was used 23 times."[9]

As her time in Germany drew to a close, Alice experienced outsize spectacle for the first time at the September 2 Sedan Day pageant, an annual celebration of war victories. At the Tempelhof parade ground, she watched for five hours as military hardware, cavalry, foot soldiers—perhaps fifty thousand troops—strutted past the kaiser, kaiserin, and crown prince. "Bands played, flags were draped over everything," in AP's description. Despite her inbred pacifism and plain ways, she found the pageantry "exhilarating," much grander than the parades and other rituals she had experienced at Swarthmore and in New York.[10]

Shortly after Sedan Day, Alice prepared to leave for Britain. She had "seen practically every thing in Berlin." More importantly, she wrote, "I can understand German very well now—almost everything & can speak well enough to get whatever I want." She packed her trunk with a new winter wardrobe acquired in the inexpensive city—"2 hats (best & everyday), one morning dress, 2 evening, 1 silk waist, 2 white waists, gloves, belts, etc."—and sent it off to England by the cheapest route. Then she suggested to her mother that, although ninety dollars remained of her trip money, "perhaps thee had better send more."[11]

In late September, Alice set off alone on the long trek to Britain. She traveled by train to the sea, then by steamer north to Grimsby on England's east coast. Her thirty-six-hour crossing was, she wrote on a postcard, the "calmest in history of ship." Once in Britain, she boarded a train going southwest. Finally, the industrial smoke of Birmingham came into view, and she knew Woodbrooke lay only a few miles ahead.[12]

The Woodbrooke study center became the first of several cutting-edge Quaker undertakings Alice experienced in England. Its program drummed in the call to useful service that Alice had already imbibed from Swarthmore as well as from Progressives at NYSP and Penn. Indeed, Woodbrooke joined a variety of attempts to forge a "new Quakerism"; founder George Cadbury, the chocolate magnate, and other influential Friends hoped to guide a debilitated British Quaker community into social activism and political involvement, an aim reminiscent of Jesse Holmes's efforts at Swarthmore. In 1903, the Cadburys donated their estate to house (and name) the experiment. The center, said the loftily worded Woodbrooke catalog, offered young people the opportunity to "more fully [qualify] themselves, spiritually, intellectually, and experimentally, for any service to which they may feel called." At Woodbrooke, Alice also discovered the limits of Quaker acceptance.[13]

Despite the continuing inconsistency of overseas mail, Alice immediately felt at home. She enjoyed the gracious, bucolic setting as well as living once more in a Quaker community, among English speakers. She could take up sports again, including biking, tennis, and ice skating. The lack of central heating proved less welcome: she wrote home asking for her furs. Still attentive to style, she told her mother, "Mine are just about like those worn here."[14]

Alice again judged herself more advanced than most of the term's forty students. Most were Quakers, women slightly outnumbering the men. British and Americans made up a majority; Norway and Holland were also well represented; and others hailed from Algeria, Syria, even Madagascar. The nine Americans underscored the continued prominence of the Philadelphia Quaker community; all, including two Swarthmore men Alice knew, claimed that area as home. Confident now of her own superior intellect and training, Alice thought the students "not a particularly brilliant crowd—some seem to have come purely for the social life—some are very bright & have done a great deal. It is much like college."[15]

She had not lost her desire to know everything. She signed up for twelve courses, choosing more German, social science, and economics courses, plus philosophy and a class on what she called "the Mohammedon religion." Her interest in her own faith proved minimal: she avoided all lectures on the Bible except for the required "Spiritual Life" course. "It is a most religious place," she told her mother, "but they let you do as you please." Alice also arranged a tutoring exchange with a German Woodbrooker; she still considered Germany a likely venue for doctoral study.[16]

If the Woodbrooke student body failed to impress her, the faculty did. "All the professors are Cambridge or Oxford men," she told her mother. In fact, three female professors (barred from taking Cambridge or Oxford degrees) taught languages during spring term; Alice's failure to note their presence underscores her predilection for the men she considered superior. George Shann had followed his working-class heritage into the Labour Party, and Alice took his course on sweatshops. Like Shann, Woodbrooke's social science instructors leaned socialist, as did most intellectuals involved in British social reform. AP thought the idealistic Shann and John St. George Heath "the two cleverest lecturers there." The tall, dark-haired Quaker convert St. George Heath, only two years her senior, loved having students who challenged him. He encouraged Alice's academic plans, thinking her "born to be a student and a teacher."[17]

Despite being drawn to male mentors, Alice was bothered by the absence of women in her field of study. Needing more intellectual stimulation than Woodbrooke offered, she routinely bicycled four miles through, she recalled, the "terrible fog in England" to take an economics course at the University of Birmingham. She found Birmingham comparable to Penn: though women comprised one-fifth of the student body, she was the sole female of twenty students in her class. "I am the first woman who ever took a course in the whole department of commerce at this Univ," she wrote her mother ruefully. "I do wish my taste had run to Greek or something in which I would have some comrades who were females." Her atypicality did not deter her; however, the Birmingham classroom and Woodbrooke's second-class female professors reminded her how tenuously women often existed in academe.[18]

All the coursework failed to satisfy Alice: she craved more practical experience, the service so many of her mentors had attempted. Even though her enthusiasm for social work had waned, if she wished to teach, she needed empirical knowledge, not just book learning. As a seasoned "visitor," Alice quickly found part-time voluntary work at the British COS. They sent her to an acutely deprived neighborhood served by the Summer Lane Settlement, an eight-year-old project founded, like many British settlements, by women. Though St. George Heath later praised Alice's "gift for learning about institutions and customs," her letters offer no details about her Summer Lane experience.[19]

Woodbrooke allowed plenty of time for social and recreational pursuits; Alice crammed these much like her courses. One student described the atmosphere as "love, unity & sunshine." The Cadburys lived nearby and often invited students to dinner, tennis parties, or excursions to local attractions. Woodbrooke's head residents, the Braithwaites, acted as nurturing parents, encouraging parties and performances for every occasion. Woodbrooke's small size and easy mixed-sex mingling, less restrictive than at Swarthmore or even Penn, allowed AP experience in more informal settings with young men, though her letters mention no one in particular. She did become close to two Dutch women.[20]

Woodbrookers loved to entertain each other. At night, everyone sat around the fire drinking cocoa and telling tales. Lively Mary Braithwaite, an American, often regaled the others with stories in Negro dialect. Braithwaite may have encouraged the "Woodbrooke Minstrels," students in blackface whose performances greatly amused the assemblage. Despite the Quaker emphasis on equality, the construct of the childlike darky remained in Britain as in America. Alice's letters did not mention Braithwaite's stories or the Minstrels, which may suggest she found such doings commonplace.[21]

Most Woodbrookers soon purchased bicycles to get around. Alice prudently rented hers until she realized its value. "I couldn't go around and do much without a bicycle," she remembered. Groups of men and women pedaled off routinely to nearby castles and historic sites. As in America, women on bicycles had ceased to surprise in Britain, but a whiff of the "new woman" still surrounded female cyclists of all classes. Since the late nineteenth century, the popularity of bicycles had helped enlarge female independence and advance questions about restrictive dress and physical activity for women. By Alice's day, the debate over cycling's effects on health had largely settled in the bicycle's favor, despite lingering concerns about morality. Long used to athletic endeavors, Alice—and many other young women—brushed off such worries.[22]

Like many privileged Americans and Britons, Woodbrookers often attended lectures for entertainment. Alice heard Winston Churchill, then a young Member of Parliament (MP), and George Bernard Shaw (she also attended a Shaw play), among others. The effect of one November lecture lingered—the night she journeyed into Birmingham to hear Christabel Pankhurst speak.[23]

She knew from newspaper accounts about the controversial reputation of the Women's Social and Political Union (WSPU); indeed, she and her mother had discussed the British suffrage group. Founded in 1903 by Emmeline Pankhurst and her daughters Christabel, Sylvia, and Adela, the WSPU emphasized action. "It is unendurable," Christabel once declared, "to think of another generation of women wasting their lives begging for the vote." The WSPU joined a long list of British suffrage groups. By late 1907, it had distinguished itself with bold tactics unknown to women beyond the laboring classes, including staging demonstrations and disrupting political meetings despite repeated arrests and imprisonment. Reporters quickly tagged the group "militant."[24]

The suffrage issue felt familiar, if distant, to Alice. She remembered attending Moorestown meetings with her mother and how the Philadelphia Yearly Meeting encouraged Hicksites to work on the issue. Her prior knowledge of the WSPU's audacity probably stoked her interest. As she recalled, "It just never entered my head NOT to go to the meeting." Her anticipation was wholly realized.[25]

Like Alice, Christabel Pankhurst did not hesitate to venture into male-identified arenas. Alice remembered her first impression of the woman: "Quite entrancing and delightful person, really very beautiful I thought." Indeed, she would have dismissed a mannish Christabel. At twenty-seven, the charismatic eldest daughter of Emmeline Pankhurst exuded grace and femininity, even sweetness, yet she could hold her own with a ready wit even in hostile crowds, a trait no doubt amplified by her legal training. Christabel Pankhurst fanned her passion for the cause with a burning indignation over being denied admittance to the English bar. Despite her best efforts that night in Birmingham, however, "she was completely shouted down." University students, Alice wrote her mother, "sang, yelled, whistled, blew horns, played rattles etc from beginning to end so that no one heard a word beyond the reporters seated beneath [Pankhurst]." The head of the university, infuriated, insisted that Pankhurst return for a more civilized debate a short time later, which AP also eagerly attended.[26]

The scene etched itself in her mind, though she mentioned it to her mother only weeks later. Her letters typically refrained from detailed descriptions except for particularly stirring occasions; the Pankhurst events clearly qualified. "It was most exciting," she wrote her mother. "People tried to eject some of the [cat-calling] ringleaders & then there was a fight—the police had a lively time—It was worse than what we read about." She knew that the WSPU courted such strife: "At all the political meetings the women make a big rumpus & are put out."[27]

Watching men silence the formidable Christabel Pankhurst became a crystallizing moment in Alice Paul's existence. Judging from her later remarks, Alice unconsciously crafted a myth around the Pankhurst speech. "Any normal person I think, seeing the people who were working for what you always believed in treated in this way would be very much aroused," she offered years later. "I just wanted to align myself with them, to join them, of course." Despite the imagined epiphany, Alice Paul did not toss aside her carefully laid plans. There is little evidence that she changed anything about her life at this time, in fact.[28]

If she toyed then with the idea of taking up suffrage work, several factors discouraged her. One hint of such a plan appears in a letter from St. George Heath, suggesting he discouraged her: "I never took to the idea of your going to do practical work," he wrote, "except perhaps for a short time." Alice had discarded social work as a career, so St. George Heath could have been referring to suffrage activism. AP wrote her mother that most Woodbrooke faculty disapproved of the Pankhursts, another disincentive to join the movement. And at least one supervisor at Summer Lane worked prominently for a more conventional suffrage society, which might have also deterred Alice. She also needed to consider her mother: would she support Alice financially while she worked to gain British women the vote? AP's letters hint that her mother already fretted about the added expenses of her daughter's "scholarship" year.[29]

She did not join the Pankhursts at this time, but the myth she later spun around Christabel's speech suggests that the event led Alice to recognize, for the first time, her own personal stake in the suffrage cause. The Quaker belief in equality provided the foundation of that consciousness, but her experience with graduate education had sharpened her awareness. Christabel Pankhurst—denied the professional status she had earned—became a proxy for Alice herself; as she witnessed this ambitious woman struggle with the unruly crowd, she could see herself contending in a male-centered environment—whether at Penn, Birmingham, or potentially in Germany. If she then considered doing suffrage work, the "heart and soul convert" of memory ultimately leaned on her innate prudence and decided to tuck away her newfound zeal, unclear how she could manage it. The Pankhurst speech gestated within her until even more profound events rekindled her desire.[30]

Alice's letters home record the intensifying emotional pull of her British life. She now rarely mentioned home or queried her mother about goings-on, unlike her letters from Germany. In the fall of 1907, she seemed to feel her separation from her books more keenly than from her family. When she realized how inexpensively books could be shipped, she asked for a few volumes to use in Woodbrooke classes. Then, in lieu of Christmas gifts, she appealed for old favorites, mostly poetry, to read in her spare time. Her list included Lanier, Dunbar, Milton, Burns, and Wordsworth, as well as Dante and Homer. "Don't send them if it costs much," AP wrote, allowing that her mother's idea of thrift might differ, "for I can get them all at the Library in Birmingham." Her precious books provided sustenance and a whisper of home. The only hint of homesickness appeared in her signoff: "Alice" now often became "With love, Alice."[31]

Over the Woodbrooke holiday break, Alice traveled to London to see the sights and acquire more practical experience. She stayed at the Canning Town Settlement for Women Workers, by her own account "one of the most famous [settlements] in London." The project served a desperately poor area along the north side of the Thames. The settlement had largely emptied out for the holidays, so Alice could board for a short while, a safer prospect than finding a room in the neighborhood.[32]

The settlement became her jumping-off point for a daring and apparently spontaneous adventure. She spent her first days pursuing activities typical of the privileged: visiting London sights and, one evening with two other Americans, attending Shakespeare's *As You Like It*. She found London, though twice the population, "not half so rushing and busy" as New York. After ten days exploring the city and Canning Town, she undertook a dramatically different plan. "I took a room with one of the COS cases near Canningtown [sic]," she wrote her mother (after the fact), and looked for sweatshop work. The other settlement residents thought her "mad."[33]

Alice, not unlike Shakespeare's Rosalind, wanted to try on another identity. The juxtaposition of this bold move a month after she saw Christabel Pankhurst seems no accident; we glimpse her growing desire to shape her own life course. She had likely read of other privileged women's experiments with menial work. The chronicle of American Maud Younger's days as a "millionaire waitress" appeared in the March 1907 *McClure's*. And Alice may have learned from George Shann's lectures about socialist intellectual Beatrice Webb's 1902 account of working as a trouser finisher in East London.[34]

So Alice Paul pretended to join the laboring class. Though she was unquestionably a voyeur, her venture required considerably more nerve than settlement work. She set out in costume. "I dressed as a working girl—they gave me the clothes at the Settlement," she wrote. After finding no work at a jam factory, she "went to the rubber factory—there were about 40 girls waiting in the yard. The foreman came out & looked at us as though we were so many cows" (a sentiment uncannily close to one of Younger's). "Then he beckoned to me & asked me where I had worked etc & took me on." She went on, "I suppose it was because I was larger than the others," looking well fed.[35]

Alice took the enervating labor in stride. Her athleticism and knowledge that the job was temporary both helped. She worked a twelve-hour day threading cords into automobile tires. The fastest workers might take home five dollars a week. "I worked from 6 a.m. to 6 p.m. with a half hour at 8 for breakfast & an hour at noon." The week plunged her into a life her parents spared her from living, a life she could peel off like she doffed her work clothes.

The experience was largely self-serving. Her one complaint—"We could not sit down while at the factory"—suggests that she connected to some degree with other workers, though she discussed no one in particular. Understanding working conditions from the inside surely amplified her expertise. Nevertheless, one letter home indicates that her underlying goal was to try on independence. "I got my own food & supported myself on my wages," she wrote. Impressed by her pluck, the settlement house headworker offered her a room and board scholarship, similar to her status at Woodbrooke. She declined, wanting to finish what she had started at the Quaker community.[36]

A short time into the new Woodbrooke term, Alice's desire to be self-supporting became a possibility. In February, the Quaker head of a London district COS, Lucy Gardner, spoke at Woodbrooke and ended up offering Alice a job. From COS contacts, Gardner knew of AP's Summer Lane work and perhaps also of her Canning Town venture. Alice decided to accept this offer for several reasons. First of all, Gardner proposed an actual salary. "$300 a year, which will just cover board & lodging there with a little toward laundry. It is a wretched salary but it is all they pay," Alice explained to her mother. Second, the job offered administrative experience, as assistant to Gardner, rather than settlement work. And she could start after the term ended.[37]

Despite these pluses, she had to win over her mother. Alice's letters suggest Mrs. Paul felt unenthusiastic about her daughter's plan to spend another year abroad. Her eldest pushed back: "I think that going to the London C.O.S. is a very good plan. I have always wanted to spend about a year in COS for it is the best way to understand social work & see all sides of it for the work is so extremely varied." Alice then aimed squarely at her mother's Quaker frugality and pragmatism: "By this plan I can support myself or nearly do so & at the same time be learning a great deal of practical work." Finally, her mother accepted the idea.[38]

As the Woodbrooke term ended, Alice thought ahead to living in London. The other American Woodbrookers planned to return home or travel. As AP realized how full-time work would constrain her time and activities, she felt "very much as though I were going to prison for a year." She grabbed a last taste of freedom: a visit to France with her Dutch friend from Woodbrooke, Mietza Heldring.[39]

On the two friends' tour of northern France, Alice again seemed intent on self-sufficiency. The contrast between her autonomy and her companion's is striking. Mietza, the daughter of a wealthy Dutch Reform pastor, had never traveled without a chaperone. Once on the continent, she rode the train between destinations, while Alice cycled, a common practice for English visitors, though few women rode solo. "The roads are splendid," Alice wrote her mother, but Mietza lacked the strength to cycle her way. Moreover, one train left so early that "Miss Heldring was afraid to go alone in the train & so I went with her." After her friend returned to London Alice cycled the seventy miles to Paris. She found a student hostel near the Sorbonne and lingered for a week, sightseeing and socializing with the many English-speaking boarders. At week's end, she boarded the train for London and her job at the Dalston COS.[40]

As in her earlier settlement work, her living conditions buffered her from the miseries of neighborhood life. London's Dalston district lacked the desperate poverty of Canning Town, three miles to the south. Nevertheless, rows of oppressive brick tenements lined the streets, many without indoor plumbing. Too many families lived in one small dark damp room; those better off made do with income comparable to Alice's "wretched" $300 salary. By contrast, AP lived with Lucy Gardner in a small house that included the COS office; Gardner worked mostly outside the office. "It was very nice," Alice later recalled. "She had a housekeeper and you got all your meals there."[41]

In Dalston, Alice took on significant responsibility, juggling never-ending duties. There her formidable work ethic emerged. The COS district offices operated as clearinghouses to organize existing relief efforts. Every day, Alice wrote nearly two dozen letters, visited the homes of clients, oversaw various agents and volunteers of both sexes, and kept the accounts. "Every spare moment I have I spend in trying to get new volunteer workers," she wrote her mother. She also reviewed cases with supervisors each week. She even took on after-hours work teaching an evening class and assisting with a girls' club. She worked so relentlessly, Alice wrote, "that I scarcely have time to see anything that is going on in London or even read the papers."[42]

She managed some socializing and sightseeing, but she missed a fuller life. She dined several times with Woodbrooke friends and visited historic Toynbee Hall, the first settlement house. She maintained her correspondence with family and friends such as her Penn roommates, Carrie and Clara. "I feel as though I were wasting the heyday of my youth working so hard when I hear of the good times thee has," she wrote Helen. "I have not danced, except once with some old woman at a Settlement, since I left [Woodbrooke] nor been swimming, or rowing, or sailing, or skating or anything."[43]

As the summer progressed, Alice gained confidence, even arrogance, about her administrative abilities. She judged three of her helpers incompetent, making "such mistakes all day long till I nearly go out of my mind." Miss Gardner proved "hard to suit," reminding AP of her Aunt Hannah, "so I am most pleased that she approves of me so far" (Gardner had discharged two previous assistants).[44]

An unexpected change in living arrangements led her back to the suffrage movement. In late June, Gardner suggested she could live in the nearby Hoxton settlement, a fifteen-minute ride on her newly acquired secondhand bicycle. Alice moved to Hoxton to live with six other women and assist both male and female residents after her Dalston work. She wrote little about the settlement; living in Hoxton became opportune for another reason: the head of the settlement was an ardent suffragist.[45]

She learned from the Hoxton head worker about two upcoming suffrage processions aimed at demonstrating women's desire to vote to the British government. She had never heard of a parade for suffrage; indeed, such events were still novel in England. Alice had refrained from any suffrage involvement since attending the Christabel Pankhurst speech six months earlier. The Pankhursts' organization—the WSPU—planned one parade, and a more moderate umbrella group—the National Union of Women's Suffrage Societies (NUWSS)—the other. Perhaps recalling her exhilaration at the German Sedan Day extravaganza, Alice decided to march in both.[46]

Fortuitously for Alice Paul, the curtain was rising on what British suffrage leader-cum-historian Ray Strachey later called "The Great Days" of the woman suffrage struggle. Advocates felt poised to win the vote for England's women after its self-governing colonies of New Zealand and Australia granted suffrage in 1893 and 1902. In Britain, women had voted in local elections since 1869, but decades of concerted effort across the political spectrum failed to secure further gains. The property qualification for voting complicated the struggle—and some men still lacked the franchise in 1908. Opting for the easier target, most woman suffrage champions advocated *equal* suffrage (women voting on the same qualified basis as men) rather than *adult* suffrage (a vote for every adult man and woman). A new generation of suffrage leaders and activists had recently reinvigorated the movement.[47]

Most English suffragists allied themselves with one of the two largest national societies. The NUWSS used familiar methods to influence and elect pro-suffrage MPs. The "militant" WSPU, on the other hand, attempted increasingly controversial tactics, which Alice had followed in the newspapers for years. Britons energized by the disruptive politics had tripled the WSPU's funds in the past year. Since the beginning of 1908, numerous arrests had followed WSPU attempts to charge Parliament.[48]

The two groups' differing approaches increasingly placed them at odds. However, when Alice signed up to march, the NUWSS and the WSPU still cooperated in many ways and even worked together occasionally. NUWSS leader Millicent Fawcett told the *London Times* that "no rivalry or hostility" existed between the two groups, though Emmeline Pankhurst had once likened the NUWSS to "a beetle on its back." Despite the WSPU's radical tactics, all British suffrage groups aimed to effect constitutional reform and many women belonged to or participated in both WSPU and NUWSS. Many, like Alice, marched in two successive suffrage demonstrations that June.[49]

A recent statement by the new prime minister galvanized suffragists into planning highly visible responses—right on Parliament's doorstep. The Right Honourable H. H. Asquith, a woman suffrage opponent, claimed that a show of "strong and undoubted support" might influence him to include votes for women in a forthcoming reform bill. The NUWSS set its procession for Saturday, June 13; the WSPU's parade would follow on Sunday, June 21. Both groups expected larger turnouts than at the NUWSS's first parade, held in February 1907.[50]

That infamous NUWSS "Mud March" had attracted three thousand women. Despite drenching rain, women strode with purpose from Hyde Park to the Strand while their long skirts trailed in the mud. Curious throngs gawked, many wondering what to think of women—particularly middle-class and titled women who ordinarily avoided the public gaze—marching in the streets. The public shaming and derision many marchers feared did not come to pass. As Strachey wrote, "They walked, and nothing happened." In fact, journalists remarked on the women's courage and determination. Camaraderie bloomed, abetted by women of the laboring classes long accustomed to marching for workers' rights. In the aftermath, many suffragists became convinced of the strategic value of publicly demonstrating allegiance to the cause. Sixteen months later, the NUWSS savored the opportunity to show its strength.[51]

On the gray and breezy early afternoon of Saturday, June 13, Alice emerged from the Embankment tube station to find thousands of women massing. Stewards wearing the NUWSS colors—red and white—busily organized great sections of marchers behind colorful banners and pennants. Working women of all sorts lined up. International delegations formed, including a healthy American contingent led by suffrage leader Anna Howard Shaw. A steward guided Alice to her appointed section. Precisely at three o'clock, leaders assumed their places behind a grand flowing NUWSS banner and the marchers stepped off.[52]

The multicolored leviathan snaked its way two miles through the London streets to the Royal Albert Hall. The women's light summer dresses, vivid academic robes, and brilliant banners created a stream of vibrant hues. Alice now joined the pageantry she had once merely observed. Most spectators accorded the women tolerance, if not respect. Even the anti-suffrage *London Times* applauded the "quiet, dignified earnestness of the demonstrators." Ninety minutes later, the parade reached the hall and marchers flowed in for a rousing celebration.[53]

The first WSPU rally a week later dwarfed the NUWSS effort. The Pankhursts' ambitious plan called for seven processions, each converging on Hyde Park from a different direction, as if thousands of suffragists swept all of London before them. Again near the Embankment station that Sunday afternoon, Alice found her place in the contingent led by Christabel Pankhurst and WSPU treasurer Emmeline Pethick-Lawrence. Pethick-Lawrence had dreamed up the idea of distinctive colors—white, purple, and green—and now a flurry of white dresses caught the sun; great silk banners and hundreds of smaller cotton ones, flags, pennants, ribbons, and sashes in purple and green glistened. Alice's unit set off on cue behind the two leaders and an eight-by-ten-foot silk banner that claimed moral authority for the WSPU: "Rebellion to Tyrants is Obedience to God."

The meticulous planning was evident from start to finish. The *New York Times*, stalwardly against suffrage, later complimented the "totally unexpected genius for organization." Amid throngs of spectators, WSPU marshals hastened the marchers onward. At Hyde Park, hundreds of thousands awaited them, the curious mingling with committed partisans. The seven separate parades arrived and thirty thousand marchers fanned out to twenty platforms around the park to be inspired by fiery speakers. At Pethick-Lawrence's stage, Alice felt "thrilled beyond words by [the] marvelous speech." Then, a final victorious bugle blast signaled every voice to shout one ear-splitting cry, "Votes for Women! Votes for Women! Votes for Women!"[54]

Alice stored details of both processions in her memory, little knowing she would find ample use for them. Organizers of both marches relied on the powerful, even disturbing effect of a mixed gender message: an almost-military precision coupled with a stereotypically feminine talent for display. The WSPU raised a small fortune and utilized every possible mode of publicity beforehand: handbills and posters, canvassing and open-air meetings, and of course newspaper coverage. They mastered details like scrutinizing Hyde Park for platform placement and unforeseen obstacles; they arranged police protection. The only uncontrollable element—the weather—turned up in their favor.[55]

The spectacle immersed Alice in a cause larger than herself, a cause driven by and for women. It allowed her to express the outrage she felt in Birmingham at attempts to silence Christabel Pankhurst and, by extension, herself. Her Quaker heritage contributed the principle of gender equality. But her own ambition and newfound awareness of gender ultimately brought her to realize that she was personally invested in suffrage. Joining the WSPU became another step toward truly owning her life. "I still remember my thrill," she recalled, "at getting a beautiful letter welcoming me into their ranks."[56]

Alice Paul had no intention of changing her academic goals, nor did she anticipate how her involvement with the Pankhursts would reshape her expectations. She began by attending WSPU weekly meetings.[57] As she absorbed the real-world politics of such meetings and reawakened her academic fascination with political action, she unwittingly prepared herself for a different life course. For the Pankhursts' meetings were lessons in the day-to-day shaping of political protest.

Despite joining the WSPU, Alice needed to continue with her paid work. However, when Gardner decided to leave her post in the fall, AP—"so tired that I could scarcely eat"—saw an opportunity to move on to a less-exhausting prospect. Gardner helped her secure part-time work at the Quaker-run Peel Institute, a non-resident settlement. The work would allow Alice more WSPU time as well as the opportunity to attend classes at the London School of Economics (LSE).[58]

As the summer of 1908 ebbed, family drew her attention. Her favorite cousin Susanna Parry came to London on holiday with her family. Alice's aunt wrote Tacie Paul that Alice seemed "very happy and well, but does not know when she is coming home." The Parrys brought distressing news from Moorestown. Helen was reconsidering a decision to transfer from Swarthmore to Wellesley. Alice rushed to rectify the situation; she now rued her own delayed entry into the wide world. "There is nothing I regret more than having spent 4 yrs at one college," she wrote, probably a surprising admission to her mother. To Helen, Alice detailed the advantages of Wellesley, known to her only secondhand.[59]

Alice followed up her letter to Helen with another, one unusually revealing about her belief system. All the Quaker exhortations about practicality, all her Progressive professors' calls to serve: these teachings nested deeply in Alice Paul's consciousness. "Surely thee must realize," she wrote Helen, "that we are practically what our environment makes us." She believed her own exploratory process to be fundamental. "I wish thee would realize the seriousness of these years," she went on. "They are an opportunity in which to increase one's efficiency & power of becoming a useful member of society."[60]

Alice also advised Helen on how to construct herself as a woman. She believed exemplary women exuded intelligence and refinement. She termed a mutual acquaintance "my ideal of a woman [because of] her sweet refined manner, her splendid mind, wide reading and knowledge." She discouraged her sister from being influenced by "slangy, uncultured, rather half refined girls who [have] not a very big view of life." And she stressed that the refinement, the "big view" of life, came earned.[61]

Alice's ideal reflected her class sensibilities and the approval given higher education and life exploration in both the Quaker community and parts of mainstream society. She had internalized Dean Bond's exhortations about women venturing into new realms needing to guard their reputation. Like other "new women," Alice rejected the still-current notion that knowledge and experience unsexed women. Her conception of gender-appropriate activity was broad, and thus she embraced behaviors—marching in suffrage parades, biking solo through France—that few would term "refined." Yet she disdained the informality of speech and conduct increasingly emblematic of her peers. Aspirations often conflict with reality; these contradictions expose a young woman struggling to reconcile her existing belief system with the pull of her ambition. In terms of her private conduct, Alice held herself to her ideal her entire life. Nevertheless, as she pursued autonomy and ambition, her notion of proper female comportment in public expanded noticeably.

As the Dalston job ended and Alice anticipated attending the acclaimed LSE and working at the Peel Institute, she also took another step toward independence, hoping to allow herself more time abroad. Rather than live in a rooming house, she rented two unfurnished but well-lit attic rooms for $1.25 a week at 31 Red Lion Street near Peel, purchasing furniture she intended to sell later. She hoped to find a roommate to share costs; that plan failed and she struggled to afford the place herself. Supporting herself became a less likely prospect. Nevertheless, she remembered the space fondly as "the first little home I ever fixed up."[62]

Her work at Peel proved disheartening. In the afternoons that fall, Alice pulled on her hat and walked the two short blocks down congested Clerkenwell Road to the Peel Institute, trying to keep the hem of her long skirt above the street dust and dirt. She visited the desperate and helped with youth club activities and the evening women's school. The ever-present, grinding indigence began to wear her down. Only a few weeks in, she wrote, "Peel is a dead place. I spend my time looking after babies and old women." Years later, Alice only remembered the constant burial of children. Indeed, infant mortality in the area at the time stood at 33 percent, double the national norm. She wrote her brother Parry that she enjoyed the music and games of the Sunday school most, as a welcome respite from the weekday routine.[63]

Her expectations of free time proved premature. She struggled to attend even the two morning LSE lectures. In an environment where she had so often excelled, she feared losing her place. "I am rather afraid that I won't have any time to read or study as Peel takes so much time," she told her mother, "& then I'll get the reputation of being stupid which is a disadvantage but still I am going to try it—so far

I haven't read anything." Once she determined to push through, prepared or not, she liked LSE "more each time I go there."[64]

The LSE provided an invigorating contrast to the Peel Institute. When she could get away, Alice walked or rode the scant mile southwest down to Clare Market off the Strand, to the imposing brick structure that housed the progressive school. The Pankhursts' Clement's Inn offices stood conveniently next door. At the LSE, Alice found many women and foreign nationals among the sixteen hundred students, though few other Americans. She felt at home in the Common Room where she studied or wrote letters by the fire in between lectures. More than that, she found other students "very bright & up to date. It is a most stimulating atmosphere."[65]

As at Swarthmore and NYSP, Alice attended LSE at a propitious time: the school had become the center of gravity for British sociology. Her courses exposed her to some of the leading lights in the social sciences, including L. T. Hobhouse and LSE founder Sidney Webb. Both were molding the discipline of sociology and shaping the infant Labour Party; Alice received a strong dose of the party's democratic socialist thinking. Exposed to Labour politics from WSPU meetings as well, AP grew intrigued enough to attend an occasional meeting of the Fabian Society, which had co-founded Labour and created LSE, and whose members included, at one time, Emmeline Pankhurst.[66]

Alice loved the atmosphere at LSE and tried valiantly to keep up with classes but struggled to attend lectures amid her Peel work and the novel but wearisome task of living on her own. She wanted to experience life as others in Clerkenwell lived it, to see "the life of an ordinary person and all the handicaps and troubles and so on that they had." She lived without servants for the first time, cleaning, washing, and killing vermin. She hauled water up several stories from the well. Hampered by her lack of culinary knowledge and equipment, she prepared only her breakfast, confining herself to bread, butter, and fruit; she purchased lunch and dinner inexpensively at the school's refectory.[67]

Like many privileged and educated women of the era, Alice's class values thwarted her search for self-determination. She was open to self-sacrifice but balked at compromising her class identity. Her wardrobe needed attention, in particular. In England, where dress connoted status even more than in America, less-than-presentable clothing branded one in undesirable ways. By late October, Alice gave up on self-sufficiency and wrote home for more funds. "Could thee send me some more money," she wrote her mother. "I want to buy a winter suit and hat & have used up all thee sent last time."[68]

Mrs. Paul parceled money out, perhaps unconsciously setting up a power struggle with her strong-willed daughter. It is unclear whether Tacie Paul used money to communicate her resistance to her daughter's continuing interest in

England or simply to underscore her own frugality. One can only imagine how this contest might have played out if her husband still lived. At any rate, funds arrived before long, and Alice purchased a wine-colored suit as well as hat and shoes. "I don't feel quite so delapidated [sic] as I have been," she wrote home in thanks.[69]

She looked more respectable now, especially for the Fabian Society, WSPU meetings, and social occasions. Alice still seemed intent to cram as many varied experiences as possible into her time in Britain. Her letters do not suggest a preference for suffrage activity, though she did not share everything with her mother. She worked at Peel, attended LSE, and helped the Pankhursts with a mass mailing. She also socialized with two other Woodbrooke grads, a man and woman, living in London.[70]

By November, Alice's frustration with the surfeit of Peel work, lack of study time, and bare-bones living peaked. "It will soon be Thanksgiving," she wrote her mother with longing. "I'm afraid I'm getting home sick & tired of being away. Isn't it strange—about the first time I've felt so." She quickly moved on to another topic, not wishing to dwell on the negative or, perhaps, not wanting to provide her mother with an opening to suggest returning. A week later, however, Alice found time to write both her younger brother and sister. She sounded happier, for she had secured a roommate through her Woodbrooke connections and her financial concerns abated for a time.[71]

Nonetheless, Tacie Paul seized upon AP's homesickness as an opening to persuade her to return home to teach. Alice appealed to her mother's belief in education: "Have just gotten thy letter in which thee tells me to not waste my strength on people of the slums. Well I am not doing it for their sakes but in order to learn about conditions myself." Whether Alice accepted her mother's class prejudice is unclear from her reply. Her mother wondered whether Alice might teach at Wellesley, a more appropriate situation by her lights, but AP held out for more exploration abroad. "As to going to Wellesley I don't know enough—I could hardly expect to get such a position till I had my Doctor's degree. Of course I could come back to America next year and take the degree after one more year's work—That is in 1910." She went on, "But if thee can afford I would rather spend more time about it & know more in the end."[72]

Alice considered her options as her term at Peel ended. Acceding to her mother's wishes would make her life easier, but she continued to seek ways to lessen her dependence on family funds and, by extension, the approval of her mother. Even without maternal prompting, Alice felt done with social work. "I've seen [it] pretty thoroughly in London," she wrote, "& don't feel that I want to spend any more time on it." She wanted to continue studying at LSE without the distractions of work—"it simply results in getting no studying done." One contingency plan became teaching in France or Germany to gather funds, if Mrs. Paul could not or would not keep her at LSE. Another was seeking Swarthmore's prestigious Lippincott Fellowship, which provided alumni with funds for graduate study abroad.[73]

Alice's class sensibilities again trumped her desire for self-reliance. The catalyst was accepting an invitation to spend the holidays in Holland with Mietza Heldring. She knew the Heldring family moved in court society; "I'm rather afraid my clothes won't be good enough," she told her mother. Unused to the experience of being the poor mouse, her anxiety peaked and she pressed her mother repeatedly for more funds in one letter. Her time with the Heldrings in Amsterdam became a whirl of concerts and fetes, theater and galleries. "I don't know when I've spent a happier two weeks," she wrote. "But it is awful to be here without money." She borrowed small amounts from her friends. She petulantly wrote home again that she needed "something when I land in London. It has been rather unfortunate not having any money for I have needed gloves etc badly but could not buy any." To her "great relief," money finally arrived before she returned to London.[74]

As she closed out her holiday, Alice sought her mother's approval for her plans, justifying herself in case the delay in forthcoming funds signaled her mother's displeasure. She made known her decision to find even cheaper rooms. Then she elaborated her scenario for the near future. "I am going to do nothing now but study and take my PHD [sic] and teach," she wrote. With Tacie's admonitions still fresh in her mind, she added tartly, "I suppose this will suit thee." The Lippincott prize could finance her doctoral studies in Germany or Switzerland for two years. "The German degree is the best to have in the world," she told Mrs. Paul, "as it is the hardest to get." Without the Lippincott, other American fellowships might suffice. Then, Alice maintained, "I will settle down & teach for the rest of my days." She squeezed in a postscript underscoring the need to stay abroad: "One cannot get a degree at a German Univ. unless one has studied there (that is in Germany itself) at least two years." None of Mrs. Paul's letters survive, but apparently she accepted the plan.[75]

Alice looked for new quarters. She and Nellie Molenaar, a Dutch student at Woodbrooke who was also entering the LSE, planned to room together. They found a suitable boarding house in Bloomsbury at 22-24 Gordon Street, within a twenty-minute walk of the LSE and close to the British Museum. The busy, tree-lined, thoroughly middle-class area was a welcome change. At a shared six dollars a week for a double room and two daily meals (fire and hot baths extra), the new place proved affordable and offered a lively mix of young Friends, students, teachers, and even an MP.[76]

Freed from social work, Alice turned her attention to her further education and the money needed to fund it. Of course, she planned to live frugally, but she now eschewed living like ordinary folk and accepted family funds when necessary. She thanked her mother for sending fifty dollars, then proceeded to detail anticipated expenses for the LSE term, concluding, "So I ought to have more money for books, clothes, etc." She could now do more than attend lectures; she wanted to participate in seminars and write papers so that professors might take her measure as a student. She needed their recommendations for her Lippincott Fellowship application.[77]

Alice had so far avoided mention of her suffrage activities in letters home, despite six months of attending WSPU meetings and celebrations. In late January 1909, Alice finally revealed her WSPU membership to her mother, though not the extent of her activities. "I have joined the 'suffragettes'—the militant party," she announced, later adding, "They are the ones who have really brought their question to the fore" amid "much comment and criticism."[78]

Her wariness underlines the fragility of her situation. She had fared poorly in her attempts at self-sufficiency. Thus, her life abroad could be brought to an immediate halt by a parental command to return home. It was one thing to describe attending a Pankhurst lecture, quite another to be regularly engaged with the controversial suffragettes, as they were labeled by the press. She hid her deepening involvement with the WSPU, indeed her apprenticeship in the Pankhurst school of protest.

Rachel Barrett, a former science teacher Alice encountered at LSE, drew the young Quaker into active WSPU participation. The two women met in a Hobhouse class; AP recalled the spirited Barrett's analytical skills and fortitude. The Welsh suffragist was "recuperating" from full-time WSPU organizing by pursuing her doctorate—an overachieving attitude that Alice recognized. One day, she remembered, Barrett "asked me if I would go out and help her in selling their paper, *Votes for Women*, in the street. So I did."[79]

The Pankhursts had grown the WSPU newspaper into a bullhorn for militant suffrage. After only two years, they sold thirty thousand copies weekly, many thanks to young, sometimes privileged, women hawking them on busy street corners. The widely distributed papers offered a kind of community both to current and prospective members, an imaginary place for the sharing of political views, as well as real space when women sold, shared, and discussed news.[80]

Alice now became more than a face in the WSPU crowd; she stepped out on (a corner of) the militant suffrage stage. Newspaper selling proved a more solitary and potentially threatening experience, unlike the marches where units of women shielded each other. Sellers became symbols of women claiming a

political identity in male territory, redrawing the boundaries of social convention. The thirtyish Barrett quickly revealed her seasoned skills. Alice recalled her
own awe of "how very bold and good she was" and, by comparison, "how very
timid and unsuccessful I was." She thought, "I didn't seem to be very brave by
nature." Despite her habitual self-effacement, Alice demonstrated courage simply
by undertaking the task.[81]

She had never attempted anything as confrontational as selling newspapers
on the streets of London. Standing in the gutter as vendor laws required, *Votes
for Women* sellers faced a whole gamut of responses. Women commonly reported
verbal and physical harassment. One recounted "a woman cursing me horribly"
as well as a "nasty taxi driver with a diabolical grin" whose cab forced her to the
pavement. By contrast, encouragement from all classes buoyed sellers' spirits.
"The real working men are so decent," wrote one seller, also noting a pretty young
woman who purchased the penny paper for her mother, declaring, "We are all
suffragists."[82]

Alice's desire for mastery probably overrode her reserve, with Barrett at her
side. Her experiences visiting destitute families accorded her some level of ease on
the public streets. But Barrett's expertise helped calm fears and arouse her competitive nature. We do not know AP's particular experience, but she found selling
Votes for Women palatable enough to continue, and soon proved herself enough to
be asked to take on more challenging duties.

Her poise on the street drew notice. Even seasoned organizers dreaded public
speaking so much that the WSPU eventually offered training in elocution and
dealing with harassment. Alice had school experience with debating and public
address, though she preferred to avoid the spotlight. As she recalled, "they began
to ask me to speak outdoors" at street meetings. "Naturally they asked anybody,
as I have always tried to do in our movement—to ask anybody to do anything that
I could get them to do." And, once again, Alice agreed. At first, she appeared at
street corner meetings, in neighborhood squares, and Tube or train stations; later,
she spoke at indoor meetings. She first took on the neophyte role of introducing
the main speaker, "someone who was an experienced speaker and would give you
a little confidence so that you'd know you didn't have to go on; you could stop in
a minute."[83]

Alice soon became the seasoned speaker at meetings, a feat she downplayed
sixty years later. "All we had to do was to tell what the movement was doing that
week, what they were trying to do," she recalled. She had forgotten the hostility
that went with the territory; hooligans routinely roughed up women. The public often presumed women straying beyond conventionally female territory to be
legitimate targets. WSPU speakers brought along makeshift platforms to ensure

they had the advantage of height for returning verbal fire or dodging rotten produce or stones.[84]

Alice Paul's willingness to undertake such work records her deepening commitment to the WSPU. By this time, she recognized that behaving unconven-
tionally in public courted bodily harm and charges of indecency, not to mention
parental disapprobation. Indeed, news-selling hardly squared with her own
refined ideal. Many avid WSPU members of AP's age and class declined to sell
papers or speak in public. The fictionalized novice in one contemporaneous novel
agreed to line up *Votes for Women* sellers and newsagents: "I feel that I ought to
go with these women myself," the narrator demurred, "but somehow I cannot
summon up sufficient courage to do it." The Pankhursts published many tales of
heroic paper-sellers, attempting to counter the all-too-real ordeals common to
the work.[85]

Alice's omission of her more dubious pursuits from her letters home suggests
how tentatively she stepped into unknown territory. She held one advantage: she
was an American with no reputation to uphold before family close at hand. She
did know Woodbrooke disapproval well and likely refrained from mentioning
her involvement to Woodbrookers stopping in London. And she gave no indication that her roommate Nellie joined her advocacy.

Alice maintained her school work and social life even as she expanded her
WSPU role. Negotiating the London streets in snow, rain, and heavy fog—one
day, she wrote, "It was blacker than night all day long"—gave her plenty of exercise. She spent a good deal of time studying at the library of the nearby British
Museum and made several trips further afield to the National Gallery. She
attended a play currently animating the British populace, *An Englishman's Home*,
and became acutely conscious of the possibility of war. "Thousands and thousands
of men have enlisted as volunteers," she wrote home. Women joined a voluntary
nursing corps. "There is a feeling in the air that war will come with Germany," she
wrote, "unless the English make themselves so strong that Germany will not dare
to fight."[86]

She stole a few minutes here and there to keep in touch with American friends
in Europe. Her Penn roommate Clara Thompson was studying in Italy and a
Swarthmore classmate and settlement house worker, Lydia Lewis, took a rest cure
in Rome. Rest cures were less common in the early twentieth century than in
previous decades, but a significant portion of privileged women found intense
volunteer work strained their constitution; family and physicians often encouraged them in that belief. Alice's vigor stood in stark contrast to such stories. Lewis
felt well enough to travel to London in late March, and the two women visited
Oxford.[87]

Alice continued to respond cautiously to her mother's queries about British suffrage. She offered her analysis of the difference between suffragists and suffragettes ("the latter have pursued militant methods") and the commonalities among various groups. She omitted her selling of *Votes for Women* on the street or her speaking at open-air meetings. When writing to her mother, she cast herself as a spectator, telling her "the excitement over the question is really amusing."[88]

As the first spring blooms faded, her plans started to fall apart. She had applied to Swarthmore for the Lippincott Fellowship and, as an afterthought, applied for a Penn fellowship as backup. However, the Penn application arrived too late. Her former professor Carl Kelsey held out hope for some sort of special grant. "Let me know what your minimum necessities are," he wrote supportively. By mid-April, there was still no word from Swarthmore. "They certainly are taking a long time to make up their mind," Alice fretted. She grew downright peevish after her mother apparently warned her that she might not receive the coveted award: "Thee says thee does not think they will give it to me. I wonder why thee advised me to apply then." In May, she wrote Swarthmore to inquire and waited impatiently as the mails criss-crossed the Atlantic.[89]

Everything seemed to go awry at once. Her glasses broke, she needed dental work, and the landlady abruptly raised the rent for tourist season. She and Nellie decided to move and finally located other, less convenient rooms west of Hyde Park. Funds once more grew scarce. Summer term fees came due and Alice needed clothes. She had just received one hundred dollars from home, and now she needed more. "I hope I am not spending too much," she wrote, treading carefully on her mother's fiscal nerves. "It seems as though I am always asking for it but $100 does not go far."[90]

Despite the strain of waiting, Alice felt confident about her Lippincott application. Her academic record seemed superior to those of other applicants and she had experienced a variety of workplaces. A doctorate earned in Germany was the most prestigious education anyone could acquire; there was no reason for the Swarthmore fellowship committee to quibble there. It seemed unlikely that any other candidate of comparable age matched her in experience, language preparation, and academic work. So she told herself.[91]

Suddenly the wait ended with Swarthmore choosing someone else for the Lippincott Fellowship. They chose Mary Janney ('06). Unversed in rejection, an anguished Alice wrote her mother, "I was not surprised at not getting the fellowship but I was astounded that I should lose it to Mary Janney. She was not considered at all bright at Swarthmore—is about the level of [cousin] Susannah Parry for instance in brains I had always thought—at least that is her reputation." Accustomed to a place among the best and brightest, Alice searched for an explanation. She rejected family connections, political intrigue, and even Helen leaving Swarthmore. She finally decided that the Swarthmore faculty had little faith in her talents.

> So they must apparently think that I have very little ability if they prefer Mary Janney to me & therefore I will never apply to them again. If I had lost to a very clever person I would have thought it due to the strength of my opponent & it might have been worth while trying again. But when you lose to such a very weak opponent it seems to me clear that your own position must be exceedingly weak. I will certainly never have an easier person to compete with than Mary Janney so if I can't beat her it is useless to try against anyone else.[92]

Alice did not blame herself, as women often do when confronted with defeat. Her reaction was more typically male: she pointed the finger at outside forces, at Swarthmore for failing to recognize her abilities. Her self-esteem remained intact, despite the psychological blow. Indeed, in her confidence, she neglected to consider the possibility that Swarthmore's appraisal of Janney might differ from her own.

She cast about for a way to satisfy her ambition and still appease her mother. Mrs. Paul sent the Lippincott results with a letter flatly telling her peripatetic daughter to come home. Alice reviewed her options but not before lashing out at her mother: "I'm sorry thee thinks I have spent too much. When one has no idea of what one's income is it is impossible to form any idea of what one ought to spend." As to the future, "if thee wants me to earn money," she could teach in Germany or America—American schools paid more. However, "if I teach school I am not getting on in my own work." Alice held out for her original goal of the doctorate, but through independent study, "unless thee needs the money I think I had better stay at home next year & study by myself." She felt so disappointed that she stopped attending LSE classes. As she waited for her mother's response and prepared to leave London, the Pankhursts entered the conversation.[93]

They wanted Alice to join a June 29 deputation to Prime Minister Asquith, this one led by Emmeline Pankhurst herself. Asquith invariably refused the deputations, despite the presence of a suffrage bill in Parliament. Alice understood, she recalled, "You would be under some danger of being arrested and imprisoned, so you must not accept this invitation unless you were willing to do this." Arrest seemed a far cry from street-corner speeches.[94]

The WSPU aimed to assert woman's right to be heard—a right that now resonated to Alice's very core. But at what cost to her social standing, to her family relations? Would defying propriety accomplish anything? We will never know—and perhaps Alice Paul never knew—the full provenance of her decision, except that it came amid the most profound failure of her life. We have her recollection: "I remember hesitating the longest time and writing the letter and not being able to get enough courage to post it and going up and walking around the post office wondering whether I dare put this in." She debated using an assumed name—"I thought all my family and everybody I knew would object"—and discarded the idea. Finally, her ambition stymied, the cautious Alice Paul seized the moment. Her despair supplied what she lacked in certainty. "So at last I got up enough courage to post my letter, saying I would go."[95]

4

"A New and More Heroic Plane"

DEVOTING HERSELF TO feminist advocacy unexpectedly awakened Alice Paul's deep-seated connection to her familial, Quaker, and historical past and gave her a political identity. Before leaving Britain in January 1910, an unusually emotional Alice addressed her compatriots in a stirring farewell to her time spent with the WSPU. As she spoke, the narrative rooting her impassioned commitment bubbled up. She underscored the inherently male role she had assumed. "As an American citizen," she told the audience, she "had often longed to be one of those who had fought in the revolution instead of being merely a descendant."[1] By calling up US history before her British audience, she implicitly connected the American and British suffrage movements, despite her previous lack of interest in her native country's suffrage activism.

Six months before the January speech, Alice Paul's decision to risk arrest in the wake of a wrenching failure began to reshape every day of her future. Her charismatic authority as an American suffrage leader grew out of the six months she spent as an itinerant organizer for the Pankhursts' WSPU. Her exploits during these months became a proving ground that legitimized her subsequent American role, inspired her followers, and, most importantly, gave her the confidence to lead. She launched and drove her leadership out of the bedrock of resolve and political acumen she built and the expanded strategic repertoire she acquired during these months.

Her subsequent letters home demonstrate her deep cognizance of the Pankhursts' philosophy and tactics as well as her intensifying attachment to their cause. She understood the value of individual conscience from Quaker and American history; the Pankhursts showed her its power. She tested her academic expertise in political science on the real world, learning how to read political opportunity and strategic efficacy, and adapted to the requisite physicality of WSPU action as if learning a new sport. The freedom the Pankhursts gave their itinerant workers enhanced her motivation along with her skills, while teamwork offered immediate support, feedback, and ready access to movement veterans. She felt loath to conclude the most fervent experience of her young life and repeatedly rebuffed her mother's insistence that she return to America.

After initiating confrontational tactics in 1907, the Pankhursts became highly successful at drawing attention to the suffrage cause. *Votes for Women* and frequent rallies sustained the faithful and lured converts like Alice; disruptions at political events and deputations to Parliament invited arrest and, more importantly, debate that reverberated from the street to the courts into the press. Imprisonments only amplified the debate. The Pankhursts epitomized their definition of militancy—active opposition to a national government that excluded women—with their battle cry, "Deeds, not Words." Their day-to-day expression of militancy evolved, consciously informed by centuries of radical protest. As Emmeline Pankhurst asserted in one speech, "Nothing has ever been got out of the British Parliament without something very nearly approaching a revolution."[2]

The Pankhursts mined deep veins of social and political reform. For women's ends, they refashioned rhetoric and political action ranging back to the Magna Carta and as far afield as South Africa. Emmeline Pankhurst and her late husband, Richard, longtime activists, had raised their daughters to follow in their footsteps. Their eldest daughter, Christabel, worked with them on socialist causes through the Independent Labour Party (ILP) and the Fabian Society; the Pankhurst home became a gathering place for leftists of all persuasions. Emmeline and Christabel turned away from these connections after they threatened WSPU autonomy; nevertheless, the pages of the weekly *Votes for Women* attested that many of their practices sprang from leftist forms of political challenge. Some strains of protest gained particular strength from Quaker experience.[3]

In England, as in America, Quakers engaged with suffrage represented the leading edge of the faith. One English Quaker suggested that "the very fact of unquestioned equality" within the Friends' religious principles delayed the recognition of the suffrage issue, some Friends being "slow in realizing the need of many others who have not that equality." In both Britain and America, women gained policy-making—if not real—equality within Quakerism only after a lengthy struggle; despite the substantial majority of female members, the Friends as a religious body hesitated to endorse suffrage officially.[4]

Certainly, the Pankhursts' belief that moral authority trumped the letter of the law held a clear appeal for Friends. However, Alice Paul was unusual among Quakers in her willingness to join WSPU protests. The experience of Alice Clark, a longtime activist, suggests a common response to the WSPU. Clark, eleven years AP's senior, belonged to the mainstream suffrage alliance. She appeared at a few WSPU events (along with other family members), but she did not formally join. In 1906, Clark told a Union critic, "My Quaker descent made me feel that it was rather an admirable thing to go to prison for one's principles." However, Clark never went to prison, and by mid-1908 she could not countenance increasingly "offensive" tactics; she continued to express support but never participated again, believing forceful tactics violated the age-old Quaker peace testimony. Alice Paul tolerated a higher level of aggression than Clark, for reasons her letters never discuss.[5]

We can also only speculate about why she accepted the consciously military-style WSPU hierarchy to which some members had objected. In line with their focus on action, the Pankhursts reached beyond the democratic conventions of suffragists to craft an organization built for speed, efficiency, and control—quite different from the Quaker practice of consensus. One disaffected WSPU group argued in 1907 for more inclusive decision-making and defected after Emmeline Pankhurst spurned their proposals and abolished her group's constitution. "The WSPU is not hampered by a complexity of rules," Mrs. Pankhurst later declared. "We have no constitution and by-laws; nothing to be amended or tinkered with or quarreled over at an annual meeting." Most members supported her, agreeing that "the WSPU is simply a suffrage army in the field. It is purely a volunteer army, and no one is obliged to remain in it." Alice apparently respected that logic and was willing to follow the Pankhursts' lead.[6]

Hierarchy notwithstanding, enterprising followers often informed and at times led WSPU practice. Christabel Pankhurst acknowledged as much: "Our organizers and members," she wrote later, "often astonished themselves and their friends by their ability and initiative." For instance, when two women threw stones at 10 Downing Street in 1908 in retaliation for police roughness, the Pankhursts embraced the token violence. Mrs. Pankhurst herself soon concentrated on being the public face of the WSPU, ceding day-to-day decision-making to Christabel and co-leaders Emmeline and Frederick Pethick-Lawrence (called the "triumvirate"). The 1907 splinter group reconstituted itself as the Women's Freedom League (WFL), and became known for its nonviolent form of militancy, tactics AP later emulated.[7]

By the summer of 1909, the Pankhursts' frustration mounted. Their campaign to punish the government party (the Liberal political party in power) had successfully ratcheted up debate; nevertheless, Parliament came no closer to granting equal suffrage. Instead, Prime Minister Asquith announced a decision to refuse all future suffrage deputations, including the WSPU's.[8]

The WSPU leaders resolved to test their right to petition the prime minister. Alice agreed to risk arrest for this June 29 event, the Pankhursts' largest deputation to date. When *Votes for Women* termed petitioning an "instrument of remonstrance," AP no doubt recalled her familial connection to that signal petition in American Quaker history, the 1657 Flushing Remonstrance. In both 1657 and in 1909, a moral law demanded redress. The sacred British right of petition spoke to remedying grievances and, inextricably, to immunity from sanction. Yet police had routinely arrested suffragettes in earlier deputations. The WSPU determined to challenge the constitutionality of the arrests.[9]

The Pankhursts sent artist Marion Wallace Dunlop, a descendant of the Scottish patriot William Wallace, to the main Parliament entrance to underscore the principle involved. Dunlop stamped a violet notice of the event on the wall along with a pointed excerpt from the 1689 Bill of Rights:

> It is the right of the Subject
> to petition the king,
> and all commitments and prosecutions
> for such petitioning are illegal.

Dunlop's arrest and subsequent imprisonment generated the anticipated press, and the stage was set for the Pankhursts' distinctive brand of constitutional theater.[10]

Dramatizing women's exclusion allowed the Pankhursts to demonstrate their belief in constitutional government simultaneously with their challenge of its authority; they reimagined the act of citizenship. At the same time, the protest presented a powerful symbolic tableau of Woman seeking access to the body politic. Parliament's increasingly violent resistance to change, in the Pankhursts' logic, obliged progressively more forceful tactics. The militants declared themselves actors in the political sphere and engaged citizens in the process of claiming their rights, not unlike the barons who demanded the Magna Carta in 1215 or, in the present day, Russian peasants revolting or Indians rebelling against South African rule. As Christabel wrote the previous year, "Those who are outside the Constitution have no ordinary means of securing admission; and therefore they must try extraordinary means." Just as a locked-out homeowner would break a window to gain entry, she wrote, "British women, who find the doors of the Constitution barred against them, are prepared to force their way in as best they can." Alice later employed a similar metaphor. Mrs. Pankhurst couched the idea in more positive terms. "We are here not because we are law-breakers," she argued, "we are here in our efforts to become law-makers."[11]

The Pankhursts prepared for the June 29 deputation in their usual meticulous fashion. The Marion Dunlop publicity, augmented by advance notice in *Votes for Women* and on pavements and broadsides posted all over London, focused public attention; the Pankhursts realized early on the value of ballyhoo for spiking interest. The deputation players received point-by-point instructions. "They told us *just* what to do, where to meet, what to wear, how to act, everything," an aged Alice still recalled. Veterans told new volunteers to expect to be kicked, pushed, or knocked down by the police; they encouraged them to wear padding.

The tip brought to many minds the previous year's Albert Hall meeting when hall stewards seized suffragettes who dared to interrupt speakers, then "bumped them down the steps of the orchestra [and] dragged them over chairs by the hair." This time, in self-defense, some women created papier-mâché armor to wear under thick athletic jerseys; Alice devised cushioning by winding fat black ropes of spinners' cotton wool around her body.[12]

By seven thirty that evening, perhaps fifty thousand onlookers (AP saw "millions") expectantly crowded the streets around Parliament as Alice joined the pre-event rally in Caxton Hall, a favorite staging area of the Pankhursts. The rally did more than line up protesters, however; it fired up the women's courage and solidarity for facing the predictable violence. Alice attended enough of these rallies to master their craft. The WSPU fife and drum corps played and the packed hall vibrated with green, white, and purple banners. Yet the mood felt tense as the women double-checked their padding and contemplated the drama awaiting them. From the narrow stage, Emmeline Pethick-Lawrence and Christabel Pankhurst reassured the faithful of their virtue; one witness compared the assembly to "a service of dedication." Duly fortified, the lead group filed out to "The Marseillaise" ("To arms!"), while others awaited their turn silently. Alice knew that Mrs. Pankhurst had declared that the prime minister's failure to grant an interview would lead them to use "every possible effort to gain entrance" to the House of Commons.[13]

Both the Pankhursts and the government carefully choreographed the spectacle. The WSPU planned to send forth not one, but a series of deputations; if the authorities rebuffed the initial group, another would start off, and so on. At eight o'clock, a horsewoman announced the formal protest, her black bowler and riding habit enlivened by a "Votes for Women" sash. Emmeline Pankhurst and her deputation of eight then pushed through the crowd along Victoria Street. As they neared Parliament Square, mounted police held back the throng and their counterparts on foot lined the perimeter of the square and every entrance to Parliament, some three thousand police all told. Curious MPs left the House and stood hatless by the police barricades.

Police officials escorted Mrs. Pankhurst—"pale," wrote one supporter, "but proud and perfectly calm, with that look of courage and persistency on her face"—and her group through the cleared square to the Commons entrance. Officials presented her with another rejection from Prime Minister Asquith, whereupon Mrs. Pankhurst insisted the women had "come here in the assertion of a right." Asked to leave, she replied, "I am firmly resolved to stand here until I am received." When a police inspector began to push the group back, Mrs. Pankhurst lightly struck him, an assault, strictly speaking, that ensured immediate arrest and thereby protected the two elderly women in her group.[14]

The arrests prompted the second act of the drama, a tableau symbolizing woman's persistence. Sixteen deputations pressed forward, one by one, into what a newspaper called a "maelstrom of shouting and swaying humanity." The women were told, according to Alice, to "try to force our way through the police lines into the house [sic] of Commons." AP's location is not clear, but her subsequent description suggests a good vantage point. "It was really an awful scene," she wrote her mother. "We were all padded as though for a football match—it is a wonder that no one was killed." She went on:

> The suffragettes threw themselves against the lines of police & forced their way through once or twice only to be captured in a few minutes. Behind them was the crowd yelling & shouting & pushing them on but afraid to take any part for fear of being arrested. The police grabbed the suffragettes by the throats & threw them flat on their backs over & over again.

Alice's team pushed through the lines and the police shoved them back. "The mounted police rode us down again & again," she recounted breathlessly. "Finally when the police could not drive the women back or control the scene," the suffragettes were arrested.[15]

The demonstration required Alice to expand her notion of womanly behavior and acquire a new set of skills, skills that went beyond those needed in parades, paper-selling, or open-air meetings. The required level of self-possession and raw courage proved far beyond her earlier activities, beyond anything a privileged woman might anticipate encountering. While she had dealt with verbal hostility and occasional physical aggression, in Parliament Square a higher level of belligerence emanated not from the public, whom officers for the most part held back, but from the police. They countered the women's pushing with shoving; horses ramped up the physical threat. How much rough handling Alice withstood is not clear. Her narration, often in third person, as if she witnessed rather than endured the combat, hints at the psychological impact of being knocked about. Some of her restraint, however, was probably intended to deflect alarm from her mother.

Unintentionally, Alice's arrest became a comic high point. Journalist Laurence Housman, standing just outside the Commons doors, noticed one well-stuffed figure in her tightly buttoned coat. "The rough handling began," he later wrote, and "the buttons (strained beyond endurance) broke from their moorings in swift succession, and the padding like the entrails of some woolly monster emerged roll upon roll ... The crowd was, of course, highly diverted. 'Oh, Look at the stuffing!' was the cry. Immediately she became a popular favourite; and, as she went off under arrest carrying her coils with her, opinion was in her favour, and cheers followed her."[16]

Alice did not witness the third act of the constitutional drama. While she and other suffragettes recovered in a nearby police station, several audacious women made their way to nearby government offices, where they wrapped petitions around small stones with string and cautiously threw the stones through darkened windows in contempt of a government that battered and excluded them. Christabel Pankhurst quickly endorsed the token violence.[17]

Oblivious to the stone throwers, Alice watched in dismay as suffragettes entered the police station. "The scene was one awful nightmare," she wrote afterward, her detachment slipping briefly. "I never shall forget the women as they were brought into the police station half fainting & their clothes torn to pieces. It was dreadful." She soon discovered an LSE classmate among the detainees and another American woman named Lucy Burns, in London expressly for the protest. "She had a little United States flag of some type on her suit," Alice recalled, "and so I went up to her to introduce myself—we were the only two Americans there." As several hours of agitation in the square ebbed, more than one hundred women and a few men sat under arrest. Police held Alice and her cohorts until Parliament adjourned at 1 a.m.; arraigned them in, she later wrote, "a common police court with drunks, thieves, & disorderlies"; then released them on their own recognizance.[18]

In Moorestown, New Jersey, Tacie Paul opened the latest letter from London, unprepared for the news. "Dear Mamma," her eldest wrote, "On Tuesday I went on a deputation of the Suffragettes to the House of Commons & 108 of us were arrested." She knew Alice had joined the militants, but arrested? What about the promise to come home? Her daughter now divulged that she had joined the Pankhursts, not a few months earlier, as a previous letter claimed, but a year earlier. "I never did anything militant till now," Alice insisted, "for I could not risk having to give up my work, in case of being sent to prison."[19]

Tacie Paul found herself outmaneuvered, and Alice probably foresaw this in making the decision to join the deputation. She assured her mother, and perhaps herself, that her unconventional behavior was temporary: she still planned to return and study for her doctorate. "So I will come home as soon as this trial is over—I cannot come before," AP told her mother after describing the protest. "And if I am sent to prison I will come as soon as I am released." The sentence, Alice thought, might be six weeks. She staved off parental disapproval by asking for money for her return home. From her mother's perspective, the situation looked like a fait accompli.

The nine-page letter Alice wrote after her arrest recorded her identification with the Pankhursts' righteous indignation. The detail and emotional underpinning of her account of the demonstration contrast markedly with her earlier letters, which breezily skip from one incident to the next. She both confessed a transgression to her mother and passionately tried to convince her that the cause she had joined was just. She drew no comparison with the American suffrage movement, or indeed American politics, but embraced the Pankhursts' effort as her own.

Alice was engaged at a visceral and intellectual level. She vigorously denounced the prime minister's position as "incomprehensible," her outrage tinged with class attitude. "He told us that almost all his time is taken up in receiving deputations of men, & yet he will not receive [one] from women who need it much more for the men also have their representatives in parliament [sic]." She added, "And yet he receives rough hooligans representing the unemployed, & representatives on any subject however trifling as far as practical politics goes such as vivisection." Alice sized up the prime minister as a political opponent, much as she later took the measure of an American president. "It seems to be a matter of pride with him," she concluded, "never to yield anything to women."[20]

Since Alice now awaited trial, her mother had little choice but to accept the delay in her return. But the account Mrs. Paul wrote during her daughter's last months in Britain suggests that Alice had convinced her mother of the import of the Pankhursts' demonstrations. Tacie Paul knew the Quaker history of dissent, even on her own family tree. If the protest AP described was not exactly the nonviolent resistance Friends had historically embraced, neither could her actions be termed "violent." Certainly, Quakers of old accepted imprisonment rather than disown their beliefs. Mrs. Paul stood for suffrage herself; indeed, she had introduced her eldest to the suffrage cause. She decided to keep the *Votes for Women* and news photos Alice sent for safekeeping and cabled money for the ticket home.

Alice's post-protest missive to her mother revealed the competing forces at play in her mind. The fact that she withheld her militant involvement from her mother until she faced the possibility of a prison term underscores her trepidation at venturing outside accepted Quaker and female mores. Her apparent fearlessness in a dangerous and frightening situation may have been a reluctance to admit fear, especially to a disapproving parent. The elated tone of the letter suggests that political fervor met her emotional needs at this vulnerable time. Indeed, such a radical shift in her careful plans and conception of herself required vulnerability. She later described her sense of fulfillment as satisfying a hunger to connect with her Quaker progenitors, who had figured in the political culture the Pankhursts drew upon.

While Alice and the other protestors awaited their July 9 trial, two other developments shaped AP's thinking about effective protest. First, gentle, middle-aged Marion Dunlop, serving a one-month sentence for defacement, refused all nourishment after authorities denied the usual WSPU request for political prisoner status. Taken aback by the move, prison officials tried tempting her with food. Asked what she wanted to eat, the prisoner reportedly declared: "My determination." Dunlop grew weaker—"they felt her pulses every half hour," Alice said—and the authorities' anxiety deepened. Finally, after she had gone four days without food, they released her. One WSPU organizer later observed, "The Government had not had experience of hunger-strikes then, and the Cabinet, being far more afraid of death than any Suffragette, let them out once the doctor's report was unsatisfactory."[21]

Indeed, the Pankhursts quickly realized that hunger striking offered a compelling tactic. Fasting strengthened the WSPU demand for political prisoner status and embarrassed the government, not only by the early release but doubly when the WSPU heavily publicized the prisoners' experiences. Most importantly, hunger striking won suffragettes shorter terms in jail. And the symbolism of women wasting away for want of a basic right was powerful. The Pankhursts lauded Dunlop as a hero. The word passed quickly to Alice. "All the Suffragette prisoners after this are going to make the same or some other resistance until they are either released or given [political prisoner] treatment," she wrote her mother. She went on confidently, "They will soon force the authorities to treat them as political prisoners."[22] Her prediction pointed up her naiveté in the world of political protest. By the end of her time with the Pankhursts, however, Alice understood enough about the tactic of hunger striking to employ it herself in coming years.

While the Dunlop saga unfolded, another group of militants exercised their own right to petition. The WFL, which splintered off from the WSPU in 1907, acquired a reputation for nonviolent militancy. Alice Paul later borrowed more from the WFL's passive-aggressive approach than the WSPU's more strenuous one. The WFL made its own request to petition the prime minister; he rebuffed them too. As the Commons sat down for its evening session on July 5, eight WFL members brandishing a petition silently took up stations at the public entrance, asking after the prime minister each time Big Ben chimed the quarter-hour. The women remained until the Commons adjourned at four in the morning; the next day the WFL announced its plan to continue its "Siege of Westminster" until Asquith granted them an audience. After waiting a few long days in vain, the sentinels moved to 10 Downing Street, where officers promptly arrested them for obstructing access to the official residence. Alice monitored the WFL protest in the days before her trial, telling her mother about "another & milder suffrage society." The siege persisted, despite repeated arrests, into the fall.[23]

The WFL offered a womanly alternative to the Pankhursts' brand of militancy. The quiet dignity of the Westminster siege implicitly confronted the notion that a political woman inevitably unsexed herself with defiant postures. The WFL, drawing on Milton, characterized itself as a "peaceful band of women 'who only

stand and wait'; we have neither invited nor created disorder." The group stressed
its womanly qualities, drawing explicit as well as implicit comparisons to the earlier WSPU protest. Alice recognized the political ploy; some of her later political
choices seem influenced by the WFL's skill at manipulating the WSPU image for
its own benefit. In July 1909, the WFL's attempt to play off the WSPU's unruliness
failed to alter the result. The siege, nevertheless, drove home a larger point: the
government denied women's petitions whether they obeyed or broke the law.²⁴

The July 9 trial offered another opportunity for the Pankhursts to exhibit
their facility at using courtrooms as spectacle: an occasion—thanks to press
coverage—to drive home their version of the truth for an audience far beyond
the courtroom. Alice gleaned only secondhand knowledge of WSPU court tactics this time, because she sat outside the Bow Street courtroom. She wrote her
mother that during Emmeline Pankhurst's and another leader's trial, "the rest of
us were kept in a big billiard room over the police court. Their trial lasted nearly
all day." Alice explained that the WSPU used the leaders' trials as tests, "as our
case depends on this same point." She understood the goal and the use of the
pronoun "we" underlined her accord: "We are hoping that we will all be acquitted
& that it will be shown that Mr. Asquith (prime minister) was the one who took
illegal action & not we."²⁵ All too soon, her own trials would offer the opportunity to use similar tactics.

Competing narratives formed the core of the trial argument. Alice thought
the verdict "the greatest success the Suffragettes have ever had yet." Charged with
interfering with police duties, Mrs. Pankhurst asserted her right to petition and
labeled her arrest unconstitutional. In the end, the magistrate ruled the presenting of petitions legal; compelling the prime minister to receive deputations he
judged illegal. He thus found the suffragettes guilty. Nevertheless, he noted, the
importance of the point of law encouraged an appeal. "Before," Alice wrote, the
suffragettes "have always been bundled off as drunks and disorderlies. Now their
case is recognized as involving a great constitutional issue. It is a pity," she went on
caustically, "that some 400 women should have been imprisoned before the rea-
sonableness of the Suffragettes' contention penetrated the heads of the Judges."
Believing her narrative had temporarily won the day, Emmeline Pankhurst
accepted the right to appeal and no one went to prison that day. The fourteen
stone throwers received an immediate sentence a few days later; they promptly
declared a hunger strike.²⁶

Alice and Lucy Burns became acquainted during their hours awaiting the
trial's outcome in the upstairs billiard room. AP recalled, "We became very good
friends." The two shared a privileged upbringing and a graduate education. Like
William Paul, Lucy's father worked as a banker. Six years Alice's senior, Lucy had
studied abroad at the University of Berlin from 1906 to 1908, which meant she

had lived there during AP's time in Berlin. Alice's small-town upbringing differed from Lucy's childhood in the prosperous part of Brooklyn; Lucy's Catholicism, a faith disdained by Tacie Paul, did not faze Alice.[27]

The two young Americans soon realized their common problem: the trial appeal delayed a final verdict for months. Alice quickly assured her mother that she was not trapped in England. The two women approached Emmeline Pankhurst, who "told us we could leave the country any time we had to & when the trial came on they would explain to the magistrate that we had gone & the union would pay our fine if there were a fine."[28]

Thrilled to be part of the WSPU's finest hour, Alice felt more committed to her new advocacy than to her careful life plan. Her freedom restored, she went south to the magnificent Surrey Hill countryside for the weekend with companions from her "band of 6 on the deputation." She grew reflective amid the natural beauty. "I'm becoming so passionately fond of England that I'll be heart broken to leave it if I stay much longer," she wrote her mother wistfully. Nevertheless, Alice conceded, her words sounding rote, "It is quite time that I should come home.... As soon as I get thy money I will pay for my passage home." Her words betrayed her misgivings: "I can really study there much better than in Europe or at a University because other places there is so much going on that one feels one should not miss."[29]

Alice did book passage home. However, the urge to continue with the Pankhursts proved compelling. When the WSPU asked her to help disrupt an important meeting in Norwich, she agreed, telling herself she had time before her ship sailed. Clearly, the emotional intensity of the past two weeks had deepened the young Quaker's sense of loyalty; she knew the Pankhursts now counted on her. As she later said, "Once you were arrested, and they saw you were perfectly willing to be arrested—I mean you didn't disclaim all connections with the movement—from that time on you were asked to do more and more. They had so few people they could send to do anything." She had undoubtedly encountered many WSPU members who balked at joining demonstrations or risking arrest. Those like AP, who willingly stepped up, saw themselves as a distaff version of Shakespeare's band of brothers. The Pankhursts' facility for identifying "women of the right spirit" stayed with Alice.[30]

Her settlement house work had exposed her to many less privileged women; while organizing for the Pankhursts, she became accustomed to working under and alongside them. She soon joined two other activists bumping along in a horse-drawn WSPU carriage adorned with suffrage flags on her way northeast to Norwich. The Pankhursts typically teamed a veteran with novices: Louisa Cullen, a married woman of thirty-three who left school at fourteen to work, led the expedition. Cullen had taken part in nearly every type of protest and organizing the

WSPU offered, and Alice may have known her already from the July deputation. The third woman, Kathleen Jarvis, may have been the "parlor maid" Alice recalled as inexperienced, but she was "as enthusiastic as I was." The Pankhursts directed the three to provoke Winston Churchill, now a dapper thirty-five-year-old cabinet minister, who planned to address a Norwich audience the following Monday evening.[31]

WSPU advocates had disrupted ministers' speeches for four years, and officials now banned them from political meetings. Nevertheless, cabinet ministers proved relatively accessible compared to the prime minister and, as representatives of the government, still allowed suffragettes to challenge the party in power. As AP remembered, the Pankhursts "conceived this plan to publicly ask all the cabinet members what they were going to do about votes for women."[32]

The tang of salt air signaled their approach to Norwich, a city of one hundred thousand residents some ten miles west of the North Sea. It was an ancient town with charming historic buildings and cobbled streets. The artisans who built the town had a long history of dissenting politics and nonconformist religion. The three women arrived at the meeting site, storied St. Andrews' Hall, a centuries-old friary at the center of town. They eyed the generous plaza outside the hall's main doors, perfect for staging a demonstration.[33]

The suffragettes had four days to "rouse the town." The pace felt frenetic; organizers not uncommonly withdrew from exhaustion. Alice seemed to thrive, however. With Cullen's guidance, she learned how to create anticipation for the main protest, drawing on techniques she had already grasped for selling papers and gathering a crowd. The meetings she and the others organized drew larger and more responsive crowds each day. The women urged the townspeople, as Alice wrote, to "come in your thousands" to Churchill's speech. Local skepticism gradually faded and the evening meetings began to draw workers and tradespeople. Cullen soon boasted of "very large and extremely sympathetic" meetings.[34]

The WSPU's reputation had preceded the three activists, and the Norwich authorities' attempts to thwart the protest forced some recalculations. But the suffragettes already knew how to bob and weave. Officials first denied permission for the Churchill demonstration, prompting the women to move their start time from eight o'clock to five o'clock. Then, over the weekend, officials successfully stymied their plans to gain entry to the hall. When Alice mingled with tourists around the ancient hall, calling through the locked doors for entrèe, a caretaker cracked the door to explain, "The Suffragettes are about, and they mustn't get in." She found no other access. Cullen telephoned London for reinforcements, "some who would not be readily recognized as suffragettes."[35]

The run-up to Churchill's speech seemed promising. The suffragettes arrived on their open wagon around five o'clock the afternoon of July 26; some 250 people awaited them. After rousing speeches by Cullen and Jarvis, the three women left, only to reappear shortly after eight o'clock that evening. A throng of several thousand now swarmed St. Andrews' Plain, "many of them," one reporter observed, "anxious for a sight of the distinguished statesman, and others hoping for a little fun with the Suffragettes." Police arrived from all over the county to ensure "a straight path to the door" for those holding the requisite tickets; "a battalion of stewards [kept] watch and ward within."[36]

Alice now embraced the roughness of forcible entry like any other athletic challenge. "We called to the people to help us break into the meeting & then jumped out," she later wrote. "They opened a passage right to the doors & we rushed on—at the door were a great force of police who had linked arms to resist the onslaught of the crowd. In addition the door was locked & great iron gates also barred the entrance." The three came close to forcing their way in, but police quickly arrested and hustled them off, as the crowd continued to charge the doors. Unbeknownst to the police, WSPU reinforcements had secured tickets and sat waiting for a chance to interrupt Churchill.[37]

Winston Churchill felt wary of the WSPU. Pankhurst supporters had interrupted meeting after meeting during two elections for his Manchester seat; local satirists so ridiculed Churchill's remarks at one such event that he refused to be "henpecked into a question of such importance." (The rising political star did support adult suffrage, considered too radical by many.) Churchill, despite his glamorous pedigree, went down to defeat the second time; some doubted the WSPU claim to a rout, though the victor thanked the women. Parliament bigwigs quickly set him up in another seat in Dundee, Scotland. At Norwich, the minister chose to arrive and leave the back way.[38]

The Right Honourable Winston Churchill determined to speak "only about the Budget" that evening. He had not counted on the din from outside. A short while into his speech, the commotion grew so loud that Churchill finally stopped to note with a patronizing smile the "great distinction between a reasonable argument and incoherent clamor." He picked up his thread but then a male voice cut in loudly: "Why tax voteless women?" As the WSPU heckler walked out, another sprang up to cry, "Votes for Women!" Stewards closed in instantly and ejected the man. Churchill resumed speaking. A third cry rang out. One supporter straining to hear the speech grew angrier by the moment. He later told Alice, "There was such hell outside that I could scarcely hear a word that the speaker said." Indeed, the suffragettes' arrest only emboldened the crowd to keep charging the doors.[39]

The three WSPU comrades sat nearby in an anteroom, listening to the "roar and tumult" and feeling pleased with themselves. Alice wrote her mother, already thinking as a strategist, "I thought the demonstration of June 29 in London was effective but it was mild compared to this for here the people were all gathered in one spot & they got quite beyond the control of the police." Six policemen stood guard over the three women, and stewards stood nearby. "They even had to put the lights out in the building where we were kept so as to make the crowd think we had gone & the police hoped that then they would stop," Alice said. "So we sat there with our six policemen guarding us, in absolute darkness for over an hour."[40]

Officials declined to jail the women. After the crowd thinned, the authorities "charged us with having incited the crowd to riot and I, in addition" wrote Alice—a little puffed up in a most unQuakerly way—"with having assaulted the police." She appreciated the lack of "fearful scuffling" like the June 29 protest, a belated acknowledgment of her unease with the violence. Released after police declined to prosecute them, the three suffragettes rushed in vain to the train station to intercept Churchill's leave-taking. They failed to identify the private rail car where the minister sat waiting to depart with all the blinds down.[41]

Not everyone agreed with Alice that the event was a success. One local reporter wrote that nothing disturbed the meeting despite the fact that the police felt "sorely tried." Another paper's columnist thought the suffragettes presented "not altogether unreasonable claims," but felt "more and more convinced that these street demonstrations do the cause of woman suffrage much harm." He added that the police presence also caused more harm than good.[42]

The effectiveness of the demonstration lay again in the symbolism of competing narratives, a language in which Alice quickly gained fluency. When suffragettes forced Churchill and meeting officials to consider canceling, moving, or proceeding with a speech under exasperating conditions, they threatened male-dominated political affairs. The great fifteenth-century hall doors came to represent the age-old barriers to women's full citizenship. And the more vigorously the press insisted on the suffragettes' failure, the more the women (and readers and onlookers) claimed success. Alice acquired the knack of declaring victory at opportune moments.[43]

The most galling point for Alice was confessing to her mother that she had missed the ship home. "I had to cancel my passage because I was again arrested," she began cautiously. By the time the suffragettes drove their horses back to London on Tuesday, little time remained to pack and take the train to Liverpool by sail time Wednesday. Alice probably hoped for this on some level, but she knew that her mother would not appreciate the delay. She assured the frugal Mrs. Paul that she reclaimed her ticket deposit, "so I did not lose anything"; furthermore, the WSPU paid her expenses for Norwich. Alice went on to regale her mother with her Norwich exploits and noted others' arrests and releases at a similar WSPU protest in Northampton. "The government is evidently at its wit's end & dare not send any more to prison," she contended, "now that they all go on the hunger strike." Her judgment, again premature, did not conceal her sense of pride and triumph. Her sorely pressed mother, who was all set to welcome her home, received her daughter's letter the day before the steamship docked.[44]

By the time she returned from Norwich, Alice had become the "heart and soul convert" of her memory. She wrote her mother, "I will engage my passage again & let thee know as soon as possible," but, rather than do so, she continued working with the Pankhursts. Mrs. Paul chose to indulge Alice rather than cut her funds off. She probably wondered if her daughter was ever coming home.

Both Alice and Lucy Burns likely appeared a few days later for the July 29 WSPU "At Home." The mass meeting honored the stone throwers turned hunger strikers from the June House of Commons deputation. The Pankhursts had expertly honed the tactic of lauding those who took on the most difficult work. Alice learned to craft similar performances to build loyalty.[45]

This type of WSPU rally attracted a variety of spectators, including outlanders. The Pankhursts' celebrity drew some. As Frederick Pethick-Lawrence observed, "American women 'doing' London considered their visit incomplete" if they did not attend a Pankhurst rally. The Pankhursts welcomed onlookers, seizing any opportunity to preach beyond the choir. WSPU veterans understood the complexities of popular attraction. "The strange thing with the public," one working-class organizer observed trenchantly, "was that they did not like to see or read about Militancy, but they loved being told about it." She surmised, "Why women wanted the Vote was tame, dull, uninteresting. How women would get it was exciting, romantic, and amusing."[46]

Curious suffragists also attended WSPU meetings, much as Alice had initially. AP later encountered many Americans with firsthand experience of the Pankhursts. Travelers spread the word about the Pankhursts, and the most widely read American suffrage paper, the *Woman's Journal*, often featured WSPU content. The Pankhursts' more sensational exploits appeared in both British and American newspapers. Also, Elizabeth Cady Stanton's daughter, Harriot Stanton Blatch, had lived in England until 1902 and, in the years since her return to America, served as an important contact for Mrs. Pankhurst. Alice and Lucy stood out in the WSPU not so much as Americans but for the depth of their involvement. The two likely drew their own set of rubberneckers at the July 29 rally: the *Woman's Journal* had announced their arrests at the House of Commons, under the sedate heading "Activities of College Women."[47]

One guest at the rally listened very closely. Forty-year-old Mohandas Gandhi was visiting London in his capacity as a leader of the Indian civil rights movement in South Africa; he had borne insult and imprisonment during fifteen years spent developing his philosophy of passive resistance or, as he said in Hindi, *satyagraha*. On an earlier trip to London, Gandhi extolled the suffragette commitment, echoing the WSPU battle cry, "They are bound to succeed and gain the franchise, because deeds are better than words."[48]

Gandhi met Emmeline Pankhurst after the July 29 meeting and wrote at length about the WSPU's impressive organization and fundraising. "We have much to learn from the suffragettes," he advised his readers. The willingness to suffer imprisonment or even death, he believed, became an invincible "soul force." "If we want freedom," Gandhi wrote, "we shall not gain it by killing or injuring others (i.e., by the use of brute force) but by dying or submitting ourselves to suffering (i.e., by the use of soul force)." Gandhi later took issue with tactics like stone throwing, insisting that successful movements held "no room for impatience." The purity of nonviolent suffering, he believed, would ultimately win the day. Alice Paul came to agree with him. Her own sacrifices underlay her later appeal.[49]

Too immersed in the struggle to go home, Alice agreed to join Lucy at another cabinet member's speech the next evening. Chancellor of the Exchequer David Lloyd-George planned to address an audience in Limehouse in west London. Alice and Lucy played limited but timely roles, urging the crowd to burst through the meeting-hall doors. Eleven other women completed the team, including veteran Emily Wilding Davison. Unlike in Norwich, the police did not simply detain and charge the protestors; they arrested them. After a brief appearance the next day, the magistrate ordered all thirteen to serve from one day to two months or pay fines. Alice received fourteen days. All the women refused to pay fines and prepared themselves for London's prison for women, Holloway Gaol. Alice somehow tucked her court judgment away for safekeeping; she wanted to remember the day she went to prison.[50]

Votes for Women had published many prisoner accounts, so Alice had some inkling of what happened next. Nevertheless, she probably shuddered to see the grim horse-drawn "Black Maria" arriving; one suffragette compared it to "the hull of a great dead ship." The women stepped up and climbed in, one by one. As the van rumbled off to the north of London, the women lightened their mood by making "a flag of two [WSPU] regalia tied on the end of an umbrella; this we hoisted through a hole in the roof, and so, unnoticed by the police, we were able to display our colours all the way to Holloway." If one learned nothing else from the Pankhursts, the value of publicity became an instinct. As an earlier detainee observed, "Wherever you see the colours you know we are there and you know our meaning." The prisoners arrived at Her Majesty's Prison, Holloway, and Alice climbed down to see an imposing 1850s-era castellated structure featuring three stories of medieval-looking windows, not unlike many British castles she had once toured.[51]

The customary WSPU demand for political prisoner status began Alice's introduction to another facet of the Pankhurst challenge of state—that is, male—authority: the hunger strike. Young Mary Leigh, the most experienced of the group, told the prison's governor that she and the other clearly political detainees "could not consent to be treated as second-class offenders." Marion Dunlop's refusal of food and her prompt release only weeks earlier suggested, Emmeline Pankhurst later wrote, "a new and more heroic plane" for the WSPU, a long-sought solution to the authorities treating suffragettes as criminals.[52]

Prior to 1908, magistrates sentenced suffrage detainees to the "first division," a prison status designed for minor offenders. The first division commonly held political prisoners and allowed them privileges such as keeping books and writing materials, wearing their own clothing, and visiting with friends. The second division housed criminals, and the third kept hardened criminals. After early 1908, as Alice explained, "the government tried to stamp the movement out by putting us in the 2nd division where drunkards, thieves, etc. are put." Suffragettes of every class status felt the affront, believing their lofty motives accorded them moral authority. The insult did not end their agitation; nevertheless, the Pankhursts felt forced to accept such treatment until Dunlop showed them another way. "After 1 ½ years of argument," Alice wrote, "they saw that argument was of no avail & that the only thing was to resist."[53]

Alice and the other women knew how to respond when Holloway's governor refused them first division status. "We, of course, demanded proper treatment, refused to change our clothes or be inspected, or to go to our cells," one of the group reported to *Votes for Women*. "We were surrounded by wardresses, but linked arms and resisted with all our might, Mrs. Leigh rallying us with her cries of '*Never Surrender!*'" The governor intended to perform his court-ordered duty. He threatened to use force and summoned additional wardresses, warning the suffragettes darkly that male attendants might follow. The scrappy rebels fought to hold their own and shouted encouragement to each other. If the melee felt less glorious than the later *Votes for Women* accounts, the women understood their roles, as did the authorities.[54]

The Pankhursts encouraged resistance, realizing that it mitigated the inevitable feelings of powerlessness. Alice dived into this new experience like the others, fighting back as matrons dragged her to a cell. Warders outnumbered and overwhelmed the prisoners, forcing their linked arms apart. "Eventually," one woman recounted, "we were overpowered, resisting to the last." The matrons shoved a protesting AP into a cell and the steel door clanged shut. Immediately, Alice "began to destroy as much property as possible," a protest against both the rough treatment and the lack of ventilation. She made no mention of Quaker pacifism in later telling her mother she "broke every pane in my window—40 panes they tell me." She heard glass breaking in the cells around her. And she knew punishment would follow.[55]

The governor ordered the remaining women, including Lucy Burns, to don prison garb. Each and every one refused. "One determined opponent got a good grip on my hair," Lucy disclosed, "and all the others lending a willing hand, I was fairly bolted across the court into a punishment cell." There, Lucy "lay down to rest, and was just beginning to be at peace, when the door opened, a long file of wardresses came in, and before I [Lucy] had time to raise my head they fell upon me and fairly ripped my clothes off, leaving me lying on the floor only half covered and very much battered in body and bruised in spirit."[56]

Alice and the other window smashers maintained their roles, even as guards carried them to solitary confinement. "They tore off all our clothes & left us with only prison clothes," AP wrote her mother. She honored the group pledge to refuse the prison garments. "I sat there for about 2 hours with nothing on," she reported impassively. She could not bring herself to write how excruciatingly vulnerable, how defenseless she undoubtedly felt as a woman raised to wear layer upon layer of clothing, in accordance with the propriety of the time. The Pankhursts' script demanded extraordinary fortitude.[57]

Once she recovered from the shock of her nakedness, Alice examined the narrow brick-walled solitary cell, scarcely wide enough to allow her to spread her arms. She already shivered on the cold stone floor. She smelled sewage, almost tasted the dankness. This window resisted her attempts to smash it; its opaque and dingy panes let in scant light. Below the window, the cell seemed clean enough; she knew vermin were common though. A plank bed stood on one side, a stool and metal dishes by the opposite wall. A small shelf in one corner held a stained water mug, soap and towel, toothbrush, comb and brush. She heard the woman in the next cell and, faintly, others singing or calling out. London's East End held worse; however, she never experienced confinement there. After two hours of shivering nakedness, "they brought me a blanket so I remained wrapped up in a blanket until I was released."[58]

Suffragettes' accounts of imprisonment in *Votes for Women* became part of the Pankhursts' strategy to embarrass the government while challenging its use of excessive force. As Sylvia Pankhurst later wrote pointedly, "Suffering born for a cause begets sympathy with that cause and coercion arouses sympathy with the coerced." The women's accounts formed one piece of an overall political strategy and thus may have overdramatized or embellished actual events. Nonetheless, Alice's subsequent letter home, while not as detailed, corroborates the basics of those published accounts.[59]

Undaunted by solitary confinement, Alice joined the others in a hunger strike—now a pivotal tactic in the WSPU's challenge to the British government. The prisoners believed that their voluntary hardship gained adherents for the cause and discredited governmental authority. Hunger strikes embodied political resistance in a way easily communicated to the public. Furthermore, the idea of intentional fasting was familiar in many religious traditions. The hunger strike thus suited the moral tenor of the Pankhursts' quest and allowed them to emphasize the womanliness of the prisoners.[60]

Alice embraced voluntary starvation as a political weapon; nevertheless, throughout both her British and American imprisonments, she declined, for the most part, to turn her personal ordeal into a feminist spectacle. She never turned the particulars of her experience into political fodder for *Votes for Women*. For a woman who later milked spectacles for any political leverage, her reluctance seems surprising. The answer to this apparent contradiction may lie in her Quaker heritage. Friends historically held selfless suffering in awe; Moorestown Quakers in the early twentieth century, on the other hand, more likely viewed hunger striking as "unseemly" conduct, antithetical to Quaker propriety. As with so much of that heritage, Alice fashioned a hybrid path, striking with the others but avoiding the *Votes for Women* display of the experience.[61]

The reality of the hunger strike was dreadful. Alice told her mother simply that they "all refused all food," taking only water. The first couple of days, solidarity buoyed the women. They sang and called to each other. Lucy often sang to herself, every song she knew, finding it "good exercise, and cheering," she later wrote. She carefully omitted singing "Home Sweet Home." Inexorably, hunger faded as weakness set in. Severe headaches, depression, even delirium followed. One prisoner in AP's group felt tremendous hunger only on one day; another felt ravenous and dreamed of elaborate banquets until she "grew too weak to care." Although she drank water, Alice too felt lethargy gradually overwhelming any desire to eat.[62]

Lucy mostly feared loss of control. Indeed, violations to the women's bodies began with the police buffeting during protests; the rough handling continued in prison. Lucy wrote, "The worst thing to endure was the fear of being overpowered." She feared betraying solidarity with personal inadequacy. "I was afraid I might become unconscious and have something poured down my throat—or that I might walk in my sleep (under pressure of hunger) and take the food which was left overnight in the room." Lucy worried about some of her companions, perhaps thinking of Alice, who seemed "very young and not at all strong."[63]

As Lucy's account indicates, suffragettes often viewed the physical and emotional challenge of solitary confinement as a test of their value to the cause. Measuring up could mean a renewed sense of strength and self-confidence. Our knowledge of Alice's particular experience is slight: the women who recounted their prison days never mentioned her, and her letter home offered no further details.

Nevertheless, she did not lack psychological resources. She felt comfortable on her own after living independently in the slums, fending for herself, working in the midst of destitution. She knew few songs, but her wide knowledge of literature, especially poetry and Dickens, gave her plenty of stories to rehearse. Furthermore, her ease with silent worship provided a spiritual tool to counter the long hours. She relished testing her boundaries, though the passivity of the hunger strike seemed more feminine than much of her work with the Pankhursts.

Alice's later willingness to repeat the hunger strike suggests that she felt a sense of empowerment during the long days in Holloway, perhaps similar to that described by a WSPU compatriot. Three months earlier, Emmeline Pethick-Lawrence called prison "a place of many surprises." "You go to Holloway thinking that it is a place of imprisonment and restriction," she wrote, "and you find that it is a place of release and deliverance." She found her prison days allowed her "release from all fear." That release felt profound. "When you have lost fear, then for the first time you begin to feel the wings of your soul. You are afraid of no abyss, of no height, of no depth." Pethick-Lawrence felt, "I was able, in my solitary cell, to think of all these things and to look them in the face." Certainly, she constructed her prison stint positively to bolster suffragette courage and calm fears. Her account, nevertheless, underscores the self-mastery involved—a discipline Alice held in high regard.[64]

The suffragettes' strategy to reduce their prison time paid off. Authorities released two women on medical grounds on the fourth day. That evening, according to Alice, "the doctor ordered me to be taken to the hospital of the prison. I could not walk so they carried me on a litter." The following evening, Thursday, August 5, she was set free after serving only five of fourteen days: "They gave me a dose of brandy & sent me home in a cab with a wardress." The prison governor also released Lucy, Emily Davison, and three others, freeing the remaining women the following day. As one suffragette declared, "Thus once again women have proved themselves stronger than the government." Undeniably, the British government had yet to figure out how to counter the mighty weapon of the hunger strike; in a few years, the American government felt similarly nonplussed.[65]

WSPU staff immediately took the unbowed Alice to the home of two suffragette caretakers. The Pankhursts assumed the responsibility of helping their martyrs regain their health, drawing on their network of well-heeled supporters. The recovery process thus offers a window into a lesser-known aspect of the Pankhursts' operation, one which Alice also emulated. A day after her release, she felt well enough to write her mother. "Two Suffragette ladies are entertaining me & another girl who came out with me." She preferred the arrangement to returning to her rented room, "for there was no one to look after me there. A lady doctor comes to see me—also a Suffragette—She is a consulting physician only & one of the most prominent in London." Alice lay confined to her bed, she said, "but will be alright in a week." Her mother probably hoped for a sign that her daughter might come home now. Instead, Alice seemed undeterred by her trial. She wrote, "I shall go on the hunger strike again I think."[66]

A week later, a re-energized Alice Paul readied herself for new missions. When Emmeline Pankhurst asked AP and Lucy to join her on a speaking tour, Alice felt "overjoyed" and immediately agreed, as did Lucy. They usually glimpsed Mrs. Pankhurst from afar. She spent much of her time proselytizing around Great Britain, while Christabel handled the daily WSPU administration. Mrs. Pankhurst planned a US lecture tour in the fall and probably anticipated getting questions about the two Americans. Hence the invitation. For Alice and Lucy, the trip offered a rare intimate opportunity with the charismatic leader. As the women set off to the north, Alice sent a photograph on to her mother for safekeeping. "I am in the picture next to Mrs. Pankhurst," she wrote. "They are having a campaign in Scotland now & we are going up to help."[67]

5

"A Little Stone in a Big Mosaic"

JUST RIDING IN the WSPU touring car made the trip worthwhile. Alice's journey with Mrs. Pankhurst became one source of inspiration for the 1915 cross-country automobile tour she later spun to great effect. The official motorcar carried meaning along with its passengers. The Pankhursts' brand-new Austin featured the WSPU colors: a narrow purple stripe lined the green body, and white spokes accented the wheels. Inside, the leather upholstery shone purple and green. Alice gawked at the uniformed driver. "Nobody had ever *seen* a woman chauffeur," she recalled. "It was unusual for a woman to drive a car but to have a woman chauffeur—!"[1]

The road trip and other more limited encounters with Emmeline Pankhurst gave Alice a glimpse of charismatic power in a womanly cast. Alice found her leader "very fearless, amazingly courageous I thought, unselfish, selfless"[2]—qualities others later admired in AP herself. Mrs. Pankhurst's love of beauty and respect for propriety meshed easily with AP's sensibilities, despite Pankhurst's more modest upbringing. Mrs. Pankhurst also embodied contradictions some later saw in Alice Paul: the widow's feminine refinement and dignity stood in stark relief to her raw courage and fiery rhetoric. Her desire for control at times overpowered her easy graciousness, as when some followers pushed for a more democratic WSPU. Alice ultimately fashioned her own leadership role as a hybrid of Christabel Pankhurst's role as administrator and chief strategist, and Mrs. Pankhurst's as WSPU evangelist. After her road trip with Mrs. Pankhurst, Alice began to test her own mettle as a leader.

Alice and Lucy's interest in passing muster and the former's ever-present craving for knowledge spurred them to take full advantage of their time with Emmeline Pankhurst, though we know little about their interaction. For four days, the touring car jostled north along narrow roads rutted by hooves and wagon wheels. "Great meetings had been arranged for Mrs. Pankhurst," AP remembered, "and she would make one of her great speeches to enormous crowds; and then we would go on to the next stopping place." Alice heartily agreed with most observers that Pankhurst was "a *marvelous* speaker, a very moving speaker." They slept in hotels—Alice assured her mother that she spent money only for lodging—or homes, as in Newcastle, where "a family of suffragettes entertained us." Mrs.

Pankhurst allowed sightseeing, so they toured cathedrals and Sherwood Forest. On the fifth "delightful" day, they crossed the border into Scotland and headed for Edinburgh.[3]

The Pankhursts had worked at building a presence in Scotland, a country with a historic and richly earned reputation for independence. Since 1906, WSPU organizers had busied themselves canvassing Scottish cities and towns in the populated southern regions. Three years later, WSPU activities flourished, alongside those of other suffrage groups. The Scottish votes-for-women movement was thriving.[4]

So far, the Scottish reaction to the Pankhursts felt much like the English response. Two years earlier, the WSPU organized the country's first suffrage procession in Edinburgh. Newspapers published generally favorable accounts, one noting the "ladylike" behavior of two thousand marchers, while Edinburghers—characteristically—watched the parade undemonstratively. Heckling at political meetings, routine practice for Scottish men, drew a different reaction. The first time a suffragette interrupted a meeting in Scotland, stewards unceremoniously tossed her out, much as in England. Glasgow suffrage leaders soon warned female hecklers against spoiling their identities, risking "that much-prized virtue—respectability. She gives up friendships that she values; often she renounces all her past life."[5]

The week of Alice's arrival, *Votes for Women*, the WSPU magazine, sought volunteers to organize another Edinburgh procession. The procession "will be organised on an impressive scale, and will entail considerable cost." Alice and Lucy agreed to help plan the day. But first, Mrs. Pankhurst and her two American companions sped off to Glasgow, where another cabinet minister planned to speak.[6]

Alice headed for a city seemingly made to order for suffragettes. Rumbling westward across Scotland's narrow waist to the river Clyde, she, Lucy, and Mrs. Pankhurst saw the murky air rising up first, enveloping a highly industrialized city that still boasted many well-kept historic buildings and green spaces. As a people, Glaswegians stood apart from the reserved Edinburghers; they were instinctively rebels. Cutting the coat to suit the cloth, WSPU organizers planned a demonstration in Glasgow and saved the beautiful parade and pageant for Edinburgh.[7]

The travelers located WSPU's Bath Street headquarters and laid plans for disrupting Lord Crewe's speech the next night. He would speak at St. Andrew's Halls, a massive venue accommodating several stages. As before, the suffragettes had to enter the meeting surreptitiously; tickets read "for gentlemen only." Alice and Lucy walked the eight blocks west from headquarters to reconnoiter. They found a magnificent colonnaded edifice with entrances on four sides, all guarded. Three stories of sandstone defied climbing. However, they might use materials from an adjacent library construction site to gain window or roof access under cover of night. With that tentative plan, they withdrew until evening.[8]

By the time she arrived in Scotland, Alice seemed intent on demonstrating her allegiance to the cause. Her athletic prowess became her advantage that night. AP and two comrades approached the hall around one o'clock in the morning, street lamps lighting their way with an eerie glow. They entered the construction area, only to be spotted by the night watchman. Her companions retreated, but Alice just ran out of sight. She gave a typically unembellished account of what happened next:

> I managed to get on to some sheds, and from there on to the roof of St. Andrew's Hall [sic]. I lay down there to wait till night to get into the hall through one of the windows, as I knew that during the day the hall would be thoroughly searched and there would be no chance of concealment. About two o'clock rain began to fall heavily and I was soon soaked. I did not mind that, however, and when daylight came on I lay on the roof face downwards. I had a black cloak on, and I did not think I could be seen.

As the *Glasgow Herald* noted, her stunt was both dangerous and daring, an act underscoring her fearlessness as well as her ingenuity. *Votes for Women* called the feat "splendid devotion."[9]

Alice thought herself safely hidden on the roof. She sustained herself by munching on chocolates stored in her pockets. Shortly after dawn, she recounted,

> I was surprised to hear shouting and whistling, and looking up, I saw a number of workmen watching me through one of the library windows. Pretty soon I heard someone climbing on to the roof, and a workman made his appearance. I explained to him that I was a suffragist, that I wanted to get into Lord Crewe's meeting at night, and I asked him not to give me away and also to request his mates not to do so. The workmen behaved like bricks and took no notice of me.

Two hours later, a workman on another crew noticed and alerted police. They found Alice in "a woefully chilled and drenched condition. I had to come down," she said ruefully. She only regretted failing in her mission.[10]

Her bold if foolhardy stunt heightened the Pankhursts' usual focus on women's exclusion that evening, a night Alice found "thrilling." An elaborate search for other concealed suffragettes preceded the event. Once the minister's speech began, "listeners were constantly reminded," wrote one reporter, "that lively scenes were being enacted outside the hall." The crowd, estimated at six thousand including "a considerable hooligan element," largely supported the suffragettes. Alice and Lucy became the first arrests as four compatriots rushed one entrance, flying a "Votes for Women" banner. Mrs. Pankhurst, who observed from afar, posted bail.[11]

The Scottish police showed more forbearance than the English. The next morning, a mix-up about appearances led to warrants being issued for the women's arrest. Neither the suffragettes nor the police took that news too seriously. As Alice wrote her mother, "It would be a big expense for them to hunt all over Scotland for us & besides they hate to send Suffragettes to prison up in the provinces & in Scotland." So Mrs. Pankhurst bade farewell to the two Americans and set off on a fortnight's speaking tour in the Highlands, leaving Alice and Lucy to return to Edinburgh. Glasgow was not the last place Alice would profit from Scottish tolerance.[12]

Alice savored both the adventure and the travel, staving off her mother's concern. She wrote Mrs. Paul about the beauty of Edinburgh, noting "where Mary Queen of Scots lived" and the cool and rainy weather. "I am very glad to have this chance of seeing Scotland," she said. She consciously preserved memories, sending home copies of *Votes for Women* and other memorabilia with instructions for safekeeping. She also wanted her mother to understand her passion. Weeks before Emmeline Pankhurst left for her American tour, she urged Tacie, "Do be sure to hear her above all things. Thee may never have another chance." Yet Mrs. Paul's anxiety began to grate on her daughter. Alice tried to reassure her mother and conceal her own impatience. "Thy last letter was doleful. There is no reason to worry about me. I am perfectly well," she wrote crisply. Mrs. Paul continued to send money, but AP needed little of it, since the WSPU paid most of her expenses. This fact probably helped Tacie accept Alice's desire to stay on.[13]

In Scotland, Alice became adept at itinerant organizing and broadened her expertise by assisting with plans for the October procession. Over the next weeks, she spent some time in Edinburgh, though her letters did not discuss her planning activities. To introduce the WSPU to new audiences, she traveled to nearby towns, settling into a nomadic existence and coming to know the fishing villages and industrial towns of southeast Scotland quite well. Along the way, she learned how to establish a working relationship with other, often working-class, suffragettes and how to size up unfamiliar locales quickly. She organized open-air and drawing-room meetings, overcame hecklers at times, and sought recruits. In mid-September, *Votes for Women* reported on the "very encouraging reception" the town of Fife gave Alice and Florence Macauley, a WSPU veteran and bookseller's daughter.[14]

Alice's work for the Pankhursts exposed her to a wide spectrum of public reaction and forced her to adapt swiftly to the unexpected—both valuable skills in

the years to come. Fortunately, most crowds were orderly. The coastal town of
Burntisland turned out to be a grueling exception. Alice arrived in mid-afternoon,
the first suffragette ever in town, and made arrangements for an outdoor event,
chalking sidewalks and posting broadsides to advertise. Macauley showed up just
before the eight o'clock meeting that evening. "She had hardly begun when some
boys began to throw eggs, cabbages, etc at her & kept it up the whole time," Alice
reported. "I did not speak at all. I was certainly glad—it was the worst meeting
I've ever been to. Miss Macaulay had to take her coat to the cleaners this morning." Alice chose to take the "fearful meeting" in stride, as if recharging her commitment to the WSPU. The next day, she headed north to Dundee for another
cabinet minister's address.[15]

Dundee, a manufacturing seaport and Scotland's third largest city, was no
stranger to the WSPU. Four English and Scottish suffragettes plus Lucy Burns
preceded AP and busied themselves publicizing their plans. Alice took a room at
Lamb's Hotel and joined them. Her compatriots briefed her on the WSPU's past
history in the town, beginning in the spring of 1908, when suffragettes crowded
into Dundee as Churchill sought to regain a seat in Parliament after (some said)
the WSPU engineered the loss of his Manchester sinecure. The Dundonians had
tolerated protests and the police practiced restraint. Now, officials steeled themselves for renewed protests. "Alas! there are more cunning devices in Suffragette
tactics than are dreamt of in Liberal men's philosophy," a local reporter mused.[16]

After her "fearful" experience in Burntisland, Alice showed greater willingness
to take the lead. As expected, all six suffragettes outdid themselves on September
13 at Kinnaird Hall. Emboldened by previous capers (including AP's), one woman
hid on the rooftop for hours. Lucy and a comrade spoke before a thousand people
and then marched down the street to the hall entrance, meeting up with Alice.
Perhaps forty police stood on guard; "the giants in the force" defended the
doors. The three women rushed the entry and the crowd pushed forward. Police
arrested Lucy and a second woman; somehow, AP eluded officers. However, she
soon reappeared to lead the throng in charging the doors again and again, crying
"Votes for Women!" The police line held. Suddenly, one door opened as people
left and Alice edged forward to slip in; guards instantly grabbed her. "Her arrest,"
one journalist reported, "was accompanied by scenes of the wildest excitement."
She had demonstrated a new level of aplomb.[17]

The police seemed reluctant to charge them. Lucy grew impatient with the
officials' hesitation and proceeded to smash a window with a convenient ink-
pot. Alice joined in, using stones concealed in her coat. She felt no compunction
about this sort of vandalism and later opined that panes of glass held nothing
sacred. Ultimately, police charged Alice, Lucy, and WSPU veteran Edith New

with breaching the peace and "malicious damage." Mindful of the earlier Glasgow mix-up, all three refused to post bail and spent the night in jail.[18]

Despite her rumpled appearance, Alice displayed her new level of self-assurance in a crowded court the next morning. Both Americans admitted their guilt and offered standard WSPU explanations for their actions. Lucy, described as "confident and semi-defiant," explained the failure of constitutional methods. The alternative meant unconstitutional methods or abandoning the fight. "Give up the fight we cannot and never will, and we hold the Liberal Government responsible," she argued.

Alice then stepped up with her blue hat firmly in place and emphasized the higher law she obeyed. She had committed no "moral offense," she declared. Every woman had a duty "to bring pressure to bear on Cabinet Ministers." She bore "no qualms of conscience" about breaking technical laws. The government excluded women from making the laws; therefore, they "delighted in breaking them." (Later, in America, she revised her thinking on the joy of lawbreaking.) The judge lectured them about trying to advance political claims through illegal means, then sentenced Lucy and Alice to ten days in prison; Edith received seven.[19]

If Alice wearied of arrests, her experience in Dundee surrounded her with an atmosphere of unity that could only bolster her resolve. The three prisoners became a cause célèbre and Dundee quickly emerged as the locus of the Scottish suffrage movement. "We were the first Suffragettes ever sentenced in Scotland & all Scotland seemed roused by it," Alice wrote her mother excitedly. Many Dundonians rallied around the women, and the daily press reports of prisoner status shifted between bemused and respectful, if not approving. Even as the women walked out of court, a crowd of supporters "raised hearty cheers, and, surging round them, escorted the ladies to their lodgings." In further solidarity, the Dundee Women's Freedom League immediately protested the sentence, and WSPU leaders in Scotland rushed to Dundee.[20]

Dundee Prison offered another test of Alice's psychological strength and commitment, but it proved a breeze compared to Holloway. Officials treated the suffragettes respectfully, though as criminals. Once they "had their tub," the three prisoners—under protest—accepted prison clothing. After Lucy began breaking windows, authorities calmly moved all three to "the strongest cells in the establishment, where they could do very little damage to property." The prison commissioners advised "no punishment but simply defensive steps." AP and the others refused all food and work; that conduct landed them in solitary confinement, without exercise privileges. For Alice, simply being clothed improved the prison experience.[21]

Support increased daily for the imprisoned suffragettes, though the prisoners had little inkling. In the streets, newsboys hawked their papers using placards blaring, "Dundee Hunger Strikers—Will They be Released?" Adela Pankhurst arrived and headlined a public gathering attended by thousands that evening. After a brief rally, she and a "mass of cheering men and women" surrounded the prison, thundering their support through its walls. Alice said the din sounded like a riot.[22]

Despite treating the detainees more civilly, prison authorities hewed the government line on their release. The Pankhursts emphasized the mild treatment in the media and on the streets, framing Dundee as a victory. After the usual four days, officials released the weakened activists on medical grounds. Cheers greeted their arrival at Lamb's Hotel, where nourishment awaited them. Doctors judged Alice's and Lucy's pulses particularly weak; two hunger strikes in six weeks had taken their toll. Emmeline Pankhurst lauded the hunger strikers that night to an overflow crowd in the largest meeting space in Dundee. Adela hammered the point home in *Votes for Women*: "The Government must get a new set of officials in Scottish prisons if they want to carry out their usual policy of tyranny and torture; those in Dundee are above their influence." The Pankhursts held up Dundee as a clear moral victory. Alice memorized the adroit strategic feint.[23]

Public support for the suffragettes outlasted their imprisonment. After two days at Lamb's, the three suffragettes recuperated at the Abbeythune estate thirty miles north of Dundee. "A lady who has a big country house sent a motor car for us," Alice wrote her mother in delight. "She (Miss MacGregor) lives in a big sort of park & it is one mile from her front gate to her front door." Once they felt stronger, the convalescents walked around the estate. Alice's lasting memory of Abbeythune was MacGregor's shocked expression when the women set off the first time. "Miss MacGregor was very much embarrassed," Alice recalled. "She said, 'You know, no lady goes out without having a hat and a coat and gloves and so on. I wouldn't want anybody to go out from my house without being properly gowned.'" Some proprieties seemed eternal.[24]

The usually vigorous Alice glimpsed a frailer self following her second hunger strike. In a rare concession of vulnerability, she wrote her mother after two weeks that, unlike her earlier week-long recovery, "I have been a great deal more ill after this hunger strike than after the first." Lucy and Edith New returned to organizing; Alice stayed at Abbeythune another week.[25]

By the end of September, she became keenly aware that she had avoided a far worse fate. The British government began to counter the hunger strike using "hospital treatment," their euphemism for forcible feeding, to compel prisoners to serve their full sentences. Horrified, the Pankhursts denounced the action and created a firestorm of condemnation. One hundred sixteen physicians signed a petition criticizing the practice as "absolutely beastly and revolting." Two support-ive journalists resigned from the pro-government *Daily News*, writing, "We can-not denounce torture in Russia and support it in England." Alice told her mother the news, writing, "The last time [forcible feeding] was ever done in England (so it was stated in parliament) was in 1872 to a man prisoner & the prisoner died from the effect." A pro-suffrage MP attempted to bring the question before the Commons; other MPs laughed. The suffragettes viewed forcible feeding as physi-cal, even sexual, violation, and the Pankhursts framed the procedure in those terms. Alice shuddered to read the details. "I am certainly glad we escaped it," she wrote.[26]

The Pankhursts had a keen grasp of the psychological needs of their followers and ceremonies extolling the nobility of suffering for the cause were well known to all three suffragettes. Alice forgot about frailty and new fears when the Pankhursts and Dundonian suffragists feted the three suffragette warriors. On September 29, she wrote, "The women of Dundee gave us a dinner at Lamb's Hotel." Twenty-five speakers lauded the three hunger strikers. Afterward, "General" Flora Drummond presented each of them with the Pankhursts' version of high military honors. Designed by Sylvia Pankhurst, the silver brooch represented a prison gateway, a symbol similar to the Parliament portcullis; the iconic WSPU arrow pointing skyward was superimposed on the gateway. Won over by the gesture, Alice trea-sured her brooch all her life and later designed one like it for her own troops.[27]

While each former prisoner rose to take the spotlight, Alice claimed the opportunity to practice a leading role. Lucy had a light touch, allowing that she became "very hungry." Alice, by contrast, offered polemic, dwelling "at consider-able length with the arguments in favour of women's suffrage and the methods which they pursued." She justified the women's militant behavior as "bringing to bear on the Cabinet the pressure to which these gentlemen were most suscep-tible." She closed with a jest, claiming the mayor's presence signaled "his seal of approval," a point which the audience applauded. The young woman who once resisted public speaking had come a long way.[28]

Early in October 1909, Alice returned to Edinburgh to assist with the impending procession. She soon realized that working on the inside to orga-nize a parade was wholly different from experiencing two London processions. Unfortunately, none of her surviving letters offers any clues about her assigned tasks or even whether she herself marched. She recalled vaguely many years later that "both Lucy Burns and I spent our time helping in every way we could." At minimum, however, she gained a sense of the overall plan of organization and how the WSPU put together a massive spectacle in a few weeks' time, a challenge she would take on herself in less than four years.[29]

The Edinburgh extravaganza came off in unexpected sunshine on October 9. Alice wrote, "There was a long procession, women pipers, a pageant of famous

Scottish women etc." Colors ablaze, the grand spectacle of perhaps two thousand marchers raised historic Princes Street to a whole new magnificence. Some banners bore a Scottish flavor, as in "Ye maun tramp on the Scotch Thistle," and "A guid cause makes a strong arm." Thousands lined the street to watch, most with a quiet dignity echoing that of the participants.[30]

An incident following the procession suggests that Alice's experiences as a suffragette had intensified her sense of injustice. She became incensed at male university students who made a "fearful row" when Mrs. Pankhurst and others spoke after the parade. "It is incomprehensible," she wrote her mother, "why the students can go to any meeting—ours or anyone else's & make such a disturbance that no one can hear a speaker—but if a woman gets up quietly and asks a sensible question on a serious political issue she is at once thrown out of the building & often sent to prison." Her comment is disingenuous—suffragettes seldom spoke up quietly; nevertheless, the disparity of treatment seemed undeniable.[31]

Her righteous anger remained evident a few days later in Berwick-on-Tweed, just south of the Scottish border. She and other suffragettes interrupted the local MP's speech at a fundraising bazaar, a nonpolitical event likely chosen for its surprise value. Berwick officials proved less forgiving than those in Scotland. One by one the women disrupted the MP's address, and one by one stewards dragged them out. Alice, in hat and veil, grabbed the rails of a flower stall before speaking out; men promptly seized her and tried to gag her. She "refused to move, but she was speedily overpowered," according to one account. "She fought every inch of the ground to the door, however, and her elbow punches temporarily disabled one of the stewards." Alice became the only woman arrested that day, and even sixty years later, she recalled the police propelling her "through the streets of Berwick to the police station holding my hands behind me." She felt "so blazingly angry." She fumed through a three-hour lockup, but officials decided not to charge her.[32]

Alice learned that her exploits had reached her mother's ears only after she returned to London. She dived vigorously into WSPU's local efforts, demonstrating at an election rally and making three speeches a day. Two weeks went by during which she barely scribbled a few lines to her mother. A few days after Emmeline Pankhurst disembarked in New York amid much ballyhoo, someone showed Mrs. Paul the headline of the *Philadelphia Press*:

> MISS ALICE PAUL
> JAILED IN LONDON
> Beautiful New Jersey Girl,
> A Settlement Worker,
> Locked Up as a Suffragette
> HER FRIENDS INDIGNANT

"I went over to Moorestown for the mail," Mrs. Paul later wrote, "& people stopped me on the street...I had heard nothing of it." Inadvertently, Alice chose a bad time to forego letter writing. She sent her Berwick news on October 31, nearly a week after an account had appeared in Philadelphia. An enterprising reporter had cabled the story, using "her friends" as sources and erring in many details, including the location of the arrest.[33]

The *Moorestown Republican* defended the honor of one of its most prominent families and framed the story as a mistaken arrest. Alice was not a "vote-seeking rioter" but a "soft-voiced and quiet mannered uplifter of the poor," the reporter wrote. "The cablegrams," he went on, "created much excitement here in Moorestown when the news became noised about. From the dispatches it appears Miss Paul was attending a charity fair and that her arrest was entirely unwarranted as she was creating no disturbance and the following morning she was released." The article underscored the family's distinguished forebears, including Alice's late father.[34]

Mrs. Paul took a different tack in preserving Alice's class identity; she embraced WSPU activities as entirely appropriate. She acknowledged that her daughter acted as a suffragette but insisted, "I am not worried about Alice." She noted that Helen Paul, now attending Wellesley, "had a long talk" with Emmeline Pankhurst after her Boston lecture. The WSPU leader assured Helen that the suffragettes numbered among the "most influential and cultured women" in Britain.[35]

Alice carried on, oblivious to her notoriety abroad. By early November 1909, after enduring five arrests and two prison terms with brio, she earned a prestigious mission: protesting at one of the grandest and most heavily guarded affairs of the year, the annual Lord Mayor's Banquet in London's historic Guildhall. Traditionally, the entire cabinet attended the event and the prime minister presented a major address. Finding a way into the banquet hall challenged suffragette ingenuity, but success would mean extraordinary publicity.

The protestors' efforts promised arrest, imprisonment, hunger striking, and the most recent government reprisal: forcible feeding. One of AP's Limehouse comrades, Emily Wilding Davison, had resisted the feeding by barricading herself in her cell. Prison officials responded by turning a fire hose upon her until water rose six inches deep. Despite that and other horror stories, Alice agreed to the Guildhall protest, as did Lucy Burns.[36]

As usual, the demonstration involved multiple fronts. Alice and a middle-aged nurse named Amelia Brown planned to masquerade as charwomen, hoping the invisibility of the workaday domestic offered a way into the hall. In addition, the

WSPU assigned Lucy Burns to appear in evening dress with a male escort to gain access to the banquet itself. However, the cautious banquet organizers required two documents for entry, so the ticket held by her escort might be insufficient. As Alice recalled, "If Lucy, down on the floor, didn't get her words heard, at least they would hear [ours] from above."[37]

At dawn on November 9, Alice and Amelia joined the dozens of charwomen trudging with buckets and brushes through the streets of the "Square Mile," as Londoners called the ancient inner city. AP wore a faded blue garment borrowed from a compatriot. The two "chars" blended in with other scrubwomen approaching the Guildhall doors. The guard gave them nary a glance. Inside, where constables patrolled, they hid under benches when someone approached. "I remember they came in and searched just where we were crouching down," Alice recalled, "and they even touched my hair." After concealing themselves the entire day, the two women crept up a spiral staircase to the glassed-in gallery overhanging the banquet hall and opposite the head table. There, they awaited opportunity.[38]

At seven o'clock, looking tall and regal on the arm of her escort, Lucy walked into the hall. MP Arthur Henderson, leader of the Labour Party, handed over their ticket and told guards he had left the second document behind. As a guard consulted the list of invitees, Winston Churchill arrived and Lucy saw her chance. "Miss Burns immediately stepped forward," Henderson reported later to the *London Times*, "and asked Winston how he dared to be going in to a banquet while [a suffragette] was still in prison. I did not catch what he said in reply, but I saw him turn away." Some American newspapers embellished the story and reported Lucy grabbing Churchill by the shoulders "as if to push him back" and screaming, "How dare you come to a banquet while the Government is torturing political prisoners?" Henderson, however, claimed there was "no commotion"; officials asked him to escort Lucy out, "which I did."[39]

Alice and Amelia had more success. They waited until the Lord Mayor rose to toast the king. Brown, shoe in hand, quickly punched out a pane of glass and the two shouted "Votes for Women! Votes for Women!" Unfortunately, they misjudged the acoustics in the cavernous hall and their cries sounded faint to most banqueters. Mrs. Asquith looked rather alarmed. The prime minister, who, according to one observer, "must be prepared by this time for almost anything on the part of the militant suffragettes," appeared undisturbed. The two suffragettes continued shouting as the police rushed up to the gallery, arrested them, and marched them off to the police station. After posting bail, they were temporarily released. The story made the front page of the *New York Times* and other US newspapers the next morning, before American reporters realized their countrywomen were involved.[40]

Alice confidently assailed the court during her sentencing the following day. Officials charged the two activists with committing willful damage and secreting themselves for an unlawful purpose. Nurse Brown veered from the WSPU script and pleaded guilty. AP remained stalwart. Furthermore, she intended to have her say: "I should like to explain," she began, "that we feel we have broken no moral law whatsoever in doing this. We feel that it is incumbent on every woman to rebel against the state of political subjection in which we are placed." The magistrate interrupted her to complain about "hysterical creatures" trying to "promote the movement." "You said you would *allow* us to give an explanation," Alice shot back.

"You don't seem to me to *have* any plea or justification for your conduct," he retorted.

"I should be only too delighted to give it...", AP ventured, but the magistrate cut her off. He had judged men who justifiably called "the attention of the public to their distress and want," but these two well-educated women suffered no such distress and certainly knew better. He assessed a fine or a month at hard labor for each woman; both chose the prison term.[41]

Holloway Gaol seemed much as Alice had left it. The authorities refused to treat the suffragettes as political prisoners. The two women refused to be treated otherwise and declared a hunger strike. WSPU headquarters later gave out the story that both female and male warders were required to force Alice into prison garb. Once in her cell, she awaited the anticipated forcible feeding.[42]

According to accounts in *Votes for Women*, she knew the feeding would be her most difficult ordeal. But nothing happened the first day. The second day passed. "We took no food," Alice later told her mother, "& they let us starve till the third day." That morning, "the wardresses came in & dragged me out of bed & wrapped me in blankets & carried me into the next cell & put me in a chair," Alice wrote. The most horrific experience of her young life began.[43]

In the world outside Holloway, Alice became infamous. Attention in the British press was fleeting; American newspapers, however, sustained the story for weeks. Mrs. Pankhurst was lecturing in major East Coast cities (she began a Carnegie Hall address with "I am what you call a hooligan") and interest in the English suffragettes seemed keener than usual. Reporters quickly connected earlier stories about AP's Berwick protest with the Guildhall demonstration. In November alone, the *New York Times* printed five stories about the protest and its aftermath. A *Times* reporter quoted Christabel Pankhurst calling Alice "a very valued member"; the same correspondent defined AP as a "very earnest young woman" and a "capital public speaker," with "numberless friends" in London.[44]

As the story circulated in American newspapers, errors and exaggerations emerged. One shoe breaking a window at the Guildhall became multiple windows, "a shower of stones," or bricks. Some called Alice the "originator" of the hunger strike. The editor of the *Woman's Journal*, prominent suffragist Alice Stone Blackwell, criticized the *Times* for its "systematic scattering of falsehoods."[45]

The newspapers broke the Guildhall story while Mrs. Pankhurst was visiting Philadelphia. While she exploited the coverage to decry press hyperbole and claim the righteousness of the cause, her opponents used the story to their advantage. The six-month-old Pennsylvania Association Opposed to Woman Suffrage announced a protest campaign. Women needed to focus on the home, they maintained. "She should strive for domestic perfection, instead of marching about, trying to force her political opinions on respectable gentlemen or," they added pointedly, "starving herself in prison."[46]

Alice's arrangement to allay her mother's worry with postdated letters backfired once the press identified her. Journalists besieged Mrs. Paul and played up (or made up) her displeasure, while underscoring AP's "distinguished" family. Alice's mother, according to the *Philadelphia Bulletin*, became "agitated" when told of her daughter's latest arrest. She allegedly insisted, "Alice is such a mild-mannered girl." According to the *Newark Evening News*, Mrs. Paul said, "It's awful if Alice has to stay in jail a month. I am afraid the girl has let her enthusiasm for the cause run away with her judgment." Another Philadelphia area paper noted "Miss Paul's Home Folks Disapprove," and quoted Mrs. Paul asserting, "I heard Mrs. Pankhurst in Philadelphia Monday afternoon, and I can readily understand how she has the power of influencing women to her cause."[47]

Some reporters conflated the Guildhall protest with recent evidence of increasing violence by militant suffragettes. To be sure, in the fall of 1909, WSPU members more frequently threw stones and, in a few cases, bricks or roof slates. Two WFL women poured liquid into ballot boxes during a local election. Other WFL members were observed practicing at a shooting range. The introduction of forcible feeding began to spawn more determined resistance from a minority of suffragettes, controversial acts within the WSPU and the WFL and beyond. Newspapers interested in this angle publicized a November 13 incident in which a suffragette confronted Winston Churchill and struck him in the face. The *New York Times* editorialized on the pattern, including Alice among the stone throwers. "The madness grows," the editors asserted, "and as it grows the revulsion of feeling in England toward woman suffrage grows, too." Many Americans felt the same way. Destructive acts weakened suffragette claims to moral authority.[48]

To the dismay of American suffragists like Blackwell, newspapers like the *Times* used such incidents to revisit the canards about women in public and indirectly damn the suffrage cause. The *Philadelphia Inquirer* used Alice's proud academic record against her. "She was very studious," one article read, and "became a veritable bookworm." The reporter went on to say, "There is some fear that Miss

Paul's mind has become weakened by her constant study." The article also claimed Mrs. Paul complained of her daughter's "unseemly conduct." The *Times* opined that suffragette "actions in public lately have been of a sort that indicate a dangerous insane state." The editors cautioned: "Votes are withheld from men who are violently insane."⁴⁹

Back in Holloway Gaol, the trauma of forcible feeding became so profound for Alice that she needed to distance herself from the telling. "One feels," she wrote impersonally, "as though one were an animal about to be vivisected." Her resistance worsened the process. "At first they merely held me," she later wrote her mother, "but after a few times they tied me to a chair as my struggles made it difficult to feed me." She fought the procedure as vigorously as she could, as instructed by the WSPU. "They usually tied me down by a sheet around the abdomen & by another around the lungs. This latter is drawn so tightly that it is impossible to get a good breath." Thus, while immobilizing her made administering the feeding easier for prison staff, it compounded Alice's pain. "One wardress sat astride the knees & held that part of the body quiet. One wardress stood on each side & held the arm and hand." Even the doctor needed to assist in restraining her.

> One of the doctors stood behind & pulled my head back till it was parallel with the ground. He held it in this position by means of a towel drawn tightly around the throat & when I tried to move, he drew the towel so tight that it compressed the windpipe & made it almost impossible to breathe—with his other hand he held my chin in a rigid position. Then the other doctor put the tube down through the nostril. When they have finally secured you in this position you can scarcely budge.⁵⁰

Pouring a mixture of milk and eggs down a tube into an inmate's stomach seems deceptively simple; the trickiest part was the tube insertion. Alice became overwhelmed by the sense of violation, the feeling of "being strangled or suffocated."

> [The tube] very rarely went down the first time. It would usually go about three fourths of the way through the head & then he would be unable to push it any further. He would push as though he were trying to drive a stake into the ground but it would not budge so he would pull it out again & grease it again & then by the other nostril. Usually the same thing happened again & he would again draw it out & again grease it & try another time. Usually it went down the 3rd time, sometimes the fourth, sometimes the fifth and once the sixth. When it finally emerges from the head into the throat it very often causes a choking & gasping for breath.

The doctor then poured down the nourishing liquid. "While the tube is going through the nasal passage it is exceedingly painful & only less so as it is being withdrawn. I never went through it without the tears streaming down my face & often moaned from beginning to end & sometimes cried aloud."[51]

Only after ten days did the doctor use a nasal spray to deaden Alice's pain. The irritation increased over time "because the nostrils become more inflamed. Three times my head was held so far back that the tube came out between the lips instead of going down the throat. I then clenched my teeth & the doctor forced them open with some metal instrument." Alice Paul endured forcible feeding nearly twice a day, a total of fifty-five times during her November 1909 prison term.[52]

Holloway officials kept her incommunicado; they did, however, acknowledge the feedings to the press and the WSPU. Frustrated by her continued reliance on the press for news, Alice's mother nevertheless came out strongly in support of her daughter and, by extension, the Pankhursts. "[Alice] should have been treated as a political prisoner," she told one Philadelphia correspondent. "I think it is an outrage that she has been forcibly fed and been subjected to this indecent treatment, and we are greatly enraged over this."[53]

By "we," Tacie Paul meant all the extended family and friends whose letters stuffed the Paul mailbox. Merely one of the surviving messages suggests disapproval, though perhaps Mrs. Paul retained only those praising her daughter. A Quaker couple with a son near Alice's age wrote Tacie with empathy, objecting to "publicity that has utterly failed to be quite fair to thy daughter's heroic work" and reminding her that all reforms "are tabooed in their early stages." On the other hand, a friend of AP's felt "sure the report isn't correct for I don't believe Alice would do so." A cousin wished only that she herself "had been in England to do likewise, Except [sic] that I should have fallen far, far short of the required courage." One particularly cheering letter came from a Quaker just back from England, where he had spoken with suffragettes. He placed Alice's actions in the Quaker tradition of "suffering," linking her behavior to "the sturdy stand our far away ancestors took for what they believed to be right."[54]

Alice's Uncle Mickle Paul in Philadelphia proudly claimed her as a true Paul. Three decades earlier, Mickle had mentored Alice's father in business; he later dabbled in politics. Elderly now, and a recent widower, he nonetheless wrote that when Alice returned home, "I would like you all to take dinner with me—so that I can hear her tell the tale of suffering & endurance." Applauding his niece for being true to the family's values, he went on: "She is brave, brainy & energetic & hence has a wide field of usefulness here. It is cause for pride to find that there is yet the spirit of progress & independent thought—and in individual responsibility—that marked the family in earlier days—still in the head & heart of one of its members."[55]

The Pauls still heard no news from Alice and very little about her situation. Mrs. Paul cabled the WSPU and heard back from a recently released suffragette who applauded AP's bravery but knew little. AP herself could not write. "The last letter I received from Alice was written just about the time she was put in jail," her mother told the *Philadelphia Ledger*. Shortly before Thanksgiving, Mrs. Paul decided, "I must do something." She appealed to the American ambassador in London. A nephew cabled the embassy in Mickle's name: "American Alice Paul Holloway Jail deserving proper protection." Mrs. Paul wrote the ambassador and Christabel Pankhurst as well.[56]

Suffragist support blossomed. Emmeline Pankhurst urged her American audiences to appeal to President Taft on Alice's behalf. In New York, sympathetic women quickly formed Washington and London commissions. New York City suffrage leader Harriot Stanton Blatch, then stopping in London, headed the New York group. The Washington commission sought an interview with the president. "There was great indignation at the treatment of Miss Paul and many letters were sent to President Taft," Mrs. Pankhurst reported in one speech.[57]

The *Ledger* insisted the US government would not intervene. "Her alleged offense was not political, but simply against public peace, and whatever punishment she gets will be municipal." That surmise proved correct. On November 30, the American ambassador replied to the Pauls that the British government insisted Alice received "a fair and open trial and awarded the same punishment which has been repeatedly awarded to English subjects for similar offences." That being the case, "the Embassy is entirely without authority or power to interfere." Unfortunately, the ambassador mailed rather than cabled his reply. It arrived in Moorestown the day after Alice's prison term ended, along with Christabel Pankhurst's note lauding her courage and unselfishness.[58]

On December 9, 1909, Alice was freed, after serving her entire term of thirty days. Her cable, "Well. Returning Soon," arrived. Mrs. Paul trusted Christabel's assurance that her daughter would be "most tenderly cared for." Two wardresses accompanied Alice and Amelia Brown to the home of Henrietta and Ernest Löwy, wealthy supporters of the WSPU. AP spoke briefly to reporters. "Although palpably ill, Miss Paul was cheerful," wrote the *New York Times* correspondent, "telling me she did not regret her conduct and was prepared to repeat it again if necessary. She was unable to undergo the ordeal of an interview." Later that day, however, Alice released a statement briefly describing her experience and crowing, "I didn't give in."[59]

The next day, she felt well enough to write home. In fact, she claimed, "I feel as well as when I went in," an unlikely story aimed at consoling her mother. She insisted that she had gained weight in jail (probably from fluid retention). The suffragette doctor visited daily and "she says that [the prison experience] has not done me any harm but I had better lie in bed for a few days & then I will be perfectly well." She appreciated the pleasant surroundings; "it is most delightful lying here in bed by a big open fire." She told Mrs. Paul about the postdated letters and regretted "thee was so worried."[60]

Alice felt astounded at all the hubbub and lamented all the press: "How did they get my photograph and to know anything about my history?" She reiterated what Mrs. Paul heard from Emmeline Pankhurst about press distortion. "It is pure imagination," Alice swore, "to talk about the prison resounding with my screams. Many other women" took the feedings, she wrote. "Why should not I?" She quickly grew impatient with her mother's concern. "I can't see why you were so excited." Mrs. Paul likely smiled at what followed, though. "I will not do it again," her daughter conceded, "as I think I have done enough."

The English debate over forcible feeding reignited a day later, when a respected hospital administrator wrote the *London Times* deploring the practice. He echoed other doctors' concerns about the suffering involved, including "ulceration of the nasal mucous membrane, retching, vomiting, and depression." Furthermore, the alleged "violence of women excited by feelings of political injustice is amply punished by imprisonment with a few days starvation." He, like the Pankhursts, blamed the Home Secretary, who "flattered himself that the mental, moral, and physical suffering inflicted by his orders...would break down the prisoner's resolution. It did not. It broke down the prisoner's health." Indeed, Alice Paul's health languished for years. "This treatment of female political agitators," the administrator predicted, would be "looked back upon by our children with the pity that succeeding generations bestow upon the crude ignorance of their forefathers."[61]

Alice spent nearly a month in bed. She spent the days reading and writing letters and chatting with suffragette visitors. Mrs. Löwy wrote Alice's mother. "I can tell you your daughter has charmed us all & we feel as if we had known her all our lives. She is so sweet & jolly." The English mother reassured the American mother: "I quite thought I should have an invalid to look after but apart from a careful diet for 2 days, she is wonderfully well & seems very happy. Of course she wants to do some more hard work for The Cause." Löwy commended Alice's spirit and added, "We are all very keen here but as yet none of us have had the courage to go through what your daughter has gone through."[62]

Alice soon reneged on her promise to return home. After two weeks, she did not feel well enough to appear at a meeting lauding recent prisoners, though she went outside for short periods. However, she grew ready, at least in spirit, to resume working for the Pankhursts: "I want to work during the general election which ends about Jan 18th," she wrote her mother. "I have never seen a general election & may never have another chance." Nevertheless, she added, "I am really coming home as soon as it is over." She insisted, "I have made up my mind absolutely & positively to not go to prison again."[63]

Alice could not work yet, but she agreed to help publicize the brutality of forcible feeding (despite her contention to her mother that "there is nothing so very alarming about being forcibly fed"). While this seemed unlikely to change anything, AP said, the Pankhursts supported any tactic to "give more publicity to forcible feeding & perhaps help a little to bring it to an end."[64]

By the end of December, Alice had enough emotional distance to describe forcible feeding to her mother and justify her own experience. "It is barbarous," she admitted. The middle-aged Amelia Brown's "gastric trouble" had become so debilitating that she gave up her nursing job. "The nervous strain is the worst part of it all," AP decided. "I think after four or five months of it one would be seriously unstrung nervously." Nevertheless, she felt "much amused" when Woodbrooke's Mrs. Braithwaite wrote to suggest AP was "led astray."[65]

Enduring the feedings became essential, Alice believed, to gaining a sense of ownership in the struggle. The suffering held the virtue of "making the situation more acute & consequently bringing it to an end sooner. It has been successful in achieving the end we had in view. That is—the suffrage question has become more serious & insistent upon a solution than ever before." Alice viewed her actions as consistent with her Quaker heritage and defended them as such to her mother, "It is simply a policy of passive resistance & as a Quaker thee ought to approve of that."[66]

She finally gave up plans to linger in England. "I am not waiting for the election," she wrote. "My heart is not going just right so the doctor insists on my sitting still most of the time & that makes me useless as far as election work goes." She seemed less certain now about her physical condition, adding, "I will be perfectly well I think." Her main feeling was the disappointment: "I am sorry to miss the election." She also turned down Christabel Pankhurst's tempting offer to work as a full-time WSPU organizer. Lucy accepted the same offer; assigned to Edinburgh, she remained another two years. "I knew," said Alice later, "[that] if I stopped now to be an organizer, I would never go back to school." She decided "to finish up my academic work and take a degree. I thought it was perhaps the best thing to do. So I came home. By myself." Alice scheduled passage out of Liverpool in early January. "No one but thee knows I am coming," she told her mother, "so if thee does not say anything about it no reporters will get to know. I hope I will never have to see my name in the paper again."[67]

Alice used the time in prison and in recuperation to think deeply about her involvement with the Pankhursts. On January 3, 1910, she gave her farewell speech to her suffragette comrades at a meeting in St. James's Hall, standing—still weak—to deliver what one listener later described as "a great fighting speech." She clearly felt loath to leave the struggle. "As an American citizen," *Votes for Women* reported her words, she "had often longed to be one of those who had fought in the revolution instead of being merely a descendant, and so in her heart she pitied the coming generation who would be daughters and granddaughters of the women revolutionaries, but would not have had the privilege themselves of taking part in this great war."[68]

In the 1970s, Alice Paul repeatedly brought up a conversation she had with WSPU colleague Emily Wilding Davison in 1910, shortly before sailing for home. At the time, Davison had distinguished herself in the WSPU by successfully suing the officials who tried to break her hunger strike by fire-hosing. Alice remembered Davison saying, " 'Oh, it is so wonderful you are going to America. Think what all you can accomplish.' And I said, 'Oh my goodness, I couldn't accomplish anything. *Anything.* I just did what I was asked to do, whatever is useful. Just a little stone in a big mosaic.' " Davison insisted, "Oh, any person, *any person* can accomplish enormous amounts, if she is just determined to do it." According to the aged Alice, she considered further suffrage involvement only at Davison's urging: "And so I thought about that all the time I was going home—thinking, Well now, maybe I could do something." Davison's subsequent infamy probably merged with AP's memory of this encounter. In 1913, Davison demonstrated her fervent suffragism by running in front of a racehorse with a votes-for-women banner; the horse trampled her to death.[69]

Sixty years later, Alice was still rationalizing her ambition. Out of her memory of Davison, she fashioned a creation myth for herself that removed any need for AP to own her personal ambition. The WSPU had given her a taste of women claiming power for themselves, offering a vision beyond Quaker humility and the societal blunting of female possibility. Alice had already pushed against boundaries with her educational ambitions. The Davison story hints that, in January 1910, despite her apparent reversion to earlier academic plans, she was already thinking about how to sustain the intellectual and emotional passion of her time with the Pankhursts.

After Alice left England, the Pankhursts' claim on public sympathy declined as escalating numbers of violent acts came to define their image. While arson, petty vandalism, window smashing, and other forms of property destruction formed a small part of the WSPU's overall militancy, such actions drew the lion's share of press attention, especially in America.[70] The Pankhursts continued to inspire Alice, but their reputation would cloud her future.

"We Came, They Saw, We Conquered!"

ON JANUARY 6, 1910, Alice Paul boarded the *Haverford* in Liverpool and endured a stormy Atlantic crossing, made even more trying because of her fragile health. Physiologically, she seemed far from the robust, energetic young woman who ventured into Europe three years earlier. And the transformation was more than physical.[1]

Now twenty-five, she had vaulted onto a new plain of self-assurance. Travel and study had challenged her intellect and enlarged her perspective on the world. However, her time organizing for the Pankhursts had truly invigorated her. She had tested herself against extraordinary demands on her mind and body, in the process awakening her desire for heroic struggle. She returned to America determined to complete her academic goal but also cautiously exploring and preparing for a life devoted to political activism. By the end of 1912, she had chosen a new direction and a worthy ambition.

When her ship finally docked, Alice entered an America where many suffrage supporters thrilled to the drama of the British fight, especially as mediated through emissaries like Emmeline Pankhurst. "Never, until these women appeared, telling, with rare eloquence, their stories of struggle, arrest and imprisonment, had the vote appeared such an incomparable treasure," wrote journalist Rheta Childe Dorr in 1910. "Never before, except among a few enthusiasts, had there existed any feeling that suffrage was a thing to fight for, suffer for, even to die for." Though the American suffrage movement had won limited success, few imagined British methods taking hold.[2]

Unlike Britain's profusion of national suffrage groups, a single body had presided over the American movement since 1890: the National American Woman Suffrage Association (NAWSA). Susan B. Anthony, a towering and universally beloved figure, had presided as president until 1900. (The other renowned figure in the women's rights movement, Elizabeth Cady Stanton, grew too radical for many supporters by the last years of her life. She died in 1902.) Anthony's presidency balanced federal and state activities, petitioning Congress annually to pass an amendment to the US Constitution giving American women the vote, while also mounting initiatives at the state level. During Anthony's last years at

the helm, four victories in western states during the 1890s raised hopes that subsequent years had dashed.

After 1904, when Anna Howard Shaw, a medical doctor and one of the first
women to be ordained a Methodist minister, assumed the National's leadership
at the age of fifty-three, she concentrated on state-based offensives. Even before
"Aunt Susan's" death in 1906, Shaw placed the constitutional amendment on the
back burner, wary of taking on the racial politics of a resurgent Jim Crow South
and convinced, like most suffragists, that only a dozen or more state victories
would prompt federal action. By early 1910, NAWSA's membership ballooned to
one hundred thousand, but the last state success was a distant memory, fourteen
years in the past. Shaw struggled to stay relevant.[3]

Winning the vote became vital to disparate groups of women as the new
century unfolded. Wage-earning, often immigrant, women, who proved willing
to strike for better conditions, realized the vote could further workplace goals.
Women coming of age and streaming into colleges and voluntary reform work
began to consider voting requisite to their own development. For Progressive
leaders like Jane Addams, woman suffrage became a way to achieve a long list of
desired urban reforms. As women in many spheres declared the vote a necessity,
NAWSA membership grew and grew restive; one state leader termed the discontent "a fever that brings recovery."[4]

At dusk on January 20, Alice Paul walked down the Philadelphia gangplank looking tired and thin but happy. She walked straight into her celebrity.
Local reporters and photographers swamped her greeting party, Mrs. Paul and
fifteen-year-old Parry. Despite her surprise, Alice patiently answered questions
and removed her glasses to pose for pictures. The photograph adorning the
front page of the *Public Ledger* the next day showed a bemused Alice wearing a
lace-trimmed high collar and cuffs to set off her brown tailored suit and a fashionable beaver tricorn hat as wide as her shoulders. Reporters thought this cultured
image clashed with reality: As one wrote, "There is nothing about Miss Paul's
appearance that would lead one to suppose that she could possibly raise disturbance enough" to be imprisoned. Surprised at the British lilt to his sister's speech,
Parry asked, "Doesn't she talk queer, Mother?" Mrs. Paul agreed.[5]

As reporters fired questions, Alice's replies suggested that, contrary to her creation myth, she felt more than capable of joining the American suffrage cause,
though she knew little of its current state. "Will you take part in the movement
here?" one journalist queried. "I didn't know there was any movement here," she
said. "But if the opportunity arises I shall certainly do what I can."

She already sounded like a leader. Reporters then told her about well-to-
do American women working for suffrage. "Your suffrage movement," she
responded, betraying her continued allegiance abroad, "will not get far so long

as its patronage is limited to society women. It must be a universal movement, in which all women must join and work for the common cause." Reporters mentioned the ongoing shirtwaist workers' strikes in Philadelphia and New York City, in which socialites allied themselves with picketing factory women. Alice approved: "'We really are living in a new sort of era,' she declared, 'when it will be necessary for women to vote because of their knowledge. They can no longer be held down, because they are no longer ignorant.'" She felt that American women would win the vote sooner than the British. "Over here the conditions are freer," she believed, especially in the press. She took the common view that militancy would not serve the United States. "'But,' she warned, 'If it becomes necessary to fight to win, I believe in fighting.'"[6]

Later that night, she sank into her very own bed in her very own room at Paulsdale, a setting at once familiar and strange. The next morning, as she looked around, much about her childhood home appeared the same: the oil lamps, the relatively new piano, the family portraits, the sheep grazing on the lawn, the fresh air, the quiet. Paulsdale still functioned as a working farm. Like Alice, her family had moved on. The house seemed emptier: Will and Helen now were away at college. Mrs. Paul busily managed the farm and Paul properties. Gregarious Parry, fascinated with the newfangled Model T, kept his mother and now Alice company.[7]

Physiologically, she recovered slowly. "Her heart is beating too rapidly from 90 to 100," her mother recorded, "& she has no appetite." Her sense of smell had faded. The heartbeat eventually decreased, but her digestive system gave her problems for years to come. Nonetheless, Alice refused to be frail and fought back against her physical limitations.[8]

As she reoriented herself at home, the attitudes of family and friends toward her British suffragism filtered in. Some of the older men in her extended family disdained her exploits, though a few, like Uncle Mickle Paul, continued to support her. Other family members responded to Alice's return positively, though less warmly. Cousins Susanna and Beulah Parry appreciated her contribution without approving of the method. Tacie's best friend, Tacy Lippincott, remained so but felt a woman's place in the home more important than politics. In 1920, a family history described AP as acquiring "considerable notoriety, not enviable."[9]

Even Alice's siblings differed in their assessments of her activities. Helen, busy at Wellesley, now proudly recognized two types of suffrage campaigning: "Alice's or plain." Parry likewise admired her. Brother Will, on the other hand, home in Moorestown by March, was reportedly less than proud of Alice, perhaps modeling himself after what he took to be his late father's probable view. "He just thought she was too active—and in public view and all," one relation recalled.[10] Will's attitude underscores how her father's death reshaped her possibilities.

Attending First Day meeting with her family required some delicacy. Alice found herself in a tricky position with Moorestown's Hicksites: liberty of conscience was fundamental to the Quaker faith. Still, the *Rules of Discipline* warned against embarrassing the Society of Friends with "immoral or disorderly conduct" or "unseemly practices as shall occasion public scandal." The Hicksite Yearly Meeting's encouragement of suffrage work did not have vigorous protesting in mind. More conservative Hicksites took an even more circumscribed view of appropriate behavior, especially for women. Alice's memory in old age that everyone "looked rather askance, rather embarrassed", probably records the reaction of these Friends. Nevertheless, by 1910, disownment—once common for infractions—became unusual, partly because liberal Hicksites became more dominant and more reluctant to exclude members, especially younger ones. So AP remained within the Moorestown meeting, although some elders may have informally admonished her.[11]

Alice embraced her newfound celebrity, though her ambition at this juncture appears no larger than recounting her British experiences; as in England, she thought long and hard about changes in course. Area newspapers and the nationally distributed *Woman's Journal* trumpeted her return, and speaking invitations soon arrived from suffrage groups in New Jersey, New York, and Philadelphia, some offering honoraria. Alice hurried to repair and replace her worn clothes so she could present herself properly. Her desire to contribute and to prolong her British involvement, if only indirectly, overrode her distaste for the spotlight.[12]

Alice debuted as a suffrage lecturer less than a week after coming home and quickly came to know movers and shakers associated with the American effort. Her conversations with them became her schooling in the current state of American suffrage. In addition, her speaking engagements and the press they generated gave her a presence in the national suffrage community.

Philadelphia groups claimed her first. The bolder tactics long used in western states and now surfacing in a few eastern cities were starting to influence suffrage activity in the conservative City of Brotherly Love. There, hewing to long-standing NAWSA tradition, the movement was nonpartisan, educational, and gender appropriate. Friends, though not representative of Quakers at large, often took a prominent role. Since 1869, the Pennsylvania NAWSA chapter held sway; several new independent groups and even newer discussions of novel methods began to reflect experimentation in other cities. Meetings still typically convened in members' homes; however, for a special event, some organizations rented space and invited outside speakers.[13]

Alice encountered both enthusiasm for and apprehension about Pankhurst-style politics in her first speaking engagements. At the College Club on Locust Street, she found a former graduate school colleague also preaching social action: Scott Nearing, an avid suffragist and a shirtwaist strike ally, now taught at Penn and Swarthmore. He gave a brief address that evening, as did the elderly Jane Campbell, one of the leading suffragists in the area. Alice repeated her gangplank remarks about the connection between her own activism and that of striking shirtwaist workers. The shirtwaist picketers, she said, brought to mind last summer's "siege of Westminster," in which the WFL sent silent pickets to the entrance of Parliament.[14]

The next day, on Campbell's own turf—the county-level NAWSA—the audience expected Alice to justify militancy. "Do you think the suffragettes like their own methods, or want to pursue violent tactics?" she asked. "The price they are paying for their freedom is terribly dear, but they are convinced that only the methods of war and practical politics will ever win their cause." The Pankhursts succeeded, she claimed, by making votes for women "the most burning question in Europe today," a phenomenon this older audience could scarcely imagine. "No one has ever been injured in the suffrage cause, except the suffragettes," AP emphasized, knowing this fact spoke volumes to listening Quakers. Some women became "permanently hurt and broken in health, but for that," she declared, "they care nothing." Her prior speaking experience paid off: one reporter wrote of her "quiet eloquence, a vivid pictorial power, a fund of logic and occasional touches of stinging sarcasm."[15]

Alice reluctantly agreed to describe her forcible feeding. The listeners reacted with "quivers of indignation" and "motherly tenderness." She emphasized the psychological torture, sparing this audience's and her own discomfort about acknowledging the physical and sexual connotations of the feedings. "The mental agony, had it lasted longer," she said, "would probably have driven me mad. Living in daily dread of this operation," she confessed, "was the worst kind of suffering I have ever endured."[16]

Jane Campbell took Alice Paul's measure over the course of the two presentations and judged her decorous enough to mute anyone's doubts about her involvement with the Pankhursts. Alice recalled that Campbell approached her afterward and said, "You know, when we asked you, we didn't know who you were or what sort of person you were or whether you were wild and fanatical. Now we see what sort of a person you are and we'd like you to go on our committee." Campbell knew that both the state and county NAWSA chapters planned to establish formal headquarters and, following a New York effort, begin organizing work in voting wards. AP agreed to serve on the executive committee.[17]

Alice acquired a skewed view of the American suffrage movement in Philadelphia, but she became a significant voice in promoting a broader view of activism to the city's suffragists. She simultaneously defended the Pankhursts' tactics and emphasized the need to enter the political realm. Appearing before another newborn Philadelphia suffrage league, she encouraged local plans to organize by ward. The British situation was not suited for such work, she said, reiterating the idea that the British and American systems of governance demanded different efforts. "Here men do not throw stones through windows to accomplish their purpose. They organize and form a machine. And that is what we must do to accomplish the establishment of equal suffrage." Her vision stretched well beyond nonpartisan ward organizing.[18]

In early February, Alice returned to New York City for the first time since her settlement house days and found suffrage activism quite different than in Philadelphia. Some New York advocates had embraced labor organizing tactics borrowed from the Pankhursts and suffragists in the American West. Most prominently, Harriot Stanton Blatch's Equality League of Self-Supporting Women, founded after a 1907 visit from a British suffragette, actively recruited industrial workers as well as the usual elites. Mrs. Blatch, the daughter of Elizabeth Cady Stanton, used street-corner organizing and open-air meetings. Carrie Chapman Catt, a veteran of several western state campaigns, founded the Woman Suffrage Party, a quasi-machine devoted to bridging traditional suffrage work and conventional politics.[19]

An even bolder group than the Equality League crystallized the sentiment many "new women" felt. The group behind the short-lived *American Suffragette* journal proudly adopted the British "-ette" identity to distinguish their provocative approach. A *suffragist*, they contended, "plods along in the beaten track made by the great pioneers of the movement and contents herself with methods conservative." The *suffragette*, on the other hand, "realizes the ineffectiveness of tea-table and drawing-room chat." Impatience was her watchword. "The Suffragette is unwilling to wait for the ballot another sixty years. She wants it *now* and she wants it *quick!*"[20]

Alice spoke in New York at Mrs. Blatch's invitation, which gave her the opportunity to thank Blatch for pressuring British officials about AP's release a few months earlier. Alice's newfound self-assurance probably shrank before Blatch: the latter's short, matronly stature and salt-and-pepper waves belied a commanding presence. Blatch also had thirty years on AP. In the years to come, however, Harriot Blatch became a powerful, if mercurial, ally. Blatch's efforts had not persuaded the New York press to look kindly on the militancy of the WSPU. While the Philadelphia press had generally played up Alice as newsworthy and credible, New York reporters denigrated not only her activities but the woman herself. The subhead on one article promised "Details of the Glad Life in Holloway Jail." Alice appeared rather odd to this scribe: "a little figure in a queer shade of green velvet, a genteel sort of a necklace, brown hair, nose glasses, low shoes and lisle thread stockings." Another reporter belittled AP as one who "could not break herself of the habit of shouting '*Votes for women*' whenever it chanced to occur to her." Despite his disparaging attitude, the first writer became struck by Alice's imperturbability. "Some women have made more of a fuss about missing the Fifth avenue coach than Alice Paul did over her seven arrests, her three imprisonments, and her rather annoying way of being subjected to nourishment."[21]

A few days after returning from New York, Alice laid out the full sweep of her outlook on women's status. On February 9, she appeared at a Philadelphia symposium on "The Significance of the Woman Suffrage Movement," sponsored by the influential Penn-based American Academy of Political and Social Science. The event allowed AP to reacquaint herself with the range of arguments for and against woman suffrage and to expand her connections with prominent suffragists. Furthermore, the symposium gave her a platform to put forth an expansive view rather than one focused narrowly on her suffrage work in Britain.[22]

The other invited speakers included political, religious, and social leaders on both sides of the suffrage issue; AP was the youngest (by nearly twenty-five years) and the most obscure. She knew Carl Kelsey, her Penn advisor. She remembered Unitarian minister Anna Garlin Spencer from the NYSP. And she met NAWSA president Anna Howard Shaw, a magnetic orator, for the first time.[23]

Altogether, the speakers provided a glimpse of the contemporary debate over suffrage. Shaw cogently pointed out that women were "just as much a part of the 'governed' as men." Spencer focused on the theme Progressive reformers often invoked: women stood prepared to enter the public arena because of their voluntary work in families, schools, and hospitals. Maud Nathan, founder of the National Consumers' League, added that the indirect influence of voluntary work and social networks could not match the power of the vote for directly influencing public policy. The part-Cherokee senator from the new state of Oklahoma, Robert L. Owen, brought in the wage-earning woman's perspective, calling equal pay for equal work the "first great reason" for woman suffrage. On the other hand, for anti-suffrage leader Louise Caldwell Jones, women already enjoyed equality; she believed private life far outweighed voting in importance. Similarly, minister and reformer Charles Parkhurst insisted that woman's genius lay in her sensibilities, not in her logic.[24]

Alice's speech revealed that the suffrage struggle was now foremost in her mind. Ostensibly about British suffragism, her talk rested on the tenets of turn-of-the-century Progressivism, but even more on her enhanced level of awareness occasioned by returning to her homeland. As she regained her physical strength and assessed her years in Britain, she saw America with fresh eyes and puzzled her way forward. Her symposium address makes clear that Alice was synthesizing her academic knowledge with her experience in settlement houses and political activism. Like others analyzing women's status at the dawn of the twentieth century, she connected shifting cultural mores and expanded work and educational opportunities with the suffrage struggle. The speech suggests that neither social work nor academic work now animated Alice Paul; suffrage became *the* job worth tackling. The Academy published the symposium addresses, circulating her name widely.

Alice grounded her speech in specifics about Britain, but she knew her ideas applied to America as well. She took the view, common among Progressives, that evolution always pushed forward and built her optimism on the changes in women's social and economic life. The Industrial Revolution had drawn millions of women into the labor market, she noted, while others finally wore down barriers to higher education and the professions. Female volunteers stood at the forefront of most social reforms. (Notably, she did not challenge the acceptability of paid work for privileged women like herself.) "The giving of the ballot," she declared, "would be but the public recognition of the change which social forces have brought about." After a woman entered the political realm, she said, "demanding the ballot for herself was but a natural step."

While the early part of her speech implicitly accepted class distinctions, she then confronted class attitudes. She believed political activism promised to destroy outmoded ideas about gender and social standing. The prejudice that constructed women as appendages to men still held fast, though she believed this to be less so in America than in Britain. "This old idea of women as created solely in order to minister to man is akin to the idea that the working man's whole purpose in the world is to contribute to the happiness of the upper classes," she observed tartly. "Both ideas have been hard to kill." As a Quaker well schooled in the virtues of inner struggle, Alice rejoiced that the battle for suffrage in Britain came hard-fought, for "the struggle has done much to help women throw off their mental bondage." She surely spoke from personal experience of the "great spirit of rebellion" such contests kindled. She had learned, in Gandhi's later phrase, "You must become the change you wish to see in the world."[25]

In less than three weeks, Alice Paul emerged as a presence in the suffrage community. Her lecture suggests that, during these weeks, she convinced herself of the need to engage with the American suffrage cause. Her speaking engagements allowed her to work out and expound on her views about woman's status. Indeed, these speeches soon became implicit forums on the urgency of suffrage, with herself as the most important audience.

The evening after the Penn conference, Alice faced a different and perhaps her toughest audience: her Moorestown friends and neighbors. The Young Friends' Association asked her to discuss her British activism at her alma mater, the Friends School. One attendee recalled, "Every one in town went." Actually, five hundred people packed the auditorium. If not most of the town's four thousand residents, at least most Quakers attended. AP strained to project her low voice to the back row.[26]

Anticipating criticism, she took a defensive posture in her address. As her sister later remarked of Moorestown, "We are all so wretchedly well-to-do, we dread anything disturbing, even an idea." Alice first told her audience they should not judge the Pankhursts based on the American press, whose stories about the suffragettes were rife with distortion. She invoked Florence Nightingale and American abolitionists as examples of earlier reformers who used unorthodox methods to overcome great odds. The crowd sat silently as she spoke "earnestly and rapidly, but without heat or bitterness," according to the *Friends' Intelligencer.* Alice presented the militant position, emphasizing, "Women representing all classes are fighting for the ballot. They are in deadly earnest." Window smashing was an age-old political tactic in Britain, and suffragettes had used it sparingly. She talked about prisoners being treated as the "scum of London" but eschewed describing the forcible feeding. Finally, she noted the suffragette' maxim so familiar to this faith-grounded audience: "Resistance to tyranny is obedience to God."

Moorestown Quakers seemed bent more on courtesy than calumny this night. Hearty applause and even a cheer or two rang through the hall. Then, "James C. Stiles created a sensation," the *Public Ledger* reported, "by asking Miss Paul if she thought it a Christian act to break a window, and if God would approve of it." "Sit down, Jimmy, sit down!" another man interjected. Alice felt weary of this sort of question. "Miss Paul promptly replied," said the *Ledger*, "that she saw no particular sanctity in a pane of glass, and that she herself had broken forty-eight." Her response undercut the elevated status which the broken windows had assumed in some minds. Cheers rang out and the crowd broke up; old friends gathered around AP. Alice no doubt breathed a sigh of relief.[27]

Her growing reputation produced continued opportunities to appear before suffrage audiences. A suffragist in one of her Philadelphia audiences wrote to the *Women's Journal* to recommend strongly that other groups invite AP to speak. "She disarms all prejudice and creates a healthful sympathy which reacts for suffrage. The Philadelphia League reports a hundred new members through Mrs. Pankhurst and Miss Paul." Invitations continued to come in. Most notably, those organizing the April 1910 NAWSA convention invited Alice to speak.[28]

An interest in political tactics animated the NAWSA faithful as they gathered in Washington for their annual meeting. President Taft agreed to welcome the delegates; his presence, despite his doubts about women voting, hinted that politicians were noticing the burgeoning suffrage ranks. Indeed, many state delegations announced plans to lobby candidates and voters. The convention had nixed attempts to encourage public advocacy two years earlier; by contrast, the 1910 delegates sanctioned lobbying, street-corner meetings, and poll watching.

One Quaker speaker wrote later about the unusual number of younger women influencing the group's direction; their interest, he wrote, "rather runs over to the agitator side of the propaganda."[29]

At this time of rising expectations among suffragists, the NAWSA leadership was in disarray. True, the recently established headquarters in New York City allowed greater exposure and easier coordination with chapters. Socialite and philanthropist Alva Belmont, the force behind the new offices, also funded them in part. Despite support from other wealthy donors, however, the organization had little to spare after collecting $21,000 over the previous year. During the convention, simmering discontent about Anna Howard Shaw's direction and administration of the National erupted. Several prominent figures resigned from the executive board in protest against Shaw's failure to set clear policy and take methodical action. This became the first of several reshufflings over the next five years.[30]

The 1910 NAWSA convention was Alice Paul's coming-out party for the national suffrage audience. She reconnected with Shaw and Harriot Blatch and met other leading lights such as Carrie Chapman Catt, a former NAWSA president, now head of the International Suffrage Alliance. The delegates at the convention, however, were the backbone of the movement. They formally or informally led chapters and set direction locally. Many had read about her, and they now had the occasion to size her up in person. For Alice, the convention provided a chance to gauge the overall temper of American suffrage. She also took full advantage of the opportunity to mollify those leery of the WSPU's methods.[31]

Her stirring speech on the British militants fit the restless tone of the convention. She offered the Pankhurstian narrative of courageous women versus contemptible politicians in a way designed to spur listeners to action. Reviewing the long British pursuit of the vote and "the magnificent struggle for political freedom" under the Pankhursts, she said, "Women who have grown grey in the suffrage cause have told me they had almost lost hope." The window breaking that some Americans decried was a long-established "symbolic act of rebellion," she observed, linking the history of British and American activism, "just as our fathers held the Boston tea-party as an act of protest."

She went on to reassure her audience that—as most of them (and she herself) believed—American politicians would never treat suffragists as shamefully as the British. The British government, not the Pankhursts, had perpetrated the real violence (forcible feeding), to which the WSPU simply reacted with passive resistance. She welcomed the American situation, where elected officials received suffragists courteously. The experienced hands in the audience knew this to be true and also knew that most politicians subsequently ignored them. Alice insisted, however, that an American victory lay just out of reach. Her optimism struck a welcome chord.[32]

One speech at the convention hastened Alice's movement toward a different career path. NAWSA official Frances Squire Potter issued an urgent call for up-to-date research on state and federal laws pertaining to women. Potter's call seems more than coincidental to the work on women's legal status Alice began that summer, research that would become her doctoral thesis. Investigating women's legal status gave AP a deeper understanding of the long American suffrage effort and presaged her lifelong interest in the law as it pertained to women.[33]

On the last day of the convention, Alice glimpsed the current state of the national leadership at the annual suffrage hearings before both Senate and House committees, currently the only federal effort by the National. AP probably joined those squeezing into new and spacious Senate hearing rooms for a performance long familiar to both parties. Shaw and other NAWSA leaders first presented suffrage petitions with 404,825 signatures to both houses. Addressing the Senate suffrage committee, Shaw declared, "It is not revolutionary on our part to ask a share in our Government." She introduced the speakers; several Senators responded in kind. The chairman thanked the women; his promises of careful attention to a woman suffrage amendment were his last attention to the subject. The House Judiciary Committee reacted the same way. Neither committee bothered to report out the amendment resolution, favorably or otherwise. NAWSA, for its part, discussed no further action other than scheduling a repeat performance the following year. To Alice, the National leadership's languor seemed a world away from Britain, where the Pankhursts always had another political gambit in mind.[34]

An unexpected coda to the convention suggested that Alice had now transferred her suffrage allegiance to the American movement. A middle-aged convention attendee felt so impressed by the young Quaker that she gave her a life membership in NAWSA. This woman's local suffrage club had petitioned Taft over AP's imprisonment in late 1909. Alice wrote, "I can hardly tell you how touched I am by this great and most unexpected honor." She felt proud, she wrote with a careful use of the possessive, to be a life member of "our association. May I be a worthy one!"[35]

In May 1910, Harriot Stanton Blatch pulled off the first large-scale suffrage parade in America, an event consciously modeled after WSPU processions and intended to signal the arrival of militancy in the United States. She likely invited Alice, who certainly joined the marchers in spirit, if not in person. This time, the redoubtable Blatch proceeded over the objections of her state suffrage association and NAWSA, both of which believed a Pankhurst-style event would reverse the political gains of the past two generations. Shaw finally agreed to ride in one of the parade motorcars and make a speech, despite serious doubts about "so radical a demonstration"; philanthropist Alva Belmont and Carrie Chapman Catt both pleaded illness.[36]

Several hundred women did march, many with the same apprehension British women felt. As the *New York Times* noted, "Many of them had never taken part in anything of the kind before and were resolute, but a good deal scared." "We felt we must do it for the Cause," one participant said, recalling her "palpating emotions." At first, participant Inez Gilmore wrote, a marcher felt "every spectator's eye is glued to you." A mounted police guard eased fears, as the city's myriad suffrage groups walked or rode down Fifth Avenue amid thousands of curious, mostly male onlookers. The women waved banners and flags in yellow, the traditional American suffrage color. "You find yourself floating about in a sea of women," Gilmore continued, "enjoying a new, strange almost unanalyzable emotion—a sense of triumph such as you have never known in all your life." Blatch repeated her parade success in 1911 and 1912, prompting one writer to dub her the "Mrs. Pankhurst of America." Nevertheless, Blatch showed no inclination to extend her purview beyond New York.[37]

Home at Paulsdale during the summer, Alice continued to regain her strength while she reacquainted herself with her family. Helen's college roommate, Myra McNally, visited Paulsdale that summer and became struck by the plain ways of the Paul homestead. A silent grace preceded meals; the use of *thee* and *thy* rendered conversation "gentler, more intimate." Myra noticed the absence of dancing, though she joined the family singing around the piano and playing parlor games like charades. "Helen admired her older sister tremendously," McNally thought, though Alice seldom socialized with the younger women. However, one fine day everyone climbed into the Pauls' new—and first—touring machine, one with a convertible top, and Parry drove them to the Atlantic City beach.[38]

That summer, Alice also joined in an effort to push more Quakers toward activism. Twenty American alumni of Woodbrooke reunited to highlight social reform at nearby Haverford College, an Orthodox Quaker institution. Organizers asked Alice to give a special evening lecture, which one listener later called the "most fervent" of the day.[39]

Her speech made clear she had acquired a sense of mission that, though secular, nonetheless grew out of her nonconformist Quaker heritage. She joined her Woodbrooke colleagues in urging Friends to look beyond their faith community to serve the needs of the wider society. After earlier speakers lashed out at a complacent faith, Alice took an inspirational approach, one that drew on both her pride in being a Quaker and her dismay at the faith's stolidity, notably about gender. "There is no religious body," she declared, "which has more splendid principles and traditions of democracy than has ours." She spoke of young Friends like herself wanting to uphold "unsullied the character which has been handed down to us." The spirit of the founders had withered, she said, and offered a pointed example from her own experience. A Friend she knew, a woman "most punctilious as to plainness of speech and garb," heard of the needs "of a certain reform movement." "Yet her first question was, 'What sort of people are taking this up— what is their social caste—are they *ladies?*'" Alice believed too many Friends were "clinging to the letter which killeth and losing the spirit which maketh alive."

Alice's deepest hopes for herself form the subtext of the Haverford speech. *She*, not just Friends at large, wondered, "Why should we be so impotent compared to the early Friends?" She well knew that "these are just as stirring times" as the inspiring campaigns of old in which Friends proved influential. As she closed, she laid bare her desire to cleave to her Quaker heritage. Her own path looked clear, she seemed to say, but she felt reluctant to forsake Quakerism or be forsaken by the faith; rather, she wanted Friends to live up to the long-cherished ideals of their Society. She wanted them to be "worthy of the great traditions which we have inherited" and be "more valiant soldiers in humanity's cause than ever before." Alice called on members of her faith to join her on the path to social activism, but she refused to wait for the Society of Friends to catch up. Indeed, on an institutional level, that prospect languished for years to come.[40]

Alice re-entered the University of Pennsylvania in early 1911, joining old friends and noticeably more women students than in 1907. She moved into rooms near campus, living again with Clara Thompson, who was back from Italy to finish her doctoral work. After missing the deadline in 1909, Alice now won a doctoral fellowship from Penn. The fellowship paid all expenses for her final graduate year, including room and board. Accepting the Moore Fellowship, designed for candidates in education, indicated that AP still envisioned a teaching career for herself, either alongside suffrage work or afterward.[41]

Though the Penn trustees still declined to welcome female undergraduates to all departments, women in the graduate school population now totaled close to ninety, one for every five males. Most women still focused on the humanities. Alice became the odd woman out once again—the only one to integrate political science with sociology and economics.[42]

She renewed her acquaintance with mentors like Simon Patten and Carl Kelsey, but became more focused intellectually on her political science work with Leo Rowe and Ellery Stowell. Both Rowe and Stowell were early internationalists pursuing diplomatic as well as scholarly work; they surely influenced the international work Alice undertook later in life. Stowell, just ten years AP's senior and perhaps a bit smitten, remembered her as "a brilliant student" with "a fine taste in dress."[43]

While she had identified mentors among Penn's professors early in her master's training, she now drew male admirers from the instructor ranks. Scott

Nearing may have introduced Alice to colleagues, though he disapproved of her
exploits in Britain. Postdoctoral fellow Howard Gray Brownson asked Alice to
dinner and a Eugene Debs lecture: "It occurred to me," he wrote, that "you might
be interested in hearing him. If you could arrange it I should like to have you take
dinner with me Saturday and then attend the meeting." The invitation dates from
several months *after* both left Penn, hinting at a continuing friendship between
the two scholars; indeed Brownson and another Penn colleague contacted Alice
years later in Washington.[44]

One man at Penn seemed enamored with her. Carl William Parker Jr., a
Cornell graduate, co-taught a political economy course with Nearing. Parker
(known as William) hailed from a small town north of Albany, New York. Like
Alice, he was born in 1885 to a prosperous farm family. He left Penn late in 1911 to
do doctoral work at Columbia.[45]

The familiar tone of Parker's letters to Alice is exceptional among all her
correspondents. Only his end of the communication survived. "I was in the
Adirondacks," he wrote, "when I had the pleasant surprise of a letter (think of
it) from you. I had begun to think my occasional missives must be boring to so
world renowned a figure." He seemed put out by her lack of reciprocity. Alice had
written about completing her doctorate. No one else teased her, but he poked fun
at her self-effacing persona: "'By great good luck I took my degree.' Ha! Modest
violet! How surprised everyone must have been!" He admired her though. "You
have a tremendous constitution," he told her, "and if you only don't break yourself
to pieces, you will conquer the world." He hoped they could see each other in
New York and continue corresponding as well. He closed, "I shall always look
for you." We do not know whether the correspondence continued from 1912, but
William Parker would turn up in Alice Paul's life again.[46]

Amid classes and research, she found some time for suffrage work and other
friends. She began to integrate doctoral research on woman's legal status into
speeches as early as December 1910, when she told a local suffrage group that
state laws restricting married women "should be done away with." She had not
lost contact with British suffragists. Sylvia Pankhurst toured the nation in March
1911, and Alice met with her at the Philadelphia speech, shortly before the horrific
Triangle Shirtwaist Factory fire on March 25 in New York. Alice and Henrietta
Löwy still corresponded. Löwy, who had nursed AP after her forcible feeding,
sent love and thanked AP for sending a photograph ("the best I have of you").
Mrs. Löwy found the courage to be imprisoned herself in late 1910 and thought,
"We are in sight of the Vote now." She added ruefully, perhaps giving Alice pause,
"We have always thought that haven't we?"[47]

After her Penn semester concluded, Alice felt ready to test her leadership skills.
She and Lucy Burns approached the Pennsylvania NAWSA chapter (PWSA)

about a summer open-air campaign, and the group agreed to the idea. Since the 1910 convention, when delegates voted in favor of open-air meetings, several state chapters had tried them, including New Jersey. Illinois sent speakers touring in automobiles and found it the "most effective legislative suffrage work we have ever done here." Appropriating labor methods offered access to new audiences, yet exposed suffragists to often arbitrary enforcement of laws protecting freedom of assembly. Nonetheless, in Philadelphia, the pecuniary advantages of the open air won over hesitant members. As one organizer wrote, "No rent, no paid speakers (a luxury we indulged in occasionally), no notices to be sent to members, practically no expense at all."[48] And they could pass the hat at meetings too.

Alice wanted the help of Lucy Burns in her first foray into American suffrage organizing. The two WSPU veterans reunited in the summer of 1911 when Lucy returned to America to visit her family. She worked now as the Edinburgh WSPU organizer. The two friends had much to discuss, including the news that a suffrage bill in Parliament looked promising; militants had declared a truce to await the outcome. The American news also seemed encouraging and not only for the interest in new tactics; in November 1910, women in Washington State won suffrage, the first such victory in fourteen years. Excited about American possibilities, Lucy agreed to help AP in Philadelphia for a week.[49]

Alice now drew on all she learned organizing for the Pankhursts. She planned street-corner meetings twice a week from late July through late September and every night the first week. Twenty-three-year-old Caroline Katzenstein, the PWSA secretary, later described the lead-off event and her own apprehension. AP assembled a small band of recruits, including a middle-aged Quaker PWSA officer, a young wage earner, and a thirtyish lawyer and her sister, as well as Caroline Katzenstein and Lucy. They sent no advance notices. "No one knew better than Miss Paul the possible consequences," Katzenstein wrote.[50]

While Alice later advocated only passive resistance, in 1911 she still valued physical defiance, even—or perhaps especially—in the Quaker city. As the group rode a nearly empty trolley to the first meeting site, she told them, "If the police threaten to arrest us and we offer no resistance, it will mean the end of open-air suffrage meetings in Philadelphia." Katzenstein presumed she meant physical resistance, and no one objected, though they all remembered belligerent authorities arresting hundreds of striking Philadelphia waistmakers the previous year. This night, the neophytes wished to avoid trouble. Alice and Lucy probably hoped otherwise: tumult always improved the press coverage. The suffragists reached their destination at Front and Dauphin, an industrial area, and the women stepped out to find their hired horse, cart, and driver; the cart served as rostrum. As the moment approached, Katzenstein noticed a constable walking his beat.[51]

Alice failed to recognize the uneasiness some in the troop felt; in Britain, her protest companions had matched her own fortitude. Nonetheless, she lost no one. Katzenstein looked at the officer and looked at her comrades and thought "it might be a very unequal combat." Statuesque Lucy promised to be their best weapon; Katzenstein recalled that "her irresistible smile should have disarmed any policeman, no matter what his size." The other Quaker among them, the PWSA officer Mary Morgan, felt protected by her status. She quietly told Katzenstein to avoid arrest and telephone Morgan's husband, a newspaper editor, if the group required bail.[52]

No one needed bail. "We came, they saw, we conquered!" Katzenstein exclaimed. Despite her experience, Alice gave the starring roles to others; she opened the meeting and introduced Morgan, then Lucy and the lawyer. A curious crowd soon gathered, perhaps three hundred spectators, including many young working women. The surprised constable either saw no reason to interfere or feared being outnumbered. When Katzenstein telephoned the eight local newspapers that night, she found "more interest at the city desks than I had ever before been able to arouse." Alice wrote the *Woman's Journal* to announce the start of Philadelphia's open-air campaign. Though not much by British standards, the open-air campaign proceeded through the summer, without the hostilities that had marked the shirt-waist strike or the violence that beset British suffrage workers.[53]

Two factors underlay the success of AP's first campaign: the absence of an opposing entity like the waist manufacturers determined to shut down the suffrage meetings and the presence of prominent women like Morgan. Consequently, city officials took a cautious approach and the citizens of Philadelphia became accepting of women's right to assemble, if not their right to vote.

Alice did not urge nonresistance; rather, she willed struggle to occur. The occasion never presented itself; jeering and laughter erupted at times, but neither spectators nor police abused anyone physically. Verbal hostility often bubbled up: Alice faced down a male crowd of hundreds one evening on City Hall Plaza and won them over. As a patronizing *Bulletin* reporter wrote, "Head back, eyes flashing and with determination in every line of her firm little chin, she argued her cause." When a drunk disrupted her, "half a score of men, some well dressed, others in short sleeves" quickly hustled him off.[54]

Like the reporters covering her return to America, the *Bulletin* correspondent felt confounded by the notion of a privileged female agitator. "Tall and gracefully slender, with fine eyes and beautiful teeth, she is smartly gowned. Last night, over a cool summer frock, she wore a pongee coat with brass buttons. A big, broad-brimmed hat with Paris all over it, crowned her small head." For Alice and other suffragists trying similar campaigns around the country, the contradiction became another tool for opening minds.[55]

Alice had never led a campaign in Britain, but she demonstrated a capacity for leadership and an ability to utilize her experience with the Pankhursts. She paid attention to costs, making sure organizers sold literature and took up collections at each meeting. She kept the press interested with stunts like sending Katzenstein and Morgan at dawn to chalk the sidewalks of the city center with "Votes for Women!" She moved any willing volunteer onto the meeting platform, overwhelming any reluctance. In the no-nonsense fashion that became her trademark, she persuaded Katzenstein to join the speaker corps. When the young woman demurred, saying she was "going through the tortures of the damned," Alice "didn't come over and try to comfort me and she did not try to make the task seem a light one. She answered simply in her calm, imperturbable way, 'We've all done that.'" She encouraged Katzenstein to start by introducing speakers, so the press had other names to use. The tactic had worked for AP herself in Britain and it served well for Katzenstein, who worked with Alice Paul from then on.[56]

The coup de grâce of the Philadelphia summer campaign, this first Alice Paul production, was a monster rally, its importance as much symbolic as real. The Pankhursts knew the importance of location, and Alice clearly had acquired the knack as well. She persuaded a series of city officials to grant her hallowed ground for the September event: Independence Square, the so-called Birthplace of Liberty, where the Declaration of Independence and US Constitution were crafted. Those documents gave women no voice, but provided the foundation of their appeal. Alice claimed the meeting was the first of its kind for women, but a few Philadelphians probably remembered July 4, 1876, when Susan B. Anthony, denied a place in a centennial gala, read a Declaration of Rights for Women to a crowd just off the square. In 1911, the mayoral election also scheduled for September 30 lent the suffrage rally added symbolic weight; while men went to the polls, women gathered to demonstrate their worthiness as citizens.[57]

Alice's plan resembled one of the WSPU's outdoor rallies. The day went off without an obvious hitch, quite a feat for a neophyte organizing an event involving thousands. She drew on her suffrage contacts to bring in, as she recalled, "the most illustrious people we could get," notably Anna Howard Shaw and New York socialite-activist Inez Milholland. Eighteen orators, including AP herself, engaged a crowd of two thousand and sparred with skeptics from five rickety platforms. By the end of the day, PWSA found itself the beneficiary of a great deal of publicity and a summer campaign netting $117.63. AP's grand plans, unfortunately, exceeded available funds and she dug into her own pocket and appealed in the *Friends' Intelligencer* to "those who sympathize." Nevertheless, she had tested her wings as a suffrage leader and found them surprisingly sturdy.[58]

With the successful open-air campaign concluded, Alice returned to her immediate goal: completing her doctoral degree. She focused her dissertation on women's legal status in Pennsylvania, inspired by Frances Potter's call for such studies at the NAWSA convention. (Her home state of New Jersey already planned to publish a booklet detailing state laws.) Toward that end, she dug into both legal and social history, tracking the course of Pennsylvania jurisprudence over three centuries and connecting it to her broader knowledge of American and British history.

Alice sought not simply to compile current law relating to women but to understand how women's status evolved. After summarizing laws from the 1600s to the present day, as well as changes in women's lives through the centuries, she observed that progress came as "a series of minute, slowly wrought modifications." She pointedly noted that women's status in Pennsylvania benefited historically from "the strong Quaker element," concluding that the biggest obstacle to advances in woman's status was "general indifference and even quiet opposition." Opposition came from women and men alike; she saw no "sex struggle" or male conspiracy. As more women moved into paid labor as a result of the Industrial Revolution and concomitantly participated more in public life, their legal status also began to change. As women's status slowly improved, she thought, more grew indignant about the remaining discrimination. Court interpretations of some newer laws rendered them all but void; nonetheless, like a good Progressive, Alice found no steps backward in her history.

Alice's conclusion validated the possibility of carving out a continuing public role for herself. Those women, she wrote, who enjoyed "the greatest freedom" with "no personal grievances" historically led the way (presumably another nod to the Quakers), while those with the most to gain often proved indifferent or even hostile. She blamed the "self-sacrificing quality in woman's nature" for their showing less "zeal in their own cause" than the causes of others and cited the abolition movement as an example. In particular, she adopted the Stanton-Anthony view that abolition-bred suffrage advocates weakened the cause in 1866 by favoring African American over simultaneous female and black enfranchisement. Even in 1910, she felt, women's rights advocates worked more for benefits they saw accruing to other women, not themselves.

Alice was in essence talking about herself, recognizing her privilege and dismissing any discrimination she had herself experienced. Her statement that "the movement for improving [women's] legal status has been essentially an altruistic one" suggests that she sought justification for her own ambition from female role models who upheld the great Quaker traditions for being, in her earlier phrase, "valiant soldiers in humanity's cause."[59]

By the end of May, Alice completed her doctorate. She joined another woman and thirty-two men receiving doctoral degrees in 1912, conservative Penn lagging behind the national average of 10 percent of doctorates awarded to women. Alice chose never to use the honorific she earned, following the Quaker preference for more egalitarian address; she continued as "Miss Paul." Advisor Carl Kelsey praised her final examination and wondered what she planned next: would she be teaching next year?[60]

Precisely when Alice decided to pursue full-time suffrage activism is unclear. Only indirect evidence survives. In her 1911 open-air campaign, she experimented with organizing in her own right. She later sought validation for advocacy in her dissertation. Both show her increasing identification with feminism rather than academia, but neither proves she wanted to devote all her energies to suffrage instead of teaching and ancillary suffrage work. However, a 1913 letter suggests that AP's recognition of the uncommon courage required for full-time dedication to a cause ultimately swayed her. Empowered by her British exploits, she felt confident she fit the bill, taking her own advice to find zeal in a cause for women. As she wrote her Swarthmore chum Mabel Vernon, "There are plenty of people to teach school."[61]

Indeed, suffrage groups were competing for Alice's proven speaking and organizing skills. Jane Campbell wrote several times to ask AP to undertake another summer campaign; "Everyone says," she insisted, "if we only 'secure Alice Paul' for the 'open airs,' they will be a success." Harriot Blatch thought AP could be her group's very first salaried political organizer, and the Ohio chapter of NAWSA wanted her to organize its referendum campaign. NAWSA planned its annual convention for Philadelphia in November 1912, and Dora Lewis, chair of local arrangements, sought AP's assistance as well. Alice had probably met Lewis, a society matron-cum-reformer, during the previous summer's open-air campaign. Unfortunately, by the time she matriculated, Alice felt in no shape to accept anyone's offer.[62]

The cost to Alice's health from the hunger strikes and forcible feeding became increasingly clear. In the rush to finish classes, exams, and her dissertation, she exhausted herself. Campbell wrote in late June hoping she felt "well enough and sufficiently rested to read this letter." In July, Lewis hoped "to hear you have color in your cheeks"; early August still found her voicing much the same sentiment. AP continued to push herself relentlessly, as she had habitually done for years, but the consequence no longer became simply a couple of good nights' rest; she now needed weeks to recover. At twenty-seven, she had lost her youthful resilience.[63]

In the fall, Alice joined with Mrs. Lewis to help plan the November NAWSA convention; she saw a chance to organize a grand procession. The two women quickly formed a lifelong bond, though the gray-haired Lewis was nearly twenty-five years AP's senior. Thanks to her refined aspirations, Alice often developed affinities with older women and Lewis became the closest of these. Mrs. Lewis had involved herself with suffrage, as well as the shirtwaist strikers and prison reform, despite or because of her distinguished Philadelphia lineage. The sadness in her eyes came hard earned; her husband had died early in their marriage rescuing a child from an oncoming train. Lewis held a high opinion of Alice's judgment and developed a deep affection for the younger woman. The two activists first envisioned a procession, but Alice did not want to compete once New York City suffragists announced a torchlight parade for early November; she held her ideas in abeyance.[64]

She was already looking beyond the NAWSA convention, having concluded that "the time had come for pressing the Federal [suffrage] amendment." Naïve about American politicking despite her academic knowledge, Alice presumed the amendment process offered the fastest route to woman suffrage. She found few prominent suffragists who agreed. NAWSA board member Mary Ware Dennett thought pushing vigorously for a constitutional amendment "a rather foolish idea." Harriot Stanton Blatch, a more obvious ally, called the idea "premature." Blatch, like many, believed that suffragists needed to win a big eastern state like New York before a suffrage amendment would become viable.[65]

Alice decided to seek help again from Lucy Burns. By mid-1912, Lucy became frustrated by pettiness among Edinburgh suffragettes; she gave up her position with the Pankhursts and returned home for good. The situation in England had deteriorated, so she perhaps felt discouraged as well. Alice journeyed out to a Burns retreat at Bellport, Long Island, Lucy later hopped the train to Moorestown, and the two former suffragettes talked about what a Washington focus might accomplish. Lucy wondered if Alice's health could withstand the rigors of an intense campaign.[66]

Once she persuaded Lucy, Alice kept working her connections. Blatch proved "very helpful," she recalled, "and offered to take me to see Miss Jane Addams." AP thought Addams (NAWSA vice president) might have some leverage; some spoke of the noted reformer as Shaw's possible successor. Blatch introduced Alice to Addams and privately urged Addams to use her influence on AP's behalf.[67]

Everything came together in late November 1912 at the NAWSA convention in Philadelphia. Jane Addams quickly suggested that Alice be appointed to the National's Congressional Committee (CC). She explained that the CC, established only in 1910, served as a nominal effort to maintain a Washington presence on behalf of a constitutional amendment. The 1912 chair, Elizabeth Thacher Kent, wealthy wife of Progressive congressman William Kent (Independent, CA), accepted the job under duress, since she believed in the state-by-state method of winning the vote. When leaders assured her they saw "no danger of the amendment being passed," she agreed to the task and dutifully arranged the annual Capitol Hill hearing. NAWSA gave Kent ten dollars for expenses; she returned change at year's end.[68]

Now, the National's board sought a new Congressional chair. Addams suggested the committee would dovetail nicely with AP's interest in pushing the federal amendment. Alice agreed, since she had failed to persuade Blatch or NAWSA to shift focus. As she recalled, "I decided that the only way to get it done was to endeavor to do it myself." Addams consented to support her plan at a forthcoming board meeting.[69]

Even with the support of Jane Addams, gaining approval of the NAWSA governing board became complicated. The executive board strained to tamp down the effects of Shaw's administrative weaknesses. An increasingly unwieldy organization, the National at this juncture followed more than it led. Pressure from the rank-and-file contributed to significant turnover on the executive board both in 1910 and 1911. Member expectations of NAWSA only increased after Oregon, Arizona, and Kansas women won the vote in November 1912. Board officers seldom thought alike, however, and some found AP's association with the Pankhursts controversial. Alice hoped that Addams's mediating abilities could overcome any reluctance.[70]

Alice and Lucy volunteered themselves for a new Congressional Committee, with AP as chair. They suggested starting their tenure with a flourish: a grand suffrage procession in Washington at the time of Woodrow Wilson's presidential inauguration. Addams urged approval, but other officers countered that Washington, DC, groups already planned a suffrage contingent in the Wilson inaugural parade. And who had the money for such lavish plans? NAWSA helped finance ongoing state campaigns. After lengthy discussion, the board agreed to appoint both women to the new year's committee providing Alice lived in Washington, DC, and the two women raised the money needed for both working and living expenses. The board directed the two to work out the most feasible plan for an inaugural event with District suffragists and present it at the next board meeting. Clearly, the board intended to keep the two Pankhurst enthusiasts on a short leash.[71]

Alice immediately began packing and raising money from Quaker, suffrage, and personal contacts. Dora Lewis offered to help and started with a check of her own. The heads of local suffrage leagues gave, as did prominent Quaker women. Alice approached cousins, old Swarthmore classmates, even women from her former Arch Street boarding house. The response gratified her. Over just two days, she raised more than $300 in cash and pledges, about $7,000 in today's dollars. With the idea of a glorious procession in her mind, she boarded the train for Washington.[72]

7

"A Procession of Our Own"

ALICE ARRIVED IN Washington, DC, on December 10, 1912, with a sense of urgency. She made her way across town from the vast new Union Station to 1827 I Street, a boarding house catering to Quakers. A small third-floor room functioned as her home and headquarters for now. She and Lucy Burns hoped a year would suffice to win a constitutional woman suffrage amendment. She chuckled in later life, "You can see we had our heads in the bushes."[1]

Alice Paul's failure to persuade more seasoned workers like Harriot Blatch to take up federal work on suffrage ultimately prompted her own action. Stepping into the vacuum of leadership, she vaulted suffrage into the national spotlight with a grand procession, effectively reviving the amendment drive. She built on her historical good fortune by claiming space on America's street, Pennsylvania Avenue, and muscling her way into the limelight of a presidential inauguration.

Alice's appeal as a leader became evident from her first months in Washington. Though always goal oriented, she now adopted a singlemindedness that many admired but few emulated. She subsumed her personal life with her political ambition and drove toward her goal relentlessly to the detriment of her health. Her physique, progressively thinner since her prison terms, became increasingly delicate, lending her an air of vulnerability; her characteristic self-deprecation reinforced that appeal. She won over those wary of the taint of militancy with a strategic capacity honed over ten years of study and exploration. From this amalgam of strength, savvy, and delicacy, her authority emerged.

The March 1913 suffrage procession became a defining moment for Alice Paul, one requiring her to negotiate the cultural complexities surrounding woman's place in the public realm. Against great odds, she managed to wade through complicated, at times perverse, territory and construct the event on her own terms. Alice's skill in executing this short-term vision provided the foundation to pursue her long-term constitutional ambition.

Although Alice's initial naiveté quickly evaporated, her sense of impatience and determination drew in like-minded others. Though Washington's suffrage community resembled conservative Philadelphia's, Alice found women of all ages who welcomed her initiative. She remembered starting out "unimportant, poor, without any reputation, any friends, or anything." Using an old NAWSA list, she began contacting prominent Washington members and working, she thought, "for quite a good many days before I found a single one." In fact, AP was far from unknown thanks to her convention appearances, speaking engagements, and press coverage. Her 1913 receipt book shows that, despite the outdated list, she not only found suffragists but also raised $250 by the end of her third day. Naysayers abounded. As she wrote a supporter in 1914, she kept hearing "that no one was interested in suffrage because this was a Congressional and Diplomatic city; with no industrial or commercial population; that parades, open-air speaking, or demonstrations of any kind, would alienate the few who were interested, and so on."[2]

Most of the women she attracted had served as local suffrage leaders; these included the chairs of earlier NAWSA Congressional Committees. Alice formed working alliances with District groups with the help of attorney Florence Etheridge and schoolteacher Elsie Hill, both heads of DC suffrage societies; their membership lists and personal contacts offered access to many potential recruits and donors. Hill, a Vassar graduate and the daughter of a Connecticut congressman, became a lifelong friend and colleague. Etheridge introduced Alice to congressional wife Elizabeth Kent, the woman who dutifully returned part of her ten-dollar budget as chair of the 1912 CC. No stranger to assertive tactics, Kent had marched in Harriot Blatch's 1910 parade and joined California's 1911 open-air campaign, despite her moneyed friends' disapproval. She welcomed Alice warmly and invited her to Christmas dinner; Kent's contacts and capital helped open many doors.[3]

Despite limited managerial experience, Alice deftly used these early contacts to lay the foundation for a working organization. Once she learned of 1911 CC chair and attorney Emma Gillett's reputation as a shrewd money manager, she asked the doughty suffrage veteran to be treasurer of the new CC. She later called on NAWSA member Helen Hamilton Gardener, a retired author and journalist. Gardener, AP remembered, seemed "very displeased that a young whipper-snapper such as myself" should head the National's congressional efforts. Alice refused to be intimidated. Graciously, she offered the older woman a sop for her dignity, asking her to serve as press chairman. Gardener agreed.[4]

Years later Alice recalled her hesitation about making financial commitments, yet her own receipt book records how readily she took to fundraising. Her straightforward appeals for money became legendary. Historian Inez Irwin recounted how AP knocked on Nina Allender's door one day. Allender remembered her "slim dress and a little purple hat." Alice spoke with the artist and her mother frankly, without "the small talk or the persiflage which distinguishes most social occasions. When the door closed, a few moments later," according to Irwin, "mother and daughter looked at each other in amazement." Both had agreed to monthly pledges toward office rent. Very quickly, AP raised enough money to rent office space on F Street, adjacent to Gillett's law office.[5]

Alice envisioned an even grander display than she considered for the 1912 NAWSA convention, yet the National's board stalled on making a final decision about the timing and type of event. Corresponding secretary Mary Ware Dennett advised AP that some board members regretted "the rather precipitate vote regarding the Congressional Committee." Fortunately, the upcoming board meeting in Chicago meant ally Jane Addams would join the discussion on the revised proposal. Alice knew she held more than Addams's support on the inside: Dora Lewis promised to "put your work before [Shaw] as strongly as I am able." Nonetheless, AP realized she needed to make a convincing case for her vision.[6]

Alice put her persuasive skills to work and adroitly exerted control over the board decision. She wrote a powerful argument for abandoning the idea of a mere suffrage contingent (as District women had proposed), preemptively rebutted objections, and steered the NAWSA officers toward her own goal. All her Washington contacts believed participating in the inaugural to be "inadvisable and impracticable," she began by acknowledging. She ticked off the reasons: the opposition of the police chief; the need to attract scores of marchers in a limited time, since inaugurals usually prohibited floats; a lengthy marching route. Furthermore, military men typically marched en masse; a contingent of untrained women would suffer by comparison. Finally, some potential donors balked at contributing out of fear that the inaugural, while nominally nonpartisan, would be perceived as the revels of the triumphant Democratic party. The preponderance of evidence against a suffrage contingent seemed overwhelming, Alice wrote.[7]

She then convinced the board that she had the means to accomplish a clear goal. A suffrage contingent in the customary inaugural parade "would not give our cause much prominence," she continued, subtly enveloping the board in her view; a contingent would "signify acquiescence in the present order of things." Like the Pankhursts, she wanted to stage women's exclusion, wanted spectators to see with their own eyes that "one-half of the people have not participated in choosing the ruler who is being installed." Her vision: "a procession of our own" offering "concrete evidence of our spirit of protest at our disenfranchisement." She added that Washington suffragists raised objections only about the limited time to prepare and the possibility of bad weather, both factors for a suffrage contingent as well.[8]

Despite prior misgivings, the board recognized the fait accompli Alice handed them. She concluded with a stunning revelation for a board always fretting about money. In fewer than ten days, she had raised $1,351, some of it pledged only for an autonomous procession. (Dennett later wrote that the officers "gasped in admiration" at the funds raised, which AP fudged by $300.) They immediately wired their endorsement of a NAWSA suffrage procession on March 3, one day prior to Wilson's inauguration. They set one catch: all the money Alice raised needed to be funneled through the NAWSA treasurer in New York City.[9]

With board approval, Alice's vision of a national suffrage procession came into focus. A joint procession committee was created from District suffragists and the CC with AP and Lucy Burns—the only official full-time volunteers—co-chairing the operation and dozens of subcommittees finessing the myriad details. They asked NAWSA to appoint Dora Lewis and Crystal Eastman Benedict, a Vassar classmate of Lucy's, to the new CC. Since neither lived in Washington, they functioned as fundraisers and consultants.[10]

From the start, Alice accepted that her own commitment exceeded that of Lucy Burns. Lucy came to Washington before Christmas for two days of committee decisions and left to spend the holidays with her family.[11] Quite possibly, she had an understanding with Alice about her level of engagement. The two women's outlooks had diverged since their time together in Britain. Now nearly thirty-five, Lucy felt the pull of her close family after spending six years abroad. Alice, by contrast, relished her new single-minded focus on the suffrage amendment; she drew emotional support from her colleagues.

The success of Alice's early efforts became readily apparent at the formal opening of the new NAWSA CC headquarters on January 2, 1913. An hour beforehand, people had already stepped down to the garden-level entrance at 1420 F Street NW; soon all 130 borrowed chairs filled up and newcomers were left to stand. They scanned the long and narrow front room opening onto the busy shopping street near the White House. Large display windows framed the door, drawing in light and curious eyes; the back area held two small rooms and a courtyard beyond.[12]

Alice positioned herself outside the spotlight as the director, rather than the star. Sensitive to criticisms about outsiders from her days in Scotland, she left most of the talking to Washingtonians. After an introduction by Elizabeth Kent, Alice spoke in her earnest, direct way about furthering a suffrage amendment, giving due deference to the late Susan B. Anthony's years of diligent work toward the same end. Indeed, she now had the privilege of working at Anthony's one-time desk, proffered by a former secretary. Her praise of Anthony was sincere but also a shrewd bid to transfer the fond memories many held of "Aunt Susan" to the current undertaking. Press chairman Helen Gardener spoke next. The former skeptic had changed her tune: she praised NAWSA's appointment of Alice and emphasized that "the time is ripe, the harvest is ready" for suffrage work in the nation's capital. Pageantry director Glenna Smith Tinnin then unveiled the grand plan.[13]

The procession committee planned to wed beauty and spectacle to drive home a powerful political message. Their conception drew on Harriot Blatch's New York parades. However, Alice and Lucy clearly provided the overarching vision, extracted from the Pankhursts. Unlike the marcher-heavy Blatch events, they promised mounted heralds and horsewomen, bands, brigades, floats, and automobiles. In addition to the procession and rally, planners also intended to simultaneously stage an elaborate pageant on the cascading steps of the Treasury building.[14]

The plan gathered momentum as word of mouth and a press hungry for inauguration stories spread news of the ambitious endeavor. Reporters soon found a "suffragists' beehive" on F Street, visitors, including prominent Washingtonians, streaming in and out. About twenty volunteers worked feverishly on any given day. Four typewriters clacked away and telephones rang constantly. Women sold suffrage literature and buttons. Others phoned anyone they thought likely to house one or more marchers for a night or two. The few mainstays, including Kent and Gardener, worked at their own desks. Gardener's press operation ran at full throttle; she gave interviews and mailed out dozens of press releases, stories, and photographs twice daily. The only paid workers in the office, three stenographers, labored alongside the volunteers.[15]

Alice tried to work in one of the small, cold back rooms. When the door opened, one reporter caught a glimpse of AP's "purple velvet hat pulled closely down over her hair and her hands thrust far into a big black fox muff." Interruptions became routine and she quickly became frustrated with the merely curious: "The offices have been so crowded with visitors," she wrote Mary Ware Dennett in mid-January, "that we have scarcely been able to get any work accomplished." She began to use greeters to put visitors, regardless of status, to work.[16]

The procession effort attracted volunteers beyond the city's suffrage groups, particularly young women. Young Rosa Deans Barr of the District, "only fifteen I a coming suffragett," asked if she could march—"when I am older intend to take an active part in the movement" [sic]. Alice nudged her toward involvement: "Perhaps you can get some of your friends to march also," she wrote, or help with expenses. She charmed young Mary Foster, an art student. "Of all the workers whom I met," Foster recalled, "she was my favorite." Alice's "quiet smile" and "friendly interest in all with whom she came in contact" disarmed Foster. And, the young girl remembered, Alice had "a wonderful sense of humor."[17]

A dualism lay at the core of Alice's charisma. She coupled assuredness and a powerful drive with demureness, thus undercutting concerns about her militant past. She led by example: observers noticed her enormous capacity for work. As historian Inez Irwin later wrote, "She made everyone else work as hard as possible," but drove "nobody as hard as herself."[18]

Many left her presence inspired. One procession committee chair, Marie Moore Forrest, later described AP's management style to Anna Howard Shaw. "Not only does she lay out our work on broad lines," she wrote, "but often plans every little detail." The fact that Alice knew what she wanted fortified inexperienced workers like Forrest. "No committee escapes her watchful eye," Forrest went on, "and she knows very well whether the work is being neglected or not." Her force of personality often won over the frustrated. "When many of us get discouraged and falter by the wayside," wrote Forrest, "her personal magnetism and spirituelle [sic] force carry us forward and we work with renewed courage." Some, however, found Alice's straightforward, even blunt, manner off-putting.[19]

Alice's earlier contact with American suffrage groups continued to pay off as she sought help from many quarters, using others' experience to bolster her own and gathering support as she went. She queried Harriot Blatch about how she organized and financed her New York parades. Would they loan banners? She took the train to Baltimore to introduce herself to Edith Houghton Hooker, planner of another recent parade. Hooker offered advice and loaned her group's chariots and banners; she became a stalwart of the Washington work. AP also leaned on Philadelphia colleagues, Swarthmore connections, and other suffragists she had encountered at speaking engagements or doing her dissertation research.[20]

She knew she could count on Dora Lewis. While others viewed Alice as imperturbable, Lewis recognized a latent anxiety and need for approval. Lewis had worked many years in suffrage and other reform efforts, knew all the key players, and willingly used her connections on AP's behalf. From her home in Philadelphia, she raised money and urged colleagues to join the effort. Lewis was not intimidated by Alice, nor did she always agree with her younger friend—she pushed for a less costly procession, for example—but Lewis staunchly supported the ongoing effort.[21]

Lewis's steady stream of encouragement became as valuable as her experience and knowledge, and she always kept Alice's well-being in mind. She came to Washington for a few days in January, mostly, she joked, to "see that you are properly housed and fed!" When Lucy delayed returning to Washington, Lewis wrote to "hurry her up a little. I do not like to think of your carrying on that work single-handed. It is a very great burden." She soothed Alice, "Do not worry about the money. I am sure everything will come out all right."[22]

The vagaries of volunteer help left Alice wondering how everything would get done. She breathed a sigh of relief when Lucy finally returned in mid-January, took an adjacent room in AP's boarding house, and immediately took charge of several initiatives. Helen Gardener came in every day and stayed all day, but only a few other women showed that level of commitment. Local suffrage groups had never attempted anything of this scope; even Gardener complained that she had "absolutely neither time nor strength to do anything more." Many privileged women lacked experience with hard work; one committee chair resigned because "the work has been nerve racking." Alice and Lucy willingly donated their time. We have no evidence of their conversations with parents about the Washington work, but Mrs. Paul and Edward Burns both sent checks regularly for their daughters' living expenses. Nonetheless, both women would have welcomed a greater show of NAWSA support.[23]

The NAWSA board sought more than it willingly gave. The National wanted Alice to report every move the CC made, a reasonable request, but one based on a notion of congressional suffrage work in which little happened from day to day. Mary Ware Dennett served as the primary conduit for information; she wrote AP early in January "how necessary it is for the Congressional Committee to report not only all its movements but all its plans very promptly to headquarters."[24]

Alice chose not to complain about her reporting requirements. Her first six-page report described the work to date, judiciously conveying her gratitude "for any cooperation or advice" the board might offer. Betraying some anxiety, she continued, "We feel very deeply the bigness of our undertaking and want all the help that any one is willing to give." She had assumed "that you were too busy to give any attention to our work here." This conjecture on AP's part seems hardly surprising since she had heard only once from Dennett in the month since the board approved the parade. Dennett offered encouragement, saying she felt "personally so delighted with the splendid progress you have already made," and emphasized tellingly that she wanted to "spare [AP] from later being the recipient of criticism or prejudice." She made no offer of further assistance.[25]

Anna Howard Shaw's concern seemed primarily fiscal. "I may as well say," she wrote in late January, "that I think the whole thing will be too expensive to what we will get out of it." She needed funds for state campaigns. Shaw therefore stressed, "Let us march in a dignified way and let our presence symbolise the thing we seek and not be a spectacular demonstration of that which has nothing to do with suffrage and suffrage work."[26] By 1913, Shaw had watched, even marched in, several parades in America and Britain and understood their symbolic import, but she failed to make the connection between those events, the concurrent press attention, and the rising levels of interest in the suffrage movement. To her mind, the CC needed to focus on convincing Congress to pass a constitutional amendment for suffrage. Shaw could not understand how processions accomplished that.

Despite Shaw's fulminations, the National's fiscal protocols remained nebulous and frustrating for someone of Alice's scrupulous mindset. Board instructions specified that she send all funds collected through the National's treasury. However, NAWSA lacked any system to earmark and promptly disperse funds AP raised for her use in Washington; money she forwarded might easily disappear in the general NAWSA treasury or, at best, linger for an uncertain time in New York, leaving her without any cash flow.

The young Quaker had learned the value of meticulous record keeping from a tender age, harking back to her days collecting eggs. She managed thousands of dollars by the time the National's treasurer Katherine McCormick inquired vaguely in late January about her ideas for handling the money. Alice had realized what NAWSA leaders had not: at their own direction, procession planning was a joint venture between Washington's suffrage groups and the Congressional Committee. The structure gave Alice an opening to manage her own funds, albeit temporarily. The joint committee's treasurer, she told McCormick, would send NAWSA a full accounting later though she welcomed other suggestions. McCormick failed to reply further, but later recounted her embarrassment at AP's "refusal" to hand over funds.[27]

Organizing the procession required managing not only individuals but also groups with competing agendas. Some tried to manage Alice. As she handled disputes and clashes, she struggled to maintain focus on her own vision. Both her vision and her values were challenged in the days before the procession.

The District's unique status furthered Alice's national aspirations for the parade. She believed that the abbreviated time frame and the distances involved for many groups made the event unlikely to draw extraordinary numbers of marchers; the procession would attain significance more through its artistry. Yet she continually sought ways to boost the numbers by drawing on the District population. Many congressional families stayed in town most of the year; likewise, federal employees hailed from all forty-eight states and embassy denizens included women from many countries. Distant groups, therefore, might easily be represented.

Promotional efforts thus reached well beyond the suffrage societies. Like the Pankhursts and Harriot Blatch, Alice understood that the range and diversity of marchers held as much importance as aggregate numbers for communicating suffrage strength. She drew in women of all ages, including working women, and radicals. As in previous parades, male suffragists were welcome; sympathetic congressmen received special invitations. Lucy often spoke at meetings aimed at clerks in government offices, Quakers, Jewish women, Socialists, and others. Elsie Hill, in charge of the college section, appeared at area universities to urge students to march. Parlor, office, club, and street meetings took place each day for nearly two months. Alice appealed to the local superintendent to allow schoolgirls to participate. She discussed the event with at least one local African American leader, probably former National Association of Colored Women's Clubs (NACWC) president Mary Church Terrell.[28]

Despite AP's attempt to dignify the enterprise by using the term *procession* rather than *parade*, some thought women marching for a political cause was unseemly. Educated and privileged women, in particular, found the proposed demonstration—as well as the organizing—less than respectable. Despite earlier parades in a number of cities, political theater still daunted many suffragists in 1913; as in Britain, they conflated marching in the public streets with street-walking. In early February, the local women's medical society notified Alice that though its members sympathized with the suffrage cause, "the majority were not willing to take part in the parade." One congressional wife believed the procession "unbecoming work." Despite the naysayers, plenty of others found their interest piqued. By late February, the *Washington Post* described Alice calmly working at her desk amid an outer office storm of men and women signing up to march.[29]

Any national political procession was highly unusual in 1913. To be sure, military marches, inaugural parades, and even presidential funerals down Pennsylvania Avenue formed part of Washington's fabric. Yet an organized political demonstration had materialized only once before, when Coxey's Army strode into town in 1894. Jacob Coxey and his followers brought the economic distress of the 1890s directly to Congress, a "petition in boots," they called it. The ragged, hungry look of the men terrified many residents. Congressmen and journalists alike framed Coxey's protest as an assault on the capital, and ultimately, police arrested him. Yet, Coxey's Army validated Washington as a site for political protest. Twenty years later, Alice bet on the procession's potential to transform woman suffrage into a national issue.[30]

She knew the contested nature of the street from past experience. Indeed, officials around the country during the 1910s granted permits for political meetings and processions based on their reading of the potential disruptiveness of a given group's ideas and presence. By 1913, the success of suffrage parades and open-air meetings in other cities lent credibility to Alice's appeal, another gift of historical fortune. Nevertheless, she sought help in securing permits from socially prominent suffragists, aware that their participation lent respectability to the effort and tamped down notions that suffragists marching down city streets threatened public order.[31]

The District of Columbia's government operated unlike that of any other American city or state. The more than three hundred thousand residents did not elect their government: a board of three appointed commissioners, usually businessmen, ran the city. They became accountable not to the local citizenry but to Congress and the president. People grumbled regularly about the questionable efficacy of Congress-as-town-council (not to mention the president-as-mayor), but the arrangement persisted.[32]

In England and in Philadelphia, Alice observed how social connections helped negotiate power structures. During her parade preparations, she gained valuable experience employing both class and gender conventions to her advantage. She found them used against her as well. Nothing in the District's previous history with women's groups prepared officials for the forceful way she sought her goals. Her combination of relentlessness and ladylike modesty, so appealing to followers, often confounded Washington authorities. AP remembered a similar reaction to the genteel Emmeline Pankhurst. For compatriots, her determination under pressure became a source of admiration and empowerment.

She needed to face down several levels of patriarchal bureaucracy. First, she sought permission to march the day before the inauguration. Alice and prominent Washingtonians called on chief of police Major Richard Sylvester, who promptly tried to talk them out of demonstrating on March 3. The veteran officer gave his visitors the benefit of his experience. Assuming a paternal air, he explained that a "more desirable" crowd, meaning fewer young military men, would attend on March 5, the day *after* the Wilson inaugural. Alice insisted on March 3 and, persuaded by her phalanx and her vehemence, Sylvester reluctantly backed down.[33]

When she requested Pennsylvania Avenue as the procession route, he balked again. Did the ladies really want to march by all the saloons at the lower end of Pennsylvania Avenue? He expected the "riff-raff of the South" to be out in droves to toast the Virginia-born Woodrow Wilson, at the first Democratic inauguration in twenty years. Sylvester, Alice reported, "gave quite alarming pictures of what Pennsylvania Avenue was like at inauguration times." He suggested Sixteenth Street as a more respectable alternative, a street less known to visitors but one that exuded propriety and wealth. AP shot back that they did not want a "fashionable street. We want to go where the people—the so-called 'common people' are. This is not a social, it is a political organization." Sylvester wondered aloud about connections to the English militants. At that point, further discussion proved futile. Alice returned with other well-connected citizens several more times, to no avail.[34]

She then appealed to Sylvester's superior, District commissioner John Johnston, who turned out to be even less enthusiastic and more protective about the time and place. He warned a group of prominent volunteers, including Kent and Gardener, about the cold and the difficulty of controlling crowds. Perhaps, he said, they could parade later in the spring on another street? They wanted a national procession, the women quickly pointed out, not "a little side show out on Sixteenth Street somewhere in the spring." Johnston turned a deaf ear.

Discouraged and humiliated, the group reported back to Alice, telling her, "We will give up the Avenue. We can not go on meeting with this kind of thing."[35]

Alice refused to concede. "Miss Paul did not want to give up the Avenue," Gardener recalled. "None of us wanted to, but she had the courage to go on." AP intensified the pressure, lobbying House and Senate officials and alerting the newspapers, which loved the conflict. She soon wrote Dennett, "All of the Washington papers have set forth our claim to the Avenue at length." True enough, though the *Post* also highlighted Sylvester's fears with a front-page story titled "Women Scorn Danger." The *Washington Times*, AP added to Dennett, had "printed an editorial stating that there is no reason why we should not have that particular street, since men's processions have always marched there." The District commissioners pushed back, asking Congress to increase the police force because of two recent and alarming street crimes against women. Nevertheless, after the Inaugural Committee declined to object to the suffrage event (perhaps foreseeing bad press), the beleaguered commissioners signed off on a permit for Pennsylvania Avenue.[36]

Alice's ability to persevere and outlast her opponents became one of her strengths as a leader. The social alliances she won provided maneuvering space inaccessible to a less privileged leader. She resisted assumptions about class and gender that might compromise her endeavor and insisted on her own terms and boundaries. Indeed, she set would-be male protectors against each other for advantage.

She believed the Avenue worth fighting for. The broad swath of Pennsylvania Avenue, connecting the house of Congress and the presidential mansion, endures as the quintessential channel of American political might. Alice recognized that a suffrage march down the Avenue on the eve of a presidential inauguration—that real and metaphorical transfer of power—would send a cogent message: that women stood at the gateway of American politics, willing and able to stand alongside men as full-fledged citizens.

Another set-to with NAWSA revealed Alice's grasp of the importance of symbolic communication. She celebrated the Pennsylvania Avenue victory by unfurling a purple, white, and green flag outside the headquarters and soon heard from Mary Dennett, who declared the news "really disturbing." Historically, NAWSA claimed no official colors, she noted, though most associated blue or yellow with suffrage. The idea of the procession adopting the Pankhursts' colors, wrote Dennett, "will surely be offensive to a large number of our members who are hotly opposed to the militants." She urged AP to add a yellow and blue flag to the one already flying on F Street. Shaw soon chimed in that she "personally would refuse to march" under the purple, white, and green.[37]

As in earlier disputes with her mother, Alice appeared conciliatory while minimizing deviation from her chosen course, a talent she employed when she could not afford to offend her opposition. In this instance, she protested too much to be as innocent as she claimed to be. "It did not occur to us," she replied to Dennett guilelessly, that anyone would object. Probably thinking her preparations flew under NAWSA's radar, she hung out the flag and sent out banner requests to only two organizations (Blatch's and Edith Hooker's) who embraced WSPU colors as their own. While any group could fly its own colors during the parade, the hundreds loaned from the Blatch and Hooker groups would predominate, flashing, she presumably thought, a sign of solidarity to the militantly inclined. After Dennett's warning, though, Alice also placed a blue or yellow flag outside headquarters and ordered hundreds of yellow sashes and flags from the National's sales office. She modified the most identifiable procession colors—those worn by the heralds—to purple, gold, and white. She gained more than she gave up.[38]

Alice had less success with other perceived threats to her grand vision. An innovative group of New York women led by a young socialite and newfound political actor named Rosalie Jones wanted to capitalize on the attention garnered by their December hike to Albany as brown-cloaked suffrage pilgrims. Jones proposed a second hike to Washington for the parade. Only a dozen women signed on for the three-week, two-hundred-mile pilgrimage, but they hoped to attract more along the way. If Alice feared the sight of Jones's bedraggled and weary pilgrims might besmirch her vision of a dignified procession, she did not let on, perhaps hoping for additional publicity from the unorthodox trek. She met with Jones and offered her group a designated place in the marching order. However, when Jones later accepted men into the group, AP became alarmed. The presence of male reporters had caused controversy during the December hike, and Alice flatly told Jones that accepting male pilgrims was a mistake.[39]

Alice recognized that pre-parade reportage laden with sexual innuendo could damage the image of the procession and discourage women from participating. She welcomed men in the procession ranks but felt Jones was compromising their shared political purpose. If men joined the pilgrims, the expedition would possess "the character of a lark rather than of a serious crusade," she wrote Jones. Suffrage marches down public streets had gained a fragile acceptance; the prospect of women and men tramping along together in a less public setting raised questions of propriety that journalists could easily exploit. However, Alice had no control over Jones's plans and could only voice her criticism, which Jones ignored.[40]

Alice had more say about her next challenge: how much attention African American marchers would draw. Many historical accounts describe how AP first tried to exclude and then segregate black women at the back of the procession. In fact, a more complicated scenario unfolded. Nevertheless, Alice's handling of the situation exposed her inexperience with racial issues and her determination to prevent anything she deemed secondary stand in the way of her goal.

She began recruiting local African American women, but shifted course when white volunteers tried to dissuade her. Black women had marched in New York's suffrage parades and those in other northern cities. When a parade volunteer, C. L. Hunt, inquired in early January about women of color marching, Alice wrote her, "We are expecting to include them." A few days later, she viewed black participation differently, after prominent local residents like Helen Gardener discouraged the idea, and Hunt wrote that she planned to ask the *Woman's Journal* to encourage black marchers. AP hastily wrote editor Alice Stone Blackwell to dissuade her from making any such targeted appeal. However, she was not comfortable tamping down black interest:

> I am a Northern woman and have never lived in the South; moreover, I belong to a Quaker family which has always taken a stand for the rights of the negro and all of the traditions of my family and the influence of my home are such as to make me predisposed to side with, and not against, the negro in any question of racial difference. I hope, therefore, that I am viewing this present question with an unbiased mind.[41]

Washington women like Gardener believed the white community and inaugural visitors would react badly to black participation. As Gardener wrote Blackwell, "Washington is not Boston—nor even New York." She went on, "Just now the public mind in Washington is especially enflamed because of an atrocious assault on a white woman of standing by a black man." This civic mood coupled with an influx of southerners for Wilson's ascendancy augured, the Virginia-born Gardener thought, a precarious situation. She declared, "If we now thrust into our demonstration the negro question we may just as well abandon the entire undertaking for we will lose absolutely all we have gained—and more." Elizabeth Kent proposed that any black applicants "be asked to withdraw by some tactful people."[42]

Alice became convinced that black marchers, like Rosalie Jones's pilgrims, threatened her grand vision. "The prejudice against [blacks] is so strong in this section of the country," she wrote Blackwell, "that I believe a large part if not a majority of our white marchers will refuse to participate if negroes in any number formed a part of the parade." That being the case, she wrote in frustration, "as far as I can see we must have a white procession, or a negro procession, or no procession at all." The best solution was to "say nothing whatever about the question, to keep it out of the newspapers, to try to make this a purely Suffrage demonstration entirely uncomplicated by any other problems such as racial ones." Lacking any substantial experience with women of color, she failed to imagine that black women would be injured in any way by not marching. Indeed, she believed that "our winning the suffrage will be the thing that will most raise the status of negro women, as well as white women." She felt "extremely sad" that local women showed such prejudice; nonetheless, she could not ignore the potential impact on the parade.[43]

To Alice's credit, she refused to exclude women of color publicly, either for altruistic reasons or because she feared any public statement would exacerbate the situation. Blackwell concurred, writing, "While the condition fills us with indignation, we have to look the facts in the face and realize what the consequences would probably be." Dennett cautioned against letting "fear control our actions" and the importance of "living up to our principles." Like Alice, however, she believed very few black women would apply to march. None of the three suggested bringing African American suffragists into the conversation, a fact which records their presumption of white control. So after considering three options— publicly welcoming black participation, wholly excluding black women, or accepting black marchers quietly—Alice gained NAWSA approval for the third choice and kept the question out of the press.[44]

The attempt to restrain the number of black suffragists in the procession, while clearly racist, recorded very real fears shared by these three white women. Rigid cultural stereotypes governed the popular perception of African Americans as disreputable; even the black elite tried to distance themselves from such attitudes by framing their ranks as the "talented tenth." A highly visible black presence in the parade threatened to endanger the image of propriety Alice wanted to project, thus jeopardizing the event's success.

The paradoxical thinking required for Alice to condemn prejudice and simultaneously stifle black participation was all too familiar. Quakers had long espoused black equality while at the same time declining to accept blacks as members, a disparity rooted in their belief that spiritual equality differed from social equality. Likewise, Alice's own 1912 dissertation implicitly defined women as white when discussing the 1866 rupture of the women's rights community over the conflict between emphasizing black versus black and female enfranchisement. Some women's rights activists at that time supported the Fifteenth Amendment legislation, which aimed to remove racial barriers to voting; other suffragists advocated revising the amendment's proposed language in order to simultaneously strike down both racial and sex barriers. Ultimately, Congress passed the original language, focusing on enfranchising men of color. The breach in the women's movement endured for a generation, until suffragists resolved the conflict in 1890 and created NAWSA. In her dissertation, Alice wrote that (white) women now must find "zeal in their own cause."[45]

Alice's ambivalent approach to racial politics mirrored NAWSA's history with women of color. Officially, the National supported universal suffrage; however, the group's emphasis on pursuing woman suffrage state by state implicitly upheld the states' rights position of southern white supremacists. Part of NAWSA leaders' reluctance to roll out a full-bore campaign for a federal suffrage amendment was the specter of northerners insisting they support black women's suffrage alongside votes for white women. So, like the Quakers, the National tried to have it both ways. Standing for black equality would endanger NAWSA's internal dynamics, finances, and image, so its policy allowed state chapters to make their own rules about membership, thereby giving chapters license to exclude black women.[46]

When black interest in woman suffrage burgeoned in the twentieth century, many, though not all, NAWSA chapters ignored or politely turned away potential black members. African American suffragists like Terrell, backed by increasingly strong organizations and sympathetic white suffragists, regularly protested the de facto exclusion. NAWSA leaders mollified black leaders by cultivating personal relationships behind the scenes and periodically inviting speakers of color to address conventions.[47]

Nevertheless, as in other ways, change overtook NAWSA as black women became a force in their own right. After 1890, African Americans organized nationally in response to deepening anti-black violence around the nation. The black population of the District had thus far escaped the lynchings or violent intimidation all too typical in the South; even so, the local color line stood more firmly fixed in 1913 than after the Civil War, and black Washingtonians of every station faced an increasingly virulent racism. The NACWC, established in 1896, and the National Association for the Advancement of Colored People (NAACP), founded in 1909, vigorously championed black equality. Both boasted tens of thousands of members, most of them now college educated. The NACWC had cooperated with the National and at once challenged its inconsistencies for years. The arrival of the fiftieth jubilee of Emancipation in 1913 only added to the desirability of black political protest.[48]

Black women and their advocates drove the debate on the color line in the procession. Just as young educated white women like Alice felt unwilling to wait for equality, women of color felt the same impatience. They saw the March 3 suffrage procession as an opportunity. Alice considered placing black marchers in their own section between sympathetic northerners but discarded that idea after suffragist and historian Mary Beard canvassed New York's black recruits; they seemed determined to march "where they belonged," she reported to AP, "and not just where some women were willing they should march."[49]

African American suffragists of all ages proposed to march. Alice received requests from two groups of Howard University women for march assignments, one proud young woman writing, "We do not wish to enter if we must meet with discrimination on account of race affiliation." She placed the Howard women with other college women, in the same section both she and Lucy expected to join. About the same time, NACWC organizer Adella Hunt Logan, who thought the parade "one of the best yet planned," wrote Washington colleagues such as Mary Church Terrell to urge them to march. Terrell would join a number of prominent local women of color.[50]

Questions of black participation temporarily at bay, Alice concentrated on financing the procession. Her vision ultimately cost nearly $14,000 for costumes, floats, bands, lodging rentals, and office expenses. She sought funds incessantly. Hundreds of small contributions provided a broad base of support, solicited face-to-face, through the mail, or by taking up collections at hundreds of small meetings.[51]

No sizable donor seemed willing to gamble on an unproven entity. Lucy made efforts to interest the most obvious target for a major donation: Alva Vanderbilt Belmont, the fabulously rich New Yorker whose money and force of will once convinced NAWSA to set up a permanent office in Manhattan. Belmont felt drawn to assertive tactics; she had worked with Harriot Blatch and founded her own suffrage group as well. As Lucy wrote Glenna Tinnin, "she is a newspaper item;—& once here, would probably contribute." Belmont responded positively and offered her group's banners, literature, and representatives; however, her other commitments precluded a visit to Washington and she balked at making a substantial contribution before meeting CC leaders and taking their measure.[52]

In the absence of a benefactor, Alice capitalized on the entrepreneurial methods of raising money already familiar to many volunteers. The modern merchandising strategies becoming endemic to a burgeoning consumer culture proved a boon to suffrage coffers. Suffragists now routinely sold a wide variety of items to raise money, from banners, flags, and sashes for special events to fine jewelry, clothing, and movement literature. AP became familiar with such fundraising techniques during her time with the Pankhursts and in Philadelphia.

More important than the cash generated, selling merchandise bolstered group identity and fostered a sense of commitment. It also underscored the privileged base of the movement, for many working women could not often afford such discretionary purchases. For the suffrage procession, nevertheless, many marchers purchased some sort of costume or at least a hat, button, or sash to wear and a pennant or banner to carry. Alice continually ordered suffrage literature to sell for profit. She arranged for an elaborate printed parade program newsgirls sold during the event. Still, in the end, the pamphlets, programs, and wearable items never recouped their costs.[53]

Alice displayed her resourcefulness with imaginative and more lucrative schemes for raising money. She utilized proven techniques like selling seats at the pre- and post-parade rallies and in parade automobiles. Her most remunerative idea, however, was her own brainchild and feasible only because of the inaugural parade's proximity. She brokered a deal to use the inaugural reviewing stands, an arrangement necessitating complicated negotiations with the Inaugural Committee, private firms, the Treasury and the War Departments, and even one sympathetic senator. She then made a profit-sharing deal on March 3 seat sales with the stand contractors. Finally, she collaborated with Treasury officials to build a separate set of grandstands for viewing the pageant planned for the Treasury building steps and sold those seats for both the procession and the following day's inaugural parade. The grandstand project ultimately netted almost a $2,000 profit.[54]

In early February, Alice prefigured her subsequent focus on presidential power when she revisited the question of police protection with President Taft himself. Thousands planned to march in the suffrage procession, and Police Chief Sylvester had stated that, considering all inaugural and other commitments, he could spare only one hundred men for the suffrage parade. Alice knew that inadequate policing invited trouble and recalled New York's May 1912 suffrage parade, when rowdies broke up platoon formations and spectators surged into march lines. Concerned about Chief Sylvester's war stories about disruptive inaugural crowds and wary of his stonewalling, she made a direct appeal to the president. Gaining an audience with Taft proved relatively easy, thanks to Helen Gardener's social connections, which moved the two women quickly past the White House doorkeepers and Taft's male secretaries. After hearing the women's story, the president diplomatically agreed that their permit guaranteed police protection, then sent them back through the District chain of command. So much for presidential power.[55]

Another frustrating series of meetings ensued. "All that we asked," Gardener later said, "was a clear street." Sylvester refused to apply formally for more officers, and Commissioner Johnston, certain the existing arrangement would suffice, maintained his "confidence in American manhood to believe that the women would be properly taken care of." He refused to ask the War Department for federal troops, fearing such a request signaled local incompetence. AP persisted; finally the commissioners agreed to assign more officers to the parade route and forward her own petition for federal troops to the secretary of war. For his part, Secretary of War Henry Stimson reminded the commissioners that Congress had appropriated funds to maintain order during inaugural week. Protecting a procession of women hardly seemed formidable, he wrote; hence, the request for troops seemed improper. Alice doggedly barraged District offices during the entire month of February seeking some assurance of a clear parade route. She was still at it when the pilgrims arrived in town.[56]

The promotional value of the pilgrims' hike faded fast as a series of cool encounters and misunderstandings created unforeseen conflicts. Jones and her weary band—"far from alluring in their dingy brown cloaks and heavy shoes," wrote one chapfallen journalist—walked 250 publicity-filled miles in sixteen days, often through rain, snow, or mud. After they crossed the Mason-Dixon Line, Maryland, which preferred its women more ladylike, received the wayfarers coolly. Outside Baltimore, a large group of black women and men with a "Votes for Negro Women" banner tried in vain to join the hike, creating exactly the kind of publicity Alice sought to avoid. She then tried to dignify the hikers' entry into the District by sending an automobile escort (which she herself joined), but communication problems rendered the effort ineffectual. Rosalie Jones and her group trod wearily through the streets and across the Capitol grounds. As they emerged on Pennsylvania Avenue, they suddenly found the street choked with well-wishers.[57]

The pilgrims' arrival on Friday, February 28, became an ominous portent for the Monday procession, confirming Alice's worst fears. According to the *Washington Post*, "the company of brown-clad women, huddled in a little group, [was] forced to fight their way through veritable walls of shouting humanity for more than a mile" to the Congressional Committee's F Street offices. The escort car carrying Alice and Dora Lewis could only inch along. Workers inside parade headquarters frantically telephoned for more police. To everyone's considerable relief, officers on the street finally cleared a narrow path and the pilgrims were able to reach the office door.[58]

The tumultuous scene offered clear evidence of police impotence, which Alice used to her advantage. On Friday afternoon, she redoubled her efforts to secure federal troops by personally visiting the secretary of war, who maintained that the law did not permit him to act. By Sunday night, Alice was at her wit's end. Supporter Elizabeth Selden Rogers, just off the train from New York City, offered a ray of hope: Secretary Stimson was her brother-in-law. The two women made a private call on the secretary at home. Indeed, the eleventh-hour meeting did persuade Stimson to find some flexibility in the law. "Just call me up if you do have any difficulty," AP remembered his reassuring them manfully. "So," she recalled, "that relieved our minds very much." The next day, Stimson interceded with the District commissioners until they all reached an understanding about placing cavalry based at nearby Fort Myer on call.[59]

As she hustled around with more last-minute details, anticipation rose. One local observed, "The inaugural procession follows the suffrage parade in public interest as in fact." The *Post* declared Washington "suffrage mad" and the F Street headquarters "the busiest place in town." Special decorated suffrage trains from Chicago, New York, and other eastern cities steamed into Union Station. Other parade-goers boarded local trolleys and transferred through the extensive eastern and Midwest trolley systems to get to Washington. Inaugural buntings festooned federal buildings and Pennsylvania Avenue businesses. New Yorker Alberta Hill expressed the views of many on the eve of the procession: "I am looking forward to the parade," she wrote, "with as much interest as a little girl to her first party."[60]

After two months of frenetic preparations, Monday, March 3, 1913, dawned sunny and mild. Hours before the procession's scheduled three o'clock start, masses began pouring out of streetcars, and Pennsylvania Avenue crammed with would-be spectators searching for the best vantage point. Offices and stores over-looking the Avenue filled with expectant faces. The throng of parade watchers grew exponentially. At noon, police officers roped off the streets as hordes of people streamed onto the Avenue from every direction.[61]

As delegations assembled near the parade route for drill, last-minute instruc-tions from parade organizers to segregate split the Illinois delegation. Ida B. Wells-Barnett, a longtime activist on racial issues, was the sole black woman in the group. A *Chicago Tribune* reporter traveling with them described the tense scene. The head delegate announced that procession organizers "advised us to keep our delegation entirely white" because of objections raised by "eastern and southern women." The reporter identified state delegation chair Genevieve Stone, wife of an Illinois congressman, as a source for the instructions. (Some historians have named Alice, yet she had for weeks directed that interested black women be included.)[62]

The sixty Illinois women debated what to do. One pointed out that including blacks might "prejudice southern people against suffrage"; another called such a move "entirely undemocratic." Wells-Barnett stood firm. "The southern women have tried to evade the question time and again by giving some excuse or other every time it has been brought up," she declared. "If the Illinois women do not take a stand now in this great democratic parade then the colored women are lost." The delegation chair ultimately decided to follow Stone's lead. Wells-Barnett insisted on marching with the Illinois delegation or not at all. When the Illinois contin-gent re-assembled for the procession, Wells-Barnett did not appear.[63]

By early afternoon, the staging area on the US Capitol grounds teemed with thousands of marchers finding their places, their numbers and diversity vis-ibly recording the strength of the suffrage cause. Alice recalled, "We went out early, very early, to try to begin to line the people up in all the different sections." A kaleidoscope of color shifted up, down, back, and forth as state delegations, and various groups of professionals and wage earners, each costumed distinc-tively, moved into position. College women in academic gowns, including the young African Americans from Howard, assembled between the nurses and the lawyers. A Quaker group and the Men's Suffrage League found their places near the pilgrims, still cloaked in cheerless brown. Drivers carefully maneuvered floats and chariots into line. Progressives and Socialists gathered in the penultimate section, along with a few congressmen.[64]

The moment neared. Two hundred marshals repeated their mantra "to march steadily in a dignified manner, and not to talk or nod or wave to anyone in the crowd." The spring air reverberated with a cacophony of creaky wagon wheels and braying horses mingled with pipings and bleats and drum rolls as musicians warmed up. As starting time neared, lead-off riders mounted their steeds and adjusted their top hats. Behind them herald Inez Milholland, long dubbed "the most beautiful suffragette," looked resplendent in white suit and boots and a flowing blue cape. A gold tiara adorned her long dark hair; she steadied her white charger. Nearby, Alice, in academic cape and gown, conferred with the sergeant of the mounted patrol. Behind Milholland, she saw the first wagon roll into place bearing a giant boldly lettered sign, a sign leaving no question about her long-term political goal:

WE DEMAND AN AMENDMENT
TO THE UNITED STATES CONSTITUTION
ENFRANCHISING THE WOMEN OF THE COUNTRY[65]

Unlike earlier parades, the first national procession told a story: women had earned the right to vote. After the "Great Demand" float were seven sections, each led by a mounted herald, each featuring banners, floats, and marchers. The first section mostly featured floats representing countries where women voted, but groups of girls from Scandinavian countries and Belgium wearing native costumes accompanied their country's floats. Floats in the second section illustrated the status of the American suffrage struggle in 1840, 1870, 1890, and 1913; pioneering suffragists rode these wagons, displaying banners like "Justice conquering prejudice." A third section demonstrated the ways women help build a strong state. On one float, a man bearing the state on his shoulder stood alongside a woman with hands bound; "Man needs her help but she cannot give it," the legend read. AP designed the remaining sections to demonstrate the readiness of aid: a full array of professions and occupations, state delegations, and congressmen marched. Four golden chariots led contingents from NAWSA's key campaign states; the pilgrims marched before the remaining states and participants in automobiles. The narrative built toward an undeniable conclusion. As Alice wrote in the printed program, "We march today to give evidence to the world of our determination, that this simple act of justice shall be done."[66]

She designed the spectacular procession to send a complex message about women and their place in the public realm. Staging women's exclusion from the body politic, the procession suggested a new role for women while maintaining conventional assumptions about femininity. The event tied suffrage activism to America's long history of using parades to celebrate national values, implicitly wrapping participants in the flag. Many of the float tableaux underscored the noble ways women had served the country, even as they challenged the nation to live up to its ideals. This visual rhetoric lent a moral authority to the spectacle of women marching in the streets, sending a message to not only the public at large but also those suffrage opponents and adherents who opposed bold tactics. The act of marching for a political purpose, furthermore, mirrored the citizenship women sought. And the emphasis Alice placed on beauty and dignity in the procession tacitly repudiated the popular notion that politically active women became desexed harridans. It was a tricky business, essentially requiring marchers to walk a tightrope of respectability.[67]

Finally, at 3:25, the starting gun sounded. Police-driven escort vehicles formed a flying wedge to precede the procession down Pennsylvania Avenue's broad expanse; sixteen mounted officers followed. Then, the parade's grand marshal, Jane Walker Burleson, and her riding attendants nudged their horses onto Pennsylvania Avenue at First Street. Inez Milholland followed, heralding the New Woman, her standard flying the phrase from an old hymn used first by the Pankhursts, then by Harriot Blatch: "Forward into Light." Her dazzling image symbolized the procession for years to come. The audacious "Great Demand" float succeeded Milholland and then the NAWSA board came, with Anna Howard Shaw proudly walking in front. (Jane Addams, unfortunately, was abroad.) After a girls' band gaily played the "Star-Spangled Banner," Carrie Chapman Catt, head of the international suffrage alliance, led the section on woman suffrage worldwide. Alice, Lucy, and other parade directors monitored the forward movement, which seemed to slow. And then stopped.[68]

Spectators challenged suffragists' right to the street. Jane Burleson, at the head of the procession, began to notice men here and there walking into the street to hoot at the women. "They came out gradually," she later said, "then closed around us, closed around me." By the time she reached Fifth Street, "we found ourselves up against this horrible howling mob, this jeering mob." She looked in vain for the police. The automobile wedge had dispersed; the mounted police merged with the crowd. "I was absolutely alone," Burleson said later. "I was terrified. I did not know what to do." She looked back at Milholland and saw her equally surrounded by hostile spectators. Milholland, however, kept urging her steed through the mob. Burleson did the same, but progress seemed painstakingly slow.[69]

For the Washington police force, threats to the marchers looked like an assault on state power, a defiance of official manliness. Police Chief Sylvester, waiting at Union Station for President-elect Wilson to arrive, learned of unmanageable crowds on Pennsylvania Avenue at 3:10; he immediately ordered the on-call cavalry, an order not relayed, inexplicably, until 3:45. The troops, across the Potomac River beyond Arlington Cemetery, quickly mounted up and trotted off. They would not arrive until 4:30.[70]

Meanwhile, official womanhood took charge. Alice, Lucy, and committee chairs Glenda Tinnin and Patricia Street climbed into nearby motorcars to investigate. They managed only a few blocks along Pennsylvania Avenue before, Street later said, "the road was so congested that my car could not even get through it." "We kept pushing along," she said, "pushing along a little bit at a time, and asking the police officers if they would not please help us to clear the road." They finally reached a relieved Jane Burleson, who watched their cars begin to move the crowd back. "They really were the policemen of the day," she thought. Alice and the others kept urging the police to assist but, in Burleson's view, police efforts seemed fleeting. Street stood on the running board of her vehicle with a megaphone "calling on the people, asking if they would stand aside." She left her car after she saw one marcher put out her hand to keep a man back, only to be spit upon. "I asked a policeman would he not please protect this woman, and he retorted, 'There would be nothing like this happen if you would stay at home.'" Alice also left her car at times to push spectators back behind the rope lines. The women's automobiles finally wedged themselves in front of Burleson and inched their way down the avenue. Nevertheless, behind Milholland, throngs surged again into the street.[71]

Thousands of marchers struggled down Pennsylvania Avenue. The careful organization and drills went for naught. One woman thought "it was like going into the neck of a funnel." The college section started off four abreast; two blocks later, they could manage only double file. Students "inched along," said Mary Foster, "sometimes single file." Delays were frequent, one local observer counting eighteen halts. "There was a danger in it," said teacher Sarah Wallace, "that made you hold your breath and look ahead to that Treasury Building, and wonder if you would ever get there in safety."[72]

At best, the nearly six hundred police officers and special deputies became overwhelmed; at worst, they exhibited callous disregard. Officials never expected a crowd estimated at a quarter of a million people or more. One eyewitness compared the policing task to "sweep[ing] the sea back with a broom." However, the lieutenant in charge of the first blocks managed to keep his area of the avenue clear. Some other officers made admirable efforts: Helena Weed saw a black officer who intervened to prevent a woman's banner from being snatched. Nevertheless, many marchers found police unsympathetic or worse. "We were almost at the mercy of the crowd," said Janet Richards. Olive Hasbrouck complained of a mounted officer simply "looking down the street in an amused manner." Pilgrim Ernest

Stevens repeatedly asked in vain for police assistance, but "they acted in an indifferent, careless manner."[73]

In the absence of sustained police authority, marchers endured verbal assaults and, at times, physical violations. Helena Hill Weed, a veteran of other parades, expected "obscenity, absolutely indecent remarks." Others felt taken aback: physician Nellie Mark had "never heard such vulgar, obscene, scurrilous, abusive language as was hurled at us." Many felt intimidated. A Baltimore woman found herself "shoved, jostled, pushed, hooted, jeered" and suffering "many smutty propositions." Young men often broke into the march line to trip or slap the women. One rowdy dragged a blind woman out of the line completely, leaving companions to wrest her from his grasp. "The marshal in front of me was pinched by the crowd on the arm until she was black and blue," Dr. Mark recalled. "I did not know that men could be such fiends."[74]

With police protection desultory, the procession was transformed. It remained both a literal and metaphorical claiming of territory in the public domain; however, the momentum turned from offensive to defensive, from celebration to vindication. The march became a rite of passage for many individuals, as events challenged them in unanticipated ways. Young Mary Foster's group "struggled along with lumps in our throats, fighting back tears, we thought all was lost." A few women became hysterical, fainted, or even fled. Most tamped down their fear and maintained a dignified front. Abby Scott Baker stoically "neither listened nor looked." Helena Weed "felt like fighting, but I was marching with my State banner and my university colors on my cap and gown, and I thought it was due to me to be dignified." Some women held hands or stood shoulder to shoulder, silently defending their right to march. Mrs. Keppel Hall recalled, "Dignity was about the only weapon we had."[75]

The marchers felt buoyed up by those who chose active resistance. Individual spectators took it upon themselves to police the masses. Anna Howard Shaw watched horsewomen like Milholland force spectators back with their steeds. Hannah Mills saw a group of soldiers join hands to keep back the crush of people. Near the end of the parade route, a troop of Boy Scouts kept the crowd back with batons. The black drivers of one float climbed down to berate onlookers and keep them off the float. And the women helped themselves. Marshals like Janet Richards, walking at the outer edges, held out their small Votes for Women flags and appealed time and again for more space. A young woman in front of Helena Weed seemed terrified, then turned around to say loudly: "Girls, get out your hatpins; they are going to rush us." The threat subsided. Mary Troxell watched a man brush against her daughter and make "a remark so vile" that her daughter struck the man.[76]

The procession finished the last few blocks in grander fashion. At long last, as an exhausted Jane Burleson turned on Fifteenth Street toward the Treasury building and its grandstand, the cavalry arrived, horses prancing. The troops quickly moved to the sides of the street, using their horses to force the masses back. They rode along Pennsylvania Avenue in the opposite direction of the marchers, clearing block after block, to the visible relief of marchers. As dusk gathered, the colorful sections passed in review before the seated audience, telling the story of the American woman suffrage movement with (somewhat disheveled) beauty and dignity.[77]

The procession's arrival triggered the climactic moment of the pageant already unfolding on the colonnaded steps of the Treasury building. Many performers, draped only in layers of gauze, stood shivering in an icy wind as they waited for the struggling marchers to appear. Then the commanding figure of Columbia dressed in red, white, and blue velvet and silk joined Justice, Charity, Hope, and then Liberty in a whirling, exuberant dance to herald the "New Crusade" of women and sound a grace note on a frustrating day. Amid great cheers, the performers then followed the procession to nearby Memorial Continental Hall.[78]

The day became a quiet triumph for African American women. To their great if ironic relief, the black marchers whose presence was so feared were treated no worse than the whites who participated. The black men in the crowd and driving so many of the floats no doubt added to their sense of solidarity. Ida B. Wells-Barnett, after disappearing for hours, resurfaced during the parade to slip into the Illinois delegation without incident. African American women marched within the Delaware, New York, West Virginia, and Michigan sections. Two dozen Howard women showed off their academic caps and gowns alongside Mary Church Terrell and five other prominent college-educated suffragists. Other African American women marched with their sister workers or professionals. Washington activist-marcher Carrie Clifford, writing in the NAACP's *Crisis*, praised the nearly fifty black marchers for making "such an admirable showing in the first great national parade."[79]

The post-procession rally at Continental Hall became an outpouring of indignation. Weary young Mary Foster, who had struggled along for what seemed like hours, stood amazed. NAWSA leaders told her "what had happened was not a catastrophe but an unlooked-for blessing." As Alice and NAWSA leaders compared notes, they all recognized that a publicity coup awaited them; in May 1912, Blatch had parleyed police inattention to her parade into days of publicity. Washington, with congressional oversight of the District police, presented the possibility of a national forum. Anna Howard Shaw set the tone in an address offering more than her usual bite, saying, "Never was I so ashamed of our national capital before." Praising the marchers, she went on, "If anything could prove the need of the ballot, nothing could prove it more than the treatment we received today." The tired, disheveled, and angry assemblage quickly approved a resolution calling for an investigation into the causes of disorder. The next day, Harriot Stanton Blatch released her letter to President-elect Wilson, which read in part, "As you ride to-day in comfort and safety to the capital...we beg that you will not be unmindful that yesterday the Government, which is supposed to exist for the good of all, left women, while passing in peaceful procession in their demand for political freedom, at the mercy of a howling mob on the very streets which are being at this moment so efficiently officered for the protection of men." Indeed, the police lines along the inaugural parade route the next day held firm, despite two hundred fewer police in attendance.[80]

Alice was already thinking ahead. Shortly after the rally concluded, reporter and parade volunteer Winifred Mallon found her at the deserted F Street headquarters. Piles of banners, flags, and regalia haphazardly stood against walls; programs and fliers littered the tables. "Through the wreck came Alice Paul," wrote Mallon, already smitten, "the long black robes of her doctor's gown swinging from her slender shoulders, and her thin, wonderfully expressive hands in her flowing sleeves." For once, her head stood bare "and for the first time I saw the masses of her brown hair piled carelessly high on her head." Her eyes seemed "darker and larger," her exhausted visage unusually pale. Mallon vented her anger at police conduct, and AP told her about striding into the crowd herself to move them back. "The police could have stopped the disorder instantly. They had only to be determined about it." Their neglect, however, gave her fuel for the next step.[81]

Alice Paul in a pinafore at age six with her brother
William. She looked serene even as a young girl.
Alice Paul Institute

Alice's father, William Paul,
often wore a solemn look. He
overcame early struggles to
achieve business success. *Alice
Paul Institute*

Alice inherited her mother's
large brown eyes and thick, dark
hair. Tacie Parry left Swarthmore
College to marry William Paul in
1880. *Alice Paul Institute*

Alice's Swarthmore senior class basketball team gaily climbed up a ladder balanced against a lamppost to pose in their sweatshirts and bloomers. Alice is the center girl.
Division of Political History, National Museum of American History, Smithsonian Institution

Alice (standing, center) wore a long braid to pose with Moorestown relatives in 1907. *Alice Paul Institute*

was issued for Mrs. Pankhurst's arrest as soon as she came back from America but some one paid her fine against her will & without her knowledge so she will not have to go to prison. The officials in prison were very kind. I had something to read, it was not at all bad - I can't see why you were so excited - I cabled when I was released. I suppose thee got it. I will not do it again as I think I have done enough.

With love
                    alice

Alice Paul's 1908–10 letters from Britain reveal her emerging as a leader. At the end of this 1909 letter, she calms her mother's fears about her time in jail. *Schlesinger Library, Radcliffe Institute, Harvard University*

Alice (middle row, right) wears her glasses and her WSPU prison door pin in this photograph of her graduate women's club or sorority. The photo probably dates from the time of her doctoral work at Penn, around 1911. *Division of Political History, National Museum of American History, Smithsonian Institution*

Alice pinned her WSPU prison brooch on her academic cap and gown. Her doctoral hood hangs off her shoulders. *Library of Congress, Prints & Photographs Division, LC-USZ62-48792*

Alice looks uncomfortable sitting among notable parade volunteers in front of her new NAWSA office in Washington, DC, January 1913. From left, front row are Glenna Tinnin, Helen Gardener, Alice Paul, Elizabeth Kent, and Genevieve Stone. Standing in back, second from left is Nina Allender; second from right is Hazel MacKaye; on the far right is Elsie Hill. *Library of Congress, Prints & Photographs Division, LC-USZ62-49123*

The March 1913 suffrage procession starts off from the Capitol grounds. Jane Burleson and other horsewomen follow a flag-bearer and precede the float with the "Great Demand" for a suffrage amendment. *Courtesy of the Sewall-Belmont House and Museum, home of the historic National Woman's Party Collection, Washington, DC*

Lucy Burns (left) accompanied Emmeline Pankhurst (center, in furs) when she appeared in Washington, DC, in late 1913. *Library of Congress, LC-H261- 3299 [P&P]*

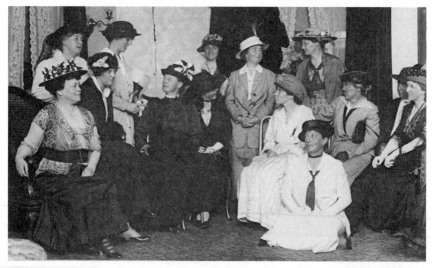

The Congressional Union's advisory council meets at the 1915 San Francisco Exposition. Seated at far left, Alva Belmont; to her immediate right, Sara Bard Field; standing just to Field's right, Doris Stevens. Seated at center right, Alice Paul; standing to AP's immediate left, Anne Martin. *Courtesy of the Sewall-Belmont House and Museum, home of the historic National Woman's Party Collection, Washington, DC*

Lucy Burns prepares to distribute leaflets from a hydroplane during the Suffrage Special stop in Seattle. Lieutenant Terah Maroney of the naval militia is the pilot in front. *Courtesy of the Sewall-Belmont House and Museum, home of the historic National Woman's Party Collection, Washington, DC*

In early 1917, banner-bearing NWP sentinels leave the White House gates after a shift on the picket line. *Courtesy of the Sewall-Belmont House and Museum, home of the historic National Woman's Party Collection, Washington, DC*

In late October 1917, a gaunt Alice Paul emerges from NWP headquarters holding a banner, on her way to be arrested at the White House gates. Dora Lewis follows her. *Library of Congress, Manuscript Division, mnwp 160029*

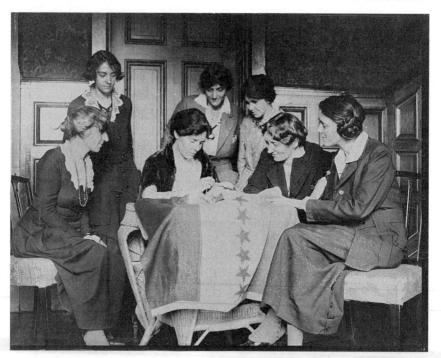

NWP organizers watch Alice sew a new star on the suffrage flag, which she used as a symbol of the progress of ratification. From left, Mabel Vernon, Elizabeth Kalb, Alice Paul, Florence Brewer Boeckel, Anita Pollitzer, Sue White, and Vivian Pierce. *Library of Congress, Manuscript Division, LC-DIG-npcc-01204*

At the May 1976 National Rally for Equal Rights, Pittsburgh ERA advocates display a message for the ailing ninety-year-old Alice Paul. *Photo by Jane Wells-Schooley, courtesy Schlesinger Library, Radcliffe Institute, Harvard University*

8

"A Dark Conspiracy"

THE MARCH PROCESSION drew abundant national press coverage. The turmoil gave the press its red meat—conflict—and newspapers from New York to Charleston to Fairbanks eagerly plucked articles from the wire services. The local press ran a wide range of stories on the spectacle, the notables involved, and the fractious crowd. Papers beyond the District focused on the "howling mob," often employing a Beauty and the Beast theme that emphasized vulnerable women at the mercy of predatory men.[1]

Inevitably, some press reports served up conventional notions about the female body. The *Washington Post* sang, "Miles of Fluttering Femininity Present Entrancing Suffrage Appeal." The male gaze objectified the suffragists. A San Francisco journalist claimed, "Not a single man among the thousands of spectators thought of votes for women." Pageant performers became "damsels in gauzy draperies of pink and rose" and "bare tootsie-wootsies." A few articles contrasted youthful beauty with aged homeliness, echoing the jeers directed at older marchers, such as "We came to see chickens, not hens," or worse. Nonetheless, the bulk of the coverage revealed that the procession successfully countered male condescension.[2]

Journalists' belief in a masculine code of ethics and in freedom of expression lay behind their widespread acknowledgment that the marchers demonstrated their worthiness as citizens. The women whose propriety some questioned became models of civic behavior—exactly the image Alice sought to create. Reporters characterized the marchers as brave and stoic, "trudging stoutly along under great difficulties" or "clos[ing] their ears to jibes and jeers." Both the image and the press response came class-bound; suffragists both presented themselves and were perceived as bourgeois. Indeed, the outrage depended on such respectability, as AP and others had foreseen.[3]

Turnabout became fair play. Women skirted convention by marching, thereby giving men license to mock; however, once unruly onlookers and police violated male ideas of chivalry, many eyewitnesses implicitly granted women permission to abandon gender expectations and fight back. Observers lauded Inez Milholland as a hero for "riding down a mob," for example, and another woman for striking a rowdy with her riding crop. The *Washington Star* called Pennsylvania Avenue "a battlefield captured by Amazons." All these conclusions tacitly acknowledged woman's freedom of assembly and, with that recognition, the notion of voting rights entered the realm of the possible.[4]

Politicians who had joined the parade brought the same point of view into Congress the day after the procession, highlighting the civil rights issue. In a brief session before the inauguration, incensed congressmen took over both the House and the Senate to vent their outrage. The House minority leader, James Mann (Republican, IL), aroused even more anger by suggesting that one put-upon woman "ought to have been at home." "She had as much right there as any one," shouted marcher John Raker (Democrat, CA). The Senate resolution calling for an investigation affirmed suffragists' right to "parade freely and unmolested." The Senate scheduled a hearing for two days later.[5]

Now the strategic capacity Alice Paul acquired in Britain came to the fore. She took advantage of the national outrage about the treatment of marchers to transform the public response into a debate on womanhood and citizenship. She knew how to exploit a public forum, especially one sanctioned by state power, to augment the meaning of a spectacle. A Senate hearing offered such an opportunity and promised to influence not only lawmakers, but the press, the public, and other suffragists.

With NAWSA approval, Alice cultivated the debate about the parade and expanded it into a forum for engaging the wider public. She fed the fire, spurring on the faithful while constructing a narrative for the press: parade disorder as an outgrowth of women's second-class citizenship. She responded to the angry letters, telegrams, and individuals pouring into headquarters by publishing calls for affidavits from marchers and for congressional action in the *Woman's Journal*. Open-air meetings kept the issue before Washingtonians; Harriot Blatch and others drew large crowds to protest meetings in New York, Boston, and other cities. The *Woman's Journal* chimed in, "Once again, the whole country is forced to see how much more effective is the little ballot, the mark of citizenship, than is the much talked of chivalry of our lawful protectors."[6]

NAWSA showered praise on Alice and Lucy. One board member gushed, "I know Washington well enough to realize what tremendous odds were against you and words cannot express the admiration I felt for your brilliant accomplishment." Despite her earlier qualms about the parade, Anna Howard Shaw now felt equally enthusiastic. Although, she wrote, "one hates to have one's work destroyed," the event "has done more for suffrage, to establish firmly those who were wavering and to bring to our ranks thousands of others." Shaw was so impressed that she loosened the purse strings, offering NAWSA funds to underwrite a protest meeting in Washington. "The National Association," she insisted, "will never cease to be grateful to you all for the splendid service you have done in its name."[7]

The Senate hearings ramped up nationwide interest, drawing even more front-page stories than the suffrage parade itself. The hearings began on March 6 and "promise[d] to be one of the most sensational conducted at the Capitol in years," according to the *Washington Post*. The power and prestige of the Senate elevated the story in reporters' minds, as did the Beauty and the Beast theme and the all-American appeal of an underdog valiantly overcoming the odds. Even the anti-suffrage *New York Times* ran the hearings story on page one.[8]

While Lucy went home for a few weeks, Alice prepared for the hearings and the national scrutiny, organizing a raft of eager and well-dressed witnesses who packed the hearing room. Like the 1910 trial she had watched the Pankhursts exploit, this hearing became an opportunity to dramatize injustice. The congressional subcommittee looked attentive, so unlike the polite toleration typical of the annual suffrage hearings. One marcher-congressman told the press: "We intend to get to the bottom of this thing if it takes us all summer." Nearly 150 women and men, including Alice, testified over two weeks in March and two more days in April.[9]

Almost unanimously, marchers insisted that few police honored their right to assemble. Alice had commissioned professional photographs of the event, now evidence of the abrogation of suffragists' rights. When a few witnesses, including a local minister, called the throng good-natured and the police sincere, an overflowing female audience shouted, "No! That isn't true!" Police Chief Sylvester minimized his own responsibility, noting the hundreds of untrained flatfoots-for-a-day. He insisted, "I did my duty" and "exhausted every effort I could" to honor the women's claim to the Avenue. "My conscience is clear," he maintained. But a police captain recounted how a *McClure's* magazine article about Alice's British militancy had been passed among the DC police, undermining Sylvester's assertions.[10]

If Alice hoped someone would be held responsible for the mistreatment of the suffrage marchers, the diplomatic conclusions of the Senate investigators disappointed her. She tried to stir the pot by telling a reporter that "the police had the tip from some power higher to let the rough characters in the city through the police lines." Though she refrained from such criticism in her testimony, the Senate committee pursued that idea; however, it found only dead ends. But it did affirm suffragists' rights as citizens on the public streets: "The line of march was not cleared," the committee's report declared, "and the parade was not protected as it should have been." The committee assigned some blame to all parties, but to no particular person. Their politic conclusions pleased no one. Nevertheless, the ten days of national attention advanced the cause more than any censure or apology.[11]

The combination of the procession and the hearings established a foothold for the suffrage amendment. Even before the hearings wrapped up, Alice began her campaign to secure an amendment to the Constitution granting all American women the right to vote. The Senate and press affirmation of women's citizenship rights allowed her to capitalize on that high note. She utilized the Pankhursts' strategy of keeping suffrage constantly before policymakers and the public and developed a keen eye for opportune moments. Her steady flow of events began with a WSPU staple: a deputation to the head of government. NAWSA leaders, accustomed to federal work that was limited to an annual hearing before Congress, struggled to maintain control of their unusually active Congressional Committee.

Alice's drive for a suffrage amendment started with the president. Both houses of Congress passed constitutional amendments, she knew; the president had no official role in the process. Nevertheless, she remembered what Penn's Henry Jones Ford taught her about the presidency. Only the president has a national mandate, Ford had asserted. Only the president could "define issues in such a way that public opinion can pass upon them decisively." The new Democratic president and former constitutional scholar, Woodrow Wilson, shared this view of presidential power. In 1908, he wrote of the chief executive's role: "His is the only national voice in affairs. Let him once win the admiration and confidence of the country, and no other single force can withstand him." Alice planned to capitalize on the president's influence to win over Congress.[12]

Perhaps she felt a kinship with Woodrow Wilson. Though born in the South, Wilson came to prominence in AP's home state of New Jersey, most recently as its governor. Both Alice and the president enjoyed the privileges accorded their race; both sought enhanced status through education. Both projected reserve, masking their emotional intensity. Like many Americans, she admired his Progressive values, despite his Democratic allegiance and her Republican heritage.[13]

Wilson, then fifty-seven, had written about the old order changing, but his generational outlook and southern upbringing kept his notion of womankind paternalistic. Only a few years before his election, he had characterized women as incapable of understanding politics and hence ill-equipped to vote. He felt certain of woman's role as a gentle nurturer of children, husband, and community. His paternalism bled into his leadership style; leaders held a responsibility to educate their public, he thought, just as fathers taught their children and husbands their wives.[14]

The first deputation to the president came in the midst of the Senate hearings, taking the press coverage in a new direction. Alice chose prominent white women for this first encounter with Wilson, implicitly underscoring the class and racial base of the suffrage movement. Three women in the group probably knew the president socially: two were related to Democratic congressmen, and another had married a well-known Wilson supporter. In Lucy's absence, Alice led the deputation herself, as NAWSA's official representative. The women would not have to fight their way in, as in London; however, Wilson offered them a mere ten minutes of his day.[15]

From this first meeting, Alice put the president on notice. Once the women were admitted to the Oval Office and introduced, Wilson invited them to sit down, motioning to a row of five chairs. The former professor sat stiffly before them. Undaunted in the president's presence, AP began the appeal by declaring suffrage "the paramount issue of the day." Several million women now voted in nine states, she pointed out; the nation should follow that example. The others followed her lead. Wilson listened politely, then told them that Congress had more pressing matters—currency, tariff reform. Alice promptly invoked fundamental principles: "But Mr. President, do you not understand that the Administration has no right to legislate for currency, tariff, and any other reform without first getting the consent of women?" Surprised at her boldness, Wilson said warily that he would carefully consider their views. In the end, Alice had to be satisfied with, as she later told the press, "making it plain to him that the women of the country are demanding action." She underscored her point by sending him two more deputations over the next three weeks, ostensibly from other suffrage groups; she also encouraged activists around the country to write him about including suffrage in his upcoming message to the new Congress.[16]

As word reached the National of ongoing CC activity, alarm bells went off. The shower of praise after the procession turned icy. Shaw chided AP, "While I realize it is necessary to move rapidly, it is also necessary to move wisely." She summoned Alice and Lucy to her home near Philadelphia. Alice and Lucy took the train to Philadelphia and set off with Dora Lewis; the *Philadelphia Record* claimed Shaw charged them with "overactivity" and "overaggressiveness." Whatever the actual criticisms, the two young women once again gained Shaw's confidence. The next day, Shaw wrote the rest of the board about their "prompt and energetic activities."[17]

After the meeting, Lucy boarded the train for Washington and Alice went home for a few days for the first time since mid-December. "I hope you are getting a beautiful rest and enjoying a week of civilization," Lucy wrote a few days later. "We are all missing you dreadfully." With AP away, Lucy had called in one of her sisters "to do what she can towards decorating the shop." She went on to brief Alice on the status of various plans. "Everything is going along all right except that we are out of money," she wrote, but insisted "we can scrape along" until AP returned.[18]

The March 1913 letter records how candidly Lucy spoke to Alice though, like nearly everyone, she always addressed letters to "Miss Paul." Her missives flashed charm and humor. The two women had apparently commiserated with each other about a common frustration of celebrity. "Your pictures are appalling," Lucy quipped, "all but one which is medium but very melancholy. It may console you to know that mine are much worse."[19]

By the time Alice returned to Washington, Lucy had planned the modest spectacle intended to dramatize their first appeal to lawmakers, timed to coincide with the opening of the new Congress. The April 7, 1913, event borrowed from the 1910 NAWSA convention, when suffragists delivered petitions bearing more than four hundred thousand signatures to Congress. AP and Lucy collected petitions and drew on District residents to identify two emissaries from each state and another representing each congressional district; messengers would petition their congressmen or senators on behalf of the suffrage amendment. AP and Lucy deliberately echoed the March 3 procession, then added flair and ritual to elevate the meaning of their ceremony for both onlookers and participants.[20]

They staged inclusion this time, imagining a day when elected officials considered women's rights of great significance. The 531 women rallied near CC headquarters, then marched down one side of Pennsylvania Avenue behind two bands. Alice helped carry the lead banner: "Nation-wide Suffrage by a Constitutional Amendment." Each white-gowned representative waved a yellow "Votes for Women" flag; state banners divided delegations. Advance press attracted large crowds who treated the women with respect, even cheers. This time, Chief Sylvester took no chances. He directed more than three hundred officers to protect the marchers, leaving the rest of the District, one local paper noted, "practically unprotected."[21]

For one radiant moment, suffragists drove the congressional agenda. The women strode through the Capitol grounds and up the steps, where, by prior arrangement, congressmen from the nine "free" states formally greeted them. Then, the women filed into the Senate and House galleries to watch the august bodies convene. As the 99th Congress opened, the petitions were ceremoniously presented in each house, followed by a pro-suffrage congressman or senator offering the very first resolution of the session, calling for the passage of a constitutional amendment to enfranchise America's women. One suffrage veteran, deeply moved, called the day "the greatest, most dignified, and most effective one single thing that has ever been done for suffrage in this country." However, suffrage resolutions had been introduced into ten Congresses since 1887 without any vote being taken.[22]

In the days following, the annual NAWSA ritual, a Senate committee hearing on the suffrage amendment, offered one more opportunity for AP and committee members to build on relationships forged with supportive congressmen during preparations for the March 3 procession and April 7 petitioning. She hoped those events and the hearing would prompt the Senate woman suffrage committee to issue a favorable report. A Democratic majority now led the committee. The House had no comparable committee, though CC volunteers worked to convince the members of the need.[23]

Alice believed that the times demanded political action rather than educational debate, but she dutifully sat in on the hearing, listening to another recital of arguments for and against woman suffrage, perhaps noting their commonalities. Many members of both the National Association Opposed to Woman Suffrage (NAOWS) and NAWSA believed women and men innately had different functions in life; they disagreed on how women should use their distinctive abilities and social roles. Womankind should advise, "consult, and cooperate with men," one anti-suffragist argued; "if she uses these rights and privileges, she does not need the ballot."

Both anti-suffragists and suffragists used fear-based arguments. Antis raised the specter of "women of differing and inferior races" voting, a racist and xenophobic argument similar to appeals some suffragists made about women's votes countering immigrant and black votes. Likewise, anti-suffragists warned against militant feminism, equating it with the "menace of socialism." Many NAWSA members shared the same fears.[24]

Alice thought she could offset qualms about militancy but wanted to convince the National to focus its energy on a suffrage amendment. In her view, that was the most economical approach to securing the vote for all American women. Passing an amendment meant persuading federal and state lawmakers. The state-by-state approach required moving bills through state legislatures and then submitting the bill to a voter referendum. In other words, suffragists needed to convert a majority of male voters in the non-suffrage states, millions of men. On the other hand, a constitutional amendment meant the persuasion could be focused on Congress and, later, state legislators—all members of the cultural elite, susceptible to political pressure, and typically more forward-looking than the average male voter. The constitutional method seemed the simpler approach.[25]

Yet even with enthusiastic backing, she knew that amending the Constitution was a formidable task requiring a two-thirds majority in both the House and Senate and subsequent ratification by three-fourths of the states. Throughout the nineteenth century, passage eluded all but three new amendments, prompting early twentieth-century observers to call the process unworkable. The spring of 1913 brought new hope to those trying to reform the Constitution, however. Two amendments were ratified: the Sixteenth Amendment established a permanent income tax and the Seventeenth, popular election of senators. The two successful crusades effectively revived hopes that constitutional amendments could serve as political remedies. Once again, Alice Paul benefited from historical good fortune.[26]

A federal suffrage amendment seemed a realistic goal in light of the Seventeenth Amendment's history. Fewer than a dozen states independently approved popular elections for senators before the amendment passed Congress, somewhat comparable to the nine "free" suffrage states in early 1913. Before passage of the Seventeenth Amendment, however, thirty-one state legislatures had also called for a constitutional amendment on direct elections; no such calls had emerged for a constitutional suffrage amendment. Southern concerns about Washington interfering with Jim Crow laws delayed enactment of the Seventeenth Amendment, and the same fear fueled southern resistance to a federal suffrage amendment. Once Congress approved the Seventeenth Amendment in 1912, however, the states ratified the measure in less than a year.[27]

As Alice rejuvenated the drive for a suffrage amendment, Harriot Blatch reignited the NAWSA debate over state and federal work. The National nominally pursued both, though federal work was given short shrift after Susan B. Anthony's death in 1906. In mid-April 1913, Blatch editorialized in her group's journal that suffragists must decide "which way" and detailed her rationale for a state focus. Blatch ally Elizabeth Rogers wrote AP, "The constitutional amendment business at this stage of the game is such nonsense." The solid block of southern Democrats would obstruct the proposal or find some way to defer it. Like many, Rogers insisted, "We must win ten states more before the time is ripe." Blatch wrote AP privately, "We here are as centered on New York [state] as you are on Washington." Winning the state's 1915 suffrage referendum was the linchpin, Blatch thought; if won, "all the states would come tumbling down like a pack of cards."[28]

Mary Dennett responded publicly to Blatch on NAWSA's (and AP's) behalf. She questioned Blatch's argument that pursuing both strategies at once meant a division of forces and funds. Faced with options, she wrote, many would choose work that spoke to them. "The whole history of suffrage work effectually disproves that there is just so much money available," she asserted. On southern Democrats, Dennett cited the recent ratification of the Sixteenth and Seventeenth Amendments as proof that the states rights ideology was crumbling. "Why," she wrote, "should suffragists be timid and hang back?"[29]

Alice Paul never faltered from her belief that a constitutional path held the most promise. With her limited experience in Washington and conviction that American politicians were more easily swayed than the British, she underestimated the power of the solid South in delaying woman suffrage. She had also not counted on the special interests dead set against women voting. In particular, since the embrace of woman suffrage by the influential temperance movement, the liquor lobby feared that women voting would herald prohibition. Nevertheless, Blatch and others miscalculated the difficulty of a New York referendum. And despite AP's inexperience, her constitutional campaign ultimately hastened the amendment's passage.

After the annual Senate hearing, Alice could let up on her frenetic pace, and she turned to long-term planning. Putting together the March 3 procession convinced her that advocacy for a suffrage amendment required a separate organization both for monetary reasons and clarity. Outside the District, CC fundraising efforts confounded many NAWSA members: some saw CC appeals as competition for their own state fundraising or assumed contributions for Washington sent directly to NAWSA headquarters would reach the CC. With the parade over and the joint procession committee disbanded, NAWSA still expected all CC monies to be funneled through the New York headquarters.[30]

Alice and Lucy had agreed to raise their own funds and wanted to control that revenue. They considered—and discarded—the idea of founding an entirely independent organization, along the lines of Harriot Blatch's group, now called the Women's Political Union, with chapters in several states. However, suffragists already associated AP and Lucy with the CC; in addition, the NAWSA brand offered unparalleled visibility and access.

They came up with a solution to address both fundraising and clarity. They created an adjunct to the Congressional Committee with "the national work as its sole object," a group affiliated with but not run by the National. The adjunct would raise and control its own funds and campaigns, while preserving the benefits of NAWSA association. Anna Shaw had approved the idea at the late March meeting in her home. After some discussion about an appropriate name, they agreed on the Congressional Union (CU). The five members of the CC (AP asked NAWSA to appoint Mary Beard as the fifth member) would also serve as the executive committee of the CU. No one involved foresaw the problems this plan would create.[31]

Alice boldly envisioned a national network of suffragists centered on winning the constitutional amendment and went about creating her desired reality. She imagined a team of workers in every state, including one paid statewide organizer. When state groups later protested that CC/CU operations interfered with their local campaigns, Alice responded that the CC/CU work would benefit state suffrage work. Much as Mary Dennett wrote about NAWSA pursuing both state and national suffrage work, AP believed more to be more.[32]

In mid-May, Alice and Lucy won their first political victory: a favorable report from the Senate woman suffrage committee, the first report of any kind in seventeen years. "We have had a hard battle to get them to meet," Alice wrote Mary Beard. Henry Ashurst (Democrat, AZ) explained the vote to the full Senate. He reminded his colleagues of the two recently ratified constitutional amendments, which "convinced the American people that our Federal Constitution is a living, breathing, dynamic force." Relying on the same notions of innate feminine qualities that many suffragists invoked, he declared that "equality or inequality of the two sexes from an intellectual standpoint" was not the issue. Since women care and sacrifice for others and the rule of law governed them as well as men, they "should not be denied a voice." He went on, "In this Republic the people constitute the Government... 'The people' includes women." Many of his colleagues doubted that.[33]

About the time the Senate formally released its history-making report, news from Britain stunned Alice. Her former comrade Emily Wilding Davison had darted onto a racetrack crowded with charging horses, attempting to place a suffrage banner over one of them, only to be trampled. Her death became a rallying cry for the WSPU. Alice had monitored the news of her erstwhile compatriots as the Pankhursts' tactics became increasingly associated with violence. Indeed, NAWSA had recently reprimanded her for sending CC delegations to Wilson administration officials on behalf of two imprisoned British militants. As she wrote one NAWSA board member, she strongly approved of the militant suffrage tactics used in England.[34]

Davison's demise affected Alice profoundly. While she was probably not surprised that the bitter frustration in Britain led to someone's death, she undoubtedly hoped American suffragists would never experience such tragedy. She now found little sympathy for the Pankhursts among Americans. As she wrote one friend, "I am sorry that we don't agree over the English suffragists. Scarcely any one agrees with me on that point, however." Like the Pankhursts, she viewed Davison as a martyr for the cause. "Afterwards," she later wrote, "when I felt lonely or inadequate, I would think of Emily, of her great courage, a constant reminder of what one person can do."[35]

In 1913, though, she had little time to reflect as nonstop organizing absorbed her time and energy. She oversaw the production of a suffrage play in late May and joined Lucy and others as the CC/CU delegation to parades in New York and Baltimore. While in New York, AP met with Mary Beard and journalist Rheta Childe Dorr about starting a weekly CU journal. Back in Washington, she sought subscribers and women to organize for the CU, approaching her Swarthmore chum Mabel Vernon to become the CU's first paid organizer. The position, she wrote Vernon, "would pay enough to enable you to live, though, of course, not much more." Alice hinted at her own decision in writing, "I do hope very much that you will take up this work and let school teaching go. There are plenty of people to teach school."[36]

Alice and Lucy's dream of prompt congressional amendment passage kept them fully engaged through the summer. "I feel certain that our bill will go through the Senate this session," AP wrote her sister Helen, confident in her ambition. Yet she and Lucy moved from their rooms at the Friends rooming house to share an apartment with Elsie Hill. Anna Howard Shaw cautioned, "Don't stay there too long in the heat. Don't rush things too hard." But the sweltering summer heat of Washington figured little into AP's plans. The Senate remained in session through the summer and so would they.[37]

Both leaders resisted enticing invitations to cooler climes. "I only wish that I could meet you again at Squirrel Inn, this summer," Alice wrote one old friend. "I still remember, with such pleasure, our talks together and the games we used to play in the evening after dinner." A friend of Lucy's invited her to Canada and wondered at "How you are whooping it up!" Lucy responded that she needed to stay in Washington until summer's end. She found the work engaging enough to distract her from the heat and humidity. Her father also tried to lure her homeward, teasing fondly, "The rest of us are living riotously. We even haunt the 'movies' now."[38]

With the favorable Senate report creating some momentum, the two leaders produced another spectacle. The plan grew out of concurrent marches on London by nonmilitant British suffragists as well as Rosalie Jones's pilgrimages. Women would converge on Washington from all directions throughout the month of July, each trek drawing attention to suffrage. "Some of the tours will be on foot, some by caravan," Alice wrote one supporter, "some by trolley, some by horseback, some by automobile, some by train, etc." These expeditions promised to arouse the public and persuade senators of the "tremendous backing" for the amendment. They would also garner attention for the new Congressional Union.[39]

The pilgrimages proved a tough sell, particularly among the privileged women Alice and Lucy counted on. July was the height of the vacation season, and most NAWSA board members retreated for the summer months, as did CC stalwarts like Elsie Hill. One New Yorker wrote, "We are having a great deal of trouble getting people to say that they will go." Tennessee's NAWSA complained about the limited time to organize the thing. Nevertheless, enough women welcomed the energy emanating from Washington to make the journey, and Alice put any available person to work arranging for housing, sending out petition blanks, and coordinating the décor for the culminating event on July 31. She found typists in such short supply that she set about learning how to use the machine herself.[40]

The day before the welcoming ceremony seemed auspicious. Alice, Lucy, and other CC/CU aides hustled around the District and nearby Hyattsville, Maryland, the site chosen for the mass rally. Large cavalcades from the mid-Atlantic states, plus Massachusetts, Maryland, and Virginia neared Washington. Most had organized still-novel automobile tours, though Virginians chose to cruise up the Potomac. Massachusetts women reported enroute, "Great gatherings—2000 last night at Lynn." Mary Dennett and the New York contingent drove, proselytizing in "as many sea-side resorts on the Jersey coast as we can." Mabel Vernon and a friend flaunted convention by "traveling in farmers' wagons and sleeping in farmhouses."[41]

Suddenly, in mid-afternoon, preparations stalled: Mother Nature swept in with the fiercest storm in Washington's recorded history. Rain and hail came in torrents; seventy-mile-per-hour winds felled trees and demolished buildings, paralyzing telephone and streetcar service. Some city streets became tangles of overturned vehicles and debris.[42]

Despite the destruction, the next morning's performance came off without a hitch. The decision to emphasize automobiles at the event cannily tied this potent symbol of modernity to the suffrage cause; using women as drivers wove novelty and an element of risk into the spectacle. With great flourish, AP, Lucy, and various dignitaries welcomed representatives from all forty-eight states (some culled from the District) in front of a large crowd at the Hyattsville ballpark. Members of the Senate suffrage committee lent a heightened sense of importance to the ceremony. Then, Alice and Lucy led a motorcar procession to the Capitol. Mounted police escorted the gaily decorated train of autos through Washington, steering through fallen trees and other obstructions. Despite the recent storm, spectators lined the streets.[43]

The real show, however, took place within the walls of the Capitol. The petitioning of elected representatives is so fundamental to the American government that the Senate has long designated "morning business" to accept petitions and memorials. In April, Alice had successfully taken over morning business on opening day to highlight the suffrage amendment. In July, with the cooperation of pro-suffrage senators, Alice exploited Senate tradition to, in essence, force a suffrage discussion onto the Senate floor, the first one since 1887.[44]

Pages delivered armloads of petitions bearing tens of thousands of names as the august body opened proceedings for the day. Many women gathered in the Senate gallery to observe. As one reporter wrote, "a cloud of femininity fluttered into the senate wing." Twenty-five senators chose to do more than present the state's petition; each of them spoke briefly, most on behalf of suffrage. After two hours, the body delayed business even further to allow all petitions to be accepted. And so, in this roundabout way, the Senate discussed suffrage.[45]

The press coverage laid bare cultural notions of woman's place, constructs assaulted by suffragists interjecting themselves into the Senate day. Most reporters thought parades one thing, interfering with the high-minded affairs of men quite another. The Associated Press wire story, front-page news even in hamlets like Titusville, Pennsylvania, belittled the action, stating that the Senate "left off its sober tariff work for more than two hours and listened to the frills and furbelows of suffrage argument." The March procession and hearing notwithstanding, cultural barriers did not fall overnight. For now, the front-page news sufficed.[46]

Alice's talent for attracting committed workers continued to be a key element in the CC/CU's accomplishments. Many found her steady gaze and plainspoken appeal compelling. "It is not through their affections that she moves [people]," Doris Stevens suggested. AP's power was intellectual but "almost never fails to win an emotional allegiance." Stevens, an Ohioan fresh from college commencement, later wrote about her own first encounter with Alice after the July pilgrimage.

> "Can't you stay on and help us with a hearing next week?" said Miss Paul.
>
> "I'm sorry," said I, "but I have promised to join a party of friends in the mountains for a summer holiday and…"
>
> "Holiday?" said she, looking straight at me. Instantly ashamed at having mentioned such a legitimate excuse, I murmured something about not having had one since before entering college.
>
> "But can't you stay?" she said.

Stevens stayed. Mabel Vernon stayed too. Historian Inez Haynes Irwin later asked Vernon how Alice "got so much work…out of amateurs." Vernon replied, "[Alice] believed we could do it and so she made us believe it." These true believers became the core of the Congressional Union.[47]

After the Senate discussion, the CC/CU pushed against the inertia in the House. Lucy spearheaded attempts to secure a suffrage committee, "a most amusing time" by her own self-assured account. She, like Alice, rejected suggestions that they moved too fast. She glibly wrote one critic, "Perhaps we would be criticized for undue haste if we asked the House to legislate this session on a Women's Suffrage bill, but the creation of a committee seems just a matter of business which would be disposed of quite easily." She added, "They have already created three new committees this session. They would not be breaking precedents in making a fourth." The Rules Committee refused requests for a hearing on creating a suffrage committee, but in the slack days of August, the CC/CU women persuaded the Rules chairman to grant an informal hearing (that is, a hearing without expectation of outcome) to representatives of the National Council of Women Voters (NCWV).[48]

The NCWV was the first attempt to capitalize upon the political promise of women voting in nine western states. Organized in 1911 by the controversial Emma Smith DeVoe of Washington State, the group foundered, though district NCWV members had nonetheless joined CC/CU events. Alice earlier amplified the public effect of deputations by sending most under the auspices of groups outside NAWSA. Now, she used the same tactic to turn up the heat on Congress, thereby breathing new life into the NCWV. "You can hardly realize the tremendous psychological effect which a convention of women voters meeting here would have," she wrote NCWV's head in urging an August gathering. She planned to manage press coverage so that the NCWV appeared to be "an enormous and powerful body" representing women voters. She persuaded Jane Addams to headline the long-sought hearing before the Rules Committee.[49]

Alice used her own speech at the mid-August NCWV convention to persuade the assemblage and the nation that the time was ripe for a suffrage constitutional amendment. Four million female voters in the West, she declared confidently, also meant that suffrage states held more than 30 percent of the vote. Therefore, she believed "the movement has reached a position which should enable it very quickly to obtain the passage of a federal amendment through Congress." The convention unanimously passed a resolution focusing the NCWV on the federal work. Since Alice largely engineered the convention, the resolution held more symbolic than literal weight.[50]

The informal hearing the next day bore unexpected fruit. After NCWV members spoke, the esteemed Addams got right to the point, saying that states' rights concerns underlay the House's avoidance of the suffrage amendment. "I don't say the House of Representatives is evading responsibility," she argued, "but it's strange that there is one burning question which cannot be brought up for discussion." Her impact seemed immediate when the Rules Committee chair suddenly decided to hold a formal hearing in early December. Unfortunately, that small step forward was the last from Congress for several months.[51]

Alice's desire for a weekly CU newspaper also continued to be frustrated. She wanted her own propaganda organ to keep supporters up to date on progress toward the amendment. In the spring she had persuaded Rheta Childe Dorr, a well-known journalist, to serve as its unsalaried editor; however, Dorr kept delaying her arrival. Alice felt so discouraged by late September that she moaned to one correspondent, "So many people have disappointed us that I hardly see how we can pull through, but I suppose we will manage somehow." Such passive-aggressive complaints usually led to AP turning inward for a solution. "We cannot postpone working on the paper any longer," she said, "so I am going to begin on preparations for it myself."[52]

With Dorr ultimately delayed until late fall, the two women corresponded about plans and Alice found herself in the unusual position of tamping down someone else's big ideas. Dorr told AP, "What we are proposing to do is very serious and ought not to be attempted in any amateurish spirit. I could not afford to lose my reputation." And she thought the CU should pay her expenses. Alice reminded her of the "modest" newspaper they had originally discussed. She did not wish to antagonize other suffrage papers or risk too much debt. Dorr, after all, could continue her other writing from Washington while editing *The Suffragist*. Alice agreed to enlarge her concept of the journal, but the accord between the two women was temporary.[53]

The weekly *Suffragist* finally premiered on November 15, 1913, boasting all the confidence and impatience of the new generation of suffragists. On the front page, Alice declared confidently that a woman suffrage amendment neared success, requiring only women standing "shoulder to shoulder behind the amendment." Lucy's inside article reiterated the urgency. "One thing we may be sure of," she argued, "until *we* ask for instant action, *no one else will ask for it.*" Alice wrote, "There is no other issue comparable in importance to the elementary question of self-government for the women of America.[54]

The debut of *The Suffragist* gave both the new Congressional Union and the amendment efforts greater visibility in the suffrage community. Within a month, the paper supported itself through advertising and boasted 1,200 paid subscriptions. Dorr's more expansive vision seemed to be paying off despite the doubling of the subscription price from fifty cents to one dollar. Like other suffrage journals, *The Suffragist* opened up space for real and imagined female political community. The CU weekly went further, however, encouraging subscribers to see themselves as agents of political change.[55]

The birth of *The Suffragist* helped promote the NAWSA convention, set for late November. Local groups had ceded their usual task of arranging the annual meeting to the CC, pleading their inability to raise the necessary funds. AP, seen as the most capable person available, acquired another responsibility. Two weeks before the convention, Alice finalized details while Lucy handled a series of open-air and indoor meetings designed to build momentum for the suffrage gathering. *The Suffragist* publicized the convention week after week.[56]

As the convention approached, fears about WSPU influence occupied NAWSA leaders, prompted by newspaper coverage of Emmeline Pankhurst's fall 1913 American tour. Despite her earlier speaking tours, immigration officials had barred Pankhurst's entry into the United States for a short time, claiming she was an undesirable alien. Mary Ware Dennett felt "really very much disturbed indeed to have the Washington papers so persistently connect the members and the work of the Congressional Committee with Mrs. Pankhurst and militancy." She wrote Alice, "It cannot fail to prejudice our prospects." Alice and Lucy refused to distance themselves from the Pankhursts, though neither one believed the violent tactics the WSPU sometimes employed would work in the United States. They avoided using the term *militant* to describe CC/CU activities. Nonetheless, a few months earlier, Alice wrote a former British comrade that she and Lucy worked "together in Washington, but our hearts are still in the WSPU." Heedless of the National's unease, Alice spent considerable time assisting Mrs. Pankhurst and arranged for her to appear in Washington a few days before NAWSA members convened.[57]

The attention Lucy attracted for chalking a meeting announcement on a sidewalk near the White House drew a swift rebuke from Anna Howard Shaw, who was equally alert to signs of militancy. Lucy had unknowingly broken the law, and the police issued a warrant for her arrest. Washington was abuzz, and papers across the country picked up the wire story. Shaw begged Lucy not to create any further ruckus. "You may think we are all a set of old fogies," she chided defensively, "and perhaps we are, but I, for one, thank heaven that I am as much of an old fogy as I am, for I think there are certain laws of order which should be followed by everybody." She added stiffly, "It requires a good deal more courage to work steadily and steadfastly for forty or fifty years to gain an end than it does to do a[n] impulsive rash thing and lose it."[58]

Lucy blithely smoothed the troubled waters, thanking the prickly NAWSA president for her communiqué. She assured Shaw that she had paid her fine, closing the case. She added that neither she nor Alice possessed a "militant spirit." "We have no occasion for it," she wrote, since they felt encouraged by their progress. When Shaw knew the two young women "a little longer and more intimately," Lucy suggested, her trust would be secure. "We think a very long time before acting, especially Miss Paul, who is I think of a very calculating and cautious temperament." She emphasized the positive: "Now it is over, and we secured nearly a week's advertising for the sum of one dollar."[59] Nonetheless, the timing of the chalking incident was unfortunate.

A week later, Emmeline Pankhurst arrived in Washington as the CU's guest. *The Suffragist* defended the British firebrand, opining that her American tour had "caused an extraordinary amount of adverse sentiment on the part of unthinking women." Though she admired Emmeline Pankhurst, Mary Dennett decried the broadly held impression of a NAWSA-WSPU linkage and regretted Pankhurst's Washington appearance. Alice stood loyally by her mentor, even presiding over the meeting at which Pankhurst spoke. *The Suffragist* acknowledged the ongoing controversy over militancy only to offer fulsome praise about Pankhurst's ability to win over skeptics. Emmeline Pankhurst, the article proclaimed, was "perhaps the greatest woman figure in the world today."[60]

A letter from her sister Helen reminded Alice of the past year's losses and gains. With the NAWSA convention opening two days after Thanksgiving, AP found no opportunity to spend the holiday with family. Helen sent on a check from Mrs. Paul ("thinking thee might want some things before the Convention") as well as details of her own plans to attend as a New Jersey delegate. Helen underscored Alice's prominence among activists: "It is a most delightful privilege to be thy sister when going to suffrage meetings—" Helen exclaimed, "thy name acts like magic—the people immediately take great interest in me & introduce me to everyone." She met Mary Beard at one meeting, who "brimm[ed] with admiration for thee. She considers thee a genius which proves her good judgment." Alice knew not everyone shared such sanguine views.[61]

The cold, steady winter rain arriving with convention delegates on Thanksgiving weekend did not lift anyone's mood. Once again, change stood at the forefront of the agenda. The *Woman's Journal* noted that "several burning questions will come up for settlement" and, anticipating the usual "tempestuous sea of excited feelings," called for reasoned debate to resolve them. The movement to set the National upon sounder fiscal ground was probably hastened by the extraordinary fundraising of the CC over the past year. On the political front, the opening rally at the Columbia Theatre signaled AP's success at turning attention toward the federal work; the assemblage called upon the president to endorse the suffrage amendment and lobby Congress on its behalf.[62]

Subtlety was not Alice's strong suit. The next morning, she welcomed several hundred conventioneers by claiming preeminence for the federal campaign, asserting that NAWSA "assembled in Washington to ask the Democratic party to enfranchise the women of America." The yellow "Great Demand" banner from the parade—"We Demand an Amendment…" hung at the back of the stage to reinforce her remarks visually. Her comments raised a few eyebrows. (Carrie Chapman Catt later claimed that many delegates viewed AP's attitude as "a dark conspiracy to capture the entire 'National' for the militant enterprise.") Alice went on to assure the assemblage cockily that "victory was at hand." After Lucy's own address that evening, she told a reporter, "Let every suffragist in the country concentrate on Congress for one day and we'd get the vote the next day."[63]

The convention forged on, showing the now-familiar signs that the NAWSA board dragged down the rank and file. Catt's stature probably helped pass higher dues requirements, though debate became long and bitter. Members seemed reluctant to accord the sprawling National more power and perhaps found NAWSA "too incompetent," Catt later mused. Still, once Alice reported that the CC/CU raised over $27,000 in the previous year, the $43,000 NAWSA income looked pathetic by comparison. Alva Belmont proposed moving NAWSA headquarters to Washington, to no avail. "The opposition of the national officers was so apparent," according to one report, "that many delegates hesitated to express their convictions for the affirmative." The fabulously wealthy Belmont, often at odds with the NAWSA leadership, started looking for new allies.[64]

When President Wilson failed to recommend woman suffrage in his speech to the new congressional session, the upshot of the long-planned hearing before the House Rules Committee seemed foreordained. The efforts of Shaw, Addams, Catt, and other eloquent speakers failed to sway the committee to recommend a separate House suffrage committee. That afternoon, however, the convention defiantly approved a massive NAWSA deputation to Wilson, which Alice joined. When the president pleaded illness, fifty-five women waited impatiently several days to see him.[65]

Wilson finally granted the suffragists an audience, only to tell them his hands were tied. He believed a House suffrage committee "a proper thing to do," and had so urged congressmen privately. Nevertheless, he could not promote suffrage legislation because to do so violated his principle of speaking only as a representative of his party, never as an individual. He had not promised suffrage as a candidate; therefore, "I am not at liberty until I speak for somebody besides myself to urge legislation upon the Congress." *The Suffragist* called the president's bluff, labeling his answer a condescending dodge.[66]

Alice was exhausted by the last day of the convention, when she stood on the stage to report on the Congressional Committee's 1913 work, but felt heartened as the delegates rose to applaud her. She could not provide separate reports for the CC and CU, she maintained, since the two groups stood "so closely allied that we must give the report as one." AP reminded the delegates of the year's accomplishments. As her detractors exchanged meaningful glances, she listed the firsts: the first majority party suffrage committee, the first unanimously favorable Senate report, the first Senate debate in twenty-six years.

Alice's success thus far led her to overreach. Shaw had discouraged her from appealing for funds to advance the amendment, but AP persisted, convinced that the convention supported her. The CC/CU had spent $25,000 to date, she said, most raised within Washington itself. She underscored the point: "The women in Washington have done more than they could have done this past year but they absolutely must have some help from the United States to carry this through." Her pale, frail appearance and enervation embodied the argument. "You have raised something like $12,000 to carry on the office in New York. Nothing has been raised to carry through the Federal Amendment which is, in my opinion, the great work before us as a nation." Unfortunately, the success of the past year had rendered her tone-deaf to an undercurrent of dismay.[67]

Former NAWSA president Carrie Chapman Catt rose magisterially at the front of the auditorium. Heads turned; whispering ceased. She confessed herself "a good deal razzle-dazzled by the situation." This Congressional Committee, she ventured, "has done everything which the National ought to do." How is it a committee of the National? As Alice listened to the powerful Catt, she may have heard the sound of the other shoe dropping. Catt's challenge marked the beginning of the end of her relationship with NAWSA.[68]

9

"We Go to Smash, or Make Good"

A DIVISION IN suffrage ranks was probably inevitable. The NAWSA convention always provided a forum for grievances; in 1913, the Congressional Union was the target. Alice and Lucy's cheeky behavior prior to and during the gathering only gave critics more ammunition. No one wanted a repeat of the discord—over whether black enfranchisement should trump woman suffrage—that drove suffragists apart between 1869 and 1890. Nevertheless, veteran activists had long feared that misguided enthusiasts of the British militants would rupture American suffrage unity. While the dispute began as an administrative inquiry, it soon exposed the real fault lines.

The National enjoyed a hard-won reputation for propriety and nonpartisanship; leaders deemed these norms essential for safeguarding personal and group standing. The disruptive behavior, violence, and partisan politics adopted by the Pankhursts could not be sanctioned, though select tactics like parades might be employed with care to placate WSPU admirers. NAWSA leaders discounted the increasingly visible minority of members—many but not all of them younger—who, like Alice, defined propriety and nonpartisanship quite differently. The National felt stifling to these women.

Immersed in the work or cavalier about the consequences, Alice Paul flaunted NAWSA customs. Once she gained approval for the independent CU, she lost sight of NAWSA's authority over Congressional Committee activities. CC/CU fundraising confused those trying to distinguish between the two groups. AP openly associated the CC/CU with Mrs. Pankhurst and published *Suffragist* articles advocating what appeared to be partisan tactics. The National's leaders responded with sanctions. Belatedly, Alice recognized the value of the NAWSA brand and fought to stay within the fold.

While on one level the NAWSA–CU conflict was about the suffrage community policing itself, on another it revealed the ambitions and insecurities of the three main personalities. Carrie Chapman Catt, the once-and-future president; Anna Howard Shaw, the embattled leader; and Alice Paul, the brash newcomer, all viewed each other with suspicion.

NAWSA members knew Carrie Chapman Catt well; older suffragists in the audience recalled her progress over twenty years. The Midwestern-bred former teacher once termed herself "not a big gun, never will be." Nonetheless, supported by a wealthy husband, she rose through the National's ranks during the 1890s. No stranger to politics, she attracted kudos for her skillful organizing and lobbying in western state campaigns and earned the esteem of the aging NAWSA president Susan B. Anthony. Catt possessed "all the external attributes of a leader," wrote Mary Gray Peck, her late-life companion, "a noble presence, a full deliberate voice, and above all, that 'gorgeous surplus called personal magnetism.'"[1]

Catt glimpsed her own history in the Congressional Committee. At the 1895 national convention, the thirty-six-year-old Catt shone, calling a more efficient and organized NAWSA the "great need of the hour." She wrote privately of suffrage as "the strongest reform represented by the weakest organization." Anthony took the criticism in stride, observing that "there never was a young woman yet" who did not think "if she had had the management of the work from the beginning, the cause would have been carried long ago." She chuckled, "I felt just so when I was young." The NAWSA leader set up an organization committee, named Catt to lead it, and gave her a generous $5,000 budget. Over five years, however, the momentum generated by the committee threatened the NAWSA board. It dissolved Catt's committee in a meeting following her triumphant 1900 election as Anthony's successor. Catt later wrote that she "cried for three hours" after that meeting and considered resigning.[2]

She did not resign but redoubled her efforts to mold NAWSA into an efficient machine. The old guard checked but failed to stall her. During these same years, she helped found and assumed the presidency of the International Woman Suffrage Alliance (IWSA). In 1904, she left the NAWSA presidency, ostensibly to rest and care for her seriously ill husband, but also frustrated by continuing resistance to her efforts. After her husband's death, Catt threw her energies into international work and founded the Woman Suffrage Party to spur political organizing in New York City. She believed suffragists could be *in* but not *of* politics by remaining nonpartisan and decorous.[3]

By late 1913, the fifty-four-year-old Catt began to turn her attention to federal work. She returned in September from a trip abroad proclaiming, "We want a Congressional amendment." She had no compunction about publicly exploiting nativist and racist fears to further her goals. For example, she opined, "It is time the Daughters of the American Revolution stopped going down on their knees to the refuse of Europe and asking for the vote." Mrs. Catt furthered her ambitions by heading up the controversial overhaul of the NAWSA constitution,[4] recognizing that Anna Shaw's shaky presidency could not resist too many more challenges. She had not counted on an equally ambitious competitor.

As Carrie Chapman Catt stood up amid the hundreds of behatted 1913 Convention delegates in the Masonic Hall in Washington, DC, she tread lightly and in the name of unity while, for her own purposes, she inserted a dangerous note into the discussion. She stomped down the CC/CU much as the National's board once stomped down her own organization committee. She first carefully stated her admiration and appreciation for the CC's important work. Why did NAWSA not fund their own committee's efforts, she wondered. Now, the CC and CU, nearly a single entity, seemed in essence a competing national organization. "The question arises," Catt interposed, "to which society are we to owe loyalty?" Her astonishing query—the infant Congressional Union rivaling the decades-old NAWSA?—slyly inserted the notion of defiance where only difference existed before.[5]

Supporters had forewarned Alice about fiscal criticism, but the source of the ambush startled her. She knew Mrs. Catt only slightly and pondered the root of Catt's apparent animosity. Unlike Shaw, Catt was clearly formidable, not a woman she and Lucy could manipulate. On the one hand, Catt put her finger on the operational weaknesses of the CC/CU arrangement with NAWSA. Alice had inadvertently opened the door to Catt's objections herself, by portraying the work of the CC and CU as hopelessly intertwined. On the other hand, Catt urged attention to the federal work. That had to be a good thing.[6]

Catt simply wanted unity, she claimed; nevertheless, she more than anyone stood to benefit if criticism overwhelmed Shaw and Alice Paul. Catt made the case for suffragists "to do our work under the direction of one Association." Everyone understood which association she meant. Elucidating the relationship of the CC and the CU seemed essential to clearing the way for the federal work, she thought. "May we have these questions answered," she concluded sweetly, "in order that we may not criticize each other and not find fault but so we may get together on one unified program that is going to carry us to success."[7]

As Catt reclaimed her seat, Jane Addams rose to defend the effort she herself had helped launch. She recalled the initial arrangement: the NAWSA board agreed to appoint Alice; Lucy and Alice agreed to raise their own operating funds. They "honorably filled their pledge," in Addams's mind. She dismissed confusion between the CC and the CU, focusing more on ends than means. She went on, "If this Committee is a committee of the National Association, the National *is* doing this work because this committee is giving its entire attention, its entire time to one thing." No one on NAWSA's board had either the time or "any such political acumen as they have displayed."[8]

Anna Howard Shaw quickly backpedaled, disclaiming any responsibility. She insisted from the dais, "We, of course, had not the remotest idea in the world what this Committee was going to do." Despite her approval of both CC and CU

activities over the past year, "the National Officers," she contended, "do not wish
to be blamed for things which they have not done."⁹

The powerful Catt's intervention brought the simmer between NAWSA and
the CC/CU to a boil. Ultimately, the delegates approved Alice's report and Catt's
subsequent motion that the CC and NAWSA cooperate in removing "all causes
of embarrassment," particularly the confusing finances.¹⁰

Ovation notwithstanding, Alice was not accustomed to public rebuke. The
one-two punch of reproach and fatigue coupled with an incipient cold finally
overwhelmed her; she took to her bed after the convention adjourned. She was
no more pleased than Catt to bump into an unexpected roadblock. Moreover,
she resented NAWSA's ungrateful attitude and would continue to resent it for
the rest of her life. Her unstinting work for the past year, she lamented decades
later, "had been a pretty big personal expense to my family and to me, as well as
taking every moment of your time and your strength and everything else." Now
Catt had entered the picture, apparently ready to charge for the amendment, but
at the same time challenging the existence of the CC/CU.¹¹

In the aftermath of the convention, Catt's query, "To which society are we to
owe loyalty?," stuck in Anna Howard Shaw's mind. Though NAWSA conventions now routinely challenged her decade-old presidency, she no doubt found
the idea that suffragists might shift their allegiance from the heretofore unrivalled
NAWSA to the upstart Congressional Union downright alarming. Shaw often
perceived threats; defensiveness about her administrative weaknesses quickly
mutated into suspicion over any difference of opinion. At sixty-six, she clung to
the top spot, driven by pride and a sense of duty to Anthony, her mentor. Once
passed over by Anthony for Catt, Shaw felt the latter's implied criticism keenly.
Still, Catt's harping on efficiency proved less dangerous than the Pankhursts
turned out to be.¹²

Shaw had long feared the Pankhursts poisoning American hopes for the
vote. Newspaper editors persisted in placing stories about the British militants
alongside those about NAWSA's work, relentlessly driving home the association
in the minds of American readers. Even the *Woman's Journal* contributed to the
problem, running frequent articles about the Pankhursts' activities, even as their
violent acts escalated. Veterans of the cause labored for years to craft a respectable
image for woman suffrage. They had long believed, like Shaw, that "no woman in
public life [could] afford to make herself conspicuous by an eccentricity of dress
and appearance. If she does so she suffers for it herself, which may *not* disturb her,
and to a greater degree, for the cause she represents, which *should* disturb her."¹³

Feeling an existential threat, Shaw moved to resolve the controversy over the
Congressional Committee and Congressional Union. She first tried to hold the
CC more firmly under NAWSA's control. Second, she sought to keep the CU

from active organizing in the states. It seems doubtful in hindsight that the ineffectual NAWSA board could authoritatively implement either of these objectives.
Nevertheless, they held a series of meetings toward those ends. As these forays
yielded only frustration, Shaw turned to the press to meet her needs, launching a
propaganda campaign to warn suffragists off the CU and away from Alice Paul.[14]

Contrary to accounts that suggest that Alice quickly broke with NAWSA,
both sides initially believed they could still work together and only reluctantly
abandoned their hopes. Shaw and the National's board sought more control;
Alice and Lucy realized that the NAWSA brand gave them needed entrée.

After a post-convention meeting failed to resolve the issues, the board summoned Alice and Lucy to New York. AP still felt so spent that Lucy appeared
alone at the December 9 meeting (one absent their advocate Jane Addams). She
rejected board proposals to assert control over the Congressional Union, since
the Union's independence was its raison d'être. Board members further decided
that the CC and CU chairmen could not be the same person. They offered the
Congressional Committee chair to Lucy—if she would resign from the Union—
and continued CC membership to Alice. After conferring with AP, Lucy declined
the CC chair, though both she and Alice agreed to continue as members. Neither
would give up their creation, the Congressional Union. Lucy wrote Shaw to offer
an olive branch: the CU could still work with a new CC chair. "I believe we could
do our work in your name without damage to the reputation" of NAWSA, she
wrote optimistically.[15]

Alice's health continued to be shaky, although she worked until mid-December
trying to resolve NAWSA's questions about CC/CU finances. "The Press says
that you have had a collapse," one longtime suffragist wrote her. "How well
I know what it is to work hard and be censured at the same time." *Suffragist* editor Rheta Dorr picked up a *Washington Star* while traveling in Paris and read
of "the breakdown I feared for Miss Paul." Dora Lewis repeatedly urged Alice
to join her in Philadelphia, where the older woman wished to supervise her rest
for a few days before AP went home for the holidays. "Your welcome is waiting," she wrote fondly. Alice first prepared independent financial reports for both
the Congressional Committee and the Union and submitted them to NAWSA
before boarding the train for Philadelphia.[16]

Lucy's peace overture failed to mollify Anna Howard Shaw, who had warmed
to the idea that the CC/CU arrangement was completely unacceptable because
of the Union's overreaching. Shaw revisited her earlier opposition to the Union
organizing state chapters. Shaw wrote the NAWSA board, "It would undermine all
existing State societies, take from them every incentive to do active Congressional
work, and build up a barrier between them and the National Association, which
it would be impossible for us to explain away." She had received complaints about

CU persistence over the objections of state suffrage officials. No organization had ever attempted to challenge NAWSA as a national presence, despite the fact that many cities, states, and regions accommodated multiple overlapping suffrage societies. The depth of Shaw's ire suggests that she now believed the Congressional Union challenge to NAWSA genuine.[17]

Shaw resolved to name a new Congressional Committee chairman who she hoped could, along with NAWSA leaders, ride herd on the CU enough to curb its state overtures. She soon identified Illinois resident Ruth Hanna McCormick, the mastermind behind NAWSA's impromptu delegation to the White House. The thirty-three-year-old daughter of the late political lobbyist Mark Hanna was also active in the Progressive Party and on the Illinois state suffrage campaign. She grew up in the political and social milieu of Washington, accustomed to easy access to the White House. Shaw declared McCormick ideal for the work. "I have great confidence in her ability," Shaw added, "to cooperate with Miss Paul and Miss Burns in such a way as to not antagonize them, and to keep their friendship."[18]

Shaw came under pressure from Washington members of the CC/CU. Parade committee chair Marie Forrest wrote Shaw of her "love and respect" for both Lucy and Alice. Lucy's tact and organizational abilities balanced AP's detail orientation and charisma, she said. Another early Washington recruit told Shaw, "It would seem a calamity if she [Alice] can not come back." "She has interested all classes," Abby Scott Baker gushed. "Miss Paul has roused deep personal loyalty in many hearts."[19]

Both sides soon lost the battle to keep suffrage dissension under wraps. In the weeks since the convention, AP and Shaw had tamped down the rumors of intramovement conflict that were turning up in a few papers. By late December, however, a misleading wire story blared: "Suffrage Mutiny over Money"; the article went on to state that Alice refused to account for CC funds. Shaw immediately corrected the press account and contacted Lucy about stopping the story. "Let it be known," she urged, "that the Congressional Union will no more stand for misrepresentation of the National Association than will Headquarters stand for misrepresentation of the Congressional Union." For once, the two factions agreed. Lucy already knew about the article. She located the reporter, who agreed to send off another story emphasizing both groups' intent to "work together in perfect harmony."[20]

Unfortunately, Alice—resting in Philadelphia—read the first article and refused to sit still for a public swipe at her probity, a bedrock value for Quakers. She immediately caught a train to New York and showed up at NAWSA headquarters with Mary Beard in tow. Angrily, she told Mary Dennett that the National was attacking her integrity after she "worked herself to death" for it. She declared heatedly that neither she nor Lucy would continue on the Congressional

Committee. NAWSA's professed innocence about the news story hardly mattered: the damage was done. The incident deepened AP's resentment.[21]

In the midst of the contention, an important ally emerged. Harriot Blatch joined the Congressional Union, even while prioritizing the New York work. She had recently affirmed her own independence from Mrs. Catt's organizing efforts in New York. She felt moved to bolster Alice and Lucy's resolve, writing AP, "Again and again I have seen vigorous young women come forward, only to be rapped on the head by the so-called leaders of our movement." She blamed NAWSA: "The National ought to have known that it either must back you financially or choke you at birth." She felt confident "you will both come out on top."[22]

Other supporters also saw the dispute in generational terms. Mary Beard, thirty-seven, had already written Alice that "the Union is winning its way to the attention of the more intelligent young women," and of the New York awareness of "the danger of siding with old fogeys." Shaw knew of the old fogey gibes and routinely met them by contrasting veterans' steadfast work with youthful impulsiveness. Twenty-one-year-old Doris Stevens, about to sign on as an organizer, wrote Lucy with swagger, "I dare say you and Miss Paul even now have a most level-headed and far-reaching scheme to outwit the Dear Ladies."[23]

NAWSA stalwarts expressed bravado as well as irritation. After further meetings in late December, Ruth McCormick puffed to Shaw about Alice and Lucy as "hot-headed young people" (actually, McCormick was a year younger than Lucy). The new CC chair was "surprised to find how weak they are in many ways, and I do not think it would take us many weeks to crush them out completely." McCormick's bluster failed to persuade Mary Dennett, who now believed that over the past year Alice "put the Union to the front and chloroformed the National."[24]

Shaw's determination to gain the upper hand became the sticking point in the continuing negotiations. NAWSA insisted on having the last word over the Congressional Union's policies and disposition of funds. Alice reportedly called the terms "not co-operation but slavery." She and Lucy balked at giving up CU independence. Still, they both thought talks were ongoing until January 3, when McCormick told the press that the two groups, while amicable, had severed all formal connections.[25]

Despite her insistence on independence, Alice feared becoming irrelevant. Dora Lewis counseled her to bypass McCormick and make a direct appeal to the NAWSA board. Toward that end, Alice began to line up influential and wealthy supporters and prepared for the first annual meeting of the Congressional Union. "If we have an extremely successful meeting and raise several thousand dollars," she wrote Lewis uneasily, "the National will realize that we are not dead, and will probably be willing to make some more possible proposition to us than that suggested by Mrs. McCormick." Money conferred power. "If we can only raise about ten or twelve thousand dollars," she believed, "they would probably be ready to agree to anything we propose." She felt determined to convince the board to maintain the CC/CU connection. "Everything depends on whether we go to them as a very weak society which has been entirely knocked out, as Dr. Shaw seems to think," she wrote, "or as a strong society with a big fund which has nothing to fear from them."[26]

She reached out to like-minded suffragists, using shared admiration for the Pankhursts to create alliances. Like the Pankhursts, Alice had at first recognized how social prestige offered leverage and realized later how much time and effort large donors could save her. She now drew on her relationship with Maryland's premier suffragist, Edith Houghton Hooker, spending a weekend at the Hooker home. A short time later, Mrs. Hooker and Alice met with Mary Beard (who had connections rather than wealth), Dora Lewis, and Hooker's wealthy sister Katharine Houghton Hepburn, a Connecticut powerhouse. This group provided ongoing financial and advisory support to the Congressional Union. In addition, Alice renewed communications with the moneyed but cantankerous Alva Vanderbilt Belmont.[27]

The wooing of Belmont, begun a year earlier, gathered urgency as the NAWSA dispute deepened. Mrs. Belmont took up suffrage work in 1908, after the death of her second husband. Already a fixture in the New York press because of her lavish entertaining and shocking divorce, she quickly became a force in suffrage circles. She underwrote NAWSA's New York headquarters, founded her own suffrage advocacy group, and financed a variety of similar endeavors, including Harriot Blatch's organization. Like the others in AP's advisory group, Belmont liked the Pankhursts and admired Alice's efforts, though attempts to involve Belmont with the 1913 parade had fizzled. Nonetheless, she agreed with Alice about the importance of the federal amendment work and had tried in vain at the convention to persuade NAWSA to move its headquarters to Washington.[28]

Alice knew the risk of an alliance. Many compared the short and squat Alva Belmont to a bulldog. Still strong willed and energetic at sixty, she liked having her own way, not unlike the woman courting her. AP's envoys to Belmont disagreed on the wisdom of collaboration. Hepburn warned Alice against including Belmont on the CU executive committee as "she is in the habit of running things absolutely" and "enjoys eternally fussing about details." Belmont's frustration with the National meant she would eventually give money anyway. After Mary Beard visited the socialite, she thought that "Mrs. Belmont is justified in not wanting to be considered merely a money bag; but she says she does not intend to interfere with you—only she wants to be asked for her opinion now and then just to be a human being." Alice hoped in vain for a substantial pledge from Belmont to announce at the annual meeting; however, Belmont wanted to meet Alice before she took out her checkbook. Reluctant to leave Washington before the big event, AP settled for a parley at a later date.[29]

Alice's anxiety about the January 11 annual meeting contrasted with Lucy's self-assurance. In letters to confidantes shortly beforehand, the two leaders considered the possible rupture with NAWSA. Lucy seemed sanguine, writing her sister breezily, "We want to show the dear old National how firmly we can stand alone." She thought the Union could raise monies "just as well without the halo of their name as with it." Alice, the chief fundraiser, approached significant change more cautiously. "I feel that our whole future depends largely upon this meeting," she wrote Lewis.[30]

No wonder Alice resisted breaking from NAWSA. The Congressional Union looked different without the National's backing. Almost all CU members had joined while NAWSA accepted the Union; many also held NAWSA cards. If the National disowned them, how many CU members would follow suit? Alice had never truly forged out on her own and built a completely independent entity: could the CU survive without NAWSA? Her ambition notwithstanding, she shrank before this unknown, especially since she remembered that the nineteenth-century discord among suffragists resulted in two rival organizations that accomplished little for decades—a chilling prospect. Thus the continuing need to do everything possible to maintain relations with the National.

The first annual meeting of the Congressional Union exemplified Alice's skill at masking hard-nosed political content in socially acceptable garb. She believed in propriety, as did Dr. Shaw but, like Emmeline Pankhurst, she also recognized its protective quality. She had used the socially prominent to build credibility for the March procession; now she depended on them to lend stature to the CU. On the afternoon of January 11, 1914, coincidentally AP's twenty-ninth birthday, designated Union ushers greeted hundreds of members arriving at the commodious home of early supporter Elizabeth Kent. The event had the air of a society fete, conveying the hoped-for sense of decorum, and the many illustrious attendees signified the integrity of the endeavor.[31]

Alice realized her hopes for an impressive showing. She recognized the need at this crucial juncture to inspire confidence in the Union's ability to forge onward and chose to do most of the talking, perhaps wary that Lucy's blitheness would send the wrong message. Her own haggard appearance likely brought to mind what one supporter termed "the self-obliteration and self-forgetfulness necessary in this work." She reiterated her plan, already announced in *The Suffragist*, to pressure the Democrats into passing the suffrage amendment. Still hopeful of a working alliance with NAWSA, she mentioned the new Congressional Committee, adding that the former CC would continue as the Congressional Union's executive committee. And the fundraising appeal, according to *The Suffragist*, raised more than $9,000 in pledges.[32]

The true fault lines in the dispute between the organizations were laid bare after Anna Howard Shaw learned of the meeting. She heard that Alice failed to differentiate the new CC from the Union. Even worse, the CU leader planned a political attack on the Democrats, by Shaw's lights a blatantly partisan and militant strategy running counter to everything NAWSA stood for. Despite her vow two weeks earlier not to publicly misrepresent the CU, Shaw exacerbated the situation. She hastened to Washington to take charge and gave a widely quoted interview accusing Union leaders of being "militant" and "un-American." In thrall to the Pankhursts, they knew "nothing of American politics," she insisted, and "are not national in spirit or in their work."[33]

Shaw's remarks exposed NAWSA fears about the Pankhursts infecting the American suffrage movement with partisan politics and improprieties. Furthermore, she labeled the CU undemocratic, with "self-appointed leaders, who allow neither voting nor criticism by their members." She knew the accusation would hit home with NAWSA's famously democratic members, though it also revealed insecurity about her own power. Worst of all, she stated, Alice and Lucy had broadcast their militancy by declaring their intention to hold the party in power—the Democrats—responsible for passing the suffrage amendment. NAWSA stood proudly "nonpartisan," Shaw proclaimed, "and we shall always help our friends."[34]

Predictably, press coverage increased after Shaw's interview, as journalists hastened to affirm the cultural cliché that women were incapable of getting along. Headlines declaring "Suffragists Clash" and "Suffragist Rivals" began to appear in major newspapers after Ruth McCormick's January 3 statement of dissociation. Even more articles blaring "Suffs Swap Hard Names" and "Suffrage Battle On" followed Shaw's remarks. The unity given such visibility in the March 1913 procession appeared to be shattering, to the advantage of those who opposed women winning the vote.[35]

Alice still feared estrangement from NAWSA. She had left Washington before Shaw arrived, stopping off with Lewis in Philadelphia before heading home for a long rest. All three women knew that Shaw opposed giving AP a hearing before the National's board; in issuing the "un-American" swipe, she seemed to be trying to sabotage any further appeal. In addition, Shaw sent Lewis a news article which claimed AP called the NAWSA leader a "dear old lady." No doubt at Lewis's suggestion, Alice replied to Shaw, denying that she had belittled her. She pointedly added that neither she nor anyone in the Union office had responded to "the criticisms of us made by you." Indeed, she maintained a policy of refusing to disparage other women in the press. Nevertheless, she wrote, "We all regret deeply your hostility toward us." Her closing seems disingenuous—"We are utterly at [a] loss to understand what we have done"—yet genuinely forlorn. She wished "that you were willing to let us work for you this year as we did last instead of compelling us to work apart from you."[36]

Shaw's horror at the proposed tactics of the Congressional Union reinvigorated her opposition. Alice's intent became a vehicle for Shaw to brand the CU as extreme. The January 1914 interview seeded the notion of the Union's militancy and AP's autocratic rule in the historical record. Of course, Shaw's concern was the immediate impact, not the historical footprint.

Shaw seized an opportunity to permanently sanction the Congressional Union. She issued a press release that denied reports of dissension and added that the Union "is not at a moment even a member [of NAWSA]." Indeed, in the wake of the convention's constitutional changes with regard to membership costs, Alice withdrew the CU as an affiliate in order to apply for a lower-cost auxiliary status. Shaw then all but rejected the new application. She encouraged members of the NAWSA executive council, composed of all state association presidents, to deny auxiliary status to the CU, because it was "trying to make itself a National organization" by organizing independently in states and adopting a partisan policy. "Any State or local society may work in the interests of conditions which are purely local, which might be contrary to the general policy of the national Association," Shaw maintained, "but a National auxiliary association, working against [NAWSA] policies and principle, involves the whole National body."[37]

Ruth McCormick underscored Shaw's preemptory excommunication of the Union, doing her best to nail the door shut. She told the press that Alice set suffrage back "at least ten years." She echoed Shaw's knock that the CU was "militant clean through" and knew nothing about politics in America. She then took the dispute to new heights, writing President Wilson an open letter that condemned the Congressional Union. NAWSA would "oppose no party as a whole," McCormick assured Wilson, "fearing lest this small group of suffragists acting under un-American and militant methods prejudice our cause."[38]

Despite the now-public censure, Alice refused to give up. She left Moorestown and headed north with Dora Lewis, determined to collect more money and support, dismissing urgings that she needed a prolonged rest. She spoke at length with Alva Belmont and, a few days later, received $5,000 and a strong endorsement. Alice felt "deeply grateful," she wrote from Boston. "Never in our wildest dreams had [we] dared to hope for such a generous contribution from anyone." For her part, Belmont became so inspired after meeting Alice that she soon raised another $1,100 from wealthy friends. It was an auspicious beginning to a relationship that ended only with Belmont's death in 1933.[39]

Alice remained persuasive on the stump, though she could not escape the acrimony. She and Dora Lewis visited CU chapters in New York, Connecticut, and Massachusetts. Everywhere, she wrote Lucy, someone from NAWSA preceded them and "prejudiced [the groups] against us," making it difficult to raise money or gain approval for coming demonstrations. Alice fretted that "people are waiting to see whether we go to smash or make good, before deciding whether or not to help us." Nevertheless, one supporter wrote Mrs. Belmont from Boston, "Miss Paul made a fine impression," and Katharine Houghton Hepburn reported to Doris Stevens that "as usual," Alice "got what she wanted." AP contented herself with implicit criticism of NAWSA. She emphasized the CU's up-to-date approach to a *Boston Journal* reporter. "We are going to try a little action," she said, echoing the Pankhurst's motto, "Deeds, not words."[40]

As Alice traveled, Union friends within the NAWSA executive council tried to sway the vote on the CU's auxiliary status. Katharine Hepburn sent out a long letter to all state presidents, reviewing the situation point by point, concluding that the Union should be "enthusiastically welcomed" as a NAWSA auxiliary. Ohio leader Harriet Taylor Upton wrote Belmont, "Letters are pouring in here begging me to vote for the reinstating of the Congressional Union. These are unnecessary for I so voted immediately." The dispute seemed all about "personal feeling," in Upton's view. Belmont was roused to action. She passed a supportive resolution through her own suffrage group; she also wrote National officials protesting their treatment of the Union.[41]

Bowing to such weighty support, the NAWSA board agreed to give Alice a new, but very brief, hearing on February 12. Anna Howard Shaw stood dead set against the hearing, telling McCormick, "I would not believe a word Miss Paul said." Shaw now viewed herself as a Christlike figure, histrionically comparing her situation to "the betrayal by Judas Iscariot." She was somewhat reconciled because the crucifixion "only added to the progress of the cause for which He died."[42]

Trusted friends and colleagues buoyed Alice up for the coming summit. Dora Lewis advised her at length about her preparations. The entire original Congressional Committee plus Katharine Hepburn agreed to attend. Shortly before leaving for New York, Alice received a cheering note from her erstwhile Penn roommate, Carrie Gauthier, saying, "I have admired the way you have weathered the storm, and still float on top. You are great, Alice."[43]

On February 12, Alice and Lucy faced off against the National's board. The two factions managed to agree on supporting a nationwide demonstration in May, but the encounter mostly hardened their divisions. The confrontation centered on three points: the CU's supposed partisanship, the accusations that AP had misappropriated funds, and public criticism of the Union in a broad sense.

Alice Paul and Anna Howard Shaw called the shots, with Lucy Burns and Ruth McCormick as seconds. The discussion exposed board misunderstandings about the Union's election policy but did not alter their opposition to it. Alice gained some ground when the board agreed to document that NAWSA did not question her integrity with regard to CC finances. On the final point of press cavil, both sides felt abused. Exasperated, Alice finally snapped, "Is the National going to take the position that its first duty is to kill the Union?" Shaw's response exposed how much Mrs. Catt's query about loyalty had rattled her. NAWSA's 100,000 members notwithstanding, Shaw shot back, "We do not intend to let the Congressional Union kill us."[44]

The failure of the summit generated regret on both sides. The NAWSA executive council punctuated the sense of finality by voting against auxiliary status for the Congressional Union, 24–54. Even Mary Dennett seemed unsure that the rupture was necessary. "I am exceedingly sorry," she wrote Alice after the vote, "that the policy of the Union has been such as to exclude it from the National Association." Indeed, board member Louise Bowen later wrote, "I always felt that [AP's] interest and her ability should have been retained." Union stalwart Mary Beard blamed Shaw for the mess. "Isn't it sad to see her end her life of struggle with hatred gleaming out of her aged eyes?" she wrote Lucy. "She doesn't know how to hold together the things she has spent forty years in building up and because she can't take the next step necessary to its growth." For her part, Alice felt simply defeated. She wrote Hepburn dejectedly, "I am afraid we made absolutely no impression on the board." Another Alice, reformer and Hull House resident Alice Hamilton, distant from the fray, wrote her sister, "There is a terrible mix up between the Congressional Union and the National Suffrage Board and everybody says the latter bungled most stupidly."[45]

Anna Howard Shaw's insecurities, further provoked by Catt, led her to construct Alice as a demagogue who was leading good suffragists astray. Shaw's paranoia was confirmed during the convention by a report that claimed Alice was stirring up trouble with her comments to journalists and other NAWSA members. AP's professed interest in unity, according to Shaw, "was the kind of desire which the lion has for the lamb, when the lion is perfectly willing to unite with the lamb, provided the lamb resides inside of it."[46]

Even so, resolution looked possible until Shaw brought the underlying tension about militancy to the fore. Her personal fears tapped into National stalwarts' fear of returning to fringe status, outside the accepted realm of womanliness, whether as eccentrics or as militants. Either way, personal reputations could be spoiled or the suffrage cause damaged. They failed to imagine other possibilities, particularly with the specter before them of the British and American public turning away from the Pankhursts in dismay.

Alice and the minority siding with the Union, younger women thinking suffrage history began with them, failed to grasp the extent of NAWSA's fears. Like all conflicts, however, the leaders of NAWSA and the Congressional Union clashed more than their followers did. AP later remembered, "Most of the people of course didn't sever their relations with the old National. They just belonged to both." As did Alice herself.[47]

In the end, NAWSA lost more than the Union did. While the debate over the conflict energized the membership, the National's leaders felt forced by the CU's continued visibility to spend time dissociating themselves publicly and policing their members privately. Women distressed by the infighting tended to blame Shaw, weakening her presidency even more. Though Alice Paul's cautious nature resisted the break, she realized after the summit that the organizing and fundraising intended to convince the National of the CU's worthiness had strengthened the Union as an independent force.

"A Great Body of Voting Women"

ALICE PAUL HAD not set out to be a suffrage outsider, but her work with the Pankhursts and her Quaker heritage burnished her ability to confront her situation. Once fully independent of NAWSA, she had free rein to exercise her more malleable senses of propriety and nonpartisanship. Her supporters among the privileged classes became a defense against the stigma now associated with the Congressional Union. Nevertheless, repercussions from the discord between NAWSA and the CU seeped into nearly every facet of the Union's activism. Confident now of her independent course, she managed the NAWSA fallout, dissent within Union ranks, and her own health problems. By the end of 1914, the CU emerged with an influence belying its size. Instead of "going to smash," Alice staged a bold fall campaign against the controlling party in Congress that rooted the Congressional Union firmly in the suffrage landscape.

Her decision to oppose the Democrats, often misunderstood as an unrealistic attempt to build a women's voting bloc, was in fact an effort to control the balance of power, though in later years it became a different sort of political exercise. However, just as Alice failed to see the NAWSA dispute coming, she also badly misjudged the National leaders' response to the Congressional Union's election policy. Anna Howard Shaw capitalized on AP's failing, painting her as dangerous and successfully banishing the Union from NAWSA. Even many in the CU struggled to understand the election policy, forcing Alice to spend much of 1914 explaining her intent to her own membership.

Alice believed she clearly communicated the nonpartisan election policy early on. In the premiere editorial of *The Suffragist*, she argued for moving suffrage from propaganda to "purely a political issue. We hope to convince the Democratic Party, now in power, that [suffrage] is the next great issue to be dealt with in Congress." Nonetheless, she maintained, "That does not mean that suffrage is a partisan measure. It is distinctly non-partisan. We call upon the Democratic Party simply because it happens at the present time to be the governing party." Alice reiterated her strategy after Woodrow Wilson insisted that he could not endorse woman suffrage ahead of his party. The president, she wrote, "puts the whole question of Federal legislation for Woman Suffrage directly up to the Democratic Party in Congress." According to AP, Wilson himself routinely pressured his own party. No naysayers came forth while the discussion focused vaguely on persuasion.[1]

NAWSA's censure rained down only after Alice clarified that persuasion meant opposition campaigning, a practice wholly unknown in the American suffrage community. At the January 11 CU meeting, she put the Democratic Party on notice, declaring her intention to campaign against its candidates, no matter their suffrage position, in the November congressional elections. She softened her proposal by encouraging the Democrats to pass the suffrage amendment before the campaign season and render her plans unnecessary. The press promptly reported "Suffragists on Warpath" and "Women Make Threat," and Shaw proclaimed the Union ignorant of American politics.[2]

Shaw meant that the American political system was unsuited for an opposition campaign like that the Pankhursts conducted against the governing party of Britain. In that nation, the political party with the greatest strength in the House of Commons forms a government and appoints ministers. A vote of no confidence can remove that ruling government at any time. In the United States, by contrast, the candidate of one political party might win the presidency but face another party's control of one or both houses of Congress. Thus, political parties seldom wielded such decisive power as in Britain.

Nevertheless, in 1914, the Democratic Party held the presidency and majorities in both houses of Congress, which gave the party extraordinary power. Democratic loyalists had thus far passed every bill President Wilson advocated. Furthermore, campaigning against suffrage allies in the party as well as foes was paramount to the success of the CU's election policy. If the CU exempted allies, those pro-suffrage congressmen would incur the wrath of their party and lose any leverage they had. So the only way the election policy worked was to campaign against the entire party.

Alice underestimated the backlash against an approach that struck many as baldly partisan, despite her insistence that a recalcitrant Republican majority in Congress would warrant the same treatment. For decades, suffragists who entered the political arena had practiced nonpartisanship, happily allying themselves with pro-suffrage politicians of any and all camps. Since politics was considered a dirty business, suffragists bolstered the womanly propriety of their public image by avoiding the mud of the partisan fray, thereby thwarting those who argued that partisan politics would besmirch women, rendering them unfeminine. Older women like Shaw remembered how NAWSA's brief 1890s alliance with the Populists helped Idaho and Colorado women win the vote; however, the Populists soon faded nationally and anti-suffrage forces used the left-leaning association to frame suffrage as a radical cause.[3]

Though opponents begged to differ, some supporters thought the CU's controversial plan vindicated when in mid-January, the Democratic-controlled House Rules Committee voted against creating a committee on woman suffrage. "Certainly, the 'party government' thesis has gained support since the vote," Mary Beard wrote Alice confidently, "even the blindest must now see the accuracy of the Union's diagnosis." Beard took on the task of persuading New Yorkers, including AP's settlement house mentor Lavinia Dock and the usually cutting-edge Harriot Stanton Blatch.[4]

A stream of letters decried the adversarial policy. "Is it true," asked Ohio's Harriet Taylor Upton, that the CU wanted to defeat Democrats "whether they are suffragists or not? If the Congressional Union carries out this plan in Ohio we simply are ruined." A District resident and Nebraska native tendered her resignation, believing it "a grave error to defy and antagonize the democratic party." Two prominent Washington men expected as speakers at an event backed out, concerned about perceptions that they sanctioned a controversial organization.[5]

Some suffragists understood placing responsibility on the controlling party's doorstep. Mary Beard and Alva Belmont grasped the idea right away. Kansas voter and journalist Lilla Day Monroe felt gratified that "some young women who understand politics are to be in the work." One admirer of Mrs. Pankhurst wrote from Minneapolis, "Your attitude in regard to the Democratic Party is much misunderstood here," and ordered fifty copies of *The Suffragist* discussion on the issue. Minds changed, particularly when they realized the CU planned to target only a few swing districts. Mary Beard crowed that she "got them all" after a Q and A with Blatch's Women's Political Union.[6]

The *Woman's Journal* aired the controversy. Katharine Hepburn defended the plan in two letters to the editor. Dr. Shaw responded with her own letter disparaging the purported nonpartisanship. The following week, Lucy explained the Union's plan at length. "The point of difference between the policy of the National Association and the Congressional Union," she maintained, "is that they hold individual Congressmen of all parties responsible for the passage of the Federal Amendment; we hold the party in power responsible."[7]

Mainstream newspapers entered the fray, recording and furthering the new-found prominence of suffrage as a national issue. Some presented both sides of the debate without editorial comment. Others took sides. A *Roanoke Times* editorial warned of the "danger of bringing women into the sphere of politics." On the other hand, *Washington Times* editor Judson Welliver, a prominent Progressive, came to the CU's defense, contrasting "ladies who are willing to fight for what they want" with those finding "such a political purpose is unduly partisan." Welliver believed the new Democratic majority in both houses made every issue, including woman suffrage, a political-party question. "The Congressional

Union ladies," he wrote, "have the argument all on their side." Welliver derided the sexism at the core of the debate. The alternative to party politics, he opined, was to "smile and simper their way to victory in this fight. They will do that about the time Gibraltar is captured with a confetti assault."[8]

When both Alice's and Lucy's efforts to clarify the election policy went for naught, they decided to downplay the plan until the fall. Over and over again, they pointed out that any party blocking suffrage would receive the same treatment. They insisted in vain, "We do not offend politicians when we press them energetically for action." By late January, Lucy began to backpedal, writing that the CU really held "no policy whatever toward any party" until they assessed the political situation in the fall. After the mid-February summit with NAWSA, Alice advised her new publicity chair, Jessie Stubbs, against further alienating people by discussing the election policy. She wrote, "I think that we have threatened enough now and do not want to say another word on this subject until somewhere near the time for putting our threats into operation." For now, at least, they put the Democrats on notice. "Have you even seen anything so delicious in your life," Stubbs wrote a friend, as "the Democratic party sitting up and taking notice of the woman suffrage movement?"[9]

Indeed, the Democratic Party attempted to dodge the prospect of Union attacks. Lucy headed the CU effort to convince the House Democratic Caucus to take up the question of a suffrage committee after the Rules Committee refused the task, though she believed the measure doomed. In fact, the caucus chose to vote instead on a substitute motion. "By a vote of 124 to 56," *The Suffragist* reported, the caucus decided that the states, not Congress, needed to act on woman suffrage. In other words, most House Democrats wanted to turn back the clock to the time before the Congressional Union, Lucy Burns, and Alice Paul. They preferred NAWSA's usual approach, which expected little of Congress and everything from the states.[10]

While the *New York Times* thought the Democrats' action "sounded the death knell" for suffrage in the current Congress, sounds of glee emanated from the CU offices on F Street. The Union had trapped the Democrats into voicing their hostility to votes for women. In *The Suffragist*, Alice interpreted the "error" in the Democratic vote for her readers. "Any question affecting citizens of more than one State is a federal question," she asserted. "It is women's business to decide by what avenue they shall seek enfranchisement." Lucy reckoned privately that the caucus's hostile action only made winning a suffrage amendment easier. Indeed, the Democrats' public shifting of responsibility for suffrage laid the foundation for the Union's plan of attack.[11]

In mid-January, Alice finally yielded to coworkers' concerns about her health and agreed to a prolonged rest. Dora Lewis prodded until AP gave in. "Tell Miss

Paul," Lewis wrote one staffer, "I am looking for her hourly, and shall send a policeman after her if she does not come soon. That hospital bed is waiting for her, also my guest room." Alice stopped off with Lewis before continuing on to Moorestown.[12]

But she found setting aside her control difficult. Her idea of rest involved considerable work; lying in her childhood bed, she continued sending in material for *The Suffragist*, keeping up with correspondence and the bank balance and managing office minutiae via assistants. She fumed at her lack of control, not only over the work at the Union but over her own health as well. When AP received the January 17 *Suffragist* containing unexpected content, her frustration mounted. She wrote Stubbs, "I shall never forgive myself for having left Washington before [the paper] was out." Stubbs agreed to take over *Suffragist* preparation until the traveling Rheta Dorr reappeared, and Alice sent her five pages of handwritten notes about preparing the next issue. The next day, she changed her mind about moving to a hospital.[13]

On January 20, she boarded the train for New York and New England, to raise funds and drum up interest in May demonstrations. "I hope I can get enough to keep us going for awhile," she wrote the CU treasurer. Dora Lewis accompanied her, perhaps concerned about a mid-trip collapse. CU staffer Emily Perry urged, "Do not put [the hospital] off too long. You have done more than your share in raising funds, and now it is but fair that the rest of us should try." Undeterred, Alice knew that no one save Lucy had yet become a sure money-raiser. She gained Alva Belmont's support and, after success in Connecticut and Massachusetts, returned to Belmont's New York mansion for an overnight visit to thank her for the badly needed funds and no doubt discuss Belmont's future role.[14]

A photograph published during her visit to Boston makes abundantly clear why so many urged her to take time off: she looked painfully thin. The three-quarters head shot revealed her jutting cheekbones and sunken eyes, a truly cadaverous appearance. Alice insisted on pushing herself, refusing to acknowledge the changes to her post-prison health. Was disregard for her own well-being the subtext of her appeal? One staff member found in her "self-obliteration and self-forgetfulness," qualities all the more affecting in the wake of Emily Wilding Davison's death six months earlier. Alice reminded Bostonian Elizabeth Evans of one recently beatified martyr. She began calling Alice "Joan of Arc."[15]

While Alice traveled, Ruth McCormick, the new NAWSA Congressional Committee head, began encouraging CU defections. Shaw's and McCormick's public charges about the CU's undemocratic ways had already prompted a dozen resignations. A group of government workers sent a letter insisting, "We cannot belong to any organization in which we have no voice." McCormick inveigled another group of District members to protest formally. The dissidents, claiming more than fifty allies, asked for a constitution, elected officers, and member-approved policies.[16]

Alice recognized the need to address Shaw's and McCormick's charges. She knew that Emmeline Pankhurst had brushed off the same autocratic accusations, proclaiming the WSPU unhampered "by a complexity of rules." Likewise, AP wanted to avoid the "immense debating society" aspect of NAWSA and keep decision making centralized so the Congressional Union could respond rapidly to new opportunities. She therefore neatly parried her own dissenters, saying she welcomed "any better plan for organization" and suggested they devise one. She wondered, nonetheless, how the CU could bring in members coast to coast "without building up state organizations, which would run counter to the state organizations and the National Association. This, of course, we do not wish to do." Indeed, her plans called only for small teams of organizers in the states.[17]

Alice and Lucy were already mulling over a constitution and some sort of advisory council. Even within the inner circle, opinions differed. Katharine Hepburn hoped "that the particular kind of work that you people have to give won't be killed now you are getting all tied up in red tape." She told Alice to "say to people simply what Mrs. Pankhurst does." Hepburn's sister Edith, by contrast, became the most forceful advocate for representative governance at a mid-January meeting of executive committee members (Lucy called it a "fight") in Alice's absence. In a letter apprising AP of developments, Lucy reported Hooker's belief that "our system had already broken down." She added dryly, "I think she meant that the role of leadership demanded extraordinary qualities, which we did not possess in quite the necessary degree." Elizabeth Kent pleaded for a basic document as "a way of keeping good faith" with members. According to a disgusted Lucy, "the discussion used up two hours," with no resolution in sight, "after which we were all much depressed."[18]

Faced with ongoing and multifaceted opposition to CU policies, Alice felt the need to buoy up the Union image. "If we fail in anything now," she told Lucy anxiously from New York, "it will be particularly difficult to get outside help again." They agreed on a deputation of working women, the first, wrote Stevens, "to wait upon any president." Bringing in new faces always energized the press. Lucy contacted recognized advocates like the Women's Trade Union League's Mary Dreier (whom AP knew from NYSP) and her sister, Margaret Dreier Robins, in Chicago. Union workers and other tradeswomen had marched in the 1913 parade, but the deputation was AP's first attempt to target this constituency directly.[19]

Two factors complicated the organizing: class attitudes and the ripple effect of the dispute between NAWSA and the CU. "The National row is back of all my difficulty" raising money, wrote Beard. And Lucy's limited experience with working-class women showed. Margaret Robins educated her about the issue of expense for working women: "It does not only mean traveling expenses but the payment of wages lost for the days of absence for each working girl." Katharine Hepburn wrote from Hartford of the "almost impossible" task, since working women had "very little money to spend traveling about the country." Lucy quickly adjusted her expectations and sent out frantic calls for travel funds as well as eleventh-hour requests for DC supporters to offer free room and board. The obstacles were overcome and, on February 1, several hundred women from ten states boarded trains bound for Washington.[20]

Although Emmeline Pankhurst sent repeated WSPU deputations to the British prime minister, Alice believed that nominally independent delegations might carry more weight in the United States. So, after prominent labor activists such as Rose Schneiderman and Rose Winslow rallied the troops, Alice joined the spectators watching the women march down New York Avenue behind a brass band. The "Great Demand" banner, Old Glory, trade standards, and state banners added a festive note. Once the delegation was in the White House, the president listened courteously but reprised his December theme. He insisted he could speak only "for what my party has declared." After that, some workers refused to shake his hand.[21]

Alice publicly used the president's remarks to underscore the importance of holding the party in power accountable. The president stood "waiting for the verdict of his party on woman suffrage," she said. "Women must learn to go on agitating" until the party in power agreed to pass the amendment. Arthur Brisbane, editor of the *Chicago Evening American*, privately expressed a different view. Wilson, he wrote Alva Belmont, "pays not the slightest attention to his party or his platform unless he feels like it."[22]

The deputation and the press response boosted morale. Lengthy stories appeared on page one or two in the Washington and Philadelphia papers and page five of the *New York Times*. Some of the working women felt transformed by the experience. The Hartford organizer raved, "Our girls were thrilled by it. How much good it did in Washington, I don't know, but certainly 33 live wires have come back to Connecticut." Lucy wrote Mary Beard that the event "gave us an immense lift and has stopped for the time being any way, all gossip."[23]

After the failure of the New York summit with the NAWSA board, Alice finally acknowledged her physiological needs. The entreaties from coworkers point to the complexity of AP's persona: the sacrifices central to her drawing power allowed followers to see her as a leader and at the same time as vulnerable. One plea incorporated the dualism: "If you look around and measure up the forces in the field, you can see how ill we can spare you," wrote a Hartford supporter. "Therefore it is your duty to us all to take good care of yourself." Dora Lewis affectionately prodded, "When are you coming? Each morning I expect to find you in my bathroom scrubbing—& each morning I am disappointed." Alice finally went overnight to Lewis and then home for several days, continuing to work all the while. Staffer Emily Perry fretted, "I trust Miss Paul really gets to the hospital tomorrow," she wrote Lewis, "for she needs building up badly, and we do want her to be well and strong, as she means everything to the cause." Alice dutifully entered the Woman's Hospital of Philadelphia, a pioneering institution founded by Quakers and operated by women. She later conceded to Harriet Upton, "I suppose I must admit that I am really not well, as I am lying in a hospital bed."[24]

She submitted to hospital care but remained driven. Rest cures became popular decades earlier as a corrective for so-called nervous women; by 1914, suffragists and other reformers adapted the practice, which emphasized prolonged inactivity and hyper-nutrition, to alleviate exhaustion. As Lewis told Lucy, "I do believe she will be made over if we can keep her in bed & under care long enough." The motherly Lewis kept a close eye on the recalcitrant patient, visiting her daily. AP worked from her bed, exchanging a daily stream of letters with Washington on office details. "I am ensconced in bed with a stenographer at my side," the frustrated AP told Lucy. "Will you not send me word as to our bank balance?," she pleaded with the treasurer. "I shall have to come back to Washington to see if you do not let me know—I am consumed with anxiety as to whether there is plenty of money on hand."[25]

CU staff, friends, and family maintained a watchful eye on the restless invalid. Helen Paul traveled back and forth from Moorestown, bringing fresh nightgowns and other necessities. Elsie Hill tried to tamp down AP's edginess: "Please behave yourself for a little while longer than you think is necessary. It will pay, you know." As the prospect of discharge grew near, Crystal Eastman Benedict, herself recently released from bed rest, empathized: "You must feel very gay now with the prospect of coming out of prison so soon." She encouraged AP to "spend most of the time eating."[26]

While Alice recuperated, her stalwarts renewed their efforts to persuade Congress, that bastion of male-dominated politics, to hear the Congressional Union's demand. Lucy, taking aim at the recent House declaration that states should decide about woman suffrage, gained a hearing before the Judiciary Committee. On March 3, the first anniversary of the 1913 procession, Mary Beard and Crystal Benedict left no doubt, as Beard later wrote AP, that the CU was "politically-minded and politically determined." Indeed, the change in tone from the usual suffrage hearing seemed startling. Historian Beard lectured the committee: "Those who say that suffrage is a purely State matter, have neither history nor political science on their side." Benedict tackled the controversy over the CU's election policy, telling Democrats the Union planned to campaign against

them because "you Democrats happen to control the Government. That's all."
Women, she said, "for the first time in the history of the country are in a position
to demand action on [the suffrage] amendment." Pass the amendment before the
fall elections, Benedict concluded: "Gentlemen, why turn us into enemies?"[27]

Alice's satisfaction with Beard's and Benedict's commanding performances
proved short lived when she learned of NAWSA's new project. At the same
hearing, Ruth McCormick introduced a rival suffrage amendment, one she had
persuaded the National's board to approve. The alternative, soon known as the
Shafroth-Palmer amendment (after its Senate and House sponsors), propped up
the states' rights argument by requiring any state to hold a suffrage referendum if
8 percent of its voters petitioned for the move. Alice thought it "incomprehensible" that NAWSA would toss aside the age-old, straightforward amendment
(soon known as the Bristow-Mondell amendment) and insert new complica-
tions into the process. The Shafroth amendment gained little traction before the
National abandoned the effort in 1915, but the dueling amendments exacerbated
the NAWSA–CU split.[28]

The National rubbed salt in the Shafroth wound by lobbying for a Senate
vote on the original suffrage amendment. NAWSA, the CU, and supportive
senators all agreed the vote would fail, yet McCormick successfully lobbied to
bring it to the Senate floor. *The Suffragist* joined some NAWSA members wondering about the precipitous vote, when the scheduled national demonstrations
in May and several state suffrage campaigns might alter enough votes to win the
Senate. The amendment lost 35–34, lacking the required two-thirds majority.
The next day, a McCormick ally introduced the rival Shafroth amendment into
the Senate.[29]

Alice monitored the action in Washington from her bed. After three weeks,
she left the hospital and continued convalescing at the Lewis home before returning to Washington. "The doctor says," Lewis wrote Lucy, "that Miss Paul ought to
be in very much better condition now." Early in April, Alice eagerly returned to F
Street, ready to plunge into work once more. Lucy had just recovered from a brief
illness herself, prompting Benedict to quip, "What will become of the Union if
we *all* retire to hospitals in various cities of the country?" She added, "Don't *work
too hard.*"[30]

Alice hoped her audacious plan for the May demonstrations would elevate the
suffrage amendment and the Union on the national stage in a way that reached
beyond press coverage. The events offered an opportunity to demonstrate suffrage unity to those fretting over newspaper accounts about the bickering.
The National's board had pledged to cooperate (the only positive result of the
February summit) and, inexplicably, agreed to focus on the original amendment.
NAWSA failed to realize that the plans allowed Alice to control the crowning

event and bid for the allegiance of activists just as the fledgling Congressional Union regained visibility after its excision from NAWSA.[31]

Alice proposed a literal and symbolic uniting of voices for suffrage. The concept, a "Mayday from ocean to ocean," even *The Suffragist* acknowledged as "almost too ambitious for realization." Her idea appears to be original. Although the Pankhursts held "Women's Mayday"—a nod to their labor origins—and American suffrage parades often occurred in May, no one had ever attempted a nationwide event. On May 2, at an appointed time, a demonstration in each and every state would demand passage of the suffrage amendment. Not simply a suffragist social or a time devoted to outreach, AP conceived the political purpose as "a whole great country making a simultaneous demand for the complete reform of the electorate." *The Suffragist* modestly foresaw "the greatest suffrage demonstration ever organized." Fortunately for Alice, Anna Howard Shaw traveled abroad that spring.[32]

The May 2 events proved a great success, despite concern over the public focus on recent military campaigns in Mexico. Parades and mass meetings in Philadelphia, Boston, and Chicago were expected, but suffragists in towns and cities as far flung as Cheyenne, Wyoming; Parkersburg, West Virginia; and Grafton, Vermont, brought off their first events. "We are walking on air," wrote Sophie Kenyon from St. Paul, Minnesota. At least three southern cities—San Antonio, Atlanta, and New Orleans—joined in. Helen Paul reported on Moorestown's event, writing that their brother Parry joined the celebration, making a large banner to hang above Main Street. Alice and Lucy spoke at a Carnegie Hall rally in New York. As suffrage landed on the front page once again, the House of Representatives took notice.[33]

On May 7, 1914, the House Judiciary Committee reported out the Bristow-Mondell amendment, and both houses of Congress stood poised to vote on a suffrage amendment for the first time in history. (The Senate Suffrage Committee had rendered a favorable report a month earlier.) "A veritable triumph," crowed *The Suffragist*, stressing that the question now was "squarely up to the Democratic Party," which controlled both houses. At this heady time, representatives from many state Maydays arrived in Washington for the culminating event.[34]

Once again, Alice utilized beauty and dignity—and ignored the dissension among movement leaders—to camouflage the serious political purpose of the event. "Nothing of hardness, or bitterness or rancor," would be on view, *The Suffragist* emphasized, "but a beautiful and a righteous discontent with a state of affairs that ought to be changed." Blessed by perfect weather, the women marched to the Capitol. Alice marched near the front with the CU executive committee, her white suit and hat enlivened by a shoulder sash in Union colors. The empowering effect of the procession only expanded when the marchers joined a chorus of hundreds of girls and women already massed on the Capitol's east steps. As resolution-carrying delegates streamed upward into the Capitol, the huge chorus voiced its endorsement, singing out the suffragist favorite, Edyth Smyth's "March of the Women": "Strong, strong—stand we at last/Fearless in faith and with sight new-given/Shoulder to shoulder and friend to friend."[35]

Congress tempered the exhilaration all too soon. The Democratic caucus accepted President Wilson's recommendations as their agenda for the rest of the session. Despite the May demonstrations and the lobbying, the caucus confined the schedule to three commerce bills. Suffragists tried repeatedly to change congressional minds—one House chairman objected to the women "coming too thick and fast"—but this frustrating state of affairs continued all summer.[36]

As Alice rolled out summer initiatives to build the CU's national presence, an abdication left her scrambling. Rheta Childe Dorr, the prominent writer who was editing *The Suffragist*, resigned, ostensibly over her lack of editorial control. Unfortunately, Dorr's journalistic pretensions had always clashed with AP's polemical needs. And her outside work often kept her from Washington, leaving others to pick up the slack. Alice, ever vigilant about expenses, welcomed the savings from one less salary and office rent. She soon decided to let go the journal's business manager as well, writing Benedict gleefully that she totaled the savings at over $3,000. She used the newfound funds to organize in summer resort areas.[37]

Two traumas dominated the nation's attention during the summer of 1914. On June 28, the assassination of Austria's Archduke Franz Ferdinand set in motion the war that many, including Alice, had seen coming. Europe's great powers declared war by early August. In Britain, the Pankhursts and the WSPU set suffrage aside and turned all their energies against the foreign foe; the British government gratefully released all suffragettes in jail. As AP and her compatriots pondered the Pankhursts' response to war, the First Lady died from kidney disease. The grieving president resisted the prospect of America entering the war. Alice hardly realized how his subsequent decisions would affect her own quest.

The stalemate with congressional Democrats made the fall implementation of the CU's controversial election policy seem increasingly likely. Accordingly, Alice set out to bolster the Union's credibility by organizing the advisory council she and Lucy had discussed for months. She appealed to notables, not only in suffrage, but in education, social work, and other reform efforts. The appeal made clear that they wanted the name recognition to boost CU visibility but valued advice and assistance as well. Indeed, some of the women already served as informal advisers.[38]

Responses re-aired the debate over the NAWSA–CU breach and the CU's planned election policy. Some allies, such as Katharine Hepburn and Inez

Milholland, now formally Milholland Boissevain, signed on at once. Milholland gushed, "I'm with you boots, saddle, and breeches!" Harriot Blatch, however, felt it "unwise" to join the advisory council, since the New York campaign required her full attention; "I could not remain dead wood upon so vital a question." But Alice finally persuaded her. Alice approached state suffrage leaders such as New Jersey's Lillian Feickert. Feickert declined. Since the NAWSA–CU debate seemed "so strained" locally, she feared harming the state work. Hepburn later withdrew for much the same reason. By August, though, more than thirty women had agreed to serve.[39]

As election season approached, Alice steeled the Congressional Union's defenses in preparation for the campaign against the Democrats. Her coffers depleted from the summer organizing, she invited the new advisory council to the seaside resort of Newport, Rhode Island, at the end of August to confer with CU staff and other supporters. Her purpose was threefold: she wanted to unite supporters firmly behind the original suffrage amendment; she hoped for an equally united front on the Union's election policy; and she needed money to finance the fall offensive.[40]

Alva Belmont had lobbied for the Newport site and Alice thought it wise to accede. Mrs. Belmont, who summered in her Marble House "cottage," wanted to show off her specially commissioned Votes for Women china and the newly built Chinese tea house on her clifftop property overlooking the Atlantic Ocean. She invited Alice to stay with her during the conference, giving the CU leader the opportunity to take in the lavish estate firsthand. More importantly, Alice could cement her ties with her wealthiest patron. AP later thanked Belmont for the "delightful memories of my stay," but she appreciated the $5,000 her benefactor pledged even more.[41]

The Newport conference drew women from seventeen states. Many advisory council members made the trip, as well as reliable friends like Blatch. WSPU veteran Annie Kenney, on an American lecture tour, addressed a garden party. Clearly, Alice still saw no need to distance herself from the Pankhursts. Social events like the party brought in hundreds more local and vacationing suffragists. All of the executive committee, save for Mary Beard and, unexpectedly, Dora Lewis, joined Alice for these crucial meetings.[42]

Beard's absence brought Alice face-to-face with an incongruity in her efforts: she welcomed everyone, but depended increasingly on the wealthy to fund her ambitious plans. Beard feared associating with Newport wealth would damage her labor credentials. Alice encouraged her to reconsider, noting that Belmont would host only two of six events at Marble House. Everything else would "be on a rather humble plane." Few local members, she said, seemed "particularly high on the social scale." She acknowledged Beard's concerns, though she thought the historian overreacted. A labor activist appeared at a Belmont conference in July, Alice reminded Beard: "I do not suppose that in any way lessened her usefulness in the labor world."[43]

Nonetheless, Alice exaggerated the accessibility of the conference. The two business sessions at Marble House were the crucial meetings, designed to focus everyone on the goal and to raise money, though the other events did allow for social mingling. Whatever AP's leanings, she found herself trapped between her Quaker egalitarianism and her interest in raising significant sums quickly. As in her dealings with African Americans, expedience trumped ideals.[44]

The crucial piece at Newport was gaining support for the controversial election policy. The conference readily stood behind the Bristow amendment, especially after Harriot Blatch declared the rival amendment "utterly ridiculous." The next day, Alice turned the spotlight on the election policy. Lucy first provided a detailed rationale for campaigning against the party in power. With one party— the Democrats—in control of Congress, no important legislation passed without their endorsement. Both the Senate and the House had displayed "one continuous course of opposition to the suffrage amendment," Lucy maintained. In other words, the Democrats were the enemy. Alice then ramped up suspense, asking journalists to leave and pledging the conferees to secrecy until mid-September on her proposal. Her flair for the dramatic seemed intact, though insiders already knew much of her plan.[45]

She wanted suffragists to control the balance of power. Without the support of the activists in her audience, Alice knew a rough road awaited her. She mustered all her debating skills, all the persuasiveness she learned on the stump in England. "How shall that enemy be attacked?" she asked. Her answer was simpler in concept than execution: women held the power to force the Democrats to pass the suffrage amendment. Four million women voters lived in the nine suffrage states, all in the western United States. Voter loyalty had declined in the last two decades: in eight of those states, voters switched parties repeatedly in congressional elections. In the most recent elections, a 10 percent difference in the vote, on average, would have altered the outcome. Therefore, if enough women in suffrage states voted against the Democratic Party in the coming elections, the Democrats "will change their attitude on suffrage. When we have once affected the result in a national election, no party will trifle with suffrage any longer."[46]

The goal seemed unassailable: to pressure the most powerful politicians into recognizing women as a potent political force. Alice acknowledged the Union's paltry war chest and army for such a daunting task. Nevertheless, CU organizers could tackle the nine states in some measure. "If the Party leaders see that some votes have been turned," she declared, "they will know that we have at last realized this power that we possess and they will know that by 1916 we will have it organized." Small efforts could prove effective, AP maintained. More than one congressman had sought their support for the coming elections. "Now if our help is valued to this extent," she told the conference, "our opposition will be feared in like degree."[47]

Alice's rhetoric promised political power and softened the unconventional behavior intrinsic to her strategy. Presenting the logic in the elite setting of Marble House rendered the notion of political opposition even more palatable. And, in many respects, the women in attendance were ready for a bold, if risky, move.

The response gratified her. Harriot Blatch, no stranger to the dramatic, rose first, perhaps by pre-arrangement. Alice understood, Blatch said, what being political meant, unlike most women. She added, "I find myself absolutely standing with the national policy." Longtime reformer Florence Kelley, whom AP knew from her settlement house days, confessed that she had dimly grasped the policy before and now found her fears "unfounded" and the plan "statesmanlike." Veteran CC member Crystal Eastman Benedict also felt uncertain before Alice's talk. She understood now that fighting anti-suffrage Democrats proved pointless "because Democrats from suffrage states do not go on record against woman suffrage." The conferees then enriched CU coffers by $2,000. In addition, a few women each offered to pay expenses for an organizer; others volunteered to go west themselves and pay their own way.[48]

After Newport, Alice still fretted about having the wherewithal to execute the Congressional Union's fall campaign successfully, her ambition ever outpacing her available funds. Without the wealthy donors she courted, her time would be entirely consumed with trolling for money. Yet she knew that the money underlay her success. Though the CU's size was less than 1 percent of NAWSA's membership in 1914, AP raised close to half the monies available to the National. Belmont contributed the most—more than $10,000 in 1914. By year's end, receipts from all donations totaled more than $37,000. But with Alice's expansive plans, the money poured out almost as soon as it flowed in.[49]

Finding the right workers became a challenge. Alice wanted two organizers in each of the nine suffrage states. Most suffragists knew their own state work; she needed women conversant with the federal work and the CU election policy. Most of all, the campaign required women who were comfortable with oppositional politics. And the CU needed nearly two months of their time—a hard sell for many women, especially wage earners.

Alice spent a frantic couple of weeks lining up workers, foraging in other friendly suffrage groups as well as among her own staff. Lucy, Doris Stevens, and Mabel Vernon topped the list of seasoned organizers; Hooker, Blatch, and Lewis each gave up capable local workers. Emmeline Pankhurst even agreed to allow Annie Kenney to organize temporarily. The more privileged women paid their own expenses. For those unable to do so, including former factory worker Rose Winslow, the CU picked up the tab or found someone who would. Alice expected all the women to raise funds as they organized in the West.[50]

The Union's 1914 campaign expected a lot of western women voters. Only a few years after most won the vote, Alice wanted them to engage in both single-issue politics and altruism. CU rhetoric called on women's loyalty to their eastern sisters and challenged them to use their newfound political agency to strike at the continued disenfranchisement of American women as a whole. She capitalized on the solidarity built up from NAWSA's successful state campaigns, hoping that and the appeal of selflessness would tip the balance of power.[51]

In mid-September, Alice launched the campaign from Washington with eleven of the hoped-for organizers. At a garden party send-off, she made the plan public, declaring, "We shall work in the suffrage states only. We shall work only against the Democratic candidates. Not because we do not like the Democrats," she noted, "but because the Democratic party has proved so effectively that it dislikes us." The next morning at Union Station, the campaigners—all white women in their twenties or thirties carrying the congressional directory, names of contacts, and campaign literature—climbed aboard a special rail car decorated with colorful suffrage banners. They rode together to Chicago, then pushed on separately or in pairs to Colorado, Kansas, Arizona, Washington, Oregon, and California. By the end of September, five more women joined the effort, adding Wyoming and Idaho to the campaign. AP relabeled the ninth state, ultraconservative Utah, as impervious to organizers.[52]

NAWSA leaders immediately circled the wagons, fearing the Congressional Union's negative campaigning would taint their cause. Anna Howard Shaw and Ruth McCormick sent letters and telegrams to the eight states defending the National's friends among the Democrats and again dissociating NAWSA from the CU. Carrie Chapman Catt dismissed the CU in the *New York Times*: "It does not follow that the cause is unjust or ridiculous just because some of its advocates are," she insisted, adding dismissively that the "semi-militant" Union did not "constitute more than one-fourth of 1 per cent" of all suffragists.[53]

Alice routinely ignored NAWSA's criticism of the CU, but she could not allow misapprehensions of the election policy to flourish. She gave up precious time to urge suffrage societies to protest Shaw's letters. To bolster the election policy's credibility, she sent out two thousand copies of a *Suffragist* appeal from Belmont that played up the altruistic angle, proclaiming "the power of women to free women" and extolling "the sisterhood of a new era." Finally, she addressed frequently asked questions directly in *The Suffragist* with a long editorial, revisiting the true nonpartisanship of the campaign and why opposing Democrats was not "ungrateful or ungracious."[54]

For the first time, she confronted the charge of militancy publicly, repeating what she told the Newport conference privately. The election policy was "not militant in the sense that it means physical violence," she wrote. "It is militant only in the sense that it is strong, positive, and energetic." Indeed, she and Lucy never used the term so associated with the Pankhursts to identify themselves; their American work seemed a far cry from the militancy practiced in Britain. Alice resisted the label, writing, "If it is militant to appeal to women to use their vote…then it is militant to appeal to men or to women to use their vote for any good end."[55]

For the American public, however, the CU's aggressiveness brought to mind nothing so much as the spectacular politics of the Pankhursts, rendered so vividly by the press until the WSPU's August turn to war work. Alice made the comparison all the more apt by adopting the Pankhursts' mantra of opposing the party in power, though the concept played out differently in the United States. Her protests notwithstanding, the militant label stuck.

Amid the controversy over the Union's tactics, Alice appreciated the constancy of its stalwarts. Mary Beard, absent from Newport, assured AP of her thorough approval of the campaign. "Your scheme seems faultless to me," she wrote, "even if no man is defeated." "In the end," supporter and western voter Cora Smith King wrote, "you will be the most cursed & the most blest woman in the country, but every body will be talking about you." She continued, presciently,

The political effect will never be unanimously agreed upon, but always subject for debate—some declaring you did no harm to the Democrats but great harm to the women's cause, & others that you are the saviour of women. But the deep inner effect will be that the party leaders in secret conference will decide to come out for suffrage *much* sooner because of the trouble you have made them.[56]

While Lucy campaigned in California, Alice remained in Washington, maintaining operations with a skeleton staff. She trolled for more workers, monitored those in the field as well as the congressional work, and managed the weekly *Suffragist*. She began asking supporters for help. "So many of our workers have gone West," she told one Massachusetts woman, "that we need people here more than usually." Alice missed the routine consulting with Lucy; she plaintively wrote Dora Lewis in late September, "Won't you come down to Washington soon?" When Lewis grew ill a short time later, she felt quite distressed—"I can hardly realize that it is possible that you can be ill." Her confidante soon entered a sanitarium for her own rest cure.[57]

Alice hoped for the Democrats' fierce opposition to the Union's campaign, in essence, their fear of women exercising political agency. Arizona organizer Jane Pincus raved, "We have created a heap of excitement among political parties and Democrats are raging mad." Doris Stevens reported from Colorado that longtime suffrage advocate Senator Charles Thomas responded to a passersby's question by swearing and "did nothing else for a solid block. After this out-burst he declared we did not represent the women, and swore some more." Outraged congressmen from Kansas wrote letters and visited the F Street office to persuade Alice to remove CU organizers from their state. Even her usually supportive Uncle Mickle, the sole Democrat in the family, complained, "Don't thee see that it is not democrats that throttle equal suffrage?"[58]

Alice stood undeterred, remembering the more violent opposition to the WSPU. She reached out to underscore her seriousness of purpose. The Congressional Union's policy remained "absolutely non-partisan," she reiterated in *The Suffragist*. She sent well-placed emissaries to each of the affected congressmen and released to the press her letter to targeted candidates. "Whatever your personal views on the subject may be," she wrote, "you are not able to make them effective owing to the opposition of the majority of your party colleagues." Therefore, she went on, "we are forced to regard you as an opponent together with the other members of your party."[59]

Many western women proved resistant to opposition politics. Some resented what they considered to be outside interference. Lucy and Rose Winslow found considerable support in California; their experience became the exception. In Idaho, the state Council of Women Voters thought eastern women should "wait in patience and faith" instead of demanding American suffrage. Likewise, Pincus wrote from Arizona, "I am trying to get before [women's] Clubs but they all plead non-political." Seasoned organizers like Doris Stevens had enough local support to hold up against intense hostility; other operatives gave in to frustration. One Wyoming organizer found only one helper after weeks of work. "She is absolutely the first soul I have met with any willingness to help in any small degree," the worker wrote AP.[60]

The resistance meant contributions became hard won. Wyoming's worker despaired, finding the local women "appallingly indifferent"; thus, "there will be no financial returns." "I don't seem to be able to raise a cent," Pincus lamented. Increasingly anxious about the bills, Alice urged organizers to persist, telling them, "Money is the backbone of our work," and "No sum is too trivial to take." One day, she carped, "If we cannot convince the people that the campaign is sufficiently worth while for them to give at least twenty-five cents toward its support that we might as well not talk to them at all."[61]

Her reach had again exceeded her grasp, at least monetarily. The CU bank account dwindled as the campaign continued. Since her efforts to encourage workers to raise money continued to fall short, Alice reluctantly turned her own energies again to raising badly needed dollars. "We have now just $3.00 left in the treasury," she advised Stubbs. "It does not seem much to send a hundred dollars to any one headquarters, but when all nine of them ask for that amount at the same time and at rather frequent intervals, it amounts to a rather alarming total." She beseeched members to fulfill outstanding pledges. "I have been calling and phoning to people all day for money, and have just gotten enough to meet the needs of the various headquarters for today," she told a Chicago donor. "I am afraid that more of them will telegraph for money tomorrow." She felt forced to leave the office for quick fundraising trips. As before, she resigned herself to the expense rather than trim her expectations, telling Stubbs, "We will have to make a success of this campaign even if it does cost a great deal and we spend the rest of our days raising money to pay for it."[62]

Election day arrived and early reports seemed largely positive. "Jubilant reports credit us share defeat Thomas [&] Seldomridge," Stevens cabled from Colorado the next day (though Thomas later won when all results were in). Another organizer wired, "We won Idaho papers credit Union with making national suffrage lively issue." On the other hand, Pincus felt certain that Arizona Democrats had overwhelmingly taken the day.[63]

Ultimately, the Congressional Union claimed a small share of the credit for the twenty-three Democratic losses in the nine suffrage states. Factoring in the usual off-year incumbent losses, Alice attributed three defeats outright to the CU's campaign work and significant influence on three more. The Union also helped reduce the majorities of three other candidates, notably that of Senator Thomas, who admitted, despite his earlier bluster, that the 1914 election became the "fight of his life." The news that women won suffrage in two new states—Nevada and Montana—only added to the exuberance; the other five NAWSA state campaigns went down to defeat.[64]

Alice jubilantly celebrated. "Our campaign has succeeded beyond my fondest hopes," she wrote Stevens. Indeed, being able to claim some credit for Democratic defeats would keep the CU's election policy viable in the eyes of wavering members and raise the organization's profile both in Congress and in the press. If Democrats, particularly pro-suffrage ones, retaliated, however, the CU's efforts would prove fruitless and NAWSA's point of view would gain credence. On this score, the Seattle organizer wrote encouragingly that the one state Democratic victor made "a public statement twice that if elected he would work for our bill in spite of the fact that I had worked against him."[65]

The CU feted the campaign crusaders at a rousing welcome-home celebration a few days later. As AP watched, Edith Hooker gloried, "We have met this afternoon to sum up our victories," and introduced Harriot Stanton Blatch. Perhaps thinking of her mother, Blatch sounded the triumphant call: "A new day has come," she proclaimed. "We women of the East at last see a great body of voting women who are going to extend to us a helping hand."[66]

For the moment, Alice took heart that the Congressional Union had proved itself a power to be reckoned with, despite its small membership. Flushed with election success, she wrote a supporter that forging the power of women voters was "one of the biggest and most important tasks that we have before us." The moral authority of that power, she thought, held the potential to light a fire under Congress.[67]

"The Voice of the New Power"

ALICE PAUL'S DREAMS of uniting suffragists behind the constitutional amendment bore fruit in 1915. In a year when the fear of American involvement in the European war distracted many suffragists, she maintained the Congressional Union's single-minded focus on passage of the federal suffrage amendment.

The CU's fall campaign yielded fruit soon after Congress reconvened in early December. The House Rules Committee, after refusing to consider suffrage for nearly a year, agreed to report out the amendment. Lucy reported that two CU lobbyists found the Rules chairman "beaming with friendliness and suspiciously eager to take immediate action on suffrage." Since the committee planned to release the long-controversial prohibition amendment as well, she guessed at the plan: "The Democrats," she wrote Stevens, "are now determined to kill off the two national proposals, as quickly as they can." Indeed, later in the month, prohibition failed to find the necessary two-thirds majority for passage; the House set a suffrage vote for early January.[1]

Before the House voted, Alice renewed her efforts to gain presidential support, building on the fall campaign with a party appeal. On January 6, 1915, nearly thirty Democratic women from fifteen states, some of them congressmen's wives, arrived at the White House flying CU colors. The president appeared cordial, if condescending, *The Suffragist* related. Consistent with his previous resistance, Wilson declared that he, like the 1914 House Democratic caucus, believed in state, not federal, action on suffrage. However, the president said nothing about states' rights in writing a female friend later that same morning. "Suffrage for women will make absolutely no change in politics," he insisted. "It is the home that will be disastrously affected. Somebody has to make the home, and who is going to do it if the women don't?"[2]

Despite the president's patriarchal views, this deputation succeeded in placing him on record at a key moment, just before the House vote. Alice told reporters that Wilson placed a "very heavy burden" on his own party. She alluded to the CU's recent campaign success in calling up the specter of future elections: "If the Democratic members of Congress make as bad a record for their party on this subject as has the President," she proclaimed, "that party cannot longer hope to receive the support of self-respecting women."[3]

Alice was determined to build on the fall campaign and empower western women to vote in the interest of all American women. She held out little hope for the House vote and for the sitting Congress. So, a few days later, she set the stage for the year at the second CU annual meeting. She reviewed the organization's "tremendous growth"—3,600 members to date. The November 1914 NAWSA victories in Montana and Nevada, she said, meant that 20 percent of all eligible voters resided in the suffrage states; in these states, she intended to maintain the CU presence. A fall political convention for women voters would harness their emerging power. She envisioned an "army of women" descending upon the new Congress in December 1915, forcing the amendment through.[4]

The first-ever House vote on woman suffrage drew suffrage activists of all persuasions despite torrential rains on January 12. Though Alice anticipated defeat, as with the Senate vote the previous March, the House vote placed the entire Congress on record about the suffrage amendment. The anti-suffragists trooped to one part of the public gallery above the House floor; while Anna Howard Shaw and National stalwarts sat by invitation in the Speaker's private gallery; and the less-favored CU flock gathered in yet another section, purple and gold sashes and banners lending a festive air to the proceedings. Alice sat in the front row and, according to the *New York Tribune*, "like the Sphinx she is, scarcely moved or made a sign, either of approval or disapproval, through the long day." (Privately, she called the day "a rather wearying experience.") Those less engrossed brought their war knitting and the click-clack of needles accompanied the prolonged debate below; denied representation in the hallowed political hall, the women interjected themselves into the deliberations with applause and murmured approval alternating with hisses.[5]

The women watching the six hours of debate grew tired, especially when anti-suffrage congressmen rehearsed both petty and exalted rationales against enfranchising half the population. The fear of women voters turning the world upside down still held sway. *The Suffragist* recapped the arguments, including that "no man would care to marry a suffragist" or a female police officer or butcher. Because of men's "respect, admiration, and reverence for womanhood," they could not stand by while She became degraded by the vote. Women "must be protected against themselves." Conscious of the ongoing fighting in Europe, one congressman acknowledged a pervasive fear that a voting womanhood might not stomach "the duty of organized murder": they would vote against war. No matter how often suffragists rejoined by pointing out the continuing right-side-upness of the suffrage states, such arguments persisted.[6]

Suffrage proponents everywhere viewed the vote in the House of Representatives as a victory, however the final tally turned out. Thirty-five years after the amendment was introduced, both houses of Congress would now have voted on the question of woman suffrage. After sixty-six congressmen spoke for or against the measure, the amendment failed by seventy-eight votes to reach the required two-thirds majority. Democrats comprised 171 of the 204 *nay* votes. Nevertheless, *The Suffragist* noted, many women witnessing the vote saw "the beginning of the end—and an end not far distant." For those congressmen voting *nay* became vulnerable targets.[7]

The House debate and vote offered further proof that the CU fall 1914 campaign affected Congress more than NAWSA's two-of-seven state victories. Although the leader of the House Democrats reiterated his party's states' rights stance on suffrage, two of his flock, attributing their lame-duck status to the Congressional Union, voted *aye*, giving more credence to the CU's fall crusade. Furthermore, Alice gained a new argument for her national focus. She editorialized in *The Suffragist* that the vote proved NAWSA's state campaigns misguided: fewer than half of congressmen from their five failed campaign states voted *aye*, some reversing previous *aye* votes because of their state's defeat of suffrage. "Not only do such campaigns dissipate strength," AP wrote, "but, as this debate and vote has indicated, they erect further barriers against the passage of the national amendment." Nevertheless, with seven successes in five years, the National had no plans to abandon state campaigns.[8]

Indeed, state legislators took notice of the historic vote. Historian and syndicated columnist Ida Husted Harper wrote that "suffragists are rubbing their eyes" in disbelief because, instead of the usual delaying tactics, state legislatures were acting before activists could "unpack their trunks and get to work." Seven states took positive action of some type by mid-February. Even the *New York Times* noted the effect of the congressional vote, calling the cascade of state moves "unprecedented in the history of the movement." Four large eastern states, among them New York and New Jersey, planned suffrage referenda for November 1915.[9]

In the wake of the House vote, Alice expanded her vision, seeing advantages to widening the CU's national presence. NAWSA resisted, believing its territory invaded. AP made no apologies; she believed the National's divisive strategy with the rival Shafroth Amendment required a firm response. In the meantime, the impediments to fundraising during the fall campaign left AP considering better ways to bring in money. Possibilities in Washington seemed tapped out. One answer came to her quickly: New York City. As she wrote Doris Stevens after the fall elections, Gotham was ripe for fundraising as well as publicity. A New York office also could maintain a closer connection with the CU's largest benefactor. Indeed, Belmont expressed delight at the idea and offered space in her own offices rent free. Alice was thrilled. "We ought to make a great success," she told Stevens, and "collect a great deal of the money there that is now going entirely to the state work."[10]

New York suffragists soon got wind of Alice's plans to open a Manhattan office and cried foul. Several major suffrage organizations already operated from the city, including NAWSA and three already competitive state groups led by Harriot Blatch, Belmont, and Carrie Chapman Catt. All were in the middle of organizing for the 1915 referendum. "Outbursts of indignation arose from all quarters at this wicked act," Lucy impishly wrote Stevens from her home in Brooklyn. She added that "everyone in authority" believed the New York referendum would fail "and it is absurd for them to go on squandering money"; the idea of "exclud[ing] national work from their territory at the same time, is the last word in reason." Lucy believed more suffrage activities meant more workers and money, not less. Yet both Lucy and Stevens felt inclined to back off for the time being. As the chief fundraiser, however, AP swayed the executive committee otherwise and Stevens opened a Manhattan headquarters in early January.[11]

NAWSA leaders had so effectively demonized Alice and the Congressional Union over the last year that many suffragists now viewed any new tactic suspiciously. Nonetheless, as with the 1914 rollout of the CU's election policy, Alice again created more problems for herself by her unwillingness to take precious time to soften up New York suffragists. On the other hand, some of those very suffragists already worked for the CU, so the idea that Union organizers invaded the city was patently false. AP's dogged focus on the task at hand consumed her sensibilities, blinding her to some of the niceties people still expected, particularly of a woman. Yet when she found it necessary, as with Alva Belmont, she seemed perfectly capable of what Lucy called "jollying up" supporters.

Alice's desperation about money prompted her to reshape her own role in the CU. Her watchful anxiety kicked in as she realized how much her plans for 1915 would require; money was "the point where we are weakest," she felt. In the weeks after she announced her 1915 plans, letters to potential donors implored, "We do not know where to turn." Only she and Lucy reliably brought in significant dollars, and Lucy had taken over *The Suffragist* in addition to overseeing the work in Congress. AP finally allayed her own fears by deciding to relinquish her position in order to spend her time raising money.[12]

Her decision alarmed the Union's inner circle but perhaps was less dramatic than it initially appeared. Alice wanted someone else to undertake the routine administrative work and talked with Edith Hooker in vain about stepping in. Belmont could think of "no one who can fill your place," a sentiment echoed by Mary Beard, who felt "grieved and in utter despair," blaming herself for not giving enough effort. Beard thought "the physical must be the only reason." However, the pragmatic AP underlined the value of changing officers frequently and "now that the work was well established and apparently going better than ever before would be a good time to hand things over to some one else."[13]

Her closest confidante, Dora Lewis, sensed less self-sacrifice in the decision than free-floating anxiety. "I wish I knew what your plan is & why you are thinking this is 'the time' to resign your leadership," she wrote Alice. "Of course you would be the leader in any case—but why even think of changes when everything is going so beautifully?" Lewis intuited that Alice needed buoying up more than anything. "I wish you were here, curled up on my bed, this minute. I want to have a good talk so much," she told AP fondly. After Alice spent a night with Lewis, the talk about resigning ceased. Lewis apparently suggested that AP could spend considerable time fundraising and organizing away from Washington without any need to resign; she began to do just that.[14]

Alice felt heartened as the New York work gained momentum from extensive press coverage of early events. Women from both Blatch's and Catt's groups joined the CU, many—like Lavinia Dock—feeling no need to focus on only one type of suffrage work, others leaving off state work. Two of Lucy's sisters, already members, now joined the volunteers. They helped with the formal CU office opening on January 20 and a mass meeting at Cooper Union in February, which the *Tribune* called "the first real political meeting held by suffragists in this city." When the advisory and executive councils met in the city in March, the press made much of the supposed territorial incursion, as usual playing up any disharmony angle. "Yesterday [CU] leaders came into the camp of the enemy," the *Herald* reported. As a matter of fact, signs beyond the CU's New York activities suggested a newly aggressive stance toward NAWSA.[15]

Alice saw an opportunity to build up the Congressional Union in the anger and dismay accompanying the National's continued support for the Shafroth Amendment. She did so by constructing the CU as superior in political savvy and implicitly bidding for the loyalty of NAWSA members. She fought first on a rhetorical front. To start off, she brilliantly elevated the stature of the original suffrage amendment by rebranding it the "Susan B. Anthony Amendment." Then *The Suffragist* assailed the National's support of the rival amendment. In one article, AP herself contrasted the "economy of time, strength, energy and money" fighting for the amendment itself as opposed to securing only a means to that end. Another piece described NAWSA as lacking "unity of purpose," a charge made for years by the National's own members, compared to the CU: "a new leadership towards union, towards co-operation, towards that complete solidarity of women."[16]

Privately, Alice encouraged prominent CU supporters to cut their ties with NAWSA. Harriot Stanton Blatch needed little help: she led a failed "dump

Shafroth" effort at the December 1914 NAWSA convention and many already anticipated her break with the National. Her Women's Political Union cut all ties in late February 1915, citing Shafroth as well as increased dues. Blatch's spokeswoman claimed the National had "practically gone to seed and needs new blood." A few weeks later, Alice instructed Doris Stevens to urge Alva Belmont to withdraw and "do so now, as this seems to be the psychological moment." She went on to emphasize the publicity value of such a move. Belmont declined, fearing criticism for bolting in the midst of the New York referendum campaign. Alice's public conduct remained more circumspect. She still refused to criticize the National in the mainstream press.[17]

The National's continuing support of the Shafroth Amendment also motivated AP to create a nationwide organization. Her thinking about the Union had evolved considerably since November—when she told people that the CU needed only a central headquarters—and even since January, when she proposed maintaining state offices. The swift response of state legislatures after the House vote suggested a warming to the suffrage cause. However, with NAWSA committed to Shafroth, the CU could no longer count on existing state groups for help. The Union needed groups, Alice wrote a supporter, that would dependably advance the work in Washington. Also, months of sporadic work with Edith Hooker on a CU constitution persuaded her that the size of the Union now required a way, she wrote Beard, to "make the groups in far away states feel some responsibility for the general work and bind them more intimately to it." The nine months before a new Congress convened presented the time to organize such groups.[18]

Alice worked through her own and others' doubts about enlarging the scope of the CU. The Union's national posture spoke only to its purpose; its members lived mostly in twelve northeast states plus the District stronghold. Citizens of Pennsylvania and New York (mostly Philadelphia and New York City), as well as the District with its residents from all states, comprised 40 percent of Union membership. Having offices in active states unquestionably boosted participation. On the other hand, such far-flung efforts drained resources. How could a relatively small group like the Union be everywhere? Alice rolled out the new plan for the advisory council in late March, after carefully arranging for some members to applaud the now self-supporting New York office.[19]

As it turned out, the advisory council proved more concerned about one aspect of the new constitution—men joining the CU—than expansion plans. Alice explained the point of more state offices and the council agreed with alacrity. She unveiled the constitution, a reluctant attempt to buttress the CU against NAWSA attacks. The document declared the Union a national and nonpartisan group, under the direction of an elected executive committee and open to any woman supporting suffrage over any political party. The only substantive objection arose over the constitution's exclusion of male members. After all, the Union boasted many male contributors and supporters. The assemblage finally agreed that men seemed unlikely to place woman suffrage before party interests, and the provision stood. Like the Pankhursts' WSPU, the Congressional Union now stood as a women-only and thus woman-controlled organization; it welcomed men as supporters but not as members.[20]

State CU offices would allow women to further invade male political territory by accosting Democratic congressmen on their own turf. Since many of the naysaying Democrats hailed from the South, the CU now needed to confront the racial implications of the Anthony Amendment. Alice approached this minefield in a highly political manner, giving southern Democrats what they wanted to hear. A *Suffragist* article titled "The Federal Amendment and the Race Problem" calmed those fearing hordes of black female voters, while avoiding any overt endorsement of either side. States "would be in exactly the same position to retain their white supremacy that they now are," the article insisted, meaning that under the Anthony Amendment, southern states could still restrict black women voting with the same qualifying tests already keeping most black men from the polls. Alice responded much the same way to private and press queries. Some Union members expected more from her.[21]

Several women protested or resigned their memberships. One District member recognized that the article's interpretation hinged on perception and bemoaned the CU contributing "even tacitly to the injustice and oppression suffered by another class." A few days later, the Miller sisters of Maryland resigned their membership and their *Suffragist* subscription over "a sinister element of indirectness and evasiveness" creeping into the Union's methods. They enclosed an editorial from the NAACP's *Crisis* excoriating Belmont for a recent speech sidestepping the question about whether a federal amendment would enfranchise black women. Belmont had replied, "We want the same voting privileges for colored women as are given colored men." Editor W. E. B. DuBois called the evasive response part of the "desperate effort" by "certain elements among the suffragists to dodge the Negro problem." The Millers agreed: "There are thousands of white people in this country whom this kind of quibbling disgusts."[22]

Alice's lengthy response to the Millers claimed ignorance about the "sinister element," and no knowledge of Belmont's speech. Nevertheless, like a politician under fire, her reply ducked the specific complaint and took the offensive:

> Having been accustomed to a long series of remonstrances and withdrawals on the part of suffragists who strongly objected to our allowing Negroes to march in our processions, participate in our meetings, deputations and banquets, and to our practice of accepting invitations to speak at meetings

arranged by Negroes, it is rather astonishing now to receive a protest from some one who feels that we are unjust in our attitude toward the Negro.[23]

AP went on to say that no article in *The Suffragist* offered an opinion on black enfranchisement and, as an organization, "we always endeavor never to express a moral judgment on any question whatever except the suffrage question." She added, "We could not divide our energy by working for any other than our one object." However, Alice decided for the first time to go on record, albeit privately, with her own views, forged out of her Quaker heritage. "Personally, I do not believe in the disfranchisement [sic] of the Negro, but I see no reason why we should not constantly point out that we are working for woman suffrage only and that the question of Negro suffrage is entirely different."[24]

Alice Paul made a Faustian bargain. To be sure, neutrality seemed impossible on the subject of southern black women voting. As Lucy wrote a supporter later, "You have no idea how timid we are about the negro problem, for of course it is with the negro that we are perpetually confronted in federal work." Indeed, NAWSA had long avoided the issue by concentrating on state efforts. Ignoring the subject angered those in the South who feared the loss of white supremacy if black women voted. Affirming that a ratified Anthony Amendment would pre-serve state power to set voter qualifications appeared to encourage the South to continue the practice, as Alice well knew. She also recognized that the federal amendment could only succeed with the votes of southern Democrats and that success would mean black women outside the South voting. Despite her personal views, she made the politically expedient, if repugnant, choice to mollify the South. AP's discomfort is evident in her request that the Millers visit the F Street office, in the hope that they could "come to an understanding and appreciation of each other's position."[25]

The uproar occasioned by opening a New York office soon expanded as CU organizers worked to set up state chapters. Alice Stone Blackwell aired NAWSA's complaints in the *Woman's Journal*, writing that the strategy "overlook[ed] the obvious drawbacks of duplicating machinery, of causing friction and ill feeling, and of disintegrating the suffrage societies now existing." She barely acknowl-edged that the Union sought state chapters mostly because of NAWSA's support of the Shafroth Amendment. She ignored the avid interest in many states for the Union's can-do attitude. Indeed, the CU's state work prompted suffragists who belonged to both groups to choose sides. Some women chose quickly and CU branches appeared in four new states by June.[26]

Carrie Chapman Catt felt particularly threatened; Alice persisted in stand-ing in her way. In April, in a widely circulated letter, Catt asked Alice to leave New York. Frustrated in her efforts to unify all the New York suffrage forces,

Catt complained that Union workers discouraged her referendum activists. She defended the state campaign—"you must realize that the winning of New York is the greatest thing which could happen to the movement"—while at once gainsaying her own work—"ours is a delicate situation but not at all hopeless." She haughtily derided the Union effort, insisting that the CU would only attract the "disgruntled" and "garner small results; but you may irritate and antagonize, to the permanent detriment of your work." She asked Alice to "withdraw your efforts at organization" until after the New York referendum in November.[27]

Alice's adroit reply failed to mollify Mrs. Catt. AP assured her that she felt "deeply interested in the success of the New York campaign and wish its success as ardently as even you can do." However, Catt was "misinformed" about the CU's work in the city. Alice intended to delay organizing a formal Union branch in the state until after the November referendum; that strategy held for all campaign states, contrary to rumor. Catt took the chairman's response as a "promise that New York is to have a free field to try its chances." She claimed to be satisfied. However, she continued to stir the pot—without AP's knowledge, Catt thought.[28]

A week later, Catt struck a false note of unity. In a note that made its way to Alice, Catt wrote Harriet Upton that the latter's Ohio suffrage group had "lost its senses" inviting both the CU and the National's revamped Congressional Committee into their state. "Our strength lies in a united band of women demanding the same thing," Catt maintained. Two organizations working for the federal amendment would be disastrous, "each one accusing the other of trickiness, unfairness and all that sort of thing." Catt kept alive the falsehood that the CU only sought to attack Democrats, claiming she could not work amid such strife. "When that time comes I [will] retire to my little chicken ranch and those who like to scrap can scrap," she guilefully declared. "I dread the time in this country, which I surely see is coming, when our forces are going to be divided up into little camps, each with its own leader and its own policy wasting strength fighting each other, instead of the enemy." Catt foresaw the future, except that only her camp would waste much of its time scrapping.[29]

As state organizing revealed continuing confusion about the Congressional Union's election policy, Alice decided more clarification was in order. Away raising money, she wrote Lucy in Washington that many people she encountered believed the CU would attack Democrats anywhere. The *Woman's Journal* exacerbated the confusion by claiming the Union's sole method was fighting the dominant Democratic party, an idea NAWSA leaders continued to circulate. AP suggested Lucy write an editorial stating unequivocally "that we are not in a political campaign now and are not defeating anyone now—that we hope our last election campaign and that organizing work that is being done now will make it

unnecessary ever to wage another election campaign." Entitled "WE ARE NOT
FIGHTING DEMOCRATS," Lucy's May 29 editorial left little to the imagination. "This is certainly no time for attacking any man or any party," she wrote.
She stressed that the Union was focused on organizing the national sentiment for
suffrage and communicating that to elected federal officials. But before the article
appeared, another controversy emerged.[30]

Alice fit a few days of rest and preparations for a lengthy fundraising tour in
the West around organizing a Philadelphia deputation to Wilson. She spent the
last week of April gathering up clothing and seeing the dentist. Dora Lewis hoped
"you are doing nothing but rest, rest." Lewis wanted to spend a night together
before AP's departure, offering to come to Moorestown if necessary. "There is
a hotel there isn't there?" she wrote. "Or is your bed big enough to let me get in
too. I'll promise to lie very still." Alice never responded to notes like these in a
comparably intimate way; however, we have only her CU correspondence with
Lewis, not the private correspondence she maintained with her confidante. She
carefully preserved all CU correspondence, anticipating historical interest, and
just as carefully shielded her personal relationships from view.[31]

In May 1915, NAWSA and the press again leveled charges of militancy at
the Congressional Union. The Union intended to utilize the long congressional interregnum by setting up deputations to congressmen in their home territories. The outcry came when Alice applied a similar strategy to the president
after he announced high-profile visits to Philadelphia and New York City. Much
as she had once tried to confront cabinet ministers for the Pankhursts, she now
wanted the American president to find women demanding suffrage everywhere
he ventured.

With a confidence earned from the success in New York and other states,
Alice decided to intensify the tenor of the CU's activities. She talked to prominent Philadelphia women about meeting with Wilson at his planned May 10
address at a city naturalization ceremony. Despite a *Suffragist* article to the contrary, she seemed to expect a presidential snub, telling Lucy to herald any refusal
of the interview "broadly so that it will give point to whatever demonstration we
arrange instead of the deputation." To raise the stakes, she sent intermediaries to
Washington to arrange the deputation in person.[32]

When Wilson spurned the emissaries, Alice's instincts proved sound. Dora
Lewis and Pennsylvania CU chairman Anna Lowenburg, a naturalized citizen,
visited the White House on each of three consecutive days, first leaving their
request and then waiting for hours, said the *Washington Post*, for "just two minutes" with the president. Wilson's private secretary Joseph Tumulty later wrote
Lewis that Wilson regretted the "inconvenience" but felt "necessarily engaged in
matters which seemed to be of consequence to the whole world"; his note reveals

both the president's awareness of Lewis's privileged status and his continued marginalization of the suffrage cause. Alice urged widespread publicity; Lucy brought in "movie men" to act out the women's dismay for newsreels.[33]

A rhetorical battle ensued among the press, NAWSA, and the Union. The press and NAWSA quickly framed the women's attempts to see the president as a "siege" of the White House. The *Washington Post* at first termed the incident a "freezeout" by Wilson, then a day later hardened its views to claim the women harassed the president. "Harassing or heckling of public men" would only arouse the same resentment as militants had faced in Britain, the *Post's* editors pontificated; the president had "larger things to occupy him now" (meaning the war in Europe). Other papers picked up the story, emphasizing "bad manners" and "pestering." Anna Howard Shaw released a statement disavowing the CU's "heckling."[34]

Lucy, a veteran of the WSPU's contests with the press, immediately recast the episode, invoking time-honored democratic principles. Her public retort to one editor questioned why "so innocent a series of actions" incited blame. To criticize the women "for their mere persistency in appealing for their rights," she shot back tartly, "shows a rather disappointing lack of imagination on the part of an American newspaper." She added, implicitly disputing the Union's militancy: "We have found it to be possible to be very patient with militant Mexicans, with militant English, and with militant Germans, who have seriously interfered not only with official etiquette but with the life and liberty of American men and women." Therefore, she said, "some of the same forebearance [sic] might be expected for the women of America who are so patiently working for independence."[35]

The aftermath of the "siege" revealed the president's intolerance of persistent women. Lucy discovered that the newsreels were scrapped "because the White House was displeased by their being taken." The vice-chairman wondered why "so much official interference" felt necessary. Indeed, the episode foreshadowed presidential attempts to control the press. In apparent compensation, the sympathetic Tumulty leaked to Lewis that Wilson planned to announce his position on suffrage well before the October referendum in his home state of New Jersey. In the years to come, Tumulty became a CU friend in the White House. And Wilson found the White House under far greater threat from persistent women.[36]

All the publicity surrounding the "siege" disappeared on May 8 when a German torpedo sank the *Lusitania*. Beyond the tragedy of the lives lost (including one hundred Americans), the *Lusitania's* fate brought the war in Europe fearfully nigh. Until this time, the national economy actually benefited from the European hostilities as American factories geared up to supply munitions to their allies. Now, many people wondered: would the president declare war? He soon used his scheduled Philadelphia appearance to affirm his intent to keep America at peace.[37]

Alice's correspondence with Lucy about the Philadelphia event reveals her keen calibration of the CU's assertiveness as well as male resistance to any perceived invasion. She abandoned any thought of disrupting the president's speech once she realized the extensive security surrounding his visit. "We are confronted with the situation of having to resort to actual militancy or doing nothing," she wrote Lucy. Philadelphia's mayor sent word "that he will protect the President from us at all costs." Their only alternative seemed to be rushing the police and military lines. For the time being, she felt, "it does not seem the moment or place to start any more aggressive tactics. ¼ of those lost on the *Lusitania* were Philadelphians and the city seems to be thinking of nothing else." She felt reluctant to cancel but believed that the president's rebuff probably created more publicity and good will for the CU than the planned deputation.[38]

Alice backed off the Philadelphia event but her letters to Lucy in May 1915 reveal that she had not discarded the idea of using "actual militancy," meaning willfully disruptive behavior. She and Lucy had discussed militant action before AP left Washington in March. She did not consider forcing an interview or a hall protest in Philadelphia to be in that category. Nevertheless, AP conceded, "militancy is not something to be started lightly and without much consideration."[39]

Alice's strategy mirrored the Pankhursts' first attempts at disruption, cunningly placing public officials on the defensive. And the president played directly into her hands. The exhilarated young Quaker who thrilled to British-style protest resurfaced for a moment as she wrote Lucy, "We want to convict [Wilson] before the country of evading us. We ought to be able to get publicity for a considerable time out of his refusing to see us and when we have exhausted the possibilities in that line and he has gotten the reputation of refusing to see suffragists, I should think we might then go further and try to make him see us." Alice charged Lucy to write it up boldly: "Do, I beg, put some righteous indignation into the account!"[40]

The calls of impropriety after a subsequent attempt to confront the president in New York gave Alice a taste of the hypervigilance overtaking American society. She oversaw two Union members' bid to relay an interview request from Mrs. Belmont, but the two women managed only to call out to Wilson as he left a social luncheon, surrounded by Secret Service agents. The women went to his next engagement but succeeded merely in leaving a written request for the interview. Despite the pro-suffrage stance of eight of ten New York dailies, press coverage mostly stressed impoliteness and imprudence; one paper even claimed a "dark plot." The suffragists rudely termed Wilson "the greatest little evader," some reporters noted, and accosted him as he left; the articles belittled the action, writing that Wilson simply smiled or laughed in response.[41]

The elite status of well-placed supporters helped fortify the CU against the social criticism for which Alice came fully prepared. She deferred comment to her most upper-class supporter—Belmont—who told the press, "We shall follow the President everywhere until he says, 'Yes' or 'No' on the suffrage question." Like Lucy's earlier justification, her rationale insisted that the Union acted in the finest First Amendment tradition: "What is the use of a republic," wondered Belmont, "if not to entitle its citizens to speak with their President?" Elizabeth Rogers followed up with a letter to the *New York Tribune*, bravely taking on the implicit anti-American swipes. "With hot-headed fools trying to plunge us into war," she wrote, this time "was a peculiarly fitting one in which to remind him of the incompleteness of our democratic government and of his passion for 'human liberty.'"[42]

Reporters eagerly covered attacks from other suffragists, whose attitude echoed the ultrapatriotic tone of news articles and presaged mainstream suffragists' response to the American entry into war. A close friend of Mrs. Catt proclaimed that "no real, earnest suffragists will endorse this action," adding that "all true patriots are thinking kindly of the President and doing their utmost to uphold him." Catt wrote the socialist *New York Call*, speaking for "99 per cent of the hundreds of thousands of suffragists of the Empire State when I declare that they unqualifiedly condemn the attempt made yesterday to harry the President." Both women cast the event as British-style militancy alien to America. "Although the denial of the vote to American women is a monstrous injustice," wrote Catt, "there is neither sense nor logic in harrying the President over it."[43]

A week later, Carrie Chapman Catt renewed her efforts to drive the Union out of New York. She privately accused Alice of going back on her word "against further mischief," addressing the letter to the CU's executive committee as well as AP. Catt claimed the CU imprudence caused "a statewide revulsion" of suffrage that threatened to endanger the November referendum bid. The public did tend to lump together all suffragists; however, Catt herself admitted earlier that the New York referendum looked iffy. Hoping that "true suffragists" made up the CU, Catt looked for Alice to cease and desist. Catt's letter caught up with AP several weeks later as she raised money in the Midwest.[44]

Alice resented Catt's underhanded tactics and was fast approaching the limit of her forbearance. She responded to Catt that she had pledged only to refrain from organizing a formal New York branch until after November. She countered the heckling charge at length, acidly questioning how CU tactics caused revulsion, "unless it came from the action of suffragists denouncing the event in the press and describing it as something very different from what it was." Alice then revealed her awareness of Catt's attempt to dissuade Ohio suffragists from working with the Union, questioning the older woman's claim to be concerned only about New York State. She finally reminded Catt that nearly all the CU's New York volunteers also worked for that state's referendum. Alice signed off with an edgy courtesy, chalking Catt's fault-finding up to misinformation. She then slyly flaunted her evidence, enclosing copies of her own May letter as well as Catt's Ohio letter "in case you may not have these letters accessible."[45]

If nothing else, Carrie Chapman Catt surely realized now that Alice, much like Harriot Blatch, would not simply fall into line behind her. The possibility of Catt's vaulting to the NAWSA presidency had increased noticeably, for the wealthy Miriam Leslie had bequeathed her a huge sum solely to advance the suffrage cause; court challenges delayed a final settlement. The Leslie money gave Mrs. Catt even greater motivation to tamp down perceived threats to the suffrage community. AP's refusal to play along came as bad news indeed for someone eyeing Shaw's shaky NAWSA reign.

The fallout from the two Wilson confrontations proved time-consuming for both Alice and Lucy, but their organization stayed strong. Renewed support from shocked members offset a handful of resignations and retreats. Both Union leaders spent considerable time responding to anxious correspondents, urging them to take press coverage with a large grain of salt and read *The Suffragist* for accurate accounts of CU activities. Nonetheless, one substantial contributor backed out and another talked of resigning. Alice's presence at the Connecticut CU convention failed to ease Katharine Hepburn's dilemma, as she tried to reconcile her Union sympathies with the opposition of the state suffrage group she led; she stepped back from active federal work. Even Alva Belmont decided that "the incident had given Mrs. Catt an unnecessary handle against us."[46]

Some members' outrage over public reaction to the demonstrations deepened their loyalty, however. In particular, the response to Catt's offensive enhanced AP's appeal because she seemed newly vulnerable. Well-placed New York advisory council members Eunice Dana Brannan and Elizabeth Rogers wrote a meticulous repudiation of Catt's letter, which they sent to all CU executive committee and advisory council members. After reading the widely circulated Catt–Paul exchange, AP's old mentor Lavinia Dock wrote Catt directly that the latter blew the Wilson incident out of proportion; better to turn against the president, she wrote, for his "shabby, seemy insult." One incensed CU organizer told a vacillating member that "the treatment of Miss Paul by certain suffragists has practically amounted to persecution."[47]

Alice spent most of the summer of 1915 traveling, leaving the stress of the Washington office behind and searching out fertile ground for the Union. The change of scene seemed to refresh her. Beyond expanding the CU, she prepared for the convention of women voters in San Francisco, planned to coincide with the Panama-Pacific International Exposition.[48]

Alice had plenty of time on trains to think about all the opprobrium. Her travels seemed ceaseless: in June alone she journeyed to Connecticut, Virginia, and back to Boston and New York, then Columbus, Ohio, and west to Wisconsin, Minnesota, and Michigan. She raised money, inaugurated new chapters, attended state conventions, and shored up loyalties, stopping only briefly in Washington to catch up on mail and spend a night with Dora Lewis. She particularly enjoyed her ten days in Wisconsin, writing Lucy, "I have never had a happier time or a more delightful trip." AP did not begrudge time spent, thinking it essential "finding the right persons," meaning prominent, but also strong-minded women, to lead the state branches. They needed to leave behind "a permanent working committee... who will really push the work and finance it."[49]

Alice set off for the West Coast in early August. She attended state conventions in Denver, Santa Fe, Salt Lake City, and Boise before going on to San Francisco. Like other first-time travelers to the West, she no doubt marveled at the spectacular vistas; losing her luggage for a while tempered the mood. And rough terrain loomed awfully close when she traveled by automobile. En route to Salt Lake, "washouts and wrecks" held her up for so long that she missed the Utah convention. Her travails warranted one line only in her missive to Lucy; more importantly, the convention was successful and the resulting state committee included "both Mormons and Gentiles" as well as women loyal to all three major political parties. Finally, late in August, the intrepid Miss Paul arrived in San Francisco, site of the Panama-Pacific International Exposition and her brainchild, the first Women Voters' Convention.[50]

Alice recognized that the Panama-Pacific Exposition presented an extraordinary opportunity to push suffrage forward on the nation's agenda. The exposition, a dreamland of color and light, commemorated the end of construction on the Panama Canal; like most world's fairs, its dominant theme rationalized science and industry as the foundation of a prosperous future. Pastel colonnaded temples towering eight to ten stories covered the six-hundred-acre site near the city's Presidio, anchored by the magnificent Tower of Jewels, which sparkled through the day and glowed like an immense flame at night. The first world's fair held in the American West, the exposition drew nineteen million visitors (including AP's brother Parry) during its ten-month run and generated endless publicity.[51]

In contrast to the 1913 suffrage parade, which staged women's exclusion from political life, the exposition allowed Alice to present the suffrage cause as a natural part of a Progressive future. The larger-than-life setting of the fair offered a perfect backdrop for AP's now-signature political theater. The CU suffrage booth, situated favorably in the Palace of Education near the fair's entrance, served as the focal point. As one organizer wrote, the booth (actually a long narrow space) looked "entirely worthy of the idea it represents," with neutral decor overlaid by the Union's festive banners as well as hanging baskets and bouquets, thanks to funds donated by Californian Elizabeth Kent. An oval portrait of Susan B. Anthony hung prominently among displays sent by chapters, one of which was a US map showing the status of woman suffrage in every state. Pride of place, however, went to the enormous chart laying out the January 1915 suffrage vote of every member of the House of Representatives. Once workers reported hundreds of visitors stopping by each day, Alice conceived the idea for a grand petition they could sign supporting the Anthony Amendment. The petition served as a political prompt, linking the Women Voters' Convention to the next Congress.[52]

Alice had started building momentum for the fair and the convention shortly after the January House vote. She sent her best organizers to San Francisco: Michigan's Margaret Whittemore, a veteran of the 1914 campaign, and Doris Stevens, who arrived for the summer. *The Suffragist* touted the exposition and the convention in nearly every issue. A variety of activities and special events, including open-air meetings and deputations to local congressmen, kept interest high. Illustrious visitor-members gave lectures on the importance of the vote. As the date of the voters' convention approached, newspapers like the *New York World* duly reported, "The trek of the suffragists from every State in the Union to San Francisco … is on in earnest now."[53]

Once again, a grand and gracious setting provided a bulwark against criticism. Delegates from the "free" and "unfree" states gathered at the exposition on September 14, the Congressional Union's purple, gold, and white banners greeting them from all the palaces and along the main Avenue of Palms: thanks to Stevens's efforts, the convention's first day was Everywoman's Day at the fair. Alice Paul left the speeches to Alva Belmont and other prominent supporters, including suffragists from China, Italy, and Persia. Belmont's speech galvanized the eight hundred suffragists at the opening luncheon. She declared, "The union of this sisterhood of woman voters is the power, politically, of the near future." The post-program reception and tea at the Kent estate in Marin County lent the proceedings the requisite womanly and privileged touch, as did the ball held the following night.[54]

Alice insisted that convention resolutions be the voice of western women whose states had accorded them the vote, thus excluding herself and NAWSA interlopers, who had heeded a call from Anna Howard Shaw to take a stand against the CU's "injurious" election policy. However, Alice avoided the controversial party-in-power rhetoric and emphasized the need to support the Susan B. Anthony Amendment rather than the rival Shafroth one. NAWSA stalwarts opposed to pledging allegiance to the Anthony Amendment ultimately proved to be a minority, most of whom could not vote. In the end, *The Suffragist* reported, Alice secured what she wanted: resolutions passed overwhelmingly in support of the Anthony Amendment as "the only direct and effective method of securing national suffrage" and proclaiming "unalterable opposition" to any other suffrage amendment.[55]

Alice conceived a novel way to further legitimize the CU as a political authority: a cross-country mission to deliver the grand petition to Congress. She realized the trip held great symbolic potential as a transcontinental drive to win suffrage. Hearing of the plan, two Swedish immigrants approached her at the fair booth and offered their car. "They had just bought it, said they were going to drive it back to Rhode Island," AP recalled. "It was the easiest and least expensive way to have a campaign: drive into a town, speak *on* the car at street corners." The notion reminded Alice of her days organizing around Britain.[56]

She persuaded Sara Bard Field, a tiny thirty-three-year-old divorcee, poet, and suffrage lecturer with young children, to undertake what Field later termed the "gasoline flight." She recalled asking whether AP realized "service stations across the country are very scarce, and you have to have a great deal of mechanical knowledge in case the car has some accident." The fearless Alice, who had only recently washed out on Utah's roads, brushed objections aside. "She said, 'Oh well, if that happens, I'm sure some good man will come along that'll help you.'" Once Field agreed, *The Suffragist* christened the travelers as "envoys," co-opting a diplomatic term to symbolize a message —the "voice of the new power, the woman's vote"—carried from "free" woman voter country to the country of men who blocked the same freedom for other women.[57]

On the final evening of the convention, Alice put the theatrical exposition setting to work to send off the envoys. "We wanted to get all the drama out of it we could," she recalled. The ceremony married the emotional wallop of a soldier's farewell with the loveliness and pageantry that, for suffragists, bespoke Woman's unique capacities. Ten thousand people gathered in the Court of Abundance beneath a starry indigo sky to cheer the envoys on their way amid the magical aura of the nighttime fairgrounds. A massive female chorus sang Field's "Woman's Hymn": "We are women clad in new power/We march to set our sisters free." As the fair lights slowly faded at midnight, raved *The Suffragist*, "orange lanterns swayed in the breeze; purple, white, and gold draperies fluttered, the blare of the band burst forth, and the great surging crowd followed the envoys to the gates." Mrs. Field and the two drivers climbed into the decorated car; a "Great Demand" banner festooned the back. With great pomp, women set the grand petition into place. "Cheers burst forth as the gates opened and the big car swung through, ending the most dramatic and significant suffrage convention that has probably ever been held in the history of the world."[58]

The envoys headed for Washington accompanied by nonstop press coverage, not to mention many bumps in the road—literally and figuratively. In Field's words, "the cross-country trip meant waking up a nation to national suffrage." The day-to-day reality felt more prosaic. Field wrote, "We get up at 6 a.m., jolt, bump, bounce, and shake over a hundred miles of awful roads, land weary to the breaking point." Small towns and cities salved their travails, greeting the envoys with wonder and, often, celebration. Field talked up the federal work everywhere they stopped and gathered more signatures for the petition. The envoys aimed for a late November arrival in Washington.[59]

Alice made her way back to Washington in just over a week, anxious about CU finances. She assigned organizers to attend to the remaining states where conventions and deputations seemed possible and cast her net out again for new blood. "Our great need is more workers of ability," she wrote one supporter. She spent much of October and November traveling back and forth between Washington, New York, and points in between, raising money, planning for the first national CU convention, and overseeing the envoys' voyage.[60]

In early November, Alice's years of prodding the National into a single-minded focus on the Anthony Amendment found recompense. First, the NAWSA board abandoned the Shafroth bill; Anna Howard Shaw bowed to internal and external critics, acknowledging the rival amendment as "not a wise measure." Furthermore, the 1915 elections badly bruised NAWSA's state-focused strategy: male voters in New Jersey, Massachusetts, Pennsylvania, and even well-organized New York nixed woman suffrage. As he had announced earlier in the fall, President Wilson traveled to his home state of New Jersey to cast his personal vote in favor of woman suffrage.[61]

The idea of suffrage unity resurfaced when Anna Howard Shaw, foreseeing another challenge to her leadership at the upcoming convention, announced she would step down as NAWSA president. With Shaw out, some wondered whether NAWSA and the Congressional Union might now work together. "Is that a pipe dream?" wrote one CU member. The *Woman's Journal* thought, "No one needs to go outside of the National Association in order to work for that amendment now." Yet many thought the CU a surer bet: Harriot Blatch immediately announced she would devote herself to federal work and the CU. And more than a thousand women of similar mind joined the Union in the week following the November elections.[62]

As the Union faithful prepared to convene in Washington, the envoys became the talk of the town. Sara Bard Field and her drivers arrived in the East after braving all manner of weather, breakdowns, and washouts. After inspiring a New York audience and raising thousands of dollars for the federal work, the envoys arrived in the nation's capital the day before the new Congress convened.[63]

The grand event welcoming the envoys to Washington seemed to herald a new day for the Anthony Amendment; as usual, Alice stayed out of the spotlight. A brilliant river of purple, white, and gold flowed down District streets as suffragists gaily rode or walked to the Capitol. Twenty women bore the massive petition bringing up the rear of the parade; they followed the envoys and a distinguished escort, including Alva Belmont, up the Capitol steps, where a group of pro-suffrage congressmen greeted them and accepted the proffered resolutions. Then the entourage moved on to the White House, where President Wilson had agreed to receive them in the East Room. He declared the petition "impressive," *The Suffragist* recounted, and promised to "consider very carefully what is right for us to do." The petitioners interpreted his cautious remark positively, since for the first time he declared his mind "open" on the suffrage question.[64]

The president's fellow Democrats were also newly attentive, revealing that they now associated political power with the CU and, by extension, with the suffrage cause. Democrats on the House Judiciary Committee quickly granted a suffrage hearing in December and showed intense interest in the Congressional Union's plans. But the dyspeptic committee chairman, Edwin Webb (Democrat, NC), questioned Alice closely, pressing her on whether the Union planned to campaign against Democrats in the 1916 elections. AP neatly sidestepped his queries, saying, "What we shall do depends upon what you do." The chairman retorted, "We will come to a better understanding of the situation if we know what you are going to do to us."[65]

The CU's new stature was underscored by its new commodious headquarters. Alva Belmont first broached the idea of renting one of Washington's converted mansions in early 1914; she and Lucy finally settled on an historic home a stone's throw from the White House in Lafayette Square. The ever-frugal AP came reluctantly to the idea, wanting to spend as little as possible for rent. But when Belmont negotiated a price equal to the Union's current office rent and offered to pay for three years, Alice agreed. CU staff hastily moved into Cameron House just before the convention.[66]

High spirits prevailed at the first convention of the burgeoning CU. As *The Suffragist* noted, Alice presided, calling the year's fruit of nineteen state chapters "tremendously reassuring" (actually, the total fell short of her initial lofty goal of forty-eight states). Nevertheless, she ventured, "We are beginning to believe that now the women of the country are going to back" the federal amendment. With the Shafroth bill abandoned and new leadership at NAWSA, she held out hope for substantial progress and agreed to meet with National representatives also convening in Washington about working together again.[67]

Unity was both sides' pipe dream. They made one last attempt to come together but quickly reached an impasse when Catt insisted the Union abandon

its election policy. Alice refused. "And up she got and walked out," AP remembered. "That was the end of the whole attempt." Catt returned to the NAWSA
convention where, disclaiming her own ambition, she rode Shaw's Shafroth
failure and her own forthcoming Leslie legacy to victory as the National's new
president. She inherited two million members from Anna Howard Shaw. Alice
remembered Catt's parting words to her—words calling to mind the grueling
trench warfare engulfing Europe in 1915—"I will fight you to the last ditch."[68]

"The Ghost at the Feast"

CAMERON HOUSE, THE new Congressional Union headquarters Lafayette Square, boasted quite a pedigree in Washington history. The "little White House" at 21 Madison Place stood so near the president's home, wrote one journalist, "you can hear the dishes rattle on the White House table when the wind is southerly." The mansion's niche between the popular Belasco Theatre and the private men's Cosmos Club ensured lots of foot traffic. Distinguished political families had occupied the imposing dwelling for nearly a century. The graceful bay-shaped entry led to drawing rooms and parlors on the first and second levels and eleven bedrooms on two upper levels. Alva Belmont, who bankrolled the move, crowed, "At last, our dreams of grandeur seem to be materializing."[1]

Though she preferred plainer quarters herself, Alice recognized that the mansion furthered important goals. To the outside world, the elegant surroundings communicated power and stature to the social and political elites crucial to their success; Dora Lewis imagined congressmen "shaking in their shoes at such an evidence of prosperity." Although the place might intimidate ordinary women, the patrician image of Cameron House belied accusations of militancy. In addition, the pragmatic AP planned to use the house to generate income. She and Lucy moved, renting rooms in Cameron House. Dora Lewis immediately leased one of the larger bedrooms for her Washington stays, and others rented for the remaining bedrooms within two months. Alice also arranged to open a tearoom on the ground floor to accommodate CU workers and passersby. She planned to rent out downstairs rooms to other local groups as well as save money on hall rentals for their own gatherings.[2]

Most critically, Cameron House enhanced the CU's ability to forge community. The intimate societies in which Alice came of age—the Swarthmore women's dorm, the College Settlement House, Woodbrooke—offered social space, which allowed bonding and opportunities for self-exploration. Cameron House now served as quasi-political, constantly shifting multipurpose space, as organizers and event participants moved in and out. Here, women bonded and became schooled in the alternative universe of the CU. Their commitment thus nurtured, many found themselves imbued with Union-style political fervor.[3]

The community had its share of tensions as well. Some of the younger women felt put upon by older hands who expected them to serve as gofers. Salaried workers and more privileged volunteers clashed. In addition, Alice established unwritten rules that guarded the refined CU image she wished the world to see. "We were never to smoke downstairs," one young organizer recalled. She and others considered this "narrow-minded and straight-laced" but acquiesced out of allegiance to AP. Likewise, every staff member knew they should not discuss anything but the Anthony Amendment with the press.[4]

Residing at Cameron House encouraged Alice to work around the clock; however, the house community also prompted a healthier existence. When her practicality led her to rent Cameron's most spartan room, Lewis urged, "Will you please use 'my' room? And I perhaps can tuck in with you when I come—may I?" AP engaged the gracious Californian Ella Dean as the house hostess, that is, housekeeper. Dean supervised daily maintenance, received visitors, and apparently kept tabs on AP. One member wrote Alice after a visit: "Perhaps the thing that pleased (and surprised) me most was that you are eating as much as three times some days and being dragged to bed ahead of the dawn. My compliments to Mrs. Dean!"[5]

The late 1915 removal of the rival Shafroth amendment from the political landscape and concomitant setbacks in NAWSA's state-focused strategy opened the door for Alice Paul to build on the CU's 1914 election success. Congressional action and press coverage recorded the Union's success at conveying the nascent power of the woman voter. First, the Senate Suffrage Committee gave the Anthony amendment a favorable report a mere six legislative days after the December hearing. The mainstream press applauded the Senate's nod to women's votes. The *Philadelphia Evening Telegraph* termed the Senate action political expediency in a presidential election year and a "special effort to win the good will of the hundreds of thousands" of female voters in the western states. The pro-suffrage *Christian Science Monitor* agreed: "States where women vote in congressional and presidential elections are not to be alienated, if it can possibly be avoided."[6]

Alice prepared to exploit both the perception and the reality of power to create a permanent structure for women's political influence. "At last, after years of waiting," she wrote in a mid-February *Suffragist* editorial, "we have reached a situation where there is 'a decided practical advantage to be gained by a dominant political party' by giving support to the suffrage amendment." She quoted a leading congressional Democrat warning his colleagues that the November election endangered their dominance. Indeed, the entire House, one-third of the Senate, and the president were standing for re-election. Suffragists needed to capitalize on this moment, she declared. "Not for another four years, and perhaps not then, shall we have another opportunity for success."[7]

The first imperative was a full-fledged organization. Twenty-nine states remained without CU chapters. The South proved most resistant—while more than three hundred members claimed a southern home, only two states in the Deep South, North and South Carolina, had mustered enough strength for a chapter. Many southern suffragists allied themselves with the Southern States Woman Suffrage Association, which decried federal suffrage action. Nevertheless, Alice believed that influential southern Democrats in Congress would respond to pressure from constituents, even non-voters. In late January, she went to Texas and then to Tennessee, Arkansas, and Kansas, joining organizers to help create new Union chapters.[8]

In her new peripatetic role, Alice accorded significant new responsibilities to trusted allies in order to allow herself to function as a roving ambassador. She enticed Anne Martin, a Pankhurst devotee who recently led the Nevada suffrage victory, to sign on as legislative chairman, leaving Lucy to focus on *The Suffragist* and administrative tasks. Martin, a former NAWSA board member, joined the executive committee of the Union as well; her NAWSA ties proved invaluable. The best of the previous fall's organizers became salaried field secretaries with regional territories. These included Pan-Pacific Exposition veteran Margaret Whittemore, Elsie Hill, and Mabel Vernon. Alice further eased her administrative burden by charging Doris Stevens with completing the CU's national structure.[9]

Newly elected NAWSA president Carrie Chapman Catt found herself in a delicate situation. She wanted to turn much of the National's energy to the Anthony amendment but feared popular conflation of NAWSA and CU efforts and the taint of militancy stigmatizing the National. So, like Anna Howard Shaw, Catt sought to define acceptable suffragist behavior as within the bounds of the National; she operated with more sophistication than Shaw, wary of alienating ambivalent members. Privately, Catt admitted to Anne Martin, "the Congressional Union has pushed the Federal Amendment to the front, no matter what anybody says about it." She pledged her "personal power" toward cooperative lobbying. Nonetheless, she promptly exacerbated the breach. In a January letter to NAWSA state presidents, Catt wrote that she hoped the two groups could "get together on some common platform." Nonetheless, the Union believed the amendment could pass now and she did not. "On this point," she demurred, "I do not know which is right." Catt then reiterated the National's condemnation of the CU's "anti-Democratic policy."[10]

Catt distanced herself from the Congressional Union, but her first acts as NAWSA president had a familiar ring. She insisted on appointing her own board, thereby gaining much the same authority Shaw had once criticized Alice for having over the "undemocratic" CU. In mid-January, as Catt publicly "sounded the trumpet call" for NAWSA members to "work with heart and soul" for the amendment, she carefully dissociated herself from any attempt to instruct western women "how to use their votes." However, she thought a meeting about "What can the West do to secure Woman Suffrage?" highly appropriate. Doris Stevens sent Catt's press release to Alice, pronouncing it "very amusing."[11]

The Union's field secretaries felt less amused. Catt planned to attend most NAWSA state conferences, so the prospect of her appearance to muddy the waters prodded CU organizers to hasten their own organizing. A Maine worker wrote the local press to head off attacks by Catt, while the National's operative there wrote Catt of the Union's strength, discouraging her from irritating the chapter. CU loyalist Lilla Day Monroe wrote Martin from Kansas, "I used to think Mrs. Catt one of the finest women in the world"; she now found Catt's tactics "criminally selfish and short-sighted." When Catt came to Massachusetts, local leader Katharine Morey struggled to keep up with the anti-CU meetings. "Mrs. Catt is here simply to kill us if she can," she wrote Lucy, "but we will die very hard."[12]

Alice refrained from a public response to Catt but consciously traveled well ahead of her over the winter. The process of building up her own organization added new depth to her influence and authority. She left a new state branch behind everywhere she traveled over the winter. In Kansas, one convert contended that "several days of Miss Paul's presence had put new life and eagerness into the old suffrage workers." Texas women, after three failed state suffrage campaigns, proved ready to sign up as well. A Tennessee reporter raved about AP's hour-long speech to an audience of 160, writing, "in her impassioned plea for solidarity among women, for the dropping of petty differences, and for the concentration of the suffrage forces upon the passage of the desired federal amendment, she stirred and aroused a desire for action in every woman within the sound of her voice."[13]

A mountain of work awaited Alice upon her return to Washington early in February. Lucy left for a month in Brooklyn, leaving AP with *The Suffragist*. With eight workers engaged in the state organizing, including the increasingly essential Doris Stevens, few office staff remained. AP urged a number of members to join the Cameron House community temporarily, stressing her "great need of aid." She entreated others to go west, anxious about finishing the suffrage state organizing before Catt's arrival. For a time, Alice even stepped in for the housekeeper, who had developed eye problems.[14]

The task of securing the funds required to underwrite her political agenda plagued her endlessly. Some organizers required salaries, and all organizing expenses drained funds; state branches struggled for self-sufficiency. Despite anxiety about making ends meet, she persisted with new plans, this time seeking donors for a publicity tour to build on the 1915 envoy expedition. Belmont promised $10,000 for 1916, but the tour alone would cost that much. The Union's capacity to devour money became well known: one Pennsylvania supporter made a tentative pledge, writing AP, "I know that where the Union is concerned a proffer of financial help is like a match to gun-powder."[15]

Remembering her own learning curve, Alice steadfastly encouraged organizers and local volunteers to develop their fundraising skills, despite repeated protestations of ineptitude. She refused to rely totally on large donors, recognizing that financial commitments of any size built loyalty. She gave one new worker an epistolary tutorial, urging her to make targeted appeals, drawing on social connections "to give in sums from one dollar up." Some aspects of the work typically raised little; therefore, "look at each piece of work as a whole and make one end of it finance another end." She mentioned that Vernon used her urban contacts in Delaware to finance rural efforts, for instance. AP felt entirely confident of the new recruit's abilities, she wrote. Raising money was "something that you will find you can do as you get more experience."[16]

Her imperturbability maintained Union momentum through continued setbacks. In February 1916, despite the earlier Senate action, the House Judiciary Committee chose to delay any discussion of woman suffrage until after the November elections. The resistance evident in their December 1915 hearing now took form. Californian Maud Younger, the new chief lobbyist for the CU, remembered one congressman bragging, "Well, we just killed Cock Robin!"—meaning the amendment was dead for the session. "Soon everyone believed it but Alice Paul," wrote Younger, "and she never believed it at all." Nonetheless, intensive lobbying and constituent pressure gained only a decision to defer *all* constitutional amendment votes until year's end. *The Suffragist* trumpeted AP's vow to "create such a powerful party of voting women" that Democrats could rebuff them no more.[17]

A boost in womanpower buoyed spirits after the committee disappointment. The Women's Political Union (WPU)—Harriot Stanton Blatch's group—voted to join the CU. With more than two thousand members, the decision meant a giant step in the New York State organizing, since key WPU members became CU district chairs. Blatch threw herself into galvanizing western women voters. She started advising Union organizers on political strategy and signed on to the CU suffrage tour planned for April. Alice treated her cautiously, concerned that the maverick suffragist would veer off course.[18]

With the Anthony amendment stalled in Congress, Alice laid the foundation for the fall 1916 western campaign against the Democrats, capitalizing on the success of the "gasoline flight." While Field's trip symbolically carried western women's voting strength to Congress and the president, this time vote-hungry envoys from the East would travel to the source of women's power in the West. Just as the 1913 procession appropriated a political party routine and tread upon conventionally male territory, the suffrage tour adapted a newfangled political practice: the campaign train tour. Theodore Roosevelt had most recently taken what we now term a whistle-stop tour; both 1916 presidential candidates soon employed the tactic. AP planned to occupy western ground first.[19]

Alice devised an ambitious crusade: twenty-two cities in suffrage states over thirty-eight days. Blatch called the itinerary "very exhaustive if not exhausting." AP tried to line up participants for two months preceding the early April send-off, seeking prominent suffragists as well as seasoned labor representatives. She felt more concern about respectability these days, newly wary of safeguarding the Union's reputation.[20]

She recognized that the public's heightened fear of war had changed the cultural landscape. In particular, the ridicule accompanying the Ford Peace Ship increased her concern for propriety. The Peace Ship delegation, led and financed by automobile magnate Henry Ford, sailed to warring Europe in late 1915 ostensibly to broker peace. Respected advocates such as Jane Addams declined to make the trip and President Wilson refused to endorse it, leaving the newspapers to deride the effort as a ship of fools. AP wrote Mary Beard of her concern about the suffrage tour being regarded like the Peace Ship, "if we are not very careful to limit it to people of considerable weight." When Beard suggested Inez Milholland, a Ford ship delegate, for the tour, Alice reiterated the "risk of being classed with" the debacle and the need for the public to view the CU trip as a "serious undertaking." She even termed the venture a "preparedness tour," echoing the language of war then flooding the country.[21]

Since the envoys needed to endure six arduous weeks on the road in a special train car, volunteers who could donate the time and (ideally) pay their own expenses proved tough to pin down. Lucy headed the party, as did Alva Belmont, always a publicity magnet. Busy with professional work and a family, Mary Beard declined, but she pushed Milholland again, telling AP that the socialite had improved considerably as a speaker; "I have quite come under her spell for the first time." She finally persuaded Alice. AP sought labor organizers but encountered resistance; Rose Winslow, a 1914 campaign veteran, finally agreed. AP's attempts to identify a well-known Jewish woman to appeal to coreligionists in the West likewise foundered. Twenty-three women would make the journey, including journalist Winifred Mallon as press officer.[22]

Alice unveiled an even grander ambition for her "Suffrage Special" at its early April send-off. As The Suffragist recounted, she wanted to take the organizing of western women voters to a level male politicians instinctively understood: the creation of a political party. She reviewed the historically close elections in many suffrage states, stressing the opportunity women held in a presidential election year to control the balance of power. In the 1916 elections, Alice wanted the

Woman's Party to be "the determining factor," like the Progressive Party in 1912. As *The Suffragist* cover caption read, "The Woman's Party for 'Suffrage First.' "[23]

Questions from the crowd abounded. Would the Woman's Party nominate candidates or lobby for suffrage planks in other party platforms? No, said Alice, the Party would "stand aloof" and force other parties to court their votes. The Party, she reiterated, existed solely to influence "the few votes that are necessary to change the result." The eastern envoys would invite women voters to organize themselves in Chicago in early June, just as all the existing political parties held their nominating conventions. With diligent work, the Woman's Party might accomplish its election goal. However, AP contended, "the threat will be enough." The amendment could pass quickly through Congress, she maintained, if congressmen recognized their self-interest.[24]

After a theatrical send-off, the Suffrage Special generated enormous publicity. The politics of the trip garnered considerably fewer column inches than human interest stories touting the "famous" visitors from the East, though both Belmont and Milholland backed out at the last minute. One Illinois editorial attributed the lack of political coverage to "danger scented in the prosecution of the national campaign so soon to begin." Despite the press treating the women more like celebrities than political actors, the tour nonetheless kept suffrage in the national consciousness.[25]

Alice recognized that many women were not ready to oppose male political candidates, but she hoped enough would rise to the challenge. As news of plans for a Woman's Party reached members far afield, she heard all the arguments for and against the endeavor, some from women voters themselves. One woman wondered whether the CU was "taking advantage of their sex," while another called the idea "energetic, virile." A Socialist woman trembled at the notion: "We cannot combat *against* men. We must work *with* them. We must affiliate with some political party." Another member, an Oregon state representative, agreed— women voters needed to work through the existing parties. In late April, Alice left the CU office in other hands and set off for Chicago to oversee Woman's Party convention preparations, keeping one ear to the ground for news of the tour.[26]

The reality of the suffrage tour ran counter to the glorious image painted in *The Suffragist*. As the envoys chugged westward, being cooped up together quickly grew tiresome. Not everyone got along ("I wish Miss Todd were in Guinea," wrote Lucy). The outside roar, the ever-present soot, and uncomfortable berths wore them down. Young Winifred Mallon told Alice, "Am very tired and dirty and dusty and my head aches and the train is jiggling fearfully." Detours and delays, sandstorms, power outages—the crusaders endured all manner of mishap. The more privileged occasionally fled to hotels for a proper bath, a night of privacy, and greater comfort. Nonetheless, they could not sidestep the grueling schedule.

The envoys often spoke half a dozen times during a full day of local stops and gatherings before climbing back on the train. "We shall be dead before we get back," Lucy predicted.[27]

The civic enthusiasm greeting the suffragists sometimes aggravated the rigors of the trip. "The people here are ruthless in their hospitality," Lucy wrote AP dryly. Locals feted them at luncheons and dinners, often providing an endless scenic tour. In Sacramento, for example, the exhausted group admired "the town, and the Capitol and them, energetically all day long." In Reno, the envoys appeared, "all dressed up and cursing," at a scheduled nine o'clock reception that evening, only to be treated to a local concert first. "At half past ten," moaned Lucy, "we spoke execrably to a remote and inattentive audience, and retired to our train after midnight in gloom."[28]

Even with exhaustion in check, the so-called flying squadron could not avoid NAWSA critics. Mrs. Catt did salute the Union tour backhandedly, by sending off a one-vehicle cross-country tour dubbed the "Golden Flier." Then she wrote or cabled NAWSA members to avoid the CU travelers, who she claimed did more harm than good. Some agreed. National members in Los Angeles tried to suppress publicity for the CU women. In both LA and Denver, Democratic women tried to interfere or absented themselves from gatherings. One prominent Denver woman penned a long letter to the *Woman's Journal* calling the CU "Republican dupes" and urging voters not to "barter [their] ballot away."[29]

Rumors and misinformation abounded. Mallon reported that many suffragists felt "badly befogged" between Catt and tales of the Woman's Party offering its own candidates. And considerable ignorance about federal work persisted in the suffrage states. "One woman," wrote Mallon, "who was bursting with friendly approval and desire to help us," talked with the group and then "turned to me, and in an undertone, being able to hold in no longer, demanded, 'What *is* the Susan B. Anthony amendment?'"[30]

As the bone-weary envoys neared Salt Lake City, they felt comforted that their efforts seemed to pay off. Most cities greeted them with open arms, if not pocketbooks. Newspaper coverage praised them, mostly generously. They signed up hundreds of new CU members, raised thousands of dollars, and piqued interest in the Woman's Party. Finally, in late May, the enervated crusaders headed back to Washington.

In Chicago during May, swamped with convention arrangements, Alice failed to anticipate the NAWSA presence at the upcoming 1916 political conventions. Her competitive instincts were aroused when Mrs. Catt announced the National's plans to hold a massive suffrage march and lobby for a suffrage plank in the Democratic platform. Catt felt too leery of southern members to ask the Democrats to endorse the Anthony amendment. Her plans threatened to overshadow the Woman's Party launch. Alice wrote one organizer of her intention to outmaneuver the NAWSA head, make her convention "dominate the suffrage world," leading the public and politicians to think "that the whole agitation is really in behalf of the national amendment."[31]

Amid so many attempts at forward motion—the tour, continued branch organizing, the congressional lobbying, the convention—the wheels started to come off the bus. Miscommunications multiplied between Washington, New York, and Chicago. Cameron House staff released a press statement suggesting that the CU had canceled the Woman's Party convention. Alerted, Alice conceded her ignorance of the bulletin; of course the convention would go on, she wrote Beard; "We are working day and night" to pull it off. She desperately needed more help in Chicago: "I do not see how we can possibly finish the work before us," she fussed, but she did not acknowledge the role her own expansive ideas played in creating problems. She wired Stevens and other organizers to join her. About the same time, Washington staff warned AP about the nearly empty bank account. The frustrated Alice appealed to Dora Lewis, writing, "I hardly know where to turn." As the Suffrage Special finally neared Washington, Alice set off to oversee their welcome.[32]

She returned to Chicago to finalize convention plans. Her presence galvanized workers: "Alice Paul arrived yesterday," Vernon wrote Martin, "so that things are speeding up a bit now." The crew in Chicago scrambled to nail down prominent speakers and accommodations as well as tickets to the Progressive and Republican conventions for some. Panic ensued when Martin and Harriot Blatch decided to skip Chicago; after several rounds of frantic telegrams, the two agreed to appear alongside Inez Milholland. And money pressures eased, particularly after a substantial contribution from new supporter Phoebe Hearst, the seventy-four-year-old widow of a Democratic senator and mother of newspaper czar William Randolph Hearst.[33]

Just when convention plans seemed in place, Mrs. Catt announced a rival NAWSA convention to coincide with the Woman's Party launch. Alice hastily wired key supporters to "leave no stone unturned to bring big delegation." She anticipated direct opposition to the new party from NAWSA: "Imperative therefore those believing national amendment make good showing." Catt claimed the NAWSA conference was announced months earlier. "We are not trying to steal anyone's thunder," she told reporters. She failed to explain why she kept the gathering from the press, though she took time to say, "I consider our method infinitely better than theirs," which she termed "anti-party politics." Catt also noted, correctly, that AP's stance on lobbying for platform planks had changed—the CU/Woman's Party now planned to best the National by pushing for an endorsement of the national amendment.[34]

As women arrived in rainy Chicago over the first weekend in June, *The Suffragist* gave the nascent party an imprimatur like no other. The thousand or so attending the Woman's Party birth learned that their beloved Susan B. Anthony had once envisioned such a development. Under the heading "Failure is Impossible"(Anthony's famed call to action), the paper quoted "Aunt Susan" advocating "hold[ing] ourselves as a balance of power to give aid and comfort to any party which shall inscribe on its banners 'Freedom to Women.' " More astute suffragists noticed that Anthony called for aiding supportive parties (plural) rather than opposing recalcitrant ones. Nonetheless, the maneuver lent a glow to the proceedings.[35]

Politicians design their conventions to inspire and invigorate the party faithful; AP's inaugural Woman's Party convention followed suit. If NAWSA and press attacks in the fall of 1916 rivaled those in the 1914 campaign, she would need stouthearted women. Monday afternoon, conventioneers shook off the raindrops and mingled with Belmont (wearing diamonds galore) and Hearst at a welcoming reception held in the modern Blackstone Hotel. They then strode into the adjacent theatre, where Maud Younger began her keynote address with a clarion call:

> We of the Woman's Party stand on the threshold of a new era. Along the road we have come many have come before, and sometimes that road was rough and sometimes it was lonely, but whether rough or smooth, always at the end the gates were barred and the women could not enter, and no key they had would open that lock. But tonight on that same threshold we stand, not pleading, not cajoling, but full of confidence that at last the key has been found by which that door may be unlocked and the entrance thrown wide open.

Alice did not choose a California voter for her main speaker by accident: the "key" Younger referenced was the power of the collective votes of western women.[36]

On Tuesday afternoon, the formal organization of the new political party commenced. The official name was to be the National Woman's Party (NWP). "The word 'National' added to anything," Belmont suggested, "seems to impress the general mind with more importance." The platform contained a single issue: passage of the Anthony amendment. Party members resolved to use their votes to promote that amendment, holding responsible any dominant party which, said *The Suffragist*, "refuses to do justice to women." In other words, the NWP continued the mission of the Congressional Union, but as an organization comprised solely of voting women. The convention quickly elected Nevada's Anne Martin as chair of the NWP, and Phoebe Hearst as vice chair. They allowed two exceptions to the voting-women-only rule: Mabel Vernon, a Martin confidante, became secretary and AP an ex-officio member.[37]

That evening, in a measure of the CU's success both in advertising and delivering women's political power, representatives of all five political parties addressed the convention. Anne Martin first reminded everyone that an average of 9 percent change in any suffrage state's vote would tip the balance of power. With that none too subtle warning, emissaries from the Prohibition, Progressive, and Socialist parties spoke. The Republican governor of Michigan then expressed his personal support for an Anthony amendment plank in his party's platform. The audience heckled the Democratic speaker, pro-suffrage Wilson intimate Dudley Field Malone, when he suggested they stop impugning the president's motives. He hinted that such criticism seemed un-American. Wilson kept the country at peace, he told them, and "great men change their minds."[38]

By design, one of the boldest suffragists in the nation rose after Malone. Self-professed Democrat Harriot Stanton Blatch rejected the implicit wink and a nod. "Mr. Malone tells us to be polite," she scoffed. "Good heavens, we have been patient and polite. We have got nothing by being polite, and it was not until we began to respect ourselves—it was not until we felt in our very souls that democracy for women was as great as democracy for men that things began to move!" As shouts of "Hear, hear!" and applause rang from the minions, the sixty-year-old pioneer defiantly pledged to deliver five hundred thousand votes against the stalling Democrats, using "every bit of energy and strength I have." Seemingly inspired by Blatch's magniloquence, Alva Belmont rose to make her own pledge: to raise $500,000 for the first Woman's Party campaign. "The whole house rose with a great shout of triumph and joy," *The Suffragist* recounted. In all likelihood, Alice sought and stage-managed both gestures.[39]

Throughout the convention, though, she remained in the background, choosing not to address those she drew to Chicago or place herself at the head of the NWP. While standing in the wings was her usual mien, she realized the importance of enfranchised women appearing to be the actors here. The focus on western women asserting their political agency implicitly rebutted those critics decrying CU interference in state activities.

Despite appearances, Alice retained control over the new enterprise. She made the decision, as in San Francisco, that only women voters could join the new party. All the organizing committees overseeing party bylaws and officer nominations included Union stalwarts like Kent and Vernon. Martin, the most visible voter in Union ranks, led the new party. Martin's arrangement with AP called for shared decision making; however, since Martin planned to spend the fall campaign in Nevada, Alice Paul essentially ran the NWP.

Many at the convention undoubtedly failed to realize her degree of control. They read AP's reserved nature as modesty, selflessness, and quintessential femininity. Near the close of one session, the assemblage called Alice to the stage for a suitable encomium. Connecticut CU state chairman Lillian Ascough spoke for the convention, underscoring AP's continuing influence. "It is to her clear vision, her genius, that is due the launching of this great new Woman's Party," Ascough began. "She has been a tireless leader, she has given her life to her work, and she has inspired in all of us not only enthusiasm and loyalty, but deep personal devotion." Three rousing cheers and a standing ovation followed. Alice could not be found.[40]

After the closing luncheon, many Union and newly minted NWP members headed out into the rain to join NAWSA's suffrage parade down Michigan Avenue to the site of the Republican convention. Alice marched, as did many others with dual membership. Some wondered why the National's parade failed to push the federal amendment: "I think Mrs. Catt has gone crazy," one woman wrote AP. Spectators watching from the warmth of buildings edging the avenue looked out on a sea of umbrellas and large soggy hats as the intrepid marched despite the driving rain.[41]

A few suffragists missed the parade in order to appear before the Republican platform committee. Inside the vast and turreted Chicago Coliseum, Mrs. Catt urged a suffrage plank. She was followed by the president of the national anti-suffrage society, who inveighed against the same plank. As the antis finished, reporters wrote, the hall doors opened and thousands of parade marchers, Alice among them, poured into the arena, "wet through and glowing with enthusiasm." They cheered Anne Martin as she rose to impress the potential of a female voting bloc upon the committee, eschewing what she saw as begging for a platform plank. Martin and prominent NWP Progressives later made a similar presentation to the Progressive platform committee; that plank, to no one's surprise, endorsed suffrage via any method. As it turned out, the Progressive Party soon fell to pieces after Theodore Roosevelt abandoned the fledgling party to support the Republican presidential nominee.[42]

The Chicago papers suggested that a first-ever Republican suffrage plank seemed imminent; indeed, like the Progressives, the Republicans vaguely "favor[ed] the extension of suffrage" without committing themselves to federal or state approaches. Both the CU/NWP and NAWSA immediately began written and personal appeals to the Republican candidate, Charles Evans Hughes, to gain a clear endorsement of their strategy. One elderly suffragist, calling the Republican plank insulting, wondered, "Is there any hope for the Democrats?"[43]

Some in the press took the new Woman's Party seriously. Denver's *Rocky Mountain News* understood Alice's intent, saying that like all third parties, the

Woman's Party would be "a party of protest. In practice it will seek to hold the balance of power, to defeat the party that is opposed to it and elect the party that promises reform. This is a policy which has gained most parliamentary reforms." The *San Francisco Bulletin* cheered the "vigorous action," calling it "quite in the spirit of the Revolutionary patriots, though without destruction of property or effusion of blood."[44]

Even the negative editorials presaged a new attentiveness. As Elizabeth Rogers wrote Lucy, "they are just beginning to believe the Woman's Party means business." Cleveland's *Plain Dealer* used Shakespeare to call up their vision of NWP as the ghost at the feast, "a new and, in the opinion of many, dangerous element" in political life, "the first direct appeal of sex solidarity through the ballot box." The editorial in the *New York Times* was predictably scathing, terming the CU/NWP the "Extreme Left" of the suffrage movement "deserted by a sense of the ridiculous." "The publicity is fine," Lucy wrote one field worker, "and we are enjoying ourselves hugely."[45]

National attention turned to St. Louis and the Democratic convention, where partisans seemed newly heedful of suffrage, thanks to the suffrage planks of their competition. Alice, Anne Martin, and a few others packed up and headed south. At the convention hall itself, appeals to the platform committee by NAWSA and the CU/NWP preceded an all-night vigil awaiting the result. Two cabinet members consulted AP and Martin, asking "What is the least you will accept?" The *Wisconsin State Journal* quoted one senator remarking about the pair: "Those two little women know more about politics than all the rest of us combined." Ultimately, the president directed the Democrats to approve a plank that pleased neither suffrage faction. Bowing to political expediency, Wilson requested formal recognition of woman suffrage for the first time but reiterated his own belief in states' rights. Catt, now favoring a combined strategy, immediately telegraphed him to provide a more "precise interpretation" of the language. Alice simply called the plank "meaningless."[46]

She believed that the demise of the Progressive Party strengthened her hand with the Democrats. Without a Progressive nominee splitting Republican-leaning voters, Woodrow Wilson's party needed to run hard to win; the West promised to be the key battleground. Democratic partisans urged the CU/NWP to accept the victory of any suffrage plank. "They realized at least," according to Alice, "that we were a factor to be reckoned with." She emphasized, "We must show that we have not been conciliated and show that we have the power to deliver those votes."[47]

In the space of three years, as the popular *Everybody's* magazine wrote, the suffrage amendment had "been taken out of cold storage and made to sizzle." For the first time in American history, the party in power and its chief rival both formally acknowledged the national importance of woman suffrage. "As a result of the recent events," the *Chicago Herald* opined, "equal suffrage goes before the country with its prestige immeasurably strengthened." More than one writer credited CU/NWP influence for the change. "Congressional action is demanded," the *New York Tribune* editorialized, "and unless it comes, look out for the hurricane."[48]

In the wake of the NWP founding, Alice cautiously moved again into confrontational tactics, pressuring both presidential candidates to endorse the Anthony amendment. On the president, AP employed her consummate sense of moment. During an outdoor address on July 4, as Wilson waxed eloquent on human liberty, Mabel Vernon, sitting on the reviewing stand a few feet away, loudly asked why he opposed federal action on woman suffrage. The president turned to look at Vernon, then replied, "That is one of the things which we will have to take counsel over later," and continued on, receiving the interruption with less consternation than his British counterparts. A Secret Service agent, however, told Vernon to stop. Vernon boldly pressed Wilson again at the close—"Answer, Mr. President, why do you oppose the national enfranchisement of women?" No answer came. But the agent reappeared to escort her off the platform. In the wake of July 4, Wilson became leery of assertive suffragists. When Mrs. Catt and a compatriot asked him for a meeting (Catt's first as NAWSA president), he asked his secretary, "Are these ladies of the 'Congressional Union' variety?"[49]

Lucy and Alice defended Vernon publicly and privately against the expected criticism. Lucy's *Suffragist* editorial, aptly titled "The Rising Tide of Discontent," asked whether a president "personally responsible for [men's] political helplessness" would respond likewise to a man. She added that the CU had "nothing to lose" since the president continued to reject federal suffrage action. Few CU/NWP members criticized Vernon's actions, underscoring Lucy's perception. One member who complained about the previous July's "heckling" in New York, now wrote, "We shall be obliged to explode a bomb now and then, no doubt." To those who regretted the incident, Alice replied pointedly, "If women do not make clear their dissatisfaction with the President's attitude there is certainly little likelihood that he will change it."[50]

In unison, Alice and Lucy carefully calibrated the uptick in direct action. They distanced themselves from the Pankhursts for the first time and defined their own brand of activism, continuing to resist the word *militant*. In a letter to the editor of the disapproving *Chicago Post*, Lucy declared that the British militants "resisted the orders of the police, held assemblies and destroyed property in defiance of the law." They might offend propriety; however, the CU/NWP chose to be law-abiding. With this declaration, Alice and Lucy drew a line in the sand in the summer of 1916, a position they never renounced in the difficult years that lay ahead.[51]

Despite weeks of multitiered effort, Charles Evans Hughes balked at venturing beyond his party's vague suffrage plank. Early in July, AP herself met with Hughes in New York (Lucy: "You won't forget to jolly him along a little, will you?") and secured his promise to endorse the Anthony amendment as the self-evident route to suffrage. After delaying another month, he announced his support for the amendment early in August, becoming the first major-party candidate to endorse the Anthony amendment. Woodrow Wilson, under pressure from his own party to match Hughes and eliminate a campaign issue, dug in his heels.[52]

With Wilson still obdurate and the House continuing to delay action on any amendment, the 1916 campaign against Democratic candidates would clearly go forward. Alice began lining up workers just after the NWP launch and urged state chairmen in the suffrage states to finish organizing congressional districts. She exceeded her ambitious goal of two operatives for each "free" state and signed up an additional corps of roving speakers, including Maud Younger, Sara Bard Field, Harriot Blatch, Rose Winslow, and Inez Milholland. Lucy took charge of Montana; Martin of Nevada. Alice planned to coordinate the effort from Chicago and New York.[53]

She believed the campaign required at least $50,000, more than a million in today's dollars. Alva Belmont pledged at the convention to raise ten times that amount; consequently, CU/NWP members assumed the organization's financial straits were history. Unbeknown to most, however, Belmont promptly set off on an extended cruise. By mid-July, funds ebbed so low that AP again began to focus on fundraising, including nudging Belmont, who stayed mostly incommunicado. The CU benefactor gave $6,000 of her own money by August and promised to begin collecting more by the fall. "In the meantime," AP wrote Edith Hooker, "our organizers are at work and all of them clamoring for more money." She hoped Hughes's support would make collecting funds easier. To Alva Belmont, she sent details of the organizing effort and probably gritted her teeth to wish the socialite "a delightful rest." A chastened Belmont began sending out appeals in late August.[54]

Alice's ambition granted her no such delightful rest during the summer, despite repeated suggestions that she do so. Her incessant working left her noticeably wan and underweight once again. A woman she met in St. Louis wanted to "put you to bed for four weeks and feed you on cream." Interest in her health proved so acute that news spread quickly of the sunburn she acquired when she traveled to Colorado.[55]

She found time to reconnect with family briefly but not with close confidante Dora Lewis. She stopped at Paulsdale, knowing that sister Helen had created a stir by both resigning from the Moorestown meeting and leaving suffrage work to devote herself to Christian Science. The New Jersey CU chairman warned AP of

"an awful black eye" for the state's work, but Helen remained firm, perhaps needing a separate identity, out of her now-famous older sibling's shadow. Lewis wrote
from her summer home in Maine, "How I wish I were with you this minute." The
two had spent precious little time together recently.[56]

In August, Alice traveled to Colorado Springs to launch the Woman's Party's
fall campaign, as the Democrats appeared to gird their defenses. The president took notice in a roundabout way by sending an ingratiating public letter
to Democratic women in Colorado. Wilson indirectly criticized Hughes for
going beyond the Republican platform and emphasized his own fidelity to the
Democratic plank—which, of course, he had authored. He praised women's interest in political questions and service and reminded them of his steadfast belief in
maintaining peace.[57]

Later in August, congressional Democrats lobbed more direct attacks on
the CU/NWP. Former supporter and pro-suffrage senator Charles Thomas
(Democrat, CO), still smarting from his near-defeat in the 1914 election,
denounced the CU/NWP at length on the floor of the Senate; several of his
colleagues followed suit. They accused the Woman's Party of raising money for
Hughes, a laughable charge, considering the CU/NWP finances. Rumors also
swirled, however, that AP's forces *sought* money from the Republicans; she
directed organizers privately to correct such misconceptions, since any party
money stood to compromise the NWP's nonpartisan stance.[58]

Meanwhile, Carrie Chapman Catt was diving into her presidency, trying to
correct the behemoth National's course. She bumped the annual convention
from December to early September in order to prepare for the fall campaign and
invited the president to address the gathering. She benefited from the foundation
AP laid for the Anthony amendment.

In his much-heralded appearance in Atlantic City, the president appealed
directly to his suffragists of choice and found them less compliant. He flattered
the delegates, complimenting their persistency. Aligning himself with the least
objectionable suffrage camp yet echoing NWP rhetoric, he claimed NAWSA
represented a movement "which has not only come to stay but has come with
conquering power." Wilson then cast out his own history on the issue, declaring
that suffrage would prevail soon and "we shall not quarrel with the method of it."
The crowd held its collective breath—the president acknowledged the possibility
of federal action. Winning suffrage, he went on, required "moving masses. It is
all very well to run ahead and beckon, but, after all, you have to wait for them to
follow." Though suffragists had proved very patient, he thought, "you can afford
a little while to wait." In a measure of how much the CU/NWP's impatience had
infected all suffragists, not even Anna Howard Shaw swallowed Wilson's patronizing. She stood up to retort that women had waited long enough—"We want

[suffrage] to come in your administration!" As the NAWSA faithful cheered that thought, the president smiled, bowed, and took his leave.[59]

Once again, Woodrow Wilson displayed his mastery of political rhetoric, especially when facing a re-election bid. *The Suffragist* quickly pointed out that "the President did not say a word on this occasion to explain how, if he favored suffrage, he has steadily opposed it in Congress; or what he would do to help it in the future." Some in the pro-suffrage press responded even more pointedly. Wilson had reached "the stage of not overtly opposing a federal amendment," said *The New Republic*, "at least during the campaign against an opponent who frankly favors it." The *Philadelphia Public Ledger* bluntly labeled the speech "weasel words." The president had been more forthcoming with Harriot Blatch in a private meeting a month earlier. "The negro question," the Virginia-born Wilson told her, precluded Democratic support for the Anthony amendment.[60]

Wilson's statement only began the commotion in Atlantic City. Mrs. Catt now told delegates that the Anthony amendment should demand their primary attention; the convention duly deemed financing state referenda secondary. States' rights advocates, particularly southern women, felt ignored. After maneuvering that vote, Catt boldly announced that her executive board would now direct all operations and hire two hundred field workers; NAWSA, she said, needed a million dollars to finance the effort, a tenfold increase from the previous budget. She instructed her minions to "let the world know where each candidate stands and then ask the voters to choose a candidate who is favorable to the Federal Amendment." This move was just a shade shy of partisan activity, though not oppositional. Catt wanted a full-bore lobbying effort in Washington, a prospect delegates heartily approved. When the dust cleared, the National and the Union were both moving in the same direction for the first time, prioritizing the Anthony amendment.[61]

The enthusiasm for what Catt called her "Winning Plan" owed much to Alice Paul. The convention recorded an astonishing shift of direction for the National. The centralization, the money, the sharper focus—Catt essentially followed the road AP hacked out of the suffrage wilderness. In addition, the new NAWSA leader, while staying out of the unwomanly muck of negative campaigning, steered away from an ineffectual nonpartisanship. Catt built on the foundation for federal action built by the much-maligned women of the Congressional Union. Furthermore, delegates who once disdained Catt's formidable organizational skills during her early turn at the NAWSA presidency now, in the light of AP's efforts, embraced them.

Alice Paul knew how much was riding on the CU's 1916 election campaign. "For three years," she wrote one supporter, "we have been saying that the women would rise in revolt at the polls this November against the Democrats if they did not pass the amendment. We are now face to face with the test of whether they will do so."[62]

She understood the arguments against holding the party in power account-able for the passage of the Anthony amendment. First of all, said opponents, the two-thirds vote needed to pass a constitutional amendment required congressio-nal votes from both parties. Opposing one of those parties might foster enough resentment to delay matters rather than hasten them. Second, Wilson and the Democrats stood for many issues that women gravitated toward, such as peace. Republicans, while more likely favoring the Anthony amendment, also repre-sented militarism and business. To vote Republican, then, many western women needed to believe that their votes against Democrats would hasten nationwide woman suffrage. CU/NWP critics believed, like Wilson, that the timing was off, particularly in the state legislatures necessary to ratify any constitutional amend-ment. Western women needed to vote as if suffrage was the preeminent issue of the day. But to many women, keeping America at peace seemed more vital in 1916.[63]

Alice Paul's logic differed. Yes, a two-thirds vote required both parties, but congressmen always voted in their own self-interest regardless of the opposition. Even though Senator Thomas felt furious at the CU, for example, the Colorado senator still advocated suffrage. More power could be demonstrated in opposi-tion, she felt, than in support. Indeed, the NWP campaign sought to convince enfranchised women to vote their own self-interest. Women's influence over peace and other issues depended on their power in the political arena; maximizing that power would only happen when all women could vote. The final argument that suffrage could not be hastened seemed self-evident—the Congressional Union's actions since 1913 had already accelerated the issue, raising it to national impor-tance for the first time. Patience might be a virtue at home; in the political arena, it meant only continued defeat.[64]

The campaign began in earnest in October, with Alice running the show from Chicago while she directed the Illinois work and simultaneously edited *The Suffragist*. While the public goal stressed defeating Wilson, the reality proved more complex. "Whether we succeed in defeating Mr. Wilson is of secondary importance," AP wrote privately. "What we must do is to show him and every other national leader that women are ready to revolt against hostility." A strong protest vote would speak loudly to either victor. However, if western women "flock to [Wilson's] support," suffragists would find it "exceedingly difficult in the next Congress to secure respectful treatment for the suffrage amendment from any party."[65]

Inez Milholland became the NWP's most effective publicity magnet. She did not fail to appear this time, as some feared, but needed a pep talk from AP about the virtues of opposition campaigning. Setting off in early October with sister

Vida as companion and *Suffragist* stringer, "the most beautiful suffragist" was to follow the usual rigorous itinerary—thirty-two cities in a month's time. Alice hastened to keep her happy, while some organizers on the scene found "the Lady Milholland" a prima donna. As one remarked from Spokane, "From raving beauties and egoists of exaggerated type 'Good Lord, deliver us.'" Nevertheless, the beautiful New Yorker drew large crowds and considerable publicity everywhere she went.[66]

The hostility from Democrats experienced in the 1914 campaign ratcheted to a new level in 1916. In Denver, workers reported "a mob howling down" Elsie Hill's speech outside a Democratic event. Vivian Pierce reported street banners in three Arizona cities cut down repeatedly and "filthy anonymous letters" to Phoenix headquarters. The acerbic Pierce wrote AP, "I may be dynamited one of these moonlight nights." Alice had her hands full in Chicago. Coworker Minnie Brooke reported organizers "bid[ding] each other a fond adieu when we start out to do anything."[67]

As usual, Alice viewed resistance as a sign of success and a spur to her efforts. When the president spoke in Chicago, she adapted the 1909 Siege of Westminster for her purposes. One hundred silent picketers, including AP herself, materialized outside the speaking venue. They embodied female endurance while holding banners mocking Wilson's Atlantic City call for patience: "President Wilson— How long do you advise us to wait?" According to one news account, the contradiction of silent protest and provocative messages angered some spectators including "a band of jeering hoodlums" who pushed "their canes and umbrellas through the signs, pulling them down and smashing them." The men trampled the demonstrators.[68]

The experience empowered some workers. Brooke, attacked a block away simply for wearing NWP colors, crowed to a coworker, "We had a most wonderful riot. Women with black faces, hair pulled awry, noses turned down and up, flag and signs torn in shreds." Returning to headquarters, another woman found an excited group "all feeling that they were Joan of Arc, while a few frantic wives telegraphed soothing messages to their husbands." As usual, AP turned the melee to her benefit, calling the scene worse than the 1913 parade mob. "Evidently [Democrats] feel keenly the weakness of Mr. Wilson's suffrage position," she told reporters.[69]

Early on, simply keeping enough organizers working bedeviled Alice. Heart and nervous ailments beset workers in Utah and Nevada; family issues called two others home. Labor advocate Rose Winslow (nerves, weakness) and Elsie Hill (bronchitis) had languished in bed since August, done in by the thin air in high-altitude states. Stevens needed injections to keep her going. When Katharine Morey became ill in Kansas a couple weeks later, her doctor advised her to go home. Though some of the women bounced back quickly, October became a jug-gling act for AP, who frantically tried to keep the crusade afloat. "I am in despair," she wired Dora Lewis.[70]

Alice suspected that paternalistic doctors exacerbated the problem. As she wired Hill, "In hands of doctor one is practically lost." To another, "I am afraid that most of our organizers would receive a similar edict from a doctor if they consulted one." Morey, whose problem turned out to be food poisoning, agreed; she told AP the doctor's advice "went in one ear and out the other." Diagnoses as nebulous as "exhaustion" and "nervousness" recorded some phy-sicians' view that strenuous work for privileged women was beyond the pale. Women could feel likewise: Beulah Amidon, a young new recruit from North Dakota, told Stevens of a coworker tamping down her own diligence: "She doesn't understand that it isn't necessarily fatal to do a good day's work seven days in succession."[71]

To be sure, reasons for caution existed. Amidon, for example, apparently tried to hide a serious illness. Desperate for money and workers, amid another impera-tive to prove herself, Alice Paul needed everyone to match her own astonishing capacity for work. Few could. Some organizers seemed well aware of the high expectations; Vernon wrote Stevens, "Poor Alice Paul has been fairly desperate, I hear, because so many of the organizers have failed her on account of illness."[72]

The publicity surrounding Inez Milholland's tour soon turned sour. Within two weeks of starting out, she started to cancel appearances, pleading tonsillitis. Trying to avoid audience recriminations, AP urged her to appear briefly, while another speaker shouldered the burden of the meetings. Milholland agreed but soon asked to "let me speak alone or not at all." Alice duly made the arrangements, later changing the schedule to allow the star speaker more rest. Should she "cancel tour return for operation or rest few days hoping to recuperate," Milholland then wired Alice. Then, "Doctor insists upon two days rest to avoid complete collapse." Alice arranged for Milholland to skip Arizona; however, "calamity for you aban-don tour." Milholland's cancellation of the earlier Suffrage Special had generated many negative headlines. AP tried to avoid these and keep her headliner by asking Milholland to simply sit quietly on the stage.[73]

Milholland felt impelled to do more than just appear. Consequently, later that evening, she fainted while attempting to make a speech in Los Angeles. An ador-ing *LA Times* reporter described the scene in the packed hall. "In the middle of an intense sentence she crumpled up like a wilted white rose and lay stark upon the platform." Carried offstage, Milholland pulled herself together and insisted on returning. "You can imagine how that 'got' people," reported Amidon. The speech continued with a wan Milholland in a chair. Afterward, the ailing luminary, said

Amidon, was "in a complete state of collapse....I guess she really has gone the limit."[74]

Alice learned a week after Milholland's collapse that the suffrage beauty was seriously ill even before the tour began. Vida Milholland confided in AP that her sister felt "quite unfit" from the start, with infected tonsils and an erratic heart. Doctors offered medication but by Salt Lake, Inez doubled or tripled the dosage. With her sister improving, Vida wondered, "Can't we in some way capitalize her illness and get some votes in that way?" She knew how masterfully the English militants won sympathy for the hunger strikers; why not follow their example? Vida added that she knew many of the "magnificent fighters" in the NWP shared Inez's health struggles. Amidon put the situation more bluntly: "After all these years to have a girl risking her life for suffrage—it's enough to make us all cynics & manhaters, only we can't afford it."[75]

Alice held out hope for her debilitated star to recover, at least enough for the final long-distance appeal planned from Chicago. "Surely she can pull through this," she wired. However, she began arranging substitutes for Inez's remaining dates. The election waited for no woman. Inez rallied but soon weakened again.[76]

Despite the Milholland calamity, the National Woman's Party became ubiquitous in the suffrage states in 1916, as fresh and familiar publicity stunts brought politics into the everyday lives of western women, encouraging them as political actors. Daily and weekly press bulletins reached hundreds of newspapers. The California campaign used "movie slides" (still pictures shown before a film) to spread the word. Elsie Hill hired a donkey cart, festooned it with signs, and sent the four-footed emissary clopping endlessly about the Denver streets. She arranged for five hundred loudspeakers on the balconies of Denver's Brown Palace hotel to receive the election-eve telephone communication from Chicago.[77]

The dramatic and unprecedented long-distance telephone hookup capped off the 1916 NWP campaign and urged enfranchised women to the polls. Characteristically, AP turned over the crowning appeal to Harriot Blatch who stepped in for Milholland. Spellbound audiences marveled as Blatch asked voting women to place suffrage first. Her call to arms—"Wilson kept us out of suffrage!"—echoed the president's campaign slogan—"He kept us out of war!" The next day in many western cities, NWP volunteers monitored polling places handing out "Vote against Wilson" flyers. With that effort, the 1916 campaign became history. While others waited for the results, Alice made plans for the future.[78]

The last organizer to "fail" Alice turned out to be Lucy herself. A nonchalant postscript on her final letter from Montana dropped a stunner: "I want to live in Brooklyn for a while." Lucy still intended to volunteer for the CU from home but decided to leave the full-time suffrage organizing in Washington to others. She later told AP that single women had done enough for suffrage; married women should pick up the slack. Alice no doubt hoped her longtime co-conspirator spoke from exhaustion and would soon return. Yet, as she told an interviewer many years later, her longtime ally was "never quite as committed as we'd like."[79]

Excitement reigned in NWP headquarters on election night as Charles Evans Hughes appeared victorious. But by dawn, Wilson had vanquished his opponent, with a 3-percent vote margin. Harriot Blatch and others blamed the Republicans for being overconfident and refusing to court the suffrage vote aggressively. "I don't think I shall ever be the same after thinking that Mr. Hughes was elected and then finding out that he wasn't," wailed loyal Margaret Whittemore from Michigan. Katharine Morey wrote of the gloom in the Boston CU office, many feeling "we might as well lie down and die."[80]

The discouraged women forgot that politics turns on perception as much as reality. Alice would have declared victory regardless of the result. After the election, she found plenty of evidence to support that conclusion. She dined in New York with a prominent Democrat, who told her the party understood the message of the NWP campaign. "He seemed to think," Alice wrote privately, "that the Democrats would have to put our Amendment through either this Session or the next in order to remove all opposition before the 1918 Congressional Election." The public (and many NWP members), she realized, saw the election simply in terms of who won or lost. "Fortunately," she went on, "it is the Democratic leaders which we have to deal with... as far as I can gather they have come out of the Campaign with a profound respect for the strength back of the National Suffrage Movement."[81]

In *The Suffragist*, Alice provided more evidence of success as well as her own political calculations. In the only state that counted women's votes separately, Illinois (where women could vote only for president), a majority of women voted for Hughes. In the western states with full woman suffrage, the male population outnumbered the female by large margins, so women's protest votes would be insufficient in any case—a fact AP somehow neglected to mention at the outset of the campaign. She had insulated the NWP effort whatever the result. She declared, "We did not endorse any candidate. We did not care who won." She added that "every Democrat" understood the NWP protest vote. "Elections are uncertain affairs," she reminded the faithful. "Organized opposition based upon a widely accepted principle must be conciliated."[82]

Inez Milholland died at the end of November at the age of thirty-one. The process of turning her into a martyr for the suffrage cause began almost immediately with a *Suffragist* cover bearing the young woman's likeness, her large eyes seeming to pierce the viewer's heart. The legend suggested a Christlike sacrifice: "As He died to make men holy, let us die to make men free." A revised version of her last words became the new battle cry: *How long must women wait for liberty?* Alice, remembering Vida's encouragement to capitalize on her sister's illness, somehow reserved the US Capitol rotunda on Christmas Day (perhaps the only day she *could* reserve it) and then proclaimed that the government "has recognized the greatness of the cause she fought for."[83]

AP began to shape the memory of a capricious and occasional suffrage celebrity into a torch illuminating the way forward. A reverential memorial pageant unfolded on December 25 in Statuary Hall, with the CU/NWP symbolically placing Inez Milholland among the heroic figures gracing the rotunda, claiming the power of that male-dominated space for themselves. One thousand invitees, including Milholland's widower, Eugen Boissevain, and the entire Milholland family, rearranged their holiday to attend. Alice modeled the service after the one held by the Pankhursts for their own martyr, AP's friend Emily Wilding Davison. She urged speakers to emphasize female solidarity: Maud Younger, for one, articulated the need to newly "consecrate ourselves to the cause of Women's Freedom, until that cause is won." Alice decided to build on the emotional climax of the Milholland memorial and the raw nerves from the 1916 campaign to launch her most powerful appeal for justice.[84]

13

"*The Young Are at the Gates*"

AS 1917 BEGAN, Alice Paul stood at the head of an organization boasting more than forty thousand members among the Congressional Union, the NWP, and affiliated branches. The power she had urged women to claim began to manifest itself amid the persistent rumbling of the European war.

President Wilson had won re-election in the face of NWP opposition, but the Democratic party signaled its readiness to consider the federal suffrage amendment. The president, however, held firm to his belief in state-by-state methods. In December, he greeted the reconvening Congress with his annual message and ignored the Anthony amendment. AP, said *The Suffragist*, decided to match his "weapon of silence" with one of her own. Mabel Vernon secured gallery tickets to the opening session and sat in the front row. As Wilson held forth on citizenship rights for the men of US-held Puerto Rico, she flung a golden banner out over the gallery rail reading, "Mr. President, what will you do for woman suffrage?" Wilson saw the banner and paused, then continued his speech, eventually quieting the buzz on the House floor. The silent protest warned both the president and Congress of the NWP's persistence. A week later, the long-resistant House Judiciary Committee reported out the Anthony amendment, positioning it for a new vote in the full House.[1]

Alice remained convinced that a presidential endorsement was the key to suffrage victory. Therefore, on January 1, 1917, she followed up the Vernon protest by sending a bold and specific request for Wilson to receive what she billed as the Milholland Memorial Delegation. The president, clearly annoyed, wrote his secretary, "I would like to avoid seeing them altogether, but if I do see them, it will be at a time of my own selection." After AP responded more humbly, he assented, bowing to the public dismay over Milholland's death.[2]

Alice ambushed Wilson, using the memorial to lobby the president. On January 9, three hundred CU/NWP members marched across Lafayette Square to the White House; AP remained at headquarters. Received in the East Room, Maud Younger and Sara Bard Field each eulogized Milholland and appealed to Wilson to prevent further sacrifice by supporting the Anthony amendment. The president, who had agreed to listen to only one speaker, responded stiffly that he expected only a memorial. Though he now personally supported woman suffrage, as ever, he awaited his party's command on the amendment. According to *The Suffragist*, Wilson insisted that his party was "more inclined than the opposition party to assist in this great cause" and hinted at his displeasure with the NWP's role in the recent election. The deputation was dumbfounded at the president's doubletalk. They walked dejectedly back to Cameron House.[3]

Anticipating Wilson's intransigence, indeed courting it, Alice orchestrated an indignation meeting after the presidential audience to launch the next phase of demonstrations. After the members of the delegation aired their pique, Harriot Stanton Blatch energized them, stressing the need for a novel approach to a president who could have led his party but had shunned acting for suffrage. "We have got to take a new departure," Blatch declared. "We have got to bring to the President, individually, day by day, week in and week out, the idea that great numbers of women want to be free, will be free, and want to know what he is going to do about it."[4]

Blatch proposed a silent vigil, an unceasing picket line at the White House through Wilson's second inaugural in March, a plan in fact already approved by the CU/NWP executive committee. "Let us stand beside the gateway where he must pass in and out," she urged, "so that he can never fail to realize that there is a tremendous earnestness and insistence back of this measure." She then asked: "Will you not be a silent sentinel of liberty and self-government?" The group pledged $3,000 and Alice, seemingly just a witness, had launched her next offensive.[5]

The idea of suffragists picketing was still novel, though not original. Choosing Blatch to set up the White House picketing was Alice's nod to the former WPU leader's 1912 use of "silent sentinels" at the New York state legislature. Dutch suffragists had recently ended a similar vigil. AP most directly modeled the White House picketing after the infamous Siege of Westminster by the British Women's Freedom League, held during her first days of organizing with the Pankhursts. The previous October, she used pickets in Chicago, an incident still fresh in many minds because of the anger directed at the demonstrators.[6]

Although most scholars describe the picketing as civil disobedience, Alice Paul felt confident that the NWP vigil would stay within the bounds of existing law. Picketing suffragists appropriated a staple of American strikes practiced by unionized working men and often accompanied by violent altercations. Female workers too had walked picket lines in recent years, sometimes enduring arrest as a consequence. After several bitter strikes, union leaders sought legal protection for participants; many interpreted the 1914 Clayton Act as deeming non-violent protest legal. Nevertheless, in an increasingly militaristic climate, the notion of defiant women protesting outside the preeminent house in the land seemed risky. For if the sentinels declined to break the law, they nonetheless would engage in social disobedience, transgressing accepted boundaries of class and gender.[7]

As before, Alice deflected criticism and masked determination with grandeur and feminine pageantry. Shortly before 10 o'clock the morning of January 10, twelve women emerged from Cameron House wearing tri-colored sashes, holding colorful flowing banners aloft. Mabel Vernon led the group; AP observed. In single file an arm's length apart, the women crossed Lafayette Square, then busy Pennsylvania Avenue, and took places before the east and west gates of the White House. The purple, white, and gold enlivened the sentinels' long dark coats and stood out against the stone and iron gates and the stark white mansion behind. Three women stood on either side of each gate, facing the street. They displayed printed swaths of silk. "Mr. President, What Will You Do for Woman Suffrage?" asked one banner; the spirit of Inez Milholland spoke through the second: "How Long Must Women Wait for Liberty?"[8]

The sentinels first drew curious or dismissive looks, no more. The president soon motored in from a golf game—and ignored them. Though Alice had instructed the women on how to handle any police interference, the White House guards looked mostly bemused. Passersby and presidential visitors laughed or paused in amazement or admiration. One picket reported, "Not one unkind or insulting word from any one." AP warned them against getting drawn into debate or personal conversation, telling them, one remembered, "exactly what words to say" to explain the vigil. Hours passed and the women wearied; fortunately, the weather stayed mild and clear. Replacements arrived in early afternoon; at five thirty, they retired for the evening. The next day, another group of twelve took up the watchful waiting.[9]

The silent sentinels intended to reclaim the stage. As calls for American entry into the war in Europe began to dominate the national discussion, Alice recognized the challenge of keeping the Anthony amendment in the public mind. She constructed the banner bearers as American Womanhood, exercising the sacred right of petition. Symbolically, they faced the nation and commanded its attention. They personified womanly virtues—patience, reserve, endurance—while sending a political message. The sentinels further challenged the brassy public image of the CU/NWP by embracing their new political weapon: silence.[10]

Alice carefully chose nonviolence in order to retain public sympathy. Her decision owed more to the recent history of the WSPU than to Quaker values. Though she would never disavow the Pankhursts, she learned from afar that their use of violent tactics only ushered in widespread disrepute. Alice now distanced herself from such political mischief. However, her instructions reveal that she expected violence from the police and, like the Pankhursts, she planned to turn that to her advantage. After Milholland's death, some women were ready for bodily sacrifice on the altar of suffrage.

The sentinels received a muted, sometimes condescending response from the press, a reaction suggesting that many journalists now accepted the inevitability of suffrage by federal action. Indeed, both the *Washington Post* and *Washington Star* placed the Anthony amendment on their lists of imminent legislation. Many papers around the country featured the vigil on the front page, but only for the first day or so. Editors at the *San Francisco Bulletin* struck a common note. They thought the pickets were "mildly hazing" the president in a friendly way. They felt sure the women did not have the heart to go any further.[11]

For critics of the vigil, including a number of Union members, the sentinels' silent decorum failed to meet their standard for propriety. In the press, hypervigilant anti-suffragists labeled the pickets a "silent invitation" to any potential assassin. Mrs. Catt immediately issued a statement bemoaning the "annoyance and embarrassment" to the president. NAWSA felt equally impatient for suffrage, she insisted, but heckling remained inappropriate; she privately called the picketing childish and futile.[12]

Alice's mailbox filled up with disparaging letters labeling the vigil silly or undignified or simply hurtful to the cause. One former supporter told the CU chairman to "use your own splendid talents for something besides circus tricks!" Michigan organizers wired of "protests all day from members." A dozen resigned. Alice's own mother wrote in dismay: "I hope thee will call it off." AP politely thanked nonmembers for sharing their views and sent each *The Suffragist* so fault-finders might "learn more of what we are attempting to do."[13]

Unlike Alice, some longtime members failed to see any political value in the silent vigil. A group of prominent New York members, including Mary Beard, urged returning to the "political method" (meaning opposition campaigns); one wrote, "We must really injure them,—not just nag them." Harriot Stanton Blatch's complaint seemed more puzzling. The mercurial Blatch was appalled to find women voters picketing—she recalled supporting only nonvoter participation. Alice felt that using voters made the possibility of electoral retribution even more trenchant. Unconvinced, Blatch resigned her position on the executive committee, though not her membership. Some New Yorkers felt mollified by AP's assertion that publicity "results immediately in discussion and discussion is the very essence of politics."[14]

Yet the hostility pouring into headquarters took its toll, particularly with Lucy gone. When a gracious letter (and check) arrived from Belmont, Alice's relief seemed palpable: "We have received almost nothing but letters of sternest reproach since we started," AP told the socialite. "It was indeed a joy to open your letter after all the other hostile ones." Alice's confidence was not unshakable, despite her serene exterior. Her doubts resurfaced in one self-deprecating note: "I am beginning to feel that our efforts are always doomed to meet with disapproval," she groaned to one correspondent. "If we could only once do something that would be popular!" In England, comrades shored up each other; without Lucy to share the burdens of leadership, AP's role became a lonelier one.[15]

She no doubt found some solace when her former Penn admirer, William Parker, appeared in Washington. Parker left his position on Wall Street and came to the District sometime in 1916 as a finance expert in the Department of Commerce. He remained until 1918. A few letters survive to indicate that Parker and Alice stepped out on a regular basis, their relationship known to staffers at Cameron House.[16]

Alice also drew strength from supporters. Despite the cavalcade of criticism, the vast majority of members stuck with Alice. Those who also admired the Pankhursts felt particularly enthusiastic. An Oregon member "deplor[ed] the necessity for such sacrifice" but found the sentinels valiant and brave and AP's "unflinching loyalty" to suffrage admirable. One District member recalled Milton: "They also serve who only stand and wait." And a New Jersey member offered "double duty" when she came to Washington. "You are a match for Woodrow," she told AP, "and he knows it."[17]

So the vigil continued, day after day, usually six days a week. The women soon discovered that, even in Washington's mild winter, standing outside for several hours numbed the bones. They endured sleet, hail, snow, and biting winds; at times, shifts were reduced to two hours. Alice drew on her fur coat and took her turn one day. The sentinels tried standing on wooden boards and later hot bricks to keep their feet warm; to thaw their insides, Mrs. Kent routinely drove up in her coupe with a thermos of hot drinks. Supporters sent warmth in the form of rain slickers, wool mittens, and hose. Even White House staff invited the sentries inside one day to warm themselves; they declined.[18]

Once the possibility of arrest seemed remote, local black women became willing to join the vigil. Alice telephoned Mary Church Terrell, who came with her daughter at least one cold day. Affluent black women, even a leader like Terrell, feared any run-in with the law would severely compromise their status. It seems likely that Terrell's presence paved the way for other black sentinels, but no evidence of their participation has survived.[19]

Alice continually refreshed the ongoing demonstration in the public eye as well as members' minds. She designated special days for college students or wage-earning women or state groups to generate hometown press. Patriotic Day allowed groups like the Woman's Relief Corps to bring American flags to mix with suffrage colors. The constant stream of new recruits through headquarters both eased and exacerbated the burden on staff and local volunteers. AP welcomed as many out-of-towners as Cameron House could hold; at times, she reported the house "crowded to the doors," with four in some bedrooms.[20]

Many of the hundreds of sentinels forged bonds, reshaping and deepening a feminist community already predicated on devotion and sacrifice. The sorority of Cameron House, the drama of the daily vigil, heady conclaves, the camaraderie of dinners and midnight snacks: all these heightened the experience. Emotions bubbled to the surface as woman after woman took her turn as banner-bearer. "An hour's silent guard in a January storm," wrote one volunteer in *The Suffragist*, "brought to you as nothing else could a realization of the years that suffragists have spent waiting." The community of Cameron House burnished the slow burn, despair or even elation the pickets felt into, as another wrote, "the thrilling warmth that simply working for a great cause brings with it," a warmth the young Alice Paul once consciously sought for herself.[21]

The ongoing vigil complicated the lobbying effort in Congress. Anne Martin oversaw the congressional effort and state letter campaigns, while Maud Younger headed the lobbying effort. A burgeoning card file held detailed information on each congressman, including nearly word-for-word accounts of each CU visit. Like Alice, both Younger and Martin felt besieged with questions about the silent sentinels and lamented the time spent responding. Martin disputed the vigil's value with NAWSA's new full-time lobbyist Maud Wood Park, who insisted the picketing lost votes for the Anthony amendment. She failed to produce any proof, however.[22]

Martin's and Younger's diligence proved essential as Alice strained to keep the vigil and other operations going without key lieutenants. She told one member of feeling "more closely confined than ever." Lucy Burns showed no sign of returning, although she took on some organizing near home. The moral support and expertise Lucy brought as a longtime comrade seemed irreplaceable. Alice kept her name on *The Suffragist* masthead but struggled to publish the weekly journal, so essential to nationwide communication, without her. In addition, Doris Stevens had yet to recover from the fall campaign and Dora Lewis was traveling in China. As Alice wrote Boston CU co-chair Katharine Morey, she felt "quite mad." She moaned to Morey's mother Agnes that she felt "already worn out and how we shall keep it up until March 4 is a problem which we cannot face with equanimity."[23]

When Stevens returned, Alice faced a new challenge: an imminent war. After the president broke off diplomatic relations with Germany in February, an American declaration of war seemed all but certain. Telegrams and letters streamed in urging AP variously to postpone suffrage activism for war work or devote the CU/NWP to peace or stay the course. Harriot Blatch thought the "national crisis" should end the vigil; Elizabeth Rogers, however, wrote, "Do

stand firm on the picketing!" Field organizers reported the populace already turning to war service.[24]

American activists faced the same choice British suffragists confronted when
England came under direct threat in 1914. Most Britons, like the Pankhursts, for-
sook advocacy for war work and a grateful public lauded their patriotism. Mrs.
Catt thought American women might reap that benefit too and be rewarded later
with the vote. She quickly announced the National's support in the event of war.
Her decision startled NAWSA members, because Catt had worked tirelessly with
the Women's Peace Party (WPP). The WPP promptly ousted her. Many pacifists
resigned from NAWSA; others remained disgruntled, finding the move high-
handed or "too evidently a bid for popular favor."[25]

Alice remained single-minded, driven by the historic Quaker commitment to
peace but, more importantly, glimpsing an opportunity. While one might support peace or war, she maintained, suffragists agreed on one thing: the need to
enfranchise women. "Never was it so urgent that women have representation in
government councils," she argued in *The Suffragist*. She urged CU/NWP members to persevere and consider the sentinels symbolic of the need for female as
well as male consent to any war. "Now above all times," she wrote, "women must
hold aloft the banner calling for full political liberty for all women." At a March
convention, members voted their support.[26]

While a whole new stream of protests and resignations greeted Alice's
announcement, new members far outweighed the defections. "It was Time
I Graduated from the National I plainly see!" crowed a Rochester woman, suggesting AP take advantage of the "psychological moment to swing any pacifists
who are now heart broken members of the National into C.U." She did; indeed,
during March, the NWP gained two hundred new members. Mary Beard further
boosted AP's claim with a *Suffragist* article pointing out that, in past American
conflicts, gratitude for women's war work had been "short lived and often shal-
low." And the vigil continued at the White House gates.[27]

As Alice organized the demonstration for Wilson's second inaugural in
March, she increasingly felt Lucy's absence. She pleaded with her to attend, citing
the need to "allay the suspicions of those who insist that we are hopelessly rent
in twain because of dissension over our 'near militant' policies." The surviving
correspondence contains no such accusations, just amazement at Lucy's continued absence; AP probably heard rumors from staff and visitors. Some undoubtedly found a deeper meaning in Lucy's desire to remain in Brooklyn than existed.
Ultimately, Lucy agreed to appear at the inaugural demonstration.[28]

For the fourth anniversary of her debut on the national stage, Alice planned
concurrent conventions for both the CU and NWP and a "monster picket" of the
White House. Three hundred delegates streamed into Washington several days

before the March 5 inaugural. The mansion soon filled to the rafters with guests, so many that—the press reported—Alice and a few others slept on the fire escape. Waking up in sleeping bags covered with snow seemed just fine, they decided, and they would happily do so again.[29]

The convention agenda included two items: how to proceed if the war was declared and whether to merge the Congressional Union and the National Woman's Party. The merger seemed inevitable, since AP essentially ran both organizations and the money for the NWP all came from CU efforts. As with the earlier CC/CU, two tightly interwoven groups confused some people. Alice also believed adding potential voters to the NWP would strengthen it, though others thought that nonvoters might blunt its political force. Her view held sway. Delegates approved the merger and upheld AP's single-minded focus on suffrage. They elected her chairman of the amalgamated CU/NWP, now called simply the National Woman's Party.[30]

Alice Paul's election underscored her heightened authority within the NWP. The charisma underlying her ascendance on the national stage had deepened as members witnessed her willingness to bear any burden for the cause. As she challenged her body to match the strength of her drive, she looked at times like a martyr in the making; Milholland's death magnified that aspect of AP's presence. Now, in the face of impending war, her desire to stay the suffrage course brought the moral authority of her Quaker values to the fore. Her stance buoyed pacifists and sharpened the distinction between NAWSA and the NWP.

The March 4 pre-inaugural demonstration dramatized the determination of the silent sentinels and the implacability of the president in unexpectedly stark fashion. Hundreds of marchers faced a biting wind and driving rain as they strode across Lafayette Square to the White House. Accompanied by a brass band, Vida Milholland shouldered a gonfalon with her sister's rallying cry ("How long?"), while young Beulah Amidon carried Inez's parade standard proclaiming "Forward into light!" The "Great Demand" banner followed and then colorful standards, pennants, and state flags. Weeks earlier, the president sent word that it was "literally impossible for me at such a crowded time" to meet another NWP delegation and, true to his word, guards locked every gate and refused to accept proffered resolutions. Undaunted, the marchers slogged around the White House grounds four times as thousands cheered them from the shelter of umbrellas. Doris Stevens later wrote that the Wilson rebuff "probably did more than any other to make women sacrifice themselves."[31]

Alice succeeded in casting Wilson as the unfeeling executive. Mother Nature's touch only enhanced the doggedness the women conveyed. In the cogent words of *The Suffragist*, "March 4, 1917 will undoubtedly long be remembered by suffragists of the nation as the day on which the author of *The New Freedom* refused to hear the demand of a great group of citizens for political liberty." The spectacle symbolized all that had gone before: "on the one side the persistent, earnest plea of spirited women demanding political liberty; on the other side the contemptuous indifference of the government." In sum, the American Revolution redux.[32]

Much of the press recorded the common view that the Anthony amendment seemed expendable in the face of war. The *Cincinnati Enquirer* mocked the logic behind continued appeals to Wilson while war threatened, viewing the demonstration as "senseless, utterly devoid of reason." Editors at the often-supportive *Philadelphia Ledger* called the spectacle "misguided," fueled by "a desperate strife for the notoriety of headlines and moving pictures, by a pseudo-martyrdom of wholly superfluous hardships."[33]

Alice turned her attention to a growing financial crisis. Income had fallen off dramatically since January and she scrambled to make her payroll. Fortunately, Belmont continued wholehearted support, but some other large contributors signaled their preference for preparedness efforts. AP set about persuading doubters and finding new donors among pacifists. She wrote an Iowa supporter, "We are really facing a test of whether we can carry out our resolution to keep on with the suffrage campaign in spite of war difficulties." She scrapped a plan for a special southern initiative for lack of funds, though she sent two organizers south.[34]

Alice's emaciated condition alarmed convention delegates. She planned to take a break after the inaugural but scrapped that idea and decided to resume the vigil when the president called in the new Congress for a special session to consider the war in Europe. Both Moreys wrote, urging her to rest for a while. The New York chairman offered a room "either for a rest for you, or to pursue your usual activities, if you must." With Lucy back in Brooklyn, and fiscal problems and criticism mounting, Alice felt she must stay on the job.[35]

As the special session opened in April, the NWP and NAWSA found something to agree upon: celebrating the first woman elected to Congress. Montana's Jeannette Rankin had participated in both organizations, and both leaders hosted a breakfast at the Shoreham Hotel before Congress convened on April 2. The thirty-seven-year-old Rankin sat on the dais, the younger Alice Paul to her left and the older Catt to her right. Rankin had friends in the NWP, though she herself now differed too much philosophically from it to join. NWP stalwarts were amazed at Catt's appearance with Alice. "We were intensely interested," Agnes Morey teased from Boston. "You might have been gobbled up by the big Catt."[36]

After the breakfast, while some joined Rankin's grand escort to the Capitol, Alice monitored the resumption of the vigil at both the White House and the Capitol. Timed to begin simultaneously, sentinels arrived at the House and Senate entrances and at the main White House gates to take up their posts. Blossoming gardens echoed the purple, white, and gold of their banners. The mood was not sublime, however. Anticipating the president's call for war, doves and hawks descended upon Washington. By contrast, the pickets stood silently.[37]

The president appeared before a joint session of Congress that evening to make his case. Wilson's thinking had evolved from his 1915 "too proud to fight" manifesto. Now, insulated from the rainy darkness outside, he insisted that "the world must be made safe for democracy." He claimed "the right is more precious than peace, and we shall fight for the things we have always carried nearest our hearts." The vigorous, flag-waving ovation following his speech belied the questions many held about entering a European war; Congress debated the war resolution for four days.[38]

On the evening of the war vote, a somber Alice Paul, prompted by her Quaker heritage to put suffrage aside briefly, paid a visit to Jeannette Rankin. Alongside a Montana NWP member, AP assured the "Lady from Montana" that they spoke as individuals, not as NWP representatives. "And so we told her," Alice recalled, "we thought it would be a tragedy for the first woman ever in Congress to vote for war; the one thing that seemed to us so clear was that the women were the peace-loving half of the world and that by giving power to women we would diminish the possibilities of war."[39]

Catt and others had already subjected Rankin, a known pacifist, to fierce pressure. Returning to the House floor, Rankin joined forty-nine others in refusing to stand for war. Nevertheless, in both houses of Congress the vast majority endorsed Wilson's view. Catt assured the reading public that Rankin did not speak for American suffragists: NAWSA did. And the National officially committed itself to the war effort.[40]

For Mrs. Catt and Alice Paul, the advent of war presented a crucible to sharpen their definition of woman's citizenship. The NAWSA leader gambled that shared sacrifice and service would lead to respect, then inclusion. However, once Congress restricted itself to emergency war measures—which did not include suffrage—Catt found herself boxed in.

Alice recognized in the call to war an opportunity to intensify her critique of the federal government's failure to enfranchise women. Her *Suffragist* ripostes to Wilson's speech pointed out the contradictions inherent in making the world "safe for democracy." "It will always be difficult to wage a war for democracy abroad," she wrote, "while democracy is denied at home." She refrained from calling the president a hypocrite, but her intent was clear. Under her direction, the sentinels exposed with increasing bite the sham of an anti-democratic president cloaking himself in American ideals.[41]

The NWP chairman was not alone in noting the contradictions. Within a few weeks of the vote for war, Michigan, Nebraska, and Rhode Island granted women presidential suffrage. "How right and fitting it would be, before the war begins," wrote the *Richmond Evening Journal*, "to put all citizens on a footing of equal rights when we are so soon to be on a footing of equal service." The *New York Sun* agreed, "In these progressive times, war for men seems to mean votes for women."[42]

After Congress declared war, banner bearers holding legends such as "Democracy must begin at Home" became the brunt of increasingly negative comments questioning their propriety and their allegiance. "You are an impossible, unpatriotic gang of women," cried one elderly gentleman, objecting to their "embarrassing" the president. A well-dressed woman accused them of setting suffrage back fifty years, echoing NAWSA jibes. The sentinels came prepared to defend themselves quietly, citing their desire that America cleave to its founding principles, pulling out copies of Wilson's own words. Calls for ending the vigil appeared in the press, one letter writer mocking their "bad manners and mad banners."[43]

Wilson himself contributed to a growing intolerance for anyone steering clear of the war. Years earlier, as a scholar and college president, he wrote, "Agitation is certainly of the essence of a constitutional system." His views transformed after he entered government service. By 1916, he proclaimed the need "to secure unity of opinion as a basis for unity of action." Well aware that prominent Progressive supporters, including Jane Addams, were pacifists, the president skillfully couched his April 1917 rationale for war in terms they could rally around, claiming American entry would "vindicate the principles of peace and justice" in the world. At the same time, he vowed to handle any disloyalty "with a firm hand of stern repression."[44]

The Wilson administration made loyalty supreme, crafting legislation and creating new agencies to ensure a united front. In February, "written or spoken statements" threatening the chief executive were criminalized. Congress rejected the press censorship in the bill Wilson sent to Congress shortly after the war vote; however, the final Espionage Act rendered illegal any attempt to interfere with the military or "promote the success of enemies." These laws were interpreted broadly by an administration intent on unity and by like-minded jurists. Wilson also created a Committee on Public Information to orchestrate devotion to the war effort. All told, these measures infused daily life with the repression he promised.[45]

Alice responded to the overheated climate by constructing NWP efforts as deeply patriotic. She anticipated more intense criticism after the war vote and, defensively, hung an American flag alongside the suffrage colors flying outside Cameron House. She declared, "Our decision to re-establish picketing is prompted by the highest patriotic motives." When the Senate Suffrage Committee yielded to NWP/NAWSA pressure to consider the Anthony amendment as a war measure, she brought in speakers already involved with war work, notably Rankin, as well as historian Mary Beard. The sentinels stood "not as women, but as Americans," an erstwhile picket (and admiral's wife) stressed. AP designed the performance not only to hasten the passage of suffrage but to distance the NWP from claims of disloyalty.[46]

Carrie Chapman Catt used the mounting criticism of the NWP and talk of suffrage as a war measure to lobby the president herself. She craftily played on Wilson's conventional views of women, implicitly presenting NAWSA as archetypal womanhood. In a private letter, she pointedly distinguished the National from the aggressive NWP and commiserated with the "overwhelming pressure" on Wilson. "It seemed to us only fair to you to wait yet a while longer and not press for suffrage during this extraordinary session," she wrote in unctuous tones. She added, "However, if this seems to you the auspicious time to make our war appeal, will you not permit [NAWSA] to carry the glad news to the women of America?"[47]

The southern-born president appreciated women who knew their place. The very next day, he replied, "You are always thoughtful and considerate, and I greatly value your generous attitude." Indeed, he wrote, "this is [not] the opportune time." He did agree to signal his approval of the long-sought House suffrage committee, calling the move "an act of fairness to the best women." This small payoff encouraged Catt to continue wooing him.[48]

The declaration of war only aggravated the NWP's financial woes and organizational difficulties. Though membership numbers climbed steadily, frustrated supporters around the country reported that many women were turning to war work. "We are in a slough of despond here in Illinois," wrote one. Alice traveled to New York City twice in April to raise funds and seek help; she met with and no doubt appealed again to Lucy, who called herself "fat and flourishing." Lucy remained at home, but Alice perked up when the long-absent Dora Lewis returned to Washington. Lewis's assistance eased the fiscal demands and Belmont helped them meet the May 1 payroll. Still, AP confided to one stalwart, "There are a few of us who can keep on...no matter what befalls, but we cannot conduct a campaign that will make much impression unless we have money."[49]

Political allies emerged to ease fears of irrelevance and elicit unexpected support from the president. Five groups, including the Prohibition, Socialist, and New Jersey state Progressive parties, allied themselves with the Woman's Party to push for immediate suffrage. J. A. H. Hopkins, the millionaire chairman of New Jersey's Progressive Party, led the group to the White House. The canny Wilson decided to choose these male leaders to carry the revelation that he believed the war altered the suffrage question. The president, like many observers, recognized how much of the war effort depended on women; he had also noticed the flurry of new activity by state legislatures, as several Midwestern states, Rhode Island, and Arkansas gave women limited suffrage rights. So Wilson now thought the Anthony amendment made sense—but the time was not yet right.[50]

As the president's position became fluid, Carrie Chapman Catt's fears about the destructive impact of the White House vigil mounted; she publicly called on Alice to withdraw the sentinels. She repeated her earlier claim that they presented "an unwarranted discourtesy to the President and a futile annoyance" to Congress. Now, however, she held decisive evidence that the vigil was "hurting our cause": one congressman refused to vote for a House suffrage committee as long as the pickets remained. AP responded privately that the congressman had long voiced his opposition. She asserted, "We have never found a vote lost by picketing." Despite the potential advantage of a response in the press, Alice, as usual, refrained from public criticism of NAWSA and, in the same vein, insisted that organizers not respond to Catt-instigated editorials.[51]

Under increasing pressure, Alice tried to hold the NWP together. In the war-frenzied West, state chairmen in Arizona and Oklahoma resigned and, in Utah and Idaho, entire state committees signed off. AP traveled south twice in the spring to bolster two organizers' tenuous efforts. They managed to found chapters in Florida and Alabama.[52]

Finances remained bleak and AP's anxious, single-minded concentration left some donors wanting. She began placing organizers only in states able to pay their salaries. When the monthly balance sheet still fell short, she again sought contributors in Philadelphia, New York, and Boston. Mary Beard reprimanded her for treating members of the New York City committee "*solely* as machines for getting money." Beard thought, "They are right in wanting a little decent appreciation personally." But niceties were never Alice's strong suit; the pressure on her now made acquiring them unlikely.[53]

In mid-June, Alice returned to Washington to assess the ongoing vigil. Cameron House still overflowed with daytrippers in town to picket, yet the war dominated the news and outrage over the vigil had receded considerably. At the same time, Wilson seemed close to declaring suffrage a war measure. They needed to keep the pressure on. Lucy, who had recently agreed to return temporarily, penned an unusual signed *Suffragist* editorial, signaling her continued involvement and calling on the NWP faithful to stand strong as an "unconquerable army." She challenged suffragists to maintain "the indomitable picket line," acknowledging the difficulty of being heard amid the warmongering.[54]

A White House visit by a Russian delegation became the moment for a newly dramatic appeal. The February 1917 revolution in Russia had spawned a provisional government and uncertainty among the Allied powers just as America entered the war. Alice knew that the Russians had instituted universal suffrage in recent local elections. She saw an opportunity to point up a contradiction: Wilson would be commending the Russians for throwing off an oppressive monarchy at the same time that he denied the vote to half the American population. She crafted the language of the new banner with care.[55]

At high noon on June 20, Lucy Burns and Dora Lewis marched across Lafayette Square with a ten-foot banner and stood proudly at the White House entry gate. A crowd gathered, taking in the accusing words quickly, some spewing out their anger just as fast. The banner told the Russian envoys that President Wilson was deceiving them in saying "we are a democracy. Help us win a world war so that democracies may survive." On the contrary, "we, the women of America, tell you that America is not a democracy," and "President Wilson is the chief opponent of [women's] national enfranchisement." The banner demanded, "Tell our government that it must liberate its people before it can claim free Russia as an ally." The Russians glimpsed the banner as their motorcar drove through the gate.

The crowd's anger spilled out. Suddenly, one man grabbed the banner and ripped the muslin completely out of its frame, startling the two bearers, who managed to keep hold of the bare supports as well as their dignity. The White House guards never left their posts, while the throng so lauded the vandal, a young architect, that he passed out his calling cards.[56]

Alice deliberately spiked the Russian banner's rhetoric. Earlier ones aimed to embarrass the president, yet none edged so close to calling the president a liar. AP had instructed the sentinels on dealing with interference from the start. Since the authorities failed to oblige, she provoked them.

The intolerance nurtured by the Wilson administration spewed out for weeks after the Russian banner incident. Accusations of disloyalty, many from other women, overwhelmed those of unladylike behavior. Some believed the Russian banner violated the Espionage Act. A Texas suffragist wrote bluntly: "Such conduct is nothing less than treason and should be treated as such." And an NWP member from Pennsylvania declared, "I am an American before I am a suffragist," and resigned. More often, members chose not to resign, even if they felt leery of the Russian banner's language.[57]

Many members, particularly those of a radical bent, reveled in the whole incident. Some stepped up for for picket duty. Crystal Eastman and her brother, editor Max Eastman, wired, "Magnificent perfect from every possible point of view." Another enthusiast concurred, "I am so tickled with the Russian picket publicity it makes me happy all over!" Alice wholeheartedly agreed, "We had a very exciting time today." Provocation still thrilled her.[58]

Praise was not limited to members. N. A. Bessaraboff, a member of the Russian mission, sent an immediate note. "From all my heart and soul I am proud," he wrote, "of the courage of American wooman [sic]." He urged them to "stay unshaken."

AP promptly released his letter to the press. A more private gratification arrived with a wire from William Parker, her Penn admirer: "Congratulations. Stick to it."[59]

While new sentinels carried out similar banners, government officials monitored NWP activities. Alerted by an informant to the first "unpatriotic" banner and preparations for additional signs, Secret Service agents went to the White House gates and later to the shop where the NWP banners were painted. Their reports reveal that the police chief inspected the banners before their delivery to Cameron House. Another agent passing the White House the following day raised the specter of armed snipers within the crowds as well as "erroneous impressions" created by press use of the term "White House riots." The Secret Service and the District police exchanged notes, then took action.[60]

The police moved to shut down the vigil. The District's police chief, Raymond Pullman, telephoned Alice about his instructions to arrest any new sentinels. Whether or not the president, Pullman's ultimate supervisor, shaped this decision remains unclear. AP told Chief Pullman that peaceful picketing was legal; Pullman reiterated his intent to arrest. After some discussion, the NWP women decided to hold fast to their right to picket. The next morning, Lucy and Katharine Morey stood at the White House gates, their banner pointedly adorned with Wilson's battle cry—"We shall fight for the things we have always held nearest to our hearts." The police demanded they surrender the banner; the women refused. Officers arrested them for obstructing traffic, then released them to await a summons to court.[61]

The authorities were feeling their way while Alice seemed to foresee each step. Indeed, her strategic capacity—in this case, her prior knowledge of potential actions on both sides—gave the NWP a clear advantage. Unaccustomed to detaining "respectable," even prominent, women, some supervisors felt unsure of their superior's expectations. AP, by contrast, confidently went off to a meeting in Philadelphia after Lucy and Morey went to the White House the second time. Over the next few days, the police briefly detained more women.[62]

In the first and subsequent trials of the suffrage pickets, Alice set in motion the courtroom strategies she and Lucy learned in Britain, tactics designed to transform court appearances into public forums. In the controlled atmosphere of the court, suffragists presented themselves as rational political beings, confounding characterizations of the sentinels as silly or threatening. Mabel Vernon acted as the group's advocate and focused attention on the legality of the silent vigil. "If you think we were performing illegally for one hundred and fifty days," she asserted, "you should have interfered before the one hundred and fifty-first day arrived."[63]

The judge disagreed, insisting the pickets were "the proximate cause of this idle curious crowd." He convicted the six, assigning each a twenty-five-dollar fine or three days in jail. As instructed, the group refused to pay the fines. Vernon, Morey, fifty-nine-year-old Lavinia Dock, a teacher, an NWP staffer, and munitions worker Annie Arniel all climbed into the patrol wagon for the trip to the District jail. They became the first women imprisoned in the United States for demanding the right to vote.[64]

The experience of jail proved a bleaker reality than the thrill of arrest and trial. Yet benevolent treatment obviated any need to declare themselves political prisoners. "We are getting the best treatment, accommodations, etc. that is ever given in jail and perhaps better," one wrote. The women were permitted to have their own clothing and towels, reading material, and food from outside. They could avoid the atrocious jail food, though not the hard beds and stifling air. They passed the long hours talking with other inmates, many of them black women, and sharing food; they even held a suffrage meeting the first night. But a cool breeze heralded the morning of their release.[65]

Alice used the release as the Pankhursts had, to highlight and deepen commitment. Members grandly escorted the freed pickets back to Cameron House in a stylish touring car, then saluted them at a breakfast garden party. Vernon called the episode "no great hardship" and urged the others on: "Do not falter! Do not give up—ever—until this work is done!" Newfound radical ally and one-time prisoner John Reed came to commend their efforts, telling them that "political action is the only hope" for the world.[66]

That day's *Suffragist* underscored the women's determination. AP's editorial threw back the language of the naysaying jingoists: "It is never unpatriotic to demand justice." In the same issue, Lavinia Dock, one of the NWP's oldest members, laid down the rallying cry: "The old stiff minds must give way," she declared. "Obstructive reactionaries must move on. The young are at the Gates!"[67]

Alice now reduced the schedule of vigils to once a week and gave each a special profile. She advertised a Fourth of July vigil and, sure enough, both spectators and police turned out in force. The sentinels carried a banner echoing the Declaration of Independence: "Governments Derive their Just Powers from the Consent of the Governed." *The Suffragist* worked up a David-and-Goliath theme for the day, posing the "little group of women" against the male authority of dozens of police. Officers arrested eleven women—including Lucy, Arniel, and Vida Milholland—gave them a summary trial, and jailed them for three days. Unfazed, Alice was overseeing plans for a similar Bastille Day demonstration when the unthinkable happened.[68]

She collapsed at Cameron House, unable to ignore persistent digestive and kidney problems any longer. Her relentless pace coupled with the earlier damage from forcible feeding finally did her in. Staff quickly moved her to early NWP recruit Cora Smith King's sanitarium in northwest Washington. As usual, Alice thought she could work through her "rest"; Hazel Hunkins read mail to her over the telephone and forwarded other letters. Her condition seemed to ease. Then the diagnosis came in: Bright's disease.[69]

Most remembered the 1914 death of the president's first wife, Ellen, from the same condition. Doctors dimly understood kidney function in 1917; they termed a range of kidney conditions "Bright's disease" and prescribed treatments such as colonic irrigation and "static" (a treatment involving electricity), both of which Alice endured. Dr. King thought AP might die within weeks or, with sufficient rest, perhaps survive another year or so.[70]

A glum executive committee—all save Alva Belmont—gathered around AP's bedside on July 13 to determine a course of action. Some wondered whether their leader would ever resume her duties, but Alice, uncomfortable with the attention, led the meeting in a businesslike manner. The committee agreed to appoint an acting chairman and quickly drafted the obvious choice: Lucy. Vernon's meeting minutes contain no other mention of Alice's illness except that the NWP wanted to pay her medical bills (she refused and paid them herself).[71]

Dora Lewis saved the day. After the meeting, Lewis insisted that Alice seek treatment at Johns Hopkins Hospital, then a Quaker institution with which Lewis's brother, the eminent physician Howard Kelly, was affiliated. Alice left for Baltimore the next day. After a few days of care, Kelly pronounced AP's first diagnosis faulty. Her digestive problems lingered, nevertheless, and she felt utterly exhausted; the doctor called for a minimum of two months' rest. Alice agreed to rest for a while and promptly boarded the train for Moorestown and her own bed. "Things did look dark for a time," a relieved Lucy wrote Belmont, "but we are greatly encouraged now."[72]

News circulated quickly about Alice's illness, although nothing appeared in *The Suffragist*—no doubt at her direction. "I heard with horror that you were in the hospital," wrote Marjorie Whittemore. "We were so distressed to hear of Miss Paul's illness," a Denver woman wrote Vernon, "not that it was the least surprising that she should break down." And William Parker regretted rushing away the last time he saw her: "Of course had I known you were really in need of a word or hand you would have had them." He was not particularly surprised to hear she was "temporarily retired" but trusted she would "come back *toute entente et bien*."[73]

Alice managed to rest for a month, refusing several invitations in order to remain at Paulsdale. Washington staff enforced her relaxation by answering what mail they could and holding the remainder. She spent time in Atlantic City with Dora Lewis in late July and welcomed her old Woodbrooke colleague Mietza

Heldring Bye at Paulsdale a few days later. Lewis went off to raise funds, no doubt at AP's urging but also to keep her charge from doing so.[74]

Alice considered other remedies for her digestive difficulties. Lewis chided her for not following up fully on the Johns Hopkins advice. She urged AP to enter another sanitarium to be taught "to intelligently understand your own difficulty." Alice, still skeptical of doctors and certain of her own mind, declined. Probably following the lead of sister Helen, now a Christian Scientist, AP decided on a Christian Science regimen with a former Quaker in Philadelphia, who later hoped "thee does feel the Truth has helped thee." Typically, AP ended the treatment prematurely, and on August 12 she returned to Washington. Lucy wrote Elizabeth Rogers, "Miss Paul came back three pounds heavier (not very much) but looking very well and quite rested. She was actually sun-burned. She is in fine feather now and the work is going at a furious pace."[75]

Alice experienced only vicariously the turning point in the picketing campaign. Bastille Day arrests set into motion a series of events that turned the tide of public opinion about the vigil and, for the first time, gained acknowledgment from the president. On July 14, shortly after AP left for Johns Hopkins, police arrested sixteen sentinels. Perhaps in a show of solidarity for Alice, six executive committee members were among the sixteen held, including Stevens, Martin, and New Jersey NWP chair Alison Hopkins.[76]

The turbulent trial of the sixteen shattered government patience. Among the observers sat Hopkins's husband, politico J. A. H. Hopkins, and Wilson appointee Dudley Field Malone, a supporter of the NWP since meeting Doris Stevens at the Chicago launch (Malone and Stevens were carrying on an illicit affair). As before, the sentinels leveraged the courtroom to advance their cause. Elizabeth Rogers argued, "We know full well that we stand here because the President of the United States refuses to give liberty to American women." Affronted by the women's defiance, the judge castigated them, insisting there was "nothing unusual" about an obstructing traffic charge. The women clearly broke the law, he said, intimating that they sought to use their sex and class standing to avoid consequences. Instead of the expected three days, he fined each woman twenty-five dollars or sixty days in prison—not at the District jail, but the Occoquan Workhouse an hour south in Virginia. Startled by the extreme ruling, the sixteen conferred, then proudly chose the prison time.[77]

Malone and Hopkins went straight to the top to vent their outrage—sixty days for obstructing traffic? Malone drove directly to the White House from the courtroom. His personal connection to Stevens notwithstanding, he felt cheated—he had stumped for the president in 1916, hinting that a re-elected Wilson would embrace suffrage. Malone protested the police actions and the sentences; the president disclaimed any personal responsibility. According to his

own account, Malone blamed the "carefully laid plans" of the District's commissioners, who he knew had consulted Wilson's secretary, Tumulty, and Secretary
of the Treasury William McAdoo (Wilson's son-in-law) about the arrests. Wilson
denied knowledge of those conversations. Malone tendered his resignation from
his post in the Customs office: an attorney, he intended to defend the NWP
instead. Wilson assured Malone that he might serve as the suffragists' counsel
without resigning and urged him to hold off.[78]

J. A. H. Hopkins talked about a political solution with the president later
that day. Wilson claimed no objection or annoyance with the picketing, according to Hopkins, and found them entirely within the law. The two men discussed
a pardon, both recognizing this answer as a temporary fix. "As you said today,"
Hopkins later wrote Wilson, "the picketing will doubtless continue" and only
passage of the Anthony amendment "will satisfy the critical situation that now
exists." Hopkins therefore offered data showing that if Wilson put his weight
behind the Anthony amendment, "it would easily pass both houses." The president promptly sent the poll to a cabinet member for verification.[79]

Woodrow Wilson saw a scandal brewing that could cast a pall on his wartime popularity. He could not afford to be seen as a bully. The shaky "obstructing
traffic" charges, Malone's veiled threat to leak his probable involvement to the
press, the likelihood that the NWP would appeal a guilty verdict: all these factors entered his decision. On July 19, he pardoned the suffrage prisoners, granting
them a consideration other dissenters had sought in vain. Having two influential
political operatives in their corner aided the jailed women, as did their gender
and the prominence of some. The pro-Wilson press rewarded him by describing
his pity and compassion for the women. "Mr. Wilson is more than lenient," wrote
the *New York Times* editors, who thought the pickets seditious. The president's
pardon also rewarded the sentinels: Wilson acknowledged their protest publicly
for the first time.[80]

The hints of presidential involvement with the arrests are belied by one District
commissioner's account. Commissioner Louis Brownlow later recalled Wilson
taking him severely to task. Brownlow claimed, "He told me that we had made
a fearful blunder, that we never ought to have indulged these women in their
desire for arrest and martyrdom, and that he had pardoned them and wanted that
to end it." Brownlow took complete responsibility for the situation but believed
the pickets' behavior "riotous." The commissioner offered his resignation. Wilson
refused it but asked Brownlow to notify him before authorizing further arrests,
"making it plain that he would never consent."[81]

The NWP quickly snatched the moral high ground from the president. The
sixteen prisoners accepted his pardon reluctantly. As Alison Hopkins wrote
Wilson, the pardon left the suffragists in an "intolerable and false position" of

being labeled law-breakers; it "in no way mitigates the injustice inflicted upon me by the violation of my constitutional civil rights." The infuriated Hopkins took a banner to the White House gates herself, standing there alone and unimpeded for ten minutes. The ailing Alice Paul, contacted by a reporter as she left Baltimore, signaled the futility of anything short of passing the Anthony amendment. "We're very much obliged to the President for pardoning the pickets but we'll be picketing again next Monday," she declared. "Picketing will continue and sooner or later he will have to do something about it."[82]

Sensitive to the sentinels' claims of moral authority, the president sought to tamp down the public debate, resenting what he viewed as the endemic sensationalism of the press. Having failed to institute press censorship with the Espionage Act, he jumped at an offer by the sympathetic editors of the *Washington Times* and *Star* to "refrain from giving the suffragette ladies any publicity." Yet the editors thought no picket news at all might encourage "unwise extremes in order to COMPEL attention." Wilson's jaundiced view of the NWP emerges in his response: the editors should not "provok[e] the less sane of these women to violent action." Rather, report the pickets' news in a "bare, colorless chronicle" away from headlines or the front pages. Wilson was not blind to his own cant: that November, he avoided meeting free-speech advocates.[83]

In Alice's absence, Lucy Burns tested the limits of presidential and police forbearance. She resumed weekly vigils after the pardon seemed to end press attention. She soon decided to muscle the spotlight back from the war news. On Friday, August 10, she carried a new banner to the White House gates, unfurling it as government workers returned from their lunch hour. The banner asked provocatively:

KAISER WILSON
Have you forgotten your sympathy with the poor Germans
because they were not self-governed?
20,000,000 American women are not self-governed.
Take the beam out of your own eye.

A small crowd seemed interested and respectful, until a male clerk ripped the banner from Lucy's hands and took off running. With police monitoring the scene, the remaining onlookers dispersed. Nevertheless, the incident became the opening salvo to a week of near-riots, carrying over to the nearby NWP offices.[84]

Alice returned to headquarters in time to witness an assault on Cameron House itself. Monday, sentinels carried "Kaiser banners" again; three times, men tore them down. The women persisted in carrying identical signs the next day but failed to reach the White House four times. The crowd grew to several thousand—mostly government clerks and soldiers—and swarmed like a mob (described as "good-natured" by some newspapers) across Lafayette Square toward headquarters. They dragged Lucy to the street as she exited the mansion with another banner. They roughed up two other staffers. The women resolutely hung Kaiser banners from the house balconies; several rowdies climbed up the balconies to rip them down, then tore the NWP standard off the house flagpole along with the Stars and Stripes. They pelted a new banner with eggs and threw stones; a bullet shot through the balcony window and careened through one room.[85]

District police again displayed uncertainty. Their inconsistent behavior suggests some officers felt caught up with the crowd despite orders and required reining in by supervisors. One outraged observer, former congressman Charles Lindbergh (Republican, MN), later wrote the president, the police "did nothing whatever to stop the mob violence but actually encouraged it by rough-handling anyone who tried to protect the women." Officers did arrest two men. Reserves arrived belatedly to disperse the crowd, about the time two women strode out the back entrance of Cameron House and succeeded in carrying a Kaiser banner to the White House gates. The police protected them as they displayed their cloth catalyst until, after an hour, a furtive onlooker snatched this banner away too.[86]

For many onlookers and police, the August banner bearers violated the contract women implicitly held with men. Their perfidious words, however silent, and their doggedness conveyed an unseemly aggressiveness which negated any expectation of chivalry. As in the 1913 procession, force now became an acceptable response to the unwomanly woman, regardless of class. Some men who eschewed violence nonetheless viewed the pickets not as women but miscreants. One observer wrote Wilson that he felt police should allow onlookers to protect the president from ridicule. Others implicitly questioned Wilson's own manliness. "Picketing can be countenanced no longer," wrote one District resident.[87]

As the pickets reappeared on the nation's front pages, the violence in Washington continued. Alice, though marginally fit, joined the others taking out Kaiser and similar banners over the next few days. For her trouble, a sailor grabbed her shoulder regalia and dragged her across the pavement; other men struck down other pickets and even a man trying to protect the women. By Thursday, police alternately joined the throng or protected the picket line. Ruffians stole or ruined scores of banners and flags that riotous week—nearly $1,500 worth by *The Suffragist*'s count.[88]

The president shrank from commandeering the situation, though he went out as usual to the theater near Cameron House twice during the riot week. Meanwhile, Joseph Tumulty and others at the White House urged Chief Pullman to act. Commissioner Brownlow, by his own account, finally stepped in. After a week, he telephoned the president to say "belligerent" pickets were attacking onlookers, with no signs of easing up on their "riotous behavior." He offered to take responsibility for ordering arrests. After a brief silence, the president replied, "with more sorrow than anger in his voice, 'The blood be on your head!'"[89]

The fact that Wilson supervised the District commissioners and ultimately held responsibility for their actions seemed to escape him; however, Brownlow's memory of the events may be self-serving and at once protective of the president. If Brownlow's account is accurate, the president feared being cast as the heavy in the press at a time when public belief in his own moral crusade—the war— seemed paramount. He recognized the untenable position the NWP forced upon the administration. Late that afternoon, officers hauled six women, including recidivist Lavinia Dock, off to Police Court, where a judge later sentenced them to thirty days at Occoquan.[90]

Alice exploited the administrative uncertainty, asserting the righteousness of the women's cause to the public and NWP members. "President Wilson has adopted the attitude of an autocratic ruler," AP told the press, "while he is asking our men to die for democracy abroad." *The Suffragist* added that Wilson had "no moral claim whatever upon [women's] allegiance."[91]

The rhetoric failed to mitigate the shock of the Kaiser banners for the dozens of members who resigned; others gloried in the episode and new members once again outpaced resignees. Alva Belmont quickly wired her wholehearted approval of the banners after the New York papers reported otherwise. A California stalwart praised, "I rejoice in all your work." Elizabeth Rogers took a more sober view: she only hoped "that all you dear women are not killed by Wilson's police."[92]

The six women arrested on August 17 became the first suffragists jailed for more than three days and the first to experience Virginia's Occoquan Workhouse. Washingtonians knew Occoquan as a model Progressive penal farm. Built in 1910 along the Potomac River, it housed prisoners in wooden barracks rather than cell blocks. Male prisoners worked the farm; female inmates typically sewed the sack-like uniforms given newcomers. One official description noted the absence of "bars or bolts or other means of physical restraint either day or night." Ironically, the lack of privacy in the wardlike barracks aggravated the suffrage prisoners' experience.[93]

Occoquan conditions quickly prompted protest. Veteran Lavinia Dock and the other five suffragists appreciated the light and air; however, many found living alongside the mostly poor, black prisoners abhorrent. The food and sanitary conditions shocked them. Coordinating with headquarters, the pickets issued demands for "separate drinking cups, clean toilet facilities," personal utensils for meals, and daily baths. *The Suffragist* insisted that the women sought no special treatment. The journal termed the pickets political prisoners, but they sought improvements simply for humanitarian reasons. Authorities initially conceded

to most of the demands and granted them quarters apart from black prisoners, implicitly acknowledging their singular status. Further protests prompted a
District investigation both into conditions and the superintendent; the politically cautious report concluded, however, that conditions seemed satisfactory
and the suffragists had "seriously embarrassed and even endangered" workhouse
operations.[94]

With the prospect of weeks in jail, the suffrage prisoners' class, race, and
gender collided with the criminal designation thrust upon them by the courts.
"Completely vanished," as one sympathetic journalist wrote, "is the identity one's
own clothes provide." Whatever their class status, the women resisted a criminal identity, maintaining the legality of picketing and asserting their right to be
treated as respectable white women. One *Suffragist* cover falsely constructed all
suffrage prisoners as highly privileged, decrying the indecency of "refined, intelligent, society women" being "thrown into the workhouse with negroes and
criminals."[95]

The prisoners' challenge of workhouse authority strengthened their defiant
posture toward the Wilson administration. Longer jail terms nevertheless opened
up the possibility of being stigmatized, not only by society at large but by family,
friends, and neighbors. In this context, the negotiations over conditions and the
praise accorded the prisoners in *The Suffragist* became tools of reassurance and
solidarity that reaffirmed their status.[96]

As more arrests followed, Alice employed her most inspirational rhetoric
for anyone wavering and fearing the consequences to her good name. In her
September 1 editorial, "Why We Keep on Picketing," she located the NWP vigil
within a larger historical context: the battle to win woman suffrage that had
engaged three generations. She then reiterated her image of the administration
as trapped by the contradiction of urging sacrifice for democracy abroad while
denying democracy at home. The Anthony amendment could easily pass now, she
averred, if Wilson pledged the power of his office in support. Then, "this victory
for democracy could be accomplished without struggle or grief, without," she
warned, "the loss of a single life." Instead, Wilson and his party sought "to intimidate those who ask for freedom." She posed women as innocent yet powerful.
"Women," she wrote, casting the pickets as female archetypes, "are determined
to go on." A few days later, police arrested another dozen pickets, including Lucy
Burns; they were sentenced to sixty days in the workhouse.[97]

These lengthy sentences had a chilling effect on the silent vigil, even for eager
volunteers. Plans for a monster protest in September with one hundred women
fell so short that Alice canceled it. Many women felt unable to leave families—
young children, ailing parents—for a month. As Sara Bard Field wrote, "My
life is not my own and there were those dependent on me who would suffer by

my going. This is my own humiliation and sorrow." Often, husbands or parents strongly disapproved. Not a few women feared the hardship of jail or disgrace.[98] As Mary Church Terrell had foreseen, black women willing to endure arrest faced a torturous situation both inside and outside prison walls; none volunteered.

Wage-earning women might lose their livelihood as well as hard-won social respect. Many could "neither afford the car-fare nor risk the chance of arrest. So many of them support families, etc.," wrote one member. Another wrote of her own employers, "They have told me that if I go, I must resign from here first, unless I can guarantee that I wont [sic] be arrested and have to spend Monday or maybe longer away from the office. Ain't it fierce?"[99]

Despite the considerable barriers, radical women stepped into the picket lines in greater numbers. Ever since the Russian banner, leftist groups themselves experiencing censorship or public scorn for their antiwar activities had increasingly found common cause with the sentinels. The socialist *New York Call* covered the vigil extensively and offered space for NWP supporters. The socialist presence in the NWP was always significant, especially among organizers. After the Kaiser banner, however, more radical women volunteered for sentinel duty, in particular wage earners with histories of radical activism in their native homelands. Among the noteworthy radicals, Polish-born activist Rose Winslow, a veteran of the Suffrage Special, joined the picket line. Self-professed anarchist Dorothy Day appeared at a November vigil, drawn by the assault on free speech. Asked about the presence of radicals among the sentinels, Alice said, "It makes no difference to us what a woman's political tendencies may be." She welcomed "women of all classes and opinions" to the picket line.[100]

The NWP did not lack for prominent mainstream support. After one of their own served time at Occoquan, several Connecticut NAWSA leaders resigned to join the NWP, among them Katharine Houghton Hepburn. Pacifist Belle Case LaFollette, wife of the antiwar senator Robert LaFollette, praised the sentinels in *LaFollette's Magazine*, reminding her Progressive readers that the pickets "have not violated the law nor committed violence." The press gave considerable coverage to one supporter, however: Dudley Field Malone. Malone lost faith in the president and insisted on resigning from his administration post in early September. His lengthy protest letter declared it "high time that men in this generation, at some cost to themselves, stood up to battle" for the Anthony amendment. Alice hailed Malone's defection the "first outward sign of doubt and disillusion within the President's own loyal inner circle." And the new publicity angle helped keep the suffrage prisoners in the public eye.[101]

As the number of incarcerated sentinels climbed, Congress took note. The Senate woman suffrage committee finally issued a favorable report in mid-September. The report, *The Suffragist* took pains to point out, came shortly after the committee chair and other senators journeyed to Occoquan to "reason" with the prisoners. Over in the House, congressmen finally debated establishing a suffrage committee, which Wilson had approved the previous spring. One anti-suffrage congressman called "monstrous" any action that appeared "to yield to the demands of some iron-jawed angels." Andrew Volstead (Republican, MN) alone took issue with the "ruthless warfare" against the pickets. He reminded the chamber of the "disgraceful attack" on the 1913 parade and declared, "it is high time that something besides cheap politics be demanded."[102]

Ultimately, the House approved the creation of a suffrage committee, with both parties voting in favor, though the Democratic vote was close. *The Suffragist* conveyed one Democratic leader's olive branch: action by the next Congress—if justified by the 1918 election results. Alice viewed both the Senate and House actions as a result of the president's change of heart on the federal suffrage amendment; she still believed Wilson held the political power to compel Congress to act.[103]

Alice found enough women willing to face imprisonment but struggled to meet other organizational exigencies. The vigil continued on a weekly basis in September and the number of suffrage prisoners in Occoquan grew to twenty-three. AP planned to end the picketing temporarily after Congress adjourned in October. With Lucy and other valuable workers in prison and some organizers ill, maintaining even bare-bones operations proved difficult. Office staff spent much of their time monitoring the prisoners' health and welfare and communicating with their families. "We are considerably handicapped," AP wrote one organizer in late September.[104]

On the other hand, donations had increased substantially after the July pardon and continued strongly into the fall. Dissatisfied with press distortions in the frenzied war climate, Alice sent speakers out touring to communicate accurate information about the silent vigil directly to the American people. In early October, with the tour dispatched, money in the bank, and Congress nearing adjournment, Alice decided that the best place for her now was prison.[105]

"Jailed for Freedom"

THE IMPRISONMENT OF Alice Paul in late 1917 increased the pressure on the Wilson administration exponentially. Unlike many of her compatriots in jail, she brought experience negotiating the political environment in and outside the jail. While the mainstream press and her own *Suffragist* capitalized on her charismatic persona for sensational ends, Alice exploited every opportunity she found to gain the upper hand. Nevertheless, she did not anticipate the depths to which an administration intent on censorship would stoop. Her self-mastery became critical to her ability to withstand imprisonment, hunger striking, and psychological hazing.

On the late afternoon of October 6, 1917, as Congress prepared to adjourn, Alice Paul emerged from Cameron House leading a procession of eleven women. They marched slowly across Lafayette Square to the White House gates. Her fur coat overwhelmed her frail figure; to one admirer, "her eyes and face really lit with exaltation of purpose." She held aloft a white standard lettered with the now-familiar cry, "Mr. President, what will you do for woman suffrage?" The other banner-bearers, young and older, followed with their purple, white, and gold regalia, colors echoed in the autumn leaves.

A crowd gathered. As the suffragists approached the gates, a young man rushed toward them, tearing down one banner; the bearer picked up the cloth and tied it to her staff as angry onlookers tore down another flag and then another. Finally, they pulled off Alice's banner, leaving her standing at the president's gate holding a bare staff. The pickets stood silent, wary. Abruptly, the police scattered the crowd as a clanging patrol wagon drove up and officers confiscated all the regalia, herding the still-silent women into the van. As with earlier groups, the sentinels were released to await a summons.[1]

At the group's appearance in police court two days later, Alice defied the court completely. She refused to enter any plea. Repeating the sentiment she first uttered in a British courtroom, she said: "We do not consider ourselves subject to this court since, as an unenfranchised class, we have nothing to do with the making of the laws." The other eleven women followed suit and not only refused to plead, but shunned calling witnesses and even refused to be sworn. The packed courtroom buzzed. Calling for order, Judge Alexander Mullowney staunchly responded that the laws bound him and, as an American, AP as well, "notwith-standing the fact that you do not recognize the law." He pronounced the women guilty of obstructing traffic. Unbeknown to the pickets, the judge had learned that the women would not demonstrate while Congress stood adjourned. As a result, he suspended all their sentences, subject to recall.[2]

Alice's decision to challenge the court's authority seems a curious one. Other detained sentinels had used the same tactic, but as a precursor to a lengthy defense of their picketing. With the increased public attention on her trial, AP could use the theater of the courtroom as the setting for an impassioned defense of the vigil and of federal action for suffrage. However, she chose to remain mostly silent, her choice perhaps reflecting internal conflict about being in the spotlight. The sus-pended sentences surprised Alice, but she swiftly adapted her strategy. First, she declared victory. "We are glad," she told the press, that the authorities have "grown wary of prosecuting women for peacefully petitioning for political liberty." Of course, she said, Mullowney's move made "glaring" the unjust incarceration of the eleven women sitting in Occoquan at that moment. Without their release, what could she do except "use our unexpected freedom to press our campaign with ever-increasing vigor." As she wrote Dora Lewis, letting "picketing drop the way it stands" became ineffectual now. The NWP should not appear cowed by the suspended sentence. Therefore, she scheduled weekly vigils into early November.[3]

By sending out more pickets, Alice dared the court to respond forcefully. Indeed, she received a summons after authorities arrested four sentinels the follow-ing week. Mullowney gave those four women the maximum sentence demanded by prosecutors: six months or a twenty-five-dollar fine. Undaunted, AP issued a statement parrying the extreme move, claiming it lit "the fire of rebellion" among the nation's women. The authorities, she said, "must be forced to realize that the demand of American women for self-government is too deep to be stamped out by sentences of any length." She recognized that her own imprisonment offered unparalleled symbolic value as well as public attention. She therefore joined three other sentinels at the White House gates on Saturday, October 20. Her banner used the president's own words to throw down the gauntlet: "The time has come to conquer or submit. For us there can be but one choice."[4]

Alice's second trial made clear how the NWP vigil challenged the authori-ties' conceptions of gender and class. Two days later, she appeared again in court, reiterating her refusal to be bound by laws in which she had no voice, though she pled "not guilty" this time. Again she remained mostly silent. Judge Mullowney finally admitted his bewilderment at the whole situation. Since the first arrests, he said, "I have not really known what to do," inadvertently revealing that the pickets confounded his notion of respectable women. He could not believe that "ladies" of this ilk believed in disobeying laws, "any such radical proposition as that." He felt equally mystified by the women's belief that they acted legally. "You force me," Mullowney concluded, "to take the most drastic means in my power to compel you to obey the law." He sentenced AP, "the ringleader," to seven months in jail.[5]

Alice had prepared for imprisonment. That morning, she dictated a few letters, leaving instructions for some, telling one organizer—ironically—to take a holiday, urging others to send protests about recent sentences to Wilson and Congress. She knew that the speakers' tour still roaming the country gave the NWP a direct line to the public; she set in motion more local publicity, notably a massive picket line for early November. With Lucy still at Occoquan, Dora Lewis agreed to manage the NWP in AP's absence and seasoned organizer Virginia Arnold took over the daily administrative work. Alice reassured her mother, "Please do not worry. It will merely be a delightful rest." She planned to work while in prison. She arranged to have her five daily newspapers delivered and advised Arnold to visit weekly with a stenographer in tow. These instructions belied journalists' expectations that she planned a hunger strike. Alice gathered some books, pulled on her fur coat, and set off to be sentenced.[6]

In the days before her sentencing, the pickets at Occoquan formally demanded treatment as political detainees, thereby raising the stakes for all the suffrage prisoners. The genesis of the women's demand is murky and stories conflict. However, the prisoners' written petition to the District commissioners followed claims of increasingly rough treatment at the workhouse and the solitary confinement of Lucy Burns. *The Suffragist* lauded the demand, claiming that "almost all civilized countries" recognized political prisoner status. AP's input in the decision to ramp up protest is unclear; nonetheless, she recognized the tactic and ran with it.[7]

Alice signaled her intention to extend the Occoquan demands before climbing into the patrol wagon on October 22. Since her punishment hardly fit the "crime," she told the press, she was clearly a political prisoner and expected to be treated as one. She felt only the "deepest indignation against an Administration which permits such gross injustice." "I am being imprisoned," she continued, "not because I obstructed traffic, but because I pointed out to President Wilson the fact that he is obstructing the progress of democracy and justice at home, while Americans fight for it abroad." With that political jab, she disappeared into the wagon for the short trip to the District jail. The next *Suffragist* cover featured a line of intrepid pickets, banners flying, marching toward a jailhouse door. The caption read: "Headquarters for the Next Six Months."[8]

The substantial jail term given the NWP leader stunned supporters around the country. In the Philadelphia office, Caroline Katzenstein wondered whether the lengthy sentence could stand: "It seems impossible." Mabel Vernon fretted, "I do think her doing time will have tremendous effect but I'm terribly depressed about her." One person voiced what many others feared to say: would the standard-bearer's lengthy absence cripple the organization? Yet the news also banished complacency. AP's "imprisonment has stirred us up," an Oregon follower wrote. And western New York members wired Alice at the jail, "Two hundred Buffalo women are with you."[9]

Alice and the three women sentenced with her joined fifteen other suffrage prisoners, including Lucy and ten other women recently transferred from Occoquan after their petition for political status. Unlike the workhouse's open barracks, the 1870s-era District jail held conventional cells, though matrons usually locked them only at night. Its proximity within the District facilitated the visiting and monitoring of prisoners. The women at headquarters also breathed easier with the pickets there rather than in Virginia. "The warden is much more humane," Arnold wrote Lucy's sister. "The matron is kindly." Officials typically permitted prisoners to wear their own clothing, receive fruit, and buy food items at the jail canteen. By October, however, privileges became highly arbitrary. Alice soon found working impossible.[10]

Despite its advantages over Occoquan, the District jail showed its age. A picket fence enclosed the dingy brick, L-shaped building, belying its function. Tall, narrow barred windows, each topped by a porthole-styled window, lined the walls. Inside, three tiers of dank steel and cement cells held the prisoners; officials housed nearly all suffragists on the upper level, effectively segregating them from the largely black population on the second tier. Frequently, two women shared a cell designed for one.[11]

Conditions were atrocious, yet far from uncommon. Dora Lewis, long involved with prison reform, rated the place three on a scale of ten. Bryn Mawr student Mary Winsor thought the six-by-nine cells were "so narrow that we could touch each side with the finger tips of outspread arms, each had an open toilet, smelling frightfully, hard mattresses on steel cots." Between the open pot (flushed from outside the cells), the dust billowing up when custodians swept the corridors, and the windows being closed from late afternoon until morning, the atmosphere became stifling. Officials turned off the heat and lights at night. In the dark, more vermin appeared. "Huge rats scrampered [sic] about," another picket charged. One woman found her bed "black with bed bugs." And the rats kept her up at night, making "such a noise fighting each other."[12]

Alice had no foreordained plan to contest the authority of her jailers who, for her purposes, became stand-ins for a government that denied women suffrage. Nonetheless, she knew the stratagems available to her and unveiled that disruptive power by degrees. She avoided breaking the law but knew the wholesale disobeying of inhumane or arbitrary rules could redound to the pickets' benefit. "We determined," AP later told Doris Stevens, "to make it impossible to keep us in jail." The barred cell doors worked to her advantage. As Winsor remembered,

" 'Solitary' confinement was not in the least solitary and a whisper could be heard all over." The privileged status of some suffrage prisoners became assumed for the entire group, likely meaning fewer consequences for disobedience. At the same time, protesting the uneven enforcement of regulations allowed the pickets to assert their resistance to the criminal label authorities foisted upon them.[13]

The first protest arose spontaneously over an appeal for fresh air. Alice joined another picket holding the rope that kept the top window open, in defiance of the matron's command to close it. In a flash, a male guard responded to the matron's call and wrested the rope from AP's fists. She then grasped the bars of a nearby cell and held on for dear life; finally, several more guards succeeded in carrying her to her cell, locking her door and those of several other participants. That night, flashing back to her glass-breaking days in Holloway Gaol, Alice joined the others in a follow-up revolt. As one later wrote, they threw shoes, "tin drinking cups, the electric light bulbs, every available article of the meagre supply in each cell" at nearby windows, succeeding only in cracking one or two. For three hours, they called for fresh air; matrons ultimately opened a few windows. Alice and her co-conspirators, however, paid for their disobedience with solitary confinement, meaning matrons kept cells locked day and night and permitted no mail or visitors.[14]

Solitary confinement failed to stop the protests. Some efforts were more successful than others. The next day, Alice initiated another drive for fresh air. Each time custodians swept the corridors, "the prisoners would be choking to the gasping point." This time, AP urged, "Throw water yourselves." The women filled their cups and tossed water repeatedly into the corridor as sweepers appeared, sending a message about sprinkling, the age-old way to reduce the dust cloud of the broom. Warden Louis Zinkhan finally ordered routine sprinkling. Repeated complaints about stifling air subsided when matrons agreed to open more windows. Appeals for privacy proved less successful; each time a prisoner hung her blanket over the front grating of her cell, matrons promptly ripped it down. As Alice pointed out, the notion of privacy in a detention facility counters "all institutional thought and habit."[15]

Nothing improved the jailhouse food. In an age before extensive food regulation and adequate refrigeration, substandard food was normal, nowhere more than in the nation's prisons; officials considered such fare suitable for criminals. In late October, denied care packages as well as canteen food, the jailed pickets made do with subsistence meals they could barely stomach. Alice remembered averting her eyes from the worm-ridden pork. From an adjacent cell, young NWP organizer Lucy Branham, a veteran of weeks at Occoquan, coached AP and the other newcomers on how to down the pork: "Shut your eyes tight, close your mouth over the pork and swallow it without chewing it." Nevertheless, Alice seldom managed to ingest the meat. The bread often seemed edible, though, especially with the occasional molasses. But minimally nourished, she grew progressively weaker. Another prisoner lost five pounds in her first five days. As she pointed out, AP "is not as husky as the rest of us."[16]

As in Britain, singing became a popular means to bolster group solidarity as well as pass the time. Alice remembered years later, "We always took our song along." The suffrage prisoners favored the British "March of the Women" ("Shoulder to shoulder, friend to friend"), which was often featured at NWP rallies and parades. Some fashioned instruments like comb-and-tissue harps to lend accompaniment. Satirical commentaries lifted their spirits: "We worried Woody-wood,/As we stood, as we stood./ . . . /We asked them for some air/ And they threw us in a lair,/. . ./Now, ladies, take the hint,/Don't quote the Presidint,/Don't quote the Presidint, as ye stand." But summoning the energy to sing, as the minutes and hours and days wore on, proved beyond the reach of some.[17]

After officials released Lucy and the other Occoquan transfers on November 3, concern mounted about Alice's health. The NWP leader sent word that she felt well despite ten days in her locked cell. She smuggled out a note with the one visitor her jailers permitted—a real estate agent consulting her about Cameron House. The man thought she looked "unusually well," her spirits seemed good, and she treasured the warmth of her fur coat. She sent him out with a detailed list of instructions for organizers. Despite these signs of normalcy, Dora Lewis felt concerned enough about AP's health that she wrote Mrs. Paul about discussing habeas corpus with the NWP attorney. Lewis's fears were only stoked when one of the Occoquan group fretted, "Alice Paul will die if kept seven months under such conditions." Munitions worker Annie Arneil cherished her last glimpse of AP: "I looked down to the lower tier," she told a welcoming audience, "and there was Miss Paul looking up with her face close to the bars. And I threw her a kiss."[18]

Actually, jail life improved for the remaining seven pickets after the Occoquan contingent's release. Left a smaller group, Alice suggested, "the authorities felt able to cope with us." The warden ended solitary confinement for those left behind, allowing them to mingle and take yard exercise. Soon after, Rose Winslow fainted outside and guards carried her back to her cell. Alice never made it to the yard— she felt too weak to climb out of bed. As she later told Stevens, "However gaily you start out in prison to keep up a rebellious protest, it is nevertheless a terribly difficult thing to do in the face of the constant cold and hunger of undernourishment." Two days later, guards locked all seven in their cells again after one woman called out a window to Elsie Hill, who had called from the yard outside the jail, since officials still excluded most visitors.[19]

Even in her weakened state, Alice found ways to continue protesting. Later that day, matrons removed both AP and Winslow to the jail hospital, placing them in the same ward until authorities realized the value of isolation. When offered fresh milk and eggs, both refused them, insisting that decent food be available to all the pickets. The argument underscored their moral authority, particularly when Alice pointed out that even murderers in the jail could enjoy canteen food.[20]

Alice reluctantly came to the realization that a hunger strike was the most powerful weapon available to her now. Some journalists predicted such a strike when she entered jail, but the NWP leader did not consider starving herself until she lay in the hospital. As with the Pankhursts, the hunger strike emerged organically. AP still contended with the toll on her health from her 1909 hunger strikes, so her reluctance seems understandable. With officials continuing to deny most basic privileges to the suffrage prisoners, however, she recognized the opportunity to force their hand and, by extension, the government's. As she wrote Lewis, "The more harsh and repressive we can make the Administration seem in these weeks before Congress opens, the better."[21]

The announcement of the hunger strike produced an immediate reaction that enabled Alice to keep communication lines open. After both she and Winslow started refusing nourishment, officials permitted Dr. Cora Smith King to see her, albeit in the presence of Dr. J. A. Gannon, the jail physician. Gannon seemed to delight in making jail more onerous for the pickets; among other things, he seized some prescription medications. AP described Gannon as the "devil incarnate," unusually strong words from the Quaker. Alice told King visitors should "refuse to be discouraged, insist on seeing her," in order to establish regular communication. She gave King messages for the NWP staff, principally urging the largest picket line possible for a planned last hurrah on November 10. King played courier in both directions, duly tucking a note from Lewis beneath AP's bedding. The reply to Lewis, which Alice knew would find a larger audience, shows her canny use of her charisma and her powerful modesty. "I had not thought of carrying [the strike] to any great length as I thought no one would know," she wrote. Now that newspapers had picked up the story, "I suppose we are committed to the plan and must go forward!"[22]

Alice's letter to Lewis also revealed clumsy and futile attempts to brainwash her. Unlike the usual graphic missive smuggled out of jail, AP's long letter contained her usual detached description of her situation. Despite a wire story claiming that jail officials were calmly "waiting for Miss Paul to get hungry enough to eat," Alice related that Gannon and two other doctors alternately told her they ordered milk and eggs for all seven pickets, threatened her with forced feeding, and hinted about removing her to a "very unpleasant place" if she did not start eating. The NWP leader rejected the idea that she and Winslow should be "fat-tened" in the hospital for a few days and then returned to the cells to starve, back and forth repeatedly, likening the ploy to similar attempts by British authorities to break Emmeline Pankhurst. Seemingly indifferent to the worst-case scenario, AP coolly observed that forced feeding over seven months offered "excellent ammunition against the Administration." Nonetheless, she believed the authori-ties would soon "concede everything we have asked."[23]

Alice's confidence depended largely on the pickets' ability to communicate their status. She knew that suffragists inside and outside had quickly learned to be inventive, often putting aside class or racial prejudices in the process. Inside, they passed notes between cells or used agreeable staff. After mail and visiting privileges were denied, the pickets convinced jail personnel or released prison-ers to carry dispatches out. One hospital scrubwoman became a regular courier, carrying notes, paper, and pencil from Cameron House to Alice and back. After officials threatened arrest, outsiders utilized more subterfuge—Stevens described one twilight visit to the grounds, skulking about, wrapped in a seedy overcoat.[24]

When Alice heard the news is unclear, but huzzahs certainly rang out at Cameron House after the elections held November 6. The second suffrage ref-erendum in New York succeeded, making the Empire State the first large "free" eastern state and adding millions to the number of women voters. One freed suf-fragist, at home recruiting more pickets, reported, "New York is very cocky over their splendid suffrage victory." After setbacks in Maine and Ohio (where voters overturned an earlier win) and the controversy over the picketing, many had pre-dicted another defeat and stood ready to blame the NWP. On the contrary, pro-claimed Elizabeth Rogers, "the Pickets did it—as they aroused the Socialists who set to and really worked for it." The ultrapatriotic, anti-suffrage *New York Times* also blamed the leftists, calling the victory a "gift from Socialism, from pacifism, from those who, consciously or with intent, serve Germany."[25]

Socialists were conspicuously absent on the platform for the NAWSA cel-ebration where a buoyant Carrie Chapman Catt immediately announced, "The fight is now for the national amendment." She hoped to tamp down remaining state initiatives and turn the limited attention of NAWSA's war workers toward Washington. Even Anna Howard Shaw, busy herself with war work, predicted "that when Congress next convenes, President Wilson will help us win the fight to pass a suffrage amendment to the Constitution." If nothing else, the New York victory could provide cover for Democrats unwilling to acknowledge pressure from the NWP as reason to vote for the Anthony amendment.[26]

Completely unbeknown to Alice, President Wilson had inquired about conditions at the jail. Wilson acted after receiving one too many protest letters about the imprisoned suffragists' plight. His right-hand man Tumulty felt the women were "being treated very harshly"; the president, however, thought such claims daft. Rejecting the secretary's opinion, he directed Tumulty to contact the District commissioners about jail conditions, "letting [them] see how very important I deem it to see that there is certainly no sufficient foundation for such statements." Did Wilson ask for an official whitewash? His dismissive attitude coupled with the ambiguous language could be interpreted as a cover-up request. Tumulty contacted newly minted commissioner Gwynne Gardiner. Eager to please, Gardiner responded boldly, sending the esteemed alienist (psychiatrist) Dr. William Alanson White, superintendent of St. Elizabeth's Hospital, the government-run mental institution, to evaluate Alice Paul.[27]

White's interview alerted Alice to the authorities' intentions. He approached her bed, asking the orderly, "Does this case talk?" AP quickly assured him that she did, saying, "Talking is our business." White asked her about suffrage, the picketing campaign, and her goals, and she obliged at length, later saying in a rare moment of immodesty, "It was one of the best speeches I ever made." Only when White scrutinized her, asking repeated questions about why she opposed the president did she grasp his meaning. "I realized with a sudden shock," AP told Stevens, that White sought to evaluate her sanity, to ferret out "symptoms of the persecution mania." That unpleasant place the doctors hinted about was the insane asylum.[28]

Alice's self-possession proved crucial to blunting Commissioner Gardiner's objective. The next day, White reappeared with Gardiner, both hoping she might be induced to eat. The doctor repeated his examination of the previous day. Alice reiterated why she refused food and the pickets' demand for political prisoner status. After the men left the star patient, White indicated, to Gardiner's probable dismay, that he found Alice quite sane and refused to transfer her to St. Elizabeth's. (He reportedly told Stevens that he found AP an "unusually gifted personality.") Gardiner reluctantly acquiesced, later telling Wilson that the protestor-in-chief seemed "perfectly calm, but very determined." More than fifty years later, Alice still felt "the greatest sense of indebtedness" to White: "It would have been so very easy for him to have given an adverse decision and I might still at this moment be in the St. Elizabeth's psychopathic ward." Indeed, the ramifications might have extended well beyond Alice Paul herself.[29]

As in Britain, fear finally drove officials to desperation. Gardiner returned and with other jail officials continued to pressure Alice to renounce the hunger strike. When she held fast, Gardiner gave the go-ahead for forced feeding. Although White found AP sane, he felt no compunction against forced feeding, which was common practice at St. Elizabeth's. White claimed that one patient there endured it "for twenty years with no ill effect." Gardiner evidently feared the NWP leader might die on his watch, clouding his new political appointment, not to mention the president's fortunes. Though she "seemed quite strong when she undertook to emphasize what she claimed as her rights," he wrote, she "is a very, very frail woman." Dr. Gannon proved more than willing to implement the feeding decision and gave the order. Matrons promptly carted Alice off on a stretcher to another part of the jail—the psychopathic ward.[30]

Gardiner successfully elicited the information Wilson required. The following day, he presented a self-serving report to the White House, saying what he thought the president wanted to hear. He reviewed his sessions with Miss Paul, conceding no evidence of "nervousness" but noting the physicians' agreement that forced nutrition now seemed imperative. Gannon reported successful feedings, claiming "no force or persuasion necessary." The suffragists misrepresented jail conditions, Gardiner maintained; the facility seemed clean and sanitary. Furthermore, he and White examined menus as well as food preparation and pronounced the quality "all that could be expected." The administration might correct the pickets' prevarications, wrote the commissioner, but he preferred to avoid controversy. The suffrage prisoners were implacable, "having beforehand a set purpose and plan to violate every rule of those institutions." The report satisfied the president: he began replying to alarmed correspondents that the pickets' treatment seemed "grossly exaggerated and misrepresented."[31]

Gardiner effectively punished Alice for thwarting his scheme. Guards locked her in a tiny room of the psychopathic ward, replacing its wooden door with a steel cell grate; they quickly boarded over one narrow barred window, leaving the second for light and air. She lay isolated, at the mercy of the loathed Dr. Gannon, who supervised the feedings. Her vitality sapped after two days without food, AP nonetheless insisted later that she fought "to my utmost strength" as the attendants pushed a tube down her throat and poured in a pint of milk and eggs. She waged the same battle, dreadfully familiar from her term in Holloway Gaol, twice each day thereafter.[32]

Gannon maliciously exacerbated Alice's situation, in essence using sleep deprivation to break her resolve. He instructed a nurse to shine a bright light over her face once an hour through the night, "a most terrible torture," she later recounted, "as it prevented my sleeping for more than a few minutes at a time." The Quaker soon learned from the nursing staff that the ward served as a way station for patients headed to St. Elizabeth's. Oblivious of White's positive conclusions, she feared the worst. Authorities denied all her requests for her own physician and lawyer or any visitors; she saw no one save jailhouse staff.[33]

Despite attempts at terrorizing her, Alice held on mentally, if not physically. As dusk approached on her second day in isolation, she heard a tentative call at the window. She rose from her bed to look out on a wondrous sight: her sister Helen and the stalwart Agnes Morey, the latter in from Boston for the next day's picketing. Desperate to determine AP's whereabouts, headquarters finally gleaned her location from an enterprising reporter. The two women felt shocked at the apparition clinging to the window sill, terribly pale and limp with exhaustion. Alice reassured them and quickly told the pair about her mental examination and her fear of confinement at St. Elizabeth's. She dictated a statement reiterating the demand for political prisoner status; her words explicitly acknowledged the many other jailed political dissenters who lacked the spotlight. "We are seeking to secure honorable conditions for the suffragists in jail," she said, "making it possible for them to live through their seven months' imprisonment and we are protecting the rights of political offenders everywhere in the nation."[34]

Helen's letter to Tacie Paul suggests the elder woman had not changed her mind about Alice's actions since her January 1917 letter asking her daughter to call off the pickets. Helen tried to shift blame for the pickets onto Lucy; her words hint at the prejudices of the Paul elders. Helen assured her mother that "everyone" believed in the principle of the protest. Lucy, however, "was at the bottom of most of these things. I have just discovered that the latter is an R. Catholic."[35]

As in Britain, Alice's self-command enabled her to distance herself from physical privation. She presented herself as indifferent to suffering. John Milholland, for example, called her a "mere network of steel nerves about a cast-iron spinal column." Her familiarity with the physiological processes of starving and forced feeding undoubtedly helped, though Winslow noted AP's palpable dread of the feedings. For those on the outside, AP cast the whole business as just "an interesting time, much more interesting," she wrote Lewis in one smuggled note, "than collecting money." She disciplined her mind to ignore the physical, to keep busy evaluating possibilities and considering what instructions she needed to send headquarters. She gleaned information from anyone she saw—doctors, matrons, trusties, or charwomen. She may have recalled Mary Winsor's mantra "Stone walls do not a prison make" and opened her secreted *Oxford Book of English Verse* to read the entire poem, coveting the line, "Minds innocent and quiet take/That for an hermitage."[36]

When NWP staff heard that officials might send Alice to St. Elizabeth's, the consternation at Cameron House reached epic proportions—no one had for a moment thought the Wilson administration would stoop to committing their leader. Dora Lewis and Lucy quickly decided to call in their most powerful weapons. Telegrams sped out to Jane Addams—"Could you possibly come to protest in person to the President?"—and to Doris Stevens—"Please persuade Malone if possible come Washington. Believe he could see Miss Paul." Messages alerted NWP supporters all over the country; as Agnes Morey wired the Massachusetts chapter: "Situation desperate." The SOS to Addams seemed off the mark, since the public had marginalized the well-known pacifist for her antiwar stance; she could do the NWP no good. Malone, on the other hand, was still an NWP attorney and, as a former Wilson intimate, their best bet to speak truth to power. While the anxious faithful awaited him, however, they went off to be arrested themselves. The circumstances required more than the usual measure of courage.[37]

Alice Paul's minions beat the bushes for weeks to line up fifty pickets for November 10, hoping to do her proud. Lucy communicated AP's desire that everyone "work unremittingly," to "show the Administration that our demand for freedom absolutely cannot be suppressed." She also reckoned fifty more disruptive prisoners would overwhelm the jailers' ability to grapple with them. As Lucy wrote, "We want all our best and bravest in line." She assured likely recruits of short sentences; judges gave only multiple offenders six months; nonetheless, with AP in jail for seven months, many women balked.[38]

Carrie Chapman Catt and Anna Howard Shaw preceded the pickets to the White House. Despite the New York success, they remained convinced that the pickets' impropriety actively damaged suffrage chances and were unwilling to exert political pressure on the president. Like black women in the 1913 procession, the pickets' visibility threatened the cause. Underscoring the importance of the New York victory, Catt beseeched the president to urge the Anthony amendment on the coming Congress to "save the expense and the long struggle" of more state referendums, the idea long championed by Alice Paul. The NAWSA leader chose not to mention the suffrage prisoners.

The president agreed to nothing, despite his respect for the National and his change of heart on federal suffrage action. Nevertheless, Catt declared herself satisfied with Wilson's "sincere friendship for our cause." Shaw spoke out once more for Wilson and against the pickets two weeks later at a state suffrage convention, decrying the "great wave of sentimentality" for the suffrage prisoners that was sweeping the nation.[39]

Indeed, the sentinels standing before the White House gates the next day noticed a more benign mood. Longtime NWP allies Elizabeth Kent, Lucy Burns, and Dora Lewis led forty-one pickets from fifteen states. Septuagenarian Mary Nolan journeyed north from Florida for the honor of picketing once more. The president noticed them—he almost motored in at the same gate, but his driver quickly swung around to the back. Lewis termed the crowd which gathered "wonderfully sympathetic for the first time"; the spectators included Tumulty. "The whole affair was conducted in the most polite and gentle fashion," according to one reporter. An embarrassed group of policemen arrested the pickets anyway, one officer allegedly pleading, "Aw, for the love of Mike be sensible."[40]

Justice officials, like the District police, felt ready to be done with the whole affair. In court two days later, Judge Mullowney, complaining that he lacked the power to deal with the situation, pronounced the entire group guilty but took sentences under "advisement." After most of the same group picketed twice more, the frustrated Mullowney finally issued sentences. Most women received thirty days, but he singled out Nolan for her age, giving her six days, and Lucy for her leadership role, giving her six months. Former congressman William Kent refused to allow his wife Elizabeth to be jailed and paid the fine over her vehement protest. Ultimately, twenty-nine more pickets made the trip to Occoquan Workhouse.[41]

In Virginia, the warden had no more patience for the suffrage prisoners. Upon their arrival at the penal farm, Dora Lewis, speaking for the group, insisted upon seeing Superintendent Whittaker; he arrived more than an hour later in an angry mood. Refusing to listen to Lewis's demand for political status, he ordered guards to seize the women and remove them to solitary confinement, beginning what the women later termed the "night of terror." Their accounts describe guards throwing the pickets, including the elderly Mary Nolan, into cells, Mrs. Lewis handled so roughly "we thought she was dead." After Lucy called around to check on the others, guards handcuffed her and threatened a straitjacket and gag. Officials denied repeated requests for counsel. Most of the pickets began a hunger strike in protest. In a particularly ominous yet bizarre turn of events, Whittaker called in a contingent of Marines to guard the compound.[42]

Meanwhile, in the District jail's psychopathic ward, Alice Paul steeled her mind to endure. The watchfulness that held her outside the moment proved a boon now, when only the feedings punctuated the colorless days and interminable nights. She saw only nurses, doctors, and attendants, except for the occasional patient peering through her bars. She heard the other inmates more often. "When one person started shrieking," she wrote in one smuggled letter, "the others usually joined in, and continued for an hour or two." Silence reigned for minutes or hours, then the screams resumed. "I have got to live through this somehow," she recalled telling herself. "I'll pretend these moans are the noise of an elevated train, beginning faintly in the distance and getting louder as it comes nearer." Any thoughts of elsewhere, though "childish devices," helped sustain her. Alice also drew comfort from the occasional kindhearted nurse, one of whom told her, "I know you are not insane."[43]

After nearly a week, her spirits rose when she saw a delegation of the November 10 pickets approaching the warden's residence. She called to the group as they mounted the steps to the warden's residence and the women rushed beneath her one open window. Amid cries from other patients, AP assured them she felt well and still resisted the forced feedings. She urged them to keep up the demand for political prisoner status, before guards chased the group away. Shortly thereafter, attendants boarded up that window, too, preventing further communication from the outside.[44]

The day after Alice's conversation with her secret visitors, Dudley Field Malone arrived to contest her isolation. As her attorney, he protested the NWP leader's confinement in the psychopathic ward and insisted on seeing her; the warden coldly refused. Zinkhan grudgingly admitted him only after Malone threatened a writ of habeas corpus. Alice's spirits rose when Malone appeared; they talked for ninety minutes. The outraged Malone then read the riot act to Warden Zinkhan, firmly establishing Alice's right to see counsel and demanding that officials remove her from the psychopathic ward. He further told the warden that he could either "make himself famous" by giving the pickets political prisoner status and privileges or be "discredited as a fool before the country." "Mr. Malone has such a delightful sense of humor," Helen wrote her mother. The next day, attendants carried Alice back to the hospital. Beulah Amidon, hearing the sorry tale from Malone, smuggled a note to Winslow, "We wept all of us, but we glory in you."[45]

Attention turned to alleviating the Occoquan situation. The NWP's local attorney, Matthew O'Brien, finally succeeded in seeing Dora Lewis and Lucy after three days, and then only after getting a court order. Their reports and that of Mary Nolan, released after her six days, convinced the horrified staff at headquarters that only actually filing for habeas corpus could relieve the incendiary situation at Occoquan. O'Brien gained a hearing for November 23, nearly a week later.[46]

Between the situation at Occoquan and Alice's week in the psychopathic ward, alarm bells rang all over the country. Some newspapers started to speak out against the treatment accorded the suffrage prisoners. A longtime *New York Tribune* critic suggested the NWP's allegations required impartial investigation. Editors at the *Philadelphia Ledger* wrote that the suffragists' "unwisdom offers no excuse for the ruthless severity with which the pickets have been treated." Protest meetings held by Maud Younger, Anne Martin, and others in every region drew larger and larger crowds, although in some southern locales, organizers fought to secure meeting space.[47]

Some women opposed to picketing nevertheless recoiled at the treatment accorded the pickets. An Indianapolis suffragist reiterated her lack of sympathy for the prisoners but acknowledged, "I am sorry indeed that [they] cannot be justly treated." Longtime NWP member Mary Beard, a vehement critic of picketing, put together the "Committee of One Thousand Women" (mostly working women), whose representatives tried (and failed) to meet with Wilson to protest the pickets' treatment.[48]

Not everyone revised their views; some still found the picketing morally bankrupt, unwomanly, even self-indulgent, and thus deserving of punishment. The late October and November picketing still brought the NWP mailbox a handful of contemptuous letters each week. "You are, once again, trying to take advantage of the fact that you are women, and resenting the treatment you therefore receive in war times," opined a Texas woman. From Maine, a NAWSA member wrote that the pickets were "more fit for the insane asylum than any of their inmates." Such letters, however, all but stopped after mid-November.[49]

Woodrow Wilson continued to avert his eyes. Some of his own friends and supporters appealed to him now, one saying the situation was becoming "painful for other women to stand by and watch." Dr. Howard Kelly, Alice's erstwhile physician, declared himself "heartily in accord" with Wilson's policies, including the sentencing of the pickets. "I cannot, however," he wrote, "ignore the constant complaints of injustice and discrimination and cruel treatment." "An extraordinary amount of lying" has occurred, the president insisted, denying any "real harshness" in the treatment.[50]

To be sure, plenty of other issues commanded presidential attention: the ongoing war, the overthrow of the new government in Russia, and a coal crisis and impending railroad strike at home. Yet Wilson carried on much as before, golfing and usually taking a long drive each day, attending the theater twice a week. A rumor circulated in mid-November that he had convened a meeting with the District commissioners to discuss the pickets. The protestors' situation remained crystal clear in the chief executive's mind: the women had "offended against an ordinance of the District and are undergoing the punishment appropriate in the circumstances." Joseph Tumulty, who talked to a far wider range of people than Wilson did, believed the president willfully ignorant. He warned Wilson that "the time is soon coming when we will have to seriously consider this matter."[51]

As November 23 approached, Cameron House staff anticipated a victory from the habeas corpus hearing. Attorney O'Brien's connections yielded the news of preparation at the District jail for the Occoquan prisoners' arrival, so at the very least staff expected a transfer out of Occoquan if not outright dismissal of the charges. Both sides knew of an earlier verdict declaring a male prisoner's transfer from the jail to Occoquan illegal. To boost spirits further, two more congressmen issued public statements of protest about the pickets' treatment. The administration countered by releasing the Gardiner whitewash.[52]

The hearing exposed a vigilant administration applying political pressure. The litigants assembled on Friday, November 23, in Alexandria, Virginia, just across the District line. Superintendent Whittaker brought the pickets, which the habeas corpus writ forced him to produce, and they joined reporters, spectators, and, surprisingly, Warden Zinkhan from the District jail. Zinkhan's presence suggests prior behind-the-scenes decision making, or at least the expectation that this judgment would find Occoquan an illegal transfer point for District prisoners. US District Court judge Edmund Waddill, "a mild mannered, sweet-voiced southern gentleman," according to one reporter, felt alarmed by the writ's description of the women's treatment, calling it "bloodcurdling" if true. The appearance of the lethargic prisoners hinted as much: the reporter thought most seemed so weakened from their hunger strike that they took scant notice of the proceedings. The next day, Waddill had a sudden change of heart and disallowed testimony on conditions at Occoquan.

However, that decision came after he pronounced the transfer of the pickets to the workhouse illegal, "without semblance of authority or legal process." Any further inquiry into Occoquan was thus deemed fruitless, since the prisoners were leaving. Whittaker's intent to appeal entitled the pickets to be free on bail. However, with the exception of three women nearing collapse, the prisoners chose to finish their sentences in the District.[53]

On Saturday evening, as the Occoquan pickets joined the three suffragists remaining in the cramped cells of the District jail, Alice remained on hunger strike in the adjacent hospital building. She was still isolated from Rose Winslow, although the two managed some communication between their wards. After continued attempts by NWP staff to visit by way of the windows, Dr. Gannon ordered their third window nailed shut; air seeped only through the top of a single window. Alice thought Gannon seemed "determined to deprive me of air" because the pickets demanded fresh air as political prisoners. The warden still denied mail, reading material, and visitors (including counsel), though true to the authorities' consistent inconsistency, they permitted both occasionally. Forced feeding continued twice a day for Alice and Winslow; now Lucy and Dora Lewis joined the list.[54]

Shortly after the Occoquan group arrived at the District jail, the warden welcomed an unexpected visitor and gave him full access to the suffrage prisoners, even those in isolation. David Lawrence, a prominent *New York Post* columnist and recognized friend of the administration, spent several hours there, talking primarily with Lucy and later with Alice Paul. The journalist looked around and discussed jail conditions with both women; Lucy later termed his attitude "frankly antagonistic."[55]

Alice, well aware of Lawrence's connection to Wilson, happily discussed the status of the suffrage amendment with him. Lawrence expected the legislation to pass the House during the coming session because of the groundbreaking New York victory. AP felt gratified, taking the journalist's presence and comments as an indication that the administration was coming around. Days later, she said so publicly, and the story quickly ballooned out of control to the point where Lawrence became an emissary from the president himself. Certainly, the timing of the visit was intriguing: Lawrence came soon after Tumulty's warning to the president about addressing the situation.[56]

David Lawrence's gendered lens resembled the president's in its seemingly respectful yet condescending approach. The journalist wrote about his visit in his next column, published Tuesday, November 27. The article appeared in the usual commanding front-page position. Lawrence alternately admired the suffrage prisoners and belittled them, sometimes both at once; overall, he viewed them as "emotionally inclined women." Lucy talked eloquently, he wrote, and AP was "rhetorically aggressive," with "enough energy to talk a blue streak for an hour"— a pointed contradiction of any notion that she was near death.

He paternalistically hesitated to dispute their views. "There's an age-old rule about arguing with a woman," he reminded readers. He defended them in a back-handed way, stating his disbelief that they "would lend themselves to intrigues with anarchists or German plotters"; yet they failed to realize how their actions might endanger the president. He further agreed that some jail conditions might be improved but felt more sympathy for the jailers, for whom "the pickets had made life miserable." One red flag springs up: little of the discussion with Alice about suffrage appears in the column. Lawrence did tell AP, he averred, that any future picketing, if even necessary, should be at the Capitol, since "the President already has done enough to show he's interested in the cause."[57]

The Tuesday that Lawrence's column appeared, officials abruptly released all the suffrage prisoners. Judge Mullowney apparently became concerned on Monday about their health. "I understand," he wrote Warden Zinkhan cryptically, "there are certain prisoners in your custody" whose health would be endangered by further time in jail. He made no mention of the pickets, suggesting some additional communication between the two. Zinkhan responded Tuesday with the names of the twenty-two prisoners on hunger strike and recommended prompt action. Hours later, without explanation, the warden freed Alice and twenty-one other women, some too weak to walk. Zinkhan pronounced himself "greatly relieved" and wrote the judge Wednesday suggesting that the remainder be released as well. He ushered those eight women out before night fell. As an exceedingly frail Alice Paul left her hospital bed, she mustered the strength to declare, "We are put out of jail as we were put in—at the whim of the government. They tried to terrorize and suppress us. They could not, so they freed us."[58]

Alice's explanation sounded as good as anyone else's. Mullowney refused comment. Neither the District commissioners nor the White House had anything to say. The *Chicago Tribune*, however, pointed out that with Congress convening the next week, the authorities had forestalled threatened investigations. Wilson's friends drove the situation, according to a Philadelphia paper. In Washington, the *Post* kept its tongue firmly in cheek and suggested that the judge invoked the constitutional prohibition against "cruel and unusual punishments"—on behalf of the jailers. Other newspapers left the mystery intact. Of course, the timing guaranteed a warm spot in some hearts—the next day was Thanksgiving.[59]

The appearance of David Lawrence's column on the day of Alice's release raises more questions about his role in the pickets' deliverance. If the White House—more likely Tumulty than Wilson—sent Lawrence, why dignify the jailed pickets with a long, albeit conflicted treatise? The column ran right next to the release story on the front page. If Lawrence served as emissary, why alert keen-eyed readers by publishing the column as the release happened? These and other questions about the freeing of the pickets cannot be answered, because the principals left no paper trail.

Four months later, the pickets received a measure of dispensation. Early in March, the District Court of Appeals ruled on two appeals filed after the August riots and arrests. The judge, ruling narrowly, found the government's case against the pickets "too vague, general, and uncertain," failing to meet the requirements of due process. In other words, the District provided insufficient evidence that the pickets obstructed traffic. In the absence of sufficient proof, the judge could not rule on the question of guilt or innocence. Therefore, the court reversed the guilty verdicts and ordered the cases dismissed.[60]

The NWP immediately declared "complete vindication," even though the court dismissed the cases because of lack of proof, rather than the pickets' guilt or innocence. Alice probably realized the decision's limited scope but recognized another opportunity to declare victory. NWP members happily leapt to conclusions. Dora Lewis, like many, interpreted the ruling as total absolution. She wrote Alice, "Of course we knew that we would win, but it's good to have the world know our immaculate character."[61]

Some pickets became embittered about the damage to their respectability. Amelia Himes Walker, a Swarthmore classmate of AP's, welcomed the court decision but believed a damage lawsuit "the only way for our conduct to be vindicated thro' the public press, as a governmental apology would be thought a joke—were there such things as governmental apologies." Indeed, a number of women did file damage suits totaling $800,000 against the District commissioners and wardens Whittaker and Zinkhan. Even successful lawsuits, however, could not repair Walker's reputation. "The damage done most of us cannot be estimated in money," she confessed, decrying her many alienated friends and neighbors.[62]

Upon her release from the District jail, an unrepentant Alice Paul declared the NWP ready to enter the breach again. "We hope that no more demonstrations will be necessary," she told reporters. "But what we do depends entirely upon what the Administration does." She pronounced the picketing campaign successful. "Administration leaders told us to wait patiently until the end of the war," she pointed out. "Now they prophecy suffrage at the session opening in December. That is a gain, perhaps of many years, the saving of many years of women's energy when it is so greatly needed." With that, she retreated to Cameron House. Well wishes poured in from supporters, including one from Alva Belmont, who rejoiced "to have you all once more among us."[63]

15

"Not a Gift, but a Triumph"

THOUGH SOME BELIEVED that Alice Paul had bested Woodrow Wilson when the administration released all suffrage prisoners, Alice herself held no illusions. She maintained her conviction that presidential pressure was the key to the passage of the Anthony amendment; her belief would be put to the test in 1918.

Recuperation became the first order of business. As one picket wrote, "I find that one does not soon recover." Tall, strong Lucy, down thirty pounds after back-to-back imprisonments, immediately traveled home to Brooklyn to convalesce. Rose Winslow required a trained nurse. Late in December, AP sought a restful spot for her erstwhile hospital mate at a supporter's beach home, feeling that the NWP "ought to look after her." Cameron House also was transformed into a recovery ward.[1]

Alice herself was largely incapacitated for three weeks, neglecting even to keep family informed. Her mother finally wrote, ten days after her release, "We are anxious to hear how thee is & how thee stood the ordeal." A plaintive note from Helen two weeks later—"How is thee by this time—drop us a line now and then"—finally prompted Alice to wire hastily saying "Merry Christmas" and that work kept her in Washington.[2]

The healthy staff cared for freed pickets while they prepared to vacate the premises, an unexpected consequence of the picketing campaign. Early in 1917, the owners of Cameron House had objected to the NWP's notoriety and withdrawn its lease; Dora Lewis stalled them for nearly a year. The NWP found a new home across Lafayette Square, but it was unavailable until the new year, so they moved to temporary quarters at 822 Connecticut Avenue, just north of the square. Somehow, the migration happened in time to welcome advisory council members and state chairmen to a conference beginning December 6.[3]

The four-day gathering claimed the picketing crusade as a victory and anticipated future success. Conference chair Elizabeth Rogers, after a brief introduction by the recuperating AP, trumpeted the year's progress. "They have tried everything they could, and yet what has happened to us?" she exclaimed. The NWP boasted fifteen hundred new members; the "few we have lost," she suggested (actually about two hundred), "haven't perhaps understood us." Donations exceeded the previous year's by $7,000. The news that Congress planned another vote on suffrage topped even that for excitement. The informational component of the conference paled, however, next to its emotional heft.[4]

Events celebrating the commitment and sacrifices of the pickets validated their efforts and implicitly refuted critics of the White House vigil. A celebratory banquet held under twinkling lights, amid purple and gold blossoms, flags, and battle-worn banners, extolled the sentinels' unconquerable spirit. A noticeably thinner Lucy offered a tribute to Alice, "who led our forces into jail." The next day, the crowning spectacle at the Belasco Theatre, a favorite Wilson haunt, turned thousands away.[5]

The pageant of former prisoners featured eighty-nine former pickets. Alice joined the processional, the women striding two by two down the inner aisles and climbing to the stage. Recalling Emmeline Pankhurst's gift of prison door brooches, AP had arranged for a similar cell-door replica for each "prisoner of freedom." The subsequent largesse, though probably exaggerated, nevertheless recorded the extraordinary depth of feeling in the hall: *The Suffragist* claimed pledges of more than $86,000 for the NWP's continuing efforts.[6]

Alice retreated to her bed for another week, as friends and supporters heaped praise and concern on her, even arousing a touch of self-pity. Organizer Margaret Whittemore wrote of her relief and impatience to see her: "Please never go into such danger, again," she urged. "You are too valuable." Elsie Hill, a friend from the start, sent "my affection and wholehearted admiration for what you have done not only for those of us who have the real happiness of being associated with you but for all women." Former Penn classmate Clara Thompson wrote lovingly from her academic post at Rockford College, hoping "you are going to be very good to yourself for a little while now," encouraging her friend to take time off.[7]

Convalescing at Cameron House made Alice a bit melancholy about the road not taken. "Will you not tell me something about your own work and life?" she answered her professorial chum. "I feel so removed from you and often wonder how the world is going with you. My own life is entirely limited by what appears in 'The Suffragist,' so that I have nothing about which to write."[8]

Her recuperation acquired urgency when the new Congress acted on the Anthony amendment. Shortly after Congress convened, Alice received word that the House intended to vote on suffrage; indeed, NWP lobbyists estimated fifty more affirmative votes since January 1917. To her dismay, the judiciary committee attached a rider to the bill, specifying a time limit of seven years for ratification. AP quickly issued a statement denouncing the rider, knowing that the tactic only encouraged the opposition to wait them out. She sought counsel from the dean of Harvard Law School on the matter; he assured her the Supreme Court would not give the idea "aid or comfort."[9]

Suffragists' hopes swelled when the prohibition amendment cleared the House in December after earlier passage by the Senate. The history of the movement to ban alcohol had often paralleled the suffrage cause; many women viewed temperance—and later, prohibition—as a means of protecting women and children from the ravages of alcohol abuse. As AP's *Suffragist* editorial noted, prohibition not only set a fresh precedent for amending the Constitution, but also took "the ground from under the states rights argument." Retribution might help too: "They say the 'wets' are so mad," Lewis wrote Caroline Katzenstein, "that many of them will vote for us in order to 'put it over' the Southern members," conservatives who abandoned their customary states' rights cry to support prohibition.[10]

Despite these auspicious signs, Alice left nothing to chance. She refused all pleas for further rest and hunkered down, working round the clock to secure the House vote. Committed votes on the Democratic side still fell short, while more than two-thirds of Republicans favored the measure. AP continued to believe that only the president's influence could sway the necessary Democratic votes. "A word from him," she maintained to the press, "and suffrage will pass the House. Without his influence the result of the vote is doubtful." She warned that women voters in the western states would use the 1918 elections to avenge any delay in nationwide suffrage.[11]

Advocates on both sides of the suffrage issue now joined her in looking toward presidential influence. The president heard from anti-suffragists imploring him to uphold states' rights. Suffragists flooded the White House with pleas for support, and Democratic women also besieged the president. Despite the NWP's few concrete results in 1916, some Democrats took AP's threat about the 1918 elections seriously. They warned Wilson that another defeat for the amendment endangered the Democratic House majority. "You, and you alone," a Kansas congressman stressed, "can save the situation."[12]

Nevertheless, timing mattered. Wilson's focus as the new year dawned was his fourteen-point peace plan, the centerpiece initiative of his second term; his congressional address was scheduled two days before the suffrage vote. He sought to avoid drawing attention away from his plan. To petitioners, he continued feigning powerlessness. "The most I have felt at liberty to do," he replied, was "give my advice to members of Congress when they have asked for it." Amendment supporters, however, saw their opening and quickly organized a delegation, mostly of wavering Democrats. After some urging by Tumulty, Wilson bowed to political realities and grudgingly made room in his schedule the day before the vote.[13]

On January 9, 1918, Woodrow Wilson told the visiting Democratic congressmen that the Anthony amendment was "an act of right and justice." Though a private endorsement, the president allowed the congressmen to announce his support to the press. The news traveled with lightning speed, making the front page of many newspapers the day of the vote and causing even pessimistic observers to predict success. The *New York Sun* thought Wilson had cannily waited for "the psychological moment." The *Baltimore Sun* said bluntly: "The President has succumbed to the pickets." Alice believed the president acted to forestall voter retribution in the 1918 congressional elections and to eliminate the threat of more picketing. She told reporters that the president's approval made a House victory inevitable.[14]

The next morning, charwomen still soaping the Capitol floors looked up to find suffragists already lining up for gallery seats. Many had stuffed sandwiches in their coat pockets and prepared to spend the day. The House Speaker gave Mrs. Catt and NAWSA officials pride of place in his gallery, while Alice, Lucy, and other NWP stalwarts filled the east gallery. The debate commenced shortly after eleven o'clock that morning and droned on for hours, rehearsing all the familiar arguments against the amendment. Jeannette Rankin echoed AP's rhetoric, stressing the need to not only make the world safe for democracy, but America too. If the amendment failed, said Rankin, "How shall we explain to [women] the meaning of democracy?"[15]

As the afternoon shadows lengthened, Alice slipped out of the House gallery and returned to work, apparently confident of the result and always thinking ahead. Vote counters frantically looking for absentees felt less confident. One elderly congressman finally appeared with a broken shoulder; two climbed out of hospital beds to be present. A New York member arrived on the floor despite the overnight death of his wife, an avid suffragist. At five o'clock, the House addressed riders to the bill, including the seven-year time limit. After a majority, but not a two-thirds majority, voted down that limitation, alarmed whispers rose from the gallery. Would they have enough votes for the two-thirds required to pass a constitutional amendment?[16]

The first roll call for the Anthony amendment came and went and the second began, seeking any members failing to answer. Just when victory seemed at hand, an opponent shouted for a recapitulation of the count. The women in the gallery waited breathlessly. Finally, the announcement: 136 opposed, 274 in favor. The suffrage amendment passed the House with exactly the two-thirds majority required, forty years to the day after the amendment's first introduction into Congress. Six of those votes proved directly attributable to Wilson's eleventh-hour endorsement.[17]

Cheers and applause consumed the House floor and gallery. Suffragists embraced each other and wept with joy. As the jubilant multitude passed out of the House gallery, Lucy, Dora Lewis, Doris Stevens, Maud Younger, Anne Martin—seemingly everyone save Alice—joined the impromptu singing, starting with "Glory, glory, hallelujah." In the chill of the evening, the NWP women trooped joyfully back to headquarters. They found Alice Paul hunkered over her desk, according to Younger. She looked up. "Eleven to win before we can pass the Senate."[18]

The next day, Alice's thirty-second birthday, congratulations poured into headquarters. J. A. H. Hopkins wrote: "The women of the country have you and the pickets to thank." Insiders felt euphoric. "You and I know that the Pickets did it, Don't we?," one field operative crowed. New Yorker Ethel Adamson agreed. Long critical of the picketing, she now offered nothing but praise: "We all know WHO PASSED THE FEDERAL AMENDMENT," she wrote. "It was little Alice Paul."[19]

In the "Victory Number" of *The Suffragist*, Alice declared, "The President himself was finally forced to pay tribute" to "the political balance of power" women represented. And, she added, the House vote vindicated the idea of holding the party in power responsible. Mentioning the pickets only indirectly, she maintained that the Democrats and Wilson acted to save their party's seats in the 1918 elections.[20]

The press also emphasized the political expediency of the vote, motivated by an evenly divided House. Since Wilson declined to speak publicly, opined the *New York Herald*, opportunism seemed "the only possible conclusion" for his "about-face." "It is not a question as to whether or not Democrats will kindly condescend to let women vote," the *Washington Times* suggested. "The question is, will the women consent to let Democrats stay in power?" Even the staunchly opposed *New York Times* concurred, though the editors insisted that "in the presence of war, woman suffrage is but a piffling and sub-minor matter."[21]

Mysterious quantity or no, the potential suffrage vote had loomed large in the collective mind of the House, particularly on the Democratic side. Although NAWSA compiled a blacklist in 1916, it still declined to campaign against anyone. Only the NWP devoted time and resources to political pressure. During 1917, the pickets kept suffrage in the public eye despite the war and forced the administration into an embarrassing position. Democratic congressmen did not fear NAWSA coming after them in the 1918 elections: they feared the National Woman's Party.

An analysis of the vote records the significant change in Democratic votes since the 1915 House vote. The amendment failed by 78 votes in 1915; three years later, Republicans overwhelmingly voted *aye*—165 to 33—while Democrats managed only a scant majority—104 to 102. The opposition continued to flourish in the South, the site of seven of eight states with most or all of their delegation opposing the amendment. Southern resistance proved only part of the story, however. Two-thirds of the large Ohio and Massachusetts delegations voted against the amendment; Pennsylvania and Alice's home state of New Jersey tallied another sixteen *nay* votes. The push for the Senate vote, then, would not focus solely on the South.[22]

In mid-February, NWP staff moved to 14 Jackson Place, directly across the park from Cameron House. The four-story mansion, like so many around the square, boasted a long and impressive history. With its distinctive white stone facade and graceful portico, the house allowed ample offices as well as bedroom and auditorium space. After painting and papering and decorating, the NWP would once again boast a dignified headquarters-cum-lodgings-cum-sanctuary. They even had hot water on demand, a real luxury.[23]

The decorating of Alice's bedroom in the mansion occasioned a rivalry that speaks to her galvanizing effect on some younger operatives. As usual, she chose one of the smaller rooms for herself, a room lacking even a good light. Organizer Julia Emory, working in Maine, pushed AP to fix up what she called a "Hell-hole" but, she wrote Alice, "don't forget to leave your painting for me to do." A wealthy supporter overcame AP's resistance to spending money on herself by donating specifically for the renovation of her room. Soon, visiting former picket Natalie Gray reported AP joining Maud Younger and others "having the time of their lives planning for color schemes, arrangement of furniture, etc." Alice wanted an entirely white room, including furniture, a desire suggesting she sought to recreate the restful, if sterile, environment of her two infirmary stints. Gray purchased some paint before she left for home and began covering the walls with white, expecting Emory to be "very peeved!!" Gray felt ecstatic when, to her surprise, "Miss Paul kissed me good-by and *walked all the way* down to the *front door*!! with me."[24]

Alice's surprising affection for Gray may have reflected her need to draw even more emotional sustenance from her work relationships. William Parker remained in Washington through 1918; he and Alice probably continued to see each other, though no other record of their meetings survived. However, his relationship with AP had spanned five years. Quite possibly, he proposed before leaving Washington and Alice turned him down. Her decision was all too common at the time for ambitious women, who saw little possibility of combining outside work and marriage. Bryn Mawr president M. Carey Thomas wrote about the "cruel handicap" accomplished women endured: "They have spent half a lifetime in fitting themselves for their chosen work and then may be asked to choose between it and marriage. No one can estimate the number of women who remain unmarried in revolt before such a horrible alternative." After the war, Parker returned to Wall Street. He never married.[25]

Alice maintained her commitment to the impressive political machine she had built by 1918. Despite the constant scrambling for funds, the NWP's paid staff rivaled that of NAWSA itself. Support staff included five stenographers and two switchboard operators as well as a manservant and maid (the man was paid 20 percent more). Salaried personnel, including *The Suffragist* staff and the press office, totaled thirteen. Fourteen field operatives drew salaries and expenses, nearly all paid by state branches by early 1918. Alice and some department heads, of course, worked full time but were paid only for any expenses. Nevertheless, the organization paid out over $1,800 in salaries alone each month. During 1917, the NWP spent $131,000, most of it raised not from membership fees, *Suffragist* sales, or bequests, but from hard-won donations. Little wonder Alice always fretted about money.[26]

She and many other suffragists believed a Senate victory easily possible in the fourteen months before the 65th Congress adjourned in March 1919. However, uncertainty and unexpected vacancies complicated attempts to schedule a vote. The design of the Senate also contributed to the delay. The equal representation given each state meant more power for less populous states, like some in the South. Senate rules, furthermore, allowed for dilatory tactics such as unlimited speechifying. Indeed, opponents filibustered when the Anthony amendment came up in late June. In mid-July, the Senate recessed until fall.[27]

Alice refrained from new demonstrations through the spring and summer of 1918, counting on lobbying and the pressure of the fall elections to prompt movement. However, she had accustomed her troops to bolder action. A Colorado stalwart voiced a common frustration: "Do suggest something fierce for us to do," she wrote. Wilson's continued recalcitrance only fueled their impatience. He wrote or met privately with a few senators but failed to change any votes. Despite his faith in strong presidential directives, he shied away from publicly endorsing suffrage, though both NAWSA and NWP urged him to do so. By late April, Ethel Adamson advised AP of the widespread feeling in New York "that something more drastic ought to be done to stir the president to action."[28]

Alice's forbearance lasted until the summer Senate recess. She then launched plans for a new demonstration and toured the mid-Atlantic to rouse support and raise funds. Most members trusted AP's political judgment by now, though a few felt it was politically risky to continue targeting Wilson. Alice planned to ramp up the pressure on the president, just not at the White House gates.

She designed a new protest to rivet public attention once again. The NWP would now demonstrate across from the White House in Lafayette Square. The statue of Lafayette offered a fresh opportunity to invoke founding principles by reminding the nation of the Frenchman who, said *The Suffragist*, "defied his King and his government" to serve an infant republic. Lafayette, like the suffragists, fought for freedom. The protest would symbolically link the suffrage cause to the present war's alliance with the French. AP made special efforts to recruit munitions and Red Cross volunteers, counting on the legitimizing presence of war workers to stave off jingoists and rowdies alike. She did not assume that the pickets' March 1918 court victory made the NWP any less controversial.[29]

Indeed, Alice defied attempts to suppress the meeting. Police interference seemed a distinct possibility, but not because the NWP set out to break the law. For the past few months, officials had denied them permits even for routine street meetings. This time, Alice chose not to seek a permit and told participants to expect arrest. When Chief Pullman and Colonel C. S. Ridley of the War Department wrote to advise that she needed a permit, she told both men that her legal counsel believed otherwise. She did not say that after the pickets' successful appeal she believed the odds of arrest slim.[30]

As Alice faced down the authorities, 14 Jackson Place filled up with dozens of eager recruits for the demonstration. It felt like old-home week for the jail veterans. They greeted each other like long-lost relatives, crowding into every available bedroom and closet. Alice and Julia Emory slept on the roof, soon the site of late night parties, as women came up to breathe in cool evening breezes. The camaraderie especially warmed the organizers who so often, as Elsie Hill wrote, lived in an "awful jumble" traveling, speaking, organizing, and raising money for suffrage.[31]

At mid-afternoon on a sweltering August 6—Inez Milholland's birthday—a pageant commenced with all the flair now expected of Alice Paul. Nearly one hundred women assembled in the mansion, dressed in their crisp summer whites, bareheaded in the heat. One suffragist held the American flag aloft and led others carrying the tricolor or banners with the fallen Inez's war cry, "How long must women wait for liberty?" The women marched along the square's perimeter, then turned to approach the tall bronze figure of Lafayette facing the White House. As the tricolors fluttered, the suffragists took positions around the monument and immediately attracted a curious crowd, including police officers.[32]

Dora Lewis stepped onto the base of the statue and began to speak about a "war for liberty and democracy," but officers quickly cut in and arrested her as well as other women nearby. After a moment of shock, another protestor took Lewis's place, only to be seized, then another and another. (Elsie Hill quipped at her trial: "During my years of suffrage work I've been told and re-told that women's place is on a pedestal; and the first time I get on one, I'm arrested.") Alice, observing from behind the crowd, also found herself in police hands. Forty-eight women with flags and banners climbed into paddy wagons, a place all too familiar for most.[33]

The administration seemed no more adept at handling the protesting suffragists, despite the events of 1917 and the successful March 1918 appeal. The US attorney rejected the initial unlawful assembly charges but failed to find an appropriate one—"I have had no orders," he complained—and postponed the cases for one

week. As one New York editor complained, "severity has become impossible since
the courts upset the workhouse sentences for 'picketing.'" Alice, however, now
believed authorities would find some way to jail them. Meanwhile, many of the
same women joined demonstrations on August 12 and 14; the police arrested the
participants but, amid the uncertainty, soon released them.[34]

Senate Republicans exploited the arrests for their own political ends, while
congressional Democrats found common cause in criticizing the protest and
defending the president. The Senate minority whip claimed the Democrats
sought to silence the "indignation of women"; he called on the majority party to
cease blocking a vote on suffrage. The Democrats responded with a Senate discussion on August 8 during which pro-suffrage senators labeled the demonstration
"misdirected enthusiasm" and "un-American."[35]

NAWSA tried to redirect the attention given the protest. Presidential lobbyist
Helen Gardener alerted the White House to the situation and, craftily, sneaked in
a bit of reverse psychology. The NWP "are really frightened I think," she wrote,
"lest the President's influence with the Senators may now put it 'over the top' during this session." NAWSA historian Ida Harper declared in the *New York World*
that the NWP sought credit for moving the amendment along, credit that only
the National, the "official authority" for suffrage, deserved.[36]

As Alice suspected, officials leveled charges against the protestors the following week. A judge released women whom police failed to identify, then convicted
the twenty-six remaining for either "holding a meeting on public grounds" or
"climbing a statue." Sentences ranged from five to fifteen days; AP, as an observer,
received ten. Police took them to an abandoned workhouse on the District jail
grounds that authorities, *The Suffragist* reported, "found too unsanitary in 1909
for ordinary criminals." All but two elderly women immediately began a hunger
strike to demand the rights of political prisoners.[37]

The administration insisted on reprising past mistakes. Conditions in the
abandoned workhouse proved the worst Alice had experienced. The stench of the
damp and dark five-by-seven basement cells with open toilets was oppressive; fortunately, matrons rarely locked them. The stagnant air in a long-deserted building
became nauseating. Elsie Hill termed the place "a ghastly coffin." Soon, the entire
group grew violently ill from tainted water flowing through the rusty pipes. The
hated Dr. Gannon refused hunger strikers medical treatment, exacerbating the
situation.[38]

Officials beat a quick retreat. They released all the prisoners unconditionally
after five days, the timing coinciding suspiciously with the president's return, said
the press, from his "best rest in years." The same day, Colonel Ridley wrote AP,
granting permission for park demonstrations, though he warned that "good order
must prevail." Alice responded crisply to Ridley, pleased "that our meetings are

no longer to be interfered with." She added pointedly that she had postponed the next demonstration due to the condition of so many former prisoners.[39]

Briefly gratifying news followed. Four days after the suffragists' release, a Republican caucus called for an immediate vote on woman suffrage. While those behind the resolution sought to quash the amendment, *The Suffragist* noted, the call focused attention on the necessity of Democrats bringing the measure to the floor. The Democratic leaders of the Senate responded only with silence. Aware that senators felt the pressure of the coming elections, Alice wanted a vote; NAWSA took the same position. Determined to push through the stalemate, AP scheduled the next demonstration in Lafayette Square for September 16 and set off to raise funds in New York.[40]

Her September 16 initiative was to be even bolder, but she encountered opposition from unexpected quarters. In the aftermath of the administration's retreat, several key allies hesitated to support the audacious action Alice planned. Belmont wrote anxiously that AP's new idea seemed "rather a dangerous thing to do." Even Dora Lewis felt nervous, writing AP three times and warning her about allowing "anything being said that would mean getting arrested." She believed, "It has been run to the ground now, and I am *sure* is poor policy." Alice trusted her own instincts and found enough other support to forge ahead, despite warnings that more controversy could impair fundraising at a time when lack of money was, again, handicapping the NWP's efforts.[41]

The silent procession from Jackson Place to Lafayette Square seemed familiar at first, except for the early evening step-off, timed to follow an earlier NAWSA meeting of Democratic women with the president. Alice took Lewis's suggestion and included already familiar banners such as "Mr. President, what will you do for woman suffrage?" Women dressed in white, bearing the purple, white, and gold. One woman held a flaming torch aloft in the twilight. While many of the most seasoned protestors were absent, younger enthusiasts still felt game. With Alice again observing, the marchers made their way to the Lafayette statue and assembled what she termed an "exceedingly beautiful" tableau. The police observed quietly, told only to maintain order. The crowd seemed friendly. Lucy Branham stepped forward for the main event.[42]

Once again, Alice gave an elite and feminine gloss to an age-old mode of protest. The cover of the week's *Suffragist* tipped off NWP members: "To the Woman Voter," the legend read, "Start the Home Fires Burning." Taking inspiration from the popular war tune implicitly linked the demonstration with the war effort. "We want action," Branham proclaimed, echoing the Pankhursts' motto, "Deeds, not words." "The torch which I hold symbolizes the burning indignation of women who for a hundred years have been given words without action." She held aloft the president's statement—"I shall do all that I can"—to the Democratic women.

Branham took "these empty words" and burned them on the spot, emulating, she cried, "the ancient fights for liberty." The mood of the crowd surrounding her contrasted starkly with that of one year ago: they applauded this incendiary act and even began to pass the women bills and coins in support. No one was arrested.[43]

The women's audacity, coupled with the NAWSA presidential delegation, found swift reward. One day later, the Senate suffrage committee placed the Anthony amendment on the calendar for September 26, despite its chairman having declared himself "powerless" the previous day. Alice felt unusually confident, writing Lewis about the vote, "It looks as though it would go through this time." Mrs. Catt too believed the amendment had votes to spare. Hopeful activists once more filled the Senate galleries on the twenty-sixth only to be treated to days of further debate on the issue. Those outside Washington waited. One wrote, "I can scarcely endure life" until the vote.[44]

As the Senate vote stalled, Wilson's son-in-law, Treasury secretary William McAdoo, approached him about the situation, suggesting an address in the midst of the Senate debate. The president balked at such a highly unorthodox step, fearing a hostile reaction. McAdoo stressed the elections six weeks hence, countering that, even if the attempt failed, it would bolster pro-suffrage candidates. Either way, Democratic electoral chances improved. Maintaining Democratic congressional majorities assured Wilson of more votes for his treasured League of Nations proposal. Swayed by the prospect of sustained party power rather than any vision of equality, Woodrow Wilson, at long last, agreed to publicly endorse the Susan B. Anthony amendment.[45]

The Senate scarcely received notice of Wilson's arrival when he appeared the following day, flanked impressively by the First Lady and the entire cabinet save the one suffrage opponent. Speaking with his usual eloquence, the president declared woman suffrage "vitally essential" to winning the war. His own conversion came through "many, many channels," although, he insisted, NWP protests played no part: "The voices of foolish and intemperate agitators do not reach me." In the end, however, the last-minute presidential appeal failed to sway even one man. The Senate defeated the Anthony amendment by two votes as, *The Suffragist* grieved, "the quiet women sat above counting the enemies of democracy."[46]

Alice now faced a credibility crisis. Had her emphasis on the power of the presidency been wrong-headed? Would women still follow her lead after Wilson's public advocacy went for naught? She quickly penned a signed editorial in *The Suffragist* that addressed the question head-on. She applauded Wilson's public endorsement; nevertheless, she wrote, "the President's support was too reluctantly and tardily given." He failed to fight "with the vigor he has put behind other measures" (an idea she had advanced for months) and consequently, the

Democrats faltered. "If the President," she wrote, "really means that the passage of this amendment is necessary as a spiritual weapon for the conduct of the war, he will put all the power of his high office into securing this weapon."[47]

In truth, many people had believed that the eleventh-hour presidential address would win the necessary votes. Many observers attributed Wilson's presidential success to his strong leadership of the Democratic Party. Since early 1917, Congress had granted nearly every measure the president deemed necessary for the war effort. The *New York Times* reported that pro-suffrage senators themselves depended on the president's clout with his own party. To be sure, southern Democrats remained intransigent, despite their respect for him. Wilson also failed to sway three Delaware and Ohio votes.[48]

Alice weighed her strategic possibilities. Suffragists had until March 4, 1919, to win the Senate after amendment proponents maneuvered to allow a second vote. Without Senate passage in the sitting Congress, however, the legislation would start from square one in the new Congress. AP organized a picketing campaign at the Senate to keep the members mindful of the Anthony amendment. Her primary focus, however, was the Senate elections. Three organizers covered the suffrage states of the West to encourage voters both male and female to vote against Democrats for delaying nationwide woman suffrage.[49]

In addition, her first eastern campaign gave Alice the chance to prove the NWP nonpartisan, a symbolic victory, if nothing else. She directed her strongest efforts at elections to fill Senate vacancies in New Jersey and New Hampshire, both seats previously held by suffrage opponents. From these two contests, Alice hoped to secure the necessary two votes. Democratic contenders in both states strongly supported the Anthony amendment, so AP threw NWP support behind them.[50]

When the November returns came in, Alice found that the NWP campaigns against Democrats joined a general routing of the president's party. She claimed a victory for suffrage, calling the results "a strong rebuke" for the Democrats' failure. The new Republican majorities in both houses assured passage in the next Congress and, AP thought, demonstrated to the Democrats of the sitting Congress the futility of opposition. Though NWP campaigns in New Jersey and New Hampshire, which were centered on short-term replacements in the current Congress, fell short, other vacancy elections gained one, possibly two, votes.[51]

Even with the necessary support, motivating the Senate to vote again promised to be "not a trifling contest." Indeed, the political environment had shifted. An armistice ended the war on November 11, and the congressional plate filled up with the business of peace and reconstruction. The Senate, "glad to have [suffrage] out of the way," needed to be become uncomfortable once more, Alice believed.[52]

A second vote looked probable after the president urged it in his usual address to the returning Congress in December. Alice took this moment to come down with the flu, which raged everywhere, and the steadfast Dora Lewis tried to keep the patient in bed for a few days. Lucy, earlier qualms allayed, took over the planning for what she billed as a "last appeal" to the Senate and one "positively guaranteed not to result in imprisonment." A final rally proved alluring to many members; no dissent emerged this time. One former picket wired that she was coming "if I have to crawl."[53]

In the days before the planned demonstration, the outlook for a new vote dimmed: anti-suffrage forces in both parties maneuvered to keep the issue off the Senate calendar. A stronger, edgier protest seemed clearly required. The president was beyond their reach, however. He had sailed to Europe for the peace conference, playing the "apostle of democracy for the world," as *The Suffragist* scoffed, "yet American women are still denied democracy."[54]

Alice unveiled NWP outrage on the anniversary of the Boston Tea Party. At dusk on December 16, several hundred women joined a procession to the Lafayette statue. Fifty women carrying torches formed the heart of the pageant. A gossamer mist embraced each figure, lending a spectral air to the darkening scene. The event attracted the usual crowd of government clerks and passersby—and police. Alice watched from a distance as the torchbearers took up places behind a large park urn in front of the statue.[55]

Speaker after speaker sent a literal and symbolic message to the leader of the Democratic party. "We burn in shame and indignation" that Wilson spoke abroad for democracy while it languished at home, declared one. Russia and England had enfranchised women, while American women waited. "Mr. President," another cried to the throng, "the paper currency of liberty which you hand to women is worthless fuel until it is backed by the gold of action." With these words, they began tossing the president's words on freedom—speeches, books, messages to Congress—into the urn as the flames flickered in the twilight.[56]

This demonstration stands among Alice's most theatrical creations, replete with a complex and layered imagery. On the one hand, the drama continued the association of suffrage with the war, the destructive force of fire (guns, bombs) used for constructive ends. The burning "shame and indignation" wedded the destructive force of disgrace with the constructive energy of women's anger. The source of that anger itself became fuel; Wilson's words literally sustained the women's protest.[57]

Alice took the risk of appealing to a president focusing on peacemaking, but perhaps no greater risk than Wilson himself took by sailing off to Europe for two months, the first president to leave the country for an unexpected period while in office. She counted on the American public's war fatigue and disenchantment

with the leader who presided over it. A bold protest might just engender unprecedented attention and support. After a working Christmas, during which Alice
and a few other remaining headquarters staff contented themselves with dinner
before the drawing room fire, she refashioned the central idea of burning Wilson's
words and came up with a fresh and striking incarnation.[58]

On New Year's Day 1919—the year she named Victory New Year—Alice inaugurated a perpetual "watchfire of freedom," drawing on ancient rituals of eternal
flame. *The Suffragist* revealed the plan to maintain a fire near the White House
ready "to consume every outburst of the President on freedom until his advocacy
of freedom has been translated into support of political freedom for American
women." AP's use of the term *watchfire* drew once more on wartime and patriotic associations. The constancy of the flame connoted the vigilance necessary to
keep suffrage in the president's and the public's consciousness. She drew the large
ornamental urn before the Lafayette statue into service again and women carried a smaller urn to the pickets' once-customary spot at the White House gates.
The crowning touch: an enormous bell appeared on the second-floor balcony of
headquarters to sound the changing of the guard and announce the arrival of new
words to burn. Each peal also brought to mind familiar calls to worship and to
mourn, as well as the ominous warning of a buoy in the night.[59]

Alice Paul launched a renewed drive to "keep the home fires burning" and
drive official tolerance to the breaking point. In the late afternoon of New Year's
Day, a dignified contingent walked to the White House. Dora Lewis, convinced
of the efficacy of this type of protest, christened the sidewalk urn, building a fire
to consign her offerings with wood said to be from Philadelphia's Independence
Square. But the most provocative incendiary was the banner calmly rolled out
by two demonstrators; it accused the president of "deceiving the world when he
appears as the prophet of democracy."[60]

As with earlier such banners, the legend incited a swift response. Lewis began
to explain the protest to a growing crowd when a group of servicemen rushed
toward her, knocking down some women, overturning the burning urn, and
stamping out the blaze. Alice anticipated as much and, poised for action across
the street at the park urn, quickly lit another fire. Police promptly arrested AP
and the two women with her but released them when officials failed to find an
appropriate charge. The protestors quickly rekindled the fire.[61]

Maintaining the flame twenty-four hours a day proved challenging but offered
fresh opportunities for what Dora Lewis called "the wonderful comradeship of
this struggle." Police officials reluctantly offered a permit for the park fire but
failed to prevent mischief-makers in the crowds from overturning or dousing the
flames. The women kept a third urn at the ready to ensure that one flame endured.
The night watch could be trying or uplifting. AP had Julia Emory and Annie

Arneil for companions the first night in the park; the three wore yellow slickers to ward off a heavy downpour.[62]

Despite issuing a permit for the NWP's perpetual "liberty fire," police officials soon reconsidered, leaving Alice scrambling to adapt. Constables reverted to arresting women on January 4. They detained eleven protestors, including AP, over three days. All were later tried and convicted of the hitherto-unknown crime of starting a fire after sundown in the park. Their sentences ranged from five to ten days. Facing an unforeseen shortage of troops, Alice quickly sent for Lucy and Mabel Vernon to take charge of the demonstrations.[63]

The two veterans pared the protest down. The women now set a White House fire for each new Wilson speech abroad; a torch burning outside headquarters stood in for the perpetual flame. The bell still tolled (to the dismay of the neighbors). Urgent calls sped out for state delegations to bring native wood, rekindle the flames—and risk arrest. Less than sixty days remained until the sitting Congress adjourned March 4.[64]

Police carted off Alice and the others to the District jail, which reportedly received a thorough cleaning before their arrival. Grateful for short sentences and confinement in the jail proper, as opposed to its abandoned counterpart, the prisoners accommodated themselves as best they could. Warden Zinkhan refused them both visitors and mail, denying AP permission to see her mother and sister, en route to Florida for the winter (apparently inured to the idea of Alice in jail). In addition, matrons confiscated books and extra blankets. Undaunted, the women promptly declared a hunger strike and passed the hours talking, sleeping, composing parodies to familiar tunes, and, for some, studying the habits of the cockroaches and rats. Despite their spirit, as one wrote, "the jail was real. And it was not funny."[65]

The ongoing demonstrations were AP's most visible but not her only strategy to win a second Senate vote. Upon her release, looking to one journalist "very thin, emaciated nearly," she returned to monitoring state and national efforts as well as the periodic watchfire protests. She urged members to send cables to the president in Europe and encourage state legislatures to pass resolutions supporting the Anthony amendment. The resolutions could sway recalcitrant senators and hasten the pace of state ratification. NAWSA applied similar pressure. By early February, twenty-four states had passed such resolutions or similar petitions, with less than a month remaining until Congress adjourned. By that time, police had jailed sixty more women.[66]

With time running out, the Democrats tried once more to call their willful members to account. The president cabled key senators to urge passage and the Democratic caucus met to preach the virtues of political expediency. Southern Democrats largely resisted appeals to party welfare, feeling greater political danger in their one-party states from white supremacists. Alice personally lobbied the one suffrage state holdout, "lion of the Senate" William Borah (Republican, ID), for months; the powerful Borah remained elusive. Finally, Democratic leaders scheduled another vote for February 10, 1919.[67]

Alice planned a demonstration on the ninth to apply one more turn of the screw, an "action more drastic," *The Suffragist* declared, "than the burning of the President's useless, impotent words." NAWSA lobbyist Maud Wood Park caught wind of the protest and gave District officials advance warning; nevertheless, the event took place as scheduled.[68]

The bell tolled as sixty protestors marched with banners flying from Jackson Place. Two held what looked like a small scarecrow. The women made their way to the White House sidewalk through masses of people and lines of bluecoats, formed a tableau with the urn at the center, quickly built a fire, and dropped an effigy of Woodrow Wilson into the flames. The lead speaker had barely launched into her speech when police arrested her and, in short order, thirty-eight other demonstrators, while a crowd watched silently. Finally, the police stopped arrests and the remaining two dozen women collected themselves, marched slowly back to headquarters, ensured that the torch out front continued to burn, and walked inside. The tolling of the bell ceased.[69]

Although the dramatic protest received front-page coverage in many newspapers, reaction ranged from scorn to apathy. In the aftermath of the war, the press no longer equated suffrage protests with radical unrest. As a Colorado member noted about a Denver editorial, "We are only 'hysteria sisters' now; then we were dangerous agitators." Indeed, the *Brooklyn Eagle* compared the "suffragettes" to the "witches of old Salem" and the *New York Sun* wondered "whether the authors of this outrage on decency are mad or merely lawless." In areas more distant from Washington, however, organizers reported minimal response from the news dailies or the populace.[70]

Among NWP members, however, this protest drew more dissension than any other. Two dozen people resigned or dropped *The Suffragist*; others simply gave Alice an earful before and after the ninth. The board of the Detroit chapter thought the idea "bad judgement and undignified," and Maine members objected to the "grave mistake." Even the stalwart Lavinia Dock felt dismayed, writing that some New York supporters shuddered "because it approaches so terribly to lynching. I feel it's the first mistake that has been made." The demonstration hinted at common cause with southern Democrats, she thought, thereby alienating many others. On the other hand, a Chicago member wrote AP, "How can you always hit the nail on the head exactly at the psychological moment!" A Louisiana member agreed, wiring that the protest worked "better than fifty years of conservative work."[71]

Burning President Wilson in effigy came as close as Alice ever would to violence. Despite the long political history of effigy burning, this NWP act seemed directed at Wilson personally rather than in his presidential role. In addition, AP should have anticipated the racial overtones some detected; though lynchings had peaked twenty years earlier, violence against blacks surged in the postwar period, causing one House Republican to introduce an anti-lynching bill. In her desire to top her own distinctive protests, her judgment finally lapsed.

Neither the effigy burning nor the entirety of Senate suffrage supporters forestalled another defeat for the Anthony amendment the following day. Only one vote changed, that of a South Carolina Democrat briefly filling a vacant seat. Thus, the Senate vote failed by a single *yea*. Carrie Chapman Catt finally agreed with Alice Paul: she blamed the defeat on the Democrats.[72]

Alice did not miss a beat after the effigy controversy, determined to keep the Anthony amendment in the public mind. She wanted to confront the president directly once more, but cautious officials stymied her efforts. She succeeded in sending off a "Prison Special" train tour one week after the failed Senate vote. The women, including Lucy, Elizabeth Rogers, and elderly Mary Nolan, often appeared in replicas of the drab prison garb and showed lantern slides to bring their experiences to life. The month-long tour rumbled first through the southern states and then west to California before returning east.[73]

Despite attempts to formulate a compromise suffrage amendment, the 65th Congress adjourned on March 4, 1919, without passage. Republicans blocked a number of major bills, including suffrage, in an attempt to force Wilson to call a special session of the new Republican-controlled Congress immediately, well before the official December 1919 opening. Pro-suffrage Democrats reacted furiously at the lost opportunity, knowing how eagerly Republicans would take credit for woman suffrage in the new Congress.

Suffragists simply felt disgusted. Dora Lewis and Maud Younger, at the Capitol to witness the Senate's "dying night," gained solace from an unexpected source: a southern Democratic congressman. "Your being so annoying and persistent and troublesome," he told them, "is what put the suffrage amendment on the map. It is like the cinder in your eye, you have to get rid of it.... This amendment is going through ten years sooner than it ever would have done without you."[74]

Both Alice and Carrie Chapman Catt knew that the Anthony amendment had the required votes in the next Congress, with its new Republican majority. Even the notoriously anti-amendment *New York Times* conceded that "triumph is but postponed."[75]

While Alice urged others to rest and recuperate, she remained vigilant. She returned to Washington "looking very much fatigued," according to Dora Lewis. "I wish I could take her off for a little rest," she wrote Katzenstein, "but know well that she will not go away for pleasure before the amendment is passed." AP wrote with palpable longing about the "air of comfort and repose" in family photographs sent by one former picket. Shaking off weariness, she boarded the train for New York shortly before the weary denizens of the Prison Special pulled into their final stop on March 10.[76]

A mass meeting at Carnegie Hall celebrated the suffrage tour; more importantly, it raised money. As Alva Belmont presided over the speechifying, an anxious Alice may well have walked from box to box, speaking *sotto voce* to potentially major donors. Her money-gathering efforts reflected skyrocketing income tax rates; the 1918 Revenue Act set the maximum rate at 77 percent, rendering large donations increasingly scarce. Meeting pledges totaled $3,500, not nearly enough to meet NWP debt ($10,000) or fund the ratification drive. "We can do nothing on the next Congress," AP insisted, until the financial situation eased. Accordingly, she remained in New York City for several days raising funds and then set off elsewhere for more of the same.[77]

By mid-April, Alice felt "almost in despair" over money. "As fast as we raise money," she wrote Margaret Whittemore, "our bills seem to increase." Despite her efforts over the last month, NWP branches unable to pay Prison Special or other bills appealed for funds. The debt, as a result, remained $10,000. The situation eased a bit when Alice finally received a $1,500 bequest from the estate of Jessie Anthony, a second cousin of Susan B. Anthony, after months of correspondence with an executor in California. However, the nonexistent bank balance precluded Alice hiring additional organizers for the ratification effort. She continued to urge branches to take on the expense.[78]

Early in May, faced with mounting transatlantic pressure not only from Republicans and suffragists but from cabinet members concerned about languishing postwar appropriations, the president cabled his acquiescence to a special session of the new Congress. He also secured the last necessary suffrage vote from a newly elected senator traveling in Europe, a man who owed his seat to Wilson. Two other Republican senators quickly signed on as well, giving vote counters some leeway.[79]

The Anthony amendment had gained momentum in the months after the Armistice. By 1919, twenty-eight states had passed full or presidential suffrage for women. The argument that women were essential to the war effort became opportune, as politicians sought to appease suffragists and encourage thousands of female war workers to yield their jobs to the men returning from the front. Moreover, women in much of Europe and Scandinavia had won suffrage; British women over thirty also voted in the aftermath of the war. America lagged behind.

After all the agonized waiting, the end came swiftly. On May 19, 1919, the 66th Congress convened with a large Republican majority in the House and a smaller one in the Senate. The House passed the Anthony amendment two days later, not by the minimum two-thirds, but with forty-two votes to spare, a testament to the momentum suffrage had acquired. The Senate followed suit on June 4. All attempts to change or amend the Anthony amendment with time limits or state enforcement provisions went down to defeat in both houses.[80]

All suffragists rejoiced and congratulations poured into NWP headquarters. Alice did not attend the final vote. She had already set off to inaugurate the ratification campaign. Her victory statement from St. Paul underscored her belief in an assertive approach to the suffrage campaign. It was also a long-suppressed sigh: "Women who have taken part in the long struggle for freedom feel today the full relief of the victory," she declared. "Freedom has come not as a gift but as a triumph, and it is therefore a spiritual as well as a political freedom which women receive."[81]

Suffragists believed ratification would be swift. Alice expressed confidence about women voting in the next presidential election; Carrie Chapman Catt expected women to vote in 1920 as well. Both leaders hoped the Anthony amendment would equal or better the prohibition amendment's thirteen-month record. Quick passage seemed assured in more than two dozen states where women already voted; getting to the requisite three-quarters of the states—thirty-six in all—seemed eminently doable.[82]

Many commentators in the press agreed that the federal amendment had gathered force. The *New York Tribune* cited the "irresistible force of the popular will" and declared "the whole nation is ready for the move and persuaded of its necessity." The *Philadelphia Bulletin* thought neither party wished voters to see them as delaying ratification. Even in the deep South, the *Atlanta Constitution* said, "Woman Suffrage is coming regardless of what any one state can do to prevent it, and there is nothing to be gained by opposing it. Georgia might as well get on the 'band wagon'—for the procession is passing."[83]

At first, states clamored to join the procession and the pace of ratification exceeded expectation. Wisconsin and Michigan vied for first place; only a dash to Washington by the father of NWP stalwart Ada James secured Wisconsin's blue ribbon. Eleven states, collectively holding more than 50 percent of the nation's population, ratified during the first month after the June 4 Senate vote.[84]

Despite the rapid pace, Alice realized that state obstacles might derail suffrage indefinitely. Every state with a sitting legislative body had now ratified the amendment. Even if all thirteen state legislatures convening by early 1920 ratified, twelve additional states needed to call special sessions to meet the fall 1920 ratification goal. Suffragists thus needed to lobby many governors about special sessions before canvassing legislators. AP had poured a lot of money and energy into initiating and maintaining state NWP chapters over the years, and now she relied on those women.[85]

Financial contingencies reshaped the organizing staff and the campaign itself. Alice still worked as the fundraiser-in-chief and spent much of June on the road visiting state chapters to raise money for ratification campaigns. To conserve funds, she limited the number of ongoing state campaigns and reduced the number of paid organizers, turning to women like Mary Winsor and Dora Lewis, who could forego salary and work for expenses only. Gone were the radical wage earners who fired up the election campaigns—the elite waged the final battle. By mid-July, they ran campaigns in four southern and five northeast and western states.[86]

Alice wracked her brain for a way to keep NWP efforts before the public, a visual symbol as cogent as the picket at the White House gate or the guardian of the eternal flame. Her answer, "The Betsy Ross of Suffrage," appeared on the cover of the July 19 *Suffragist*. Alice herself posed as the legendary seamstress of the American flag, taking an uncharacteristic turn in the spotlight as she embodied the American Woman waiting for suffrage. She quickly stepped out of the limelight: the NWP issued a similar photograph to celebrate each state or group of states ratifying. All featured other staff members in the iconic role.

The Betsy Ross image itself contrasted markedly to the previous January's vigilant soldier of suffrage or the 1917 silent sentinel. The Ross image also connoted watchfulness, but in a startlingly different mode. Alice had evoked the nation's founding principles since 1913 and patriotic imagery since the onset of war. Now, appropriating a national icon allowed her to construct ratification as quintessentially American, following the path hacked out by the founders. Alice became the incarnation of watchful waiting, patiently sewing on star after star as the process of ratification unfolded. She appeared as a domestic archetype: woman seated, wielding just the familiar threaded needle, eyes dropped demurely on the household chore. Like its namesake icon, the Betsy Ross photograph celebrated the virtues of traditional republican womanhood.

Such a conventional image seems an odd pose for assertive suffragists. Do not fear, the photograph seems to say: women, satisfied with their approaching victory, now return to their age-old parlor pursuits, never again to irritate. Yet melting into domestic bliss was far from the minds of the "new" women of the NWP. Perhaps Alice crafted this message with hard-line resisters in mind—anti-suffragists, male and female—to reassure them that the world would keep spinning even when women submitted their ballots.

The possibility of rest disappeared after Alice fell ill briefly and the bank balance sank even lower. Dora Lewis wrote her from Maine, "Couldn't you run up to me just for a week?" she urged. "Bring your bathing suit." Instead, Alice set off to New York City to raise money. She did allow herself a fleeting holiday in late October. She spent a day with Elsie Hill in Connecticut, talking business but also motoring through the countryside, insulated against the fall chill with a borrowed union suit and wool stockings. Alice wrote her friend, "You gave me a very delightful holiday, which I shall long remember."[87]

The less frenetic pace allowed her the mental space to look ahead at a future for the NWP: another amendment, perhaps, to remove remaining discrimination against women, or some sort of endowment for mothers. She ruminated on her own future and looked up old friends. If Alice contemplated a teaching career after 1920, Lucy Burns's experience may have dissuaded her. Lucy Burns sought teaching work even before ratification, but retreated after encountering complaints about her notoriety. AP did consider studying law and thought about returning to Europe with Elsie Hill. All this assumed that ratification would succeed.[88]

As the new year dawned, state legislatures convened around the country, many in special session, and the ratification march became a gallop. AP's politically divided home state of New Jersey ratified in February, after being given up for dead months earlier. "I shall be very much surprised if New Jersey ever ratifies," state chairman Alison Hopkins declared in August. Alice initially agreed, but after several southern states defeated the amendment, she realized they needed every possible northern state. AP herself journeyed to Trenton to strategize with floor leaders, realizing that anti-suffrage forces were massing.[89]

By late March 1920, the count stood at thirty-five states in favor, one to go. The onus to bring in the last state lay with the Republicans. As Alice explained in the March *Suffragist*, "the last states in the control of the Democrats, which offer any chance of ratification, have acted." Republicans controlled the remaining three possibilities—Connecticut, Delaware, and Vermont. Suffragists needed just one of these states to ratify. Nonetheless, Alice and many others feared that winning the thirty-sixth state could take as long as the final vote in the US Senate. If women wanted to vote for the next president in November, what with state registration deadlines, the "perfect 36th" needed to ratify very soon. The two New England states had anti-suffrage governors and the odds of one calling a special session seemed slim. So all eyes focused on one of the smallest states in the Union: Delaware. Yet after two months of drama, Delaware defeated the Anthony amendment on May 5.[90]

Alice did not fear ultimate defeat, but a delay of a year or two now seemed all too possible. She focused all her attention on ratification. By contrast, Carrie Chapman Catt's plans rushed ahead of reality. Catt held a victory convention in mid-February, during the Delaware fight, proclaiming "the struggle is over." She launched NAWSA's successor, the nonpartisan League of Women Voters. With the last state still in question, she sailed off for the International Woman Suffrage Alliance convention, entrusting ratification work to her lieutenants.[91]

In mid-June, Tennessee emerged as a possible thirty-sixth state, as the result of a hard-fought court decision allowing the governor to call a special session of the legislature. "Just when all seemed lost in the fight for our enfranchisement, another chance has come," Alice wrote supporters. Since the mid-South state had recently passed presidential suffrage for women, the situation seemed very hopeful. Sue Shelton White, a Tennessee native and former NAWSA member, managed NWP efforts in the heavily Democratic state. Several other organizers from southern states joined her; these native daughters offset any lingering resentment from Democrats. Carrie Chapman Catt, back from Europe, went to Nashville to oversee the National's efforts. Alice took charge of NWP strategy from Washington.[92]

Suffragists called the battle in Tennessee "Armageddon." The opposition proved fierce and determined. As Alice wrote a supporter in early August, "there are men from whom we have signed pledges to support ratification in their own handwriting who now state they have changed their minds. There must be some cause for this extraordinary defection but we are not sure what it is." She learned that the opposition was a hasty coalition of anti-suffragists and upholders of states' rights, plus liquor and railroad interests who feared the woman voter.[93]

She longed to be on the scene in Tennessee, but felt unable to leave Washington: "I will come to Tennessee the moment I can raise enough money to keep work going while I am away." By the time that happened, a vote seemed imminent and leaving pointless. She urged White to send a rush wire with the news.[94]

On August 18, 1920, the Tennessee legislature ratified the Nineteenth Amendment after young Harry Burn changed his vote. He promised his mother and the suffragists to vote *aye* if the count came down to a single vote; his fellow antis practically chased him out of town afterward. A week later, on August 26, Secretary of State Bainbridge Colby evaded both suffrage factions and signed the final proclamation certifying the Nineteenth Amendment in the privacy of his home. A short while later, Alice Paul stepped out on the balcony of Jackson Place to the cheers of supporters and movie men below and unfurled her colorful suffrage flag, now perfect with thirty-six stars.[95]

Epilogue

ALICE PAUL COULD not step into her future just yet. Feeling the weight of pecuniary responsibilities, she insisted on eliminating the National Woman Party's $12,000 debt before she rested. She closed headquarters by the end of August 1920. Along with Maud Younger, she moved into the "tiniest apartment we could get," she remembered, and set about raising money. "At last the suffrage battle is won," she wrote her stalwart legions, "but it is not paid for."[1]

In November, she voted quietly by absentee ballot, joining the millions of American women voting for the first time. Anna Howard Shaw was not among those at the ballot box; she died during the ratification campaign in July 1919. Those women fortunate to celebrate the final victory of the seventy-two-year struggle for woman suffrage also did not include southern black women, who, to no one's surprise, faced state-imposed barriers to voting. True enfranchisement for all African Americans languished until the 1960s. Yet the increasing numbers of black women living in northern states did vote and, with the able support of the NAACP and the NACWC, began to build a foundation for full political participation.

It is ironic that historians routinely credit President Woodrow Wilson with woman suffrage, since he embraced the Anthony amendment so late and even then reluctantly. In reality, the long-awaited suffrage victory became possible because of many complex factors. Women had prepared the ground for decades by asserting their right to inclusion in a whole host of public roles. Wage earners taking up new jobs created by industrialization swelled the suffrage ranks after the turn of the century, as did the "new women" seeking higher levels of education: all saw the vote as part of a larger struggle for equal treatment. The onset of war necessitated a wide range of female contributions on war and home fronts, opportunities from which many suffragists profited. The successful 1910s campaigns in the western American states gave the national suffrage movement powerful examples of the equal franchise in action as well as staunch congressional allies who worked with both NAWSA and the NWP. Furthermore, when the British "rewarded" their women over age thirty with the vote after the war, they set an important precedent.

With so many factors advancing the suffrage cause, it may seem that the final victory after the war was inevitable; it was not. The British waited until 1930 to give younger women the franchise. In America, the Progressive enthusiasm that fueled so much reform in the early twentieth century was already fading in the economic and political disruptions which followed the war. Without ongoing suffrage advocacy, particularly the highly visible NWP pressure, the Anthony amendment might have lingered in Congress for years.

Alice Paul's contributions to the victory and to the history of political struggle are manifold. From March 1913 onward, she provided the momentum for the amendment campaign. By 1915, she had built a foundation for the Anthony amendment that redounded to the benefit of both the NWP and NAWSA. She challenged notions of gender propriety from the first, especially by pioneering the feminist use of opposition campaigning. She introduced nonviolent political protest to America and gained visibility with modern methods of promotion; her spectacles were the first successful political demonstrations in Washington. Finally, she gave us the iconic images of woman suffrage—the 1913 procession, the silent vigil of 1917, the 1918 watchfire protests—images that speak to the persistence, the courage, and the fortitude of every brand of suffragist.

The presence of Alice Paul reshaped the suffrage landscape. Unwittingly, she exposed the tensions within NAWSA about militant action. The subsequent debate within the suffrage community over basic principles led to a realignment around NAWSA and the CU that ultimately furthered both groups. Without Alice in the picture, another Pankhurst enthusiast would likely have emerged at the national level; the probability of that person having AP's compelling constellation of leadership qualities is slim. The tumult might have crippled the National or resulted in a far more destructive rupture. On the other hand, the Shafroth amendment might not have materialized without Alice, but that ruinous venture owed as much to Anna Howard Shaw's ineffectualness as to the CU threat. Indeed, Alice Paul's presence threw the leadership trajectories of both Shaw and Carrie Chapman Catt off course, while their actions mostly accelerated and focused her direction.

Discussions of Alice Paul's personal style tend to overshadow her achievements during the suffrage era. Until that period, ambitious women had few leadership opportunities, so it is no accident that suffrage drew a series of powerful and even controversial women, including Elizabeth Cady Stanton, Susan B. Anthony, and Carrie Chapman Catt herself. To be sure, Alice Paul came to relish her own power base. She retained the casual racial, religious, and class prejudices she learned at home, while at the same time she recognized the struggles of disadvantaged groups. She often reached past her prejudices to form working partnerships; like many, however, she felt most comfortable with people much like herself. She controlled the NWP more than anyone else, thereby alienating some, but also successfully managed dissent and salved the egos of any number of strong women in the process.

Despite Alice's efforts to craft a historical legacy for the NWP, the NAWSA narrative gained sway. During the ratification campaign, AP set Doris Stevens to work on an NWP history and opened up her meticulous files for research. Inez Irwin approached AP about a similar book about the same time and also benefited from the files. Stevens's book, *Jailed for Freedom*, became available in September 1920, the first published history of the suffrage movement's final years. Irwin's *Story of the Woman's Party* followed in 1921. Both books nevertheless idealized both Alice Paul and the NWP. When the last volume of the monumental *History of Woman Suffrage* appeared in 1922, its dispassionate, though no less biased prose became the movement narrative.[2] Consequently, the students who reinvigorated nonviolent protest at a Greensboro, North Carolina, lunch counter in 1956 knew nothing of Alice Paul; they cited Gandhi as inspiration.

The divisions of the suffrage years persisted. NAWSA's success at portraying Alice and the NWP as a disruptive force carried over into the 1920s. After AP persuaded the NWP to advocate for the equal rights amendment (ERA) she wrote in 1923, labor advocates immediately opposed the idea, concerned that a pro-business administration would gut protections for wage-earning women gained over decades of effort; with some justification, they believed the ERA would nullify protective legislation. Former NAWSA activists and others opposed the ERA, refreshing the divisive NWP image in Americans' minds.[3] The post-1920 policy divisions endured until Congress swept away protective legislation with the Civil Rights Act of 1964. Congress passed the ERA in 1972 but, despite AP's warning and supporters' efforts, opponents successfully appended a time limit. By 1982, when the ratification period ended, the amendment still needed three more states to ratify.

Alice did not confine herself to ERA advocacy after 1920. She spent time abroad, working to improve the legal status of women internationally. She founded the World Woman's Party in 1938 and early in the 1940s arranged safe passage out of German-occupied Europe for several feminist leaders. She returned to the United States in 1941 to continue both ERA and international work. NWP advocacy helped gain provisions for the equal rights of women in both the United Nations Charter and 1948 Universal Declaration of Human Rights. Alice and NWP later persuaded lawmakers to include a clause against sex discrimination in Title VII of the Civil Rights Act of 1964.

Alice Paul became the only suffrage leader to witness the resurgence of feminism in the 1960s. A living link to the century of struggle for the vote, she was embraced by both historians and ERA activists. Before her death in 1977 at the age of ninety-two, she saw thirty-five states ratify the ERA. She had difficulty understanding the priorities of some of the new feminists; topics such as abortion were not broached publicly in earlier times. She believed equality before the law preeminent. Indeed, Alice would condemn the twenty-first-century politicians who link her name to the anti-abortion cause; she confined her public advocacy solely to legal equality for women.

After 1920, Alice Paul led a less single-minded existence, and her life resumed more conventional rhythms. By all accounts, she chose to live independent of any life partner. The inheritance left by her mother allowed her to continue living simply and focusing on political work without the need to earn money. She found companionship in her work life, though she maintained family ties and relationships with friends such as Mietza Heldring Bye and Clara Thompson. She cultivated the younger generation, inviting her nephew and the children of cousins to visit in Washington and later at her New England home. Her most enduring friendship, that with Elsie Hill, continued throughout the latter's marriage and motherhood until Hill's death in 1970. There is no evidence that Alice kept in touch with William Parker or Lucy Burns.

The health problems Alice endured because of repeated forced feedings largely subsided after the stressful years pushing through the Anthony amendment. She returned to a weight more typical of her college years. However, she became a vegetarian after the suffrage years, perhaps after too many encounters with tainted meat. Her sense of smell, diminished after her time in Britain, may have sustained permanent damage. She told Amelia Fry, "Food simply isn't important to me."[4]

Alice had traveled a great distance from her sheltered Quaker roots and yet not very far at all. Her demeanor and invocation of moral power communicated a Quaker identity, but her use of spectacle and publicity—plus her challenge of official authority in pursuit of a cause—contradicted Friendly precepts about unseemly conduct and public scandal. Her relationship with her birthright community, and theirs with her, remained ambivalent. She remained a member of the Moorestown Meeting all her life. Though no longer interested in the spiritual community, she nonetheless lived by the core values of the Friends.

Alice Paul enjoyed what few women of her time achieved: a life of her own. She gave up her youthful desire for financial autonomy but largely achieved it by managing her inheritance well and living frugally. Among the heirlooms Alice inherited were the portraits of her forebears that had hung at Paulsdale in her youth, symbols of the commitment to Quaker values and to history that underlay her work for the equality of women.[5] She first claimed power by pursuing her own potential, then made it her life's work to claim power for all women.

Notes

All AP letters are from APP, unless otherwise indicated.
All microfilm citations are NWPP II, unless otherwise noted.

ABBREVIATIONS

AF	Amelia Roberts Fry Papers
AP	Alice Paul
APBC	Alice Paul Book Collection
API	Alice Paul Institute
APP	Alice Paul Papers
CAP	"Conversations with Alice Paul," Paul/Fry oral history
CUA	Columbia University Archives
DC	[Dundee] *Courier*
DN	*Daily News* [New York]
DP	*Daily Pennsylvanian*
DS	Doris Stevens
FHL	Friends Historical Library
FI	*Friends' Intelligencer*
FND	Facere Non Dicere Society
FSC	Friends School Catalogue
GH	*Glasgow Herald*
HP	Helen Paul
HSB	Harriot Stanton Blatch
HWS	*History of Woman Suffrage*
LB	Lucy Burns
LC	Library of Congress
MFS	Moorestown Friends School Archives
NAWSA	National American Woman Suffrage Association Records
NM	*Norfolk Mercury*
NWPP I	National Woman's Party Papers, Group I microfilm

NWPP II	National Woman's Party Papers, Group II microfilm
NWPP III	National Woman's Party Papers, Group III microfilm
NYT	*New York Times*
PB	*Philadelphia Bulletin*
PI	*Philadelphia Inquirer*
PJ	*People's Journal*
PL	*Philadelphia Public Ledger*
PP	Parry Paul
SC	Swarthmore College
SCC	Swarthmore College Catalogue
SL	Schlesinger Library, Harvard University
SOHP	Suffragists Oral History Project
SUFF	*The Suffragist*
TL	*Times of London*
TP	Tacie Paul
UPA	University of Pennsylvania Archives
VFW	*Votes for Women* (WSPU weekly)
WA	Woodbrooke Archives
WES	*Washington (DC) Evening Star*
WJ	*Woman's Journal*
WP	*Washington Post*
WT	*Washington Times*
WWP	Woodrow Wilson Papers

INTRODUCTION

1. "Conversations with Alice Paul" (CAP), interview by Amelia Fry, Suffragists Oral History Project, Bancroft Library, 1975, 47–48, available at http://bancroft.berkeley.edu/ROHO/projects/suffragist/; N.a., "Miss Paul," *Votes for Women*, 7 January 1910, 236.

2. "Miss Paul"; Linda K. Kerber, *No Constitutional Right to Be Ladies* (New York: Hill & Wang, 1998), 305.

3. See, for example, William L. O'Neill, *Everyone Was Brave* (New York: Quadrangle, 1969), 127–30, 202–4; William H. Chafe, *The American Woman* (New York: Oxford University Press, 1972), 19, 114; and Jean H. Baker, *Sisters* (New York: Hill & Wang, 2006), 232.

4. CAP, 142–46.

5. Max Weber, "The Three Pure Types of Legitimate Rule," in *The Essential Weber*, ed. Sam Whimster (New York: Psychology Press, 2004), 138–42.

6. Marshall Ganz, "Why David Sometimes Wins," in *The Psychology of Leadership*, ed. David M. Messick and Roderick M. Kramer (New York: Psychology Press, 2004), 209–38.

7. Inez H. Irwin, *The Story of Alice Paul* (Fairfax, VA: Denlinger's, 1977), 15.

CHAPTER 1

1. CAP, 6; Abstracts of Daily Journals, 1870–1907, Philadelphia, RG27, National Archives.

2. CAP, 280–84; AP DAR Application, December 1935, AF.

3. Thomas D. Hamm, *The Quakers in America* (New York: Columbia University Press, 2006), 45–46; "In Memoriam" (n.p.: Stuckey, 1882), 46–49, AF; E. M. Woodward and John F. Hageman, *History of Burlington and Mercer Counties, New Jersey* (Philadelphia: Everts & Peck, 1883), 301–2.

4. David Hackett Fischer, *Albion's Seed* (New York: Oxford University Press, 1991), 427; Barry Levy, *Quakers and the American Family* (New York: Oxford University Press, 1988), 58–59; "Singing and Worship," *FI*, 30 August 1902, 545–46.

5. Hamm, *Quakers in America*, 102; Myra McNally interview, 20–21 March 1982, 7.

6. Hamm, *Quakers in America*, 106; James Walvin, *Money and Morals* (London: John Murray, 1999), 34–35, 42; Don Yoder, "The Cultural Impact of Quakerism," *New Jersey Folklife* 15 (1990): 4–5.

7. Hamm, *Quakers in America*, 42–45, 61; Larry Ingle, *Quakers in Conflict* (Knoxville: University of Tennessee Press, 1986), 40–46, 247–49; AP to HP, 19 March 1909, Folder 159, APP.

8. Hamm, *Quakers in America*, 40–45; Thomas D. Hamm, "The Hicksite Quaker World, 1875–1900," *Quaker History* (Fall 2000): 20–24; Margaret Hope Bacon, *Mothers of Feminism* (New York: Harper & Row, 1986), 102–11; Bacon, Guilford College conference remarks on AP, June 1982, AF.

9. Philip S. Benjamin, *The Philadelphia Quakers in the Industrial Age, 1865–1920* (Philadelphia: Temple University Press, 1976), 156, 235; Levy, *Quakers and the American Family*; Bacon, *Mothers*, 179.

10. "Committee," *Alumni Register*, SC Bulletin 32-4, 1935, 16–17; Barbara Miller Solomon, *In the Company of Educated Women* (New Haven, CT: Yale University Press, 1985), 64.

11. Woodward and Hageman, *History of Burlington*, 303; Tacie Paul portrait, Paul photo album, API; "Miss Paul Puzzles Mother," *NYT*, 13 November 1909.

12. N.a., *Atlas of Burlington County, NJ* (Philadelphia: J. D. Scott, 1876); Chalkley Matlack family history, 1920, AF; Paul family album, API; CAP, 6–7.

13. "Bank President Dead," Folder 214, APP; Matlack history, ibid.; Bruce Laurie and Mark Schmitz, "Manufacture and Productivity," in *Philadelphia*, ed. Theodore Hershberg (New York: Oxford University Press, 1981), 45, 52.

14. Walvin, *Money and Morals*, 42.

15. Deed Books, Burlington County Clerk; CAP, 8, 16; William Parry to William M. Paul, 30 October 1882, AF; James C. Purdy, *Moorestown Old and New* (Moorestown Historical Society, 1885/1976), 107–9; Walter Gardiner interview, 3, and Engle Conrow interview, 15, both 16 September 1980.

16. William Paul obituaries, Folder 214, APP; Richard Robbins interview, 12 February 1981, 23; Levy, *Quakers and the American Family*, 72–74.

17. Anne Herendeen, "What the Hometown Thinks of Alice Paul," *Everybody's* 41 (October 1919): 45.

18. CAP, 15–16; New Jersey State Census data, Mt. Laurel Township, 1885 and 1895, 40, 47.

19. 1900 U.S. Census data for Mt. Laurel, 13; Steven Mintz and Susan Kellogg, *Domestic Revolutions* (New York: Free Press, 1989), xix; Jerry W. Frost, "As the Twig Is Bent," *Quaker History* 60 (Autumn 1971): 86–87.

20. CAP, 8; Myra McNally interview, 21; Conrow interview, 20; Margaret Jones interview, 22 March 1980, 25; Feyerherm Map of Paul Farm c. 1900, AF; William Kingston, *Moorestown's Third Century* (n.p.: Kingston, 1982), 51; Egg tally book remnant, AF.

21. CAP, 15–16; Frost, "As the Twig Is Bent," 86–87; Hamm, "Hicksite," 31; Engle Conrow et al. interview, 23.

22. APBC, API; Hamm, "Hicksite," 23.

23. McNally interview, 7.

24. "Singing and Worship," 546 (see n. 4 above).

25. CAP, 15; Jones interview, 36; Conrow interview, 3, 21; [Tacie P. Paul], "Family Heirlooms" & "Real Estate and Investments," both Folder 201, APP; Robyn Fivush, Jennifer G. Bohanek, and Marshall Duke, "The Intergenerational Self," in *Self Continuity*, ed. F. Sani (New York: Psychology Press, 2008), 131–43; Robyn Fivush et al. "Do You Know…" *Journal of Family Life* (23 February 2010), http://www.journaloffamilylife.org/doyouknow.html#.

26. "Memorial of Abigail R. Paul," *FI*, 23 July 1898, 515–16.

27. Photograph, AP with brother 1901, API.

28. Friends High School and Kindergarten Booklets, 1891–1892 to 1901–1902, MFS; Purdy, *Moorestown Old and New*, 94–100.

29. Purdy, *Moorestown Old and New*, 94–100; Jones interview, 24.

30. 1891–92 Friends School Catalogue (FSC), 5–10; 1894–95 FSC, 6–9; 1898–99 FSC, 11; all MFS. Conrow et al. interview, 29–31.

31. 1891–92 FSC, 6, 24–25; 1894–95 FSC, 8–9; AP Moorestown (Chester) Report Record, 1893–94, MFS; Hamm, "Hicksite," 17.

32. Purdy, *Moorestown Old and New*, 49, 54, 138, 182–83; Kingston, *Moorestown's Third Century*, 16–17, 20, 109; Jones interview, 34.

33. One later photograph shows her teeth; *Boston Journal*, January 28, 1914, UPA; Conrow et al. interview, 27; May Roberts Taylor, *Gently, Sister, Gently* (n.p.: 1975), 19; Kingston, *Moorestown's Third Century*, 119.

34. Minutes 1894–1902, Facere Non Dicere Society (FND); "VIF II (2)" FND Paper; both MFS. *History of Woman Suffrage*, ed. Elizabeth Cady Stanton et al., vol. 6, 1900–1920 (New York: Fowler & Wells, 1922), 412–13; Benjamin, *Philadelphia Quakers*, 166; CAP, 31a.

35. CAP, 16; Purdy, *Moorestown Old and New*, 104–7.

36. Christopher Darlington, "Moorestown Free Library" (unpublished manuscript, 1975), 16–20, Moorestown Library archives; Purdy, *Moorestown Old and New*, 106; Benjamin, *Philadelphia Quakers*, 31–32.

37. Hamm, "Hicksite," 23; Myra McNally to Fry, 4 April 1982, AF.

38. 1901–2 FSC, 9–10; APBC.

39. Judy Berman et al., "Alice Paul '01," *Moorestown Friends News*, Spring 1977, 8.

40. Solomon, *Educated Women*, 63–65; John D'Emilio and Estelle B. Freedman, *Intimate Matters* (Chicago: University of Chicago Press, 2012), 190.

41. CAP, 6; "Committee," *Alumni Register*, SC Bulletin 32-4, 1935, 16–17; Richard Robbins to Fry, 21 October 1986, AF.

42. 1901–2 SC Catalogue (SCC), 26–28; 1902–3 SCC, 14, 24, MFS.

43. Bond to "Esteemed Friend," 15 June 1901, in AP 1901 Journal, Folder 14, APP.

44. William Hull, "Twenty-Five Years," Box 33, Hull Papers, FHL, 28.

45. AP 1901–2 Journal, 18 September; SC Student Records microfilm, 1898–1906, FHL.

46. Louise Fahnstock (Poole), "Memories" (Unpub., c. 1979), 15–16, AF; Philip M. Hicks in *Swarthmore Remembered*, ed. Maralyn Orbison Gillespie, Swarthmore College, 1964, 2–3.

47. Poole, "Memories," 20; SC Student Records microfilm, 1898–1906, FHL; Powell photograph, API.

48. AP to TP, 12 July [actually August] 1907, APP; Poole, "Memories," 15–17; Agnes Giesecke interview, 3–5; Eliza Walker McFarland Diary, 18 September 1901, in possession of Corona Machemer, NYC; 1902–3 SCC, 27, FHL.

49. "What Should Go in the Freshman Trunk," *New York Times Magazine*, 9 September 1906; Rob Schorman, *Selling Style* (Philadelphia: University of Pennsylvania Press, 2003), 47, 51–54; Anna Pettit Brommell, "The Unscheduled Course," in Gillespie, *Swarthmore Remembered*, 11.

50. AP to HP, summer 1907, Folder 159, APP; Giesecke interview, 3–4.

51. AP Journal, 19 and 29 September 1901.

52. CAP, 26–27; Brommell, 10; Hull, "History of SC, 1869–1902," 48–50, Box 32, Hull Papers, FHL.

53. CAP, 26–27.

54. CAP, 27.

55. Homer D. Babbidge, Jr., "Swarthmore College" (PhD diss., Yale University, 1963), 148–51; Emily Cooper Johnson, *Dean Bond of Swarthmore* (Philadelphia: J. B. Lippincott Co., 1927), 119–20, 136–39, 150–53, 187–88; Bond, "Care of the College," *FI*, 26 April 1902, 266.

56. CAP, 27; Babbidge, "Swarthmore College."

57. Babbidge, "Swarthmore College," 144; Bond, *Journal, 1901–03*, Bond Papers, Series 1, FHL.

58. Bond, *Journal*, ibid.

59. Hull, "Twenty-Five Years," Box 33, Hull Papers, FHL, 4; Babbidge, "Swarthmore College," 173; Solomon, *Educated Women*, 58–59; M. Carey Thomas, "Present Tendencies," *Educational Review* (January 1908), 72, 74–75.

60. CAP, 17–18; 1901–2 SCC, supplement; Student Records, FHL.

61. AP Journal, 3, 12, and 15 October, 7 December 1901; 25–29 January 1902; AP transcript, SC.

62. 1901–2 SCC; Hicks (see n. 46 above); Johnson, *Dean Bond of Swarthmore*, 124–25; Giesecke interview, 7; Solomon, *Educated Women*, 135–36.

63. AP Journal, 17 October 1901.

64. AP Journal, 5 November 1901; 24 April and 16 May 1902.

65. Johnson, *Dean Bond of Swarthmore*, 125; Robert B. Zoellick, *The Swain Years* (Swarthmore, PA: Swarthmore College, 1975), 48–49.

66. AP Journal, 6, 13, and 20 October, 3 November, all 1901.

67. D'Emilio and Freedman, *Intimate Matters*, 189–94.

68. Ibid.; AP Journal, 24 and 27 September, 21 October and *passim*; Giesecke interview, 5; "College Girls' Larks and Pranks," *Ladies' Home Journal*, March 1900, 8.

69. Esther Garwood Couch to Fry, 14 February 1979, AF; AP Journal 24 and 27 September 1901.

70. Bond to "Esteemed Friend," November 1901; "Swarthmore College [Absence Notice]," 23 November 1901, both in Journal; AP Journal, 27 January 1902.

71. Student Records, FHL; AP Journal, 1 and 18 December 1901, 19 and 31 January, 1 March, 20 and 21 April, all 1902.

72. AP Journal, 5 and 27 October, 7, 14, and 17 November, all 1901; 16 and 19 January, 19 April, 6 May, all 1902.

73. McFarland Diary, 20 September, 25 November 1901 and passim; List in AP Journal; Student Records, FHL.

74. AP Journal, 14 and 31 October, 5 and 16 November, 6 December, all 1901.

75. AP Journal, 21 and 28 September, 9 and 12 October, 2, 9, and 27 November, 1 and 14 December, all 1901; 12 April 1902.

76. AP Journal, 9, 11, 18, and 25–31 January 1902; AP transcript, Student Records, FHL.

77. AP Journal, 22 and 27 September 1901 (includes dance card).

78. CAP, 15–16; AP Journal, weight letter, 21 and 27 September 1901, *passim*; Giesecke interview, 18.

79. AP Journal, 26 [25] April 1902; W. W. Stokes et al. to Respected Friend, 28 April 1902, Folder 210, APP; Conrow et al. interview, 6.

CHAPTER 2

1. "Bank President Dead," Folder 214, APP; Matlack history (see chap. 1, n. 12).

2. Conrow interview, 16 September 1980, 16; McNally interview, 20–21 March 1982, 28.

3. CAP, 7–8; AP Journal, 4–10 May 1902.

4. Peter Filene, *Him/Her/Self* (New York: New American Library, 1975), 18–19; Henry B. Biller, *Fathers and Families* (Santa Barbara, CA: ABC-CLIO, 1993), 199–200.

5. AP Journal, 17 May and 7–9 June 1902; *Halcyon 1903* [SC Yearbook], FHL, 127.

6. Robert Zoellick, "The Swain Years, 1902–1921," *SC Bulletin*, July 1976, 4–5; Bond Journal, 9 February, 12 March, 17 and 24 September, all 1903.

7. SC, Student Record for AP, FHL Caroline Rittenhouse to Fry, 1979, AF; Richard Robbins to Fry, 8 April 1992, AF.

8. SC, Student Record for AP; Hicks, *Swarthmore Remembered*, 4; Fahnstock (Poole), "Memories," 22; CAP, 18.

9. Benjamin, *Philadelphia Quakers*, 176 (see chap. 1, n. 9).

10. CAP 18, 31; *Halcyon 1906*, FHL, 22; Axel R. Schäfer, *American Progressives and German Social Reform, 1875–1920* (Stuttgart: Franz Steiner Verlag, 2000), 106–7.

11. Zoellick, "The Swain Years, 1902–1921," 43; McFarland Diary, 23 October and 5 December 1902, 7 January 1903; "Swarthmore College," *FI*, 1 November 1902, 701; "Call of the 20th Century," *FI*, 17 January 1903, 13; Mabel Vernon, "The Suffrage Campaign," 1975 interview by Amelia Fry, 17–18, SOHP.

12. CAP, 26; *Halcyon 1904*, FHL, 116; *Halcyon 1906*, FHL, 32.

13. *Halcyon 1905*, FHL, 172, 189.

14. SC Alumni Register 1935, FHL, 108; Elizabeth Lippincott in Conrow et al., interview by Amelia Fry, 1979.

15. CAP, 24; Vernon, "The Suffrage Campaign," vi; "Swarthmore College Notes," *FI*, 30 April 1904, 284; "Swarthmore College Notes," *FI*, 1 April 1905, 206.

16. "Opening Day," *FI*, 24 September 1904, 611–12; CAP, 31.

17. CAP, 19; "Swarthmore College Notes," *FI*, 26 March 1904, 284; "Swarthmore College Notes," *FI*, 7 March 1903, 206; Walter I. Trattner, *From Poor Law to Welfare State* (New York: Free Press, 1998), 240–41.

18. CAP, 24–25; "Class Day Exercises," n.d., 1905 Clipping Scrapbook, FHL.

19. "Swarthmore Commencement," *FI*, 17 June 1905, 375; CAP, 31; SC Alumni Register 1935, 108; "Swarthmore College Notes," *FI*, 20 May 1905, 317.

20. APBC, API; Addams quoted in Barbara Sicherman, *Well-Read Lives* (Chapel Hill: University of North Carolina Press, 2010), 157.

21. AP to TP, Folder 31, APP, September 1905.

22. Ibid.

23. Mary Simkhovitch, *Neighborhood* (New York: Norton, 1938), 60.

24. AP, *Sketch of the New York College Settlement* (School of Philanthropy, 1905–6), 13, Folder 20, APP.

25. Jane E. Robbins, "The First Year," *Survey*, 24 February 1912, 1800–1812, quoted in Harry P. Kraus, *The Settlement House Movement* (New York: Arno, 1980), 71; Simkhovitch, *Neighborhood*, 60–61; AP to PP, Jewish New Year's, 30 September 1905; AP to TP, October 1905.

26. AP to TP, September and October 1905.

27. AP to TP, September, October, and 8 November 1905; AP to PP, 30 September 1905.

28. AP to TP, October 1905.

29. CAP, 437.

30. AP to PP, 30 September 1905.

31. AP to TP, 8 November 1905.

32. "New York School of Philanthropy," *Charities*, 3 June 1905, 785; Ruth Scannel, "A History of the Charity Organization Society" (master's thesis, Columbia University, 1937); *NYSP Handbook*, 1904–5, 1, 25, and passim, CUA.

33. CAP, 438; *Alumni Register, 1898–1911* (NYSP, June 1912), CUA.

34. *NYSP Handbook*, 5–9 and passim; CAP, 19, 22, 190; Alice Paul interview by Marjory Nelson, 36–38.

35. AP Transcript, NYSP Registrar, Columbia School of Social Work; CAP, 19; *NYSP Handbook*, 16, 33–38; AP to PP, 30 September 1905.

36. Robbins, "The First Year," 72; AP to PP, 30 September 1905; AP, *Sketch*, 11, 14–16, 19–20; AP to TP, 8 November 1905.

37. AP to PP, 30 September 1905; AP, *Sketch*, 19.

38. AP, *Sketch*, 21–23; Robbins, "The First Year," 68–105.

39. AP, *Sketch*, 21–23.

40. AP to TP, 30 June 1906.

41. CAP, 20–21.

42. CAP, 21; Linda Eisenmann, *Historical Dictionary of Women in the United States* (Westport, CT: Greenwood, 1998), 177–78.

43. CAP, 23–24; Fasciculus, Department of Philosophy, 1906–1907 (University of Pennsylvania, April 1906), vi; Student Records for AP and Clara Thompson, UPA; Thompson 1923 Appointment Bureau Registration, UPA.

44. "Student Totals Omit Auditors," *Catalogue 1906–7* (University of Pennsylvania, 1907); Edward Potts Cheyney, *History of the University of Pennsylvania, 1740–1940* (Philadelphia: University of Pennsylvania Press, 1940), 303–8; Solomon, *Educated Women*, 133.

45. Fasciculus, 27; CAP, 23.

46. *Catalogue 1906–7*, 627–51.

47. Martin Meyerson and Dilys Pegler Winegrad, *Gladly Learn and Gladly Teach* (Philadelphia: University of Pennsylvania Press, 1978), 8, 205–6; Amey A. Hutchins and Penn Archives, *University of Pennsylvania* (Mt. Pleasant,

SC: Arcadia, 2004), 11, 15, 44; George Erasmus Nitzsche, *University of Pennsylvania* (Philadelphia: International Printing, 1918), 204.

48. CAP, 22; Rexford G. Tugwell, "Simon Patten," *Journal of Political Economy* (April 1923): 154.

49. Tugwell, "Simon Patten," 182, 191–93.

50. Allen Johnson and Dumas Malone, eds., "Henry Jones Ford," *DAB* 3 (New York: Scribner's, 1958), 515–16; Helene Silverberg, "A Government of Women," in *Gender and American Social Science*, ed. Silverberg (Princeton, NJ: Princeton University Press, 1998), 171–73.

51. See Ford's note here for his dim view of women: Henry Jones Ford, *The Rise and Growth of American Politics* (New York: Macmillan, 1911), 354, 376; Silverberg, "A Government of Women," 157, 162–63.

52. Ford, *Rise and Growth*, 328.

53. Ibid., 279, 283.

54. "Mask and Wig Club," *Daily Pennsylvanian (DP)*, 19 March 1907, 1; "Dr. James T. Young," *DP*, 9 November 1906, 1; "Dr. H. R. Bates," *DP*, 26 November 1906, 1.

55. Scott Nearing later gained fame as a political activist. *Catalogue, 1906–7* (see n. 44 above).

56. "J. R. S.," "Philadelphia Politics," *FI*, 16 February 1907, 106; "University Men Active," *DP*, 7 November 1906, 1.

57. Benjamin, *Philadelphia Quakers*, 155–56 (see chap. 1, n. 9); "Moorestown Friends," *FI*, 9 March 1907, 153–54; William Mickle Paul obituary, *Friends Journal*, 1959, 92.

58. Penn Student Record for AP; "Woodbrooke," *FI*, 16 February 1907, 102; CAP, 23–24; Carrie Gauthier to AP, 11 June 1907, Folder 44, APP.

59. TP, Account of AP in Britain, c. 1909–10, Folder 210, APP; CAP, 43.

CHAPTER 3

1. AP to TP, 8 July and 4 August 1907.

2. Ibid.

3. AP to TP, 17 July and 4 August 1907.

4. AP to TP, 17 and 21 July 1907.

5. AP to TP, c. 28 July 1907; Patricia M. Mazon, *Gender and the Modern Research University* (Palo Alto, CA: Stanford University Press, 2003), 120–21, 126–27, 137–38.

6. AP to TP, 4 August 1907.

7. AP to TP, 21 July and 12 July [August] 1907.

8. AP to TP, c. 28 July 1907.

9. AP to HP, summer 1907; AP to TP, 4 and 26 August, 2 September, all 1907.

10. AP to TP, 2 September 1907.

11. AP to TP, c. 15 September 1907.

12. AP to TP, c. 15 September and 20 July [September], both 1907.

13. Thomas C. Kennedy, *British Quakerism, 1860–1920* (New York: Oxford University Press, 2001), 183–91; N.a.,"Woodbrooke Settlement," October 1907, 5–6, Folder 127, APP.

14. AP to TP, 20 July [September] 1907.

15. "List of Students, Autumn Term, 1907," Woodbrooke Archives (WA); "Woodbrooke Students," Spring 1908, WA; Kennedy, *British Quakerism*, 190; AP to TP, c. 7 October and 17 November, both 1907.

16. AP to TP, c. 7 October 1907, and attached "Programme of Lectures"; AP to TP, October 1907, "Mr. Littleboy."

17. AP to TP, c. 7 October 1907; Woodbrooke Log, Spring 1908, WA; H. G. Wood, "Warden and Staff," in Robert Davis, ed., *Woodbrooke, 1903–1953* (London: Bannisdale, 1953), 39–40; John St. George Heath to Dear Sir, 3 March 1909; St. George Heath to AP, 3 March 1909.

18. CAP, 31; AP to TP, November 1907, "I am writing"; Carol Dyhouse, *Students* (London: Routledge, 2006), 4, table 1.1.

19. CAP, 32; AP to TP, October 1907, "Mr. Littleboy"; St. George Heath reference, 3 March 1909, Folder 29, APP.

20. D. Oliver, in Woodbrooke Log, Spring 1908, WA, 2, 20.

21. Wood, "Warden and Staff," 35–36; Oliver, Woodbrooke Log, 22.

22. AP to TP, 7 October and Fall, "Two men", 1907; CAP, 35; David V. Herlihy, *Bicycle: The History* (New Haven, CT: Yale University Press, 2004), 287, 315–16, 344–45.

23. AP to TP, 9 February and 2 March 1908.

24. AP to TP, November 1907, "Enclosed"; Emmeline Pankhurst, *My Own Story* (London: Virago, 1979), 37, quoting Christabel.

25. AP, interview by Midge MacKenzie, 1 April 1973, 4, AF.

26. CAP, 32–34; Henry W. Nevinson, *Fire of Life* (London: Nisbet, 1935), 252–53; AP to TP, 12 December 1907.

27. AP to TP, 12 December 1907.

28. AP, interview by Midge MacKenzie, 4–5.

29. St. George Heath to AP, see n. 17; AP to TP, 10 November 1909; "Administrative History," Scrapbook of [Cecile Matheson], The Women's Library, UK.

30. CAP, 34.

31. AP to TP, 12 December 1907.

32. AP to TP, 28 December 1907; George Shann and Edward Cadbury, *Sweating* (London: Headley Bros., 1907), 19–20.

33. AP to TP, 20 January 1908.

34. Maud Younger, "Diary of an Amateur Waitress," *McClure's*, March 1907, 543–52; Ellen Ross, ed., *Slum Travelers* (Berkeley: University of California Press, 2007), 138, 262–63; Beatrice Webb, "Diary of an Investigator," in Beatrice and

Sidney Webb, *Problems of Modern Industry* (London: Longman, Green, rev. ed. 1902), 1–19.

35. Younger wrote, "Sometimes [the manager] looked me over as though I were a horse, while I stood by, boiling with rage"; "Diary," 543; AP to TP, 20 January 1908.

36. AP to TP, 20 January 1908.

37. AP to TP, 9 February 1908; CAP, 34.

38. AP to TP, 15 March 1908.

39. AP to TP, 2 and 15 March 1908.

40. AP to TP, 13 and 19 April, 6 May, all 1908; CAP, 34–36.

41. Ross, *Slum Travelers*, 284; AP to TP, 9 February 1908; CAP, 36; Jack London, *People of the Abyss* (New York: Macmillan, 1903), 25–26.

42. AP to TP, 25 May and c. August–September 1908; Frank Watson, *Charity Organization Society Movement* (New York: Macmillan, 1922), 60.

43. AP to HP, mid-Aug 1908; AP to TP, 21 August 1908.

44. AP to TP, August–September 1908.

45. AP to TP, 3 August 1908; CAP, 37.

46. CAP, 38; AP to TP, 3 August 1908.

47. Ray Strachey, *Struggle* (New York: Duffield & Co., 1930), 302; Harold L. Smith, *The British Women's Suffrage Campaign, 1866–1928* (Edinburgh Gate, Harlow, UK: Pearson Education, 2007), 10–11, 16–20, 28.

48. Smith, *Suffrage Campaign*, 21–22, 34, 37, 39–40.

49. Ibid., 24–28; Fawcett quoted in Patricia G. Harrison, *Connecting Links: The British and American Woman Suffrage Movements, 1900–1914* (Westport, CT: Praeger, 2000), 78; Pankhurst quoted in Lisa Tickner, *The Spectacle of Women* (Chicago: University of Chicago Press, 1988), 8.

50. E. Sylvia Pankhurst, *The Suffragette: The History of the Women's Militant Suffrage Movement, 1905–1910* (London: Sturgis & Walton, 1911), 234.

51. Tickner, *Spectacle*, 74–78; Strachey, *Struggle*, 306.

52. Millicent Fawcett, "Woman Suffrage Procession," *TL*, 13 June 1908; Tickner, *Spectacle*, 81–91; AP to TP, 26 June 1908.

53. N.a.,"Women and the Suffrage," *TL*, 15 June 1908.

54. N.a.,"Demonstration," *TL*, 22 June 1908; N.a., "London in Ferment," *NYT*, 22 June 1908; Andrew Rosen, *Rise Up, Women!* (London: Routledge & Kegan Paul, 1974), 103–5; CAP, 38–39; Tickner, *Spectacle*, 91–98.

55. Tickner, *Spectacle*, 91.

56. CAP, 39–40.

57. Ibid.

58. AP to TP, c. August–September 1908 and 21 August 1908; AP to Helen, 10 August 1908; CAP, 40.

59. Beulah Parry to TP, 25 August 1908; AP to TP, August–September 1908; AP to HP, mid-August 1908, #1.

60. AP to HP, mid-August 1908, #2.

61. Ibid.

62. AP to TP, 5 October 1908; CAP, 40, 47.

63. AP to TP, 22 October 1908; Mackenzie interview, 3; Joseph Edwards, *Reformers' Year Book 1909* (Brighton, Sussex: Harvester, 1909), 129–31; AP to PP, 25 November 1908; AP to HP, 25 November 1908.

64. AP to TP, 22 October and 2 November 1908.

65. LSE building sketch, 1900, LSE information office; AP to TP, 19 and 22 October 1908.

66. Ralf Dahrendorf, *History of the London School* (London: Oxford University Press, 1995), 104–5; AP to TP, 8 December 1908.

67. CAP, 47; AP to TP, 5 October 1908.

68. Paul Thompson, *The Edwardians* (London: Granada, 1975), 297; AP to TP, 22 October, 2 and 17 November, all 1908.

69. AP to TP, 17 November 1908; AP to HP, 25 November 1908.

70. AP to TP, 22 October, 2 and 17 November, all 1908.

71. AP to TP, 17 November 1908; AP to HP, 25 November 1908; AP to PP, 25 November 1908.

72. AP to TP, 12 December 1908.

73. AP to TP, 8 December 1908.

74. AP to TP, 8 December 1908, 2 and 7 January 1909.

75. AP to TP, 7 January 1909.

76. AP to TP, 14 and 22 January 1909.

77. AP to TP, 7 and 14 January 1909.

78. AP to TP, 14 January and 17 March 1909.

79. CAP, 44–45; Elizabeth Crawford, *The Women's Suffrage Movement: A Reference Guide, 1866–1928* (London: Routledge, 2001), 35.

80. Michelle Elizabeth Tusan, *Women Making News: Gender and Journalism in Modern Britain* (Champaign: University of Illinois Press, 2005), 2–3.

81. CAP, 45; Martha Vicinus, *Independent Women: Work and Community for Single Women, 1850–1920* (Chicago: University of Chicago Press, 1985), 262–65.

82. Jessie Anthony, "Diary of a Newsy," 7, 14, 21, and 28 July 1911, Anthony Family Papers, Huntington Library; Maria DiCenzo, "Gutter Politics," *Women's History Review* (2003): 27; June Purvis, " 'Deeds, not Words,' " in *Votes for Women*, ed. Purvis and Sandra Stanley Holton (London: Routledge, 2000), 138–39.

83. Krista Cowman, *Women of the Right Spirit: Paid Organisers of the Women's Social and Political Union (WSPU), 1904–18* (Manchester: Manchester University Press, 2007), 32; CAP, 45–46.

84. Vicinus, *Independent Women*, 262–65; Purvis, " 'Deeds,' " 138.

85. DiCenzo, "Gutter Politics," 22–24; Purvis, " 'Deeds,' " 138; Katharine Roberts, *Pages from the Diary of a Militant Suffragette* (New York: Garden City Press, 1910), 25.

86. AP to HP, 19 March 1909, Folder 159; AP to PP, 30 January 1909, Folder 182; I. F. Clarke, *The Great War with Germany, 1890–1914: Fictions and Fantasies of the War-to-Come* (Liverpool: Liverpool University Press, 1997), 17–18; AP to TP, 9 March 1908.

87. AP to TP, 14 January, 17 and c. 31 March, 2 April, all 1909.

88. AP to TP, 4 (?) and 17 March 1909.

89. Kelsey to AP, 11 and 31 March 1909; AP to TP, 13 April 1909.

90. AP to TP, 21 April and 11 May 1909.

91. AP to HP, 19 March 1909; AP to TP, 5 June 1909.

92. AP to TP, 5 June 1909.

93. AP to TP, 5 June 1909; TP account (see chap. 2, n. 59); AP Student Record, LSE.

94. AP to TP, c. 1 July 1909; CAP, 47–48.

95. CAP, 48.

CHAPTER 4

1. "Miss Paul," *VFW*, 7 January 1910, 236.

2. Laura E. Nym Mayhall, *The Militant Suffrage Movement* (New York: Oxford University Press, 2003), 36–37, 48, 51–52; E. Pankhurst, speech of 21 October 1913, quoted in Martin Pugh, *March of the Women* (London: Oxford University Press, 2000), 172.

3. Jane Purvis, "Emmeline Pankhurst," in Sandra Stanley Holton and Jane Purvis, eds., *Votes for Women* (London: Routledge, 2000), 115–16; Sandra Stanley Holton, "From Anti-Slavery to Suffrage Militancy," in *Suffrage and Beyond*, ed. Caroline Daley and Melanie Nolan (New York: New York University Press, 1994), 228–29.

4. Kennedy, *British Quakerism*, 227–36, 275, 368 (see chap. 3, n. 13); *Free Church Suffrage Times*, November 1913, quoted in Sophia A. van Wingerden, *Women's Suffrage Movement in Britain, 1866–1928* (New York: Macmillan, 1999), 112–13.

5. Holton, "From Anti-Slavery," 214–16, 221–23; Holton, "'On the Horns of a Dilemma,'" in *Suffrage Days*, ed. Holton (London: Routledge, 1996), 161–71; Mayhall, *Militant Suffrage*, 98–99; Kennedy, *British Quakerism*, 230–31, 244–45.

6. E. Pankhurst, *My Own Story*, 59 (see chap. 3, n. 24).

7. C. Pankhurst, *Unshackled* (London: Cresset Women's Voices, 1987), 83; Purvis, "Emmeline Pankhurst," 116–19.

8. Rosen, *Rise Up, Women!*, 116–17 (see chap. 3, n. 54); E. Pankhurst, *My Own Story*, 136; AP to TP, c. 1 July 1909.

9. *VFW*, 2 July 1909, quoted in Mayhall, *Militant Suffrage*, 56, also 48, 52, 56.

10. Mayhall, *Militant Suffrage*, 52; Rosen, *Rise Up, Women!*, 118–19.

11. Mayhall, *Militant Suffrage*, 40–46; C. Pankhurst in *VFW*, 10 September 1908, quoted in Mayhall, *Militant Suffrage*, 45; E. Pankhurst, quoted in Purvis, "Emmeline Pankhurst," 120.

12. AP to TP, c. 1 July 1909; CAP, 48; Antonia Raeburn, *The Militant Suffragettes* (London: New English Library, 1974), 104; Laurence Housman, *The Unexpected Years* (Indianapolis, IN: Bobbs-Merrill, 1936), 226–27.

13. Antonia Raeburn, *The Suffragette View* (New York: St. Martin's, 1976), 32; Betty Balfour, ed., *Letters of Constance Lytton* (London: W. Heinemann, 1925), 167–68; Rosen, *Rise Up, Women!*, 118; S. Pankhurst, *The Suffragette*, 383–84 (see chap. 3, n. 50); E. Pankhurst quoted in Mayhall, *Militant Suffrage*, 53.

14. S. Pankhurst, *The Suffragette*, 379–80, 383–85; Henry W. Nevinson quoted in June Purvis, *Emmeline Pankhurst* (London: Routledge, 2004), 129; Mayhall, *Militant Suffrage*, 53.

15. *Daily Chronicle*, 30 June 1909, quoted in Purvis, *Pankhurst*, 130; AP to TP, c. 1 July 1909.

16. AP to TP, c. 1 July 1909; Housman, *Unexpected Years*, 226–27.

17. E. Pankhurst, *My Own Story*, 142; Purvis, *Pankhurst*, 130; "122 Arrests," *Daily News*, 30 June 1909, 14.

18. AP to TP, c. 1 July 1909; CAP, 48.

19. TP, Account of AP in Britain (see chap. 2, n. 59); AP to TP, c. 1 July 1909.

20. TP, Account of AP.

21. S. Pankhurst, *The Suffragette*, 391–92; AP to TP, 10 July 1909; Annie Kenney, *Memories of a Militant* (London: E. Arnold & Co., 1924), 145–46.

22. Mayhall, *Militant Suffrage*, 56–57; AP to TP, c. 1 July 1909.

23. Mayhall, *Militant Suffrage*, 56–57; AP to TP, 10 July 1909.

24. *Women's Franchise*, 8 July 1909, quoted in Mayhall, *Militant Suffrage*, 57; Mayhall, *Militant Suffrage*, 56–57.

25. AP to TP, 10 July 1909; Mayhall, *Militant Suffrage*, 76–77.

26. AP to TP, 10 July 1909; "Right of Petition," *Daily News*, 10 July 1909, 15 in Suffrage Scrapbook 150.82/1013, Museum of London; Purvis, *Pankhurst*, 130–31; Mayhall, *Militant Suffrage*, 56.

27. AP to TP, c. 1 and 10 July 1909; Sidney R. Bland, "'Never Quite as Committed as We'd Like,'" *Journal of Long Island History* 17 (Summer 1981): 6.

28. The appeal affirmed the ruling; Purvis, *Pankhurst*, 131, AP to TP, 10 July 1909.

29. AP to TP, 27 July 1909.

30. MacKenzie interview, 6; Emmeline Pethick-Lawrence quoted in Cowman, *Right Spirit*, 30 (see chap. 3, n. 83).

31. AP to TP, 27 July 1909; Crawford, *Suffrage Movement*, 154–55 (see chap. 3, n. 79); Robert S. Gallagher, "'I Was Arrested Of Course…,'" *American Heritage*, February 1974, 18.

32. Gallagher, "'I Was Arrested,'" 18.

33. Michael Shaw and Cliff Middleton, *Norwich Old and New* (Wakefield: EP Ltd., 1974), 29; N.a., *Cassell's Gazetteer* (London: Cassell, 1905), 45–46.

34. "At Norwich," *VFW*, 30 July 1909, 1012; AP to TP, 27 July 1909; Cowman, *Right Spirit*, 56.

35. "At Norwich," ibid.; "Trouble," *Norfolk Mercury (NM)*, 30 July 1909.

36. "Civis" and "Notes," *Norfolk Weekly Standard*, 30 July 1909; "Trouble," *Norfolk Mercury*.

37. "Mr. Winston Churchill," *NM*, 28 July 1909; AP to TP, 27 July 1909.

38. S. Pankhurst, *The Suffragette*, 45–47, 224–47; Rosen, *Rise Up, Women!*, 101–2.

39. "Civis," *Norfolk Weekly Standard*; "Churchill," *NM*; "At Norwich," *VFW*; AP to TP, 27 July 1909.

40. AP to TP, 27 July 1909.

41. "Trouble," *NM*; "Churchill" and "At Norwich," both *VFW*; AP to TP, 27 July 1909.

42. "Civis," *Norfolk Weekly Standard*; "Churchill," *VFW*.

43. See Mayhall, *Militant Suffrage*, 49–50.

44. AP to TP, 27 July 1909; TP, Account of AP.

45. "Hunger Strikers," *VFW*, 6 August 1909, 1043.

46. Emmeline Pethick-Lawrence, *Fate Has Been Kind* (London: Hutchinson, 1943), 71; Kenney, *Memories*, 147–48.

47. Harrison, *Connecting Links*, 53–55, 98–99, 103–4 (see chap. 3, n. 49); "Activities of College Women," *WJ*, 17 July 1909, 116.

48. James D. Hunt, *Gandhi in London* (Delhi: Promilla, 1978), 102, 137–39.

49. Mahatma Gandhi, London Letter, 30 July 1909, in *Collected Works of Mahatma Gandhi* (*CWMG*) 9 (New Delhi: Government of India, 1999), 452–55; London Letter, 25 September 1909, *CWMG* 10, 117; London Letter, 1 October 1909, *CWMG*, 133–34.

50. Crawford, *Suffrage Movement*, 159, 388; "Mr. Lloyd-George at Limehouse," *TL*, 31 July 1909, 1; "At Limehouse," *VFW*, 6 August 1909, 1040–41; "Woman Suffrage," *TL*, 2 August 1909, 8; Court judgment, Folder 222, APP.

51. Constance Lytton and Jane Warton, *Prisons and Prisoners: Some Personal Experiences* (New York: Doran, 1914), 60, 64–66; "Stories of the Holloway Mutiny," *VFW*, 27 August 1909, 1104–5; Holloway Prison, Google Images.

52. "The 'Hunger Strike,'" *VFW*, 13 August 1909, 1061; Purvis, "Pankhurst," 121, 145.

53. Mayhall, *Militant Suffrage*, 101; AP to TP, c. 7 August 1909.

54. "Hunger Strike" and "The Spirit That Upheld Us," *VFW*, 20 August 1909, 1081.

55. AP to TP, c. 7 August 1909; "Hunger Strike," "Spirit," and "Mutiny," *VFW*; S. Pankhurst, *The Suffragette*, 409–10.

56. "Spirit," *VFW*.

57. AP to TP, c. 7 August 1909.

58. Ibid.; Lytton and Warton, *Prisons*, 86; "Hunger Strike," "Spirit," and "Mutiny," *VFW*; Raeburn, *View*, 42.

59. S. Pankhurst, *The Suffragette*, 412; Mayhall, *Militant Suffrage*, 101.

60. "Mutiny," *VFW*; E. Pankhurst, *My Own Story*, 153.

61. *Rules of Discipline* (Philadelphia: Hicksite Yearly Meeting, 1894), 51–55.

62. AP to TP, c. 7 August 1909; David Brown, "Starving Somalis," *WP*, 4 January 1993, 1; "Spirit," *VFW*.

63. "Spirit," *VFW*.

64. "Welcome," *WJ*, 15 May 1909, 79.

65. AP to TP, c. 7 August 1909; "Hunger Strike," *VFW*.

66. AP to TP, ibid.

67. CAP, 51; Purvis, *Pankhurst*, 99; AP to TP, 13 August 1909.

CHAPTER 5

1. Raeburn, *Militant*, 94–95 (see chap. 4, n. 12); Raeburn, *View*, 39 (see chap. 4, n. 13); Rosen, *Rise*, 116 (see chap. 4, n. 38); CAP, 51.

2. Mackenzie interview, 12.

3. AP to TP, 17/18 August 1909; CAP, 51.

4. Leah Leneman, *A Guid Cause: The Women's Suffrage Movement in Scotland* (Aberdeen: Aberdeen University Press, 1991), 2, 39, 71–90.

5. Ibid., 41–42, 48–49.

6. "Scottish Demonstration," *VFW*, 27 August 1909, 1115; CAP, 51.

7. S. Pankhurst, *The Suffragette*, 377 (see chap. 3, n. 50); Iain Finlayson, *The Scots* (New York: Atheneum, 1987), 27–30.

8. *Annual Glasgow Directory, 1909–1910* (Glasgow: J. Graham, 1909), 755.

9. "Suffragist Activity," *Glasgow Herald* (*GH*), 21 August 1909; "Scottish Demonstration," *VFW*.

10. "Suffragist Activity," *GH*; "Scottish Demonstration," *VFW*.

11. "Scottish Demonstration," *VFW*; "Suffragist Activity," *GH*; "Suffragist Disturbance," *GH*, 23 August 1909; "Suffragists and Glasgow Police," *GH*, 25 August 1909; AP to TP, 21 August 1909.

12. "Suffragists and Glasgow Police," *GH*; AP to TP, 21 August 1909.

13. AP to TP, 18, 21, and 31 August 1909 and 7 September 1909.

14. AP to TP, 31 August and 3 and 7 September 1909; "Scotland," *VFW*, 10 September 1909, 1164; Leneman, *Guid Cause*, 263.

15. AP to TP, 7 September 1909.

16. AP to TP, 12 September 1909; Francis H. Groome, *Ordnance Gazetteer of Scotland* (Edinburgh: Edinburgh & Jack, 1901), 412–13; Leneman, *Guid Cause*, 61–62; "Bellman's Budget," *People's Journal* (*PJ*), 18 September 1909; "Nobody Saw Miss Kelly," *[Dundee] Courier* (*DC*), 14 September 1909; "Miss Kelley," *DC*, 15 September 1909.

17. "Suffragette on Roof," *PJ*, 18 September 1909; "Unprecedented Scenes," *VFW*, 17 September 1909.

18. "Unprecedented," *VFW*; "Suffragette on Roof," *PJ*.

19. "Unprecedented," *VFW*; "Suffragette on Roof," *PJ*.

20. AP to TP, 25 September 1909; "Hunger Strike," *DC*, 15 September 1909; "Three Suffragettes," *DC*, 16 September 1909; "Three Cheers," *DC*, 17 September 1909; Adela Pankhurst, "How Dundee Supported the Cause," *VFW*, 24 September 1909, 1202.

21. "Miss Kelley," *DC*; "Suffragette on Roof," *PJ*; Leneman, *Guid Cause*, 80.

22. A. Pankhurst, "Dundee"; AP to TP, 25 September 1909; Leneman, *Guid Cause*, 80.

23. A. Pankhurst, "Dundee"; AP to TP, 25 September 1909.

24. AP to TP, 25 September 1909; CAP, 54.

25. AP to TP, 30 September 1909.

26. Raeburn, *Militant*, 116–19; "The Dangers of Forcible Feeding," *VFW*, 8 October 1909, 19; E. Pankhurst, *My Own Story*, 156–57; AP to TP, 30 September 1909.

27. AP to TP, 25 and 30 September 1909; "Dangers," *VFW*.

28. "The Hunger Strikers," *PJ*, 2 October 1909.

29. AP to TP, 11 October 1909; CAP, 55.

30. AP to TP, 11 October 1909; "A Great Political Pageant," *VFW*, 15 October 1909, 42; "Suffragist Demonstration," *The Scotsman*, 11 October 1909.

31. AP to TP, 11 October 1909.

32. "Opening Ceremony," *Berwick Journal*, 14 October 1909; "Suffragist Disturbance," *Berwick Mercury*, 16 October 1909; "Miss Paul's Release," *VFW*, 22 October 1909, 53.

33. AP to TP, 31 October 1909; "Miss Alice Paul," *Philadelphia Press*, c. 25 October 1909, Folder 226, APP; Tacie Paul account (see chap. 2, n. 59).

34. "Suffering for the Cause," *Moorestown Republican*, November 1909, Folder 226, APP.

35. Ibid.

36. S. Pankhurst, *The Suffragette*, 454–55.

37. CAP, 55–56; "Two Americans in Guildhall Exploit," *NYT*, 12 November 1909.

38. Fry notes on Guildhall, AF; "Miss Paul Tells Jail Experience," 19 December 1909, UPA; CAP, 56.

39. S. Pankhurst, *The Suffragette Movement: An Intimate Account of Persons and Ideals* (London: Longmans, Green, 1931), 314–16; "Two Americans," *NYT*, 12 November 1909, "Guildhall Banquet/Speech," *TL*, 10 November 1909; "Local Girl Jailed in Suffrage Fight," *PB*, 11 November 1909.

40. "Local Girl," *PB*; "Lord Mayor's Feast Stoned," *NYT*, 10 November 1909; "Guildhall Banquet," *TL*.

41. "Guild Hall," *VFW*, 12 November 1909, 84.

42. "Miss Paul's Friends Seek Her Release," *NYT*, 22 November 1909.

43. AP to TP, 27 December 1909.

44. AP to TP, 10 December 1909; "Suffragettes Sentenced," *NYT*, 11 November 1909.

45. "Miss Paul in a London Jail," *Newark Evening News*, 12 November 1909, Clippings Collection, Newark Library; "Miss Paul Stirs London," Folder 210, APP; "Moorestown," *Mount Holly (NJ) Herald*, 13 November 1909, API; "Alice Paul Refuses London Prison Food," *PB*, 13 November 1909; "Distorted News about Suffragettes," *NYT*, 14 November 1909.

46. "Plan to Oppose Votes for Women," *Philadelphia Inquirer (PI)*, 15 November 1909.

47. AP to TP, 10 December 1909; "Miss Paul's Home Folks," *PB*, 13 November 1909; "Miss Alice Paul in Suffragette Row," *PB*, 11 November 1909; "Miss Paul Puzzles Mother," *NYT*, 13 November 1909; "Miss Paul in a London Jail," *Newark Evening News*.

48. "Distorted News," *NYT*; Rosen, *Rise*, 121–27; Mayhall, *Militant Suffrage*, 77–78.

49. "Jersey Woman Is Jailed in London," *PI*, 11 November 1909, 2; "Distorted News," *NYT*.

50. AP to TP, 27 December 1909.

51. Ibid.

52. Ibid.

53. "Mrs. Paul Alarmed," *PL*, 21 November 1909.

54. Marshall D. Swisher to TP, 19 November; Ella S. Johnson to TP, 11 November; Caroline Hadley Robinson to TP, 29 November; John P. Leeds to Dear Friend, 29 November; all 1909, Folder 210, APP.

55. Mickle Paul to TP, c. 20 November 1909, Folder 210, APP.

56. Tacie Paul account; *PL*, 21 November 1909; "Mrs. Pankhurst," *WJ*, 11 December 1909, 199; Mabel Tuke to Mrs. Paul, 15 November; Howard M. Paul to Aunt Tacie, 20 November; Mickle Paul to Tacie, 13 December; all 1909, Folder 210, APP.

57. "Mrs. Pankhurst Has a Day of Triumph," *NYT*, 30 November 1909; AP to Belle Squire, 24 July 1913, Reel 3, NWPP II; "Mrs. Paul Alarmed," *PL*.

58. Whitelaw Reid to Madam and C. Pankhurst to Mrs. Paul, both 30 November 1909, Folder 226, APP.

59. AP to Mrs. Paul, 9 December 1909; TP, Account of AP (see chap. 2, n. 59); Crawford, *Woman Suffrage Movement*, 359–60; "Miss Paul Describes Feeding," *NYT*, 10 December 1909.

60. AP to TP, 10 December 1909.

61. "Letter," *TL*, 11 December 1909, 4; "Decry Forcible Feeding," *VFW*, 24 December 1909, 197.

62. AP to TP, 15 December 1909; [Henrietta] Löwy to Mrs. Paul, 15 December 1909, Folder 210, APP.

63. AP to TP, 17 and 22 December 1909.

64. AP to TP, 22 December 1909.

65. Ibid.

66. Ibid.

67. Ibid.; Mackenzie interview, 19; CAP, 59.

68. "Miss Paul," *VFW*, 7 January 1910, 236; S. Pankhurst, *The Suffragette*, 478.

69. Mackenzie interview, 19.

70. Mayhall, *Militant Suffrage*, 112–13.

CHAPTER 6

1. "Shipping News," *PL*, 21 January 1910, 14b.

2. Rheta Childe Dorr, *What Eight Million Women Want* (Boston: Small, Maynard, 1910), 297; "Militant Methods," *WJ*, October 1909, 174.

3. Ida Husted Harper, ed., *History of Woman Suffrage, 1900–20*, Vol. 5 (New York: Fowler and Wells, 1922), 437 (hereafter *HWS*)

4. Nancy F. Cott, *The Grounding of Modern Feminism* (New Haven, CT: Yale University Press, 1987), 31.

5. TP, Account of AP (see chap. 2, n. 59); "Miss Paul Expected," 20 January 1910, Folder 226, APP; "Miss Alice Paul Back," *PL*, 21 January 1910; Miller NAWSA Scrapbook #8, 133, LC.

6. "Miss Alice Paul Back," *PL*.

7. Herendeen, "Hometown," 127–28 (chap. 1, n. 17); Conrow interview, 16.

8. TP, Account of AP; McNally interview, 14–15.

9. CAP, 334–35; Conrow et al. interview, 4–5; L. M. Robbins to Fry, 3 March 1992; Calvin Robbins, Jr. to Fry, 12 April 1991; Matlack history (see chap. 1, n. 12).

10. Margaret Jones interview; Myra McNally interview.

11. *Rules of Discipline*, 49–50, 54, 56 (see chap. 4, n. 61); Benjamin, *Philadelphia Quakers*, 75, 170 (see chap. 1, n. 9); CAP, 319.

12. TP, Account of AP; "Miss Alice Paul," *WJ*, 29 January 1910, 19; CAP, 62, 444.

13. Henrietta Krone, "Dauntless Women" (PhD diss., Penn, 1946), 10–11, 16; Jennie B. Roessing, "Equal Suffrage Campaign," *Annals of the American Academy* (1914): 153.

14. "Miss Paul Tells Experience," *PL*, 27 January 1910; "Miss Alice Paul Dined," *PB*, January 30, 1910; Penn *Catalogue, 1910–11*.

15. "Tube-Fed Militant," January 1910, Folder 226, APP.

16. Ibid.

17. CAP, 60; Caroline Katzenstein, *Lifting the Curtain* (Philadelphia: Dorrance, 1955), 24–26, 40.

18. "Suffragists Organize," Folder 226, APP.

19. Ellen Carol DuBois, "Working Women, Class Relations," *Journal of American History* (June 1987): 47–52, 55–57; DuBois, *Harriot Stanton Blatch and the Winning of Woman Suffrage* (New Haven, CT: Yale University Press, 1999), 159–60; Rebecca J. Mead, *How the Vote Was Won* (New York: New York University Press, 2004), 64–66, 82, 88.

20. Sofia M. Loebinger, "Suffragist and Suffragette," *American Suffragette* 1 (June 1909): 5–6.

21. "Suffrage 'At Homes,'" *WJ*, 5 March 1910, 38; "American Girl," [St. Louis] *Globe Democrat*, 6 February 1910; "Precisely How It Feels," 6 February 1910, both UPA.

22. Cheyney, *History*, 289 (see chap. 2, n. 44).

23. Alice Paul, "The Woman Suffrage Movement in Britain," in "Significance of the Woman Suffrage Movement," supplement, *Annals of the American Academy of Political and Social Science* 35 (July 1910): 5.

24. Ibid., 6–9, 10–15, 16–22, 33–37.

25. Ibid., 23–27.

26. Herendeen, "Hometown," 127–28.

27. "Miss Paul in Home Town," *PL*, 11 February 1910; Conrow et al. interview, 16; "Woman Suffrage at Moorestown," *FI*, 19 February 1910, 121–22.

28. "The College Girl Suffragists," *WJ*, 19 February 1910, 30; "Programme," *WJ*, 12 March 1910, 42.

29. Eleanor Flexner and Ellen Fitzpatrick, *Century of Struggle* (Cambridge, MA: Belknap Press of Harvard University Press, 1996), 250; Cott, *Grounding*, 26–27; *HWS*, 269, 273, 289–90; "H. W. W.," *FI*, 30 April 1910, 279.

30. Flexner and Fitzpatrick, *Century*, 250–51; "Row in Convention," *WP*, 19 April 1910; *HWS*, 276, 282; Sara Hunter Graham, *Woman Suffrage and the New Democracy* (New Haven, CT: Yale University Press, 1996), 52.

31. CAP, 61–62; "Programme," *WJ*.

32. "Miss Alice Paul's Address," *WJ*, 7 May 1910, 76.

33. *HWS*, 282.

34. *HWS*, 275, 291–309.

35. Miller Scrapbook #8, 24, 134, LC.

36. A 1908 California parade drew two hundred women; Mead, *How the Vote*, 128. Jennifer Borda, "Woman Suffrage Parades," *Western Journal of Communication* (Winter 2002): 31–33; DuBois, *Harriet Stanton Blatch*, 101–3, 111–12; Blatch and Alma Lutz, *Challenging Years* (New York: G. P. Putnam's Sons, 1940), 132–33.

37. "Suffrage Parade Has Police Guard," *NYT*, 22 May 1910; Delight W. Dodyk, "Education and Agitation: The Woman Suffrage Movement in New Jersey" (PhD diss., Rutgers University, 1997), 317; Inez Haynes Gilmore, "The Women's March," *WJ*, 4 May 1912, 141.

38. McNally interview, 20–22.

39. Woodbroke, *FI*, 19 March 1910, 187; Haverford Conference, *FI*, 17 July 1910, 451.

40. AP, "The Church and Social Problems," *FI*, 20 August 1910, 513–15; Benjamin, *Philadelphia Quakers*, 176–84.

41. McKirdy to AP, 29 July 1911, and Kelsey to AP, 17 April 1912, both Folder 21, APP; Penn *Catalogue, 1910–11*, 735; Penn Alumni Society, *Alumni Catalogue* (1917), 1050; Penn *Catalogue, 1911–12*, 644–68, 723.

42. CAP, 320; Fasciculus, Department of Philosophy, 1910–11 (University of Pennsylvania, April 1910), 28; Cheyney, *History*, 305; AP, Penn Student Record, 1910–12, UPA.

43. AP, Penn Student Record; Linda Mallon and Anita Sama, *Franklin's Daughters: Vol. 1* (Philadelphia: University of Pennsylvania Press, 2001), 25.

44. Penn *Catalogue, 1910–11*, 184, 333; *Catalogue, 1911–12*, 664; Brownson to AP, 20 September 1912, Folder 38, APP; Brownson to AP, 16 November 1917, Reel 52; Linn Seiler to AP, 29 October 1920, Reel 83.

45. No correspondence is extant from the time both Parker and Alice studied at Penn. Entry for William H. Parker family, 1900 US Census for Queensburytown, NY; Penn *Catalogue, 1910–11*, 225.

46. Parker to AP, 15 September 1912, Folder 38, APP.

47. "Miss Paul Urges 'Freedom,'" *PB*, 15 December 1910; "Sylvia Pankhurst," *WJ*, 25 March 1911, 95; Löwy to AP, 7 September 1911, Folder 38, APP.

48. Katzenstein, *Lifting the Curtain*, 40; CAP, 60–61; Dodyk, "Education and Agitation," 293; "Illinois," *WJ*, 9 July 1910, 111; Linda Lumsden, *Rampant Women* (Knoxville: University of Tennessee Press, 1997), 31, 36.

49. Katzenstein, *Lifting the Curtain*, 41; Mayhall, *Militant Suffrage*, 104; S. Pankhurst, *Suffragette Movement*, 338–40 (chap. 5, n. 39).

50. Katzenstein, *Lifting the Curtain*, 43.

51. Ibid., 43–44; CAP, 61; Daniel Sidorick, "The 'Girl Army,'" *PA History* 71-3 (2004): 344.

52. Katzenstein, *Lifting the Curtain*, 44–45.

53. Ibid., 45–46; "Women Speak from Wagon," *PL*, 26 July 1911, 1; "Pennsylvania," *WJ*, 5 August 1911.

54. Katzenstein, *Lifting the Curtain*, 47–52; "Outdoor Suffrage Meeting," *PL*, 27 July 1911; "Alice Paul Wins Debate," *PB*, 29 July 1911.

55. "Alice Paul Wins," *PB*.

56. Katzenstein, *Lifting the Curtain*, 49–50.

57. Ibid., 52–53; "Suffrage in Independence Square," *PL*, 30 September 1911, 6; CAP, 63; Lumsden, *Rampant Women*, pp. xxix–xxx.

58. CAP, 63; "Open-Air Suffrage Meetings," *FI*, 23 September 1911, 601; Joan M. Martino, "Lost Mosaic Piece," 24, API; Katzenstein, *Lifting the Curtain*, 52–53; "Suffrage Rally Draws Thousands," *PL*, 1 October 1911, 6.

59. AP, "The Legal Position of Women in Pennsylvania" (PhD diss., University of Pennsylvania, 1912), 123–24, 144–45, 254–63.

60. Solomon, *Educated Women*, 133; *Program*, 19 June 1912, Commencement Collection (UPG 7), Box 4, UPA.

61. AP to Vernon, 21 April 1913, Reel 2.

62. Campbell to AP, 2 and 12 April, 24 June, and 2 July, all 1912; Eleanor Brannan to AP, 11 February 1912; Ida Porter Boyer to AP, 6 June 1912; Lewis to AP, 8 July 1912, all Folder 227, APP.

63. Campbell to AP, 24 June 1912; Lewis to AP, 8 July 1912 and 5 August 1912.

64. Lewis to AP, 8 July 1912 and 5 August 1912; Folder 227, APP; CAP, 63; Nelson interview, 32–33.

65. AP to Dora Lewis, 24 October 1913, Reel 5.
66. AP to Eunice R. Oberly, 6 March 1914, Reel 8; Christabel Pankhurst to Janie Allan, 26 May 1914, Allan Papers, Acc. 4498/3, National Library of Scotland; Irwin, *Story of Alice Paul*, 13, 16 (see intro, n. 7).
67. Irwin, *Story of Alice Paul*, 13; Blatch and Lutz, *Challenging Years*, 194–95.
68. AP to Dora Lewis, 24 October 1913; *HWS*, 319–20, 339; "Elizabeth Thacher Kent," 7, 9, Women's Suffrage Series, Claremont College Libraries; CAP, 64–65.
69. Nelson interview, 42.
70. *HWS*, 282, 324.
71. Mary Dennett to AP, 5 December 1912; AP to NAWSA Board, 16 December 1912; both Reel 1. *HWS*, 378; CAP, 64–65; "May March," *WJ*, 14 December 1912, 400.
72. Receipt Book, Folder 236, APP.

CHAPTER 7

1. Sina Stanton and Julie Sharpless, "Friends Meeting" (DC Friends Meeting, 1965), 3; Receipt Book, Folder 236, APP; CAP, 65; Alice Paul, interview by Marjory Nelson, 41.
2. CAP, 66, 327–28; AP to Gertrude Hunter, 16 October 1914, Reel 13.
3. CAP, 66–68; 1913 Procession Program, Folder 239, APP; Biographical Notes, Folder 671, Elsie M. Hill Papers, Vassar College; Receipt Book, Folder 236, APP; "Elizabeth Kent," 6–7 (see chap. 6, n. 68).
4. CAP, 66–69; Katzenstein, *Lifting the Curtain*, 49–50; Receipt Book, Folder 236, APP.
5. Irwin, *Story of Alice Paul*, 20 (see intro., n. 7); CAP, 68.
6. Dennett to AP, 16 December 1912; Lewis to AP, 17 December 1912, both Reel 1.
7. AP to Board, 16 December 1912, Reel 1.
8. Ibid.
9. Mary Ware Dennett to AP, 18 and 30 December 1912, Reel 1; Receipt Book, Folder 236, APP.
10. Lewis to AP, 17 December 1912 and 1 January 1913; AP to Benedict, 31 December 1912, all Reel 1; AP to Board, 16 December 1912.
11. AP to Benedict, 31 December 1912.
12. "Shape Plans for Mammoth Parade," *WJ*, 11 January 1913, 9; AP to Dennett, 6 January 1913, Reel 1; Irwin, *Story of Alice Paul*, 22; 1913 photo available at hdl.loc .gov/loc.pnp/hec.02087, LC.
13. "Shape Plans," *WJ*, 9, 15; "Philadelphia Girl Suffrage Dynamo," *Philadelphia Record*, 26 January 1913, UPA; AP to Dennett, 6 January 1913, Reel 1; CAP, 289.
14. "Shape Plans," *WJ*, 15; Receipt Book, Folder 236, APP; Winifred Mallon, "Went on Hunger Strike" [NY] *Morning Telegraph*, 11 November 1917.

15. The stenographers' impressions are, sadly, lost to us. CAP, 78–79; AP to Dennett, 6 January 1913; Gardener to Dennett, 6 January 1913; and George Bowerman to LB, 3 February 1913, all Reel 1. "Philadelphia Girl," *Philadelphia Record*; "Beehive of the Suffragist Hums," *NY World*, 26 January 1913, Reels 166, NWPP I.

16. Mallon, "Hunger Strike"; "Philadelphia Girl," *Philadelphia Record*; AP to Dennett, 11 January 1913, Reel 1; Irwin, *Story of Alice Paul*, 22–23.

17. Barr to Madam, 10 January 1913; AP to Barr, 11 January 1913; Hourwich to Head, 17 February 1913; AP to Hourwich, 23 February 1913, all Reel 1. Mary U. Foster Baughman, "The Day 'Those Creatures' Shook a City" (Unpub., 1963), Folder 279, APP; Rebecca Hourwich Reyher, "Search and Struggle for Equality and Independence," interview by Amelia Fry and Fern Ingersoll, n.p., SOHP, http://bancroft.berkeley.edu/ROHO/projects/suffragist/.

18. Irwin, *Story of Alice Paul*, 16, 23–26; Gardener to Dennett, 6 January 1913.

19. Forrest to Shaw, 23 November 1913, Reel 33, NAWSA.

20. Caroline Lexow to AP, 23 December 1912; Marion Townsend to AP, 26 December 1912; AP to Hooker, 6 January 1913; AP to Hooker, 12 February 1913; Katzenstein to AP, 6 January 1913; Ruth Verlenden to AP, n.d.; Lowenburg to AP, n.d.; and AP to McCulloch, 7 January 1913, all Reel 1.

21. AP to Lewis, 20 January 1913; Lewis to AP, 3 January 1913, both Reel 1.

22. Lewis to AP, 17 December 1912; 1, 7, and 30 January 1913, all Reel 1.

23. "Motive for Pageant," *WP*, 13 January 1913; Gardener to Dennett, 6 January 1913; Elnora Folkmar to AP, 10 February 1913; Shaw to State Presidents, 30 December 1912, all Reel 1.

24. Dennett to AP, 4 January 1913, Reel 1.

25. AP to Dennett, 6 January 1913, Reel 1.

26. Shaw to AP, 22 January 1913, Reel 1.

27. McCormick to AP, 24 January 1913; AP to McCormick, 28 January 1913, both Reel 1.

28. AP to Elizabeth Hyde, 3 February 1913; AP to Dennett, 11 January 1913; Smith to AP, 8 February 1913; Meeting Chair to Ottenberg, 28 January 1913; AP to Agnes Ryan, 13 January 1913; and Harry O. Hill to AP, 20 February 1913, all Reel 1; CAP, 132, 323; "Suffragists Plan Big Reception," *WP*, 26 February 1913.

29. Louise Taylor-Jones to AP, 7 February 1913, Reel 1; Ellen Maury Slayden, *Washington Wife* (New York: Harper & Row, 1963), 194; "Suffragists Plan," *WP*.

30. Lucy G. Barber, *Marching on Washington* (Berkeley: University of California Press, 2002), 4–5; 12; 27; 43; 45; 231, n. 6.

31. Lumsden, *Rampant Women*, 78–79 (see chap. 6, n. 48).

32. Constance McLaughlin Green, *Washington* (Princeton, NJ: Princeton University Press, 1962), 35, 186, 313.

33. AP to Dennett, 6 January 1913, Reel 1; S. Doc. 63-1-#53 (1913), "Suffrage Parade Hearings," at 131–32, 136–38.

34. S. Doc. 63-1-#53 (1913), at 132.

35. Ibid., at 441–42.

36. Ibid., at 451; "Women Scorn Danger," *WP*, 6 January 1913; "City Short of Police," *WP*, 9 January 1913; Sylvester to AP, 9 January 1913, Reel 1; "Avenue for Pageant," *WP*, 10 January 1913.

37. "Avenue for Pageant," *WP*; Dennett to AP, 3 February 1913; Shaw to AP, 24 February 1913, both Reel 1.

38. Dennett to AP, 3 and 19 February 1913; AP to Dennett, 6 and 25 February 1913, all Reel 1.

39. AP to Jones, 2 and 26 January 1913; AP to Dennett, 11 January 1913; Jones to AP, 20 January 1913; AP to Katzenstein, 25 January 1913, all Reel 1.

40. AP to Jones, 26 January 1913.

41. Hunt to AP, January 1913; AP to Blackwell, 15 January 1913, both Reel 1.

42. Constance McLaughlin Green, *The Secret City* (Princeton, NJ: Princeton University Press, 1967), 156–69; Gardener to Blackwell, 14 January 1913; Dennett to AP, 14 January 1913, both Reel 1.

43. AP to Blackwell, 15 January 1913; CAP, 133.

44. AP to Blackwell, ibid.; AP to Dennett, 15 January 1913; Blackwell to AP, 23 January 1913; and AP to Blackwell, 26 January 1913, all Reel 1; Dennett to AP, 14 January 1913.

45. Hamm, *Quakers in America*, 170–71; AP Penn thesis, 144–45, 254–63 (see chap. 6, n. 59).

46. Graham, *Woman Suffrage*, 22–24 (see chap. 6, n. 30); Suzanne M. Marilley, *Woman Suffrage and the Origins of Liberal Feminism* (Cambridge, MA: Harvard University Press, 1996), 175–78.

47. Graham, ibid.

48. Rosalyn Terborg-Penn, *African American Women in the Struggle for the Vote, 1850–1920* (Bloomington: Indiana University Press, 1998), 89–92; Green, *Secret City*, 169; Jacqueline M. Moore, *Leading the Race* (Charlottesville: University of Virginia Press), 158–59, 191–93, 202–4.

49. Beard to AP, January 1913, cited in Sidney R. Bland, "New Life in an Old Movement," *Records of the Columbia Historical Society* (1971–72): 666.

50. Marie I. Hardwick to Glenna S. Tinnin, 23 January 1913; AP to Hardwick, 28 January 1913; Nellie M. Quander to AP, 17 February 1913; AP to Quander, 23 February 1913, all Reel 1. "Politics," and "Suffrage Paraders," *The Crisis*, April 1913, 267, 296; Logan to Emily Howland, 10 February 1913, and Gillett to Howland, 5 February 1913, both Reel 8, Howland Papers, Cornell Archives.

51. E. M. Gillett to Shaw, 16 April 1913, "Financial Records," Reel 124, NWPP I.

52. Caroline Reilly to LB, 28 and 30 January 1913; Belmont to Tinnin, 15 February 1913; and Belmont to AP, 3 and 6 January 1913, all Reel 1.

53. Margaret Finnegan, *Selling Suffrage* (New York: Columbia University Press, 1999), 2, 111–38; Gillett to Shaw, 16 April 1913, "Financial Records," Reel 124, NWPP I.

54. AP to Laura Crozer, 7 February 1913; AP to Inaugural Committee, 23 January 1913; Wm. C. Eustis to AP, 24 January 1913; Robt. Shaw Oliver to Hon. George Sutherland, 25 January 1913; Wm. C. Eustis to AP, 25 January 1913; Wm. S. Riley to AP, 27 January 1913; AP to J. W. Wilmuth, 29 January 1913; and J. O. Johnston to Anna Jenness-Miller, 14 February 1913, all Reel 1.

55. "Urge Taft to Assist," *WP*, 5 February 1913; "Suffragists Want Guard," [No ID], Reel 166, NWPP I.

56. S. Doc. 63-1-#53, at vi, 132–35, 140–41, 116, 232–34, 452.

57. Slayden, *Washington Wife*, 194; "Negro Recruits Put Hikers in Quandary," *NY Sun*, 27 February 1913; "Just Like the Men!" *NY Tribune*, 1 March 1913; and "Wilson Message Taken from Angry Pilgrims," *NY Tribune*, 28 February 1913, all Reel 166, NWPP I. "Throngs Greet Pilgrims' Entry," *WP*, 1 March 1913.

58. S. Doc. 63-1-#53, at 125–26; "Throngs Greet," *WP*.

59. S. Doc. 63-1-#53, at 118–20, 133–34; CAP, 76–77; Eliz. Rogers to AP, 5 March 1913, Reel 2.

60. Slayden, *Washington Wife*, 194; "Throngs Greet," *WP*; "Suffragists Take City for Pageant," *WP*, 2 March 1913; Political Equality League to Shaw, 28 February 1913; and Hill to AP, February 1913, both Reel 1.

61. "5000 Women in Suffrage Parade," *Baltimore Sun*, 4 March 1913.

62. NAWSA to AP, 28 February 1913, Reel 1; "Colored Women to March," *WP*, 2 March 1913.

63. "Illinois Women Feature Parade," *Chicago Tribune*, 4 March 1913, 3; Wanda A. Hendricks, "Ida B. Wells Barnett," in Marjorie Spruill Wheeler, ed., *One Woman, One Vote* (Troutdale, OR: NewSage Press, 1995), 269; 1913 Procession program, 18 (see n. 3).

64. "Suffrage Parade Will Form," *WP*, 2 March 1913; CAP, 77; Annual Report draft, 1913, Reel 87, NWPP I.

65. "Suffrage Parade," ibid.; Annual Report, ibid.; S. Doc. 63-1-#53, at 115, 609–10; "300 Women Hurt in Parade Crush," *NY Sun*, 4 March 1913, Reel 59, NAWSA.

66. 1913 Procession Program (see n. 3).

67. Lumsden, *Rampant Women*, 70–71, 86–90; Mayhall, *Militant Suffrage*, 57, 84, 89–90 (see chap. 4, n.2).

68. Dennett to AP, 26 February 1913, Reel 1; "Suffrage Parade," *WP*; S. Doc. 63-1-#53, at 609–10.

69. S. Doc. 63-1-#53, at 496–99; "5000 Women in Suffrage Parade," *Baltimore Sun*.

70. S. Doc. 63-1-#53, at 121, 155–56.

71. S. Doc. 63-1-#53, at 69–70, 498–99; Mallon, "Hunger Strike" (see n. 14 above).

72. S. Doc. 63-1-#53, at 15, 27, 35, 49, 72, 113, 375, 342, 471; Baughman (see n. 17 above).

73. S. Doc. 63-1-#53, at 176, 275, 376, 742; "300 Women Hurt," *NY Sun*.

74. S. Doc. 63-1-#53, at 27, 66–68, 224, 279, 291, 461, 465, 508, 509; "Women Battle Hostile Mobs in Capital Parade," *NY Tribune*, 4 March 1913, Reel 166, NWPP I.

75. Baughman (see note 17); "300 Women Hurt"; S. Doc. 63-1-#53, at 24, 41, 45, 69, 72–73, 456, 467–68.

76. Shaw quoted in "Say They were Mobbed," *NYT*, 5 March 1913; S. Doc. 63-1-#53, at 26, 37, 41, 116, 288, 460, 508.

77. S. Doc. 63-1-#53, at 24, 28, 130, 504; "5,000 Women March, Beset by Crowds," *NYT*, 4 March 1913, 4–5; CAP, 78.

78. "Barefooted Women in Gauze, Despite Cold," *WP*, 4 March 1913, 10; "5,000 Women," *NYT*.

79. *The Crisis*, April 1913, 297; Bertha Pitts Campbell, interview by AF, 16 September 1981, 3; "300 Women Hurt," *NY Sun*.

80. Baughman; "Howling Mobs Jeer at Women Marchers" *[Charleston, SC] News and Courier*, 4 March 1913, 1; "Mrs. Blatch Calls Police Inefficient," *NYT*, 6 May 1912, Reel 166, NWPP I; "Censure for the Police," *Chicago Tribune*, 4 March 1913; "Wilson Sworn in as President," *NYT*, 5 March 1913, 2.

81. Mallon, "Hunger Strike" (see n. 14 above).

CHAPTER 8

1. Linda Lumsden, "Beauty and the Beasts," *Journalism & Mass Communication Quarterly* 77-3 (Autumn 2000): 595–96.

2. "Woman's Beauty, Grace and Art Bewilder the Capital" and "100 Are in Hospital," *WP*, 4 March 1913; "300 Women Hurt" (see chap. 7, n. 65); "Women Battle Hostile Mobs in Capital Parade," *NY Tribune*, 4 March 1913, Reel 166, NWPP I; Lumsden, "Beauty," 598–99.

3. Lumsden, "Beauty," 598–602; "Mobs at Capital Defy Police," *Chicago Tribune*, 4 March 1913; "Women's Beauty," *WP*.

4. Lumsden, "Beauty," 598–602; "Mobs," *Chicago Tribune*.

5. "Parade Quiz Is Coming," *Chicago Daily News*, 4 March 1913; Lumsden, "Beauty," 597–98.

6. "Women in Protest Against Police," *Stevens Point Daily Journal*, 5 March 1913; "Paraders Protest Police Conduct," *NY Tribune*, 5 March 1913, Reel 166, NWPP I; AP, "Tell What You Saw Yourself," *WJ*, 22 March 1913, 89; Shaw to AP, 7 March 1913, Reel 2; "Senators Denounce Insults to Paraders," *NY Tribune*, 10 March 1913; "Parade Struggles On to Victory," *WJ*, 8 March 1913, 78.

7. Susan Fitzgerald to AP, 4 March 1913; Shaw to AP, 6 March 1913, all Reel 2.

8. Lumsden, "Beauty," 596; "Police Must Explain," *WP*, 6 March 1913.

9. AP to Lewis, 21 March 1913, Reel 2; CAP, 80–81; "Begin Police Grill," *WP*, 5 March 1913.

10. "Begin Police Grill," *WP*; S. Doc. 63-1-#53 (1913), at 39–41, 94, 131–35, 166–67, 537; "Chief Blames Men," *WP*, 9 March 1913, 1; "Senators Denounce Insults," *NY Tribune*, 10 March 1913.

11. Some accounts claim Sylvester lost his job over the parade debacle. He retired under pressure in 1915; "Chief Sylvester Out," *NYT*, 6 March 1915; "Begin Police Grill," *WP*; S. Doc. 63-1-#53 (1913), at xv–xvi.

12. Linda G. Ford, *Iron-Jawed Angels: The Suffrage Militancy of the National Woman's Party, 1913–1920* (Lanham, MD: University Press of America, 1991), 283; Woodrow Wilson, *Constitutional Government* (New York: Columbia University Press, 1908), 68.

13. CAP, 92.

14. John Milton Cooper, *Woodrow Wilson* (New York: Knopf, 2009), 29, 69, 98, 174, 252; Baker, *Sisters*, 186 (see intro., n. 3).

15. AP to Lewis, 21 March 1913.

16. "Too Busy for Women," *WP*, 18 March 1913; Doris Stevens, *Jailed for Freedom* (New York: Schocken Books, 1976), 22–23; AP to "Dear Suffragist," 18 March 1913, Reel 2.

17. Shaw to AP, 21 March 1913; AP to Belmont, 21 March 1913; Lewis to AP, 23 March 1913; Shaw to Executive Committee, 27 March 1913, all Reel 2; "Suffragist Army Divided," *Philadelphia Record*, 26 March 1913.

18. LB to AP, 28 March 1913, Reel 2.

19. Irwin, *Story of Alice Paul*, 18 (see intro., n. 7); LB to AP, 28 March 1913, Reel 2.

20. *HWS*, 275; "Impressive March of Suffrage 531," *NYT*, 8 April 1913, 7.

21. Harriet Laidlaw to AP, 11 April 1913, Reel 2; "Women Win Point," *WP*, 8 April 1913; Petitions Comm. to Blatch, 21 March 1913, Reel 1 and "1914 Report," Reel 87, both NWPP I.

22. "Impressive March," *NYT*; "Women Win Point," *WP*; Laidlaw to AP, ibid.

23. "Votes for Women Fought by Women," *Atlanta Constitution*, 20 April 1913; Shaw to AP, 15 April 1913, Reel 2.

24. "Hearings before the Committee on Woman Suffrage" (Washington, DC: Government Printing Office, 1913), 19 April 1913, 5–6, 7, 17.

25. "Federal Work the Economical Way," *SUFF*, 15 November 1913, 4.

26. David E. Kyvig, *Explicit and Authentic Acts* (Lawrence: University Press of Kansas, 1996), 192–94.

27. Kyvig, *Explicit and Authentic*, 213, 234.

28. Rogers to AP, 5 March 1913; Dennett to Editor, 25 April 1913, both Reel 2; Blatch to AP, 26 August 1913, Reel 1, NWPP I.

29. Dennett to Editor, 25 April 1913, Reel 2.

30. CAP, 100–101.

31. CAP, ibid.; AP to NAWSA Board, 16 April 1913, Reel 2; "1914 Report," 10; AP to Dennett, 1 April 1913, Reel 2; AP to Rheta Childe Dorr, 13 May 1913, and AP to Dennett, 24 June 1913, both Reel 3.

32. Ellen H. E. Price to AP, 3 June 1913; AP to Price, 4 June 1913; AP to Blackwell, 7 May 1913; AP to Beard, 13 May 1913, all Reel 3.

33. *HWS*, 626; AP to Beard, 13 May 1913, Reel 3; "Senators for Suffrage," *NYT*, 15 May 1913; "Suffrage Wins in Senate Committee," *NY Tribune*, 14 June 1913.

34. "Burying a Heroine," *WJ*, 21 June 1913, 196; Dennett to AP, 21 April 1913, Reel 2; AP to Katharine McCormick, 5 May 1913, Reel 3.

35. AP to Margaret Newlin, 10 May 1913, Reel 3; AP to Jane Wells Schooley, 27 August 1976, AF files.

36. AP to Beard, 13 May 1913, Reel 3; AP to "Dear Suffragist," 18 March 1913; Laidlaw to LB, 17 May 1913, Reel 3; AP to Vernon, 21 April 1913, Reel 2.

37. AP to Helen Paul, 8 July 1913; Shaw to AP, 1 May 1913, both Reel 3.

38. Marion B. Cothren to LB, late July 1913 and LB to Cothren, 2 August 1913, both Box 1, Folder 1, NWPP III; AP to Newlin, 10 May 1913, and Edward Burns to LB, 23 May 1913, both Reel 3.

39. AP to Harriet Upton, 21 June 1913, Reel 3; Tickner, *Spectacle*, 141–47 (see chap. 3, n. 49).

40. H. Laidlaw to Emma Brooks, 8 July 1913; Dennett to AP, 1 July 1913; AP to Hill, 2 July 1913; Sarah Elliott to AP, 24 June 1913; AP to Katzenstein, 8 July 1913; and AP to HP, 8 July 1913, all Reel 3.

41. M. A. Fraser to "Anyone," 18 July 1913, and Dennett to AP, 21 July 1913, both Reel 3; "All in Readiness for Suffrage Plea," *Washington Evening Star (WES)*, 30 July 1913.

42. "Heavy Rain and Electric Storm Hits City," *WES*, 30 July 1913; "Capital's Storm Losses High," *WES*, 31 July 1913.

43. "Capital's Storm," *WES*; Katharine H. Adams and Michael L. Keene, *Alice Paul and the American Suffrage Campaign* (Champaign: University of Illinois Press, 2007), 99.

44. Christopher M. Davis, "Flow of Business," July 2005, senate.gov/reference.

45. 63 Cong. Rec. 155 (1913), 15–46.

46. "Nation's Women Petition Senate for the Ballot," *WES*, 31 July 1913; "Suffragists Are Given Hearing by Gallant Senate," *Titusville (PA) Herald*, 1 August 1913; "1914 Report," 12.

47. Stevens, *Jailed for Freedom*, 11; Irwin, *Story of Alice Paul*, 24.

48. LB to AP, 28 March 1913; LB to Dr. Harvey Wiley, 24 July 1913; LB to Mrs. B. D. Hasbrouck, 15 July 1913, both Reel 3; Mead, *How the Vote*, 117–18 (see chap. 6, n. 19).

49. Jennifer M. Ross-Nazzal, *Winning the West for Women* (Seattle: University of Washington Press, 2011), 136–38, 143–45; AP to Emma Smith DeVoe, 24 June 1913, Reel 3; AP to James Laidlaw, 21 August 1913, Reel 4.

50. "National Women Meet," *WES*, 13 August 1913; "Ovation by Audience Given Miss Addams," *WES*, 16 August 1913; "Program," 14 August 1913, Reel 4.

51. "Women Plead for House Committee," *WES*, 14 August 1913.

52. AP to Dorr, 13 May 1913, and AP to HP, 19 June 1913, both Reel 3; AP to Jessie Hardy Stubbs, 25 September 1913 (2), both Reel 4.

53. AP to Dorr, ibid.; Dorr to AP, 26 August 1913, and AP to Dorr, 3 September 1913, both Reel 4; AP to Beard, 30 October 1913, Reel 5; "Subscription Price," *SUFF*, 6 December 1913, 27.

54. AP, "Foreword," and LB, "A Federal Amendment Now," *SUFF*, 15 November 1913, 1, 3.

55. "Report on Congressional Work," *SUFF*, 6 December 1913, 39; AP to Joan Wickham, 24 September 1913, Reel 4; Tusan, *Women Making News*, 2–3 (see chap. 3, n. 80); Belinda A. Stillion Southard, *Militant Citizenship: Rhetorical Strategies of the National Woman's Party, 1913–1920* (College Station: Texas A&M University Press, 2011), 100.

56. AP to Ada James, 2 October 1913, Reel 4; Dennett to Lewis, 23 May 1913, Reel 3; "Program, November 15 to 22," *SUFF*, 15 November 1913, 8; "Program for Week," *SUFF*, 22 November 1913, 10.

57. Dennett to AP, 30 October 1913, Reel 5; AP to Florence Macauley, 10 July 1913, Reel 3; Mabel Vernon to AP, 15 October 1913, Reel 5; Rheta Dorr, "Mrs. Pankhurst," *SUFF*, 22 November 1913, 14.

58. Shaw to LB, 19 November 1913, Reel 5; "Lucy Burns to Be Courted for Chalking," *Waterloo Times-Tribune*, 21 November 1913; Bland, "Never Quite," 9.

59. LB to Shaw, 21 November 1913, Reel 5.

60. Dorr, Mrs. Pankhurst; "President Decides Case," *NYT*, 21 October 1913; "Congressional Union Campaign," *SUFF*, 29 November 1913, 18, 19; Dennett to AP, 30 October 1913, Reel 4.

61. HP to AP, 17 November 1913, Reel 5.

62. "Oil on the Waters," *WJ*, 29 November 1913, 380; "Minutes," *45th Annual Report of NAWSA,* 107, Reel 58, NAWSA; "See Victory Near at Hand," *WJ*, 6 December 1913, 392.

63. "See Victory," *WJ*; Catt and Nettie Rogers Shuler, *Woman Suffrage and Politics* (New York: Scribner's, 1926), 244; "Budget Overawes Woman Suffragists," *NY Tribune*, 30 November 1913, Reel 166, NWPP I.

64. Katzenstein, *Lifting the Curtain*, 114 (see chap. 6, n. 17); *HWS*, 381; "Facts for Delegates," Convention 1913, Reel 58; "Miss Paul Then Presented Her Report," Reel 32; Treasurer's Statement, 1913–14, Reel 33, all NAWSA.

65. "Minutes," NAWSA Convention, 106; "Suffrage Congress Would See Wilson," *NYT*, 4 December 1913; *HWS*, 397.

66. "A Suffrage Delegation," *SUFF*, 13 December 1913, 37–38; "The President and the Suffragists," *Literary Digest*, 20 December 1913, 1209–10.

67. "Miss Paul Then" (see n. 64); "Suffragists Camp on Wilson's Trail," *NYT*, 6 December 1913.

68. "Miss Paul Then."

CHAPTER 9

1. Jacqueline Van Voris, *Carrie Chapman Catt: A Public Life* (New York: Feminist Press, 1987), 30; Mary Gray Peck, *Carrie Chapman Catt* (New York: H. W. Wilson, 1944), 58; Mead, *How the Vote*, 64–66, 88 (see chap. 6, n. 19).

2. Van Voris, *Catt*, 43, 50; *HWS*, 8–9; Peck, *Carrie*, 239.

3. Van Voris, *Catt*, 57–59; Robert Booth Fowler, *Carrie Catt: Feminist Politician* (Boston: Northeastern University Press, 1986), 22.

4. "Mrs. Catt Returns," *NY Sun*, 20 September 1913, Reel 167, NWPP I; *HWS*, 372.

5. "Miss Paul Then Presented Her Report," Reel 32, NAWSA; Peck, *Carrie*, 239.

6. CAP, 115; Beard to AP, 20 November 1913; AP to Lewis, 4 November 1913, both Reel 5.

7. "Miss Paul Then."

8. "Miss Paul Then"; *HWS*, 381.

9. "Miss Paul Then."

10. Ibid.; *HWS*, 381; *45th Annual Report*, 114 (see chap. 8, n. 62); A. E. R., "CU Makes Fine Showing," *WJ*, 13 December 1913, 393; Elizabeth Evans, "The Point of Issue," 5, Reel 9; Katharine H. Hepburn to AP, 27 January 1914, Reel 33, NAWSA.

11. CAP, 102; Dennett to AP, 15 December 1913, Reel 6.

12. "Anna Howard Shaw," in *Notable American Women*, ed. Edward T. James et al. (Cambridge, MA: Harvard University Press), 2:276; Shaw to Lucy Anthony, April 1914, Shaw Papers, Reel 17, Women's Rights Collection.

13. *Current Opinion*, December 1915, quoted in Wil A. Linkugel and Martha Solomon, *Anna Howard Shaw: Suffrage Orator and Social Reformer* (Westport, CT: Greenwood, 1991), 12.

14. "At the Last Business Session," Reel 32; "Minutes," 9 December 1913, Reel 58; both NAWSA. Shaw to AP, 6 December 1913; LB to Shaw, 17 December 1913; AP to Dennett, 31 December 1913, all Reel 6.

15. Harriet Taylor Upton to AP, 20 December 1913; Dorr to LB, 30 December 1913; Lewis to AP, 11 December 1913, all Reel 6.

16. Shaw to Official Board, 18 December 1913, Reel 34, NAWSA.

17. Ibid.; Kristie Miller, *Ruth Hanna McCormick: A Life in Politics, 1880–1944* (Albuquerque: University of New Mexico Press, 1992), 85, 95.

18. Forrest to Shaw, 23 November 1913, Reel 33; Baker to Shaw, 14 December 1913, Reel 32, both NAWSA.

19. "Avert Suffrage Row," *WP*, 6 December 1913, Reel 167, NWPP I; Shaw to LB, 20 December 1913; LB to Shaw, 23 December 1913, both Reel 6.

20. "At the Last," 18 (see n. 14); Dennett to LB, 22 December 1913, Reel 6.

21. HSB to AP, 29 November 1913, and HSB to LB, 22 December 1913, both Reel 1, NWPP I.

22. Beard to AP, 2 December 1913, Reel 6; Stevens to LB, 30 December 1913, Reel 6.

23. McCormick to Shaw, 1 January 1914, Reel 33; Dennett to McCormick, 8 January 1914, Reel 32, both NAWSA.

24. Evans, "Point of Issue," 4; LB to Shaw, 3 January 1914, and AP to Lewis, 5 January 1914, both Reel 6; "Fair Friends Apart," *WP*, 3 January 1914; "Random Notes," 12 February 1914, 33–34, Reel 33, NAWSA.

25. AP to Lewis, 5 January 1914, Reel 6.

26. Ibid.; AP to Hooker, 6 January 1914; AP to Hepburn, 6 January 1914; AP to Page, 6 January 1914, all Reel 6.

27. Peter Geidel, "Alva E. Belmont" (PhD diss., Columbia University, 1993), 126–28.

28. Hepburn to AP and Hepburn to Hooker, both 15 January 1914; Beard to LB, 9 January 1914; AP to Beard, 9 January 1914, all Reel 6.

29. LB to Mrs. Benjamin [Mary Burns] Reiley, 7 January 1914; AP to Lewis, 8 January 1914, both Reel 6.

30. See esp. AP to Lewis, 8 January 1914.

31. "Opening Meeting," *SUFF*, 17 January 1914, 5–7.

32. Ibid.; Emily Perry to Shaw, 20 December 1913, Reel 6; "Executive Committee," *SUFF*, 10 January 1914, 2.

33. Antoinette Funk to Dennett, 13 January 1914, Reel 33, NAWSA; "Suffs Swap Hard Names," *NY Evening Mail*, 15 January 1914, Reel 167, NWPP I; "Fair Rivals," *WP*, 15 January 1914.

34. "Suffragist Rivals," *NYT*, 5 January 1914, Reel 167, NWPP I; "Suffs Swap," *NY Evening Mail*.

35. "Suffragists Clash," *NY Herald*, 4 January 1914; "Suffrage Clash Is Denied," *NY Sun*, 6 January 1914, both Reel 167, NWPP I; "Suffragist Rivals," *NYT*.

36. Shaw to Board, 14 January 1914, Reel 34, NAWSA; AP to Shaw, 17 January 1914, Reel 7.

37. "No 'Rift Within the Lute,'" *PL*, 20 January 1914, 14; Graham, *Woman Suffrage*, 87 (see chap. 6, n. 30); Shaw to Council, 22 January 1914, Reel 34; "Synopsis of Correspondence," 24–25, Reel 33, both NAWSA.

38. "Mrs. McCormick Says," 29 January, Reel 7; "'No War,' She Writes," *WP*, 29 January 1914.

39. Belmont to AP, 23 January 1914, and Belmont to LB, 20 February 1914, both Reel 7; AP to Belmont, 27 January 1914, Reel 113, NWPP I.

40. AP to LB, 25 January 1914, Reel 7; *PL*, "Dr. Shaw Ridicules Suffrage Threat," *PL*, 19 January 1914, 12; Page to Belmont, 29 January 1914, Reel 113, NWPP I; "Suffrage Battle On," 28 January 1914, UPA.

41. Hepburn to AP, 27 January 1914, and Belmont to Sara Algeo, 7 February 1914, both Reel 33, NAWSA; AP to Hepburn, 9 February 1914, Reel 7; Upton to Belmont, 31 January 1914, Reel 1, NWPP I.

42. Dennett to Paul, 7 February 1914, Reel 7; McCormick to Shaw, 3 February 1914, Reel 33, and Shaw to Ruth McCormick, 5 February 1914, Reel 34, both NAWSA.

43. DL to AP, 9 February 1914, and Gauthier to AP, 10 February 1914, both Reel 7.

44. "Random Notes," Reel 33, NAWSA.
45. Dennett to AP, 19 February 1914; AP to Hepburn, 14 February 1914; Beard to LB, February 1914, all Reel 7; Louise de Koven Bowen, *Growing Up with a City* (New York: Macmillan, 1926), 159; Barbara Sicherman, *Alice Hamilton* (Cambridge, MA: Harvard University Press, 1984), 173–74.
46. Shaw to Forrest, 31 March 1914, Reel 8.
47. CAP, 321.

CHAPTER 10

1. "Salutatory," *SUFF*, 15 November 1913, 6; "The President's Message," *SUFF*, 13 December 1913, 28; "The Powers of the President," *SUFF*, 17 January 1914, 36.
2. "Suffragists on Warpath," *NYT*, 12 January 1914, Reel 167, NWPP I; "Women Make Threat," *WP*, 12 January 1914.
3. Rebecca Edwards, *Angels in the Machinery: Gender in American Party Politics from the Civil War to the Progressive Era* (New York: Oxford University Press, 1997), 105–10; Mead, *How the Vote*, 12 (see chap. 6, n. 19); Jo Freeman, *We Will Be Heard: Women's Struggles for Political Power in the United States* (Lanham, MD: Rowman & Littlefield, 2008), 25, 35.
4. "Suffragists Lose in Rules Committee," *NYT*, 18 January 1914; Beard to AP, 15 January 1914, Reel 6.
5. Upton to DS, 16 January 1914; Mosshart to Stubbs, 21 January 1914; Glenn to Stubbs, 27 January 1914; Louis F. Post to NWP, 26 January 1914; Beard to LB, 17 February 1914, all Reel 7.
6. Beard to AP, 4 February 1914; Jane Potter to AP, 2 February 1914, both Reel 7; Monroe to AP/LB, 7 March 1914; Beard to LB, 8 March 1914, both Reel 8.
7. "Policy of Union," *WJ*, 31 January 1914, 35; "Mrs. Hepburn on the Union," *WJ*, 7 and 14 February 1914, 46, 54; Shaw letter, *WJ*, 14 February 1914, 54; "Lucy Burns Replies," *WJ*, 21 February 1914, 62–63.
8. LB to *Roanoke Times*, 10 March 1914, Reel 8; "Two Suffrage Committees," *NY Tribune*, 1 March 1914; Judson Welliver, "Suffrage, a Party Issue," *Washington Times*, 25 January 1914, both Reel 167, NWPP I.
9. LB to Caroline M. Cooper, 29 January; AP to Stubbs, 13 February; Stubbs to Mr. Clifford E. Parks, 28 January, all 1914, Reel 7; AP to Stubbs, 4 March 1914, Reel 8.
10. "Situation in Congress," *SUFF*, 31 January 1914, 2; "Situation in Congress," *SUFF*, 14 February 1914, 2.
11. "Blasts Suffrage Hopes," *NYT*, 5 February 1914; DS to Harriet Upton, 5 February; LB to Elizabeth Evans, 6 February; LB to Hon. Henry D. Clayton, 4 February, all 1914, Reel 7; "The Caucus Decision," *SUFF*, 7 February 1914, 2.
12. Lewis to Stubbs, 14 January 1914, Reel 6; Perry to Olive Hasbrouck, 20 January 1914, Reel 7; Perry to AP, 19 January 1914, Reel 7.

13. AP to Perry, 18 January; AP to Stubbs, 19 January, both 1914, Reel 7.

14. AP to Mary Lockwood, 19 January 1914, Box 1, Folder 2, NWPP III; Perry to AP, 20 January; AP to LB, 25 January, both 1914, Reel 7.

15. "Alice Paul," *Boston Journal*, 28 January 1914, UPA; Emily Perry to Shaw, 20 December 1913, Reel 6.

16. "'No War,' She Writes," *WP*, 29 January 1914; Anne E. Draper et al. to AP, 29 January; Florence Hedges et al. to AP, 31 January; Virginia Hitchcock to AP, 3 February, all 1914, Reel 7.

17. AP to Eunice Oberly, 6 March; AP to Hitchcock, 5 February; AP to Hitchcock, 10 February, all 1914, Reel 7.

18. Hepburn to AP, 15 January 1914, Reel 6; LB to AP, 23 January 1914, Reel 7.

19. AP to LB, 25 January; DS to Mary Kenney O'Sullivan, 20 January, both 1914, Reel 7; LB to Beard, 7 January 1914, Reel 6.

20. Beard to LB, 27 January; Robins to DS, 16 January; Hepburn to DS, 17 January; on fundraising, e.g., LB to Mrs. Toscan Bennett, 19 January, all 1914, Reel 7; "Working Women's Deputation," *SUFF*, 31 January 1914, 5.

21. "President Wilson Sees," *SUFF*, 7 February 1914, 7; "Wilson Receives Women," *Washington Times*, 2 February 1914; "Women Use Sharp Terms," *NYT*, 3 February 1914.

22. "President Wilson," *SUFF*; Brisbane to Belmont, 3 February 1914, Reel 113, NWPP I.

23. Emily Pierson to Stevens, 7 February; LB to Beard, 7 February, both 1914, Reel 7.

24. AP to LB, 18 February; Annie G. Porritt to AP, 8 February; Lewis to AP, mid-February; [Perry] to Lewis, 20 February, all 1914, Reel 7; AP to Upton, 9 March 1914, Reel 8.

25. Diana Martin, "Rest Cure Revisited," *American Journal of Psychiatry* (2007): 737–38; Lewis to LB, 23 February; AP to LB, 22 February, both 1914, Reel 7; Lewis to LB, 11 March 1914, Reel 8; AP to Lockwood, 22 February 1914, Box 1, Folder 2, NWPP III.

26. AP to Helen Paul, 26 February; Hill to AP, c. March 1; both 1914, Reel 7; Beard to AP, 12 March; Benedict to AP, 12 March, both 1914, Reel 8.

27. Beard to AP, 5 March 1914, Reel 8; "Fair Sex," *WP*, 4 March 1914; "Hearing," *SUFF*, 7 March 1914.

28. McCormick to Mrs. A. H. Potter, 6 May 1914, Reel 10; AP to Beard, 7 March 1914, Reel 8.

29. Christine A. Lunardini, *From Equal Suffrage to Equal Rights* (N.p.: Excel Press, 1986), 59; *SUFF*, 21 and 28 March 1914.

30. Lewis to LB, 11 March, Reel 8; LB to AP, 13 March 1914, Reel 8; Benedict to LB, 3 April 1914, Reel 9.

31. Funk to AP, 5 May 1914, Reel 9.

32. "Mayday," *SUFF*, 2 May 1914, 2; "Nation-Wide Demonstration," *SUFF*, 11 April 1914, 3.

33. "Greatest Suffrage Day," *SUFF*, 9 May 1914, 3; Helen to AP, 3 May 1914, Reel 9; "Suffrage Day," *NYT*, 3 May 1914, 1, 12; "Suffrage for Women," *San Antonio Light*, 3 May 1914, 3.

34. "Situation in Congress," *SUFF*, 11 April 1914, 2; "Stop Press News," *SUFF*, 9 May 1914, 1.

35. "The May Ninth Demonstration," *SUFF*, 18 April 1914, 5; "Bristow-Mondell Resolution Demanded," *SUFF*, 16 May 1914, 4–5; "Storm the Capitol," *WP*, 10 May 1914, 1; "Suffragists Ask Congress for Vote," *NYT*, 10 May 1914, 7; 1914 CU Annual Report, 25.

36. "Democratic Caucus," *SUFF*, 16 May 1914, 2; Stubbs to Blackwell, 12 June 1914, Reel 10.

37. AP to Hooker, 4 June 1914, Reel 10; AP to Benedict, 8 July 1914, Reel 11.

38. "Advisory Council," *SUFF*, 25 July 1914, 5.

39. AP to Hooker, 4 June; Boissevain to AP, 19 June; AP to Belmont, 16 June; Feickert to AP, 19 June, all 1914, Reel 10; "Advisory Council," *SUFF*, 22 August 1914, 3.

40. "Newport Conference," *SUFF*, 5 September 1914, 5–7; "Newport," *SUFF*, 12 September 1914, 5–7.

41. "Newport Conference," *SUFF*; "Chinese Tea House," *NYT*, 29 June 1914, 9; AP to Belmont, 3 September 1914, Reel 12.

42. "Newport Conference," *SUFF*.

43. AP to Beard, 18 August 1914, Reel 11.

44. "Program," *SUFF*, 22 August 1914, 6.

45. "Newport," *SUFF*, 12 September 1914.

46. Ibid.

47. Ibid.; "Putting Their Issue First," *SUFF*, 3 June 1916, 10.

48. "Newport"; AP to Lewis, 4 September 1914, Reel 12.

49. AP to Belmont, 3 September 1914, Reel 12; 1914 CU Annual Report, 59; *HWS*, 425–27.

50. AP to Lewis, 4 September; AP to Hooker, 4 September; Lewis to AP, 8 September; Kenney to AP, 25 September; AP to Caroline Katzenstein, 14 September, all 1914, Reel 12.

51. Stillion Southard, *Militant Citizenship*, 103–4 (see chap. 8, n. 55).

52. "Farewell Garden Party," *SUFF*, 19 September 1914, 4; "Still More Recruits," *SUFF*, 26 September 1914, 7.

53. AP to Lewis, 21 September; AP to Lewis, 22 September; Jane Pincus to AP, 13 October; AP to Margaret Whittemore, 12 October, all 1914, Reel 12; Catt, "Women's Votes," *NYT*, 8 October 1914.

54. AP to Belmont, 14 September; Allender to Mary H. Page, 23 September, both 1914, Reel 12; "Election Policy," *SUFF*, 26 September 1914, 4.

55. "Election Policy," ibid.

56. Beard to AP, 11 September; King to AP, October; both 1914, Reel 12.

57. AP to Lewis, 21 and 22 September; AP to Lewis, 7 October, all 1914, Reel 12.

58. Pincus to AP, 30 September; Stevens to AP, 7 October; Mickle Paul to AP, 14 October, all 1914, Reel 12; Lunardini, *From Equal Suffrage*, 66.

59. AP to Stevens, 6 October 1914, Reel 12; "To Our Opponents," *SUFF*, 3 October 1914, 3.

60. "California," *SUFF*, 24 October 1914, 6; Helena Weed to AP, 11 October; Pincus to AP, 13 October; Gertrude Hunter to AP, 15 October, all 1914, Reel 12; Mead, *How the Vote*, 134.

61. Whittemore to AP, 10 October; Lancaster to AP, 3 October; Pincus to AP, 13 October; AP to McCue, 4 October, all 1914, Reel 12.

62. AP to Stubbs, 15 October 1914, Reel 12; AP to Leonard, 21 October 1914, Reel 13; AP to Mrs. William B. Lloyd, 20 October 1914, Box 1, Folder 3, NWPP III.

63. Stubbs to AP, 3 November; Stevens to AP, 4 November; Weld[sic] to AP, 6 November; Pincus to AP, 4 November, all 1914, Reel 13.

64. CU 1914 Annual Report, 51; "Two States to Win Suffrage," *NYT*, 5 November 1914.

65. AP to Stevens, 9 November; Anna McCue to AP, 6 November, both 1914, Reel 13.

66. "Welcome Home," *SUFF*, 14 November 1914, 5; "Victorious Campaigners," *SUFF*, 21 November 1914, 5.

67. AP to Lewis, 9 November; AP to Lucretia Mitchell, 12 November, both 1914, Reel 13.

CHAPTER 11

1. LB to DS, 17 December 1914, Reel 14; "Rules Committee Permits Vote" and "Rules Committee Takes Action," *SUFF*, 19 December 1914, 2, 3; "National Prohibition" and "House Vote," *SUFF*, 26 December 1914, 2.

2. "Democratic Deputation," *SUFF*, 9 January 1915, 3; Wilson quoted in Ford, *Iron-Jawed Angels*, 64 (see chap. 8, n. 12).

3. "Women Still Hope to Convert Wilson," *Washington Times*, 7 January 1915; "President Refuses Aid to Suffragists," *NYT*, 7 January 1915, both Reel 167, NWPP I.

4. "Members" in 1915 Financial Records, Reel 126, NWPP I; "Annual Meeting," *SUFF*, 2 January 1915, 5; Annie G. Porritt, "Second Anniversary," *SUFF*, 16 January 1915, 7.

5. "Speaker Threatens to Eject Suffs," *NY Mail*, 12 January 1915; "Votes for Women Storm Congress," *NY Tribune*, 13 January 1915, both Reel 167, NWPP I; AP to Belmont, 16 January 1915, Reel 14.

6. "Woman's Movement," *SUFF*, 16 January 1915, 2.

7. "Suffrage Meets Defeat," *WP*, 12 January 1915; "Rival Suffrage Leaders," *PL*, 13 January 1915; Porritt, "Suffrage Debate," *SUFF*, 16 January 1915, 3.

8. "Reasons for Opposing Suffrage," *SUFF*, 23 January 1915, 3.

9. Ida Husted Harper, "Women Surprised," *PL*, 14 February 1915; "Gains for Suffrage," *NYT*, 14 February 1915, Reel 168, NWPP I.

10. AP to DS, 4 and 9 November 1914, both Reel 13.

11. LB to DS, 17 December 1914; DS to LB, 28 December 1914, both Reel 14; LB to Kent, 29 May 1915, Reel 16.

12. AP to Beard, 11 March 1915, Reel 15; AP to Tiffany Dyer, 5 February 1915, Reel 1, NWPP I.

13. AP to Belmont, 11 March; Belmont to AP, 26 February; Beard to AP, 5 March; AP to Beard, 11 March, all 1915, Reel 15.

14. Lewis to AP, 12 February and 2 March; AP to Lewis, 2 March, all 1915, Reel 15.

15. DS to AP, 25 January 1915, Reel 15; "Politicians in Danger," *NY Tribune*, 11 February 1915; "24 States Are Represented," *NY Herald*, 1 April 1915, both Reel 167, NWPP I.

16. "Suffragists to Push Bills," *WJ*, 23 January 1915, 32; AP to Arnold, 23 March 1915, Reel 16; AP, "The Anthony vs. the Shafroth Amendment," *SUFF*, 13 February 1915, 4; Anna [Annie] G. Porritt, "The Nationalizing of Suffrage Work," *SUFF*, 6 February 1915, 5.

17. "Suffrage Break Comes," *NY Sun*, 26 February 1915, Reel 167, NWPP I; "24 States," *NY Herald*; AP to DS, 7 March 1915, and DS to AP, 18 March 1915, both Reel 15.

18. AP to Edith Swift, 16 June 1915, Reel 17; AP to Beard, 11 March 1915, Reel 15.

19. AP to DS, 20 March; DS to AP, 22 March, both 1915, Reel 15.

20. "Beware of the Men," *NY Tribune*, 1 April 1915, Reel 167, NWPP I; "Results," *SUFF*, 3 April 1915, 5–6.

21. Stillion Southard, *Militant Citizenship*, 106 (see chap. 8, n. 55); Helena Hill Weed, "Federal Amendment," *SUFF*, 6 February 1915, 3.

22. Theresa Russell to AP, 14 February 1915; Mary J. Miller to AP, 17 February 1915, both Reel 15.

23. AP to Miller, 24 February 1915, Reel 15.

24. Ibid.

25. AP to Miller, 2 March 1915, Reel 15; LB to Leavitt Stoddard, 16 July 1915, Reel 17.

26. Alice Stone Blackwell, "Two National Programs," *WJ*, 19 June 1915, 194; "Coming Conventions," *SUFF*, 8 May 1915, 3; "Convention Plans," *SUFF*, 29 May 1915, 5.

27. Catt to AP, 12 April 1915, Reel 1, NWPP I.

28. AP to Catt, 15 April 1915, Reel 16.

29. Catt to Upton, 19 April 1915, Reel 33, NAWSA.

30. AP to LB, 5 May 1915, Reel 16; "A.S.B." [Alice Stone Blackwell], "An Unpractical Policy," *WJ*, 19 June 1915, 194; "WE ARE NOT," *SUFF*, 29 May 1915, 4.

31. AP to LB, 27 April 1915, Reel 16; Lewis to AP, 29 April 1915 and 1 May 1915, Folder 255, APP.

32. AP to LB, 4 and 10 May 1915, Reel 16.

33. Ibid.; Lewis to AP, 6 May 1915, Folder 255, APP; Tumulty to Lewis, 7 May 1915, Reel 16; "Suffrage Siege Fails," *WP*, 8 May 1915, 4.

34. "Demand," *SUFF*, 15 May 1915, 3; "Women's Siege Vain," *WP*, 7 May 1915, 1, 4; "Harassing the President," *WP*, 8 May 1915, 6; "Suffrage and Bad Manners," *Hackensack Record*, Reel 168, NWPP I; "Disavows Siege," *WP*, 8 May 1915, 4.

35. LB to Editor, *[D.C.] Star*, 8 May 1915, and LB to Editor, *[D.C.] Herald*, 7 May 1915, both Reel 16.

36. "President Wilson and Woman Suffrage," *NY Evening Post*, 7 May 1915, Reel 168, NWPP I; LB to Mr. I. P. Gillette, 10 May 1915; LB to Lewis, 10 May 1915, both Reel 16.

37. "President, Firm for Peace," *WP*, 11 May 1915, 1; Robert H. Zieger, *America's Great War* (Lanham, MD: Rowman & Littlefield, 2000), 22–25.

38. AP to LB, 10 May 1915.

39. AP to LB, 17 May 1915, Reel 16; Ford, *Iron-Jawed Angels*, 65–67.

40. AP to LB, 10 May 1915.

41. AP to LB, 17 May 1915; "Two Women Make Suffrage Appeal," *WP*, 18 May 1915, 5; Doris Faber, *Petticoat Politics* (New York: Lothrop, Lee & Shepard, 1967), 137; "Dark Plot Hatched," clipping, Reel 16 at 883; "Wilson Laughs at Suffragists," *NY Sun*, 18 May 1915, Reel 168, NWPP I.

42. "Mrs. Belmont Orders Siege," *NYT*, 28 [18] May 1915; Rogers, "'Heckling,'" *NY Tribune*, 26 May 1915, both Reel 168, NWPP I.

43. "Mrs. Belmont Orders," *NYT*; "Mrs. Catt Objects," *NY Call*, 20 May 1915; "Opposed to Militancy," *NY Call*, 23 May 1915, both Reel 168; "Decries Militant Tactics," *NY Tribune*, 19 May 1915, Reel 169, all NWPP I.

44. Catt to AP, 26 May 1915, Reel 1, NWPP I.

45. AP to Catt, 24 June 1915, Reel 1, NWPP I.

46. LB to AP, 28 May 1915; Emily Fuller to CU, 24 May 1915; Porritt to AP, 18 May 1915, Reel 16; C. M. Flanagan to AP [re Hepburn], 25 September 1915, Reel 19; Hepburn to AP, 15 June; DS to AP, 2 June, both 1915, Reel 17.

47. DS note, April 1915, Box 1, Folder 4, NWPP III; Dock to Catt, June 1915; Brannan and Rogers to "Members," 16 June 1915; Latimer to M. B. Dixon, June 1915, all Reel 17.

48. Jane Bliss Potter to AP, 18 June 1915, Reel 17.

49. "National Woman Suffrage," *SUFF*, 19 June 1915, 3; AP to LB, 18 and 24 June, 13 July 1915, all Reel 17.

50. "Miss Paul Leaves on Suffrage Tour," *Baltimore Star*, 29 July 1915, Reel 168, NWPP I; AP to LB, 6, 21, and 22 August 1915; DS to AP, 23 August 1915, all Reel 18.

51. Adams and Keene, *American Suffrage*, 103–4 (see chap. 8, n. 43).

52. "Suffrage at the Panama-Pacific Exposition," *SUFF*, 10 April 1915, 5.

53. AP to DS, 27 July 1915, Reel 1; "'Suffs' Hope for Big Results," *NY World*, 15 August 1915, Reel 169, both NWPP I.

54. "Convention," *SUFF*, 21 August 1915, 5; "Voters' Convention," *SUFF*, 25 September 1915, 5–6.

55. Shaw to Van Den Avend (circular), 24 July 1915, Reel 18; Sophie G. Meredith to Mrs. Otey, 28 September 1915, and Caroline E. Spencer to LB, 30 September 1915, both Reel 19; "Significance," *SUFF*, 2 October 1915, 4; "Women Vote Advocates," *San Francisco Bulletin*, 15 September 1915; "Tempest Today?," *Bakersfield Echo*, 16 September 1915, both Reel 169, NWPP I.

56. Southard, *Militant Citizenship*, 110; Field to LB, 28 September 1915, Reel 19.

57. "Sara Bard Field," SOHP, 303; Adams and Keene, *American Suffrage*, 106; "From Boston to New York," *SUFF*, 4 December 1915, 5.

58. Amelia Fry, "Along the Suffrage Trail," *American West* (January 1969), 16–25; CAP, 149; "Field," SOHP, 301; "Farewell to the Envoys," *SUFF*, 2 October 1915, 5; "Vote Crusaders Start East," *San Francisco Examiner*, 17 September 1915, Reel 169, NWPP I.

59. "Field," SOHP, 321, 330–34; "From San Francisco," *SUFF*, 9 October 1915, 5; Field, account for *SUFF*, 14 October 1915, Reel 19.

60. AP to Porritt, 8 October 1915, Reel 19; AP to Matilda Gardner, 26 October 1915; Ida Finney Mackrilke to Miss Latham, 29 October 1915, both Reel 20.

61. Anne Martin to AP, 4 November 1915, and Shaw to President, 5 November 1915, both Reel 20; "Wilson Indorses Woman Suffrage," *NYT*, 7 October 1915.

62. Shaw to Executive Council, 20 November 1915, Reel 21; Page to AP, 6 November 1915, Reel 20; "A. S. B." [Alice Stone Blackwell], "Two Contrasted Policies," *WJ*, 13 November 1915, 362; AP to Blatch, 24 November 1915, Reel 1; "Report of Membership," 4 December 1915, Reel 88, both NWPP I.

63. "Women Voters' Envoys," *SUFF*, 27 November 1915, 3; "From Boston," *SUFF*, 4 December 1915, 5.

64. "Envoys Present Petition," *SUFF*, 11 December 1915, 4–5; "Field," SOHP, 330–32; "Suffragists Encouraged," *Philadelphia Record*, 8 December 1915, Reel 169, NWPP I.

65. "Hearing," *SUFF*, 23 December 1915, 5; *Woman Suffrage Hearings*, 16 December 1915 and 1 February 1916 (Washington, DC: Government Printing Office, 1916), 62–65.

66. LB to AP, 23 February 1914, Reel 7; AP to Beard, 7 March 1914, Reel 8; "The 'Little White House,'" *SUFF*, 6 November 1915, 5.

67. "Meeting," December 1915, Reel 22; Graham, *New Democracy*, 86 (see chap. 6, n. 30).

68. *HWS*, 453–55; CAP, 326.

CHAPTER 12

1. "Some Traditions," *SUFF*, 8 January 1916, 5; "Suffragists at Washington," *SUFF*, 4 March 1916, 5; Belmont to AP, 31 December 1915, Reel 22.

2. "National Headquarters," *SUFF*, 11 March 1916, 9; "Organization Work," *SUFF*, 15 January 1916, 7; Lewis to AP, 30 December; AP to Mrs. John Dewey, 31 December, both 1915, Reel 22.

3. Sara M. Evans and Harry Boyte, *Free Spaces* (New York: Harper & Row, 1986), 17–20.

4. Rebecca Hourwich Reyher and AF, "Search and Struggle," SOHP.

5. Note on AP to Lewis, 29 December 1915, Reel 22; *SUFF*, 11 March 1916; Lewis to AP, 5 March; Florence Boeckel to AP, 8 March, both 1916, Reel 24.

6. "Senate Report," *SUFF*, 15 January 1916, 4; *Evening Telegraph* in "Comments," *SUFF*, 15 January 1916; *CSM* in "Comments," *SUFF*, 22 January 1916, 5.

7. "The Political Situation," *SUFF*, 12 February 1916, 4.

8. "List of Members," 4 December 1915, Reel 88, NWPP I; AP to Vernon, 13 January 1916, Reel 23.

9. "Anniversary Meeting," *SUFF*, 29 January 1916, 5; "Organization Work," *SUFF*; AP to Lewis, 13 January 1916, Reel 23.

10. Catt to Martin, 30 December 1915, Reel 22; Catt to Executive Council, 12 January 1916, Reel 23; "Suffrage Rivals," *NY Tribune*, 25 February 1916, Reel 169, NWPP I.

11. Graham, *New Democracy*, 86 (see chap. 6, n. 30); DS to AP, 19 January 1916, Reel 23.

12. Florence Whitehouse to DS, 9 February 1916; Monroe to Martin, February 1916; Agnes Morey to LB, 19 February 1916, all Reel 24; Helen Bates to Catt, 6 January 1916, Reel 33, NAWSA.

13. "Kansas Organizes," *SUFF*, 5 February 1916, 3; "Texas Members Organize," *SUFF*, 29 January 1916, 3; Knoxville quote in "Tennessee CU Organized," *SUFF*, 12 February 1916, 7.

14. AP to Beard, 14 February; AP to Josephine Miller, 10 February; AP to Mrs. Cyrus Mead, 4 March; AP to Belmont, 6 March, all 1916, Reel 24; Katharine Fisher to Beard, 17 March 1916, Reel 25.

15. Belmont to Lewis, 24 January 1916, Reel 23; Marie Kennedy to AP, 22 March 1916, Reel 25.

16. AP to Clara Louise Rowe, 23 February 1916, Reel 24.

17. "Amendment Referred," *SUFF*, 19 February 1916, 3; "Judiciary Committee," *SUFF*, 1 April 1916, 5; Maud Younger, "Revelations of a Woman Lobbyist," *McCall's*, September 1919, 7.

18. "WPU Amalgamates with Union," *SUFF*, 12 February 1916, 6; DuBois, *HSB*, 189–91 (see chap. 6, n. 19); Blatch to Martin, 18 February 1916, Reel 24; Blatch to AP, 17 March 1916, Reel 1, NWPP I.

19. "The Next Move," *SUFF*, 18 March 1916, 7; Southard, *Militant Citizenship*, 15 (see chap. 8, n. 55); Adams and Keene, *American Suffrage Campaign*, 110 (see chap. 8, n. 43).

20. Blatch to AP, 7 March 1916, Reel 1, NWPP I.

21. The recently married Milholland used her maiden name for work. AP to Beard, 4 March; AP to Mrs. Nelson Whittemore, 2 March, both 1916, Reel 24; AP to Beard, 18 March 1916, Reel 25.

22. Beard to AP, 20 March 1916, Reel 24; AP to Beard, 24 March; Vernon to AP, 23 March; AP to Mrs. J. A. H. Hopkins, 25 March, all 1916, Reel 25; Linda J. Lumsden, *Inez* (Bloomington: Indiana University Press, 2004), 141–42.

23. "Woman's Party Organizes," *SUFF*, 8 April 1916, 7; "Conference," *SUFF*, 15 April 1916, 4–5.

24. "Conference," *SUFF*; "Suffragists' Hat in the Ring," *Washington Herald*, 8 April 1916, Reel 95.

25. Thelda Baehr to V. Arnold, 7 April 1916, Reel 26; Milholland to AP, 1916, Reel 36; Evanston IL editorial in "Comments," *SUFF*, 20 May 1916, 10.

26. Fanny Burke to AP, 19 April; Adele P. Blauvelt to AP, 20 April; AP to DS, 17 April, all 1916, Reel 26; Mary Blakeley to "Women Officers," 27 April 1916, Reel 27.

27. Mallon to AP, 18 and 19 April 1916, both Reel 26; LB to AP, 29 April 1916, Reel 27.

28. LB to AP, 29 April 1916, Reel 27.

29. *HWS*, 481–82; "Mrs. Catt," *Topeka State Journal*, 12 April 1916; "Club Women," *SF Chronicle*, 21 April 1916, both Reel 95; Ellis Meredith, "An Open Letter," *WJ*, 29 April 1916; Caroline Spencer to AP, 18 April 1916, Reel 26.

30. Mallon to AP, 18 and 26 April 1916, both Reel 26.

31. "Women Voters' Party," *Chicago Tribune*, 14 April 1916, Reel 95; AP to Margery Ross, 20 April 1916, Reel 26.

32. AP to Beard, 29 April; AP to DS, 4 May; AP to Whittemore, 9 May; AP to Mrs. Alden H. Potter, 5 May, all 1916, Reel 27; AP to Mrs. Harvey C. Garber, 15 May 1916, Reel 28.

33. Vernon to Martin, 21 May; AP to Nina Allender, 27 May; Martin to AP, 26 May; Ella Riegel [re Blatch] to AP, 28 May; Thelda Baehr to Arnold, 23 May; Hearst to "Dear Madam," 27 May, all 1916, Reel 28.

34. "Mrs. Catt Here," *Chicago Herald*, 1 June 1916, Reel 168, NWPP I; AP to Mrs. Annie Porritt, 29 May; AP to Martin, 29 May, both 1916, Reel 28.

35. "Woman's Party," *Chicago Tribune*, 6 June 1916, Reel 169, NWPP I; "Failure Is Impossible," *SUFF*, 3 June 1916, 12; Blackwell, "Not Miss Anthony's Policy," *WJ*, 27 May 1916.

36. "Woman's Party," *Chicago Tribune*; "1000 Guests," *Chicago Evening American*, 6 June 1916; Report of NWP Convention, 5 June 1916, Reel 28.

37. Belmont to AP, 1 May 1916, Reel 27; "Closing Sessions," *SUFF*, 17 June 1916, 5.

38. "Closing Sessions," *SUFF*; Report of NWP Convention, Reel 28; "Women Heckle," *Chicago Tribune*, 6 June 1916 (2), Reel 169, NWPP I.

39. "Closing Sessions," *SUFF*.

40. Ibid.

41. Sarah T. Colvin to "Mrs. Wolfe," 2 June 1916, Reel 28; "Peace Overtures," *Chicago Evening Post*, 1 June 1916, Reel 169, NWPP I; Photo, *Chicago Daily News*, 8 June 1916.

42. "Suffragists Invade Convention," *NYT*, 8 June 1916; "Suffrage 'Lobby,'" *Chicago Herald*, 6 June 1916, both Reel 169, NWPP I.

43. "Progressive and Republican Parties" and "Republican Suffrage Plank," *SUFF*, 10 June 1916, 2–3; Olympia Brown to Martin, 10 June 1916, Reel 29.

44. "One Issue, One Party," *Rocky Mountain News*, c. 16 April 1916; "Americanism," *SF Bulletin*, 26 April 1916, both Reel 95.

45. Rogers to LB, 13 June 1916, Reel 29; "The Ghost at the Feast," *Plain Dealer*, June 1916, Reel 95; *Chattanooga Times* in "Comments," *SUFF*, 10 June 1916, 4; *NYT* in "Comments," *SUFF*, 8 July 1916, 8; "91 Electoral Votes," *NYT*, 18 July 1916, Reel 169, NWPP I; LB to Ella Thompson, 16 June 1916, Reel 29.

46. "Women's Party Members Here," *St. Louis Globe-Democrat*, 13 June 1916, Reel 169, NWPP I; AP, "This Precious Summer," *SUFF*, 1 July 1916, 5; *WI State Journal* in "Comments," *SUFF*, 1 July 1916, 8; "Woman Suffrage Plank," *SUFF*, 24 June 1916, 3; "Call Suffrage Plank," *NYT*, 17 June 1916; "Suffragists Denounce Plank," 16 June 1916, both Reel 95.

47. AP, "This Precious Summer."

48. Anne Herendeen, "A New Leader," *Everybody's*, July 1916, 127; "Comments," *SUFF*, 15 July 1916, 7–8.

49. Vernon interview, 62 (see chap. 2, n. 11); "President Hears Appeal," *SUFF*, 8 July 1916, 7; Note on Memo 58599, 27 July 1916, WWP.

50. "Rising Tide," *SUFF*, 15 July 1916, 5; Katharine Fisher to AP, 6 July; AP to Julian T. Carr, 11 July, both 1916, Reel 29.

51. LB to Editor, 11 July 1916, Reel 29.

52. AP to Mrs. Eugene Gray, 4 July; LB to AP, 4 July, both 1916, Reel 29; CAP, 155; "Mr. Hughes," *SUFF*, 5 August 1916, 3; "Wilson to Lose," *Chicago Herald*, 3 August 1916, Reel 169, NWPP I.

53. "Campaign Plans," *SUFF*, 22 July 1916, 7; AP to Vernon, 21 August; AP to Milholland, 19 August; AP to Lewis, 7 August, all 1916, Reel 31.

54. AP to Hooker, 25 August; AP to Belmont, 22 August; Coleman du Pont to Belmont, 30 August, all 1916, Reel 31; "Suffragists Seek Fund," *NY Sun*, 5 August 1916, Reel 169, NWPP I.

55. Jane Burr to AP, 28 August; Whittemore to AP, 19 August, both 1916, Reel 31.

56. Alison Hopkins to AP, 29 August; AP to Hopkins, 29 August; AP to Lewis, 7 August, all 1916, Reel 31.

57. "Woman's Party Conference" and "President Wilson Writes," *SUFF*, 19 August 1916, 7–8.

58. AP to Clara L. Rowe, 1 July 1916, Reel 29; "'Don't Antagonize Us,'" *SUFF*, 26 August 1916, 5; "Women in Bitter Fight," *NY Tribune*, 23 August 1916; "Suffragists Attacked," *Concord NH Patriot*, 23 August 1916, both Reel 169,

NWPP I; AP to Ella Thompson, 20 September 1916, Reel 32; AP to Kathleen Taylor, 11 October 1916, Reel 34.

59. *HWS*, 496–99.

60. "President Wilson's Record," *SUFF*, 23 September 1916, 5; Editorials in *SUFF*, 16 September 1916, 5, 8; DuBois, *HSB*, 197.

61. *HWS*, 488–89; Graham, *New Democracy*, 86–89.

62. AP to Hazard, 26 August 1916, Reel 31.

63. A. S. B. [Alice Stone Blackwell], "The Woman Voter," *WJ*, 2 September 1916.

64. AP to Mrs. Lucius Cuthbert, 23 August 1916, Reel 1, NWPP I.

65. AP to Lillian Pray Palmer, 2 October 1916, Reel 33; AP to Mrs. Robert Stevenson and AP to Carrie Harrison, both 20 September 1916, Reel 32.

66. Milholland to AP, September 1916, Reel 32; "Itinerary," Reel 33; Mackrille to DS, 14 October 1916; DS to Amidon, 19 October 1916, both Reel 34.

67. Caroline Spencer to AP, 11 October; Pierce to AP, 20 October, both 1916, Reel 34; Brooke to Elizabeth, 15 October 1916, Reel 36.

68. "Attack on Campaigners," *SUFF*, 21 October 1916, 8–9; "Anti-Wilson Women Mobbed," *NY Tribune*, 20 October 1916, Reel 169, NWPP I.

69. Brooke to Miss Crocker, 21 October; [Hill] to Martin, 20 October, both 1916, Reel 34.

70. K. Taylor to AP, 27 September; AP to Margery Ross, 28 September; AP to Lewis, 27 September, all 1916, Reel 33.

71. AP to Hill, 20 September; AP to Riegel, 21 September, both 1916, Reel 32; Morey to AP, 30 September 1916, Reel 33; Amidon to DS, 24 October 1916, Reel 34.

72. Vernon to DS, 14 October 1916, Reel 34.

73. Milholland to AP and AP to Milholland, 16 October; AP to Milholland, 18 October; Hill to Milholland, 21 October; Milholland to AP and AP to Milholland, 23 October, all 1916, Reel 34.

74. Amidon to DS, 23 and 24 October 1916, Reel 34; "Milholland Faints," *LA Times*, 24 October 1916, sec. 2, 5; Lumsden, *Inez*, 158–64.

75. Vida Milholland to AP, 30 October 1916, Reel 35; Amidon to DS, 10 October 1916, Reel 33.

76. AP to Perry, 26 and 29 October; AP to Pierce, 27 October; AP to Eastman, 28 October; Perry to P, 29 October, all 1916, Reel 35.

77. Southard, *Militant Citizenship*, 116; Morey to AP, 12 October; DS to Hunkins, 14 October; Hill to AP, 12 October, all 1916, Reel 34.

78. "Woman's Party Orator," *Chicago Tribune*, 7 November 1916, Reel 169, NWPP I; "Last Minute Activities," *SUFF*, 11 November 1916, 4.

79. LB to AP, 3 November 1916, Reel 35; Bland, "'Never Quite,'" 4 (see chap. 4, n. 27).

80. "California in Doubt," *NYT*, 8 November 1916, 1; Whittemore to AP, 13 November; Blatch to Hill, November; Morey to AP, 15 November, all 1916, Reel 35; *NYT*, 14 November 1916, Reel 169, NWPP I.

81. AP to Morey, 17 November 1916, Reel 35.

82. "The Results," *SUFF*, 11 November 1916; "The Lesson," *SUFF*, 25 November 1916, 6.

83. Amidon to Martin, 15 December 1916, Reel 36; Cover, *SUFF*, 25 November 1916, 1.

84. "National Memorial Service," *SUFF*, 30 December 1916, 7–10; Lumsden, *Inez*, 174–77; Adams and Keene, *American Suffrage Campaign*, 114–15.

CHAPTER 13

1. "Ignoring," *SUFF*, 9 December 1916, 6; "Judiciary Committee," *SUFF*, 14 December 1916, 7.

2. AP to Wilson, 1 January; Wilson to Thomas Brahany, c. 2 January; AP to Brahany, 4 January; Wilson to Tumulty, c. 5 January, all 1917, Reel 209, WWP.

3. Tumulty to AP, 8 January 1917, Reel 37; "Memorial Resolutions," *SUFF*, 17 January 1917, 4–5.

4. Ibid.

5. Ibid.; Executive Committee Minutes, 5 January 1917, Reel 38.

6. DuBois, *HSB*, 138; "Dutch Women," *SUFF*, 16 December 1916, 3.

7. Lumsden, *Rampant Women*, 115 (see chap. 6, n. 48).

8. "Suffragists Wait at White House," *SUFF*, 17 January 1917, 7–8; Irwin, *Story of Alice Paul*, 202–4 (see intro., n. 7).

9. "President Ignores Pickets," *Washington Herald*, 11 January 1917, Reel 95; Hazel Hunkins Hallinan, "Memories of Alice Paul," interview by Amelia Fry, 20 May 1979, 31–32, AF; *WP*, 11 January 1917, 1, 5.

10. Stillion Southard, *Militant Citizenship*, 136–38 (see chap. 8, n. 55).

11. "'Mildly Hazing,'" *SF Bulletin*, 12 January 1917, Reel 169, NWPP I.

12. "Charge Suffragists," *NYT*, 17 January 1917, Reel 169, NWPP I; "Mrs. Carrie Chapman Catt," *WT*, 10 January 1917, Reel 95; Catt to Dr. Francis M. Lane, 14 February 1917, Reel 39.

13. Lucia McBride to AP, 11 January; Marjory [Whittemore] to AP, 10 January; TP to AP, 13 January, all 1917, Reel 37; AP to Grace M. Johnson, 23 January 1917, Reel 38.

14. Beard et al. to Executive Committee, 13 January; Ethel Adamson to AP, 11 January; Blatch to AP, 14 January, all 1917, Reel 37; Blatch to AP, 5 February 1917, Reel 2, NWPP I; AP to Eunice Brannan, 17 January; Gardner to Mrs. Colt, 18 January, both 1917, Reel 38.

15. AP to Lewis, 16 January; AP to Belmont, 15 January; AP to Lathrop, 16 January, all 1917, Reel 37.

16. Parker Alumnus File, CUA.

17. Harriet A. Curtiss to Pierce, 13 January; Sara Lefferts to AP, 11 January, both 1917, Reel 37; Agnes Chidlow to AP, 7 February 1917, Reel 38.

18. AP to Alice Dewey, 16 January; AP to Florence Hilles, 11 January; Katzenstein to AP, 15 January, all 1917, Reel 37; "Suffragists Wait" SUFF; " 'Suff' Pickets Shiver," *Washington Herald*, 12 January 1917, Reel 95.

19. Mary Church Terrell, *A Colored Woman in a White World* (New York: G. K. Hall, 1940/96), 313, 317.

20. "Fourth Week," *SUFF*, 7 February 1917, 4; "Silent Watch," *SUFF*, 17 February 1917, 4; AP to Mrs. C. M. Gates, 13 January; AP to Lewis, 16 January, both 1917, Reel 37.

21. "State Delegations," *SUFF*, 31 January 1917, 4; Florence Boeckel, "Reflections of a Picket," *SUFF*, 3 March 1917, 6.

22. Park to Martin, 22 February; Martin to Park, 28 February, both 1917, Reel 39.

23. AP to Colvin, 8 January; AP to K. Morey and AP to A. Morey, both 12 January, all 1917, Reel 37.

24. Blatch to Martin, 3 February; Rogers to AP, 6 February; Amidon to AP, 4 February, all 1917, Reel 38.

25. Joy Young to AP, 15 February 1917, Reel 39; Van Voris, *Catt*, 144 (see chap. 9, n. 1); Lunardini, *Equal Suffrage to Equal Rights*, 113 (see chap. 10, n. 29).

26. AP, "The Present Situation," *SUFF*, 7 February 1917, 6.

27. Dudley to AP, 8 February 1917, Reel 39; Membership Report, March 1917, Reel 88, NWPP I; Mary Beard, "Women and War Service," *SUFF*, 24 February 1917, 7.

28. AP to LB, 24 February 1917, Reel 39.

29. "National Conventions," *SUFF*, 24 February 1917, 10; "Women Go to Bed on Fire Escape," *WT*, 1 March 1917, Reel 95.

30. "Conventions," *SUFF*, 10 March 1917, 3–4.

31. "Rain Soaked Picket Line," *WP*, 5 March 1917, Reel 95; Wilson to Tumulty, c. 7 February 1917, Reel 89, WWP; Stevens, *Jailed for Freedom*, 79 (see chap. 8, n. 16).

32. "The Delegation," *SUFF*, 10 March 1917, 6.

33. "Misguided," *PL*, and "Latest Spasm," *Cincinnati Enquirer*, both 7 March 1917, Reel 169, NWPP I.

34. AP to DS, 9 February 1917, Reel 39; AP to Lillian Ascough, 27 April 1917, Reel 41; AP to Florence Harsh, 27 March, AP to Adamson, 24 March, both 1917, Reel 40.

35. Sarah L. Gossard to Brannan, 13 March; K. Morey to AP, 21 March; A. Morey to AP, 23 March; Adamson to AP, 23 March, all 1917, Reel 40.

36. CAP, 173; "The Capitol Welcomes Miss Rankin," *SUFF*, 7 April 1917, 7; "Miss Rankin's Stand," *WP*, 2 April 1917; Morey to AP, 4 April 1917, Reel 41.

37. "Suffrage Sentinels," *SUFF*, 7 April 1917, 5.

38. Zieger, *America's Great War*, 52–54 (see chap. 11, n. 37).

39. CAP, 175–77; Zieger, *America's Great War*, 55–56.

40. Norma Smith, *Jeannette Rankin: America's Conscience* (Helena: Montana Historical Society, 2002), 111–13.

41. "Why Not Self-Government?," *SUFF*, 7 April 1917, 6; "War," *SUFF*, 21 April 1917, 6.

42. "Rhode Island," *SUFF*, 21 April 1917, 6; *Journal* and *Sun* in "Comments," *SUFF*, 28 April 1917, 10–11.

43. "Suffrage Problem," *South Bend Times*, 25 April 1917, Reel 168, NWPP I; Ernestine Evans, "An Hour," *SUFF*, 14 April 1917; G. Foster, "Bad Manners," *WP*, 23 April 1917, Reel 95.

44. Wilson, *Constitutional Government*, 38 (see chap. 8, n. 12); Stephen Ponder, *Managing the Press: Origins of the Media Presidency, 1897–1933* (New York: St. Martin's, 1998), 78, 93–94.

45. Geoffrey R. Stone, *Perilous Times* (New York: Norton, 2005), 146–53; Ponder, *Managing the Press*, 94.

46. AP to Adamson, 23 April 1917, Reel 41; "Woman Voters War Asset," *WP*, 26 April 1917, Reel 95; Rheta Dorr, "April 26th Hearing," *SUFF*, 28 April 1917, 8–9.

47. Catt to Wilson, 7 May 1917, Reel 210, WWP.

48. Wilson to Catt, 8 May; Wilson to Edward W. Pou, 14 May, both 1917, Reel 210, WWP.

49. Mabel L. Sippy to Martin, 26 April; LB to Arnold, 22 April; DS to AP, 27 April, all 1917, Reel 41; AP to Mrs. F. R. Hazard, 4 May 1917, Reel 42.

50. "Suffrage Committee," *Washington Star,* 13 May 1917, Reel 95; "War Conference," *SUFF*, 19 May 1917, 7.

51. Catt to AP, 24 May; AP to K. Morey, 27 May; Thompson to AP, 3 June, all 1917, Reel 43.

52. "Florida," *SUFF*, 19 May 1917, 4; "Alabama," *SUFF*, 26 May 1917, 9; Amidon to AP, 29 April 1917, Reel 41.

53. Beard to AP, 23 June 1917, Reel 44.

54. LB, "Indomitable," in *SUFF*, 9 June 1917, 6.

55. "Universal Suffrage," *SUFF*, 16 June 1917, 3; "Woman's Party Appeals," *SUFF*, 23 June 1917, 7; AP to Lillian Ascough, 21 June 1917, Reel 44.

56. CAP, 187; W. W. Grimes report, 21 June 1917, FBI Investigative Records, RG 65.2.2, file 25025, National Archives; "Woman's Party," *SUFF*.

57. Mrs. Ben Fly to NWP, 22 June; Jessie Davis to AP, 23 June; Ascough to AP, 21 June, all 1917, Reel 44.

58. Eastmans to LB, 21 June; Betsy Reyneau to AP, June; Marion May to AP, 22 June; AP to May, 21 June, all 1917, Reel 44.

59. Bessaraboff to AP/LB/Lewis, 21 June; "WP" to AP, 22 June, both 1917, Reel 44.

60. George Lillard report, 20 June; W. W. Grimes report, 21 June, both 1917, FBI Investigative Records, file 25025.

61. K. Morey to AP, 19 June; *PL*, 22 June 1917, both Reel 44; CAP, 216; Louis Brownlow, *A Passion for Anonymity* (Chicago: University of Chicago Press, 1958), 76–77.

62. "Number of Picket Arrests," Reel 55 at 203.

63. Mabel Vernon interview, 75 (see chap. 2, n. 11); "Six Suffragists," *SUFF*, 7 July 1917, 5.

64. "Six Suffragists," *SUFF*.

65. "Prison," *SUFF*, 7 July 1917, 9.

66. Ibid.

67. "Our Democratic Administration," *SUFF*, 30 June 1917, 4; Lavinia Dock, "The Young Are at the Gates," *SUFF*, 30 June 1917, 5.

68. "Blunder," *SUFF*, 7 July 1917, 6; "U.S. Convicts," *SUFF*, 14 July 1917, 4.

69. Hunkins to Anna Constable, 9 July; Hunkins to Beard, 11 July; Martin to AP, 11 July, all 1917, Reel 45.

70. King to AP, 25 July; LB to Kent, 26 July, both 1917, Reel 46; Herbert McIntosh, *Practical Handbook of Medical Electricity* (N.p.: Therapeutic, 1909), 174.

71. July 13 Minutes, Reel 114, NWPP I; King to AP, ibid.

72. Martin to Helen Vaughan, 27 July; LB to Belmont, 24 July, both 1917, Reel 46.

73. Parker probably meant "*toute ensemble et bien*," that is, "all together and well." Parker to AP, mid-July 1917, Reel 46; Whittemore to AP, 14 July; Bertha Fowler to Vernon, 18 July, both 1917, Reel 45.

74. Lewis to AP, 30 July; Mietza H. Bye to AP, 7 August, both 1917, Reel 46.

75. Lewis to AP, 3 August 1917, Reel 46; *Boyd's Philadelphia Directory 1915* (Philadelphia: C. E. Howe, 1915), 227; E. K. Beach to AP, 28 August; LB to Rogers, 24 August, both 1917, Reel 47.

76. "Protest," *SUFF*, 21 July 1917, 4–5; "Picket Arrests," n.d., Reel 55.

77. Malone served as collector of the Port of New York. "United States," *SUFF*, 21 July 1917, 7–8; Hallinan interview, 10, AF; "Suffragists Take 60-Day Sentence," *NYT*, 18 July 1917.

78. "Suffrage Pickets," *NY Herald*, 18 July 1917, Reel 169, NWPP I; Stevens, *Jailed for Freedom*, 158–62.

79. "Vindication," *SUFF*, 28 July 1917, 4; Hopkins, "An Open Letter," *SUFF*, 18 August 1917; Hopkins to Wilson, 18 July 1917, Reel 45; Brownlow, *Passion*, 76; Wilson to Albert S. Burleson, 19 July 1917, Reel 210, WWP.

80. David Lawrence, "President Pardons Suffragists," *NY Evening Post*, 20 July 1917; "Sorrows of the Sixteen," *NYT*, 20 July 1917; Sally Hunter Graham, "Woodrow Wilson, Alice Paul," *Political Science Quarterly* 98 (Winter 1983–84): 670.

81. Brownlow, *Passion*, 78–79; Thompson to Baker, 21 July 1917, Reel 45.

82. "Vindication," *SUFF*; Hopkins to Wilson, 20 July 1917, Reel 45; *Baltimore Sun*, 20 July 1917.

83. Arthur Brisbane to Wilson, 20 July; Wilson to Tumulty, July, both 1917, Reel 209, WWP; Wilson to Louis Wiley, 23 July 1917; Wilson to George Creel, 5 November 1917, quoted in Graham, "Woodrow Wilson," 672.

84. LB to Hooker, 3 August 1917, Reel 46; "Banner Calling," *NY Tribune*, 11 August 1917, Reel 169, NWPP I; "President Onlooker," *SUFF*, 18 August 1917, 7.

85. "Flags Rip," *PL*, 15 August 1917; "Pelt Cameron House," *WP*, 15 August 1917.

86. "President Onlooker," *SUFF*; Lindbergh to Wilson, 27 August 1917, Reel 47.

87. Gail Bederman, *Manliness and Civilization* (Chicago: University of Chicago Press, 1995), 158–60; Glenn B. Ralston to Wilson, 16 August; J. M. Schwartz to Wilson, 15 August, both 1917, Reel 89, WWP.

88. Graham, "Woodrow Wilson," 672, n. 29; "Mob Gets Harsher," 16 August 1917; "Police Tear Down," 17 August 1917, both Reel 169, NWPP I; "Government Versus the Pickets," *SUFF*, 25 August 1917, 5.

89. David Lawrence, "Pickets' Comic Riot," *NY Evening Post*, 17 August 1917; Brownlow, *Passion*, 77–79.

90. "Government," *SUFF*; Ray Stannard Baker and David Grayson, *American Chronicle* (New York: Scribner's Sons, 1945), 386–87.

91. "Kaiser Wilson," *SUFF*, 18 August 1917, 6.

92. Belmont to AP, 15 August; Alice Park to LB, 15 August, both 1917, Reel 46; Rogers to Stuyvesant, 24 August 1917, Reel 47.

93. George Kober, "Charitable and Reformatory Institutions," S. Doc. No. 207, Cong. Serial Set 8702 (1927), 54–63.

94. "Administration Prison," *SUFF*, 1 September 1917, 8; "Investigation," *SUFF*, 8 September 1917, 8; Kober, "Charitable and Reformatory Institutions," 58, 62–63.

95. Cover, *SUFF*, 15 September 1916; Gertrude Stevenson, "An 'Outside' Impression," *SUFF*, 8 September 1917, 5.

96. Erving Goffman, *Stigma* (New York: Touchstone, 1986), 6–10.

97. "Why," *SUFF*, 1 September 1917, 6; "Draft Day," *SUFF*, 15 September 1917, 9.

98. Sara Bard Field, "They Who Sit in Jail," *SUFF*, 15 September 1917, 5; Betty Stuyvesant to Vernon, 7 September 1917, Reel 48.

99. Judith Hara to Julia Emory, 27 September 1917, Reel 49; Elizabeth McShane to Iris Calderhead, 29 August 1917, Reel 47.

100. Ford, *Iron-Jawed*, 186–87 (see chap. 8, n. 12); 262; "Picket Arrests," Reel 55; "Pickets," *WP*, 7 October 1917, 16.

101. "Connecticut State Leaders Join," *SUFF*, 29 September 1917, 9; LaFollette, "Justice," reprinted in *SUFF*, 6 October 1917, 9; "Malone Resigns," *NYT*, 8 September 1917; "Malone Resigns," *SUFF*, 15 September 1917, 6.

102. "House Woman-Suffrage Committee Created," *SUFF*, 29 September 1917, 7.

103. "The Vote," *SUFF*, 6 October 1917, 3.

104. AP to Whittemore, 28 September 1917, Reel 49.

105. "National Woman's Party," *SUFF*, 22 September 1917, 8.

CHAPTER 14

1. Pauline Jacobson, "An Impression," *SUFF*, 13 October 1917, 4.

2. "Another Administration Retreat," *SUFF*, 13 October 1917, 5.

3. Ibid.; AP to Lewis, 12 October 1917, Reel 50.

4. "'Suffs' Defiant," *NY Evening Journal,* 19 October 1917, Reel 95; "Seven Months Sentence," *SUFF,* 27 October 1917, 4.

5. "Police Court, Oct 21 1917," Reel 50; "Seven Months," *SUFF.*

6. AP to V. Pierce, 22 October; AP to TP, 22 October; AP to Arnold, 22 October, all 1917, Reel 51.

7. "Political Prisoners," *SUFF,* 3 November 1917, 8; Stevens, *Jailed,* 177 (see chap. 8, n. 16); "Suffragists Are Charged," *PL,* 5 October 1917.

8. "Seven Months," *SUFF;* "Alice Paul," *NY Tribune,* 23 October 1917.

9. Vernon to Amidon, 23 October; Katzenstein to Amidon, 23 October; Florence Whitehouse to AP, c. 22 October; M. A. E. to Arnold, 28 October; Mrs. Preston et al., 23 October, all 1917, Reel 51.

10. Arnold to Helen Burns, 22 October; Arnold to W. Ely Ainge, 22 October, both 1917, Reel 51.

11. "District Jail, Washington DC," 1909, LC; "Send Plea," *PL,* 11 November 1917.

12. Lewis Affidavit, 28 November 1917, Reel 53; Mary Winsor, "My Prisons," Folder 5, Winsor Papers, SL; Gladys Greiner Affidavit, c. 15 November 1917, Reel 54; "Send Plea," *PL.*

13. Winsor, "My Prisons"; Stevens, *Jailed,* 215.

14. "Send Plea," *PL;* Florence Boeckel, "Why They Put Alice Paul in Jail," *SUFF,* 10 November 1917, 7.

15. "Send Plea," *PL;* "Jail Horrors," *Chicago Tribune,* 4 November 1917; Stevens, *Jailed,* 216.

16. Stevens, *Jailed,* 216; Winsor, "My Prisons," 9–10; CAP, 228; "Jail Horrors," *Chicago Tribune.*

17. Rick Honey, "Nearly Broke," *Ridgefield [CT] Press,* 6 November 1975; "Over the Top," *SUFF,* 10 November 1917, 4; "Give Jail Experiences," *WP,* 5 November 1917.

18. Lewis to TP, 2 November; "Information," 1 November, both 1917, Reel 51; "Over the Top," *SUFF.*

19. Stevens, *Jailed,* 216–17; Kate Heffelfinger to Amidon, 8 November 1917, Reel 52; AP to Lewis, 7 November 1917, Reel 53.

20. AP to Lewis, 7 November 1917, Reel 53.

21. "Hunger Strike," *NY Evening World,* 22 October 1917, Reel 169, NWPP I; AP to Lewis, 7 November 1917, Reel 53.

22. Lewis to Burns, 6 November 1917, Reel 52; AP to Lewis, 7 November 1917, Reel 53.

23. "Miss Paul, Picket," *WP,* 7 November 1917; "Alice Paul Begins," *PL,* 7 November 1917.

24. Gertrude Crocker to Amidon, 8 November 1917, Reel 52; Stevens, *Jailed,* 217–20.

25. Edith Ainge to LB, 8 November 1917; Rogers to Arnold, 7 November 1917, both Reel 52; *NYT* editor, "Non Tali Auxilio," *NYT,* 8 November 1917.

26. Mari Jo Buhle, *Women and American Socialism, 1870–1920* (Champaign: University of Illinois Press, 1981), 237; Graham, *Woman Suffrage*, 112–13 (see chap. 6, n. 30); "Cooper Union," *NY American*, 8 November 1917, Reel 95.

27. Tumulty to Wilson, 26 October; Wilson to Tumulty, c. 26 October, both 1917, Reel 210, WWP; Stevens, *Jailed*, 220.

28. Stevens, *Jailed*, 221–22.

29. Gardiner to Wilson, 9 November 1917, Reel 210, WWP; Stevens, *Jailed*, 222, 226; CAP, 230–31.

30. Stevens, *Jailed*, 222–23; Gardiner to Wilson, 9 November 1917, Reel 210, WWP.

31. Gardiner to Wilson, 9 November 1917, Reel 210, WWP; Wilson to Tumulty, mid-November 1917, Reel 210, WWP.

32. "Row over Hunger Strike," *NYT*, 10 November 1917, Reel 95.

33. Stevens, *Jailed*, 223–25; "Tube Breaking Hunger Strike," *NY Journal*, 9 November 1917, Reel 95; Lavinia Dock, "Alice Paul in Prison" and "A Note," both *SUFF*, 24 November 1917, 6–7.

34. "Insanity Threat in Jail," *Chicago Tribune*, 10 November 1917; "Pickets Charge Insanity Plot," *WP*, 10 November 1917.

35. HP to TP, 12 November 1917, Folder 210, APP.

36. "John Milholland Protests," *SUFF*, 17 November 1917, 9; AP to Lewis, 7 November 1917; Winsor, "Punishment," Folder 13, Winsor Papers, SL.

37. Morey to Jane Adams [sic], 10 November; LB to Stevens, 10 November; Morey to Olive Belches, 10 November, all 1917, Reel 52.

38. LB to Rebecca Ernst, 5 November; Lewis to Ethel Adamson, 1 November, both 1917, Reel 51; LB to Matilda Gardner, 8 November 1917, Reel 52.

39. "Women Thank Wilson," *WP*, 10 November 1917; NAWSA Press Statement, 9 November 1917, Reel 210, WWP; "Shaw Severe," *NYT*, 23 November 1917.

40. "41 Pickets," *NY American*, 11 November 1917, Reel 95; Lewis to Belmont, 13 November 1917, Reel 52; "Police Net 40 Pickets," *WP*, 11 November 1917.

41. "Forty-one Suffrage Pickets," *SUFF*, 17 November 1917, 6; Lewis to Belmont, 13 November 1917, Reel 52; "A Week," *SUFF*, 24 November 1917.

42. "A Week," *SUFF*.

43. "A Note," *SUFF*; Stevens, *Jailed*, 224–25.

44. "91 Suff Raiders," *NY World*, 12 November 1917, Reel 95.

45. A writ of habeas corpus challenges unlawful confinements, forcing authorities to produce a prisoner. HP to TP, 13 November 1917, Folder 252, APP; "The Government," *SUFF*, 24 November 1917, 5–6; Amidon to Winslow, c. 13 November 1917, Reel 53.

46. "A Week," *SUFF*; O'Brien to Stevens, 17 November 1917, Reel 52.

47. "Laying Aside Suffrage," *PL*, 13 November 1917; James Seavey, "Put to Insanity Test," *NY Tribune*, 19 November 1917, Reel 95; "Rising Tide," *SUFF*, 24 November 1917, 12.

48. Corinna Barnes to LB, 15 November 1917, Reel 52; Beard to Wilson, 12 November 1917, Reel 210, WWP.

49. [Name illegible] to LB, 15 November; Amelia Francis to LB, 18 November; Alice Bodwell to LB, 15 November, all 1917, Reel 52.

50. Vera Whitehouse to Tumulty, 16 November; Kelly to Wilson, 22 November; Wilson to Tumulty, 21 November, all 1917, Reel 210, WWP.

51. Stevens to Adamson, 16 November 1917, Reel 52; Wilson to Tumulty, 21 November 1917, Reel 210, WWP; Tumulty to Wilson, 19 November 1917, Reel 210, WWP.

52. "Verdict," *WP*, 8 November 1917; "Pickets' Charges," *NY Sun*, 23 November 1917, Reel 95.

53. James Seavey, "Pickets Leave Occoquan," *NY Tribune*, 25 November 1917, Reel 95; "Decision," 24 November 1917, Reel 52.

54. "A Note," *SUFF*; "Prison Notes," *SUFF*, 1 December 1917, 6.

55. "Jubilee Dinner," *SUFF*, 15 December 1917, 10.

56. David Lawrence, "For and Against," *NY Evening Post*, 27 November 1917; Lawrence to AP, 26 February, Reel 57; AP to Lawrence, 15 March, both 1918, Reel 58.

57. Lawrence, "For and Against," *NY Evening Post*.

58. Mullowney to Zinkhan, 26 November; Zinkhan to Mullowney, 27 November; Zinkhan to Mullowney, 28 November, all 1917, Reel 52; Lawrence, "For and Against," *NY Evening Post*; "Suffrage Pickets Freed," *NYT*, 28 November 1917.

59. "Hunger Strike Wins," *Chicago Tribune*, 28 November 1917; "Mystery in Release," *PL*, 28 November 1917; "Jail Is Calm," *WP*, 28 November 1917.

60. "The Court," *SUFF*, 10 March 1918, 6.

61. Lewis to AP, received 7 March 1918, Reel 58.

62. Walker to Lewis, 9 March 1918, Reel 58.

63. "Mystery," *PL*; Belmont to AP, 27 November 1917, Reel 52.

CHAPTER 15

1. Ada Kendall to Lewis, December; AP to Marie Kennedy, 27 December, both 1917, Reel 54; "Miss Burns Tells Suff Party Plans," *NY Journal*, 30 November 1917, Reel 95.

2. TP to AP, 8 December 1917, Reel 53; HP to AP, 23 December; AP to Tacie Paul, 24 December, both 1917, Reel 54.

3. Arnold to all depts., 26 November 1917, Reel 52; Lewis to Louise Sturtevant, 2 November 1917, Reel 51.

4. December 1917 Conference Minutes, 65, Reel 53.

5. "Jubilee Dinner," *SUFF*, 15 December 1917, 10.

6. Ibid.

7. Whittemore to AP, received 3 December; Ella Thompson to AP, 7 December, both 1917, Reel 53; Elsie Hill to AP, c. December 1917, Reel 54.

8. AP to Thompson, 21 December 1917, Reel 53.

9. AP later cautioned in vain against a time limit for the ERA. "President's Address," *NYT*, 5 December 1917; "Dry and Suff Votes," *Evening World*, 6 December 1917, Reel 95; "National Advisory Council" and "Judiciary Committee," *SUFF*, 15 December 1917, 5–6; Roscoe Pound to Amidon, 21 December 1917, Reel 53.

10. "Prohibition Amendment," *SUFF*, 22 December 1917, 8; Lewis to Katzenstein, 18 December 1917, Reel 53.

11. AP to Olive Belches, 5 January 1918, Reel 55; Martin to Rogers, 27 December 1917, Reel 54; "Judiciary Committee," *SUFF*.

12. Elizabeth Bass to Wilson, 8 January; Jouett Shouse to Wilson, 8 January, both 1918, Reel 210, PWW.

13. Wilson to Bass, 9 January; Tumulty to Wilson, 9 January, both 1918, Reel 210, PWW.

14. "On the Suffrage Amendment," *NY Tribune*, 11 January 1918, Reel 168; AP to Elle Abeel, 26 January 1918, Reel 56.

15. Younger, "Revelations," 40ff (see chap. 12, n. 17); Maud Wood Park, *Front Door Lobby* (Boston: Beacon, 1960), 137–48; "Susan B. Anthony Amendment Passes," *SUFF*, 12 January 1918, 5; James Seavey, "Suffrage Wins in the House," *NY Tribune*, 10 January 1918, Reel 95.

16. Seavey, "Suffrage Wins"; "Votes from Sick Beds," *NYT*, 11 January 1918.

17. Park, *Front Door*, 149–51; "House for Suffrage, 274 to 136," *NYT*, 11 January 1918.

18. "Suffs Sing as Amendment Passes," *NY Call*, 11 January 1918, Reel 95; Park, *Front Door*, 151–52; Younger, "Revelations," 40ff.

19. Hopkins to AP, 10 January; Alice Henkle to AP, 11 January; Adamson to AP, 10 January, all 1918, Reel 55.

20. "Comments," *SUFF*, 19 January 1918, 13.

21. Ibid.; "On the Suffrage Amendment," *NY Tribune*.

22. "How the House Voted," *NY Tribune*, 11 January 1918, Reel 95; "Analysis," *NY Tribune*, 11 January 1918, Reel 168, NWPP I; "States That Have Full and Partial Suffrage," *SUFF*, 30 January 1918, 11; Flexner and Fitzpatrick, *Century*, 283–84 (see chap. 6, n. 29).

23. "NWP Moves across Lafayette Square," *SUFF*, 5 January 1918, 6; Anna P. Thomas, "The New Home," *SUFF*, 16 February 1918, 5; Minutes, 15 February 1918, Reel 87, NWPP I.

24. Emory to AP, c. 18 February and 24 February, both 1918, Reel 57; Gray to Mother, 2 March 1918, Reel 2, NWPP I.

25. Parker Alumnus File, CUA; Thomas quoted in D'Emilio and Freedman, *Intimate Matters*, 191 (see chap. 1, n. 40).

26. Minutes, 12 April 1918, Reel 87; 1917 NWP Treasurer's Report, Reel 124, both NWPP I.

27. "Suffrage Amendment Postponed," *SUFF*, 6 July 1918, 5.

28. Spencer to Martin, 25 February 1918, Reel 57; Adamson to AP, 24 April 1918, Reel 60; Gardener to Wilson, 17 June 1918, Reel 210, PWW.

29. Alison Hopkins to AP, 1 August; AP to Katzenstein, 31 July, both 1918, Reel 63; "Lafayette and Rochambeau" and "Suffrage Demonstration," *SUFF*, 3 August 1918, 4, 5.

30. Ridley to AP, 6 August; Pullman to AP, 6 August; AP to Ridley, 6 August; AP to Pullman, 6 August; AP to Josephine Bennett, 23 July, all 1918, Reel 63.

31. Hazel Hunkins, interview by Amelia Fry, 30–31; Hill to Brannan, 11 January 1918, Reel 55; "Mandy" to Emory, 16 August; AP to Emory, 3 September, both 1918, Reel 64.

32. "Women's Protest Broken Up," *SUFF*, 17 August 1918, 5–6.

33. Ibid.; "The Pedestal," *SUFF*, 14 September 1918, 10.

34. "Militant Suffragettes," *NY Globe*, 7 August; "Discreditable," *NYT*, 8 August, both 1918, Reel 169, NWPP I; AP to Elizabeth McShane, 8 August 1918, Reel 63; "Later Demonstrations," *SUFF*, 24 August 1918, 5.

35. "Women's Protest," *SUFF*; "Woman Suffrage," 56 Cong. Rec. 9211 (1918).

36. Gardener to Rudolph Forster, 2 August 1918, Reel 210, PWW; "Says Jealousy Caused Suffragists Picketing," *NY World*, 10 August 1918, Reel 169, NWPP I.

37. "The Trial" and "In Prison," *SUFF*, 24 August 1918, 6–7.

38. "In Prison," *SUFF*; AP to Stevens, 17 August; Boeckel to Catherine Flanagan, 17 August, both 1918, Reel 64.

39. "Wilson's Outing Ideal," *NYT*, 18 August 1918; "Free 23 Suffragists," *NYT*, 21 August 1918; Ridley to AP, 20 August; AP to Ridley, 22 August, both 1918, Reel 64.

40. "Suffrage Vote," *SUFF*, 31 August 1918, 6; "Says Jealousy," *NY World*; AP to Lewis, 4 September 1918, Reel 64.

41. Belmont to AP, 9 September; Lewis to AP, 12, 13, and 14 September; AP to K. Morey, 6 September, all 1918, Reel 64.

42. "President's Words Burned," *SUFF*, 28 September 1918, 6–7; AP to Lewis, 19 September 1918, Reel 64.

43. "Suffragists Burn President's Words," *NYT*, 17 September 1918; "President's Words Burned," *SUFF*; AP to Lewis, 19 September 1918, Reel 64.

44. AP to Lewis, 19 September 1918, Reel 64; "Senate Suffrage Committee Sets Date," *SUFF*, 28 September 1918, 5; NAWSA Bulletin, 19 September 1918, Wisconsin Woman Suffrage Association, Reel 12–737, Wisconsin Historical Society; Iris Calderhead to AP, 25 September 1918, Reel 64.

45. William McAdoo, *The Crowded Years* (New York: Houghton Mifflin, 1931), 496–98.

46. "Suffrage Defeat by the Senate," *SUFF*, 12 October 1918, 8; "A Ludicrous Newspaper," *SUFF*, 19 October 1918, 10; "Wilson Makes Suffrage Appeal," *NYT*, 1 October 1918.

47. AP, "Defeat in the Senate," *SUFF*, 12 October 1918, 4.

48. "Suffrage Must Win," *SUFF*, 19 October 1918, 9; "Suffrage Beaten by the Senate," *NYT*, 2 October 1918.

49. "Women Will Protest," *SUFF*, 12 October 1918, 13.

50. "Change in the Membership," *SUFF*, 12 October 1918, 13.

51. "Election Results," *SUFF*, 9 November 1918, 6; Younger, "Election Gains," *SUFF*, 16 November 1918, 7.

52. "Miss Paul Speaks," *SUFF*, 16 November 1918, 4.

53. Boeckel to AP, 3 December; A. Morey to LB, 10 December; LB to Mrs. Robert Whitehouse, 3 December, all 1918, Reel 156.

54. Dorothy Bartlett to LB, 11 December; LB to Dear Friend, 14 December, both 1918, Reel 66; "We Turn to the President," *SUFF*, 21 December 1918, 4.

55. "American Women Burn President Wilson's Words," *SUFF*, 21 December 1918, 6–7.

56. Ibid.

57. Kate Heffelfinger, "The Demonstration," *SUFF*, 28 December 1918, 4; Stillion Southard, *Militant Citizenship*, 166–67 (see chap. 8, n. 55); Adams and Keene, *American Suffrage Campaign*, 233–34 (see chap. 8, n. 43).

58. "President Starts Abroad," *NYT*, 5 December 1918; AP to Pierce, 26 December 1918, Reel 66.

59. "New Year's," *SUFF*, 4 January 1919, 7; Adams and Keene, *American Suffrage Campaign*, 235.

60. "Watchfire," *SUFF*, 11 January 1919, 6; "First Watchfire," *NY Herald*, 2 January 1919, Reel 169, NWPP I.

61. "Watchfire," *SUFF*.

62. Ibid.; Lewis to Mary Burnham, 4 January 1919, Reel 67.

63. Vernon to State Chairmen, 6 January; LB to Mary Ingham, 7 January, both 1919, Reel 67.

64. "While Women Go," *SUFF*, 18 January 1919, 4.

65. Ibid.; HP to AP, received 9 January 1919, Reel 67; "Impressions," *SUFF*, 25 January 1919, 12–13; Ellen Winsor to *Suffragist*, January 1919, Reel 68.

66. Frederick O'Brien to Sara Field, 6 February 1920, Huntington Library, C. E. S. Wood Collection, Box 177, Folder 11; "Demanding Suffrage," *SUFF*, 25 January 1919, 6; AP to Agnes Morey, 5 January 1919, Reel 67; AP to Boeckel, 5 February 1919, Reel 69.

67. "Balk Democratic Test on Suffrage," *NYT*, 6 February 1919; Park, *Front Door Lobby*, 230.

68. "Demonstration," *SUFF*, 22 February 1919, 10–11; Park, Supplementary Notes, February 1943, Reel 32–697, NAWSA.

69. "Suffragists Burn Wilson in Effigy," *NYT*, 10 February 1919.

70. Spencer to AP, 16 February; Stevens to AP, 12 February, both 1919, Reel 69; "Suffragettes," *Brooklyn Eagle*, 10 February; "Suffragette Excesses," *NY Sun*, 11 February, both 1919, Reel 169, NWPP I.

71. Whittemore to AP, 8 February; Florence Whitehouse and Madeline Freeman to AP, 9 February; Dock to AP/LB, 11 February; Lola Lloyd to AP, 10 February; Anne Rand to AP, 11 February, all 1919, Reel 69.

72. "Senate Again Beats Suffrage," *NYT*, 11 February 1919.

73. "Prison Special," *SUFF*, 15 February 1919, 5–6.

74. Lewis to Katzenstein, 4 March 1919, Reel 69.

75. "Suffrage for Politics," *NYT*, 12 February 1919; AP to Pierce, 7 March 1919, Reel 69.

76. Lewis to Katzenstein, 8 March; AP to Pierce, 7 March, both 1919, Reel 69; AP to Heffelfinger, 13 April 1919, Reel 70.

77. "Prison Special Tour," *SUFF*, 29 March 1919, 4; John F. Witte, *The Politics and Development of the Federal Income Tax* (Madison: University of Wisconsin Press, 1986), 85; AP to Margaret Whittemore, 25 March 1919, Reel 70.

78. AP to Margaret Whittemore, 9 April; AP to I. H. Preston, 17 April; AP to Emma Wold, 25 April, all 1919, Reel 70.

79. "Suffrage Campaign," *PI*, 14 May 1919, Reel 169, NWPP I.

80. "Equal Suffrage Won," *WP*, 5 June 1919.

81. "Suffragists Rejoice," *SUFF*, 14 June 1919, 9.

82. "Woman's Party Leaders," *NY Mail*, 5 June 1919, Reel 169, NWPP I; "Suffrage Wins in Senate," *NYT*, 5 June 1919.

83. *NY Tribune* quoted in "Comments," *SUFF*, 5 July 1919, 11; *Bulletin & Constitution*, quoted in "Comments," *SUFF*, 12 July 1919, 10–11.

84. "Wisconsin First" and "When States Can Ratify," *SUFF*, 21 June 1919, 8, 5.

85. "Technical Aspects of Ratification," *SUFF*, 21 June 1919, 5.

86. "Ratification Work," *SUFF*, 19 July 1919, 5.

87. Lewis to AP, 11 August; AP to Vernon, 31 August, both 1919, Reel 73; AP to Hill, 28 October 1919, Reel 74.

88. "Militants Go Right On," *NYT Magazine*, 18 July 1920, 77; AP to Elizabeth Esherick, 2 January 1920, Reel 75; Pierce to Vernon, 27 August 1919, Reel 73; Hill to AP, 29 June 1920, Reel 79; "Lucy Burns Declines Job," *NYT*, 4 February 1918.

89. Hopkins to AP, 23 August 1919, Reel 73; "Winning New Jersey," *SUFF*, March 1920, 9–10.

90. AP, "Editorial," *SUFF*, March 1920, 3.

91. AP to Mrs. Albion Lang, 15 March; AP to Lewis, 17 March; AP to "Dear Suffragist," 20 March, all 1920, Reel 77.

92. Van Voris, *Catt*, 156–58 (see chap. 9, n. 1).

93. AP to "Dear Suffragist," 2 July; Sue White to AP, 27 June, both 1920, Reel 80.

94. AP to Mrs. Kate Hayden, 6 August 1920.

95. Pollitzer to AP, 6 August; AP to Mary Winsor, 11 August; Hill to Irwin, 12 August; AP to White, 13 August, all 1920, Reel 81.

EPILOGUE

1. Sue White to AP, 18 August 1920, Reel 81; "Colby Proclaims Woman Suffrage," *NYT*, 27 August 1920.
2. DS to AP, 14 March; Irwin to AP, received 4 March, both 1920, Reel 77; Irwin to DS, 8 November 1920, Stevens Papers 32.3, SL.
3. Lunardini, *Equal Suffrage to Equal Rights*, 162 (see chap. 10, n. 29).
4. CAP, xiii.
5. Tacie P. Paul, "Family Heirlooms," Folder 201, APP.

Bibliography of Major Sources

ARCHIVAL MATERIALS

Alice Paul Collection. Alice Paul Institute, Mount Laurel, NJ.

Alice Paul Papers. Schlesinger Library. Harvard University, Cambridge, MA.

Amelia Roberts Fry Papers. Alice Paul Institute, Mount Laurel, NJ.

Friends Historical Library. Swarthmore College, Swarthmore, PA.

Moorestown Friends School Archives. Friends School, Moorestown, NJ.

National American Woman Suffrage Association Records. Library of Congress microfilm, 1982.

National Woman's Party Papers: 1913–1974 [Group I]. Glen Rock, NJ: Microfilming Corporation of America, 1979.

National Woman's Party Papers: The Suffrage Years, 1913–1920 [Group II]. Sanford, NC: Microfilming Corporation of America, 1981.

National Woman's Party Papers. Group III. Library of Congress, Washington, DC.

Philadelphia Bulletin. Clipping collection. Temple University, Philadelphia, PA.

Swarthmore College Archives. Swarthmore College, Swarthmore, PA.

University of Pennsylvania Archives. Philadelphia, Pennsylvania.

Woodbrooke Quaker Study Centre Archives. Birmingham, England.

Woodrow Wilson Papers. Microfilm, 1973. Library of Congress, Washington, DC.

INTERVIEWS

Burns, Janet Campbell. Telephone interview by J. D. Zahniser. 10, 14, and 20 January 2011.

Conrow, Engle. Interview by Amelia Fry. 16 September 1980.

Conrow, Engle, Elizabeth Lippincott, Anita Parry, Richard Robbins, and Helen Wallace. Interview by Amelia Fry. 18 October 1978.

Gardiner, Walter. Interview by Amelia Fry. 16 September 1980.

Giesecke, Agnes. Interview by Amelia Fry. 8 October 1980.

Jones, Margaret. Interview by Margaret Hope Bacon and Amelia Fry. 22 March 1980.

McNally, Myra. Interview by Amelia Fry. 20–21 March 1982.

Paul, Alice. Interview by Amelia Fry. "Conversations with Alice Paul." Suffragists Oral History Project, Bancroft Library, 1975. http://bancroft.berkeley.edu/ROHO/projects/suffragist/.

——. Interview by Midge McKenzie. 1 April 1973.

——. Interview by Marjory Nelson. "Alice Paul: Thoughts on the ERA in 1970, on Her Early Years in the Suffrage Campaign." April/May 1971.

Robbins, Richard. Interview by Amelia Fry. 12 February 1981.

Vernon, Mabel. Interview by Amelia Fry. "Speaker for Suffrage and Petitioner for Peace." Suffragists Oral History Project, Bancroft Library, 1976.

NEWSPAPERS AND PERIODICALS

Congressional Record
Friends' Intelligencer
New York Times
Philadelphia Public Ledger
The Suffragist
Times of London
Votes for Women
Washington Post
Woman's Journal

OTHER PRIMARY SOURCES

Brownlow, Louis. *A Passion for Anonymity*. Chicago: University of Chicago Press, 1958.

"Her Pressure on Congress." *New York Times Magazine*, 2 March 1919, 71.

Herendeen, Anne. "A New Leader." *Everybody's*, July 1916, 127.

——. "What the Hometown Thinks of Alice Paul." *Everybody's*, October 1919, 45.

Husted Harper, Ida, ed. *History of Woman Suffrage, 1900–1920*. Vol. V. New York: Fowler & Wells, 1922.

Irwin, Inez H. *The Story of Alice Paul and the Woman's Party*. Original edition, 1922. Fairfax, VA: Denlinger's, 1977.

Katzenstein, Caroline. *Lifting the Curtain: The State and National Suffrage Campaigns in Pennsylvania as I Saw Them*. Philadelphia: Dorrance, 1955.

Kenney, Annie. *Memories of a Militant*. London: E. Arnold, 1924.

Mallon, Winifred. "Went on Hunger Strike." [NY] *Morning Telegraph*, 11 November 1917.

"New York School of Philanthropy." *Charities* XIV (June 1905): 785.

Pankhurst, Emmeline. *My Own Story*. London: Eveleigh Nash, 1914.

Pankhurst, E. Sylvia. *The Suffragette*. New York: Sturgis & Walton, 1911.

——. *The Suffragette Movement*. London: Longmans, Green, 1931.

Park, Maud Wood. *Front Door Lobby*. Boston: Beacon, 1960.

Paul, Alice. "The Legal Position of Women in Pennsylvania." PhD diss., University of Pennsylvania, 1912.

——. *Sketch of the New York College Settlement*. New York School of Philanthropy thesis, 1905–6. Folder 20, Alice Paul Papers.

——. "The Woman Suffrage Movement in Britain." In "Significance of the Woman Suffrage Movement," supplement to *Annals of the American Academy of Political and Social Science* 35 (July 1910): 23–27.

Slayden, Ellen Maury. *Washington Wife*. New York: Harper & Row, 1963.

Stevens, Doris. *Jailed for Freedom*. New York: Boni & Liveright, 1920. Reprinted by Schocken Books, 1976.

Younger, Maud. "Diary of an Amateur Waitress." *McClure's*, March 1907, 543–52.

——. "Revelations of a Woman Lobbyist." *McCall's*, September–November 1919.

SECONDARY SOURCES

Adams, Katherine H., and Michael L. Keene. *Alice Paul and the American Suffrage Campaign*. Champaign: University of Illinois Press, 2007.

Bacon, Margaret Hope. *Mothers of Feminism: The Story of Quaker Women in America*. Philadelphia: Friends General Conference, 1997.

Barber, Lucy G. *Marching on Washington: The Forging of an American Political Tradition*. Berkeley: University of California Press, 2002.

Benjamin, Philip S. *The Philadelphia Quakers in the Industrial Age, 1865–1920*. Philadelphia: Temple University Press, 1976.

Bland, Sidney R. " 'Never Quite as Committed as We'd Like': The Suffrage Militancy of Lucy Burns." *Journal of Long Island History* 17 (Summer 1981): 4–23.

——. "New Life in an Old Movement: Alice Paul and the Great Suffrage Parade of 1913." *Records of the Columbia Historical Society* 71/72 (1971–72): 657–78.

Blatch, Harriot Stanton, and Alma Lutz. *Challenging Years*. New York: G. P. Putnam's Sons, 1940.

Borda, Jennifer. "Woman Suffrage Parades of 1910–1913." *Western Journal of Communication* 66 (Winter 2002): 25–52.

Cheyney, Edward Potts. *History of the University of Pennsylvania, 1740–1940*. Philadelphia: University of Pennsylvania Press, 1940.

Clemens, Elisabeth S. "Politics without Party: The Organizational Accomplishments of Disenfranchised Women." *The People's Lobby*. Chicago: University of Chicago Press, 1997.

Cowman, Krista. *Women of the Right Spirit: Paid Organisers of the Women's Social and Political Union (WSPU), 1904–18*. Manchester, England: Manchester University Press, 2007.

Crawford, Elizabeth. *The Women's Suffrage Movement: A Reference Guide, 1866–1928*. London: Routledge, 2001.

Davis, Robert, ed. *Woodbrooke, 1903–1953*. London: Bannisdale, 1953.

DiCenzo, Maria. "Gutter Politics: Women Newsies and the Suffrage Press." *Women's History Review* 12, no. 1 (2003): 15–33.

Dodd, Lynda. "Sisterhood of Struggle." In *Feminist Legal History*, edited by Tracy A. Thomas and Tracy J. Boisseau, 189–205. New York: New York University Press, 2011.

DuBois, Ellen Carol. *Harriot Stanton Blatch and the Winning of Woman Suffrage*. New Haven, CT: Yale University Press, 1999.

——. "Working Women, Class Relations, and Suffrage Militance." *Journal of American History* 74 (June 1987): 34–58.

Flexner, Eleanor, and Ellen Fitzpatrick. *Century of Struggle*. Cambridge, MA: Belknap Press of Harvard University Press, 1996.

Ford, Linda G. *Iron-Jawed Angels: The Suffrage Militancy of the National Woman's Party, 1913–1920*. Lanham, MD: University Press of America, 1991.

Fry, Amelia R. "Along the Suffrage Trail." *American West* 6 (January 1969): 16–25.

Gallagher, Robert S. "'I Was Arrested Of Course...'" *American Heritage*, February 1974.

Ganz, Marshall. "Why David Sometimes Wins." In *The Psychology of Leadership*, edited by David Messick and Roderick M. Kramer, 215–49. New York: Psychology Press, 2004.

Geidel, Peter. "Alva E. Belmont". PhD diss., Columbia University, 1993.

——. "Woodrow Wilson, Alice Paul, and the Woman Suffrage Movement." *Political Science Quarterly* 98 (Winter 1983–84): 665–79.

Graham, Sally Hunter. *Woman Suffrage and the New Democracy*. New Haven, CT: Yale University Press, 1996.

Hamm, Thomas D. "The Hicksite Quaker World, 1875–1900." *Quaker History* 89 (Fall 2000): 17–41.

——. *The Quakers in America*. New York: Columbia University Press, 2006.

Hewitt, Nancy A. "The Fragmentation of Friends." In *Witnesses for Change*, edited by Elizabeth Potts Brown and Susan Mosher Stuard, 93–108. New Brunswick, NJ: Rutgers University Press, 1989.

Holton, Sandra, and June Purvis, eds. *Votes for Women*. London: Routledge, 2000.

Kingston, William. *Moorestown's Third Century*. N.p.: Kingston, 1982.

Kraditor, Aileen S. *The Ideas of the Woman Suffrage Movement, 1890–1920*. New York: Anchor Books, 1971.

Leneman, Leah. *A Guid Cause: The Women's Suffrage Movement in Scotland*. Aberdeen, Scotland: Aberdeen University Press, 1991.

Lumsden, Linda J. "Beauty and the Beasts." *Journalism & Mass Communication Quarterly* 77 (Autumn 2000): 591–611.

——. *Inez: The Life and Times of Inez Milholland*. Bloomington: Indiana University Press, 2004.

——. *Rampant Women: Suffragists and the Right of Assembly*. Knoxville: University of Tennessee Press, 1997.

Lunardini, Christine. *From Equal Suffrage to Equal Rights: Alice Paul and the National Woman's Party, 1910–1928*. N.p.: toExcel Press, an imprint of iUniverse.com, 1986.

Marilley, Suzanne M. *Woman Suffrage and the Origins of Liberal Feminism*. Cambridge, MA: Harvard University Press, 1996.

Mayhall, Laura E. Nym. *The Militant Suffrage Movement: Citizenship and Resistance in Britain, 1860–1930*. New York: Oxford University Press, 2003.

Mazon, Patricia M. *Gender and the Modern Research University*. Palo Alto, CA: Stanford University Press, 2003.

Mead, Rebecca J. *How the Vote Was Won: Woman Suffrage in the Western United States, 1868–1914*. New York: New York University Press, 2004.

Moore, Jacqueline M. *Leading the Race: The Transformation of the Black Elite in the Nation's Capital, 1880–1920*. Charlottesville: University of Virginia Press, 1999.

Purdy, James C. *Moorestown Old and New*. Moorestown, NJ: Moorestown Historical Society, 1885, reprint 1976.

Purvis, June. *Emmeline Pankhurst*. London: Routledge, 2004.

Rosen, Andrew. *Rise Up, Women! The Militant Campaign of the Women's Social and Political Union, 1903–1914*. London: Routledge & Kegan Paul, 1974.

Solomon, Barbara Miller. *In the Company of Educated Women: A History of Women and Higher Education in America*. New Haven, CT: Yale University Press, 1985.

Stillion Southard, Belinda A. *Militant Citizenship: Rhetorical Strategies of the National Woman's Party, 1913–1920*. College Station: Texas A&M University Press, 2011.

Terborg-Penn, Rosalyn. *African-American Women in the Struggle for the Vote, 1850–1920*. Bloomington: Indiana University Press, 1998.

Tickner, Lisa. *The Spectacle of Women: Imagery of the Suffrage Campaign, 1907–14*. Chicago: University of Chicago Press, 1988.

Tusan, Michelle Elizabeth. *Women Making News: Gender and Journalism in Modern Britain*. Champaign: University of Illinois Press, 2005.

Van Voris, Jacqueline. *Carrie Chapman Catt: A Public Life*. New York: Feminist Press, 1987.

Walton, Mary. *A Woman's Crusade: Alice Paul and the Battle for the Ballot*. New York: Palgrave Macmillan, 2010.

Walvin, James. *The Quakers: Money and Morals*. London: John Murray, 1999.

Ware, Susan. "The Book I Couldn't Write." *Journal of Women's History* 24 (Summer 2012): 13–36.

Weber, Max. "The Three Pure Types of Legitimate Rule." In *The Essential Weber*, edited by Sam Whimster, 138–42. New York: Psychology Press, 2004.

Yoder, Don. "The Cultural Impact of Quakerism on Southern New Jersey," *New Jersey Folklife* 15 (1990): 3–9.

Index